The Civilization of the American Indian Series

THE HOUSE OF THE GOVERNOR

THE HOUSE OF THE GOVERNOR

By Jeff Karl Kowalski

A Maya Palace at Uxmal, Yucatan, Mexico

UNIVERSITY OF OKLAHOMA PRESS : NORMAN AND LONDON

Fig. 1 (shown on pages ii and iii). House of the Governor as it appeared during an 1843 visit by Stephens and Catherwood. Engraving adapted from a drawing by Frederick Catherwood (after Stephens 1963, 1: endpiece).

Fig. 2 (shown on title page, pages iv and v). House of the Governor, eastern façade. Platform of the bicephalic jaguar throne in foreground.

Library of Congress Cataloging-in-Publication Data

Kowalski, Jeff Karl, 1951–
  The House of the Governor.

  (The Civilization of the American Indians Series; v. 176)
  Bibliography: p. 275.
  Includes index.
  1. Governor's House (Uxmal Site, Mexico) 2. Uxmal
Site (Mexico) 3. Mayas—Architecture. 4. Indians of
Mexico—Architecture. I. Title. II. Series.
F1435.1.U7K69 1987   972'.65   86–19337
ISBN 0–8061–2035–5

This book has been published with the aid of grants from the Andrew W. Mellon Foundation and the Program for Research Tools and Reference Works of the National Endowment for the Humanities, an independent Federal agency that supports the study of such fields as history, philosophy, literature, and language.

The paper in this book meets the guidelines for permanence and durability of the Committee on Production Guidelines for Book Longevity of the Council on Library Resources, Inc.

This book is dedicated to Ella Gates,
and to the memories of Floyd Gates and
Roy Whitehead

Contents

PART THREE. ARCHITECTURAL SCULPTURE

Illustrations and Maps

Fig. 3. House of the Governor, western façade, from the House of the Pigeons.

Preface

THIS BOOK is a revised and updated version of a doctoral dissertation submitted to Yale University in 1981. It includes discussions of the historiography, chronology, native history, epigraphy, function, plan and massing, visual and proportional effects, and architectural sculpture of the magnificent palace building known as the House of the Governor at the northern Maya site of Uxmal, Yucatan, Mexico.

I owe thanks to many persons for helping me complete this project. I am particularly grateful to George Kubler and Esther Pasztory, who instructed me in the critical appreciation of pre-Columbian art. During my undergraduate years at Columbia University, Esther Pasztory awakened me to the richness, beauty, and meaning of this art tradition and stimulated me to make it my area of concentration. It has been a rare privilege to work with George Kubler, who was my doctoral adviser at Yale University. His deep and wide-ranging knowledge of pre-Columbian art has served as an inspiration and a challenge. During the preparation of the dissertation he read drafts of all chapters and patiently and enthusiastically counseled me on how to improve both structure and content, enabling me to shape my research into a work of scholarship. Throughout the process of revision he has continued to be helpful in countless ways.

I also owe a special debt to Michael D. Coe and Floyd Lounsbury, also of Yale University. Michael Coe's exuberant and infectious interest in Maya iconography and Floyd Lounsbury's profound knowledge of Maya hieroglyphic writing are responsible for much of the new information I am able to provide. Floyd Lounsbury provided me with extensive comments and criticisms on chapter 5, on the hieroglyphic inscriptions at Uxmal.

Others to whom I wish to give special thanks include David H. Kelley and E. Wyllys Andrews V. David Kelley commented on my hieroglyphic interpretations, and his studies of northern Maya inscriptions have deepened my own knowledge of writing and history in this area. I have had many discussions by letter or telephone with Will Andrews regarding Puuc archaeology and chronology, and he gave me free access to relevant records at the Middle American Research Institute at Tulane University.

I would also like to thank Anthony Andrews and Joann Andrews, who graciously allowed me to use the archaeological library in their home and research center, Quinta Mari, in Mérida. During the early phases of my research H. E. D. Pollock was helpful, providing information on Puuc chronology and then-unpublished maps of Puuc ruins. Anthony Aveni and John Carlson have helped me understand the astronomical significance of the House of the Governor, and George Andrews has shared his knowledge of specific Puuc ruins and construction techniques. Rosemary Sharp and I had valuable discussions on the significance of cut-stone façades, while Donald Roberston encouraged my studies of architectural design and proportion. Information on Frans Blom's research at Uxmal was provided by Mr. Edward Hinderliter, of Media, Pennsylvania, while Ian Graham sent me preliminary drawings of several hieroglyphic monuments from the northern Maya area. I have also profited from many discussions with Joseph W. Ball regarding the archaeological ceramics of Yucatan and the native historical tradition contained in the Books of Chilam Balam.

During 1976–77 I was able to travel to Mexico thanks to funds provided by the Josef Albers Traveling Fellowship administered by Yale University. I would like to thank Eduardo Matos Moctezuma, then director of the Archivo Técnico of the Instituto Nacional de Antropología e Historia, for permitting me to review unedited reports of archaeological excavations and reconstructions undertaken at Uxmal. Dr. Alberto Ruz Lhuillier, then director of the Center for Maya Studies at the Universidad Nacional Autónoma de México, kindly answered questions concerning his work at Uxmal, and Marta Foncerrada de Molina discussed her studies of the architectural sculpture of Uxmal. For my work in Yucatan I owe a particular debt to Norberto Gonzáles Crespo, then director of the Centro Regional del Sureste of the Instituto Nacional de Antropología e Historia, in Mérida, who provided me with permits to use ladders on the House of the Governor and to survey the platform system. He also introduced my wife and me to two guides, Mario Magaña and Pedro Gongura, of Oxkutzcab, who conducted us to many smaller Puuc ruins. Alfredo Barrera Rubio, also of the Centro Regional del Sureste, provided me with air photos of Uxmal and informed me about settlement pattern studies. I also wish to thank all other members of the Instituto Nacional de Antropología e Historia who helped me obtain the permits necessary to complete my work at the House of the Governor.

During 1977–78 I was the recipient of a Robert Woods Bliss Fellowship and was privileged to work on sections of this book as a junior fellow of the Center for Pre-Columbian Studies, Dumbarton Oaks, Washington, D.C. I would like to thank Elizabeth P. Benson, then director of the center, for her help locating resources and for general discussions of my topic. I returned to Uxmal in March, 1978. I am grateful to Roy Whitehead, of Hingham, Massachusetts, for acting as my field assistant on that trip. We surveyed the platform system of the House of the Governor and thoroughly measured the building at that time.

I would also like to thank my mother, Mrs. Tid Kowalski, and my grandfather, Floyd Gates, of Tulsa, Oklahoma, who made many of the inked drawings and maps for this book. Thanks also go to Barbara Fash for providing several of the final drawings. An expert job of obtaining the best possible photographic images from my negatives or from books was done by Herb Nelson, of Northern Illinois University.

Finally, my deepest gratitude goes to my wife, Mary Fleming Kowalski, and my children, Sarah and David. My children have had to tolerate my absences while I was typing or visiting libraries. Mary accompanied me to Mexico several times, most importantly during the extended visit of 1976–77. Among other things she has been a field assistant, photographer, artist, editor, and typist. Without her help and encouragement this book would not exist.

DeKalb, Illinois   JEFF KARL KOWALSKI

THE HOUSE OF THE GOVERNOR

Fig. 4. House of the Governor, western façade and south end, from the Great Pyramid. Pyramid of the Magician in the distance, Picote column at right.

Introduction

In his important study of the Maya, the *Relación de las cosas de Yucatan*, Bishop Diego de Landa averred that "If Yucatan were to gain a name and reputation from the multitude, the grandeur and the beauty of its buildings, as other regions of the Indies have obtained these by gold, silver and riches, its glory would have spread like that of Peru and New Spain."[1]

This book is concerned with the building traditionally known as the House of the Governor at Uxmal (figs. 1–4, 199). This edifice so perfectly exemplifies the "grandeur and beauty" of which Landa speaks that it has consistently been acknowledged as the masterpiece of Maya architecture in the New World. Typical of this adulation is the homage paid to the House of the Governor by John Lloyd Stephens in 1841:

There is no rudeness or barbarity in the design or proportions; on the contrary, the whole wears an air of architectural symmetry and grandeur; and as the stranger ascends the steps and casts a bewildered eye along its open and desolate doors, it is hard to believe that he sees before him the work of a race in whose epitaph, as written by historians, they are called ignorant of art and said to have perished in the rudeness of savage life. If it stood this day on its artificial terrace in Hyde Park or the Garden of the Tuileries, it would form a new order, . . . not unworthy to stand side by side with the remains of Egyptian, Grecian and Roman art.[2]

Impressive masonry structures such as the House of the Governor are the tangible remains of a great civilization which flourished in northern Yucatan centuries before the arrival of the Spaniards. By the time Landa encountered the Maya and compiled his important record of their customs and beliefs, they had already entered into a cultural de-

cline, reflected by a lessening of quality in art and architecture. It was during the Classic period (ca. A.D. 250–900) that the ancient Maya created one of the New World's most intellectually advanced and artistically rich civilizations, centered in the lowland jungles of northern Guatemala and extending into Belize, Honduras, El Salvador, and adjacent parts of Mexico, including the Yucatan Peninsula. The Classic period witnessed the zenith of social complexity in these areas, with a host of thriving cities and carved monuments attesting the Maya's cultural achievements.

A recognizable cluster of traits distinguished the Maya from other peoples at this time. These include architecture employing the corbeled vault; the Long Count and Initial Series dating system; a hieroglyphic writing system with a mixed pictographic, logographic, and phonetic script; and a specialized stela and altar cult.[3] Although they possessed a certain cultural cohesion and individuality, the Maya were also firmly included in the wider cultural entity known as Mesoamerica, which embraced much of central and southeastern Mexico and at times reached as far south as Costa Rica and Nicaragua. The Maya were making contact, trading, and interchanging ideas with other Mesoamerican peoples throughout their history. Although Maya civilization in the south experienced an irreversible decline and collapse between about A.D. 800 to 900, there was a rapid cultural and architectural florescence during this same period in the northern Yucatan peninsula. It was at the end of this time, sometimes referred to as the Terminal Classic period, that the House of the Governor was constructed. The succeeding centuries from A.D. 900 to 1200 saw the rise to power of Chichen Itza, a vital new capital in Yucatan, where the culture and art style incorporated both traditional Maya and central Mexican "Toltec" elements. The House of the Governor, created at a critical developmental juncture, thus may be discussed not only as an exceptional aesthetic object but also as an important monument for the reconstruction of northern Maya culture history.

The concurrent rise of the northern centers and fall of the southern Maya was accompanied, and caused in part, by the growing influence of the Chontal or Putun Itza Maya. These were militarily powerful groups of Chontal-speaking peoples who occupied a gulf coast homeland from Tabasco to Champoton in Campeche, and who served as middlemen for trade between Central America and highland Mexico. Uxmal and other Puuc centers apparently participated in an important circum-peninsular trade route, supplying the Chontal with commodities (e.g., cotton, cloth, slaves) for transport to central Mexico or Veracruz, and obtaining from them elite goods along with new artistic and architectural forms and cultural and religious concepts.

Increasing wealth and trade help account for the construction of buildings as grandiose and technically superior as the House of the Governor and the Nunnery Quadrangle at Uxmal. Trading contacts also help explain the distinctive blend of innovative local stylistic features, Classic Maya forms, and foreign or "non-Classic" elements visible in Puuc architecture. Features such as the elongated range plan, tripartite architectural arrangement, mat-weave lattice, long-snouted mask panels, and dynastic human figural sculptures of the House of the Governor are based on earlier southern lowland or central Yucatan traditions. Other Uxmal edifices, such as the West Structure of the Nunnery, adorned with prominent feathered serpent sculptures, display syncretistic combinations of Maya and Mexican forms and symbols. Simultaneously, the House of the Governor and other Late Puuc structures possess characteristic local features, such

as the use of lime concrete cores covered by expertly finished masonry, and an architectonic harmony between the geometric stone mosaic sculptures and the sharply rectilinear buildings they adorn.[4]

Despite general agreement concerning the aesthetic merit of the House of the Governor, and although there exists documentary knowledge of both the building and the site dating from the sixteenth century, the edifice has almost never been treated in more than a chapter or section in general descriptions of Maya archaeology, art, or architecture.[5] Consequently, until this time the student of Precolumbian art history has had to consult a wide range of studies to form a more comprehensive view of this building. The lapse this presented in studies of Maya architecture would be comparable to a similar lack of sustained discussion of a European monument of the caliber of the Parthenon or Chartres Cathedral.

This book is an art historical monograph that supplies a more complete examination of the House of the Governor. Gaining a deeper understanding of this edifice requires recognition that it is a complex phenomenon. While it is clear that the House of the Governor is a material object (composed of stone, mortar, wood, and plaster) with a tangible existence, it is also an aesthetic object whose forms have been arranged consciously to evoke a strong visual-emotional response from the viewer. In addition it is a cultural expression, or what has rightly been termed a "persisting event,"[6] made in a particular time and place by people with a specialized world-view.

In this book I portray the House of the Governor in its richness and complexity of meaning—as a monument in which material, cultural, spiritual, and aesthetic aspects are inextricably interrelated. Such a holistic approach is as productive as it is challenging, for by examining and tying together these separate strands of meaning we will ultimately be able to form a more coherent image of the House of the Governor.

PART ONE

History and Function

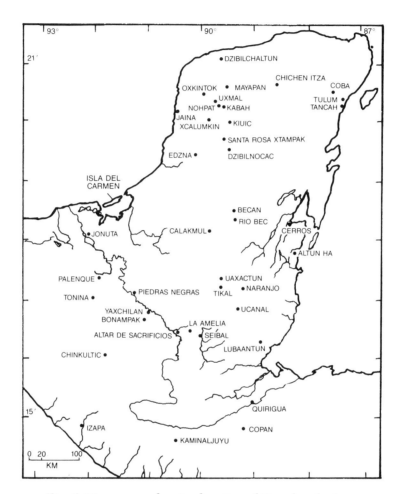

*Fig. 5. Maya area, showing location of Uxmal and other
principal sites.*

Chapter 1

Location and General Description

THE House of the Governor is the most imposing and architecturally refined single structure at Uxmal, the great Maya site of northwestern Yucatan (figs. 1–3). Uxmal lies about fifty miles south of Mérida (latitude 20°21'40"N, longitude 89°46'20"W) and is situated in a cuplike valley just south of the low range of hills known as the Puuc, which traverses the northern part of the peninsula from Maxcanu southeast toward Lake Chikankanab (fig. 4).

The central civic-ceremonial area of Uxmal covers about 250 acres, approximately a half mile north to south and 700 yards east to west (fig. 6).[1] Surrounding this central zone is a masonry wall, discovered in the nineteenth century, whose full extent has been determined only recently. This wall surrounds most of the large masonry buildings at Uxmal, although other buildings lie scattered outside, chiefly toward the south.[2]

At Uxmal the House of the Governor lies south of the Nunnery, an open-cornered quadrangle formed by four freestanding, range-type palace structures (figs. 83, 85–87). These four buildings, though forming a unified spatial composition, occupy platforms at several levels, indicative of hierarchical ranking. The principal northern building rests on the highest platform and has a castellated roof line formed of mask tiers. It is approached by a broad stairway flanked by two smaller structures that create the effect of storied architecture when viewed from the south. Occupying an intermediate level are the east and west buildings, which converge toward the north in what may be a deliberate attempt at perspective correction.[3] These two buildings resemble one another in construction and in their proportional groupings of the doorways but have different sculptural programs.

The west building features feathered-serpent imagery, while the east building carries trapezoidal arrangements of two-headed serpent bars (figs. 86, 87, 140, 186). The south building is the lowest and has a central vaulted entrance on axis with the Ball Court (fig. 99). This Ball Court occupies a concourse between the Nunnery Quadrangle and the House of the Governor. It has a narrow playing alley flanked by low, broad, slanting platforms, which are in turn backed by higher vertical walls (fig. 84). The vertical walls supported feathered serpent sculptures and had hieroglyphic rings at their centers.[4]

Northeast of the House of the Governor is the Pyramid of the Magician, a large pyramid of roughly elliptical plan with lower and upper temples built in varying styles during different periods (figs. 7, 8). The first building in the sequence is a multi-roomed range that forms part of a former quadrangle. Temple II, now encased by later construction, has colonnaded doorways and a flying façade above the rear wall. Temple III, built behind Temple II, has a sloping "mansard" upper façade. Temple IV forms the visible west façade and is reached by a steep stairway flanked by diagonally tiered masks (fig. 7), Temple IV is distinguished by a dragon-mouth entrance derived from Chenes buildings but constructed in Puuc mosaic stonework technique (fig. 8). The uppermost temple has a central chamber facing west and two flanking rooms facing east.

Southwest of the House of the Governor is the Great Pyramid, a massive mound with an ornamented temple at its summit (fig. 9). West of the Great Pyramid is the Pigeons Group (fig. 98). George Kubler has described this architectural complex as a variant of an "amphitheater court,"

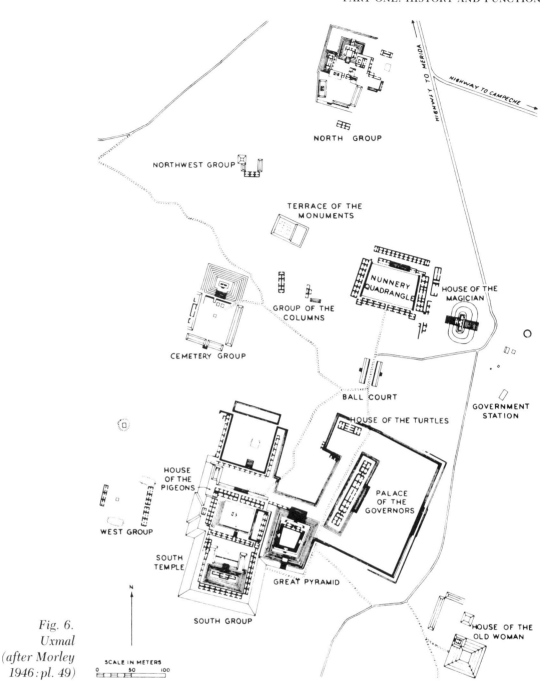

*Fig. 6.
Uxmal
(after Morley
1946:pl. 49)*

in which barrier mounds frame a courtyard on three sides while the fourth side has a dominant temple platform.[5] Tatiana Proskouriakoff and George Andrews have related the grouping to other Maya acropolises whose architecture is arranged to form a predetermined path in space leading to a goal.[6] The Pigeons Group consists of a hierarchical sequence of three courts that diminish in size as they ascend toward a south pyramid temple. Forming the northern

boundary of the second courtyard is the House of the Pigeons itself, a long, multiroomed structure with a unique nine-gabled roof comb.

Far opposite the Pigeons Group is the North Group, consisting of a northern storied pyramid with an enclosed lower court surrounded by buildings on several levels (figs. 6, 97). Between the Pigeons and the North groups is a long concourse that supports several smaller structures and the

Fig. 7. Pyramid of the Magician, west side, seen from south end of Nunnery Quadrangle.

Stela Platform. The western boundary of this concourse is defined by the Cemetery Group, named for a set of low platforms bearing glyphic inscriptions and skull and bones and "death-eye" motifs (figs. 6, 11). These platforms lie within an amphitheater court with a dominant northern pyramid. On the west barrier mound is a temple with a perforated flying façade above the front wall (fig. 10).

Southeast of the House of the Governor is the Pyramid of the Old Woman, which also commands a courtyard framed by structures and mounds (figs. 6, 33–34). At the foot of and partly covered by the later pyramid is an earlier building with simple moldings, stucco-façade decoration, and a perforated roof comb. The later temple atop the pyramid apparently was never completed. South of the House of the Governor are edifices known as the Chimez and the Phallic Temple. The Chimez is a two-storied building with upper chambers resting on a solid masonry platform surrounded by lower rooms. The Phallic Temple is named for its distinctive cornice-level downspouts shaped like phalli.[7] Still farther south are the remains of an isolated portal vault, which may have formed a terminus for a causeway linking Uxmal with Kabah (fig. 94).[8]

At Uxmal the House of the Governor itself rests on a sequence of four platforms (figs. 1, 12–13, 57). The lowest platform measures 625 feet on the east by 570 feet on the north but is only about four feet high. The second platform is elevated well above the general level of the city and is sufficiently broad and expansive that it could have accommodated comfortably large crowds, processions, dances, or rituals. It is about 25 feet high, 540 feet long on the east, and 450 feet wide. The northwest corner of this platform has an extension that projects 50 feet to the west and supports the building known as the House of the Turtles (fig. 14). The plan of this great terrace was probably determined by the alignment ultimately planned for the House of the Governor. As will be shown, the House of the Governor was purposely oriented toward certain architectural

Fig. 8. Pyramid of the Magician,
façade of the Chenes-style
Temple (Temple IV) (after Seler
1917 : abb. 94).

Fig. 9. The Great Pyramid, from the northeast.

Fig. 10. Cemetery Group, western temples.

points of interest within Uxmal and on the south-eastern horizon.[9] The second platform roughly parallels the alignment of the building, indicating that virtually the entire complex must have been conceived as a unified architectural composition.

The western boundary of the second platform was adapted so that two smaller, earlier buildings could remain in use. One of these, Structure 1, faces north and has a tripartite Chenes-type plan consisting of six chambers (fig. 12, 15). It is 71 feet 6 inches long by 23 feet 5 inches wide. This building was partly covered by the second platform of the House of the Governor and is clearly an earlier edifice. It has construction features which connect it with the Chenes architectural style that flourished south of Uxmal, and is thought to be earlier than pure Puuc buildings.[10] The sculptural program, also of Chenes inspiration, consists of a dragon mouth framing the central doorway (fig. 15) and long-snouted masks at the corners of the upper façade (fig. 156). The sculptures relied more heavily on stucco for final detail than do those of the House of the Governor. Northwest of Structure 1 is Structure 2, which is also partly covered by the second platform of the House of the Governor. This building also has Chenes construction features and originally may have had a dragon-mouth entrance like that of Structure 1[11]

The only evidence of stairways leading to the top of the second platform is located near Structures 1 and 2. Immediately south of Structure 1 is a slight western extension of the second platform, which was possibly a stairway (fig. 12). East of Structure 2 is a sloping pile of debris, which may have been another stairway to the second platform.[12] No risers are now visible, but many facing stones which could have served as risers are piled at the base. These two stairways provided the only access to the second terrace, since there is no stairway on the eastern side. Thus the approach to the House of the Governor was indirect. One would have to ascend from the

Fig. 11. Cemetery Group, detail of Platform 3.

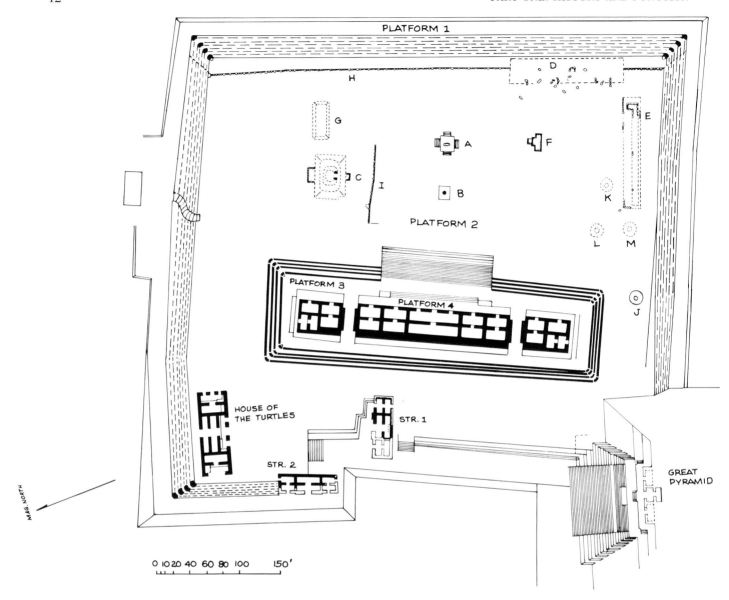

Fig. 12. Plan of platform system, House of the Governor (surveyed by Jeff Kowalski and Roy Whitehead).

rear and then walk around the north or south ends of the building before viewing the front façade.

Besides supporting the House of the Governor, the second platform also carries a number of smaller buildings and platforms. The best known of these is the exquisitely designed House of the Turtles, on the extension of the northwest corner (figs. 12, 14). This is a rectangular building, 96 feet long and 33 feet wide, composed of seven chambers. Three long rooms lie parallel to one another in the center, while two pairs of shorter transverse rooms are at the ends. The central rooms communicate with one another and have a single entrance on the north and

three on the south. At the east end are three doorways, and there were probably three doors on the west.[13] The south and east doorway groupings are carefully proportioned in balanced, hierarchical arrangements. In several of the rooms are low masonry benches.

Like the House of the Governor, the House of the Turtles is constructed with an interior core of lime concrete and superbly finished facing stones. It was undoubtedly built within a few years of the larger edifice. Although similar in construction, the House of the Turtles contrasts in the sobriety of its ornament. A plain wall rises from a simple rectan-

Fig. 13. Platform system, House of the Governor, from the Chenes-style Temple of the Pryamid of the Magician.

gular base. Between the sharply faceted three-part moldings the frieze consists of a continuous row of small columns. The structure owes its name to its only sculptures, a series of small turtles tenoned to the central member of the cornice.

The small extension of the second platform at the northwest corner supporting the House of the Turtles represents an accommodation made to the existing city plan of Uxmal, and was probably included to counterbalance the massive terrace of the Nunnery Quadrangle on the north. Since the intervening Ball Court has no end zones, the platforms of the Nunnery and the House of the Governor serve this function and could have been used as viewing stands.[14]

Directly in front of the House of the Governor is a small, radially symmetrical platform which supported a stone sculpture of a two-headed jaguar (fig. 12, Feature A). This monument was undoubtedly used as a throne by the ruler of Uxmal (figs. 16, 46).[15]

Between the jaguar sculpture and the House of the Governor is another low, quadrangular platform, about 16 inches high and 12 feet wide by 15 feet long, which supports a large, cylindrical

stone column known as the Picote (figs. 12, Feature B; 46; 54).[16] Although this column has occasionally been referred to as a phallic monument, there is no evidence to support the identification. Rather it seems to be an extremely large version of the plain, columnar-type altars common in the Puuc region.[17] A similar monument stands in front of the stairway leading to the platform supporting the Codz Poop at Kabah.

About 120 feet north-northeast of the Picote platform is a platform of moderate size that apparently supported a one-roomed building (fig. 12, Feature C). The platform is about 34 feet wide and 52 feet long and has low extensions on the north and south sides.[18] At the center of this platform is a small, ruined building about 20 feet long with some wall facing stones still standing and jambstones and cornerstones visible in the debris. There was a doorway on the south side and probably one on the north side as well. Stephens describes the discovery of two sculptured human heads in this building.[19]

At the south end of the eastern side of the second platform is a low platform about 30 feet wide, 130 feet long, and 3 feet high (fig. 12, Feature D).[20] This mound apparently supported a long building of

Fig. 14. House of the Turtles, from the southeast.

perhaps three rooms. Both on top and in front of the mound are jambstones and cylindrical column drums. This building was probably vaulted and apparently had an upper façade decorated with banded colonnettes and tau elements.

Along the southern border of the second terrace is a long, low mound about 3 feet high, 130 feet long, and 15 feet wide (fig. 12, Feature E, 44g). This platform is composed of two terraces. The lower is about 2 feet high, 15 feet wide, and 130 feet long. The upper is about 120 feet long by 4 feet 1 inch wide, with L-shaped extensions at the northeast and southeast corners. Ruppert and Smith describe this building as a house mound, and thus the upper terrace may be an interior bench.[21] The walls and roof must have been of perishable material, since no vault stones were discovered, and there is no evidence of masonry walls. Stephens describes a range of pedestals and fragments of columns in connection with this building, but he may have been referring to the columns and jambstones associated with Structure D.[22]

Between Feature E and the jaguar throne is a small, low, T-shaped platform which originally may have supported a columnar altar (fig. 12, Feature F).[23] This platform is about 7 inches high, 18 feet

east-west, and 16 feet north-south, and is constructed of cut-stone facing and a concrete core.

Feature G is a large mound of debris that appears to have been a structure. It is too destroyed for determination of its form without excavation. Feature H is a continuous line of facing stones that cross the eastern side of the second platform about 15 feet from the edge. These are considered in chapter 7. Feature I is a row of roughly faced stones which run east-west and form a low northern terrace. Toward the western end of this line is a small, semicircular grouping of stones whose function is unknown. Features J, K, L, and M are roughly circular sunken areas in the surface of the second platform. They are thought to be collapsed chultunes, artificial cisterns for the collection of rainwater. Feature N is a low, rectangular mound about 10½ feet east-west by 9 feet north-south (fig. 12).

The architect of the House of the Governor ensured that the building would be visible to the populace by raising a third long platform about 21 feet high, 370 feet long, and 90 feet wide (measured at the top) near the western edge of the second platform. This platform secures for the building a commanding height, scarcely inferior to that of the several temple pyramids at the site. Providing access

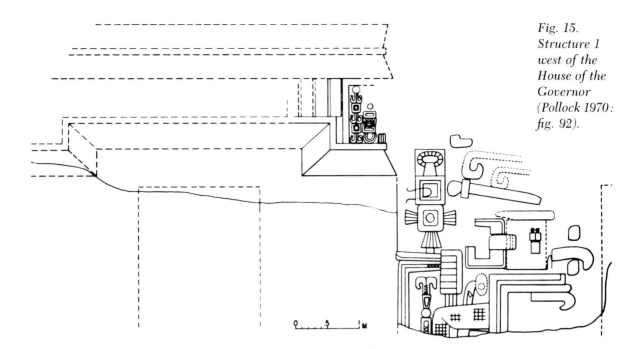

Fig. 15.
Structure 1
west of the
House of the
Governor
(Pollock 1970:
fig. 92).

Fig. 16. Jaguar throne on the second platform of the House of the Governor.

to the third platform is a broad, monumental stairway, whose ample proportions enhance the dignity of the surmounting structure. The transition between the stairway and the second terrace is softened by the widened treads of the lower three steps, a subtlety that increased the sense of connection between the upper and lower platforms (figs. 54, 55, 57). Refinements of this sort mark the House of the Governor as the product of a mature architectural tradition and a gifted architect. A fourth low building platform, lifting the House of the Governor a few feet higher, serves both as a firm foundation for the structure and as a walkway around the building (figs. 58, 59).

The sequence of platforms described above brings us to the house itself (figs. 1–4). The House of the Governor is architecture calculated to impress by external rather than internal effects. Most of the articulation, sculpture, and visual refinements are reserved for the outside of the building. The main element with which the Maya architect worked was the sculptural mass of sharply defined building blocks ordered in space. The building is composed of three bodies, which retain separateness while participating in an integrated composition. The separation into three bodies is emphasized by two tall transverse vaults. The unique aesthetic qualities of these vaults depend not solely on their grandiose dimensions but also on the fact that they were planned purposely to accentuate the three-part division of the façade by their striking contours and strong shadows (figs. 2, 16, 75–78).

In addition to the tripartite horizontal division the House of the Governor is also divided into a series of vertical registers. At the base is a podium or stylobate formed of raised bands framing alternating panels of plain masonry and engaged colonnettes (figs. 2, 3, 58). Above this the lower wall is smooth, broken only by the coffered, shadow-framed doorways. The doorways of the three pavilions mark the proportional groupings 1-2-7-2-1 and 1-2-2-3-2-2-1, the central three doorways providing entrance to the long middle chambers. The monumental eastern stairway marks a further rhythm of 3-5-3.

Both the medial and the cornice moldings of the House of the Governor consist of two outward-flaring courses separated by a rectangular string course, which is bound by a serpent interlace on the cornice (figs. 58, 173). These three-part moldings are boldly scaled and sharply cut. They cast strong shadows in the Yucatecan sunlight and bind the edifice together horizontally.

Between the medial and cornice moldings the upper façade of the House of the Governor is one of the most beautiful examples of Maya architectural sculpture extant. Thousands of separately carved stones cover the frieze with an elaborate array of motifs arranged in successive and interpenetrating layers (figs. 2–4, 54, 106, 107, 153, 173). The architect skillfully avoided letting this complex ornamentation destroy the clarity of the structure by clearly subordinating each stone and each motif to several dominant designs which govern the composition of the entire frieze. Latticework forms the background, while step frets mark diagonal rhythms. Long-snouted mask panels are stacked vertically at the corners and along the west, north, and south façades, while on the east they are also diagonally staggered in a unique manner to form five angular undulations across the frieze. The pyramidal outlines formed by the masks create canopies above a sequence of human figures who project farthest from the façade (figs. 54, 106–29). These are arranged hierarchically and culminate above the central doorway in a richly dressed figure seated against a background of diagonally tiered serpent bands (figs. 113–15).

CHAPTER 2

The Historiography of Uxmal
and the House of the Governor

UNLIKE many southern Maya cities, such as Tikal, Palenque or Yaxchilan, Uxmal has never been a truly "lost city"—references to the site are found in sources dating only about fifteen years after the conquest of Yucatan. One such reference occurs in the record of the Mani land treaty of 1557, the earliest example of the Maya language written in European script.[1] In 1557 the chiefs of the principal towns of the Xiu province of Mani, along with the rulers from several neighboring states, were called together for a meeting at Mani, the Xiu capital, in order to fix the boundaries of the province.[2] Several records of this Mani land treaty exist, including a document seen in the municipal archives of Mani by John Lloyd Stephens, who had a part of the text dealing with Uxmal translated and published. Accompanying the 1557 document was a record of a meeting held in 1556, as well as a map of the province of Mani on which Uxmal is located.[3] After listing the provincial and town governors in attendance at the meeting, and recording the places where boundaries were fixed, the document concludes ". . . Twenty-two is the number of the places marked, and they returned to raise new landmarks, by the command of the judge, Felipe Manriques, specially commissioned by his excellency the governor, when he arrived at Uxmal, accompanied by his interpreter, Gaspar Antonio [Chi]."[4]

The map accompanying these documents was copied and reproduced by Stephens. Uxmal appears toward the bottom, that is, west of Mani. The singular character of the site is conveyed in that it alone is not marked with a cross, which indicated that a town had been settled by the Spaniards. Uxmal, never occupied as a colonial town, is designated as a wholly Maya site by the roughly drawn Maya-style building that locates the ruin on the map.[5]

The Xiu Probanzas, which are family papers and claims of nobility on the part of the Xiu descendants, also contain a copy of the Mani land treaty of 1557, as well as a native map of the province (fig. 17). In large part this treaty parallels that discovered by Stephens, and it is thought to be a copy of the original Mani treaty made for the town of Yaxakumche (now a part of Oxkutzcab).[6] In addition, a transcript of the original document, mentioning Uxmal and accompanied by another copy of the map, was made on July 10, 1596. This version is known as the Mani Document, and forms part of the Crónica de Mani manuscript at Tulane University.[7] The map accompanying this document closely resembles that reproduced by Stephens, but omits the town of Ppencuyut.

Another early reference to Uxmal occurs in the Relación de Teav-Y-Tec y Tiscolum, written by Juan Bote in 1581.[8] This account, which will be examined further in chapter 4, provides important information regarding the early history and traditional founding of the city by the Xiu. The most complete sixteenth-century account of Uxmal is that of Fray Antonio de Ciudad Real, who accompanied Fray Alonso Ponce as general secretary on a tour of Yucatan in 1586.[9] Following a description of the Nunnery Quadrangle, Ciudad Real describes the House of the Governor as follows:

Besides these four buildings, there is on the south of them distant from them about an arquebus shot, another very large building built on a *mul* or hill made by hand, with abundance of buttresses on the corners, made of massive carved stones. The ascent of this *mul* is made

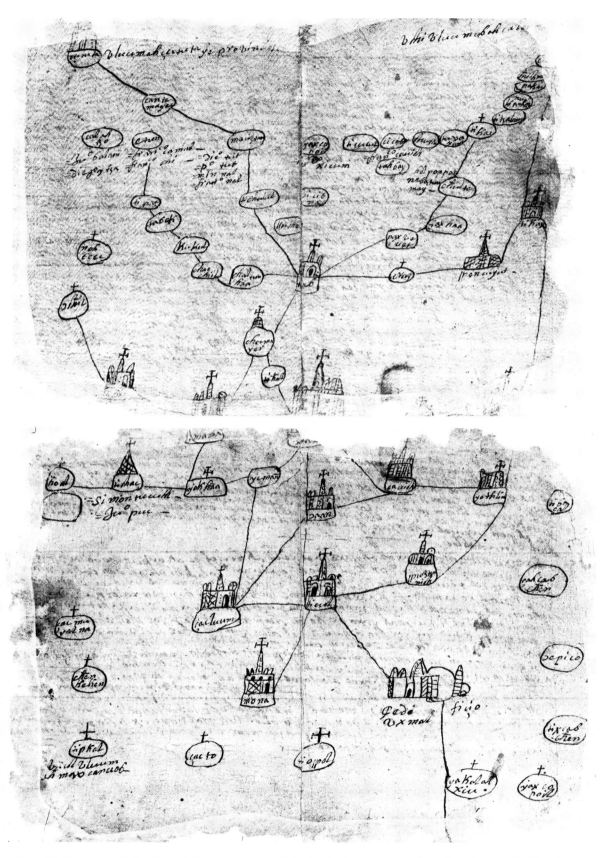

Fig. 17. Province of the Mani (photo courtesy of the Peabody Museum of Archaeology and Ethnology, Harvard University).

with difficulty, since the staircase by which the ascent is made is now almost destroyed. The building, which is raised on this *mul*, is of extraordinary sumptuousness and grandeur, and, like the others, very fine and beautiful. It has on its front, which faces the east, many figures and bodies of men and shields and of forms like the eagles which are found on the arms of the Mexicans, as well as certain characters and letters, which the Maya Indians used in old times—all carved with so great dexterity as surely to excite admiration. . . . There are in this building fifteen doors, of which eleven face the east, two on the west, and one each face the north and south, and within these doors there are twenty-four rooms arched like the others. Two of these rooms are in the northern end, and two others in the southern, while two are in the west front, and all the rest in the eastern front—all made with special accuracy and skill.[10]

Uxmal is mentioned several times in the Books of Chilam Balam of Mani and Tizimin, in which the settlement of the city is attributed to the Xiu, led by a ruler named Ah Suytok Tutul Xiu. These sources will be discussed further in chapter 4. In addition, the Chilam Balam of Chumayel also contains several references to Uxmal, its rulers, and its history.[11]

Pedro Sánchez de Aguilar, in his work on the idolatries of the Indians of Yucatan, published in 1639, refers to "the famous, great, and astounding edifices of stone and mortar, and hewn stone, and figures and statues of carved stone, which remain in *Oxumal* [Uxmal], and in *Chichiniza* [Chichen Itza], which may be seen today, and may be lived in."[12] He also suggests that these two sites had been Mexican fiefdoms for over six hundred years before the arrival of the Spaniards.

Stephens, in his search for historical materials relating to Uxmal, was able to procure the title papers of the Hacienda from Don Simon Peon, the Hacendado of Uxmal. An original deed of 1673 states that the Indians of Uxmal were "worshipping the devil in the ancient buildings which are there, having in them their idols, to which they burn copal, and performing other detestable sacrifices, as they are doing every other day notoriously and publicly."[13] This suggests that Uxmal continued to maintain an aura of sanctity, with its buildings used as shrines long after the abandonment of the site.

To Fray López de Cogolludo, who visited the ruins of Uxmal in the mid-seventeenth century, can be attributed the traditional names for the Nunnery Quadrangle and the House of the Governor. Following his description of the Nunnery ("a cloister, where these virgins lived"), he describes the House of the Governor as follows:

At the southern part of this edifice [the Nunnery] there is another which it is said were the dwelling of the lord of the land: it is not in the form of a cloister, but is made of the stone worked with the figures mentioned in the other, and there are many other smaller [houses] near here, which they say were the houses of the captains and principal lords.[14]

Cogolludo is the first writer to state specifically that the House of the Governor was the residence of a Maya lord, although Ciudad Real had stated that the ruins were formerly occupied, and had mentioned, with regard to the ring-shaped cordholders in the buildings of the Nunnery, that "the Indians say that from these rings those who lived in these buildings hung curtains and portieres."[15] Unfortunately, since Cogolludo gives no clear source for his statements, we cannot be certain whether this function of the House of the Governor represents an established native tradition or is substantially Cogolludo's own idea.[16]

During the nineteenth century many travelers journeyed to Central America exploring the Maya area and supplying descriptions of the ruins. Uxmal, being of relatively easy access from Mérida, became one of the required stops on these grand tours of Central American archaeology. Scientific knowledge of Uxmal increased during this time, as more travelers provided accurate descriptions of the buildings, accompanied by plans, drawings, and later by photographs. Accounts of the House of the Governor began to proliferate as these voyagers were impressed by the building's great size, superlative masonry, and abundance of stone sculpture.[17]

Among the earliest of the nineteenth century accounts of Uxmal is that furnished by Jean Frederic M. de Waldeck, who visited the site, which he renamed "Itzalane," in 1835. Waldeck claimed to have discovered Asiatic influence in the art of Uxmal, exemplified by the long-snouted masks that decorate the House of the Governor and other structures at the site. These he interpreted as elephant heads with curling trunks.[18] Waldeck concentrated on the Nunnery Quadrangle and the Pyramid of the Magician, and was unable to complete a drawing of the House of the Governor, although he located it on a rough map. He named the building the Temple of Fire, believing it to be "the great temple where the sacred fire was maintained by the virgins."[19] Although he expressed many such unfounded and fantastic notions, Waldeck correctly distinguished stylistic differences between the buildings of Uxmal and those of Palenque.[20]

In 1841 Baron Emmanuel de Friedrichstall, the

secretary of the Austrian diplomatic delegation to Mexico, made an exploration of the country during which he described and drew the monuments of Uxmal.[21] He briefly described the House of the Governor and its terrace system with subsidiary structures, and provided some measurements.[22]

The best of the early-nineteenth-century accounts of Uxmal and the House of the Governor is that of John Lloyd Stephens. His objective view of the ruins, accompanied by the accurate drawings of his artist-companion Frederick Catherwood, (fig. 1) stimulated an enduring interest in American archaeology, and spawned in the succeeding years a host of travelers' accounts of Uxmal, most of which rarely match the quality of Stephens's original work.

Stephens's first visit to Uxmal was in 1841 and is recounted in his book *Incidents of Travel in Central America, Chiapas, and Yucatan*. During this stay Stephens was able to view the House of the Governor, known locally as the "Casa del Gobernador":

which title, according to the naming of the Indians, indicates the principal building of the old city, the residence of the governor or the royal house. It is the grandest in position, the most stately in architecture and proportion, and the most perfect in preservation of all the structures remaining in Uxmal.[23]

Stephens measured the platforms and published the first plan of the building, as well as a drawing by Catherwood of a section of the façade.[24] He commented on the presence of smaller structures on the large platform of the House of the Governor, and also discovered a wooden lintel carved with hieroglyphic inscriptions in the outer chamber of the south end of the building.[25]

Stephens and Catherwood returned to Uxmal in 1843, during which time Stephens prepared the comprehensive account of the site that appears in his *Incidents of Travel in Yucatan*.[26] The party camped in the House of the Governor and thus Stephens had ample opportunity to observe the building and familiarize himself with its unique features. His measurements of the building are generally accurate, as are his descriptions of the interiors of the rooms.[27] Surprised by the great thickness of the rear wall of the building, Stephens determined to breach it to check for hidden passages, but discovered none. During this exploration he discovered imprints of a red-painted human hand in the mortar.[28]

Stephens decided to remove the hieroglyphic wooden lintel discovered during his earlier visit in the south end room of the building. The beam was

transported to the United States and exhibited in Catherwood's Panorama, where it was later destroyed by fire.[29] At this time Stephens also discovered the large, monolithic cylinder known as the *Picote* and unearthed the two-headed jaguar throne from a mound on the large terrace of the House of the Governor (fig. 16). He also remarked on the great number of long-snouted masks adorning the façades of the House of the Governor and the other principal buildings at Uxmal, and refuted Waldeck's theory that they represent elephants.[30]

Soon after *Incidents of Travel in Yucatan* appeared Frederick Catherwood published a series of splendid tinted engravings of various Maya ruins, including Uxmal.[31] Catherwood's drawings of both the central motif of the east façade and the east side of the southern transverse vault of the House of the Governor accurately document these features before the removal or destruction of some elements, and prior to the archaeological reconstructions undertaken by the Mexican government in this century.

Following the publication of Stephens's and Catherwood's books, numerous travelers made expeditions to Uxmal. Most provided descriptions of varying completeness, more or less accurate accounts of the ruin's historical position, opinions as the identity of the builders, and judgments of the architectural quality of the House of the Governor.[32]

In 1863 Eugène Viollet-le-Duc contributed an essay on ancient American architecture to Désiré Charnay's *Cités et Ruines Américaines*, in which Uxmal was discussed extensively.[33] Viollet-le-Duc's most notable hypothesis was that the latticework and colonnettes seen on northern Maya buildings represent stone versions of earlier wooden prototypes.[34] Charnay's own description of Uxmal in this same volume is brief and adds little to that of Stephens.[35] Charnay's greatest contributions were his photographs of Uxmal and other ruined cities. Two of these early photographs present a detailed view of the entire east façade of the House of the Governor, showing the condition of the building in the 1860s prior to any archaeological reconstruction (fig. 18).[36]

In 1867 Charles Etienne Brasseur de Bourbourg wrote several articles on the history and archaeology of Uxmal.[37] He postulated that the stone rings inside of the doorways of the House of the Governor were used to support wooden poles, from which hung fabric or mat-weave curtains. He also believed that the holes in the walls beneath the eaves served as ventilators, suggesting that the

Fig. 18. Unreconstructed eastern façade, House of the Governor, photographed prior to 1863 (after Charnay 1863: Plates 45–46).

building was a habitation (figs. 64, 71).[38] Brasseur was the first investigator to mention the fact that the large platform of the House of the Governor partly covers the remains of small vaulted apartments on the west side (Structures 1 and 2). He also mentions the presence of a stairway ascending to the House of the Turtles from the courtyard of these buildings.[39]

During the final decades of the nineteenth century, many more travelers visited and reported on Uxmal. For the most part they added nothing to the earlier descriptions of Stephens. At worst they were guilty of overly romanticizing the ruins and distorting their true history.[40] During the same period several other summaries of Uxmal were also provided, the best being those of Hubert Howe Bancroft and William H. Holmes.[41] Holmes was smitten with the grandeur of the House of the Governor, pronouncing it "the most important single structure of its class in Yucatan, and for that matter in America."[42] He was particularly intrigued by the two large transverse vaults. Although he found their form "novel and striking" he was unwilling to concede that they had been designed primarily either for architectural effect or for mere convenience in circumambulation, but rather that:

the only reasonable solution of the problem as to the function of these strange gateways is furnished by the theory that this structure was regarded as only one member—the first to be built—of a great quadrangle, and that the openings, not called for until the group was complete, were for the time being walled up.[43]

There is actually little evidence to support Holmes's idea. The presence of many smaller, contemporary structures on the second platform suggests that the House of the Governor was always intended to be the single dominant edifice (fig. 12). Further evidence for the aesthetic usage of the transverse vaults is presented in chapter 8.

During the twentieth century several Mesoamerican scholars turned their attention to Uxmal. Although some of these accounts continue the spirit of exploration and documentation begun in the preceding century, the best of them shed new light on the religious symbolism and iconography, art history, and political and cultural history of Uxmal.

Outstanding among the early twentieth-century studies of Uxmal are those of the great Mesoamericanist Eduard Seler.[44] His research on the site culminated in his monograph *Die Ruinen von Uxmal*, published in 1917. Informed by Seler's great erudition, this study remains one of the most detailed and scholarly accounts of the ruins. His descriptions of the major structures at Uxmal are scrupulously accurate, and are supplemented by numerous building plans and high-quality drawings and photographs (many of which were supplied to Seler by Teobert Maler) of architectural profiles and sculptural details (fig. 8). Seler devoted a large part of his study to a complete description of the House of the Governor and an analysis and interpretation of its architectural sculpture.[45] His descriptions, analyses, and illustrations are referred to in the following chapters.

Many other scholars also referred to Uxmal during the early twentieth century. George Byron Gordon's paper *The Serpent Motive in the Ancient Art of Central America and Mexico*, which was published in 1905 and includes an interpretation of the step-fret design, contains several references to Uxmal and the House of the Governor.[46] In 1909 Marshall Saville pointed out resemblances between the stone mosaic façades of Uxmal and those of Mitla in Oaxaca (fig. 88).[47] In the same year Sylvanus Morley made a thorough study of the Pigeons Complex at Uxmal.[48] Constantine George Rickard's volume *The Ruins of Mexico*, published in 1910, is important for its collection of early photographs of the House of the Governor.[49] Another work valuable for its photographic record is Henry Case's *Views on and of Yucatan*.[50] In 1911, Sylvanus G. Morley published an article, "Uxmal, the City of the Xius," in which he stated his basic ideas concerning the native history of Uxmal.[51]

Herbert J. Spinden, in "A Study of Maya Art" of 1913, makes numerous references to the sculptures and buildings of Uxmal.[52] In 1920, Spinden published an article on "The Stephens Sculptures from Yucatan" wherein he describes several sculptures taken from the House of the Governor and other buildings in Uxmal and Kabah. The pieces from the House of the Governor include several sections from a feathered headdress, as well as the torso and head of one of the human figures applied to the façade (figs. 19–21).[53] Two stucco portrait heads discovered at the House of the Governor were reported by Gann in 1918 (fig. 40). He also noted that the ruins of Uxmal were still venerated by the Maya of the eastern Yucatan peninsula, who refer to the "Noh Nah ti Uxmal," or "Great House of Uxmal" (possibly a reference to the House of the Governor) in their rain-making "Cha chac" ceremony.[54]

In 1921, Marshall Saville published his "Bibliographic Notes on Uxmal, Yucatan," in which he chronologically catalogued the principal references to the ancient city that had been written between 1556 and 1920. His catalogue is a valuable reference tool, since he provides summaries of and excerpts from many of the most important early accounts of the site.[55]

Danish archaeologist Frans Blom wrote several articles in the 1930s describing his researches at Uxmal.[56] Blom was the director of a Tulane University Expedition that reached Uxmal in 1930 and set up camp in the East Structure of the Nunnery.[57] No major monograph was published as a result of the Tulane expedition, but Blom nonetheless contrib-

uted to our knowledge of Uxmal. For example, he noted certain irregularities in the plan of the Nunnery Quadrangle which he believed were intentional, attributing them to architects who were "familiar with the rules of false perspective" and who arranged the buildings to make the courtyard appear deeper than it really is.[58] He also noted that the façades of the House of the Governor and other major buildings at Uxmal lean outward toward the top with what he termed a "negative batter" (figs. 101a–d).[59]

Perhaps Blom's most important discovery, made with the aid of the local caretaker Inez May, was the existence of the Stela Platform at Uxmal (figs. 6, 27). Blom noted that the presence of such stone monuments, which exhibit traits typical of the southern Maya stelae, such as bound captives, jade capes, and manikin scepters, might push the early history of Uxmal back to the sixth or seventh century. Despite his recognition of Uxmal's Late Classic occupation, Blom persisted in the then widely accepted belief that the House of the Governor was built by a "Xiu architect," and that it postdated the founding of Uxmal by the Xiu in A.D. 1007.[60]

In 1946 Morley devoted considerable attention to Uxmal in *The Ancient Maya*. Morley's greatest contribution was his exegesis of the history of Uxmal and its traditional founders, the Xiu. He viewed Uxmal's Puuc architecture as the product of a neoclassical Maya Renaissance that postdated the collapse of the Maya Old Empire, represented by the southern cities.[61] Following the historical framework supplied by the Books of Chilam Balam and other early sources, Morley attributed the foundation of Uxmal to the Xiu, a Maya-Mexican tribe that invaded Yucatan at the end of the tenth century. Although he placed excessive faith in the chronicles, while downplaying archaeological evidence that challenged his view of Uxmal as a New Empire city (e.g., the stelae discovered by Blom), Morley nevertheless furnished what has remained one of the most complete studies of the Xiu lineage in print.[62] His historical studies led him to conclude that the House of the Governor was the official residence and chief administrative center of the Xiu when they were the native rulers of Uxmal. He pronounced the House of the Governor "the most spectacular single building ever erected in the Americas in Pre-Columbian times."[63] The nature of the Xiu relationship to Uxmal is considered in detail in chapter 4.

One of the best recent discussions of the architecture of Uxmal from a stylistic and formal point of

Fig. 19 (left). Human figural sculpture from the east façade, House of the Governor (photo courtesy of the American Museum of Natural History, neg. 38617).

Fig. 20 (above). Section of a feather headdress and reptilian mask from the House of the Governor (photo courtesy of the American Museum of Natural History, neg. 38612).

Fig. 21. Headdress element with a central human skull from the east façade, House of the Governor (photo courtesy of the American Museum of Natural History, neg. 38614).

view is that of George Kubler in *The Art and Architecture of Ancient America*. He is the first scholar since Seler who has sought to develop a relative chronology for some of the principal structures at the site.[64] He views the House of the Governor as expanding upon architectural solutions developed at the Nunnery Quadrangle, and terms the building "the most refined and perhaps the last achievement of the architects of Uxmal."[65] Kubler's architectural chronology will be reexamined in chapter 3.

In 1965, Marta Foncerrada de Molina published *La Escultura Arquitectónica de Uxmal*, an excellent synthesis of what was then known archaeologically of the site, and the first sustained discussion of the architectural sculpture and iconography of Uxmal since Seler's study of 1917.[66] Her work provides an important basis for the discussion in several of the following chapters.

Throughout the twentieth century a series of reconnaissances, excavations, and reconstruction projects have been undertaken at Uxmal by Mexican archaeologists including Juan Martínez Hernández, Eduardo Noguera, Eduardo Martínez Cantón, Manuel Cirerol Sansores, José Erosa Peniche, Alberto Ruz Lhuillier, César Sáenz, Barbara Konieczna and Pablo Mayer Guala, and Alfredo Barrera Rubio. Their work and interpretations are considered throughout the text and in an appendix.

Several of the most recent discussions of the architecture of Uxmal have emphasized the principles that governed the layout and planning of the city. In his book *Die Zeremonialzentren der Maya* of 1971 Horst Hartung noted that the House of the Governor is aligned toward the first landing of the Pyramid of the Magician, and that a line drawn southeastward from the central doorway of the House of the Governor and across the jaguar throne on the great platform connects with a small mound on the horizon (fig. 46).[67] George Andrews in his *Maya Cities: Placemaking and Urbanization* suggests that the House of the Governor, the House of the Turtles, the Ball Court, and the Nunnery Quadrangle form a closely coordinated architectural complex. Thus, the layout of the Nunnery, with its elevated North Structure, was apparently designed so that the effect of a two-storied edifice would be obtained from a vantage point on the second platform of the House of the Governor.[68] Andrews also identifies the House of the Governor as the focal point of an architectural composition framed by the portal of the South Structure of the Nunnery (fig. 84).[69]

The House of the Governor is also referred to in H. E. D. Pollock's 1980 survey of Puuc architecture. His treatment of the building is brief and is important chiefly for his discussion of stone monuments associated with the structure. In addition, Pollock's volume contains a comprehensive discussion of Puuc architectural chronology that is helpful in dating the House of the Governor.[70]

CHAPTER 3

Puuc Chronology and the Dating of the House of the Governor

THE Maya word *puuc*, meaning "low range of hills," is applied specifically to the hills that cross the northern Yucatan peninsula beginning near Champoton on the west coast, reaching northeastward to Maxcanu, and from there extending southeastward toward Lake Chikankanab. In the rolling region encompassed by the Puuc hills are a host of Maya sites, the most important of which include Oxkintok, Chacmultun, Labna, Sayil, Kabah, and Uxmal. Many of the sites are characterized by a remarkably homogeneous style of architecture given the name Puuc.

The House of the Governor is the superlative example of Puuc architecture. To place it properly in time we must determine the chronological position of Puuc architecture generally, and within that broad framework determine whether the House of the Governor is an early or a late building. The exact chronological location of Puuc architecture has remained a controversial subject, but we will attempt to establish its correct date. First we will outline the essential traits of Puuc architecture and review the dates assigned to the style in several cultural-historical studies of Yucatan. Next we will review information provided by ceramics, hieroglyphic dates, sculptural style, radiocarbon dates, and studies of Early versus Late Puuc-style buildings to fix Puuc architecture in time. Finally we will consider a number of recent articles that have developed a new archaeological synthesis for the Puuc region.

The distinctive qualities of Puuc architecture are recognizable both in construction techniques and decorative treatment. In contrast to the block-wall and slab-vault construction of Early period architecture,[1] Puuc buildings have a core of lime and rubble concrete faced with finely-cut wall and vault stones (figs. 2, 64). The monolithic concrete core is the load-bearing portion of the building, so that the facing stones may fall off without causing collapse. The wall stones are well squared, pecked, and ground smooth. Joints are tight and coursing is level so no spalling is necessary. Because of the even surface, little stucco was required to cover the façades. Puuc vault stones often have a distinctive boot shape, with an inclined outer face conforming to the angle of the soffit and a tapering tenon that anchors the stone in the vault mass. Puuc vaults are not truly corbeled, since the boot-shaped stones have no bearing surface (fig. 64).[2]

The exteriors of Puuc buildings differ markedly from those of their predecessors (figs. 2, 23). In contrast to the simple one- or two-member moldings of the Early period, Puuc medial and cornice moldings often consist of two beveled members separated by a rectangular course, known as an *atadura* or binder molding.[3] More elaborate moldings of up to five or six members, sometimes including engaged colonnettes or other design elements are also known.[4] Puuc upper façades are usually vertical or, as at Uxmal and the House of the Governor, negatively battered (sloped outward slightly toward the top). Sculptural decoration was occasionally placed on the lower walls, but was normally concentrated on the upper façade, forming a contrast between the flat lower walls and the richly decorated upper zone (figs. 2, 85–87). This façade sculpture is of precarved separate stone elements which were assembled on the walls to form repetitive geometric stone mosaics. Common motifs include stepped frets, X-shaped stones combined to form lattices, engaged columns, banded columns

Fig. 22.
Sites in the
northern Maya
area.

or spools, and a number of elements used to create the typical long-snouted masks, which were often placed as accents at the corners of buildings or above doorways.[5] Although naturalistic sculpture in stone or stucco is found on some Puuc buildings, including the House of the Governor, the bulk of the sculpture is composed of a multiplanar grid of geometric elements designed to conform to an archi-

tectural aesthetic and to form sharp patterns in the hard sunlight of Yucatan.[6]

Puuc architecture, though concentrated in the area south of the Puuc hills, is distributed throughout most of the northern third of the Yucatan peninsula. Puuc-style buildings have been found in much of the northern plains region, and in the northern section of Campeche, as well as in the

Puuc region proper. On the East Coast the Puuc style is virtually absent, although some structures on Cozumel Island apparently copied Puuc decorative elements and construction techniques.[7] Pollock and Andrews IV have pointed out that although the border between the Puuc zone and the Chenes zone to the south is often indicated by a line, the two styles actually overlap geographically, with some sites (Uxmal among them) possessing both Chenes and Puuc buildings.[8]

From the early part of this century until the 1940s, concepts of Puuc chronology were dominated by the ideas of S. G. Morley, whose framework for Yucatan culture history can be summarized as follows. The historical and legendary accounts of Yucatan refer to the peopling of the peninsula by two migrations or "descents"—one from the east and one from the west. Utilizing the then-known Initial Series monuments in Yucatan, Morley constructed two routes by which the southern Maya, who were assumed to have carved the Initial Series dates, entered and colonized the peninsula. Despite the fact that dates from ten sites in the north spanned the period A.D. 455–909, Morley discounted the importance of the area and viewed it as peripheral to the Peten centers.[9]

Eventually the "Old Empire" Maya were thought to have abandoned the central area and gradually moved northward, establishing themselves en route in the Rio Bec and Chenes sites. Upon their arrival in the north, which coincided with the Toltec intrusion at Chichen Itza, they initiated a resurgence of Maya culture with Uxmal, Chichen Itza and Mayapan sharing power in the "New Empire." Relying heavily on the chronicles, Morley thus viewed Puuc architecture as the product of the "Maya Renaissance" during the League of Mayapan (A.D. 997–1194). He attributed the foundation of Uxmal to the Xiu in Katun 2 Ahau (A.D. 987–1007) and believed that "the Maya Renaissance reached its most magnificent expression at Uxmal, in the Palace of the Governors."[10]

As will be seen in chapter 4, Morley's dating of Puuc architecture and the House of the Governor relied principally on legendary and historical sources and conflicts with current archaeological evidence.

Sir J. Eric S. Thompson proposed a cultural-historical framework for Yucatan which differed considerably from that of Morley, particularly in its placement of Puuc architecture. He divided northern Maya history into four main periods: the Formative (before A.D. 320), the Initial Series (A.D. 320–900), the Mexican (A.D. 987–1204) and the Mexican Absorption (A.D. 1204–1540).[11] Unlike Morley, Thompson relied solely on archaeological data for his discussions of the Formative and Initial Series periods. He also relied more heavily on such data in his discussion of the Mexican period at Chichen Itza, although utilizing the chronicles as well. Thompson defined five regional styles in Yucatan that could be associated with the Initial Series or Classic period in the southern lowlands: Early Peten, Puuc, Chichen Maya, Rio Bec, and Chenes.[12] The Puuc, Chenes, and Rio Bec styles possess architectural and decorative characteristics so closely related that Thompson thought it impossible to study them as isolated entities. The Early Peten style differs in showing analogies with monuments in the southern lowlands, while the Puuc-related architecture of Chichen Itza was termed Chichen Maya because of minor differences in style and masonry.[13] Other scholars consider Chichen Maya style to be merely a localized variant of Puuc architecture.[14] Thompson set the chronological limits of the Puuc style from between 9.10.0.0.0 (A.D. 633) to 10.8.0.0.0 (A.D. 987), noting that the lack of X-Fine Orange and Plumbate pottery at Puuc sites seemed to indicate that they were abandoned before the beginning of the Mexican period at Chichen Itza.[15]

The work of E. W. Andrews IV at Dzibilchaltun provided the basis for a new chronological framework for northern Yucatan.[16] Stratigraphic studies led Andrews to posit four major cultural-historical periods at Dzibilchaltun, which were then extended to northern Yucatan as a whole. These were called the Formative, Early, Florescent, and Decadent periods (table 1). Andrews IV's Early period generally corresponds to the Classic period in the southern lowlands. According to Andrews IV, Morley's earlier view of northern Yucatan as having been largely unoccupied and culturally peripheral until "New Empire" times is incorrect, since during the Early period many northern centers rose to a high level of culture.[17]

During the first phase of the Early period (EPI), from A.D. 20 to 330 (or A.D. 280 to 590),[18] major architectural projects were undertaken, including two of the largest structures known to have been built by the Maya, the pyramids of Izamal and Dzilam. The Temple of the Stucco Façade at Acanceh was dated to this time, as was the complex-profiled pyramid at the same site. Early period architecture at Oxkintok can be dated by the 9.2.0.0.0 (A.D. 475) lintel found in Structure 3C6.[19]

Table 1. *Andrews IV's Placement of Major Historical Periods in Northern Yucatan According to Spinden and Goodman-Martínez-Thompson Correlations*

MAYA CALENDAR	CORRELATION AT APPROX. 12.9.0.0.0	GREGORIAN CALENDAR	CORRELATION AT APPROX 11.16.0.0.0	MAYA CALENDAR
12.15.0.0.0	COLONIAL PERIOD	A.D. 1600	COLONIAL PERIOD	12. 0.0.0.0
12.10.0.0.0	DECADENT PERIOD Second Phase (Post-Monumental)	1500	DECADENT PERIOD Second Phase (Post-Monumental)	11.15.0.0.0
12. 5.0.0.0		1400		11.10.0.0.0
12. 0.0.0.0	DECADENT PERIOD First Phase (Mayapan)	1300	DECADENT PERIOD First Phase (Mayapan)	11. 5.0.0.0
11.15.0.0.0		1200		11. 0.0.0.0
11.10.0.0.0	TRANSITION (Black-On-Cream)	1100	TRANSITION (Black-On-Cream)	10.15.0.0.0
			FLORESCENT PERIOD Second Phase (Modified)	
11. 5.0.0.0	FLORESCENT PERIOD Second Phase (Modified)	1000	FLORESCENT PERIOD First Phase (Pure)	10.10.0.0.0
11. 0.0.0.0		900		10. 5.0.0.0
10.15.0.0.0		800	TRANSITION (Tepeu 3?)	10. 0.0.0.0
10.10.0.0.0	FLORESCENT PERIOD First Phase (Pure)	700	EARLY PERIOD Second Phase (Tepeu 1-2)	9.15.0.0.0
10. 5.0.0.0		600		9.10.0.0.0
10. 0.0.0.0	TRANSITION (Tepeu 3?)	500		9. 5.0.0.0
9.15.0.0.0		400	EARLY PERIOD First Phase (Tzakol)	9. 0.0.0.0
9.10.0.0.0	EARLY PERIOD Second Phase (Tepeu 1-2)	300		8.15.0.0.0
9. 5.0.0.0		200	TRANSITION (Matzanel)	8.10.0.0.0
9. 0.0.0.0	EARLY PERIOD First Phase (Tzakol)	100		8. 5.0.0.0
8.15.0.0.0		0		8. 0.0.0.0
8.10.0.0.0	TRANSITION (Matzanel ?)	100	DZIBILCHALTUN "FORMATIVE" Phase III	7.15.0.0.0
8. 5.0.0.0	DZIBILCHALTUN "FORMATIVE" Phase III			7.10.0.0.0
8. 0.0.0.0		300		7. 5.0.0.0
7.15.0.0.0	DZIBILCHALTUN "FORMATIVE" Phase IIB	400	DZIBILCHALTUN "FORMATIVE" Phase IIB	7. 0.0.0.0
7.10.0.0.0		500		6.15.0.0.0
7. 5.0.0.0	DZIBILCHALTUN "FORMATIVE" Phase IIA	600	DZIBILCHALTUN "FORMATIVE" Phase IIA	6.10.0.0.0
7. 0.0.0.0		700		6. 5.0.0.0
6.15.0.0.0	DZIBILCHALTUN "FORMATIVE" Phase I	800	DZIBILCHALTUN "FORMATIVE" Phase I	6. 0.0.0.0
6.10.0.0.0		900		5.15.0.0.0
6. 5.0.0.0		1000		5.10.0.0.0
6. 0.0.0.0		B.C.		5. 5.0.0.0

SOURCE: after Andrews IV 1965b: Table 4.

The second phase of the Early period (EPII) corresponds to Tepeu 1 and 2 at Uaxactun, lasting from about A.D. 330 to 540 (or A.D. 590 to 800). During this phase slateware pottery and vaulted architecture appeared at the northern plains city of Dzibilchaltun and the site began its major period of growth (figs. 23, 154). Elsewhere in the north, Maya culture continued to develop in refinement, and cities begun in the first phase of the Early period, such as Oxkintok and Acanceh, continued to thrive.[20]

Succeeding the Early period was the Florescent

Fig. 23. Structure 57, Dzibilchaltun.

period, divided into two phases called Pure Florescent and Modified Florescent. According to Andrews IV, the Pure Florescent period either began about A.D. 900 and lasted into the eleventh century (GMT correlation) or began shortly after A.D. 600 and lasted until about A.D. 900 (Spinden correlation),[21] the latter being preferred by Andrews IV. The Pure Florescent might also be called the Puuc period, for this was the time when Puuc architecture characterized much of the northern part of Yucatan. Although he recognized a transition between them, Andrews IV defined Puuc and Early period architecture as two separate traditions.[22]

Andrews IV's chronology differs from that of Thompson by viewing Puuc architecture as almost wholly post-Initial Series in date.[23] His placement of the Pure Florescent period was not based primarily on inscriptional evidence, but on combined ceramic and architectural data from Dzibilchaltun. According to Andrews IV, trade ceramics show that

the second phase of the Early period at Dzibilchaltun ended at about the same time as the Tepeu 2 phase in the Peten, placed at 10.0.0.0.0 (A.D. 570 or 830). Following this he allowed for a period of architectural transition of about one hundred years, during which time there was a gradual modification from block wall to veneer wall construction, with stucco façade decoration gradually replaced by cut-stone elements. By the end of this transitional phase at Dzibilchaltun the late Tepeu trade pottery had ceased.[24] According to Andrews IV the lack of Tepeu wares in association with Pure Florescent architecture is paralleled in the Puuc region, which indicates that the southern cities were abandoned before the Puuc architectural style crystallized.

In Andrews IV's scheme the Pure Florescent period was succeeded by the Modified Florescent period between A.D. 900 and 1050. During this time there was a strong wave of influence from central Mexico, probably stemming from Tula, Hidalgo. A group of Mexican highlanders known as the Toltecs apparently established themselves at Chichen Itza through force of arms, and from there exerted political control over much of the northwestern Yucatan peninsula. Andrews IV suggests that the Puuc cities were abandoned as the result of this Toltec intrusion.[25] The exact nature of the "Toltec Empire" is open to question, but it seems certain that they enforced their will on the local Maya with military might. In the sculpture of this time at Chichen Itza the image of the warrior abounds, replacing the ruler figures or gods as a focus of attention. Accompanying this is a shifted emphasis from presentations of individual figures to serial group arrangements.[26] Various other Toltec architectural innovations include an expanded use of colonnades, the use of a battered basal zone, and serpent columns.[27]

Andrews IV calls this period Modified Florescent because he believes that, although the Mexican invaders of Chichen Itza brought a number of formal and symbolic motifs, they brought no craftsmen and utilized local artisans to carry out their programs. Thus surface forms were altered, but the craft techniques remained the same. For example, the Modified Florescent buildings of Chichen Itza employ a concrete core and cut-stone facing that is a continuation of Puuc practice.[28]

The succeeding Decadent period lasted from A.D. 1200 to 1540. Andrews IV viewed this as a time when Early period traditions reasserted themselves in Yucatan following the collapse of Chichen Itza. Filling the power vacuum was Mayapan, which controlled the northern plains, but which was itself destroyed about 1440. The following hundred years witnessed the political fragmentation of Yucatan into a number of small, warring provinces.[29]

Before examining specific categories of evidence concerning Puuc dating, we will review opinions of the two art historians, Kubler and Foncerrada de Molina, and consider the extent to which they conform to any of the chronological frameworks mentioned above.

In his 1962 survey of pre-Columbian art Kubler at times seemed willing to agree with the opinions of Thompson, but remained acutely aware of the chronological dilemma forced by Andrews IV's studies. He viewed the principal eastern Puuc ruins, including Uxmal, as having flourished during the two or three centuries before A.D. 1000,[30] but favored the Spinden correlation and the chronology proposed by Andrews IV. Kubler accepted the Cycle 9 and early Cycle 10 dates proposed for Puuc

stelae, but suggested that they might not be coeval with Puuc architecture and pottery, concluding that:

The radiocarbon dates . . . allow a correlation equating 10.3.0.0.0 with the opening decades of the seventh century, and they allow a reasonable duration for the architectural and ceramic forms of the Puuc style, without driving their date far back into Cycle 9. Our chronology, by the simple device of calling the last 300 years of Initial Series inscriptions "mid-Classic," and by retaining from orthodox chronology a Puuc period equivalent to the "Late Classic," recognizes both the stylistic autonomy of Puuc architecture and its post-Initial Series and pre-Toltec position.[31]

In the revised edition of his book Kubler's viewpoint shifts back toward that of Thompson. Although he still refers to the radiocarbon evidence supporting the alternative Spinden correlation, he abandons his "mid-Classic" placement of the Puuc Initial Series monuments and places the Puuc period coeval with the "Late Classic." This recognizes the stylistic independence of Puuc architecture while confirming its contemporaneity with the stelae and its pre-Toltec position.[32]

Marta Foncerrada's placement of Puuc architecture basically accords with that of Thompson, except she prefers to push the beginnings of Puuc architecture into the sixth century on the basis of radiocarbon dates and stratigraphy at Uxmal. Her key piece of evidence is a date of A.D. 569 ± 50 from a wooden lintel in the Lower West Temple of the Pyramid of the Magician (fig. 7).[33] This lintel is found in a pure Puuc-style building, and Foncerrada asserts that "in situating the evolved Puuc style in the sixth century, it fills the temporal vacuum between the epoch of the 9.2.0.0.0 (A.D. 475) lintel of Oxkintok and the beginning of Puuc architecture in the cities of the north of Yucatan."[34]

Many other scholars doubt that fully developed Puuc architecture began to be built as early as Foncerrada suggests. The validity of her arguments will be examined further in sections that follow.

The archaeological and art historical surveys of Morley, Thompson, Andrews IV, Kubler, and Foncerrada have provided several broad frameworks for the chronological placement of Puuc architecture. In order to test the merits of each it is necessary to examine in detail the dates for Puuc architecture and the House of the Governor indicated by ceramics, hieroglyphic inscriptions, sculptural style, radiocarbon dates, and comparisons of early and late Puuc-style buildings.

Puuc Ceramics

Ceramic studies carried out in northern Yucatan tend to support a chronological placement for Puuc architecture from between about A.D. 700 to 987, with the style's beginnings somewhat less certain than its end. Within this development there is evidence that the House of the Governor and similar Classic Puuc buildings date from between A.D. 800 to 950.

One of the most complete studies of Yucatan ceramics, including those of Uxmal, appeared in George Brainerd's *The Archaeological Ceramics of Yucatan* of 1958. He divided the culture history of Yucatan into the following periods: Formative (1500 B.C.–A.D. 100), Regional (A.D. 278–751), Florescent (A.D. 672–889/987), Mexican (A.D. 889/987-Conquest) (table 2).[35] Brainerd found that the pottery from the Puuc sites is remarkably homogeneous, with only a few sherds belonging to non-Florescent wares, and correlated this with the architectural uniformity of the region.[36] He believed that the slatewares of the Florescent period, which characterize the pottery assemblage of the Puuc centers, originated at a time when Regional monochromes were still the most common wares in other parts of Yucatan, and that there was an overlap between the two.[37] This suggests that Puuc architecture may have begun earlier in the Puuc region proper and then replaced other styles subsequently. Brainerd placed the major occupation of the Puuc cities (Kabah, Labna, Sayil, Uxmal) between A.D. 700 and 1000 and found no evidence for occupation in the Mexican period at any site.[38] He believed that "the rarity of [Peten] tradeware and of recognizable foreign traits may reflect the leading cultural position of the Puuc during this time period, at least in the Maya area."[39] This differs from and seems preferable to Andrews IV's idea that the absence of Peten tradewares indicates the post-Initial Series position of Puuc architecture.

A more recent discussion of Puuc ceramics appears in Robert Smith's *The Pottery of Mayapan* of 1971. He named the predominant ceramic assemblage represented at Uxmal and other Puuc sites the Cehpech complex. Smith placed the Cehpech complex from A.D. 800 to 1000, correlating with Tepeu 3 in the Peten.[40] During this time the principal wares in use at Uxmal were Puuc (Florescent Unslipped), Puuc (Florescent Medium) Slate, Thin Slate, Puuc Red (Florescent Medium and Thin Red) and Cauich Coarse-cream (Holactun Slateware).[41] Associated with this complex are two types

of Fine-Orangeware, Balancan (Puuc Fine Orangeware Z-type) and Altar (Y-Fine Orangeware), both of which are tradewares. These tradewares are important because they indicate which regions of Mesoamerica were in regular contact with northern Yucatan and Uxmal. The Balancan group is moderately well represented at Uxmal and is known to have originated in eastern Tabasco of southwestern Campeche. The Altar group is found in smaller quantity at Uxmal, is found occasionally at Uaxactun, and more abundantly at Altar de Sacrificios and Seibal.[42] Of 33,467 sherds collected, only a few were earlier than Cehpech, while only four sherds were attributed to the Sotuta complex, representative of the Toltec period at Chichen Itza. Smith concluded from this that the Toltecs never occupied Uxmal, although the presence of the feathered serpent in its architectural sculpture suggests some sort of Mexican influence.[43]

Uxmal ceramics have also been studied by the Mexican archaeologists engaged in reconstruction and excavation. According to Ruz, ochre slateware was the most common pottery found in all levels of Structure 1 west of the House of the Governor (figs. 12, 15), No polychrome was found, although some of the slateware forms recall Tepeu shapes.[44] Ruz suggested that the small sample of ceramics found on the surface and within the construction of the Uxmal Ball Court "reflect a typically Puuc period, prior to the Toltec phase in Yucatan." Two fragments of Fine Orangeware found at the Ball Court were believed to correspond to semispherical bowls of the Z-Fine Orange type (fig. 99).[45]

According to Sáenz, the ceramics encountered in explorations in the base of the Pyramid of the Magician date from the sixth to the tenth centuries. However, most of the pottery corresponded to the Puuc period (A.D. 800–1000).[46] This exploration also recovered several fragments of Z-Fine Orangeware and Fine Graywares. Sáenz also states that all types of ceramics from the Cehpech complex appeared in the explorations of the Great Pyramid. A few sherds of Fine Orange and Plumbate pottery were encountered also.[47] Although Plumbate pottery occurs sporadically in the ceramics of Uxmal, it appears in such limited amounts that Sáenz believes it arrived at the site through trade rather than as the result of a Toltec occupation.[48]

Further ceramic evidence for the dating of Puuc architecture comes from Dzibilchaltun, where Tepeu 2 pottery has been associated with Early period architecture. Ceramic associations at Structure 57 suggest that Early period II architecture con-

Table 2. *Comparative Chronological Chart, Northern Maya Lowlands, as Revised by Andrews V*

GREGORIAN CALENDAR	NORTHERN MAYA LOWLANDS CULTURE PERIODS	DZIBILCHALTUN CERAMIC COMPLEXES	G. W. BRAINERD CERAMIC STAGES (1958)	R. E. SMITH CERAMIC COMPLEXES (1971)	TIKAL	PALENQUE	MAYA LONG COUNT
1600	COLONIAL		COLONIAL	CHAUACA			12. 0.0.0.0
1500	DECADENT (LATE POSTCLASSIC)	CHECHEM		CHIKINCHEL			11.15.0.0.0
1400			LATE (MAYAPAN)	TASES			11.10.0.0.0
1300							11. 5.0.0.0
1200			MEXICAN MIDDLE	HOCABA			11. 0.0.0.0
1100	MODIFIED FLORESCENT (EARLY POSTCLASSIC)	ZIPCHE 2 / 1	EARLY (TOLTEC CHICHEN)	SOTUTA	? CABAN	? POST-BALUNTE	10.15.0.0.0
1000	Coast-East → Puuc						10.10.0.0.0
900	PURE FLORESCENT (TERMINAL CLASSIC)	COPO 2	(PUUC)	CEHPECH			10. 5.0.0.0
800	Puuc → North	1	FLORESCENT		EZNAB	BALUNTE	10. 0.0.0.0
700	EARLY PERIOD II (LATE CLASSIC)			(TEPEU 2) MOTUL	IMIX	MURCIELAGOS	9.15.0.0.0
600			(CHENES)	(TEPEU 1)	IK	OTOLUM	9.10.0.0.0
500	EARLY PERIOD I (EARLY CLASSIC)	PIIM	REGIONAL	COCHUAH (TZAKOL)	MANIK	MOTIEPA	9. 5.0.0.0
400							9. 0.0.0.0
300							8.15.0.0.0
200	LATE FORMATIVE	XCULUL 2 / 1	FORMATIVE	?	CIMI	PICOTA	8.10.0.0.0
100 A.D.						PRE-PICOTA	
0 B.C.					CAUAC	?	
100		KOMCHEN		TIHOSUCO (CHICANEL)			
200					CHUEN		
300	MIDDLE FORMATIVE	2			TZEC		
400							
500		NABANCHE					
600					EB		
700		1					
800							

NOTE: This chart follows a correlation of Maya and Christian calendars at 11.16.0.0.0.
SOURCE: after Andrews IV and Andrews V 1980: Table 3.

tinued to be constructed at Dzibilchaltun until about A.D. 800 (fig. 23).[49] Early period II buildings seem to date to the end of Tepeu 2, while Puuc structures, in addition to lacking Tepeu 2 trade polychromes in primary association, also contain several types of pottery not associated with the Early period II structures. This indicates to Andrews V that Puuc architecture at Dzibilchaltun postdates Tepeu 2 and began after A.D. 800.[50] This position basically accords with that of Andrews IV, who also argued that Dzibilchaltun ceramics show Florescent architecture to be a wholly post-Tepeu 2 phenomenon. The main difference is that Andrews IV thought that Puuc architecture at Dzibilchaltun began only after a 100-year long transitional period and was substantially post-Tepeu 3, not beginning until about 10.3.0.0.0 (A.D. 889) to 10.5.0.0.0 (A.D. 928).[51] Andrews V does not believe that a long transitional period is necessary, and therefore places the inception of Puuc architecture at Dzibilchaltun at 10.0.0.0.0 (A.D. 830) (table 2).[52]

The scarcity of Classic southern polychromes associated with Pure Florescent buildings at Dzibilchaltun is paralleled by the dearth of these tradewares in major eastern Puuc centers such as Uxmal. It is not quite accurate to say that no Tepeu ceramics were found at Uxmal, since a few Late Classic sherds have been identified by Smith and Sáenz, and since Smith mentions Late Classic sherds appearing beneath the platform of the House of the Governor.[53] The general absence of the tradewares is explained in part by Brainerd's suggestion that the rising political fortunes of the Puuc cities made importation of Peten wares unnecessary. Nevertheless, such trade ceramics are so rare at Uxmal and Kabah that Andrews V has suggested "the only tenable argument is that although Dzibilchaltun lags slightly behind the southern Puuc sites, the majority of buildings constructed in the Puuc style is post-10.0.0.0.0."[54] This would indicate that the House of the Governor was built sometime after A.D. 830.

The ceramics not only indicate that Pure Florescent architecture, such as the House of the Governor, is substantially post-A.D. 800, but also suggests that the cities were abandoned before A.D. 1000. Very few sherds of Plumbate or X-Fine Orangeware have been found in any of the Puuc centers. These wares are associated with the Modified Florescent Sotuta ceramic complex at Chichen Itza, dated by Smith at A.D. 1000–1200. This absence of Mexican-period pottery is generally interpreted as evidence that the Puuc architectural tradition had disappeared and its centers were depopulated before A.D. 1000.[55]

Puuc Epigraphy

Compared with the abundant dated, stone stelae, altars, and lintels at southern Maya sites, monuments with legible calendar dates in the Puuc region and northern Yucatan are fairly scarce. However, known inscriptions do provide a broad chronological framework and support the idea that the Puuc style began during the Late Classic and continued to flourish sometime through the Terminal Classic. Key dates come from Oxkintok, Xcalumkin, Chichen Itza, Labna, Nohpat, and Uxmal. The inscriptions indicate a placement of Classic Puuc buildings such as the House of the Governor in the first quarter of Cycle 10 (c. A.D. 830–928).

To begin we will survey some of the dates pertaining to the Early period in Yucatan. The best known of these is the 9.2.0.0.0 Initial Series from the lintel in Structure 3C6 at Oxkintok. Early period dates from other sites such as Coba, Tulum, and Ichpaatun run from between 9.6.10.0.0 to 9.12.10.0.0 (A.D. 564–682). These dates probably do not cover the entire duration of Early period architecture in every area of Yucatan, since the ceramic evidence from Dzibilchaltun indicates this tradition was maintained on the northern plains until the end of Tepeu 2 (c. A.D. 800). However, they do furnish a rough indication of the period when block masonry and slab vault construction was the dominant style in the peninsula.

Several scholars have suggested that the source of the Puuc tradition may lie in the western Puuc region, where there exists a class of Early Puuc-style buildings.[56] In this area the largest series of dated inscriptions comes from Edzna and Xcalumkin. Six dates at Edzna range between 9.10.0.0.0 and 9.19.0.0.0 (A.D. 633–810).[57] Several of the five stories in the pyramid at Edzna have traits associated with Early Puuc and Rio Bec architecture (fig. 28). Elsewhere at the site are buildings with finer facing masonry and three-part moldings typical of pure Puuc structures.[58] Proskouriakoff has shown that the Edzna stelae begin in Classic style, but that by 9.19.0.0.0 strong non-Classic traits become evident.[59] The architecture probably reflects the change in monumental carving style, moving from Early Puuc toward Classic Puuc forms within roughly the same span of time (A.D. 633–810).

The western Puuc site of Xcalumkin (Holactun)

has an Initial Series date of 9.15.12.6.9 7 Muluc 2
Kankin (A.D. 744) that serves to place a Puuc building in time. The date was carved on stones set in a
structure that has an important trait of Early Puuc
architecture, a single-member medial molding. The
latticework on the façade is also crude and apparently early (fig. 188).[60] We thus have an Early Puuc-
style building dated to the middle of the eighth
century.

The largest and best documented set of dated inscriptions associated with Pure Florescent architecture comes from Chichen Itza, where several structures resemble Puuc buildings in the use of stone
mosaic façade decoration, but utilize a more blocklike wall masonry. The majority of the Chichen Itza
dates were carved on stone lintels, some of which
are *in situ*, as in the second story of the Monjas,
and some of which may have been reused on later
Toltec-Maya buildings.[61] Thompson dated eleven of
these inscriptions to the third Katun of Cycle 10.
Two other dates that are not definitely tied to architecture were placed in the second Katun of Cycle
10. Together these span a period from A.D. 869 to
881.[62] A slightly later date from the Caracol perhaps
reads 10.7.0.5.1 (A.D. 968) according to Thompson,
or more probably 10.3.0.15.1 (A.D. 890) according
to Kelley.[63] Other later dates include a 10.3.17.0.0
(A.D. 906) placement for the Caracol stela proposed
by Kelley, and the date of 10.8.10.11.0 (A.D. 998)
associated with the High Priest's Grave, a Toltec-
Maya edifice.[64] The correct Long Count placement
of most of these dates is not seriously questioned,[65]
but Andrews V has commented on their significance as follows:

Although these inscriptions probably represent the approximate date of the Puuc buildings on which they occur, I doubt that the Monjas, the Temple of the Four
Lintels, the Temple of the Initial Series, and the Casa
Colorada were all constructed in twelve years. The masonry of the Casa Colorada is much rougher than that of
the others and is likely to be earlier.[66]

Andrews V's point is well taken, but we shall see
that the inscriptional data from Uxmal also suggest
that many of the site's most important buildings
were constructed during the reign of a single ruler.
However, it should be pointed out that the Monjas
dates from Chichen Itza occur in the second story
building, which was preceded by the east wing and
the Iglesia. This suggests that not all the Puuc-
related buildings at Chichen Itza need to be placed
within the twelve-year period A.D. 869–881.

Corresponding in time to the Chichen Itza in-

scriptions is the date on the underside of a mask
panel snout on the east wing of the Palace at Labna.
The glyphs have been read as Tun 13, 3 Ahau,[67]
which indicates the Long Count position 10.1.13.0.0
(A.D. 862). The section of the Palace on which this
mask is found is in the Classic Puuc style and is
definitely later than the Early Puuc-style south annex of the Palace.

A further date appears in the upper court at Nohpat. The panel on a cylindrical altar at the south
foot of the north mound bears a fairly clear inscription of 9 Tuns (winged *cauac*), 3 Ahau.[68] Following Thompson's method for determining Yucatecan
dates this would record 10.1.9.0.0, corresponding
to A.D. 858. The inscription is not associated directly with any building, but Nohpat in general is a
Classic Puuc city, so that this date probably refers
to the period during which pure Puuc buildings
were being erected.

At Uxmal itself are dates that occur on painted
capstones and the hieroglyphic monument ('Stela
17') from the Nunnery Quadrangle, and on the hieroglyphic rings of the Ball Court. Uxmal also has a
number of stelae and cylindrical altars, but unfortunately most are eroded too severely to be datable.
There are eight capstones from Uxmal that show
traces of painting; all of them are from the Nunnery
Quadrangle. Of these, only two have been illustrated in print: the painted capstone in the northwest room of the East Structure, and the painted
capstone in Building Y (the small temple flanking
the east side of the stairway of the North Structure). Drawings of both these capstones were published by Frans Blom (figs. 24–25).[69]

The capstone in the northwestern room of the
East Structure is the most important, for it contains
a calendrical inscription providing some indication
of the period of construction (fig. 24). In 1920 Morley commented on this capstone, reproducing only
the glyphs.[70] Blom later supplied a more complete
drawing differing from that of Morley in the value
given the numerical coefficient preceding the final
calendrical glyph.[71] Morley read the date as 5 Imix,
18 or 19 Kankin, falling in Tun 18 of a Katun 13,
to which he assigned the Long Count position of
11.12.17.11.1 5 Imix 19 Kankin. Spinden also accepted this data as 5 Imix 19 Kankin, occurring before the completion of a Tun 18 and a Katun 13, and
placed it at the same position in the Long Count.[72]
Recently, Kelley has accepted this reading.[73]

J. E. S. Thompson rejected the date proposed by
Morley and Spinden on several counts.[74] He noted
that Beyer had objected to the reading of the sec-

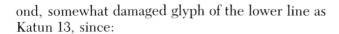

Fig. 24. Painted Capstone, East Structure, Nunnery, Uxmal (after J. E. S. Thompson 1973a:fig. 2).

Fig. 25. Painted Capstone, Building Y, Nunnery, Uxmal
(after J. E. S. Thompson 1973a:fig. 3).

ond, somewhat damaged glyph of the lower line as
Katun 13, since:

The outlines of the second hieroglyph are in complete
agreement with the contours of the hieroglyphs which
undoubtedly are representations of the day sign Ahau.
Therefore, I take the liberty of reading it this way,
namely, as 13 Ahau, and to believe that Morley interpreted some vestiges of lines in the interior of the hieroglyph arbitrarily as parts of a Tun (component of the Katun sign). A katun sign with a post-fix would be unique.[75]

Thompson further interpreted the affixes attached
to this glyph as the Ben-Ich (T168) superfix and the
bil (T130) postfix, precisely those affixes connected
with the day sign Ahau when it refers to a Katun
ending.[76] The coefficient of the second glyph is
drawn as a 12 by Blom and as a 12 or 13 by Morley,
who shows a small element between two dots that
might be either a non-numerical space filler or a
partly effaced dot. Accordingly, Thompson, following his system for interpreting Yucatecan dates,
read the inscription as 5 Imix 18 or 19 Kankin falling in a Tun 18 of a Katun ending on either 12 or 13

Ahau. These conditions are met by the Long Count
date 10.3.17.12.1 5 Imix 18 or 19 Kankin, which falls
in Tun 18 of the Katun 10.4.0.0.0 ending on 12
Ahau. According to the GMT correlation this date
would fall in the year A.D. 906,[77] and this is probably roughly contemporaneous with the construction of the East Structure.

Blom also illustrated the painted capstone from
Structure Y of the Nunnery (fig. 25).[78] The text
opens with a Calendar Round date of 4 Eb 5 Ceh
or 4 Eb 15 Ceh, the former being more probable.
Thompson believed that the Long Count dates
might be either 10.3.18.9.12 4 Eb 5 Ceh (A.D. 907)
or 10.3.8.7.12 4 Eb 15 Ceh (A.D. 897). The first of
these dates was considered preferable because it
falls only 311 days after the date commemorated on
the capstone in the East Structure.[79] Both of the
capstone dates proposed by Thompson fit well with
a radiocarbon date that has been reported for the
North Structure of the Nunnery.

Another probable date occurs on the hieroglyphic
monument ('Stela 17') from the stairway of the North
Structure of the Nunnery (fig. 85). On this monu-

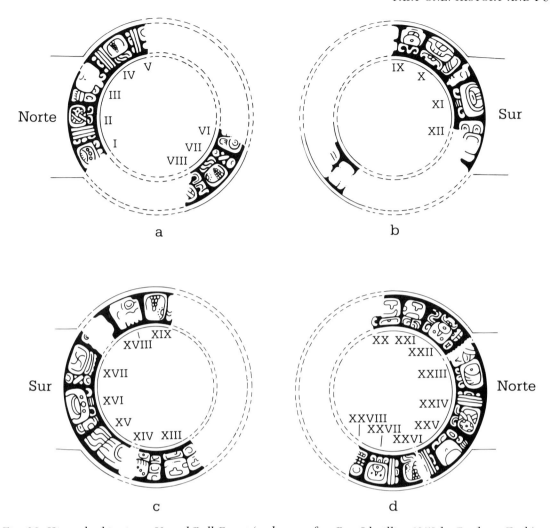

Fig. 26. Hieroglyphic rings, Uxmal Ball Court (redrawn after Ruz Lhuillier 1958 by Barbara Fash).

ment (possibly a glyphic throne) at position A5-B5 there is a Tun-Ahau date which according to Ian Graham's drawings and photographic evidence seems to refer to a Tun with a coefficient of 6 (or possibly 11), and a 12 Ahau. This would refer to a Tun 6 or above falling in a Katun ending on 12 Ahau, and the preferred Long Count positions for such a date would be 10.3.6.0.0 or 10.3.11.0.0, corresponding to A.D. 895 to 900.[80]

Another pair of dates occurs on the Ball Court rings at Uxmal (figs. 26, 99). Until recently Ruz's interpretation of these dates was accepted, placing them at 9.10.16.6.14 6 Ix 17 Pop (actually registering 16 Pop in the Puuc style) and 9.10.16.6.15 7 Men 18 Pop (actually registering 17 Pop in the Puuc style), corresponding to the year A.D. 649.[81] After reexamining the inscriptions, however, Kelley has suggested that more probable dates for these rings

would be 10.3.15.16.14 2 Ix 17 Pop (written 16 Pop) and 10.3.15.16.15 3 Men 18 Pop (written 17 Pop), corresponding to the year A.D. 905. These dates fall fewer than two years before the Nunnery capstone dates. The later placement suggests that the ring dates are approximately contemporaneous with the Ball Court, recognized as a late building at Uxmal on stylistic and iconographic grounds.[82]

As currently interpreted, all of the Uxmal dates fall in the fourth Katun of Cycle 10. These dates are especially important for the chronological placement of the House of the Governor, since the buildings they date share with it features of style, iconography, and masonry technique. The East Structure of the Nunnery, for example, has a freestanding block form like that of the House of the Governor, and both buildings share a superbly finished facing and vault masonry (figs. 2, 86). Both structures also have recessed doorways, a rare feature, and both use similar inverted tiered arrangements of serpent bands as decorative motifs on the upper façades (figs. 113, 140). These resemblances indicate that the House of the Governor dates near in time to the East Structure of the Nunnery.

The Ball Court is also generally considered to be a late Puuc building (fig. 99). Despite the A.D. 649 dates he assigned to the hieroglyphic rings, Ruz placed the court itself late in the Uxmal architectural sequence. He pointed out that the use of the feathered serpent motif on the platform walls suggested a tenth-century placement. Like the House of the Governor, the Ball Court has masonry that is very well cut and probably late. Its connections with the Ball Court and the East Structure of the Nunnery support a date from between about 10.3.0.0.0 to 10.4.0.0.0 (A.D. 889–909) for the House of the Governor.[83]

Finally, Pollock recently illustrated Uxmal Altar 4, found on the great terrace in front of the House of the Governor and perhaps bearing on the date of the building. Altar 4 carries a glyph 4 Ahau on its side. There is no accompanying information, so it is impossible to be certain whether this is merely a day-sign, a Tun ending, or a Katun ending. I am inclined, however, to take this inscription as referring to some time period roughly corresponding to the carving and dedication of the monument. Katuns 4 Ahau ended in the years A.D. 730 and 987, but on the basis of other epigraphic evidence at Uxmal neither of these dates seems likely, being too early and too late respectively. If the date is considered as a Tun ending, however, two positions seem possible: 10.3.9.0.0 4 Ahau (A.D. 898) or 10.4.2.0.0 4 Ahau (A.D. 911). Such readings are tenuous and circumstantial at best. The last of these dates, however, is about four years after the latest date on the Nunnery capstones and would be preferable if we are correct in interpreting the House of the Governor as one of the last major buildings completed at the site.

Uxmal Sculpture

The sculpture of Uxmal provides another means of dating the city and its architecture. At Uxmal, as at other Puuc sites, carved monuments are grouped away from the major buildings on a separate "stela platform."[85] The separation of buildings and monuments makes it more difficult to relate the two types of art closely. Kubler has even suggested there is no proof that the Classic stelae are coeval with the

Puuc architecture.[86] Nevertheless, Proskouriakoff has given tentative stylistic dates to the Uxmal monuments, and these certainly serve to give the time span for an elite occupation at the site. The sculptured stelae support a date for the Puuc florescence at Uxmal from between about 9.18.0.0.0 to 10.5.0.0.0 (A.D. 790–928). Furthermore, at least one of the stelae now can be tied to the architecture at the site by inscriptional evidence, and this confirms an early Cycle 10 date for the major pure Puuc buildings such as the Ball Court, Nunnery Quadrangle, and the House of the Governor.

Uxmal Stela 4 presents a figure standing on two large scrolls and perhaps holding a Manikin Scepter or possibly making a scattering gesture.[87] Proskouriakoff notes that the last calendrical glyph on Stela 4 has a coefficient of 11 and may be the day-sign Ahau. It may record the Katun ending 9.18.0.0.0 (A.D. 790).[88] She also suggests formal connections between this monument and Stela 6 at Sayil, which she gives a stylistic date of 9.19.0.0.0.

Uxmal Stelae 2 and 3 present the same subject in a similar style.[89] On each a human figure wears a headdress with a heavy enclosure around the chin, and carries a round shield, bag, and Manikin Scepter. In the upper parts of the stelae are winged figures, a motif that also appears on stelae from Jaina and Oxkintok, and resembles the compositions on Cycle 10 stelae at Ixlu and Ucanal. Proskouriakoff points out that the long sweeping plumes and the dancing pose on Stela 2 indicate that these monuments were carved no earlier than the Dynamic Phase of Late Classic art.[90] The best chronological position for these stelae is the end of Cycle 9 or the very beginning of Cycle 10.

Strong connections exist between Uxmal Stelae 11 and 14, both featuring a principal figure wearing a tremendous headdress of superimposed tiers of feathers (fig. 27).[91] Both figures carry bags and a specialized hatchet, and wear belts adorned with three human heads. Such belts are common in southern Maya art, but rarely occur in Yucatan sculpture, although one appears on the Halakal lintel (possibly dated to 10.2.0.7.9).[92] The wristlets and earplugs resemble those of Yaxchilan.

Although their protagonists are similar, the two stelae differ compositionally. Proskouriakoff notes that Stela 11 is a more static, Classic arrangement, but that Stela 14, while possessing Classic traits, also shows strong non-Classic influences.[93] Stylistic data and iconographic detail support a late date for Stela 14. Stela 9 at Chinkultic, where a similar broad, horizontal headdress and round shield with

38 PART ONE: HISTORY AND FUNCTION

Fig. 27. Stela 14, Uxmal (after Morley, Brainerd, and Sharer 1983:fig. 11.57).

pendant also occur, has been dated 9.19.0.0.0 (A.D. 810).[94] A somewhat similar headdress also appears in the murals of Room 2 at Bonampak, where it is worn by one of the three "captains." These murals date to about A.D. 800.[95] This form of headdress perhaps originated in northern Yucatan, for it also

occurs in the murals of Structure A at Mul-Chic (fig. 29). A date of A.D. 800 to 820 seems probable for these murals, and will be further supported later.

The appearance of flying figures in the upper section of Uxmal Stela 14 has parallels in the early Cycle 10 stelae from Ixlu and Ucanal,[96] while a somewhat similar figure is also found on Stela 1 from Jimbal, dating to 10.2.10.0.0 (A.D. 879).[97] Ehecatllike figures resembling those at the lower left corner of Uxmal Stela 14 are found on Seibal Stela 3, dated 10.2.5.3.10, while "Mexican" or "non-Classic" sandals provide a link with Seibal Stela 14 (ca. A.D. 870).[98] These correspondences suggest a date from between 9.19.0.0.0 to 10.4.0.0.0 for Stela 14.

Evidence presented in chapter 5 will show that Uxmal Stela 14 names and portrays a ruler designated as "Lord Chac," who is connected with inscriptions dating 10.3.18.9.12. (A.D. 907), 10.3.17.12.1 (A.D. 906), and 10.3.15.16.14 (A.D. 905). This indicates that Stela 14 probably dates from the fourth Katun of Cycle 10. Moreover, several of the occurrences of "Lord Chac's" name are associated with structures of the Nunnery and the Ball Court, considered late buildings at Uxmal. As mentioned, the House of the Governor has close architectural ties with the East Structure of the Nunnery and undoubtedly was constructed close in time. On Stela 14 "Lord Chac" stands on a bicephalic jaguar throne like that in front of the House of the Governor (fig. 16), suggesting a link between the monument and the building. Taken together, this evidence indicates a placement of about 10.3.0.0.0 to 10.4.0.0.0 (A.D. 889–909) for both the latest stelae and buildings at Uxmal. Earlier stelae, which may be placed from 9.18.0.0.0 or 9.19.0.0.0 (A.D. 790–810), may correspond to the building of earlier Puuc edifices such as the House of the Pigeons, Lower West Temple of the Pyramid of the Magician, and so forth. This again indicates a span of something over one hundred years for the major occupation of Uxmal, with the beginnings of Classic Puuc construction coming toward the end of Tepeu 2, and the last buildings, such as the House of the Governor, dating to about A.D. 889 to 909.

Puuc Radiocarbon Dating

Radiocarbon dating supplies another avenue for establishing Puuc chronology. Many of the radiocarbon determinations seem slightly aberrant, however, since they tend to run somewhat earlier than other evidence. There are eight C14 dates that pertain to the Yucatan Pure Florescent period: four from Chichen Itza, one from Sayil, and three from Uxmal. These dates range from A.D. 590 ± 50 through A.D. 900 ± 130, with the average from all sites being about A.D. 713.[99]

The four Pure Florescent dates from Chichen Itza cover a wide range of time. There is a possible Pure Florescent date of A.D. 810 ± 100 from the East Patio of the Monjas, but some doubt as to its exact provenience. Original beams from the Iglesia have given dates of 780 ± 70 and 600 ± 70; the reason for the disparity is not known. The Casa Colorada has an original beam dated to 610 ± 70. This date for the building seems early considering its 10.2.0.15.3 Calendar Round date (A.D. 869), even though Andrews V has suggested its cruder masonry might indicate construction near the beginning of the Pure Florescent.[100]

In the Puuc region proper, at Sayil, a single date of A.D. 720 ± 60 (730 ± 80, corrected)[101] comes from a beam in the Palace.[102] At Uxmal an early date of A.D. 560 ± 50 (590 ± 50, corrected)[103] has been given for a lintel from the Lower West Temple of the Pyramid of the Magician.[104] This date has been used by Foncerrada (reported as A.D. 569) to justify an early beginning for the pure Puuc style, but Andrews V has pointed out that it seems much too early "even for this early stage of the Pyramid."[105] We will consider this problem in more detail shortly. In addition, a date of 740 ± 60 (760 ± 80, corrected)[106] comes from a beam in a building to the east of the Monjas (perhaps the House of the Birds[107, 108] while a date of 885 ± 100 (900 ± 130, corrected)[109] comes from a lintel in the North Structure of the Nunnery.[110] This date from the North Structure lintel accords with Thompson's reading of the capstone date in the East Structure of the Nunnery as 10.3.17.12.1 (A.D. 906).

It is difficult to assess these radiocarbon dates' provenience or the conditions under which the wood samples were taken. They are troubling because, as Andrews V has pointed out, the average of the Pure Florescent dates from Yucatan is A.D. 713, with the Chichen Itza dates averaging about 25 years older than those from the Puuc region.[111] These early radiocarbon dates forced Andrews IV into a dilemma concerning northern Maya chronology. His studies at Dzibilchaltun and his interpretation of the Yucatecan determinations led him to favor the Spinden correlation of the Maya and Christian calendars. The Spinden correlation differs from the more widely accepted Goodman-Martínez-Thompson correlation by placing the Spanish conquest at roughly 12.9.0.0.0 in the Maya

Long Count, thus dating events in the Maya Initial Series about 256½ years earlier than the GMT, which places the conquest at roughly 11.16.0.0.0.[112] To illustrate the different placements necessitated by the two correlations, Andrews IV made a chart that we reproduce (Table 1).

It will be noted that regardless of the correlation used there is a long time of the Early period which is associated with the Initial Series period and can be placed securely in the Maya Long Count. After this the dating of events in terms of Christian chronology becomes firm only during the first phase of the Decadent period. The time span critical for the correlation problem is that falling between the end of the Initial Series period, presumed to have taken place by 10.5.0.0.0, and the beginning of the well-documented Mayapan period. This is allotted about 500 years in the Spinden correlation and about 250 years in the Goodman-Martínez-Thompson correlation.[113]

Andrews IV's belief that the Puuc cities were occupied only after the abandonment of the southern sites persuaded him to accept the Spinden correlation. As noted, he posited a long (60- to 100-year) transitional phase between the Early period Structure 57 (c. 10.0.0.0.0, or A.D. 830) and Puuc architecture at Dzibilchaltun, so that "evolved Florescent in northwestern Yucatan almost certainly appears no earlier than 10.5.0.0.0."[114]

If the Florescent period really began this late it creates a problem for the GMT correlation. Until the time Andrews IV wrote, the Florescent tradition was interpreted as substantially overlapping the Late Classic period of the southern lowlands, so that the blank zone on the time chart needed to include only the very last phases of the Classic Maya tradition and the period of Toltec influence at Chichen Itza. These events are easily accommodated by the Goodman-Martínez-Thompson correlation. Andrews IV's scheme, however, required that the entire Pure Florescent, the Modified Florescent (Toltec Chichen), and a transitional "Black-on-Cream" period defined at Dzibilchaltun be fit into the blank area.[115] In addition to the fact that this seemed to be too much history in not enough time, Andrews IV also pointed out that the majority of radiocarbon determinations from northern Yucatan seemed to favor the earlier Spinden correlation.[116]

Until recently Andrews IV's chronological dilemma has remained a thorn in the side of Maya archaeologists.[117] However, a number of new studies by Andrews V and Ball have again expressed strong support for the 11.16.0.0.0 Goodman-Martínez-Thompson correlation (table 2).[118] Andrews V, while accepting the duration of Early period masonry at Dzibilchaltun until about 10.0.0.0.0 (A.D. 830), no longer feels that a long transitional period between Early period and Puuc architecture is justified.[119] The removal of the transitional period makes it easier for the Pure Florescent period to be accommodated in the 11.16.0.0.0 correlation, since it allows time from about A.D. 830 to 950/1000 for pure Puuc development. Andrews V has further suggested that the Puuc architectural style was likely to have developed as early as 9.17.0.0.0 or 9.18.0.0.0 (A.D. 771–790) in the Puuc hills of Yucatan or southwest in Campeche.[120] This would supply a fifty-year period of Puuc evolution that need not be added to the blank spot in the Dzibilchaltun chronology, and it would move the beginnings of Puuc nearer to the early radiocarbon dates. But Andrews V has pointed out that "accepting an earlier date for the inception of the Puuc style, possibly as early as A.D. 730–770 (ca. 9.15.0.0.0—9.17.0.0.0), does not necessarily free us from the dilemma of the C14 dates, however, because these dates are mostly from structures at Uxmal, a late Puuc site."[121]

In general, aside from the northern Maya area, Maya radiocarbon dates tend to support the Goodman-Martínez-Thompson correlation. No fewer than twenty-three out of a total of sixty-three radiocarbon determinations from Tikal fall between A.D. 702 and 812.[122] These dates refer to the Tepeu phase and late monuments at Tikal, and fall far outside the end of the Classic period as proposed by Spinden. Moreover, regarding the reliability of the Yucatan dates it should be pointed out that studies of the wooden lintels of Tikal have demonstrated that radiocarbon dates may vary by 240–260 years, depending on whether the sample of wood is taken from the center or near the outer edge of the log.[123] It is unknown what kind of controls were used in obtaining the northern samples. This perhaps accounts for some of the extremely early dates such as the A.D. 560 ± 50 for the lower building of the Pyramid of the Magician at Uxmal, or the A.D. 600 at the Iglesia at Chichen Itza.

At Uxmal, for example, if the sample was taken from the interior of the log, then the true date of the Lower West Structure could be as much as 250 years later, or about A.D. 810, a date that accords much better with its developed Puuc façade (fig. 7).

Despite this possible correction, the large number of early radiocarbon determinations and the average date of A.D. 713 is still troubling. At the moment we can only agree with Andrews V that:

Perhaps the safest position to take at present is that the C14 dates indicate more of an overlap between Late Classic remains and the eastern and northern Puuc remains than do other lines of reasoning. That such an overlap did occur seems sure, but only stratigraphic excavations and more C14 determinations will define its length.[124]

Early- and Late-Puuc Architectural Style

As has been shown, Puuc architecture is generally assigned to the Florescent period in Yucatan, dating from about A.D. 770 to 1000. The construction dates of individual buildings are often matters of conjecture, however, since the establishment of an architectural chronology has relied on a few clear examples of stratigraphy combined with analyses of construction technology, architectural style, and sculptural motifs. Nevertheless, H. E. D. Pollock, George Andrews, and other scholars have sought to distinguish early and late forms of Puuc architecture with a fair degree of success.[125] We will examine some of these architectural seriations in order to place the House of the Governor in the Puuc sequence. It will be shown that there are definite differences of masonry technique and architectural style separating Early- and Late-Puuc buildings, and that within this development the House of the Governor is recognizable as a culmination of the Puuc tradition.

One of the first scholars to consider the stylistic evolution of Puuc architecture was H. E. D. Pollock. During the period from 1930 to 1951 Pollock and other Carnegie Institution of Washington researchers made an architectural survey of the area of western Yucatan and northern Campeche known as the western Puuc region. It includes such large, well-known sites as Oxkintok, Xcalumkin, and Edzna, and many other sites only reported recently.[126] Pollock was impressed both by the size and seemingly early date of Edzna, whose architecture he believed might have stimulated Puuc developments.[127] As was mentioned in the section on Puuc epigraphy, the five-story pyramid at Edzna had traits associated with Early Puuc architecture (fig. 28).[128]

Pollock's research enabled him to list features indicating an earlier date for some Puuc buildings. These features are particularly characteristic of the western Puuc sites, but appear on several eastern Puuc buildings as well. They include veneer walls with corbeled slab vaults; pyramid temples with a simple rectangular molding that steps up over the

Fig. 28. Five-Story Pyramid at Edzna.

doorways and is frequently associated with doorway columns; jambs or lintels bearing hieroglyphic inscriptions of human figures carved in low relief; and temples with roof combs or flying façades that employ stucco as a decorative medium.[129]

Proskouriakoff has also argued that it is possible to distinguish between Early- and Late-Puuc buildings. In general, she characterized Early-Puuc architecture as having "cruder workmanship and simpler ornamentation."[130] Specifically, she identified the lower west section of the Palace at Sayil as a probable Early-Puuc building.[131] This building will be discussed more fully later.

Important evidence for Puuc stratigraphy comes from Mul-Chic, a small site located between Uxmal and Kabah, where at least two clear periods of construction are distinguished. Two early buildings, A and B, sat on low platforms occupying the east and south sides of a central courtyard. Structure A is a small, one-room temple building. It has architectural characteristics which ally it with other buildings Pollock has defined as early versions of Puuc architecture. George Andrews has suggested that its constructional and decorative features closely resemble those of the Early period buildings at Oxkintok.[132] Its basal and medial moldings are simple rectangular courses, while the front façade is prolonged vertically with a perforated flying façade that supports remnants of modeled stucco figures painted in blue, red and yellow. Stucco figures of men and deer were also applied above the doorway. The construction is a facing masonry of irregular cut-stone blocks over a concrete core. The technique is not as precise as in pure Puuc structures but appears more finished than that of Structure 3C6 at Oxkintok.[133] The vault is constructed with projecting slabs covered with red stucco, rather than with the well-shaped boot stones associated

Fig. 29. Mural from the west side, south wall, Structure A, Mul-Chic (after Piña Chan 1963:lam. XII).

with later Puuc buildings. On the basis of these features, Piña Chan estimated that the building dates between A.D. 600 to 700, a placement also favored by Pollock.[134]

The early date of Structure A is confirmed by the fact that it was subsequently covered by a terraced pyramidal platform of pure Puuc construction.[135] Two other structures, E and F, are surely dated later than Structure A and have features, such as columns in doorways or a basal molding with colonnettes, that ally them more closely with typical Puuc-style buildings. It is uncertain how late in the Puuc sequence these structures date.

Within Structure A was discovered a remarkable set of mural paintings providing evidence as to the relative age of the building (fig. 29). The paintings were applied with a second coat of stucco at a somewhat later date than the erection of Structure A, but definitely antedate the later Puuc-style Structures C, E, and F. The paintings on the south wall of Structure A depict scenes of warfare, in which scantily clad warriors subdue a band of similarly attired foes. Overlooking the scene is a seated ruler holding a flint knife, and to the left are two sumptuously clad figures who wear face masks and large sombrerolike headdresses (fig. 29).[136] The paintings on the north wall depict a ruler who wears a jaguar kilt with two hanging jaguar paws.[137] At the height of his headdress and to the left there is a quetzal bird and a glyph cartouche. To the ruler's right are aides or courtiers, whose bodies are painted black and who carry obsidian knives. They wear skulls

suspended on their chests, ornate feather headdresses, capes, disk-shaped ear ornaments with tubular plugs, and interlaced leg wrappings.

Both the animated style and the bellicose subject matter of the Mul-Chic murals recall those of Bonampak, dated about A.D. 790–800,[138] while the pose of the ruler seated above the fray on the west mural corresponds remarkably with that of the ruler seated above a group of prisoners on Piedras Negras Stela 12, dated 9.18.5.0.0 (A.D. 795).[139] The headdresses worn by the Mul-Chic figures resemble that worn by the figure on Chinkultic Stela 9, dated 9.19.0.0.0 (A.D. 810),[140] and by the rulers on Uxmal Stelae 11 and 14 (fig. 27). Stela 14 is placed between 10.3.0.0.0 and 10.4.0.0.0 on the basis of its blend of Maya and Mexican features. Thus, on the basis of comparisons with other monuments, the paintings at Mul-Chic seem to have been created somewhere between 9.18.0.0.0 to 10.4.0.0.0, with an estimate of 9.19.0.0.0 to 10.0.0.0.0 probably close to the mark, considering the resemblances to Bonampak and Piedras Negras. This would put the construction date of Structure A sometime before A.D. 799, the paintings at about A.D. 800 to 820, and the subsequent buildings in the later Puuc style following somewhat later in time.

George Andrews believes the differences between Structure A and the other buildings at Mul-Chic are important because they demonstrate "the presence in the Puuc heartland of an architectural style and construction technology which clearly predate the Pure Puuc (Florescent) style."[141] Using

Fig. 30. Mirador Temple at Sayil.

Structure A at Mul-Chic as a model, Andrews examined other nearby Puuc sites to see whether they possess buildings similar in style and construction, reasoning that they also must represent Early Puuc remains. He shows that such structures are found in at least nine other Puuc sites including Uxmal, Kabah, Sayil, Sabacche, Kiuic, Chacmultun, Itzimte, and Balche. The individual buildings in this Early-Puuc style include two structures in the North Group at Uxmal, as well as the south section of the Nunnery Annex, the lower temple of the Pyramid of the Old Woman, and the temple on the west side of the Cemetery Group.[142]

Technically the Early-Puuc buildings show a lesser degree of finish and careful cutting of masonry than do later examples. Walls tend to be composed of roughly cut, semi-veneer stones which are laid in uneven courses and often show considerable variation in size and shape. Vaults are normally built of roughly dressed slabs of stone overlapped to form true corbeled vaults. Some late Early-Puuc buildings may contain boot-shaped stones. Vaults are generally low, with curved soffits, and many lack the offset below the capstones that is common in later Puuc buildings. The uneven surfaces of the corbeled vaults were finished with a thick layer of plaster.

Stylistically the Early-Puuc structures often give the impression of greater simplicity than their ornate Late Puuc descendants. Part of this seeming spareness may be due to the poor preservation of stucco sculpture. Early-Puuc buildings have simple moldings. Bases are low single member rectangular forms that project slightly from the lower wall. Medial moldings are usually simple rectangular string courses, which occasionally step up over doorways. The space above the doorway occasionally contained simple geometric decorative motifs. Often there is no upper cornice, merely an intersection of wall and roof. The lower walls are usually plain, except

Fig. 31. Three-Story Palace at Sayil (after Proskouriakoff 1963a:57).

for possible stucco sculptures. There are no decorative panels, inset colonnettes, or other cut-stone elements. The upper walls are generally vertical and are often set back slightly from the lower walls. Several upper façades show projecting stone tenons, indicating the former presence of stucco sculptures. Doorways are typically low and narrow. Stone lintels are used exclusively and the jambs are formed of single blocks like the wall-facing stones. Occasionally multiple doorways are formed by using round columns with square capitals. Many of the Early-Puuc structures have high roof structures; roof combs over the medial walls or flying façades over the front walls. These roof structures are composed entirely of rough-cut slabs and mortar and are pierced with vertical slots. They formerly were covered with painted stucco sculptures supported by stone tenons. Roof combs occasionally occur on pure Puuc buildings, but they are less popular. The later combs are constructed with well-cut facing stones over a concrete interior. In general, these Early Puuc-style buildings contrast sharply with

those of the Pure Florescent or Late-Puuc period, whose salient features were described at the beginning of this chapter.[143]

The Mirador Temple at Sayil is usually cited as an example of Early Puuc architecture, and it possesses many of the traits described above (fig. 30).[144] The Three-Story Palace at Sayil is also instructive for the differences between early and late variants of Puuc architecture (fig. 31). The western section of the lower story on the south side is probably an Early Puuc building.[145] However, despite its early traits, such as single-member basal and medial moldings, the masonry technique is essentially pure Puuc, although the finish is not as fine as that of the upper stories. Also there seems to have been a standard Puuc three-part cornice molding. According to George Andrews:

The combination of Pure Puuc technology with Early Puuc architectural and decorative features suggests that this range of rooms should be dated to the latter part of

Fig. 32. Nunnery Annex (or Northern Long Building), east side, Uxmal.

the Early Puuc period, which would make them contemporary with the late Early Puuc buildings with similar features at Uxmal and Sabacche.[146]

Contrasting in style and construction with this lower range is the uppermost story of the Palace at Sayil (fig. 31). This structure was surely the last constructed at the Palace, although it is uncertain how much time passed between the construction of the lower range and the upper story. This building has several features, such as three-part moldings and well-cut facing masonry and boot-shaped vault stones matching those of latest buildings at Uxmal, such as the House of the Governor or Nunnery structures. Above each doorway the cornice is broken by a flat panel with tenons that must have supported stucco sculptures. The use of stucco is not typical of Late-Puuc buildings, but the serrated silhouette formed by these panels resembles the periodic vertical accents provided by the mask towers of the North Structure of the Nunnery at Uxmal (fig. 85). All in all, we can see that this building surely postdates a late Early-Puuc building, and that it is the latest section of the Three-Story Palace. It also recalls several pure Puuc buildings at Uxmal, which serves to confirm the late placement of the House of the Governor in the Puuc sequence.

George Andrews has identified five buildings at Uxmal which appear to be Early Puuc in style. These include: the west wing of an L-shaped building near the base of the pyramid on the north side of the North Group;[147] the U-shaped building located near the top of the North Group pyramid; the south wing of the Nunnery Annex; the lower temple near the base of the Pyramid of the Old Woman; and the temple on the west side of the Cemetery Group.

The early qualities of the masonry at the North Group were first recognized by Seler. He placed the upper structures of the pyramid in an early period of construction at Uxmal, noting that "the entire building is simple, constructed of rough masonry, wall surface and frieze lacking any decoration, the medial molding a simple slanted projecting row of stones."[148] Despite the apparent early quality of the masonry, however, the lower story is in a more finished Puuc style, casting some doubt on the identification of the upper chambers as Early Puuc.[149]

Andrews also identifies the southern section of the Nunnery Annex as a possible Early-Puuc building. This structure is composed of two separate wings linked by a portal vault (fig. 32). The south section originally stood alone and the north section

Fig. 33. Pyramid of the Old Woman, Lower Temple, Uxmal

this instance is clear—the sharply cut facing masonry of the north building definitely postdates the slab wall construction of the south building—but it is uncertain exactly when the south structure dates.[150]

The temple on the western side of the Cemetery Group at Uxmal also has features suggestive of Early-Puuc style (fig. 10). Like other examples of Early-Puuc architecture this building has a perforated flying façade, and numerous projecting tenons on the upper façade and roof structure indicate that both were formerly covered with stucco sculpture. The medial molding seems intermediate between early and late forms, consisting of a flaring lower member and a plain rectangular upper course. A single string course separates the upper façade from the flying façade. Constructionally this building differs from other Early-Puuc structures. Vault stones are boot-shaped and both the walls and flying façade are faced with large, well-shaped veneer stones set in concrete. Because of its mixture of Early-Puuc stylistic traits and pure Puuc construction techniques, it seems possible either that this is a transitional structure or a later building that retains elements of the Early-Puuc style.[151] Recent evidence from the hieroglyphic platforms of the Cemetery Group would support a date between A.D. 850–880.[152] The Cemetery Temple points up some of the pitfalls of basing a chronology on formal seriation alone.

Important for the chronological placement of the House of the Governor is the Pyramid of the Old Woman (fig. 33–34). This group is located just southeast of the House of the Governor and contains examples of both Early- and Late-Puuc architecture in clear stratigraphic association. The two-room temple near the base of the pyramid is in the Early-Puuc style (fig. 33). This structure is surmounted by a high roof comb with rectangular slots. The construction and form of this roof comb resembles those of the Early-Puuc temples at Mul-Chic, Labna, Sayil, and Sabacche. Stone tenons project at intervals from the roof comb, indicating that it formerly bore stucco sculptures.[153] Because the vaulting is basically pure Puuc, Andrews believes that this temple's architecture is "the combination of features which seem to characterize late Early-Puuc architecture at Uxmal as well as at nearby sites."[154] Pollock recently has suggested a date from between A.D. 700 to 800.[155]

The temple is important in terms of relative chronology because it is partly covered by and was incorporated into the plan of the later large Pyra-

and the portal vault were added at a later date. The construction of the two sections differs markedly. The lower walls of the south building are formed of roughly shaped, rectangular blocks extending through the full thickness of the wall, while the walls and vaults of the north wing and connected portal vault use pure Puuc facing masonry. Both wings had a typical Puuc three-member binder molding. The upper façade of the south section is faced with large roughly cut facing stones and there are several stone tenons in the west side, suggesting former stucco decoration. The vaults employ semi-bootshaped blocks. The relative chronology in

Fig. 34. Detail of base and lower wall, Upper Temple, Pyramid of the Old Woman, Uxmal.

mid of the Old Woman. It is a stepped substructure apparently intended to support a large temple building at its summit (fig. 34). Today, however, only the foundation and lowermost portions of the walls exist. Because of the lack of debris on top of the pyramid (with no evidence of collapsed vaults) Pollock has suggested that the building was left uncompleted at the time of Uxmal's abandonment.[156] This is important because it suggests that the abandonment of the city was fairly abrupt and that a major architectural project was left unfinished. Obviously then, the unfinished temple must be one of the latest examples of architecture at Uxmal. It is thus significant that it shares many constructional features with the House of the Governor.

The building has a precisely cut, three-part basal molding consisting of projecting rectangular upper and lower members and a central member of flat panels alternating with groups of engaged colonettes. The facing stones of the walls are quite large, as at the House of the Governor, with surfaces well cut and pecked. The joints are very sharp and precise and coursing is very even. It seems probable that this building was constructed not long after structures such as the House of the Turtles or the House of the Governor. In chapter 5 we suggest that the late buildings such as the Nunnery, Ball Court, and the House of the Governor pertain to the reign of "Lord Chac," and may therefore be dated between about A.D. 875 to 925. It seems probable that the later structure atop the Pyramid of the Old Woman was erected shortly thereafter, which would place the abandonment of Uxmal between A.D. 925 to 975. Certainly by the

end of this time the local elite responsible for the city's peak could no longer have held power.

Kubler made an effort to establish a seriation of Puuc architecture at Uxmal that may now be examined to see how it conforms to the foregoing findings. He suggested that the Pyramid of the Old Woman may be the oldest edifice at the site. Presumably he is referring to the lower temple with Early Puuc traits just mentioned, though this is not clear. The North, Cemetery and Pigeon Groups are related as "amphitheater courts," and are considered "typologically earlier than the free-standing block design of the Nunnery and the Governor's Palace."[157] Kubler also suggests that:

the differences between the Pigeon Courts and the Nunnery are analogous to the differences between Monte Alban and Mitla, where we have supposed a lapse of no longer than the passage between mid-Classic and Late Classic eras, i.e. no more than six and no less than two centuries.[158]

On the basis of evidence presented thus far it does not seem necessary to allow two centuries for the span between the Pigeons Group and the Nunnery. The masonry of the Pigeons ranges is generally less fine than that of the Nunnery, and the gabled roof comb did support stucco sculptures, both of which tend to confirm its earlier placement. However, the Pigeons buildings use a pure veneer masonry and vault stones that are not as boot-shaped as those of the Nunnery, but which have tapered butts and beveled faces. Several of the ranges have three-part *atadura* moldings, and the roof comb of the House of the Pigeons is faced with a veneer, not composed of slabs as in other Early Puuc buildings. In other words, while antedating the Nunnery, the Pigeons Group is pure Puuc architecture, almost certainly dates no earlier than A.D. 750–800, and is probably later.

Kubler accepts Foncerrada's dating for the Pyramid of the Magician, believing it to have been built from the sixth through the tenth century (figs. 7–8).[159] This placement depends both on the A.D. 560 ± 50 radiocarbon date for the Lower West Temple, as well as on Foncerrada's stylistic dates for inner Temples II and III. Traits which Foncerrada considers representative of Early Puuc architecture include roof crests, inclined friezes, stucco decoration, and an absence of mosaic decoration.[160] Several of the individual structures she identifies as early, such as the Mirador Temple at Sayil and the Temple of the Old Woman at Uxmal, have been mentioned as probable Early Puuc buildings. Some of her other examples seem more doubtful, however. The Codz Poop and the Palace at Kabah and Temple II of the Pyramid of the Magician at Uxmal are classified as early because they have roof combs (fig. 158). Roof combs per se, however, need not be an early trait. The roof structures of all these buildings are divided into tiers by sharply cut, three-part moldings of stone and are constructed of a concrete core faced with well-cut stone. All have apertures given a decorative treatment of steps or step-frets.[161] This construction is like that of pure Puuc buildings and contrasts with the slab and mortar construction of earlier Puuc roof combs. Foncerrada also identifies the Palace at Kabah and Temple III of the Pyramid of the Magician at Uxmal as early because of their mansard roof profile. This is insufficient evidence for assigning a date, however, since none of the demonstrably Early-Puuc buildings (e.g., Structure A at Mul-Chic) have this feature. Moreover, an inclined frieze appears on the second story of the Monjas at Chichen Itza, and has been dated to A.D. 880 on the basis of its Cycle 10 hieroglyphic lintels (fig. 185).[162] Such evidence indicates that Temples II and III may be interpreted as pure Puuc buildings, and again casts doubt on the extremely early radiocarbon date for the Lower West Temple of the Pyramid of the Magician.

Kubler places the Nunnery Quadrangle late in the Uxmal sequence, likening it to "an improved version of the Pigeon Court."[163] Greater age is ascribed to the North Structure because it contains an older encased structure, possesses vestigial roof combs in the form of mask tiers, and has narrower vaults in heavy supporting walls (fig. 85). He cites a radiocarbon date of A.D. 893 ± 100 for this building, so he presumably places the entire quadrangle at around the turn of the tenth century, the chronological position also favored on epigraphic evidence. Using wall-to-vault span rations as a clue to age, he places the South Structure next in the sequence, followed by the East and West Structures. In general, the tendency in northern Yucatan was to increase the width of vaults over time,[164] but it is questionable whether this index can be fine-tuned to this extent. Fortunately, Kubler uses other formal evidence to support the seriation. He points out that the South Structure has its doorways variably spaced so that "the widest intervals are the central ones, diminishing toward the corners, as in Greek peripteral temples" (fig. 99).[165] Such variable rhythmic spacing of the doorways is lacking in the North Structure, but tentatively present in the East Structure, and is fully developed in the West

Structure (figs. 83, 86–87). According to Kubler "these advances in rhythmic complication correspond to the sequence suggested by the ratios of wall to span."[166]

Early dating of the main body of the South Structure seems assured, because the platforms supporting the East and West Structures abut and partly encase the South Structure (fig. 86). The dating of the North Structure is more problematical, however, since it is complicated by the fact that the present façade covers an older, encased building.[167] This allows for possible alternatives, and Kubler himself has suggested the possibility that the façade sculpture of the inner building was reused.[168] Perhaps the sequence was the Inner North, South, Outer North, East, and West Structure. Both the Inner North and South Structures lack the feature of doorways framed by an inset panel. In the North Structure the doorways take this form only when the outer façade is added. The aesthetic potential of this doorway treatment was then realized and such doors were incorporated as a further refinement in the East and West Structures of the Nunnery, and at the House of the Governor (figs. 2, 58). Such inset doorways thus serve to place the House of the Governor among the latest Puuc structures. Kubler has correctly suggested that it is "the most refined and perhaps the last achievement of the architects of Uxmal," expressing a rhythmic complexity and architectural sensibility seen in no other building at the site.[169] Although certain unfinished structures at Uxmal may postdate the House of the Governor, it was almost certainly the last major edifice completed at Uxmal.

Synthesis

Having reviewed the available ceramic, epigraphic, sculptural, architectural, and radiocarbon evidence we may now consider some of the most recent attempts to date Puuc architecture and draw some conclusions regarding the House of the Governor. E. W. Andrews V and Joseph Ball recently have discussed this problem at length in several articles and monographs.[170] They now accept the idea that the great architectural centers in the Puuc hills, such as Uxmal, were established toward the end of the eighth century.

Andrews V, though arguing for a relatively late blooming for Puuc architecture at Dzibilchaltun, suggests that the style may have developed as much as fifty years earlier, ca. 9.17.0.0.0 or 9.18.0.0.0

(A.D. 771–790) in the original homeland in the Puuc hills or to the southwest in Campeche. A pre-ninth century development at these Puuc centers is supported by Andrews V's contention that an already developed version of Puuc-style architecture spread northward to Dzibilchaltun from the Puuc hills from A.D. 800 to 830.[171] Ball has similarly suggested that there was an intrusion of Puuc-zone pottery into central-east Campeche before A.D. 830, implying a somewhat earlier development for the Cehpech ceramic configuration in the Puuc heartland.[172] This earlier placement is more consistent with the dates Brainerd proposed for his Yucatan Florescent Stage ceramics. He placed the beginning of the Puuc style, as defined by pottery, between A.D. 700 and 750 and its end at about A.D. 970. An earlier beginning date for Puuc architecture also corresponds more closely to the views of Pollock, Proskouriakoff, and others who have suggested that many of the western Puuc sites contain buildings appearing stylistically earlier than those of the major sites in the Puuc hill zone, as well as to those of George Andrews, who identifies Early Puuc structures in the eastern sites as well.

Evidence presented earlier can be made either to support or contradict Andrews V's 9.17.0.0.0 beginning date for Puuc architecture. Epigraphic evidence ties all the Late-Puuc buildings in the eastern sites to the first half of Cycle 10. The latest Puuc buildings at Uxmal, for example, are connected with dates from A.D. 895 to 907. Thus a period from A.D. 770 or 790 to 907 allows ample time for the florescence of pure Puuc architecture. It is questionable, however, whether all of the Early-Puuc structures date from this period. The Initial Series 9.15.12.6.9 (A.D. 744) at Xcalumkin is connected with a building that seems intermediate between Early-Puuc and Late-Puuc style. The dates from Edzna ranging between 9.12.0.0.0 and 9.19.0.0.0 (A.D. 633–810) are also suggestive. The five-story pyramid has stages constructed in what qualifies as a forerunner of Puuc style. Very possibly this Early Puuc-related architecture is to be connected with the earlier dates at the site. It has also been suggested that Structure A at Mul-Chic dates somewhere between A.D. 600–800. Taken together this would indicate that Early-Puuc buildings may have been erected considerably before the 9.17.0.0.0 date proposed by Andrews V. Pollock recently has proposed a date of 600–700 for what he terms Proto-Puuc (including Structure A at Mul-Chic), 700–800 for Early Puuc (including the Initial Series Building at Xcalumkin), and 800–900/950

for Late or Classic Puuc.[173] Evidence from preceding sections, taken as a whole, supports such a chronology.

If this accounts for the beginnings of Puuc architecture, what can be said about its demise? In order to understand the end of the Puuc development it is important to comment on the nature of the relationship between the Puuc sites and Chichen Itza. According to the traditional chronologies of both Thompson and Andrews IV, Puuc cities were thought to have been abandoned by about A.D. 1000 or shortly before. Their depopulation was viewed as coincident with and perhaps the result of the Toltec invasion of Chichen Itza, an event traditionally assigned to the Katun 4 Ahau (A.D. 968–987). Recently, however, a number of scholars have become dissatisfied with this linear view of Yucatecan history and have considered the possibility that the end of the Pure Florescent (Puuc) period overlapped with the rise of the Modified Florescent (Mexican-Toltec) period at Chichen Itza. Joseph Ball, for example, suggests that the traditional historical model is not necessarily correct, and that two possible alternatives exist on the basis of present evidence. The first of these Ball terms the "non-linear, partial overlap" reconstruction of Terminal Classic–Early Post-Classic culture history.[174] According to this theory Uxmal and other Puuc centers developed during the last quarter of the eighth century, rose to power, and expanded their influence onto the northern plains (Dzibilchaltun) and into the southern forests (marked by the appearance of the Xcocom Cehpech complex at Becan) by the early ninth century. Shortly before or after A.D. 900 a Maya group of western or southwestern peninsular origin established itself as an important economic and political power at Chichen Itza. According to this scheme, the Puuc centers, competing strenuously with Chichen Itza, may have endured beyond A.D. 1000. Then during the eleventh century "possibly following an infusion of new elements from central plateau Mexico, Chichen Itza succeeded in economically vanquishing the Puuc centers, thus leading to their abandonment."[175] Ball points out that this historical reconstruction corresponds well with that of Thompson, who placed the Itza occupation of Chichen Itza in A.D. 918 on the basis of ethnohistoric sources. Ball himself prefers to see Itza power in place by A.D. 866, relying on Kelley's interpretation of the Chichen Maya inscriptions to suggest that this intrusion "was accomplished by a group under the military and political leadership of one Kakupacal."[176]

Ceramic evidence also supports the possibility of a period of contemporaneity between the Puuc centers and the beginning of the "Toltec" period at Chichen Itza. Traditionally, Balancan/Altar and Silho (X) Fine Orangewares have been regarded as diagnostics of successive time periods—Balancan/Altar associated with Pure Florescent and Silho associated with Modified Florescent. At Altar de Sacrificios, however, grave-lot associations reported by R. E. W. Adams suggest that Balancan/Altar and Silho group vessels were available contemporaneously during the first half of the tenth century.[177] Recent archaeological work at Uxmal also indicates some overlap between the Cehpech and Sotuta ceramic complexes. For example, Maldonado reports finding a Silho Fine Orangeware bowl inside the east range of the Ball Court, which would indicate that Silho was being produced and traded into the Puuc cities by about A.D. 900.[178] As was mentioned, Saenz found some examples of Sotuta complex pottery types (e.g., Tohil Plumbate) during clearing and reconstruction at Uxmal. In the past Tohil Plumbate pottery has been considered an "index fossil" of the Post-Classic after A.D. 1000, while Thin Slateware has been dated to A.D. 800–1000. At Becan, where both are tradewares, Ball found the two mixed in refuse deposits, which he views as evidence that both were available simultaneously "either before or after the A.D. 1000 watershed."[179] At Izapa new data suggest the presence of Tohil Plumbate in the region by A.D. 900.[180] Ball also mentions that:

Grave lot associations observed on Isla Cerritos indicate the contemporaneous availability of Silho group Fine Orange Paste-Ware, Tohil group Plumbate ware, and either Chablekal or Tres Naciones group Fine Gray Paste-Ware, both of which traditionally are assigned pre- A.D. 1000 placements.[181]

In general this new ceramic information seems to support the idea that Post-Classic diagnostics such as Plumbate and X-Fine Orangeware may be earlier than formerly supposed. This lends weight to an earlier beginning for the Mexican period at Chichen Itza, and its partial overlap with the Puuc centers, but does not necessarily imply that the Puuc cities continued beyond A.D. 1000.

Andrews V has also proposed a partial overlap between the Pure Florescent and Modified Florescent periods. He notes that two samples of twig charcoal from Mexican style (Tlaloc censer) offerings in the Balankanche cave shrine produced radiocarbon dates of A.D. 860 ± 200. Reruns on these

samples yielded A.D. 878 ± 51 and A.D. 922 ± 42. A beam inside the south doorway of the Castillo gave an original date of A.D. 790 ± 70 and a rerun of A.D. 810. Andrews V believes that "these dates, although earlier than the A.D. 1000 date customarily assigned the Toltec arrival at Chichen, are in accord with recent suggestions that Toltec Tula may be pushed back to about A.D. 900."[182]

According to Andrews V, epigraphic evidence also supports an earlier beginning for Mexican influences at Chichen Itza.[183] As noted, the inscriptional dates associated with Chichen-Maya style buildings fall in a twelve-year period from A.D. 869 to 881, while slightly later dates of A.D. 890 and A.D. 906 may be found at the Caracol. The only known later date is that of 10.8.10.11.0 (A.D. 998) associated with the Toltec-Maya High Priest's Grave. Sabloff and Andrews recently have argued that this could imply a Toltec presence at Chichen Itza by about 10.3.0.0.0 (A.D. 889), "when Uxmal, Kabah, and probably many other Puuc sites were in full flower, although nearing the end of their florescence."[184]

Another reason for supposing a pre-A.D. 987 beginning for the Modified Florescent at Chichen Itza is the presence of Mexican features or motifs in some of the Puuc sites such as Uxmal. These include the feathered serpents on the West Structure of the Nunnery and Ball Court, and perhaps the four platforms with skulls and crossbones in the Cemetery Group and some of the figures and serpent types used as façade sculpture.[185] Proskouriakoff has commented on the Mexican flavor of Stela 14 at Uxmal. A skull and crossbones motif also appears on Structure 99 at Dzibilchaltun, while at Kabah two jambs from the Codz Poop depict warriors armed with atlatls and darts and shod in sandals like those found on figures appearing at the Great Ball Court at Chichen Itza.[186] Proskouriakoff's studies of Yucatan sculpture have also revealed the presence of non-Classic and Mexican features prior to A.D. 987.[187] Her 1971 article "On Two Inscriptions at Chichen Itza" is also suggestive of a Puuc-Modified Florescent overlap.[188] She has pointed out close resemblances between figures on a column from Structure 6E1 at Chichen and similar figures on sculptures from the Puuc region, including Uxmal Stela 14. Later it will be suggested that this column's hieroglyphic text may refer to the Uxmal ruler "Lord Chac" shown on Stela 14, which would suggest that the Modified Florescent had begun at Chichen Itza by about A.D. 900. Structure 6E1 is in the same complex as Structure 6E3 (The Temple of the Hieroglyphic Jambs), which has traditionally been identified as a Mexican style patio-quadrangle associated with a probable date of 10.2.15.2.13 (A.D. 884).[189] Whether this implies the presence of Toltecs at Chichen Itza at this date, or whether it merely reflects exceptionally strong commercial and political ties between the Itza and Toltecs is a question requiring further study.[190]

What about the end of Puuc architecture? Combined architectural, ceramic, epigraphic, and sculptural evidence from Uxmal and elsewhere certainly suggests that Pure Florescent buildings were not built long after A.D. 907. This represents the last date associated with the late East Structure of the Nunnery. Stela 14, probably the last monument erected at Uxmal, dates stylistically to about the same time. Furthermore, the presence of Lord Chac glyphs on this stela serves to connect it with the Ball Court, Nunnery, and probably the House of the Governor. I would suggest a date of around A.D. 900–915 for the House of the Governor, after which several structures at Uxmal and other Puuc sites were begun but never completed. This strongly suggests a short lapse of time, following which the Puuc centers undoubtedly were abandoned by about A.D. 925–975.[191] Thus the House of the Governor is in a real sense the final triumph of Puuc architecture.

CHAPTER 4

Uxmal and the Xiu

IN his book *The Ancient Maya*, S. G. Morley identified Uxmal as the "New Empire" capital of the Xiu, and suggested that the House of the Governor was the palace of the Xiu ruler as well as the "administrative center of the Xiu state."[1] In this chapter we will discuss the people known as the Xiu, their chronological situation and their role in the history of Uxmal. According to various native Maya and Spanish sources they are reputed to have established themselves at or "founded" Uxmal. From these same sources, and from the work of various scholars who have studied them, however, we can obtain a more accurate picture as to the positions Uxmal and the Xiu occupy in northern Maya history. It will be shown that the Xiu probably entered Yucatan long after Uxmal's abandonment, and that the claim to have "founded" the city was politically motivated.

Information regarding the city springs basically from two founts: in one case, from evidence supplied by dirt archaeology, and in the other case, from historical accounts of the founding of Uxmal and the deeds of its Tutul Xiu rulers contained in various post-conquest Maya and Spanish sources. In his recent study of the Toltecs, Nigel Davies says that any thorough understanding of happenings during the early Post-Classic period "cannot be based solely on the work of the archaeologist, nor can reliance be exclusively placed upon the historical sources; the key to any solution must lie in an apt blend of both."[2] The same caution may be applied to Uxmal, which stands between the Late Classic and the early Post-Classic periods in northern Yucatan.

The problem in synthesizing these two different types of historical evidence on Uxmal is that they often seem contradictory and irreconcilable. Early in this century investigators such as Morley were content to rely on the Maya chronicles alone to supply a consistent and straightforward history of Yucatan. Uxmal was viewed as a "New Empire" city in league with Chichen Itza and Mayapan. These literary sources continued to be accepted at face value by some scholars even after it had been demonstrated archaeologically that Uxmal, Chichen Itza, and Mayapan had their greatest florescences during different periods.

Once the disparity between the literary accounts and the archaeological record was realized, however, subsequent work relied more heavily on archaeological methods, to the extent that several recent syntheses of northern Maya prehistory barely mention the chronicles.[3]

Our task at Uxmal thus becomes bringing these two approaches together again, reviewing and examining the documentary sources in light of the archaeological evidence, and seeking to resolve, or at least explain, their points of difference. If we are unable finally to bring them into complete harmony, we will at least be able to suggest why they are often so inconsistent.

There is abundant material for the study of Maya history in northern Yucatan in the books, chronicles, relations, and other documents dating from the conquest until the seventeenth and eighteenth centuries. Our historical knowledge relies most heavily on the various traditions incorporated in the several Books of Chilam Balam, but a wealth of additional documents contain historical references often couched in prophetic or augural terms, or referred to in land disputes, lawsuits, or proofs of nobility of native Maya lords. Although these documents were written after the conquest, many of them were probably based on earlier Maya hiero-glyphic manuscripts. Such written traditions were also based on a comprehensive oral tradition transmitted from generation to generation by the priestly class before the conquest.

In addition to native Maya sources, there are also several good descriptions of Maya society and history from Spanish observers. We are able to draw information from the great descriptions of Maya life provided by Landa in his *Relación de las cosas de Yucatan*, as well as from the various *Relaciones de Yucatan* of the sixteenth century,[4] and from the histories of Herrera y Tordesillas, Lizana, Sanchez de Aguilar, and Cogolludo from the seventeenth century.

Some of the most important early accounts of the Xiu are written in the Maya language transcribed phonetically in Spanish characters. The Xiu Probanzas are documents such as letters, baptismal certificates, proofs of nobility, and family papers of the Xiu family covering the years from 1557 to 1817.[5] The Books of Chilam Balam are associated with specific towns (e.g., Chumayel, Mani, Tizimin, etc.) and contain several classes of material including Chronicles (U Kahlay Katunob), which are the most important historical sections of the Books of Chilam Balam, taking the form of a listing of events with a corresponding Katun. Although this histori-cal record is ample, it is confusing because it is based not on the Initial Series dating of the Classic period, but on the system called the Short Count, in which events are placed in time only by referring to the Katun in which they occur.[6] If a date is speci-fied only by placing it in a numbered Ahau Katun it may be repeated again after a period of 256½ years. Thus this system permits us to pinpoint a date only within a limited time. Thompson has commented on the historical value of such records:

The chronicles of the various Chilam Balams may be studied from two points of view. They may be taken as true records of Maya history in Yucatan, or they may be considered the compositions of seventeenth or eigh-teenth century re-write men, who knew very little about Maya history. In the latter case it would seem very pos-sible that these later compilers scanned the historical writings or old songs for references to Katuns and then strung these on a thread of continuous Katun endings in positions which they considered most logical. . . .

If the chronicles were composed in the manner sug-gested above it would be very easy for a reference to an event to be placed in the wrong sequence or in the wrong Katun round.[7]

We shall also see that the alterations in the Katun sequence may have been politically motivated in the case of the Xiu. In any case, it is clear that al-though the chronicles contain much of value, they must be used with caution. The most important historical chronicles are those in the Chilam Balam of Chumayel, the Chilam Balam of Tizimin, and the Chilam Balam of Mani, which is also known as the Codex Perez or Mani Manuscript.[8] The Chumayel deals primarily with the Itza, while the Tizimin and Mani pertain to the Tutul Xiu of Uxmal and the Itza.[9] Prophecies include those that supposedly foretold the coming of the Spaniards and the intro-duction of a new religion, as well as prophecies concerning the luck of the day, the Tun, or the Ka-tun. Often historical allusions were included in these augural statements.[10]

Before beginning our investigation of the Xiu proper, it is appropriate to mention two references to Uxmal that place its foundation or occupation far back in time, and which conceivably refer to the pre-Xiu occupation of the site. In the Chilam Balam of Chumayel the following statement appears:

1544 was the year . . . six hundred years and seventy-five years after the town of Chichen Itza was depopu-lated. (It was) eight hundred years and seventy years after the town of Uxmal was depopulated, after the people were driven out of its towns.[11]

This puts the abandonment of Chichen Itza in A.D. 869 and that of Uxmal in A.D. 674. A somewhat similar passage appears in the Relación of Fray Alonso Ponce of 1586 written by Fray Antonio Ciu-dad Real, where it was related by an old Indian infor-mant that more than 900 years had passed since the buildings of Uxmal had been erected. This would put the site's florescence prior to A.D. 686.[12]

It is significant that the Xiu are not mentioned in these accounts, and that the Chumayel version says the people were "driven out" of Uxmal's towns. If these passages were intended to refer to the Xiu withdrawal from Uxmal following the destruction of Mayapan, one would not expect this violent note, for as we shall see, the Xiu were supposed to have abandoned Uxmal and Mayapan voluntarily in order to found their new capital of Mani. It thus seems likely that these references describe the ar-chaeologically documented city of Uxmal.

The dates mentioned in these sources do not seem trustworthy for Uxmal, although the date for Chichen Itza is significant in light of the city's A.D. 869–881 inscriptional dates and Ball's theory that the Mexican period began there at about this time (see chapter 3). The Chumayel account of the abandonment of Uxmal is too early to accord with what is known of the site archaeologically. A more reasonable estimate would be A.D. 925–975. Nevertheless, it is possible to accept these accounts of the original Maya population of Uxmal without accepting the dates as completely factual. The antiquity of many Puuc sites is implied by the names ascribed to them at the time of the Spanish conquest. For example, Labna means "old building in ruins," Xlabpak means "old wall in ruins," and so forth. These names were applied to cities that were occupied contemporaneously with Uxmal, and according to Roys they demonstrate a rupture in the historical traditions of northern Yucatan, since the origin and history of such sites were unknown to the chroniclers of the colonial epoch.[13] It thus seems possible that the dates ascribing great antiquity to the population of Uxmal may mean something like "long ago," referring to original Maya inhabitants who had abandoned the city many years before the Xiu made claim to the site. It is also possible that the Chumayel reference was intended to refer to the actual date of the abandonment of the Puuc city of Uxmal, but that the date was placed in the wrong Katun round, since adding 256 years to A.D. 674 would put Uxmal's abandonment at A.D. 930.

We now turn from possible references to a pre-Xiu occupation of Uxmal to a discussion of the Xiu themselves, the sources for their history, and their link with Uxmal. The first reference to the Xiu in the Chilam Balam of Mani reads as follows:

This is the sequence of the katuns since they left their land, their homes at Nonoual. Four katuns and the Tutul Xiui were to the west of Suyua. The land from whence they came is Tulapan Chiconautlan. Four katuns they journeyed until they arrived here, in the company with the leader (holon) Chan Tepeu and his companions. When they left that region it was (Katun) 8 Ahau.[14]

The several place-names in this passage require comment because they refer to the Xiu place of origin (or homeland) of which one name is Nonoual. Tozzer and Barrera Vásquez equated this with the Nonoualco of the Mexican texts, signifying "the place of the dumb," "the place where a foreign language is spoken," or "the place where the language changes."[15] Attempts have been made by several scholars to locate this place geographically. Tozzer cites Torquemada, who says that Quetzalcoatl, upon his departure from Tula, went to visit other provinces and peoples whom he had sent to colo-

nize the lands of Onohualco which were near the sea and were called Yucatan, Tabasco, and Campeche.[16] Sahagún also states that "the people living in the east are not called Chichimecs but Olmecs, Uixtotin, Nonoualco."[17] Seler proposed that the general meaning of the word Nonoualco was something like "foreign speaking region" or "region where the languages change." He believed that the word stemmed from the Nahuatl root nontli or nonontli, meaning "dumb."[18] According to Seler the word was applied to the lands lying to the east of the Valley of Mexico, particularly those regions bordering the Maya area lying along the gulf coast.[19] Seler's interpretations have been generally accepted, and several other investigators such as Lehmann,[20] Jiménez Moreno,[21] and Ruz Lhuillier[22] have accepted the meaning of Nonoualco as "the land where the languages change."[23]

More recently, however, Davies has questioned Seler's translation and pointed out that several other etymologies exist. One such differing translation is that of Garibay, who points out that the adjective nontli would produce a toponym "Nononco" or "Nonpan," not Nonoualco. Garibay believes that the word derives from onoc, meaning "to be stretched out," or to be established or living in a place. Thus the meaning of Nonoualco might simply be "the inhabited place."[24]

Another possible meaning for Nonoualco has been suggested by Sullivan, who believes that the word might derive from the adverb nononcua, meaning "separately" or "independently." From nononcua a noun nononcualli could be formed, and by adding the locative suffix co the place-name Nononcualco results. Since in Nahuatl an n tends to be lost before consonants, the word Nononcualco might have become first Nonocualco, and later Nonoualco. The meaning for Nonoualco might thus be something like "place of separateness."[25]

Both Torquemada and Sahagún agree in locating Nonoualco to the east of the Valley of Mexico, but Torquemada, in applying the name to Yucatan, Tabasco, and Campeche seems to have included far too much territory under this term, since the Chilam Balam of Mani explicitly states that the Xiu entered Yucatan from this region. Moreover, Landa states that the Tutul Xiu came to Yucatan from the south, which accords reasonably well with what we are told of the Xiu homeland in the chronicles.[26]

Finally, Thompson mentions that an ancient poem concerning Quetzalcoatl's departure from Tula names Acallan as his destination, and that the places he passes through en route are listed as

Xicallango, Tlapallan, and Nonohualco.[27] This association tends to confirm the opinion of Tozzer, who believed that Nonoualco represented a border territory: "This place is generally located near Xicalango on the frontier that separates those who spoke Nahuatl from those who use Maya."[28] Regardless of the etymology then, there is general agreement that Nonoualco was located on the gulf coast of Mexico, probably embracing a large part of Tabasco, and perhaps neighboring territories in Veracruz, Campeche, and Chiapas.

The next place named mentioned is Suyua, or Zuiva as it actually appears in the Mani Chronicle.[29] On the basis of this passage, Seler located Zuiva in Tabasco,[30] suggesting a location between Xicalango and Coatzacoalcos. Seler also attempted to reconstruct the etymology and significance of the word Zuiva. He pointed out that the *Título de los Señores de Totonicapán* mentions "Pa Tulan, Pa Civan" or "In or out of Tollan, out of Civan." This text seemed to substitute Civan (gorge) for Zuiva. Seler was uncertain, however, whether this was the key to the meaning, and Davies has recently suggested that the connection seems dubious in light of the fact that both the words Zuiva and Zivan follow the name Tulan in the *Popol Vuh*. Seler also suggested that Zuiva may derive from *Zoo Paa*, the Zapotec word for west. Davies has challenged this identification, however, noting that in the Guatemalan texts Tulan is sometimes situated in the east as well as in the west, and because the word Zoo Paa does not really sound close to Zuiva.[31] Davies has proposed another possible derivation for Zuiva, which he connects with the Nahuatl words *cihua* and *cihuatlampa*, the western domain of the *cihuateteos*.[32]

Thompson also suggests that Zuiva is associated with the west, but in a different context indicating it lay to the west of Chichen Itza. The Chilam Balam of Chumayel says that the Itza came to Chichen in four divisions and the four (or possibly five) places from which they set forth are associated with world directions. The western point of origin is called Holtun Zuiva. "Holtun" is a Putun (Chontal) word meaning harbor, and Thompson identifies it as the Putun name for Puerto Escondido on the northern arm enclosing the Laguna de Términos.[33] Like Davies, he believes that the word Zuiva is of Nahuatl derivation and closely linked to the Mexican invaders of Yucatan. He suggests that Holtun Zuiva is in the Chontalpa, the river delta region in Tabasco where there was an intermingling of Mexican and Putun Maya cultures.[34] As mentioned,

Seler also believed that Zuiva was probably located between Xicalango and Coatzacoalcos.[35]

Barrera Vásquez, on the other hand, would place Zuiva slightly to the east of Nonoualco, perhaps corresponding to the present-day Isla del Carmen.[36] Krickeberg has noted that:

According to the Annals of the Cakchiquels, the tribes left their original homeland situated in the west, passing by Teocacuancu, Meahuah and Valvalxucxuc (Mexican place-names) until they arrived at Tapcu Oloman in the east, where the people of Ah Nonoualcat, Ah Xulpiti opposed them, which people "lived on the seashore and in canoes." These were conquered and the Cakchiquel tribes proceeded by canoe to a country located still farther to the east, which was that of the people of Ah Zuiva.[37]

Barrera Vásquez points out that if Tozzer is correct in associating Nonoualco with Xicalango, then Zuiva is a place further east which must be reached by canoe, seemingly a perfect description of Isla del Carmen at the eastern end of the Laguna de Términos.[38]

Finally, the Mani chronicle states that the Xiu are said to have had a homeland in "Tulapan Chiconautlan." According to Barrera Vásquez this is a Nahuatl place name which may have the meaning "the place of the nine river metropolises."[39] This might be a logical name for the intensely mercantile area in the Chontalpa and Laguna de Términos regions where we have postulated the existence of Nonoualco and Zuiva. According to Davies the notion that a Tollan was located in that region is supported by the *Toltec Elegy*, which refers to a Tollan Nonoualco.[40] On the other hand, the word Tulapan contains the root word Tula, which may serve to place the name as much in the realm of myth as history. The *Popol Vuh*, for example, describes the arrival of the Quiché tribes, after long travels, at "Tulan Zuiva, Vucub Pec, Vucub Zivan" (Tollan Zuiva, seven caves, seven ravines). The same source also mentions a "Tulan Zuiva, from whence their god came."[41] Several authors have suggested that this Tulan Zuiva of the Quichés was a kind of mythological place of origins, like the Aztec Chicomoztoc.[42]

The place-names in the Chilam Balam of Mani indicate that the Xiu entered Yucatan as foreigners from a region (Nonoualco, Zuiva or Suyua, Tulapan Chiconautlan) lying to the southwest. This is also confirmed by Landa, who writes of the origin of the Xiu:

The Indians say that numerous tribes with their chiefs

came to Yucatan from the south, and it appears that they came from Chiapas, although the Indians have no more knowledge about it. . . . And they say that these tribes wandered around in the uninhabited parts of Yucatan for forty years, without there being any water in that time except that which came from the rain, and that at the end of that time they reached the mountains which lie almost opposite the city of Mayapan and ten leagues from it. And there they began to settle and to construct very good buildings in many places; and the people of Mayapan became very good friends with them and were glad to see that they cultivated the land as the natives do; and in this way the Tutul Xiu subjected themselves to the laws of Mayapan and thus they intermarried, and as the lord Xiu of the Tutul Xius was such he came to be very much esteemed by everybody.[43]

Herrera y Tordesillas follows Landa in stating that "great companies of people," whom he later identifies as the Tutul Xiu, "entered from the south from the slopes of the sierras of Lacandon who, they were sure, were from Chiapas."[44]

Both Landa and Herrera indicate that the Xiu entered the northern part of the peninsula as foreigners. Juan Bote, the encomendero of Teav (modern Teabo), Tec (modern Tiek), and Tiscolum, states in his relación that the Xiu were of Mexican origin:

At one time all this land was under the dominion of one lord, although with change and the passage of time which have been considerable, the last lord of them was a Tutul Xiu from whom descend the natural lords of the said town of Mani of the Royal Crown and he subjected all the lords of the land more by finesse than by war. They say the first of them [the Tutul Xiu] was called Hunuitzilchac, Lord of Uxmal, a most ancient city and well renowned for its buildings, a native of Mexico. And from there he had access to all the remaining provinces, and because of his grandeur it is said of him that he was very learned in the natural sciences and in his time he taught them to cultivate the land, divided the months of the year and taught the letters which they were using in the said province of Mani when the conquerors entered this land and little by little the said Tutulxius came to command the land, very much to the liking of the natives.[45]

In this same relación it is mentioned that "the province of Mani was always at war with that of Sotuta with a lord called Nachi Cocom because of ancient animosity between the Cocoms and the Tutulxiu. The Cocoms it is said are natural lords and the Xiu foreigners."[46]

Juan de Aguilar, the ecomendero of Mama, a village near Mani, states the name Xiu is Mexican, and that they arrived as foreigners from the west. Speaking of the people of Mama, he writes:

They were subject to a lord named Tutul Xiu, a Mexican name. They say he was a foreigner from toward the west; and, having come to this province the chiefs of it by common consent raised him to be King, in view of his qualities of valor. And before he came they were subject to the Cocom, who was the natural lord of a large part of these provinces before the Tutul Xiu came.[47]

It is also implied that the Xiu were foreigners by Sánchez de Aguilar, who writes:

And if we look at the customs which they had before they became Christians, we shall discover that in their paganism they were as civilized and just as the Mexicans, whose vassals they had been six hundred years before the arrrival of the Spaniards. Of this there is only tradition and memory among them because of the famous, large and awe-inspiring buildings of lime and dressed stones, and ashlar masonry, and figures and statues of carved stone which they left in Oxumal [Uxmal] and Chichiniza [Chichen Itza], which are seen today and which could be lived in.[48]

There are other indications that the Xiu either were of Mexican origin, or had close contact with Mexican peoples before entering the peninsula. For example, Landa says that when the Xiu arrived their only weapons were the *atlatl* and darts, typical Mexican highland weapons.[49] Furthermore, one of the names on the Xiu family tree, Ah Cuat Xiu, is of Nahuat origin, *cuat* being a variant of *coatl* (fig. 35).[50] Finally, the crown worn by the founder of the Xiu lineage on the family tree closely resembles the *copilli* crown in Aztec manuscripts (fig. 35).[51]

The etymology of the word Xiu also points to a foreign origin for this tribe. Tozzer considered the name Tutul Xiu to be of Mexican origin, pointing out that Xiuhtotol signifies turquoise bird in Nahuatl. Such turquoise birds appear as adornments on the headdresses of warriors represented at Chichen Itza, although few scholars would now identify these warriors as the Xiu.[52] Brinton ascribed a Maya origin to the name, believing it to be composed of Xiu "grass or plant," Tutul (duplicated form of *tul*) "abundance, excess." He considered it likely that the name referred to those from a place with an abundance of plants. However, Brinton also considered the possibility that Tutul Xiu was a Nahuatl name composed of Xiuitl "plant, turquoise, comet, year, green or blue color," Totol "bird or fowl."[53] Roys translated the word Xiu as plant, a common term in Yucatec Maya, but he attributed to it a Nahuatl origin.[54]

From the foregoing passage in the Mani chronicle, as well as from the several Spanish sources, it is clear that the Xiu were foreigners to Yucatan, and

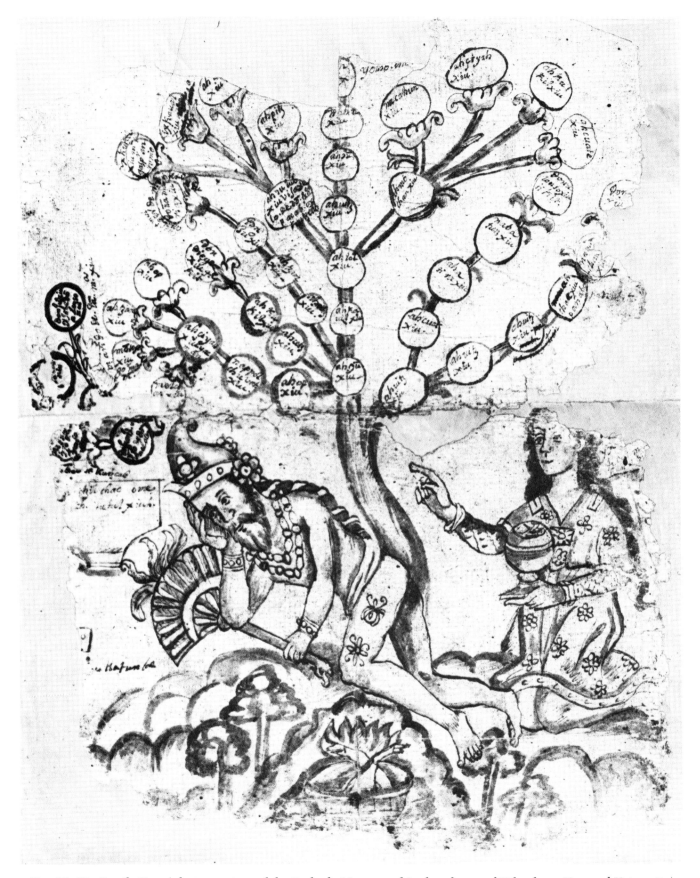

Fig. 35. Xiu Family Tree (photo courtesy of the Peabody Museum of Archaeology and Ethnology, Harvard University).

in the opinion of the conquerors they were of Mexican origin. In this regard it is important to note that Juan Bote admits that he was assisted in the preparation of his relación by Gaspar Antonio Chi, who was a native of Mani and a Xiu on his mother's side.[55] This suggests that the Xiu themselves believed they were of Mexican origin.[56] Against this, however, are the statements of Landa and Herrera linking the Xiu with Chiapas and indicating that they spoke a Maya dialect.

The notion of a "Mexican" origin should probably not be taken to imply that the Xiu were originally located in the central highlands, however, since the place-names in the Mani chronicle connect them with the southern gulf coast. In this connection, Morley suggested that whether the Xiu were originally Maya or Nahuatl, they had been living sufficiently long in the Maya-speaking region to the southwest of the peninsula to have become "thoroughly Mayanized in language and largely in culture as well."[57]

If the Xiu did come from Tabasco they might actually have had a polyglot language and mixed culture. As Thompson has pointed out, in the delta of the Grijalva River of Tabasco, Nahuat-speaking towns mingle with those of Putun or Chontal Maya speech, a situation which probably predates the conquest by several centuries.[58] This intermixture of Maya and Nahuat traditions is indicated by the name Ah Cuat Xiu mentioned earlier.

It may well be that Foncerrada's ideas concerning the cultural background of the Xiu are not far off the mark. She believes the point of departure for the Xiu migration, as well as that of the Itza, was from the southwestern region of the peninsula—southern Veracruz, Chiapas, and Tabasco. This group was non-Classic Maya, but they maintained strong contact with Maya civilization. Probably they were Chontal speakers rather than Yucatec speakers. The knowledge they had of first southern Maya and then northern Maya cultures came about as a result of trade. Foncerrada also believes that by the ninth and tenth centuries such peoples had acquired enough knowledge of Maya culture to enable them to penetrate Yucatan peacefully and to adapt to the life and culture of the region.[59] Although it is possible that this describes the situation for the Itza, and probably in broad terms for the Xiu as well, we shall see that there are strong reasons to believe that the Xiu did not enter Yucatan as early as Foncerrada suggests, but more likely came during the thirteenth or fourteenth century during the hegemony of Mayapan.

Returning now to the Mani and Tizimin chronicles, we find the Xiu journeying for some time after leaving their homes in Nonoualco:

Four Katuns they journeyed until they arrived here in company with the leader (holon) Chan Tepeu and his companions. When they left that region (peten) it was (Katun) 8 Ahau:
(Katun) 6 Ahau,
(Katun) 4 Ahau,
(Katun) 2 Ahau: fourscore and 1 year more [81], because it was Tun 1 of (Katun) 13 Ahau when they arrived here to this region (peten).
fourscore years and 1 year in all they journeyed since they left their lands and came here to the region of Chacnabiton; These are the years: 81 years (Katun) 13 Ahau;
(Katun) 8 Ahau,
(Katun) 6 Ahau,
(Katun) 4 Ahau,
(Katun) 2 Ahau, it was when he arrived at Chacnabiton, Ah Mekat Tutul Xiu [and his people] one year less than fivescore years they were in Chacnabiton; these are the years: 99 years, . . .[60]

Following this the narrative breaks off and shifts to an account of the discovery of Chichen Itza by the Itza. The Xiu narrative then resumes as follows:

In Katun 2 Ahau he established himself, Ah Suytok Tutul Xiu, at Uxmal.
(Katun) 2 Ahau,
(Katun) 13 Ahau,
(Katun) 11 Ahau,
(Katun) 9 Ahau,
(Katun) 7 Ahau,
(Katun) 5 Ahau,
(Katun) 3 Ahau,
(Katun) 1 Ahau,
(Katun) 12 Ahau: [these Katuns had passed] since he established himself, Ah Suytok Tutul Xiu, at Uxmal.
Tenscore years they reigned in the land of Uxmal in company with the halach uinicob of Chichen Itza and Mayapan. these are the years which went by when this happened: 200 years.[61]

The first passage relates that the Xiu, led by Holon Chan Tepeu, journeyed until they arrived at a place known as Chacnabiton. The location of Chacnabiton is not definitely known, but Barrera Vásquez places it in the south or southwest of the Yucatan peninsula.[62] The journey took 81 years, during the Katuns 8 Ahau, 6 Ahau, 4 Ahau, and 2 Ahau, with the Xiu arriving at Chacnabiton in the

Table 3. *Historical Chronology of the Xiu*

Short Count	Long Count Position	Christian Dates	Events (Barrera Vásquez, Morley)	Events (Tozzer, Roys, Kowalski)
Katun 5 Ahau	10.1.0.0.0	849		
Katun 3 Ahau	10.2.0.0.0	869	Xiu arrive at Nonoualco	
Katun 1 Ahau	10.3.0.0.0	889		
Katun 12 Ahau	10.4.0.0.0	909		c.905–907: Hieroglyphic references to Lord Chac (Nunnery capstones, Ball Court rings).
Katun 10 Ahau	10.5.0.0.0	928	Led by Holon Chan Tepeu, Xiu depart from Nonoualco, journey to Chacnabiton	Abandonment of Uxmal
Katun 8 Ahau	10.6.0.0.0	948		
Katun 6 Ahau	10.7.0.0.0	968		
Katun 4 Ahau	10.8.0.0.0	987		
Katun 2 Ahau	10.9.0.0.0	1007	Ah Suytok Tutul Xiu (Hun Uitzil Chac) establishes himself at Uxmal (977). League of Mayapan begins. The Xiu and their leader Ah Mekat arrive at Chacnabiton.	
Katun 13 Ahau	10.10.0.0.0	1027		
Katun 11 Ahau	10.11.0.0.0	1047		
Katun 9 Ahau	10.12.0.0.0	1066		
Katun 7 Ahau	10.13.0.0.0	1086		
Katun 5 Ahau	10.14.0.0.0	1106	Xiu remain in Chacnabiton until this time.	
Katun 3 Ahau	10.16.0.0.0	1125		Xiu arrive at Nonoualco?
Katun 1 Ahau	10.17.0.0.0	1145		
Katun 12 Ahau	10.16.0.0.0	1165		
Katun 10 Ahau	10.18.0.0.0	1185		Led by Holon Chan Tepeu the Xiu depart from Nonoualco, journey to Chacnabiton
Katun 8 Ahau	10.19.0.0.0	1204	(1194) Treachery of Hunac Ceel. End of Mayapan League.	
Katun 6 Ahau	11.0.0.0.0	1224		
Katun 4 Ahau	11.1.0.0.0	1244		
Katun 2 Ahau	11.2.0.0.0	1263		Xiu and their leader Ah Mekat arrive at Chacnabiton. Foundation of Mayapan. (Edmonson suggests Ah Suytok Tutul Xiu establishes himself at Uxmal and enters into "joint government" with Mayapan).
Katun 13 Ahau	11.3.0.0.0	1283		
Katun 11 Ahau	11.4.0.0.0	1303		
Katun 9 Ahau	11.5.0.0.0	1323		
Katun 7 Ahau	11.6.0.0.0	1342		
Katun 5 Ahau	11.7.0.0.0	1362		Xiu remain in Chacnabiton until this time.
Katun 3 Ahau	11.8.0.0.0	1382		Cocom assume power at Mayapan. Birth of Ah Suytok Tutul Xiu.
Katun 1 Ahau	11.9.0.0.0	1401		
Katun 12 Ahau	11.10.0.0.0	1421		
Katun 10 Ahau	11.11.0.0.0	1441		Ah Suytok Tutul Xiu establishes himself at Uxmal. Xiu enter into "joint government" with Cocom at Mayapan.
Katun 8 Ahau	11.12.0.0.0	1461	Abandonment of Mayapan in plot led by Ah Xupan Xiu. Foundation of Mani.	Hunan Ceel Episode. Abandonment of Mayapan. Death of Ah Suytok Tutul Xiu (Hun Uitzil Chac). Assumption of power by priest Ah Xupan Nauat. Foundation of Mani.
Katun 6 Ahau	11.13.0.0.0	1480		
Katun 4 Ahau	11.14.0.0.0	1500		
Katun 2 Ahau	11.15.0.0.0	1520		
Katun 13 Ahau	11.16.0.0.0	1539	Massacre of Xiu lords at Otzmal (1536).	Massacre of Xiu lords at Otzmal (1536).

first Tun of Katun 13 Ahau. Barrera Vásquez and Morley agree that this period is from the beginning of 10.6.0.0.0 (A.D. 928) through 10.9.1.0.0 (A.D. 1008) (see table 3).[63] After arriving at Chacnabiton, the Xiu and their leader, Ah Mekat Tutul Xiu,[64] stayed in this place some 99 years, from the beginning of Katun 13 Ahau (10.10.0.0.0, A.D. 1007–1027) to the end of Katun 5 Ahau (10.14.0.0.0, A.D. 1086–1106). It must be said, however, that this correlation of Katuns with Christian chronology is somewhat arbitrary. Thus the Katun 8 Ahau during which the Xiu began their travels out of Nonoualco to Chacnabiton could also refer to the Katun 8 Ahau corresponding to A.D. 1185–1204, a placement favored by Roys and by the writer.[65]

In the second part of the Mani chronicle we are told that Ah Suytok Tutul Xiu established himself at Uxmal in a Katun 2 Ahau. Brinton's translation of this passage, which differs slightly from that of Barrera Vásquez, is given below:

In the Katun the second Ahau Ahcuitok Tutul Xiu founded (the city of) Uxmal; the second ahau, the thirteenth ahau, the eleventh ahau, the ninth ahau, the seventh ahau, the fifth ahau, the third ahau, the first ahau, the twelfth ahau, the tenth ahau; ten score years they ruled with the governor of Chichen Itza and Mayapan; these are the years 200.[66]

The two translations of the Maya text differ only slightly, with Barrera Vásquez saying that Ah Suytok Tutul Xiu "established himself" in Uxmal, while Brinton states less equivocally that Ahcuitok Tutul Xiu "founded" Uxmal.[67] The difference hinges on the Yucatec Maya word heɔcicab. The verb stem of this word is heɔ, which is defined in the Pio Pérez dictionary as "apoyar, sellar, asertar con firmeza// Eligir lugar. Fundar, establecer usos" (to confirm, to conclude, to assert or establish with firmeza//To choose a place. To found, to establish customs).[68] The San Francisco dictionary defines the phrase Heɔ luum, which is similar to heɔcicab, as "poblar, tomar posesión, eligir lugar" (to populate or settle, to take possession, to choose a place or land).[69] These definitions do not resolve the difference between Barrera Vásquez and Brinton, since both the meanings "to found" and "to establish oneself" seem appropriate for the word heɔcicab. The definition of Heɔ luum is important, however, because it suggests that Ah Suytok Tutul Xiu merely may have settled at or taken possession of Uxmal, possibly at a time after its original inhabitants had abandoned it.

Before moving to a discussion of the dating of the

Xiu "foundation" of Uxmal it will be helpful to examine further the identity of its "founder." Both the Mani and Tizimin chronicles give the name of this figure as Ah Suytok Tutul Xiu.[70] On the other hand, Juan Bote, in the relación of Teav, Tec, and Tiscolum, states that the first lord of the Xiu at Uxmal was named Hunuitzilchac. This is the only mention of this person in the Spanish sources. In the early Maya record, however, there are six references to Hun Uitzil Chac in three sources: the Chilam Balam of Mani, the Chilam Balam of Tizimin, and the Xiu family tree (Document 3 of the Xiu Family Papers).

In the Chilam Balam of Mani two different passages contain this name. The first reads "In this book of the Seven Generations, the priest Chilam Balam saw it and he read the roll of the Katun with the priest Napuc Tun, the priest of the Hun Uitzil Chac of Uxmal."[71] The second reads "I, Ah Kauil (Chel) and Napuc Tun and Ah Xupan Nauat the priests of the *halach uinic* Ah Hun Uitzil Chac Tutul Xiu at the villa of Uxmal in the land, the district, there in the province of Mayapan, Mai[a], Cu[zamil]."[72]

The Chilam Balam of Tizimin contains two very similar passages in which Napuc Tun, Ah Kauil Chel, and Ah Xupan Nauat are named as the priests of Hun Uitzil Chac of Uxmal, in the land of Mayapan.[73]

The third native source mentioning Hun Uitzil Chac is the Xiu family tree (fig. 35). There the name appears twice: once at the foot of the tree identifying the founder of the Xiu family line, where it appears in association with a possible Katun 3 Ahau;[74] and again, in the legend referring to the woman at the lower right, an Yx . . . of Ticul, who is said to be the wife of Hun Uitzil Chac.[75]

At this point let us summarize briefly. From the Spanish sources we learn that the Xiu came from the south (Landa) or west (Juan de Aguilar), that they were of "Mexican" origin (Juan Bote, Sánchez de Aguilar inferentially) although Landa indicates that they spoke a Maya dialect, and that they founded their capital at Uxmal (Landa inferentially) under Hun Uitzil Chac (Juan Bote). Native Maya sources are not explicit on the first two points, but give many details about the Xiu entry into Yucatan and the foundation of Uxmal. According to the chronicles Uxmal was established by Ah Suytok Tutul Xiu, while Bote described the first lord of Uxmal as Hun Uitzil Chac, which is supported by his placement on the Xiu family tree. Because both of these names are associated with the Tutul Xiu founder of Uxmal, Morley has suggested that they refer to the same man. He believes that the *paal* (patrilineal) name of the Xiu leader was Ah Suytok, but that he was also called Hun Uitzil Chac, which was his *coco*, a nickname or title.[76]

In the Mani chronicle it is stated that Ah Suytok Tutul Xiu "founded" or established himself at Uxmal in a Katun 2 Ahau. Barrera Vásquez and Morley place this Katun 2 Ahau at 10.9.0.0.0, or between A.D. 987–1007, believing that toward the end of the 81-year period when the first group of the Xiu were traveling between Nonoualco and Chacnabíton (A.D. 928–1008) another group of the same tribe, led by Ah Suytok Tutul Xiu, occupied the city of Uxmal in the Puuc hill country (table 3).[77] Morley pointed out that a date of A.D. 987–1007 for the foundation of Uxmal is in general agreement with statements made by Landa and Sanchez de Aguilar. Landa attributed the destruction of Mayapan to the greed of the Cocom family, who brought in Mexican mercenaries (the Ah Canul) from Tabasco to oppress the people. The Tutul Xiu ruler opposed this tyranny, and, acting in concert with other nobles, killed the Cocom ruler and all his sons except for one who was away on a trading mission. According to Landa "who said that they had been unjustly driven out, and the Xius lasted so long that after having been in that city [Mayapan] for more than five hundred years, they abandoned it and left it desolate, each one going to his own land."[78]

Since according to the Maya chronicles Mayapan was abandoned in a Katun 8 Ahau between A.D. 1441 and 1461, an occupation of more than five hundred years would place its foundation before about A.D. 950. Morley interprets the reference as pertaining to the Xiu as well as to the Cocom. It is unlikely, however, that the Xiu were living at Mayapan as long as the Cocom, since both Landa and Juan de Aguilar state that they arrived in Yucatan during the Cocom rule of Mayapan. Furthermore, Gaspar Antonio Chi relates that Mayapan had been inhabited only 260 years before its abandonment. As we have seen, Sanchez de Aguilar says that the people of Uxmal and Chichen Itza had been subjects of the Mexicans for over six hundred years prior to the arrival of the Spanish, that is from as early as A.D. 917–942.

Morley's date of A.D. 987–1007 for the Xiu "foundation" of Uxmal seems impossible to accept in the face of archaeological evidence. Uxmal was certainly occupied several centuries before this date, and at the time in question it was undoubtedly an abandoned city, with only the still extant buildings such as the House of the Governor bearing witness to its former glory.

The "foundation" of Uxmal is referred to in the Chilam Balam of Tizimin in a different way than in the Mani. According to Brinton's translation, the Tizimin reads "[Katun] 10 Ahau; Ah Zuitok Tutulxiu founded Uxmal; ten score years passed since they established the territory of Uxmal.[79]

The same passage is given by Barrera Vásquez as follows: "(Katun) 10 Ahau, . . . he established himself, Ah Suytok Tutul Xiu, at Uxmal. Tenscore years, they reigned in the land of Uxmal . . ."[80]

Barrera Vásquez and Morley interpret this passage as placing the foundation of Uxmal in the same period of A.D. 987–1007 referred to in the Mani chronicle (table 3).[81] Morley believes that the Katun 10 Ahau referred to is not the foundation date of Uxmal, but rather the katun reached by counting up the "tenscore years" that had passed since the Xiu had reigned in Uxmal. Counting back tenscore years (approximately ten Katuns) from Katun 10 Ahau would place the establishment of Uxmal in a Katun 2 Ahau.[82] Thus, Barrera Vásquez and Morley, and Foncerrada as well, agree in placing the date of the foundation of Uxmal, at least according to the written sources, in Katun 2 Ahau corresponding to A.D. 987–1007.[83]

The *U Kahlay Katunob* from the Chilam Balam of Mani, aside from referring to the "foundation" of Uxmal by Ah Suytok Tutul Xiu, also indicate that there was a joint government of some sort among Mayapan, Chichen Itza, and Uxmal following the establishment of the latter city. Brinton translated this passage as follows:

In the katun the second ahau Ahcuitok Tutulxiu founded (the city of) Uxmal; the second ahau, the thirteenth ahau, the eleventh ahau, the ninth ahau, the seventh ahau, the fifth ahau, the third ahau, the first ahau, the twelfth ahau the tenth ahau; ten score years they ruled with the governor of Chichen Itza and Mayapan; these were years . . . 200.[84]

Because of this passage there has been a tendency to link Uxmal, Chichen Itza, and Mayapan together by virtue of their common membership in what Brinton termed the "League of Mayapan."[85] According to Morley this was the period of the "New Empire" or the "Maya Renaissance," a time of "peace, prosperity and architectural pre-eminence" (table 3).[86] In fact, however, the native Maya sources tell us nothing about the Xiu during this 200-year period. It is only during the hegemony of Mayapan that they reappear.

Although the passage in the Mani chronicle has been used to support the idea of a "League of Mayapan" during the period from A.D. 987 to 1185, Tozzer and Roys felt, on the basis of archaeological evidence and other historical references, that this political association was relatively unimportant and existed only for a short time at a later date.[87]

Archaeologically it is impossible to support the idea of a unified political league among Uxmal, Chichen Itza, and Mayapan during the period A.D. 987–1185. As we have seen in chapter 3, Uxmal was abandoned by this time, while Mayapan did not become an important center until the end of this period or perhaps later. Pollock has summarized Mayapan's chronological position as follows:

It is . . . apparently not until the end of the Middle Mexican or the beginning of the Late Mexican times that pottery was made and used in quantity. . . . Finally, it was the Late Mexican sub-stage that saw Mayapan in full flower, with most of the architecture being erected and pottery being made at this time.[88]

Because of this archaeological evidence, Roys and Tozzer have suggested the documentary evidence shows that events which are supposed to have been responsible for the dissolution of the League of Mayapan took place in the fifteenth century rather than in the twelfth century (table 3). The central cause of the breakup of the Mayapan league is what Roys termed the "Hunac Ceel Episode."[89] Strife is said to have begun when Hunac Ceel, a ruler of Mayapan, treacherously concocted a love potion with the plumeria flower, which caused Chac-Xib-Chac, the ruler of Chichen Itza, to covet the bride of Ah Ulil, the ruler of Izamal. While attending the wedding ceremonies Chac Xib Chac was persuaded to smell the magic flower and abducted the bride. This insult led to the destruction of Chichen Itza and the expulsion of the Itza. The Izamal ruler apparently had a further grievance against Chac-Xib-Chac, since he or his people had been forced to give sons as sacrifices to Hapay Can ("Sucking Snake"), a serpent god at Chichen Itza.[90]

The Mani chronicle specifies a Tun 10 of Katun 8 Ahau as the time when Chac-Xib-Chac was driven out because of the treachery of Hunac Ceel, the *halach uinic* of Mayapan "the fortress."[91] The passage reads as follows:

(Katun) 8 Ahau, he abandoned, (he) the *halach uinic* of Chichen Itza of the Itza men, their homes for a second time, because of the treachery (plot) of Hunac Ceel Cauich. against Chac Xib Chac of Chichen Itza, because of the plot of Hunac Ceel, *halach uinic* of Mayapan

Ichpa. Fourscore years and 10 more have passed. In Tun 10 of (Katun) 8 Ahau was the year in which they were dispersed because of Ah Sinteut Chan and Tzuntecum and Taxcal and Pantemit, Xuchueuet and Itzcuat and Cacaltecat. These are the names of the men, and seven men of Mayapan.[92]

Barrera Vásquez and Morley, and even Roys in an earlier work,[93] placed the Tun 10 of Katun 8 Ahau in question at A.D. 1194 (table 3), suggesting that following the abandonment of Chichen Itza by Chac-Xib-Chac and the Itza, Mayapan became politically preeminent in the peninsula. This reconstruction was also accepted by Thompson.[94] He later revised his views on the League of Mayapan, but continued to support the idea that Hunac Ceel drove the Itza from Chichen Itza in A.D. 1185–1204, after which they traveled south to Lake Peten.[95]

Roys, however, points out that the abandonment of Chichen Itza in a Katun 8 Ahau corresponding to A.D. 1185–1204 is unlikely. Since Mayapan figures so prominently in most accounts of the expulsion, and the event could scarcely have occurred before the founding and florescence of that city. On the basis of the Chumayel second chronicle, Roys places the foundation of Mayapan in a Katun 13 Ahau corresponding to A.D. 1263–1283.[97] Thus the end of Chichen Itza must have taken place after that date, at a time when Mayapan had actually become an important power.

Further evidence for a later expulsion of the Itza comes from Fray Bartolomé de Fuensalida. In 1618 Fuensalida made a visit to the Itza town of Tayasal in Lake Peten, Guatemala. While there, he was told by the Itza that they had fled from Chichen Itza in an "age" or Katun called 8 Ahau, some hundred years before the arrival of the Spaniards in Yucatan. They said that they departed both because of prophecies that people would come from the east to dominate the land, and because of the abduction of a bride during the wedding party of a more powerful neighbor,[98] an obvious reference to the Hunac Ceel episode. The Itza of Lake Peten place the incident one hundred years before the conquest, which would make it about A.D. 1417–1442. The latter date falls within the Katun 8 Ahau from A.D. 1441–1461, supporting the idea that the Hunac Ceel episode occurred near the fall of Mayapan.[99]

Another reference suggesting a late date for Hunac Ceel occurs in the Chilam Balam of Tizimin, which reads:

(Katun) 8 Ahau was when it occurred at Chichen, when the ruler of the people of Uxmal was painted. Then oc-

curred the trampling on the back of Chac-xib-chac by Ah
Nacxit Kukulcan; then came the general questioning of
the Ah Itza . . . occurred [to] Ah Ulil Itzmal. This, then,
was the time when he [Ah-Chac-xib-chac] sniffed [at the
plumeria], when he was deceived, because a sin was
committed against Ah Ulil Ahau, against the woman, the
wife of his fellow ruler. . . . Miserable is his soul when
he [Chac-xib-chac] under-goes his misery here at Izamal, deceived by the sin of the ruler of the Canul.[100]

According to Roys, one of the most important implications of this passage is that the "sin of the ruler
of the Canul" (u keban yahau canul) is virtually the
same as the "treachery of Hunac Ceel (u keban
than Hunac Ceel) mentioned in the chronicles.
This suggests that Hunac Ceel was one of the Ah
Canul or Canul, the Mexican mercenaries of the
Cocom ruler at Mayapan.[101] Landa's account indicates that the introduction of the Ah Canul did not
occur until near the end of Cocom leadership at
Mayapan, and was one of the provocations leading
to the revolt of the resident rulers under the leadership of the Xiu.[102] Thus, if Hunac Ceel was a Canul
he must be associated with the end of Mayapan.

Still another reference suggesting a late date for
the Hunac Ceel episode appears in the Chilam
Balam of Mani as follows:

Now Katun 11 Ahau, according to its reign, was when the
foreigners entered our land here, in order to bring us
into Christianity. It then began, as they say, but it was
Katun 8 Ahau, before the coming of the foreigners. This
was when occurred the introduction of the treachery to
them, the holy men, [a term applied to the Itza in the
chronicles] . . . of treachery to them [keban than]. They
understood the arrival of the time of the opening of the
13-cluster plumeria flower through the agency of Hunac
Ceel, halach uinic of Mayapan within the walls [of Maya-
pan]. It was he who caused the plumeria to come forth to
his [Chac-xib-chac's] nose, so that he would desire the
woman. Now this was because the time drew near, the
arrival of the time, the Katun given to them by their
great rulers. These were Cetzalcuat [Quetzalcoatl], Ah
Buluc Am ['11 Spider'], as he was called by their priests
and their wise men. This was Montezuma.[103]

This passage suggests that the Katun 8 Ahau associated with Hunac Ceel's treachery should be located near to the Spanish entry into Yucatan.
Furthermore, the Montezuma mentioned in this
passage is presumably Montezuma the Elder, who
reigned from 1440 to 1468. Both of these indicate
that the Katun 8 Ahau linked with Hunac Ceel and
the Itza abandonment of Chichen Itza fell from A.D.
1441 to 1461.[104]

If Roys is correct in his chronological placement

of the Hunac Ceel episode, which seems quite
probable, then the "League of Mayapan" must be
understood as something quite different from the
powerful political alliance formed of the equal part-
ners of Uxmal, Chichen Itza, and Mayapan envisioned by Brinton, Barrera Vasquez, and Morley.
Nevertheless, it does seem possible that some sort
of "league" may have existed, and that it may have
included the Xiu of Uxmal and the inhabitants of
Chichen Itza, though it seems likely that this political association was short-lived and occurred toward
the end of Mayapan's hegemony (table 3).[105] The nature of the Xiu participation in the government
of Mayapan differs according to the source con-
sulted. Some sources refer to the Tutul Xiu as the
supreme ruler at Mayapan, while others seemingly
more trustworthy indicate that the Xiu managed to
rise to a position of prominence and influence in
what might be called a kind of "joint government."

A strongly pro-Xiu source is the 1582 relación of
Gaspar Antonio Chi, which states:

This province of Yucatan, which is (called Maya by the
natives) was governed in former times (by one supreme
lord; and the) last descendant of these was a Tutul Xiu,
(who was the lord of Mani. His capital a) very populous
city (named Mayapan) and by wars and (disagreements
between him and his vassals they came to lose) the said
custom. (They resolved upon the destruction of Mayapan and razed the) city about the year of the Lord (one
thousand four hundred and twenty,) two hundred and
sixty years (after its foundation) . . .[106]

Statements that the Xiu once ruled supreme at
Mayapan also are found in several of the Relaciones
de Yucatan. In the relación of Dzan, Panabch'en,
and Muna (in the Xiu province of Mani) it is said of
Mayapan that "In this city the absolute lord was Tutul Xiu, from whom descend the lords of the said
province of Mani."[107] A similar assertion of Xiu superiority is made in the relación of Tekal, to be
cited later. In reality, however, the statements in
these relaciones also may be ascribed to Gaspar Antonio Chi, since it is known that he collaborated in
the preparation of at least twelve of the relaciones
from western Yucatan.[108] Although he was extremely
well informed about the pre-conquest history of
Yucatan, Chi cannot be considered an absolutely
trustworthy source because he was himself a Xiu on
his mother's side and was related to two Xiu nobles
who were murdered at Otzmal by the Cocom during an attempted Xiu pilgrimage to the Sacred
Cenote of Chichen Itza in 1536.[109] There was thus a
natural enmity between Chi and the Cocom, which

apparently led him to exaggerate the importance of his own Xiu ancestors in certain instances. Gaspar Antonio Chi also was seeking a pension from the Crown of Spain at about the time the relaciones were written, which also might have prompted him to inflate the prestige of the Xiu lineage.[110]

Gaspar Antonio Chi's accounts of Xiu superiority are contradicted by Landa, who states that the Xiu were latecomers to Yucatan and that they were the instigators of the rebellion, which overthrew the Cocom rulers of a joint government at Mayapan.[111] Landa seems to be a less biased source than Gaspar Antonio Chi on this matter. It is known that Landa obtained information at an earlier date both from Gaspar Antonio Chi and from Nachi Cocom, the ruler of Sotuta.[112] Landa's account is also confirmed by Fray Antonio de Ciudad Real, who states that the Cocom ruler, not the Xiu, was the supreme head of the joint government at Mayapan at the time of its destruction.[113]

In general, these accounts seem to present a more balanced picture of the Xiu than does Gaspar Antonio Chi. They indicate that after a relatively late entry into the peninsula the Xiu were able to establish a niche for themselves in the government of Mayapan, although they remained subservient to the Cocom until the fall of the city.

Because of the insurmountable inconsistencies between the Barrera Vasquez and Morley interpretation of the chronicles and the archaeological evidence, and because of the strong evidence that the Mayapan League and the Hunac Ceel episode are associated with the end of Mayapan, Roys and Tozzer do not accept the Mani chronicle's statement that Uxmal was founded in the Katun 2 Ahau corresponding to A.D. 987–1007. Instead, they prefer to take the Tizimin reference, in which Ah Suytok Tutul Xiu is said to have founded Uxmal in a Katun 10 Ahau, at face value. Roys interprets this as referring not to the Katun 10 Ahau ending in A.D. 928 or 1185, but rather to the one from A.D. 1421 to 1441, immediately preceding the Katun 8 Ahau (A.D. 1441–1461) in which Mayapan was abandoned (table 3).[114]

Another possible alternative has been proposed by Edmonson, who places the establishment of the land of Uxmal by "Zuytok, a Tutul Xiu of Uxmal" in Katun 2 Ahau corresponding to A.D. 1244–1263.[115] The Xiu then ruled in some type of joint government until the treachery of Hunac Ceel and the fall of Mayapan in Katun 8 Ahau. Edmonson's recent interpretation has the merit of keeping the "foundation" of Uxmal in a Katun 2

Ahau, which is the date definitely stated in the Chilam Balam of Mani. However, there also are ample grounds for accepting Roys' suggestion the Xiu were relative latecomers to Yucatan. Not the least of these is the fact that virtually all sources connect the Xiu with the hegemony and downfall of Mayapan. We have seen, for example, that according to Landa and Herrera y Tordesillas the entrance of the Xiu into Yucatan and their rise to power is said to have occurred after the Cocom family had assumed power at Mayapan.[116] A similar reference occurs in the relación of Mama, where it is said that the people of Yucatan were "subject to the Cocom, who was the natural lord of a large part of these provinces before the Tutul Xiu came."[117]

These references convincingly connect the Xiu's entrance into Yucatan with the Cocom overlordship of Mayapan. Roys has argued persuasively that the Cocom family assumed power at Mayapan as the result of a revolution against another faction of the Itza in a Katun 3 Ahau corresponding to A.D. 1362–1382.[118] It thus seems likely that the Xiu did not enter northern Yucatan until later (table 3).

Even more important in this regard is the relación of Tekal (located north of Izamal), which suggests that the first Tutul Xiu ruler to enter the lands of Mayapan was still living when it was abandoned. The report reads as follows:

At one time all this land was under one lord, in the time when the lords of Chichen Itza reigned; and their lordship endured more than 200 years. After much time, the city of Mayapan was settled, where the absolute lord was one whom they called Tutul Xiu, from whom descend the natural lords of the town of Mani of the Royal Crown. This one took all the land more by strategy than by war; and he gave laws, determined the ceremonies and rites that he had, and he taught letters and ordained his lordships and knighthoods. And the tribute which they gave him was no more than a certain acknowledgement of a [turkey] hen each, and a little maize at the time of the harvest. And after his death, and even before it, there were other lords in every province. And they did not take tribute from their vassals more than what the latter wished to give, except that they served them with their persons and arms in war, whenever the occasion offered. And so at the conquest of these provinces [by the Spaniards] there were already many lords and caciques. In every province there were lords, because after the destruction of Mayapan, an ancient city where the Tutul Xiu was lord, there was no enduring peace in these provinces; but each province had its cacique and lord. and so the conquerors found it.[119]

This relación suggests that the destruction of Mayapan and the breakup of the country into small *cacicazqos* occurred even before the death of the Tutul Xiu. According to Roys:

This comes from Xiu sources [Gaspar Antonio Chi], and implies that the Xiu arrived in northern Yucatan, established themselves in the "joint government" (*mul tepal*) at Mayapan, and overthrew the city within, or almost within the reign of a single ruler.[120]

For this reason he feels confident in placing the "foundation" of Uxmal in the Katun 10 Ahau immediately preceding the Katun 8 Ahau (1441–1461) when Mayapan was destroyed, and therefore identifies the Tutul Xiu ruler who conspired against the Cocom with the Ah Suytok Tutul Xiu mentioned in the chronicles, and with Hun Uitzil Chac (table 3).[121] The identification of the Tutul Xiu ruler at Mayapan with Hun Uitzil Chac is strengthened by the description in the Tekal relación of the Tutul Xiu as one who "took all the land more by strategy than by war," who gave laws, determined ceremonies and rites, and taught letters. This description is remarkably close to that of Hun Uitzil Chac Tutul Xiu given by Juan Bote in the relación of Teav, Tec y Tiscolum, and seems to refer to the same person.

Another reference that may connect Hun Uitzil Chac with the abandonment of Mayapan occurs in the Chilam Balam of Chumayel. This account links a Xiu priest and a personage named Uxmal Chac with Hunac Ceel of Mayapan and Chac-Xib-Chac of Chichen Itza.[122] As we have seen, Roys has shown that there are strong reasons for placing the Hunac Ceel episode in the Katun 8 Ahau that fell in A.D. 1441–1461. Since Bote states that Hun Uitzil Chac was the lord of Uxmal it seems probable that the name Uxmal Chac is a shorthand reference to the same person. If so, this would again indicate that the Xiu "first lord" of the Uxmal was still living at or around the time of the fall of Mayapan.

Earlier it was mentioned that Hun Uitzil Chac appears at the base of the Xiu family tree as the progenitor of the Xiu lineage (fig. 35). The genealogical and chronological information contained on this tree has been interpreted differently by Morley and Roys. Above Hun Uitzil Chac in the first generation are two males identified as Ah Ɔun I (left) and Ah Uitz (right). Morley believes that these two figures are brothers and were sons of Ah Xupan Xiu, whom he identifies as "the last halach uinic of Uxmal, he who had led the Maya chieftains against the halach uinic of Mayapan at the beginning of Katun 8 Ahau, ca. 1441. . . ."[123] Between the time of Hun Uitzil Chac, who according to Morley founded

Uxmal in A.D. 987–1007, and the births of Ah Ɔun I and Ah Uitz, Morley posits 19 generations of Xiu rulers whose names were not preserved and whose history is a blank.

Roys' interpretation of the material contained in the Xiu family tree differs considerably from that of Morley. He notes that the tree places Hun Uitzil Chac in the fifth generation before the Spanish conquest.[124] If Morley's hypothetical missing generations are eliminated this would put Hun Uitzil Chac in the first half of the fifteenth century, precisely the time when Roys has posited the entry of the Xiu into northern Yucatan during the Katun 10 Ahau corresponding to A.D. 1421–1441. Aside from obviating the need for missing generations, Roys' theory also corresponds to the late entry of the Xiu confirmed by other sources. Edmonson's recent proposal associating the establishment of Uxmal by Ah Zuytok in Katun 2 Ahau (A.D. 1243–1263) is more plausible than that of Morley, but it fails to account for the fact that no figure named Ah Zuytok appears on the family tree preceding Hun Uitzil Chac.[125]

Morley mentions an Ah Xupan Xiu as the last ruler of Uxmal. This individual is mentioned in the relación of Cansahcab in the following terms:

In the time of their heathendom the Indians had a lord who was called Mayapan, I mean the city where they resided. It was settled by a lord who was named Ah Xupan, from whom descend the lords of Mani of the Royal Crown, who was called the Tutul Xiu. . . . after the destruction of Mayapan, an ancient city where the said Ah Xupan was lord, there was no perfect peace. And there he had a servant Mo Ch'el, and [the latter] so devoted himself to letters that they later have him the name Kin Ch'el, which means priest.[126]

With regard to these references to Ah Xupan it is important to note that later in the Cansahcab relación he is referred to in terms similar to those in the relación of Tekal, that is, as "one who took all the land more by strategy than by war." This similar description suggested to Roys the possibility that the unspecified Tutul Xiu who first gained power bore the names Ah Xupan Tutul Xiu, Ah Suytok Tutul Xiu, and Hun Uitzil Chac Tutul Xiu, or that more probably the names refer to two rulers, one who "established" Uxmal and the other who overthrew Mayapan.[127]

Roys' second suggestion seems preferable, and is supported by evidence in the prophecies for the Tuns in the books of Chilam Balam of Mani and Tizimin, where the following passage occurs:

8 Muluc on 1 Pop is the sunken stone, when we arrived, I Ah Kauil Ch'el with Napuc Tun and Ah Xupan Nauat, the priests of the great *halach uinic*, Hun-Uitzil-Chac Tutul Xiu at [the villa of] Uxmal in the land [the province, the jurisdiction] of Mayapan, Maya Cuzamil.[128]

This passage is important because it mentions an Ah Xupan Nauat as the priest of Hun Uitzil Chac of Uxmal. This suggests that this Ah Xupan must have held a position of considerable confidence and prestige in the Xiu government. Moreover, we are told here that Uxmal lies in the jurisdiction of Mayapan, again supporting the idea that Hun Uitzil Chac was lord of Uxmal during the hegemony of Mayapan.

In light of the foregoing evidence, I suggest the following interpretation of Uxmal's history under the Xiu. Either Uxmal was "established" by Ah Suytok Tutul Xiu in the Katun 2 Ahau from A.D. 1243 to 1263, or Hun Uitzil Chac, who also was known as Ah Suytok Tutul Xiu, "founded" Uxmal during the Katun 10 Ahau from A.D. 1421 to 1441. At any rate, Hun Uitzil Chac was definitely the "first lord" of the city at this point. By the time of Mayapan's abandonment, however, he was either unable actually to govern for some reason, or else was recently deceased (cf. the confusion over the status of the Tutul Xiu in the relación of Tekal: "after his death, and even before it, there were other lords in every province"). Furthermore, it is possible that Hun Uitzil Chac's sons on the family tree, Ah Ɔun I and Ah Uitz, were too young or inexperienced to govern at the time of the sack of the city.[129] Thus power may have passed temporarily to Ah Xupan Nauat, a trusted advisor and priest of Hun Uitzil Chac, who served as regent until the younger Xiu could assume power. This theory is strengthened by the fact that Ah Xupan Xiu does not appear as the father of Ah Ɔun I or Ah Uitz on the Xiu family tree. If Morley's theory were correct we would expect to see an Ah Xupan interposed between Hun Uitzil Chac and the later generations. It seems inconceivable that if Ah Xupan was in the direct line of descent, and if he had been the ruler of the Xiu people at the time of the fall of Mayapan, that he would have been omitted from the family tree.

After the abandonment of Mayapan the Xiu's relationship with Uxmal seems to have been less important. In the aftermath of the destruction of the Cocom dynasty the Xiu founded a new capital at Mani. The events following the sack of Mayapan are described as follows by Herrera y Tordesillas:

All his people followed Ah Xiu, lord of the Tutulxius, and he settled in Mani, which means "now it is over," as if to say, "let us make a new book." And they settled their pueblos in such a way that they made a great province which is called Tutulxiu today.[130]

As Roys has noted, it seems natural that following their successful coup the Xiu would have moved away from the waterless region of Uxmal and taken control of the well-populated area to the south of Mayapan.[131]

After the foundation of Mani, Uxmal ceased to be the titular capital of the Xiu, but seems to have remained an important Xiu shrine site, as is suggested by the continued use of the ruined buildings for rituals up until the seventeenth century.[132]

The foregoing evidence makes the nature of the Xiu relationship with Uxmal more clear and comprehensible than it has sometimes been in the past. Not long ago it was possible for Barrera Vasquez and Morley to suggest that the Xiu actually founded Uxmal in a Katun 2 Ahau corresponding to A.D. 987–1007. Even more recently Marta Foncerrada, pointing out the Classic date of the site, rejected the Xiu as the true founders of the city, but nevertheless accepted the date of A.D. 987–1007 as marking the approximate time of a possible Xiu presence at the site. The Mexican iconographic elements at Uxmal, such as the plumed serpents on the West Structure of the Nunnery, were thus interpreted as evidence that the Xiu had actually redesigned and altered the sculptural program of the site.[133] Such an interpretation seems untenable, however, in view of the strong evidence that links the Xiu with the final days of Mayapan. If we are to detect an actual Xiu presence at Uxmal it is probably reflected by sporadic finds of later Post-Classic pottery and shoddy construction of the type reported by Ruz.[134]

Why then did the Xiu claim such a link with an already deserted archaeological city? The answer does not seem difficult to discover. We have seen that after the Spanish conquest the Xiu spokesman, Gaspar Antonio Chi, was quite willing to inflate the honor and prestige of his lineage, even if enhancing his own reputation meant distorting the facts of Yucatecan pre-conquest history. Thus, Gaspar Antonio claimed for the Xiu the overlordship of Mayapan, even though several other less biased sources state definitely that this city was in the hands of the Cocom family. It therefore seems likely that something of the same sort may account for the Xiu claim to have "founded" or established themselves at Uxmal.

From other sources we have seen that the Xiu, like the Itza, were considered foreigners by the original Maya inhabitants of Yucatan. Yet by the time of the conquest, and even before, during the sack of Mayapan, they had begun to identify themselves as the true champions of the Maya against their Cocom oppressors. Thus, in recounting their own history the Xiu probably exaggerated their antiquity and nobility in the peninsula by locating themselves at and purporting to have founded Uxmal, undoutedly still widely recognized as one of the most powerful cities in Yucatan during an earlier period. Since the ruins of Uxmal were located near the western border of the province of Mani the association probably seemed natural and reasonable. Parallels to this practice of seeking added distinction and legitimacy can be found elsewhere in Mesoamerican history. The most notable example occurred among the Mexica, who adopted the name Culhua to imply that they were the legitimate heirs to the Toltec imperial heritage as it was derived through the lords of Culhuacan.[135] From this study it is clear that the Xiu clearly did not found Uxmal, but that the city may have helped to found the Xiu, by providing them with a legitimacy they otherwise did not possess. For the Xiu the enduring majesty and grandeur of the House of the Governor and other buildings at Uxmal became a symbol of the power and nobility they avidly sought and finally gained.

Chapter 5

A Historical Interpretation of the Inscriptions of Uxmal

IF the Xiu were not the original founders of Uxmal then who actually lived at and governed the archaeological site? One of the most fruitful avenues for identifying the rulers of the city is the body of hieroglyphic inscriptions at Uxmal. During the past twenty-five years dramatic discoveries have been made in the interpretation of Maya hieroglyphic writing. As a result of the efforts of many scholars the glyphic inscriptions on the monuments, which were formerly thought to pertain exclusively to calendrical, astronomical, and ritual matters,[1] are now recognized as recording history, centering on the principal events in the lives of the rulers of the Maya sites.[2]

The prime monument for the study of Maya history at Uxmal is a small, cylindrical altar (Altar 10) discovered slightly to the south of the House of the Governor (figs. 36–37).[3] This monument now stands in the courtyard of the church known as the Ermita in Mérida. The best indication that the inscription on Uxmal Altar 10 is historical is provided by the presence of emblem glyphs at positions B2, A4 and B5. Such emblem glyphs are known to name specific Maya sites, and Berlin defined them as consisting of the following principal parts: (1) A principal element (main sign) that varies from site to site, with two constant groups of affixes attached, (2) the so-called "Ben-Ich" superfix; and (3) a prefix of the so-called "water group" as defined by Thompson.[5]

On Uxmal Alter 10 the glyph at B2 definitely has the water group prefix.[6] The upper part of the prefix is the cutaway shell motif (T38), but here it is perhaps combined with the T39 prefix, a variant which has a circle with an infixed hook or spiral.[7] The lower part of the prefix has a dotted band which is an essential element of several variants of the water group prefix (T35, T40). Glyph B2 also has a version of the diagnostic Ben-Ich superfix.[8] The postfix is apparently the comb element (T25).[9] The subfix is unreadable due to erosion.

The main sign at B2 is the face of a young man wearing a large circular earplug and a close-fitting cap, or cloth strip around the head. Above the earplug is a dotted form that may represent an animal ear (jaguar?). This main sign vaguely recalls several of the personified variants of the day-sign Ahau, but this identification remains uncertain.[10]

The second emblem glyph on Uxmal Altar 10 occurs at position A4 (fig. 37). The prefix seems to be a less typical variant of the water group prefix, here containing a simplified version of a God C head as the upper element (T41). The lower part of the prefix contains a long spiral, as in the emblem glyph at B2, but lacks the dots commonly found.[11] The correspondence in form between A4 and B2 suggests that the spiral element was considered an acceptable substitute for the more standard form of the water group prefix. The superfix is again a variant of the Ben-Ich superfix, and the postfix is probably T130, which often appears with emblem glyphs.

The main sign at A4 consists of a circular cartouche containing a vertical band that intersects a diagonal band. As the main sign appears now it closely resembles the glyph T518a or T518b, called the "Muluc Variant" by Thompson.[12] If the diagonal band originally continued across the cartouche then the closest parallel would seem to be glyph T73b or T73a, the so-called Hel glyph.[13] This alternative seems less likely, however.[14]

The third emblem glyph on Uxmal Altar 10 appears at position B5 (fig. 37). The water group prefix is either absent or badly eroded, but the superfix

Fig. 37 (above). Hieroglyphic panel on side of Uxmal Altar 10 (drawing by Barbara Fash).

Fig. 36 (left). Uxmal Altar 10 (after Holmes 1895–1897: plate VII).

is definitely the Ben-Ich superfix. Here the "Ich" or *po* element has an inscribed cross, much like that of the first emblem glyph at B2.

The main sign of the third emblem glyph is difficult to make out, but might have been a cartouche, again containing a vertical band with a horizontal element behind.[15] A possible parallel for this form would seem to be glyph T518c, another of the so-called Muluc Variants.[16] This main sign then may be only a slight variant of that seen at A4. Supporting this possibility is the fact that another example of this Muluc Variant glyph, accompanied by a Ben-

Ich superfix, occurs on one of the painted capstones from the Nunnery Quadrangle at Uxmal (fig. 27). More will be said about this example later.[17]

At other sites where dynastic content has been demonstrated in the inscriptions, the names of rulers and their associated titles often stand in a clause that immediately precedes an emblem glyph. This suggests that the glyphs found at this position on Uxmal Altar 10 might also be personal names or titles. This suppostition is confirmed in glyph A5, which precedes the final emblem glyph, and which is clearly a female name or title (fig. 37). The main

sign of this glyph is a left-facing human head in profile, with the small rounded forelock and strand of
hair curled around the ear which Proskouriakoff has
identified as the diagnostic traits of female name
glyphs at several sites.[18] The prefix seems to be a
variant of the T110 "Bone" glyph.[19] Glyph A5 thus
names a woman who is connected in some way with
the emblem glyph at B5. Because the Bone element is prominent, a nickname of "Lady Bone"
seems appropriate.

Our initial assumption, that the name glyphs
should precede the emblem glyphs, has been borne
out in one instance, strengthening the possibility
that the same rule may hold true for the other two
examples as well. Preceding the first emblem glyph
at position A2 is a glyph that is readily identifiable
to students of the Maya codices, for it is the name
glyph of God B, the Yucatec rain god Chac (T668)
(fig. 159).[20] The main sign is a cartouche with the
features of a face; a small earplug, a mouth with an
undulating line at the rear, and a T-shaped eye that
resembles the *Ik* sign and is a diagnostic of God B's
glyph. The postfix is T103, a standard postfix for the
name of the rain god, occurring often in the Dresden Codex.[21] Thus this glyph is definitely a name,
since it occurs frequently as the name of God B in
the codices. In this instance, however, it seems
likely that it is not the rain god himself who is being
named, but rather a human ruler who has adopted
the name of God B as his personal name or title.

Several lines of evidence support this identification of the God B glyph as the name or title or a
human ruler. First of all, in most Maya dynastic inscriptions, glyphs that name male rulers or nobles
usually take zoomorphic or abstract forms such as
jaguar, shield, serpent-jaguar, "sky," etc.[22] The use
of the God B glyph as a ruler's name at Uxmal would
be consonant with this trend.

There is also evidence that several of the Late
Classic rulers of Tikal may have incorporated the
name of the rain god in their personal name phrases.
Tikal Ruler A has a part of his name phrase a glyph
with a T561 sky prefix and a T1030 long-snouted
head main sign (fig. 168-gl; H8).[23] Ruler B has in his
name phrase a similar glyph consisting of the T16
"yax with darkened sun" and T561c sky elements as
prefixes and another variant of the T1030 long-
snouted head as main sign (fig. 168-gl; E9). Kubler
has suggested that possible names for Ruler A and
Ruler B might be "Sky-Rain" and "Sun-Sky-Rain"
respectively, interpreting the T1030 long-snouted
head main sign as a rain god glyph.[24] The use at
Tikal of what is probably the name glyph of the rain

god in rulers' name phrases suggests that the God B
glyph at Uxmal may also have been used as a personal name or title.

The most persuasive evidence supporting the
identification of the God B glyph on Uxmal Altar 10
as a ruler's name comes from the Maya chronicles, wherein references are made to several pre-
conquest Maya lords who took the name of the rain
god. Both the Chilam Balam of Mani and the Chilam Balam of Chumayel make reference to a ruler
of Chichen Itza named Chac-Xib-Chac.[25] Chac-Xib-
Chac was said by Landa to be one of the names of
the Red Bacab, and Roys believes that it was actually the name of the red rain god who lived in the
east.[26] That a Chichen ruler bore the name of Chac-
Xib-Chac suggested to Roys that: "Here we have an
important personage bearing the name of the rain-
god, and we may infer that he figured as the representative of the god."[27]

For Uxmal itself there is the evidence that an important ruler, Hun Uitzil Chac, bore the name of
the rain god. The most important reference to this
personage occurs in the 1581 relación of Teabo,
where Hun Uitzil Chac is said to be the founder
and first lord of the city.[28] Further references to
Hun Uitzil Chac occur in the Chilam Balam of
Mani, the Chilam Balam of Tizimin, and the Xiu
family tree of the Xiu Family Papers (fig. 35).[29]

In the region where Uxmal is located are many
detached hills known locally as Uitz, from which
the entire region takes its name.[30] Roys believes
that the title Hun Uitzil Chac therefore may mean
something like "ruler of the hill country."[31] He has
also suggested that the word *chac* in the name
probably refers to the Yucatec rain god.[32] It is also
possible that the name Hun Uitzil Chac may mean
"the unique (Hun) rain god (Chac) of the hill country (Uitzil)," an appropriate title for a ruler supposed to have founded Uxmal.[33]

The foregoing evidence indicates that God B
glyph on Uxmal Altar 10 is the name or title of a human ruler connected with the emblem glyph at B2.
The documented use of a rain god title at Uxmal
suggests that this God B glyph may refer to a ruler
of that site, although there is no reason to suppose
that it refers to Hun Uitzil Chac himself, who lived
during the period of Mayapan's supremacy. For convenience, this ruler will be designated "Lord Chac."

The final name glyph on Uxmal Altar 10 would be
expected at position B3, before the second emblem
glyph at A4 (fig. 37). There are apparently two main
signs here. The first of these appears to be a head-
form glyph, with recognizable mouth, circular eye

and a rounded triangular "ear" with three internal spots. There is some indication that a T-form, like that seen as the eye on the T668 God B glyph, may be been carved inside the circular eye. This suggests that the glyph may mix God B characteristics with those of another glyph. The spotted "ear" on the glyph resembles the spotted tympanum on the frog "uinal" glyph.[34] The subfix is probably T84, the same element that occurs beneath the female head glyph at A5. The second main sign seems to be a variant of the T507 "Spotted Kan" glyph.[35] This glyphic compound is probably the name or title of a male ruler associated with the following emblem glyph. Since one of the main signs of his name seems to combine features of both the Yucatec rain god and the "uinal" glyph, he may be referred to as "Lord Chac-Uinal-Kan."[36]

Appearing at positions A3 and B4 on Uxmal Altar 10 are two identical glyphic compounds (T17: 565a: ?), the main sign of which is one of the so-called "Serpent-Segment" glyphs (fig. 37). These identical glyphs appear before the names of both Lord Chac-Uinal-Kan and Lady Bone, and are interposed between their name glyphs and that of Lord Chac. This suggests that they refer to some sort of similar relationship existing between Lady Bone and Lord Chac, and Lord Chac-Uinal-Kan and Lord Chac. The most common relationship of this kind is the parent-child relationship. The glyphic compound might be interpreted as having some meaning like "the child or offspring of."[37] Thus the final eight glyphs on Uxmal Altar 10 apparently name a Lord Chac, who is perhaps a ruler of Uxmal, as well as a Lord Chac-Uinal-Kan and a Lady Bone, both from an as yet undetermined site or sites, who are declared to be the parents of Lord Chac.[38]

Uxmal Altar 10 opens at A1 with a glyphic compound whose main sign is the Imix glyph (T501) (fig. 37). The prefix is T13, and the subfix is a knotted element (T60), below which are two dots.[39] The glyph at B1 is probably a title connected with the Lord Chac's God B name glyph at A2. It has a T552 crossed bands main sign, with a T122 prefix and a damaged subfix which appears to consist of three dots. The crossed bands main sign has two indentations near the base which give it the appearance of an inverted jar. The T122 prefix consists of two scrolls which in several contexts are thought to represent smoke or flame.[40]

The first two glyphs on Uxmal Altar 10 are significant because they also appear on Stela 14 at Uxmal, providing a clue to the content of the inscription on

Fig. 38. Inscription of Stela 14, Uxmal (drawing by Barbara Fash).

the stela (figs. 27, 38). The inscription on Stela 14 is arranged in a single column to the left of the principal figure. The first glyph is the same as that on Uxmal Altar 10, with a T13 prefix, a T501 Imix main sign, and a T60 subfix resembling a knotted element. The second glyph is the same smoking crossed bands on inverted jar glyph seen in position B1 on Altar 10. The third glyph is somewhat worn, but it is apparently composed of the T668 main sign with the T103 subfix and a unidentifiable prefix. In other words, this is the name glyph of God B or Chac, the same glyph at position A2 on Altar 10. The T668 main sign is very faint, but both Morley's photo of Stela 14 and my own show a T-shaped infix in the eye position, which is the crucial diagnostic element of the glyph.[41] The subfix is reasonably clear as T103, and since this occurs so commonly as a part of God B's name glyph it serves to confirm the identification of the main sign.

At this point we have seen that the first two glyphs on Stela 14 duplicate those on Uxmal Altar 10, and that these are followed by the name glyph of God B on both monuments, suggesting that the two texts refer to the same subject. This indicates that the God B glyph on Stela 14 refers to the same human ruler whom we have designated Lord Chac, and whose name appears coupled with an emblem glyph on the Altar.

The only name glyph evident on Stela 14 is that of "Lord Chac." This is important, since this text is coupled with a image that depicts a richly clad Maya lord wearing a huge, stacked feather headdress and standing on a two-headed jaguar pedestal. We can assume that the name glyph in the inscription refers to the principal figure on the stela, and that Stela 14 therefore presents a portrait of

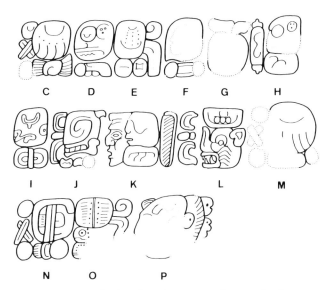

Fig. 39. Hieroglyphic band at top of Uxmal Altar 10 (drawing by Barbara Fash).

Lord Chac, whom we can also assume to have been a ruler of Uxmal, since his image appears on a monument at that site and since he stands on a bicephalic jaguar throne like that found in the platform in front of the House of the Governor (fig. 16). With the ruler on Stela 14 identified as Lord Chac we may now safely identify the emblem glyph following his name at position B2 on Altar 10 as an emblem glyph of Uxmal.

From Stela 14 we will return to Uxmal Altar 10 and consider the hieroglyphs on the band running around the top of the monument, where we again find references to Lord Chac, Lord Chac-Uinal-Kan, and possibly to Lady Bone as well (fig. 39). The text opens at position C, above the upper left-hand corner of the side panel, with the same Imix compound (T13: 501: 60) seen at A1. Following at D and E is the name glyph of Lord Chac-Uinal-Kan.[42]

The main sign of the glyph at position F is badly damaged, but the subfix is evidently the same T110 "Bone" element that accompanies the female head in the name glyph of Lady Bone at A5. It is possible, but by no means certain, that she is referred to here.[43] Glyph G is almost completely obliterated.

At position H we have another possible reference to Lord Chac-Uinal-Kan. Though damaged, the main sign takes a different prefix and subfix. The prefix may be a variant of T184, which has been shown to be an important title or honorific coupled with rulers' names at Palenque.[44] The subfix does not seem to be the T184 or T187 seen in other ex-

amples of Lord Chac-Uinal-Kan's name glyph. Following this glyph at position I is Lord Chac's name glyph, T668:102, appearing in virtually identical form to the reference at A1 on the Altar and on Stela 14.[45]

Having established the presence of emblem glyphs and personal names or titles in the inscriptions on Uxmal Altar 10 and Stela 14, we may now scan the other hieroglyphic texts of Uxmal to see if these characters and places are referred to elsewhere at the site.

On the painted capstone from Building Y of the Nunnery Quadrangle the glyph of God B appears in a register below a figural panel (fig. 25). The text concludes with what is apparently T168:518a. This final glyph has two important components of the emblem glyphs that appear at positions A4 and B5 on Uxmal Altar 10: the Ben-Ich (*ahpo*) superfix and the Muluc Variant main sign. This suggests that this glyph is a condensed form of the emblem glyphs on the Altar.[46] If this is indeed an emblem glyph then it suggests that the preceding God B glyph refers to the historical ruler Lord Chac rather than to the rain god. In this case, however, Lord Chac's name appears not in association with the emblem glyph coupled with his name on Uxmal Altar 10, but rather with the emblem glyph associated with his parents. This suggests one of two possibilities: either that this Muluc Variant emblem glyph is that of another site, from which come the parents of Lord Chac, and of which Lord Chac is also a ruler or in some other way connected; or that this emblem glyph also refers to Uxmal itself, the site having more than one emblem glyph. This last option is possible, since southern cities such as Palenque and Yaxchilan are known to possess more than one emblem glyph.[47]

The Building Y capstone thus seems to name Lord Chac and links him with the site of his parents. Aside from its historical content, this capstone is also important because it contains a Calendar Round date read by Thompson as 4 Eb 5 Ceh, for which he proposed a Long Count date of 10.3. 18.9.12 (A.D. 907).[48] The Building Y capstone is similar in theme and style to another painted capstone from the East Structure of the Nunnery. Thompson reads the date on this capstone as 10.3. 17.12.1 5 Imix 18 Kankin (A.D. 906) (fig. 24). Assuming that Thompson's readings are correct, this enables us to place the reign Lord Chac roughly in time.[49]

On the two hieroglyphic rings from the Ball Court at Uxmal there are six God B name glyphs

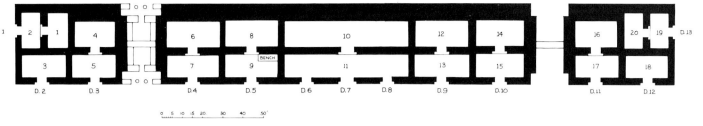

Fig. 41. Plan of the House of the Governor.

and art historians. The major drawback to the term is that it has been defined rather loosely, and is applied to a wide range of building types whose major feature in common is that they are distinguished from "temples." Pollock provides a standard differentiation between palaces and temples as follows:

Temples and shrines in their most typical forms, because of the restricted interior arrangements and exalted location of the former, and the diminutive size of the latter, seem fairly certainly to have housed the esoteric rite of a select priesthood, . . . whereas the term "palace" is used primarily for multiroomed structures that most often rest on relatively low substructures.[16]

Confusion surrounds the term palace because it is sometimes used with an implied functional meaning, and sometimes as a simple descriptive term for a more-or-less constant building type. To avoid misunderstanding, it has been proposed that the term "range-type structure" be used to describe such long, multiroomed buildings. In this sense, "rang-

ing" refers to series of vaulted rooms, with their longitudinal axes in a single line, sharing common end walls (figs. 42, 81).[17] This term is value-neutral and emphasizes the form of the building without implying its function, but it is unwieldly. Therefore we will use the word palace to describe such buildings, but with the understanding that the term refers to form not function.

Students of Maya architecture and archaeology have divided into two main camps regarding the function of Maya palaces. Some scholars hold that the palaces were not used as residences, but rather were important public buildings which may have been used for administrative purposes, for storage of ritual objects, and perhaps from time to time as temporary quarters for priests and novitiates. Adherents of this point of view often have interpreted the Maya sites as "ceremonial centers" that were largely vacant throughout much of the year.

Other scholars argue that the palaces were used as permanent residences, as housing for Maya

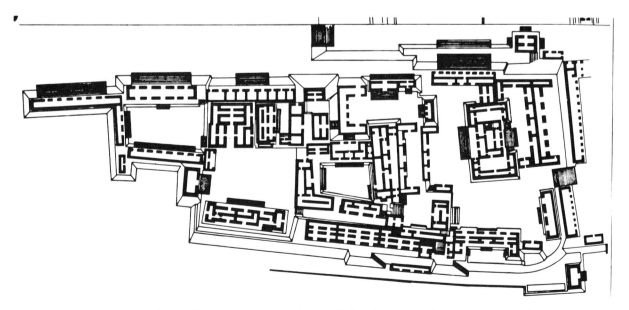

Fig. 42. Plan of the Central Acropolis at Tikal (after G. Andrews 1975:fig. 13).

nobles and priests, and have viewed Maya sites as true cities or urban centers. During the past twenty years some scholars have proposed multiple functions for Maya palaces. In this concept the buildings could have been used both as dwellings and as administrative centers, and perhaps had other functions as well. To consider properly the function of the House of the Governor we must evaluate some of the major arguments regarding the use of palaces as residences.

The writer who voices most effectively the anti-residential point of view is J. E. S. Thompson. In *The Rise and Fall of Maya Civilization* he states emphatically that the masonry palace buildings were unsuited for permanent habitation, having no chimneys or regular windows, and being prone to dampness.[18] Thompson argues that the palaces could only have been used for secret rites, or for the storage of ritual paraphernalia. He also interprets the masonry benches found in many palaces as negative evidence, since they often occupy much of the floor space, making living inconvenient. Burials sometimes found beneath the floors he views as interments of sacrificial victims. Heretofore such burials often had been interpreted as evidence for residence, since Landa mentions that it was the custom in Yucatan to bury the dead beneath the floors of houses.[19] Thompson, then, maintains that because of the general discomfort of the stone palaces the Maya priests and nobles must have lived in thatch-roofed houses near an outer perimeter of the ceremonial center.[20]

Thompson's arguments are among the most fully developed and convincing, but several other scholars have joined him in this opinion. Linton Satterthwaite argued that the Piedras Negras palaces were not used as dwellings because of the lack of evidence of eating and sleeping, the general discomfort of the interiors, and the difficulties of transporting drinking water from the Usumacinta River to the Acropolis (fig. 45).[21] Satterthwaite believed that some of the buildings at Piedras Negras contained rooms that were used for formal audiences. Structure J-6 contained a bench with a thin decorative backscreen similar to that seen on Wall Panel ('Lintel') 3 of Piedras Negras, where it is clearly being used as a throne during an important meeting.[22]

Some of Thompson's and Satterthwaite's objections no longer seem valid. Their judgements concerning the comfort of the palaces have been criticized as being ethnocentric, and it has been pointed out that other social considerations, such as a desire

for prestige, could have outweighed the value of comfort in the design of elite dwellings.[23] Satterthwaite's arguments concerning eating, sleeping, and water supply seem more cogent, since it is obvious that if food remains or an obvious bed were found in a Maya building it would be strong evidence for residence. However, it does not necessarily follow that lack of such evidence proves the palaces were not used as living quarters. A desire to keep rooms clean, coupled with a staff of servants, could account for a lack of food remains or broken pottery. Moreover, Landa tells us that Maya houses were annually cleaned at the time of the conquest. The subject of beds and other furniture will be considered elsewhere.

Evon Z. Vogt also argued against Maya palaces being used as permanent residences by the Maya elite. Based on his ethnographic work in the highland Chiapas community of Zinacantan, he supposed that the lowland Maya settlement pattern, as defined by Bullard and Willey,[24] conforms to the pattern in Chiapas. There a ceremonial center or "vacant town" is surrounded by outlying hamlets or *parajes*, whose inhabitants engage in a cyclical delegation of religious-administrative duties according to a system known as the cargo.[25] Vogt viewed the basic ancient Maya settlement pattern as one of "dispersed hamlets (where the bulk of the population lives) surrounding ceremonial centers (of various types and sizes) that are either controlled by religious officials (priests) or at least served as foci for ritual activity for people living in the hamlets."[26]

In the major Classic centers Vogt envisioned a two-tiered social structure. At the upper level was a permanent hierarchy of priests, who were served by minor functionaries such as artists and craftsmen. At a lower level were minor religious officials serving terms on a rotating basis.[27] Although he saw some permanent rulers in the sites, he viewed them principally as religious foci with priests conducting rituals on behalf of their dependent districts, pointing to the great number of temple buildings as evidence for the basically religious nature of Maya centers. Palace buildings thus were seen as periodically occupied, ritual structures associated with the temples, rather than as sumptuous residences.[28] Recent epigraphic research, which has revealed the dynastic history of several Maya sites, has cast doubt on Vogt's attempts to draw direct parallels between the Zinacantan cargo system and the governmental structures of the Classic Maya.

Various students of Maya architecture have argued that the palaces were used as housing for the Maya nobility. One of the earliest scholars to suggest a residential use for Maya palaces was A. M. Tozzer. In his report on Tikal, Tozzer refers to the palaces of the Central Acropolis and elsewhere at the site as "residential type" buildings (fig. 42).[29] Tozzer's interpretation of the residential function of the palaces rested fundamentally on their dissimilarity from temples, for which sacred functions were assumed, and on an intuitive feeling that their multiroomed form indicated use as living quarters. Writing about the same time as Tozzer, Herbert Spinden also was inclined to interpret the Maya palaces as permanent dwelling places.[30] However, he also noted the extreme difficulty in drawing a hard and fast line between "palace" and "temple," pointing out the merging of religious and secular components in buildings like the Monjas at Chichen Itza (figs. 137, 185).[31] A similar viewpoint was expressed by H. E. D. Pollock in his study of the architecture of Coba.[32]

Several years later, in his 1965 article on Maya architecture, Pollock retreated somewhat from his earlier views on the residential function of palaces. He points out that excavations at Uaxactun indicated that some palaces had a "domiciliary as well as a religious function," but that several of those at Piedras Negras apparently were meeting places or audience halls rather than residences.[33] Pollock also cautions against automatically applying the descriptions of sixteenth-century Maya town planning and building usage in northern Yucatan to the context of Late Classic times.[34] Morley classified Maya palaces as buildings for which residential functions were assumed.[35] Morley believed that the House of the Governor was probably the administrative center of the Xiu province, as well as the residence of the Xiu family during their occupation of Uxmal.[36] As we have seen in chapter 4, Morley's attribution of the building's function is inadequate because it is based largely on his reading of ethnohistoric sources, such as the books of Chilam Balam of Tizimin and Mani, rather than on archaeology.

One of the strongest advocates of palaces as residences was A. L. Smith. In his 1950 report on Uaxactun he described a religious center with perishable houses of the "common people" in the outskirts and the temples and palaces in the center. He maintained that the palaces were mainly residential, but acknowledged the difficulties of making absolute distinctions between temples and palaces.[37] Smith's judgement of the function of the Uaxactun palaces became more cautious in his later report on

Mayapan.[38] Here he argued that the multiroomed buildings should be considered "partly residential" (fig. 43). Certain structures at Mayapan also were interpreted as residential and were divided into two main groups: "Dwellings of the Wealthy" and "Dwellings of the Poor." These distinctions of rank were drawn from Landa's descriptions of Maya house types.[39]

William R. Bullard's studies of settlement patterns in northeastern Peten led him to believe that groups of priests, rulers, and administrators held office and lived in the core of the major Maya ceremonial centers. He argued that this governing elite "lived in the often enormous palace-type buildings" which occur near the center of such sites.[40] His analyses also led him to conclude that other governors lived in similar masonry structures scattered in centers surrounding the major sites.

George Kubler, like Pollock, has cautioned against the simple division of Maya buildings into two classes of "temples" and "palaces," noting that types often merge with or grade into one another. He points out, however, that variations in the building plans and massing, sensitive organization of public space, and the differences of height among the edifices suggest that a professional corps of architects and some sort of typology existed.[41] Although recognizing the difficulties involved, Kubler is willing to ascribe residential uses to several individual palace buildings in the southern Maya area.[42]

In northern Yucatan during the Late and Terminal Classic periods Kubler believes that building innovations "reflect major changes in Maya life" and that "habitations rather than temples were the aim."[43] He implies that the palaces of Yucatan were used as permanent residences having new architectural forms such as columns in doorways to improve lighting, or specialized vault stones permitting wide vault spans and hence more living space (fig. 31).[44] Despite his general advocacy of residence, Kubler is reluctant to pin down the function of formal palace groups like the Nunnery Quadrangle at Uxmal, whose buildings he believes ". . . may have been palace groups, or institutional dwellings, or even mere concourse centers with surrounding chambers for official ceremonies and storage."[45]

Peter Harrison's study of the Central Acropolis at Tikal is one of the most comprehensive attempts to establish the function of Maya palaces (fig. 42). After careful analysis, he concluded that some buildings in the Central Acropolis were used as residential quarters during the Late Classic period. The structures he found most suited to domestic use

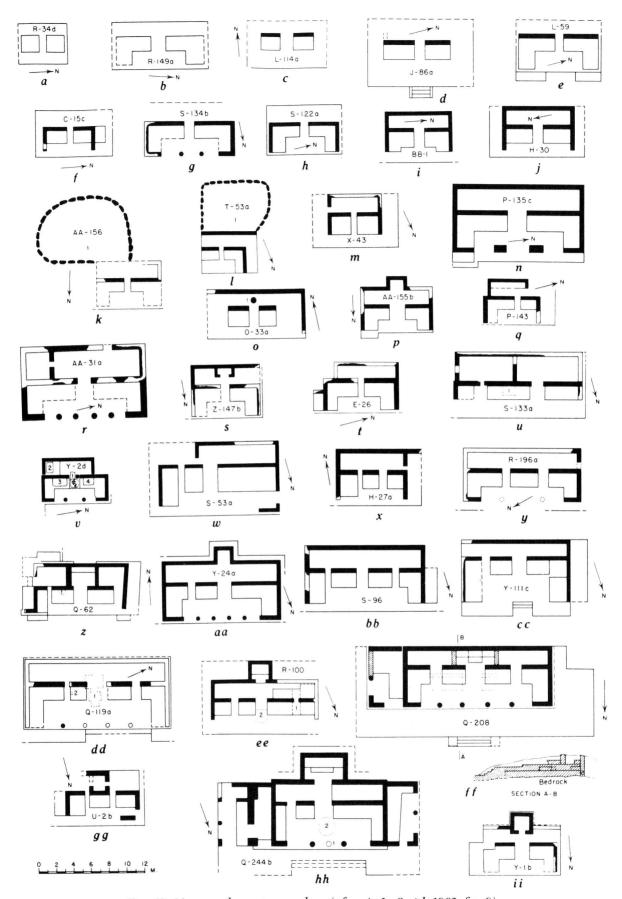

Fig. 43. Mayapan house types, plans (after A. L. Smith 1962: fig. 8).

were what he termed tandem/transverse or tandem buildings. These are long palaces with two or more corbeled ranges, sometimes with transverse rooms or wings attached at the ends.[46] The floor plans of these buildings bear a close resemblance to that of the House of the Governor, and it seems possible that these Tikal palaces may have served as distant models for the Uxmal buildings.[47] (See chapter 8.) At Tikal only one of the tandem/transverse buildings, Structure 5D-46, was interpreted as a family residence, while eight other palaces of this type were interpreted as priestly residences or colleges.[48] Within the residential buildings not all the rooms necessarily were used as "living rooms." Certain chambers, due to their placement, internal features, or size, may have been used as private oratories or public reception rooms.[49]

Though he does not believe that all the buildings were used as housing, Harrison concludes that the Central Acropolis was used for continuous residence and that features such as the large numbers of rooms, growth by addition, windows, evidence of alterations made to insure privacy and direct traffic flow, and bed "benches" show that the buildings were suitable for permanent living.[50] He calculates that about 200 people may have been occupying the Central Acropolis on a full-time basis at the end of the Late Classic period in A.D. 750.[51] Whether similar form implies similar function at Uxmal is not certain, but the Tikal data are suggestive of residence as a possible use for the House of the Governor.

Recently David Potter has suggested that the palace-type Structure IV at Becan may have been an elite residence. Structure IV is an imposing building with a southern monumental stairway leading to an elevated courtyard surrounded by apartments.[52] According to Potter, the private and protected nature of the Level 3 rooms and those surrounding the upper courtyard hints at a residential use.[53] His investigations have also shown that the upper rooms have built-in benches and are associated with domestic features such as fireplaces and drains that serve tilted floors. These drains may have been used as baths. Many built-in niches or "cupboards" which could have been used to store perishable furnishings were found also.[54]

R. E. W. Adams also argues that the "palaces" were actually used as "more or less sumptuous hierarchical residences."[55] He reasons that the multi-roomed buildings in the major centers would have been able to house relatively small numbers of people compared to the overall population. The

large masonry structures represent major community construction efforts, presumably organized by an elite class. Because their space is limited, and because they presuppose hierarchical organization, Adams believes that only the Maya elite would have had access to such buildings as permanent residences.

Like Harrison, Adams suggests that many of the benches in Maya palaces were used as living and sleeping spaces (noting that artistic evidence from Bonampak and elsewhere confirms this). Adams also points out that rooms with benches often contain built-in cupboards, as at Becan and Uaxactun. Interpreting the benches as the "primary living space" in the palaces, and assuming that they served as sleeping platforms for the Maya elite, Adams estimates the palace populations at Late Classic Uaxactun at between 150 and 200 persons.[56]

Adams counters objections to the cramped space, lack of light, and damp musty qualities of the palaces by pointing out that the Maya's ideas of comfort may have contrasted with our own, and that many of the discomforts would have been eliminated when the buildings were properly maintained during the Classic period. We can assume that Classic-period rulers could have called on a constant supply of servant labor for such tasks as plastering walls, roofs, and courtyards, as well as cleaning the interiors of the palaces. Adams concludes that:

Dry, cool inside, and with the use of broad benches as primary living areas, and furnished and decorated with small items of wooden furniture, skins, mats, ceramics are quite plausible elite dwellings. Other functions such as administration, storage, and academic are less convincingly inferred, but probable considering the inferred occupations of persons of high rank who presumably had control over these buildings.[57]

While it is true that the interiors of some Maya palaces can be very dark today because of their small doors and general lack of windows, it is likely that the interiors would have been lighter when properly plastered. Nearly every Maya palace structure shows traces of plaster covering the walls and vault soffits. This plaster not only gives an attractive "finish" to the rooms, concealing the imperfections of the joinery in the underlying masonry, but also provides large surfaces to reflect light. Regarding lighting it should be mentioned that when Father Avendaño was visiting the Itza at Tayasal he noticed the poor lighting in the interior of the house of Canek, the "King" of the Itza.[58] This suggests that for the Maya lords of the sixteenth century, darkness was not considered a serious obstacle to permanent habitation, even in upper-class dwellings.[59]

The "use-neutral" quality of Maya interiors has sometimes been cited as evidence against their having served as residences. Use-neutral refers to the fact that rooms are often similar in size and rarely contain any built-in furnishings that are unequivocally related to daily living. The House of the Governor fits into this category (fig. 41). It has virtually nothing that distinguishes the interior of one room from that of another, save for changes in size. These size differences are mostly minor, with the exception of the two long central rooms. The only sign of a built-in feature occurs in Room 9, where a low platform is constructed against the northwest corner (fig. 69). This sparse quality of interiors need not mean that the spaces were considered unlivable by the Maya, however. There is little evidence for permanent sitting furniture in Maya art. In scenes on sculpture or polychrome pottery, upper-class figures are commonly shown sitting crosslegged directly on the floor, on terraces, benches, or on daises. The mural from Structure B-XIII at Uaxactun, for example, shows a building that may be a palace, in cross section, with figures seated directly on the floor and without any furniture.[60] Occasionally figures appear seated on thrones, examples of which have been found at sites such as Uxmal, Chichen Itza, Piedras Negras, and Palenque. Maya rulers often sit on cushions or bolsters, coverings of skins, textiles, or matting (figs. 143a, 194).[61] At Tikal Harrison inferred that beds of perishable materials such as wood must have been used during the Late Classic period at the Central Acropolis.[62] It seems probable that either framework beds with coverings, or mats and skins spread on the floor could have been used to provide sleeping space in the House of the Governor.

Thus far we have seen several instances, as described by Harrison, Potter, and Adams, in which a residential function can be fairly confidently ascribed to Maya palaces at Tikal, Becan, and Uaxactun. These studies suggest in a general way that a possible function for the House of the Governor may have been residence. Aside from these general indications of residential palace function, however, a more specific argument can be made by comparing the basic community structure of Uxmal with that of Mayapan; at both a formal continuum from upper-class to lower-class housing seems to exist.

To illustrate the nature of the formal relationship suggested here we will first describe the house types of Mayapan, for which there is more abundant archaeological and ethnohistorical evidence. Houses at Mayapan range from simple to quite sumptuous forms, but share a number of traits. In the Mayapan house type there is normally a front room open on one side and often containing benches. One or more doorways in a medial wall connect the front chamber with a more enclosed and private back room (fig. 43). This house type is essentially the same as that described by Landa,[63] who in several passages indicates that the houses of the lords sometimes were made of solid masonry.[64] J. E. S. Thompson has described an example, known as Structure Q-208, of such a higher-class house at Mayapan (fig. 43ff). Because of the size, masonry quality, and associated ceramics and sculpture, Thompson interpreted this building as the residence of a noble family, with a private shrine devoted to the diving god.[65]

In many instances, as in the case of Structure Q-208, the presumed residences of the elite at Mayapan appear to be more imposing versions of what otherwise seems to be the typical dwelling. Upper-class dwellings are normally larger and more ornate, located nearer the center of the site, and roofed either with corbeled vaulting or beam and mortar roofing. Usually, the basic floor plan is retained, indicating a shared pattern between the houses of commoners and rulers.

It is possible that a common tradition also existed in earlier times, specifically at Puuc sites such as Uxmal. In order to verify this, however, we must examine what is known about settlement pattern and house types at Uxmal and compare the plans of less pretentious houses with those of the Puuc palaces.

Early work on Puuc residential buildings at Labna was done by E. H. Thompson, but little was said about the specific form of these houses.[66] During the 1950s Karl Ruppert and A. L. Smith studied and reported on several residential clusters at Uxmal, Kabah, Sayil, and Chacchob (fig. 44).[67] The most common type of house found at Uxmal is either a singleroomed building with a single doorway, or a range building composed of a series of adjoining single rooms each with its own doorway.[68] Most apparently had perishable roofs. Some of these buildings had built-in benches, while others lacked them. This again suggests that benches were not considered indispensable for daily living.

Several of the house structures at Uxmal have floor plans which seem similar to, though much simpler than, that of the House of the Governor.

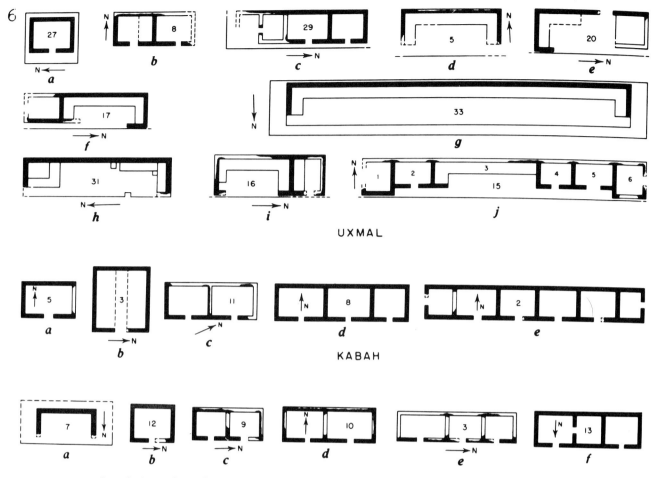

Fig. 44. Uxmal, Kabah, and Sayil house types, plans (top to bottom) (after Ruppert and Smith 1957:figs. 3–5).

This is also true of many of the houses at Kabah, Sayil, and Chacchob (fig. 44). Uxmal Structures 8 and 29 consist of strings of adjacent rooms, and Structure 29 had a doorway connecting the southernmost room with the room next to it. Although Ruppert and Smith note that this feature is unusual for buildings of this plan, it is found in the House of the Governor and is not uncommon in other Puuc palaces.[69]

Recently the I.N.A.H. Centro Regional del Sureste has been conducting studies of the community structure and settlement pattern in a residential sector about two kilometers north of the civic-ceremonial center of Uxmal. Features such as chultunes and metates demonstrate that most of this area contained habitations. The map of this zone reveals several types of structures, ranging from rectangular vaulted buildings to small, round or apsidal foundations for huts. Significantly, three of the larger, more durable houses discovered consist of arrangements of small, rectangular rooms set adjacent to one another, each with a separate entrance.[70] These house types conform to the general Puuc pattern outlined by Ruppert and Smith.

The studies of Ruppert and Smith and the Centro Regional del Sureste show that lower-class Puuc dwellings exhibit formal parallels with larger, more permanent palace buildings such as the House of the Governor; this is particularly apparent in the several examples of range buildings. Thus, it seems that the same kind of formal continuum we saw at Mayapan also existed in the Puuc region, despite the fact that the basic house type involved underwent considerable change from the Late Classic period to the late Post-Classic period. The existence of these shared features between the houses of commoners and nobles, however, suggests that we can extrapolate successfully from the Mayapan material to that of Uxmal. In Mayapan there was a basic similarity of plan between the houses of the

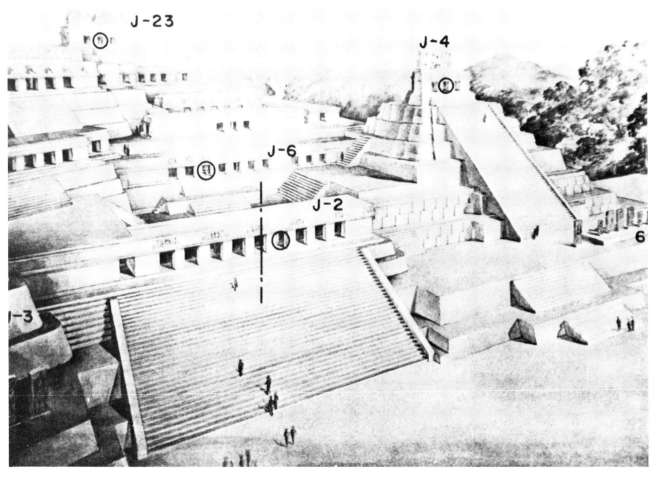

Fig. 45. Piedras Negras, Acropolis showing position of Structure J-6 and associated throne (after Proskouriakoff 1963a:17, with additions after Hartung 1971:Plate 10A).

poor and the houses of the nobility, although the size and quality of construction and decoration varied with wealth and prestige. At Uxmal the common dwellings surrounding the center of the site appear to have the same basic plan as the palace buildings such as the structures of the Nunnery Quadrangle and the House of the Governor (figs. 41, 83). This formal similarity implies a functional similarity as well. It thus seems logical to suppose that the House of the Governor, with its long range of rooms, is a more grandiose version of the typical Puuc house, and served as the dwelling of the ruler of Uxmal.

On the great platform of the House of the Governor there are four roughly circular depressions, probably chultunes, that have collapsed and are now partly filled with rubble and debris (fig. 12—Features, J, K, L, M). In northern Yucatan chultunes are artificial subterranean cisterns, whose purpose was to store rainwater runoff. As noted above, such cisterns are often located in the courtyards or in the large platfroms and terraces in front of residential complexes or larger buildings in the Puuc region.[71] George Brainerd has estimated that the chultunes in one of the larger centers could have supplied between 2000 to 6000 people annually,[72] and it has been further estimated that the runoff water from the main plaza of Uxmal alone could have sustained a population of 5000 during the six-month dry season.[73]

Study of the hieroglyphic inscriptions of Uxmal indicated that one of the most important rulers, Lord Chac, was in power when the House of the Governor was constructed. It later will be shown that it was probably his portrait that appeared above the central doorway. It seems reasonable to assume that the dynastic rulers of the Maya cities would have desired dwellings that reflected their power and magnificence. In light of the associations between Lord Chac and the House of the Governor it seems that Cogolludo named the building more appropriately than he knew, for it was probably the residence of one of the greatest lords of Uxmal.

In addition to serving as a dwelling, it is likely that the House of the Governor had broader and more public functions as well. Clemency Coggins has defined a specialized palace type that occurs at several southern Maya sites, and seems to have been used primarily for administrative rather than residential purposes.[74] The clearest example of such a palace is Structure J-6 at Piedras Negras (fig. 45). In the northwestern part of Piedras Negras the Acropolis supports thirteen long range-type palace structures grouped around six courts. Below to the southeast is a large plaza from which a broad monumental stairway leads up toward the Acropolis. At the stairway's summit is Structure J-2, a double-ranged building through which one passes to enter Court 1. From Court 1 a stairway opposite Structure J-2 leads up to Structure J-6, a long single-range building with a room centered on the stairway. Satterthwaite noted that Structure J-2, the long portico, held an important position overlooking the West Group Plaza, but that upon passing through J-2, Structure J-6, with its megalithic stairway and richly decorated stucco facade would have "burst on the observer."[75] Culminating the sequence, the doorway in J-6 centered on the two successive stairways, was an elaborately carved stone hieroglyphic throne in a special vaulted niche.[76]

Proskouriakoff has associated several stelae on Structure 0–13 at Piedras Negras with this throne and its dates [9.17.15.0.0].[77] Probably also related to this throne is the scene on Wall Panel ('Lintel') 3 from the site, which portrays a Maya ruler whom Proskouriakoff has identified as "Bat Jaguar" holding a formal audience seated on a throne that closely resembles that found in Structure J-6.[78]

Proskouriakoff's discovery that the stelae of Piedras Negras were erected to commemorate the inauguration and principal events in the lives of rulers is important for an understanding of the throne in Structure J-6. This is particularly so since the Chilam Balam of Chumayel refers to the accession rites of a new ruler involving the "construction of the stairway" and his seating in the "house on high."[79] The evidence of the dynastic structure of Classic Maya society suggested to Coggins that:

The building J-6, with its associated dated throne, in conjunction with this passage from the Chilam Balam,

suggests that some sort of structure was erected for the inauguration of a new ruler. It seems possible, in this case, that it may have been this palace-type structure which was actually used as an audience chamber by the ruler, as depicted on Lintel 3.[80]

Coggins has pointed out a few other examples where thrones occupied a place of honor in important palace buildings. At Piedras Negras, for example, in Structure J-18 a bench found in the center of the west gallery might be a throne, since the wall behind it was decorated. In House E of the Palace at Palenque is a wall relief and painted decoration over a place that probably originally held a bench or throne. (fig. 147).[81] Coggins believes that the recurrent representations in Classic Maya art of rulers seated on thrones or benches and surrounded by other figures suggest that the holding of formal audiences was a common occurrence at that time. She further suggests that:

There is one type of palace building which is approached by an important stairway leading to a central doorway and to an axially placed throne. This palace type faces outward towards a public area, and at least in the throne room was probably not intended to be lived in. It was, instead, the principal public room of the palace.[82]

The House of the Governor incorporates several of the features described in connection the specialized palace type. It is approached by broad central staircases that lead to large central chambers (figs. 12, 54). The spaciousness of these rooms suggests that they would have been suitable for the type of formal audience depicted on Wall Panel ('Lintel') 3 at Piedras Negras. Above the central doorway is a naturalistic sculpture of a seated human figure who wears the trappings of rulership (fig. 113). We will see that this motif shares important features with the accessional stelae of Piedras Negras, and that this figure may be a formalized portrait of Lord Chac of Uxmal. The building itself commands a broad public platform and a jaguar throne was placed axially in front of the stairways (fig. 16). The throne, although not inside of the building, is intimately associated with it, being placed directly in front of the central door. The above features indicate that the House of the Governor, aside from serving as a residence, functioned as one of the chief administrative centers at Uxmal.

The House of the Governor also seems to have been designed to serve as an astronomical observatory and was probably connected in some way with the cult of the planet Venus. Anthony Aveni has pointed out that most of the structures at Ux-

Fig. 46. Mound at Nohpat seen from central doorway of the House of the Governor.

mal are oriented approximately 9° off the cardinal directions, in a clockwise sense.[83] The House of the Governor, however, deviates from this orientation, being skewed about 20° clockwise relative to the common axis. Horst Hartung has pointed out the existence of a small mound that rises above the relatively featureless horizon directly in front of the House of the Governor, and Aveni found this mound to be part of Nohpat, an extensive site first described by Stephens (fig. 46).[84]

The Nohpat mound is located so that a line almost perfectly perpendicular to the façade of the House of the Governor passes from the central doorway, out over the base of the Picote column, over the center of the platform of the bicephalic jaguar throne, and then extends to meet the mound on the horizon. Aveni has reckoned that this alignment points almost exactly to the azimuth of Venus rise when the planet attained its maximum southerly declination around the year A.D. 750.[85] A variation of 200 years would still result in a fit of this alignment to within 30 mintues of arc of the Venus rise position. On the basis of architectural style and its ties with monuments such as Stela 14, a date of about A.D. 900 for the House of the Governor seems likely. This fits comfortably within Aveni's 200-year latitude, suggesting that Venus would have risen "as an impressive spectacle above the flat Yucatecan horizon" directly over the Nohpat mound when viewed from the House of the Governor's central doorway.[86]

Tending to confirm the astronomical significance of the House of the Governor's orientation is the iconographic evidence from Uxmal indicating that the city's rulers were well aware of the motions of Venus. At the House of the Governor each of the mask panels has suborbital plates adorned with "venus symbols" formed of two disks separated by a curvilinear band (fig. 151). Venus symbols also appear on the doorway mask of the Chenes Temple of the Pyramid of the Magician, and on the masks of the East Structure of the Nunnery (fig. 8). Seler pointed out that the bar and dot numeral eight appears on the lower lid of the Chenes Temple doorway mask. He interpreted this as a reference to the Maya's knowledge of the correspondence between eight vague 365-day years and five Venus synodic periods of 584 days. Based on this interest in Venus at Uxmal, Seler suggested that the House of the Governor was a residence for priests dedicated to the cult of this planet.[87] There is now better evidence indicating that the building was actually the residence of the ruler of Uxmal and his family, as well as a major seat of power and administrative center. This does not conflict with the general astronomical interpretations presented by either Aveni or Seler, however, as the Classic Maya elite were vitally concerned with astronomical phenomena, particularly with the synodic period of Venus.

PART TWO

Architecture

CHAPTER 7

Construction

ERECTING an edifice of the dimensions and durability of the House of the Governor was a formidable task for the Maya architects and masons of Uxmal equipped only with an inventory of tools fashioned of organic materials and stone. Having no draft animals, they were forced to rely on their own strength for the difficult labor of moving hundreds of tons of stone from the quarries to the building site. The delicate work of creating the smooth surfaces of facing blocks or the intricate incised designs on pieces of stone mosaic was accomplished by the steady hands and trained eyes of expert masons and sculptors.

Building Tools and Instruments

Among the most useful and numerous implements in the mason's tool kit at Uxmal were the various stone axes, celts, points, hammers, and mauls used to shape the limestone facing blocks and to break stones for fill. No collection of lithic artifacts has been published from Uxmal, but the similarities in masonry style between Uxmal and Chichen Itza suggest that the stone-cutting tools at Uxmal were much like those of the latter site. At Chichen Itza the most common tools were pecking stones fashioned from globular pebbles, from which spalls had been struck off to produce a jagged cutting edge on one side. Such stones were made from nodules of flint that occur in the native limestone.[1] Grooved hammers, made of flint or hard limestone, and hafted to a wooden handle, were also used.[2] Both the hammers and the pecking stones were probably used for roughing out large stones to the desired shape.

More finished work was executed with smaller celts, fashioned from a tough and durable, imported, greenish or black dioritic stone.[3] Probably also designed for finer work are the bifacial adzes of chert found in a Pure Florescent offering at Muna, Yucatan.[4] Stemmed, triangular, and teardrop-shaped chisels of chert from Dzibilchaltun may be included in this category of fine stone-working tools.[5] Fine-line engraving, of the type seen on the sculptured mosaic elements applied to the façade of the House of the Governor, was probably carried out with small splinters or chips of local flint, chert, hard limestone,[6] or perhaps with pointed gravers like those found at Dzibilchaltun.[7]

Fine smoothing of surfaces may have been done with blocks or points of *cholul* wood, which Landa mentions as being extremely hard and used for the manufacture of native weapons.[8] Surfaces also may have been ground smooth with abrading stones like those of igneous rock found at Dzibilchaltun.[9]

Implements for the preparation and application of stucco may have been fashioned from potsherds, gourds, and wood.[10] Wooden paddles and spreaders, as well as vegetable fiber brushes, may have been used for applying stucco,[11] while the final smoothing and burnishing was done with various pebble-shaped, brick-shaped, and banana-shaped smoothers of limestone found at Muna, Dzibilchaltun, and Mayapan.[12]

Morris believed that the architects at Chichen Itza had no leveling device more accurate than the unaided human eye, since platforms terraces, floors, and cornices are rarely truly horizontal.[13] A survey of the base of the House of the Governor reveals that it also deviates markedly from true horizontal (fig. 47).[14] The Maya of Uxmal also appar-

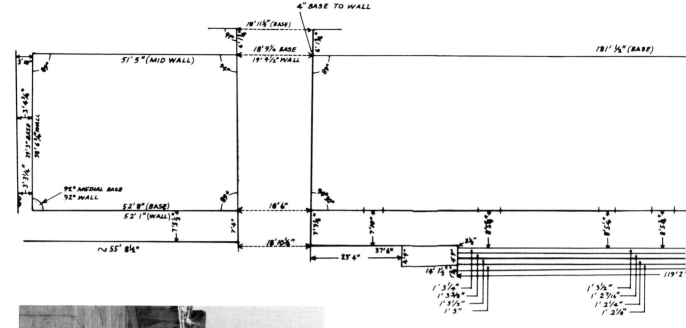

SOUTH END OF UPPER
TERRACE STAIR, HOUSE OF
THE GOVERNOR—ELEVATION

Fig. 47. View from southeast corner along east façade, House of the Governor, showing irregularities from horizontal.

ently either lacked any mechanical or mathematical means for turning a right angle, or had no interest in obtaining precise squareness in individual buildings.[15] Almost every "right" angle measured at the House of the Governor is actually somewhat more or less than 90°, varying within a range of about 86°–94° (fig. 48). Maya builders apparently knew the use of the plumb bob and line, for building corners often are aligned vertically and masonry courses, though not exactly horizontal, often are quite straight over long distances.[16] The symmetry of the House of the Governor suggests that cords or ropes were also used as measuring devices.[17]

Sources of Building Stone

Obtaining sufficient quantities of building stone presented no great problems to the builders of the House of the Governor; the entire surrounding region is composed of limestone strata offering stone of various compositions and qualities. The exact location of stone quarries used in constructing the

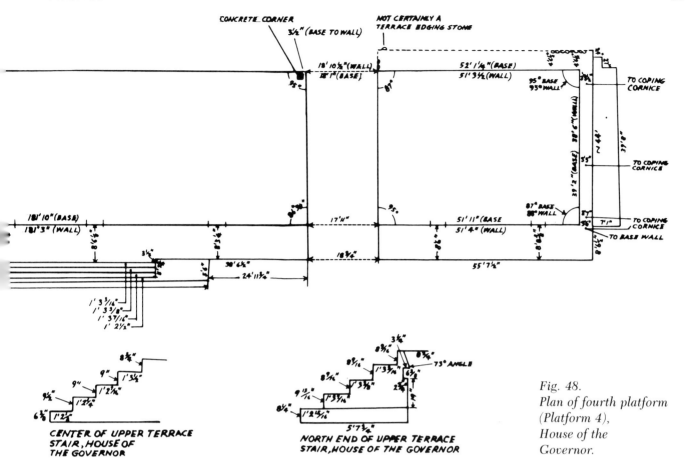

Fig. 48.
Plan of fourth platform
(Platform 4),
House of the
Governor.

House of the Governor is unknown, but the quarrying techniques probably did not vary much from those utilized at Chichen Itza, where the slopes of natural sinkholes or low areas were excavated to obtain already-loose material for fill and in mortar preparation.[18] Loose surface stone gathered from the surrounding region must also have been used heavily for this purpose at Uxmal.

Outcroppings of local limestone caprock were the preferred locations of quarries for facing stones. Ledges were undercut by mining the softer *sascab* (white earth), a soft breccia or conglomerate that often lay beneath, after which irregular limestone blocks were broken off along natural joints in the stone. Rough blocks were then shaped by laborious hammering, pecking, and abrasion for use according to their intended position in the structure. Great amounts of waste material were produced by this method, but this stone scrap could be used in fill and making concrete. Many of the specialized stones used in the construction of walls and vaults probably were cut to specification at the quarry.[19] Special types or qualities of stone were also se-

lected for special purposes. At Chichen Itza, for example, Morris noted that the vault capstones were selected from a natural stratum of very hard limestone, which had not been observed in a known quarry.[20] A similar type of slab-like limestone was used for the capstones of the House of the Governor. Different qualities of stone were also selected for the exterior or interior of a building. At the House of the Governor the blocks that face the two large transverse vaults differ in color from the blocks revetting the soffits (fig. 49). The exterior stones are a whitish to pinkish fine-grained limestone of almost marblelike consistency, while the soffit stones are a yellowish-orange limestone with pockets or seams of reddish stone.

Plaster and Stucco Preparation

During the construction of the House of the Governor large amounts of slaked lime were produced. Lime plaster was used as a mortar, mixed with rough limestone to form the concrete hearting of

Fig. 49. House of the Governor, west side of south transverse vault, showing different masonry quality.

terrace fills and wall cores. Mixed with sascab or used alone it provided a hard and durable coating for floors and roofing, and formed a handsome stucco covering for walls, vaults, and façade sculpture.

The preparation of the slaked lime used in mortar and stucco involves burning limestone in a special *calera* or outdoor hearth, a process described in detail by Morris.[21] Such a burning produces a quantity of lime powder from five to six times the bulk of the original limestone. This powder can be used immediately, but is usually aged before use to prevent cracking. To make mortar the slaked lime is mixed with water and sascab.[22] The water needed was probably obtained from artificially surfaced *aguadas*, such as the "Chenchan," located west of Uxmal. Substructures were normally constructed with a "lean" mortar of one part lime to four parts sascab, while walls had a ratio of one to one and a

half. Surfaces such as roofs, which required special hardness, might consist of nearly pure lime stucco that was treated for impermeability with a liquid obtained from the bark of the *chocom* tree.[23]

Mosaic Elements

The sculptured stone, mosaic elements of the façade apparently were produced away from the project.[24] Andrews IV suggested that different ones may have been produced at different villages whose members sold the components to architects at various sites.[25] Rosemary Sharp elaborated this idea to argue that this distribution of labor was an "artificial symbiosis" involving the production of stone pieces for Puuc façades.[26] She believes that such work was assigned by an elite in order to maintain social integration among the various Puuc communities.[27]

It does seem probable that the majority of the sculptured elements were carved away from the project, but Andrews IV's and Sharp's ideas that specific designs were manufactured in separate villages is harder to accept. If this were true then there should be a wide uniformity in design and size. Although Sharp mentions a few examples of interchangeable elements from Labna, Kabah, and Dzibilnocac,[28] measurements taken at a large number of Puuc sites indicate that it is rare to find such uniformity between sites. This is true not only of the more complicated forms such as mask panels, but also of simple elements such as lattice Xs or serrated bands. This nonuniformity suggests that the mosaic elements were not mass-produced in single centers, but rather that complete sets of elements were made for single building campaigns. The work was probably carried out at or near the local quarry of each site, in order to avoid transporting extra stone to a village and then moving the finished piece elsewhere.

Architects

There is no certain knowledge regarding the architect or architects of the House of the Governor. Unfortunately, no name of a Maya Imhotep or Ictinos has been preserved, but the evidence of the Puuc buildings themselves suggests that the architects were men whose position corresponded roughly to that of a medieval master mason. The differing plans, façade treatments, and iconographic pro-

Fig. 50. House of the Governor seen from Pyramid of the Old Woman.

grams found in Puuc structures suggest that the basic idea was determined by the secular rulers and their priests, and that the architect was expected to embody the plan in the accepted architectural style. As in Gothic architecture, the basic canons of the Puuc style were known to all, but within those strictures there was room for experimentation and individual creativity. The differences from one site to another suggest a professional rivalry, as varying schools arose and different building types and decorative schemes gained popularity. Like the master masons, the Puuc architects, perhaps accompanied by a trusted group of masons, carpenters, and sculptors, probably moved throughout the region. They were likely trained in masonry and/or sculpture, and also must have had some knowledge of Maya iconography and mathematics. Their engineering and design knowledge was basically empirical, however, as they were relying on what had always worked structurally and what had been observed in other buildings.

Construction Time

On the basis of careful computations of the amounts of fill, masonry, facing stone, and stone sculpture found at Uxmal, and after observing typical labor techniques and recording average work times for modern Maya masons and sculptors at Ticul, Yucatan, Charles J. Erasmus estimated that the entire Uxmal civic-ceremonial center could have been built comfortably within a 250-year period by 1200 heads of households working 40 days a year. More specifically, he demonstrated that "Without exceeding the 40 man-days per family per year, the Nunnery could have been built in thirteen and one half years. With a little enthusiasm (80 days per year), it could have been finished in less than seven years."[29]

Following the formulas provided in Erasmus' article, construction times for the House of the Governor and its supporting platforms can be estimated as follows. Assuming that 1200 heads of households worked 40 days per year, the platform system (Platforms 2, 3, and 4) could have been completed within 28 years. With 1200 men working 40 days per year the buildings of the House of the Governor could have been built within five years. On the basis of the recent settlement pattern survey carried out at Uxmal it seems possible that populations in the Puuc area were fairly dense. If one posits that 2000 heads of households (implying a total supporting population of only 10,000) contributed 80 days of labor per year, the platform system could have been built in about eight and a half years, while the House of the Governor itself could have been completed in only a year and a half.[30]

The Site and Platform System

The Site

The first consideration in the construction of the House of the Governor was the selection of the building site. The position of the building's terrace system seems to have been determined partly by topographic requirements (figs. 13, 50). The terrain at Uxmal slopes gradually upward to the southeast from the Ball Court. Several limestone ridges, one of which overhangs a shallow cavern, are visible to the southeast of the Ball Court and north of the House of the Governor. The architects thus took advantage of this natural elevation in locating the platforms.[31] The use of such natural ridges or eminences is common in Maya architecture and apparently reflects a desire to obtain a well-drained, secure foundation, as well as to gain an elevated position for major buildings.[32]

Once chosen, the site had to be cleared of forest growth to establish the boundaries of the platform system. Part of the area beneath the large lower platform already may have been cleared when building operations began, for two buildings of earlier Chenes-style construction were partly covered by the west side of the large second platform, whose contour was adapted so that these buildings could remain in use (figs. 3, 12).[33] It is possible that other earlier structures existed to the east of these Chenes-style buildings. If so, they would have been covered by the construction of the second platform of the House of the Governor. Trenching and excavation of the platform would be required to verify the presence of such earlier structures.

Platform 1

The lowest platform (Platform 1) of the House of the Governor is extensive but quite low (figs. 1, 12). It is approximately 625 feet long on the east side and 570 feet on the north.[34] The platform is approximately 3–4 feet high at its edges, but varies in height according to the natural elevation of the terrain. Platform 1 traces a boundary of a more or less uniform width of about 15 feet around the entire base of the second massive platform. This lowest platform seems to have been constructed to obtain a uniformly level foundation for the second platform.

The boundaries of Platform 1 presumably were established by setting the corners and laying connecting courses of terracing masonry between the corners to form a perimeter that was roughly leveled with rubble fill. The corners of this platform were formed of massive blocks of limestone with well-dressed and smoothed outer faces. The backs of these blocks are less finished, tapering inward to form a wedge-shape. The connecting masonry courses are composed of smaller stones that re-

semble the veneer facing stones used to face typical Florescent period walls. These stones are roughly cut and squared on the face, while the back of the stone is very roughly shaped. The facing wall of the platform is set in a conglomerate of rough stones mixed with a mortar of lime, sascab, and probably earth. The joints between the facing stones are chinked with smaller slabs and flakes of limestone. The fill of the outer platform probably consists of a mixture of mortar and rough, unshaped stones, but less mortar and more earth may have been used to fill the interstices between the larger rocks toward the center.[35] Judging from the visible surface of this platform, it appears that the stones used for fill decreased gradually in size toward the top, so that the surface is a well smoothed plane of pebbles. Originally this may have been covered with a smooth layer of lime mortar and sascab.[36]

Platform 2

The second platform (Platform 2) is a high and massive masonry structure whose upper surface forms a vast plaza that supports not only the House of the Governor, but a host of smaller buildings and platforms as well, including the House of the Turtles and the two small platforms of the Picote and the Jaguar Throne (figs. 12, 14, 16). Measured at the top, this platform is some 540 feet long on its eastern side and 450 feet wide (fig. 12).[37] At the northeast corner of the platform an arm extends westward some 50 feet beyond the main body in order to accommodate the House of the Turtles, so that the width along the northern edge is 500 feet.

Platform 2 rises in four terraces to a height of about 25 feet (figs. 13, 51).[38] Each of the terraces is built in a manner similar to that described for the lowest platform. The corners consist of huge rounded stones,[39] about 3 feet 6 inches across the face, between which are laid courses of smaller, roughly squared facing blocks (fig. 51). The facing blocks resemble, but are considerably larger than and not as well shaped as, those used in the wall construction of the House of the Governor itself.

This great platform was constructed in two separate building programs. During a survey of the platform in March of 1978, a row of facing stones running north–south was discovered some 15 feet west of the eastern edge (fig. 12–feature H). This line of stones was traced northward from the center of the platform to the northern edge, where the feature was revealed as the eastern face of an earlier platform phase. A break between this earlier platform

Fig. 51. House of the Governor, southeast corner of second platform (Platform 2).

Fig. 52. House of the Governor, corner stones fifteen feet from northeast corner of second platform (Platform 2). House of the Turtles in background.

and the additional section is indicated by the presence of several large, rounded corner stones visible both at the top of the platform and farther down in its north face (fig. 52).[40] A similar line of facing stones was discovered at the southern edge of the platform. Thus, as originally constructed, the second platform reached some 15 feet less to the east than at present, and the platform was extended 15 feet at a later date. The reasons for this extension are unclear, but the separation between the older and newer sections of the platform continues beneath a long, low structure built along the east side of the platform at the south end. This suggests that the addition was planned to accommodate this structure, perhaps to insure that it did not crowd the plaza in front of the House of the Governor.

Platform 2 was filled with a mixture of limestone boulders and rocks, and mortar of lime, sascab, and earth. Today the upper surface of the platform is a fairly level plain of small rocks and pebbles. Originally it probably was covered with a smooth layer of lime plaster and sascab, but few traces of this flooring exist.

Platform 3

The third platform (Platform 3), upon which the House of the Governor stands, is located toward the western side of the second platform (figs. 12–13, 50). At the top this platform is 370 feet long by 90 feet wide.[41] The platform was built in four slightly inclined terraces and rises to a height of 21 feet. The terraces are built like those described previously, with large rounded corner stones and connecting courses of facing masonry (figs. 53,

Fig. 53. House of the Governor, southwest corner of third platform (Platform 3).

Fig. 54. Monumental stairway, House of the Governor. Picote column in foreground.

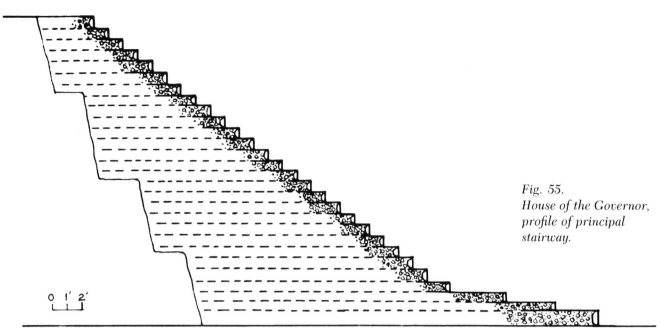

Fig. 55.
House of the Governor,
profile of principal
stairway.

0 1' 2'

Fig. 56. North side of principal stairway, House of the
Governor.

56). The facing blocks are slightly smaller and are more carefully cut and smoothed than those of the lower platforms. No facing masonry remains on the fourth or upper terrace, but the visible interior face of this terrace is well finished with rough stones laid in moderately straight courses, which indicates that the terrace facing masonry was applied only after completion of the solid masonry core of the platform.[42]

The Monumental Stairway

A grand stairway ascends from the plaza of the second platform to the top of the third platform (figs. 54–55, 57). This stairway is some 135 feet wide and has 28 steps.[43] It apparently was constructed with a variant of the technique used to construct the walls of the House of the Governor. The cornerstones for each step were set and connected with a course of well-squared and smoothed facing stones which served as risers. These riser stones are more carefully cut and finished than the facing stones of the Platform 3 and are comparable in quality to the facing stones of the House of the Governor. The area behind the risers was filled and leveled with a mixture of lime mortar, sascab, and crushed stone, with the stairway probably rising one course at a time. At the point where the sides of the stairway connect with the four terraces of Platform 3, the stairway's facing stones abut those of the terraces. The terraces continue some distance behind the stairway

Fig. 57. House of the Governor from Pyramid of the Magician, showing building platform and monumental stairway.

Fig. 58. House of the Governor, eastern façade from the north, showing building platform (Platform 4).

Fig. 59. House of the Governor, north end showing building platform (Platform 4) with northern extension. Basal corner mask in foreground. Cemetery Group in background.

Fig. 60. House of the Governor, mask panel at northeast corner of the fourth platform (Platform 4).

(fig. 56). It seems doubtful, however, that the terrace facing continues the full distance behind the stairway. More likely, the stairway was applied directly to the terrace core. Following construction of the uppermost riser, the entire stairway probably was coated with lime plaster or stucco. This stucco would have been tamped and smoothed on each step to provide a durable tread, and also would have concealed the joints between the stairway facing stones.

Platform 4

The fourth platform (Platform 4) originally was not a single platform, but rather a series of three low platforms which support the three separate buildings of the House of the Governor (figs. 48, 57–59). Because it directly sustained the House of the Governor, this platform may be called the building platform.[44] It is, on the average, 3 feet 6 inches high, and forms a walkway around the three buildings, except at the passageways through the two large

transverse vaults. These walkways are approximately 8 feet wide at the front of the building, 3 feet 6 inches at the ends, and 5½ to 6 feet at the rear. The building platform is constructed with carefully cut and faced veneer masonry, behind which is a rubble and concrete core. The platform is capped with a two-member decorative cornice, composed of a vertical string course and an upper sloping course (fig. 58).

At the base of each of the north corners of the northern building platform is a long-snouted mask composed of carved stone mosaic. The northeastern corner mask is still fully intact, while the northwestern example is only partly preserved (figs. 59–60).[45] These masks seem to have been applied originally as finishing elements at the base of the northernmost and southernmost corners of the building platform. The lower portions subsequently were covered by periodic replasterings of the floor of the third terrace,[46] and by an accumulation of debris.

Our best evidence for the terrace flooring tech-

Fig. 61. House of the Governor, section of flooring at base of west side.

niques employed comes from Platform 4. At a distance of 9½ feet north from the southern edge of the base of the west side of the central building, a well-preserved patch of the original floor remains (fig. 61). The patch is about 2 feet 11 inches long at the base of the building and projects about 8 inches therefrom. This preserved floor reveals that the lower level of the platform is formed of large, unshaped stones mixed with smaller stones and a mortar of lime, sascab, and crushed stone. Above this, beginning at a depth of about 3 inches from the surface, is a layer of lime and sascab mortar mixed with smaller stones and fine rubble. A capping layer about ¾ to ½ inches thick of lime and sascab mortar

mixed with finely crushed limestone was then applied. This layer was well smoothed and continues beneath the House of the Governor, forming the principal foundation of the building (fig. 62).[47] The surface layer of the final floor of smoothed stucco is brownish to orange-buff in color and is highly burnished.

A central stairway projects from the east side (front) of Platform 4, providing access from the top of the third platform to the House of the Governor (figs. 48, 58). This stairway is formed of five steps of complex plan. The lowest tread projects some 14 feet beyond the main body of the stairway at each side. The total width of the lowest step is 133 feet 4 inches, nearly matching that of the monumental stairway, while the upper four steps have a width of 105 feet 8 inches. This stairway was constructed in the same fashion as the monumental stairway, with the risers aligned and set one course at a time, the interior filled with small unshaped

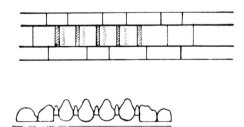

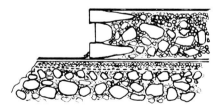

Fig. 62. Base of House of the Governor: elevation, plan, and section.

Fig. 63. House of the Governor, south side of passage through north transverse vault.

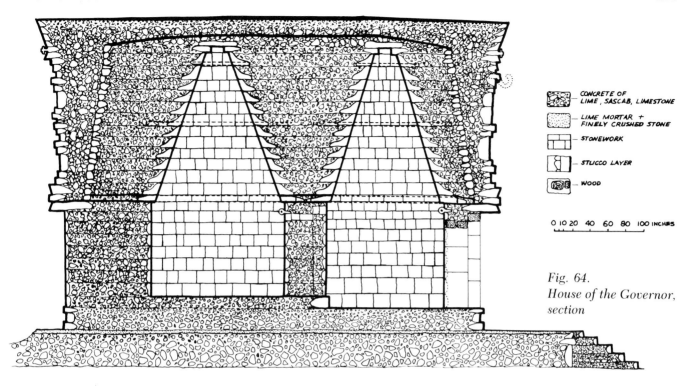

CONCRETE OF
LIME , SASCAB, LIMESTONE

LIME MORTAR +
FINELY CRUSHED STONE

STONEWORK

STUCCO LAYER

WOOD

0 10 20 40 60 80 100 INCHES

Fig. 64.
House of the Governor,
section

stones and mortar, and the whole structure covered with a coating of stucco.

House of the Governor

Base

The House of the Governor rests upon a basal molding formed of upper and lower rectangular string courses bounding an alternating series of flat panels and groups of four inset colonnettes (figs. 58–59, 62). This molding originally encircled the entire base of the building except along the walls forming the passageways of the two large transverse vaults. There the molding is merely a slight outset at the level of the top of the base (fig. 63).[48]

Each of the rectangular, faced stones of the lower course has a moderately long, slablike tenon that ties into the concrete core behind (fig. 62). These stones are about 7 inches high but their lengths vary considerably. Above this the second course is recessed some 3½ inches. The flat sections are constructed of well-cut and faced, rectangular stones, about 10½ inches in height and varied in length. These stones are quite similar to the tilelike facing stones that cover the lower wall of the House of the Governor, but where these stones adjoin a group of recessed colonnettes the sides of the stones are

also well squared. Presumably the tops and bottoms of such stones are finished as well, so as to provide a smooth, level surface for the support of the upper course. The groups of colonnettes are formed of two elements: small wedge-shaped pieces of stone with rectangular faces that serve as spacers, and the colonnettes themselves which are half-cylinders with wedge-shaped tenons at the rear. The colonnettes are, on average, 10½ inches high and 8¼ inches in diameter. The colonnettes also have flat tops that serve to support the upper course. The upper course is a carefully cut and smoothed, rectangular string course. Long, tapering, tongue-shaped tenons anchor these blocks in the concrete hearting. This course is about 6 inches high and the length of the individual stones varies.

The area behind the basal molding was filled to the top of the upper course with a mixture of lime and sascab mortar and rough limestone. Smaller stones were used near the top to obtain a more even and regular surface. The entire floor was covered with a thick layer of plaster mixed with finely crushed sascab and the surface was smoothed. This became the general floor level of the outer rooms of the House of the Governor (fig. 64). The base, with its molding and concrete core, thus serves with the building platform as the principal foundation for the entire structure. No other more secure or solid foundations were ever laid.[49] It is quite likely that the lack of firm footings cause differential settling in the building, particularly in the south wing which slopes downward toward the south (fig. 47).[50]

Following the construction of this general floor level a secondary floor was added, forming a step up into each of the rear rooms of the building (fig. 64). This upper level was formed by pouring a mixture of lime and sascab mortar and limestone to the height of a row of rectangular stone blocks that runs across the base of the rear wall of each exterior room. These blocks are about 8 inches high and only slightly wider. This interior step to the rear rooms was an originally planned feature, not an addition, for the lowest course of the facing stones in the walls of the interior rooms rests upon this upper floor rather than being partly covered by it (fig. 64).[51] The upper floor was also covered with a smooth surface of plaster and sascab, and the entire base was probably allowed to dry thoroughly before wall construction began.

Lower Walls

Once the base of the building was completed, construction began on the lower walls. The position and width of each doorway and the location of the corners were first determined, and the lower courses of the door jambs and cornerstones were set in place.[52] At the House of the Governor a shallow inset forms a frame or embrasure around each of the doorways (figs. 2, 54, 58, 64). The inner door jambs are formed of large monoliths whose widths equal that of the inner jamb (average width 2 feet 6 inches) and whose heights vary from somewhat over one third to one quarter that of the doorway. These inner jamb stones are precisely cut and smoothed on their outer faces, as well as on the top and bottom. Their corners are crisply cut to form sharp angles that approximate 90°. The backs of the stones, which were set into the wall and are not visible, were roughly carved in a convex shape. The inset panels of the doorways are composed of large blocks of stone. These are carved on the two exterior faces, which meet to form a sharp corner, as well as on the top and bottom. The rear of these blocks was also a roughly shaped, convex form. The corner stones of the building are the same general shape as the blocks of the doorway frames. The bottoms and tops of these blocks are rarely exactly perpendicular to the vertical faces, so that in most cases the blocks were leveled by inserting small limestone spalls beneath the bases.[53]

Fig. 65. *House of the Governor, interior doorway*

With the lower jambs in position work could begin on the lower course of the walls. At the House of the Governor the walls were built one course at a time, with the entire lower course laid and allowed to set up before work was begun on the second course. Evidence for this technique of wall construction is visible in the interior doorways,[54] where the large jamb stones have fallen and revealed a cross-section of the wall interiors, and where the lintels have fallen from above the doorways with the resultant partial collapse of sections of the vault masonry above (figs. 64–65). In each interior doorway several horizontal cracks of seams are visible, each occurring at the level of the top of a masonry course. From this it is clear that the so-called veneer type walls of the building were laid one course at a time, with the facing blocks used as forms between which an aggregate concrete of lime, sascab, and rough stone was poured and packed. Each layer of concrete was roughly smoothed and allowed to set before construction was begun on the next course.[55] The facing blocks are exceptionally well cut and squared with flat faces smoothed by chipping and pecking. These blocks are generally only about half as deep as they are high and wide, with the back of block tapering inward to form a roughly convex surface. The facing stones do not have flattened upper, lower, or lateral surfaces and serve no true bearing function, so that the stones resemble plates laid on the surface of the building and form a sheathing over the concrete core. Because the facing stones are so carefully squared, they fit tightly and form a smooth planar surface that wholly conceals the concrete hearting within.[56] Because of its appearance, this type of masonry has been referred to as a veneer, but technically it is a form masonry, since the facing stones must be set in place before the concrete hearting can be poured.

The horizontal coursing of the facing stones is very straight, suggesting that the masons may have used a taut line or string to determine the upper edge of each stone.[57] Either the upper edge of each stone would have been trimmed during construction to bring it to the established level, or the height of a course would have been determined at the quarry by cutting a series of facing stones to a pre-established height by means of a template or standard unit of measurement.[58]

The lower wall was thus carried upward by courses to the level of the vault spring. The spring-point is located at the same height as the top of the lower, bevelled course of the medial molding (fig. 64). This bevelled course is formed of large stones, well cut and dressed on the outer faces and with long tapering tongues of stone at the back that tail deeply into the concrete hearting (figs. 64, 66). These long tenons serve an important structural purpose, since the lower course of the medial molding supports the sculptured frieze that later was applied above.[59] At the height of the vault spring and the top of the lower course of medial molding, the concrete core of the wall was carefully smoothed and a thin capping of lime plaster was applied (fig. 64). This finishing layer suggests that the entire lower wall zone was permitted to dry thoroughly before further construction was begun on the vaults and upper façade.[60]

Because the walls of the interior rooms were constructed from the height of the raised floor level, their wall courses are not always level with those of the outer rooms. Consequently, a narrow course of rectangular stones was often used as a lev-

Fig. 66. House of the Governor, end wall of room.

Fig. 67. House of the Governor, vault construction above interior doorway.

Fig. 68. House of the Governor, zapote wood lintel.

eling layer to bring the top of the wall to a uniform height (figs. 64, 67).

Doorways

As noted, each of the doorways was built with a recessed panel forming a frame. The inner jambs are composed of large stone blocks, each of which is the width of the entire jamb and is squared on the three outer faces. The corners of the frames are shafts of stone squared on two sides. As the wall rose by courses, additional jamb and cornerstones were set until the desired height of the doorway was reached. At the top of the inner jamb stone the concrete core was leveled, and behind the jamb stone the wall was finished with two rectangular facing stones, thus creating a shelf above the jamb on each side of the door (figs. 64–65). Long rectangular beams of zapote wood were then placed on these shelves to span the doorway (fig. 68). At the top of the embrasure cornerstones, similar shelves were constructed and a wooden lintel was laid across. These cornerstones were carried eight inches higher than the inner jambs, creating a frame around the doorway at the top as well as at the sides.

All of the doorway lintels were carved from zapote wood. Prior to the building's restoration in the 1950s, all wooden supports had collapsed, resulting in the deterioration of large sections of masonry above each doorway.[61] Wood was probably employed rather than stone because the five-foot spans were so great.[62] The economic incentive for wooden lintels was negligible, since the labor required to shape a zapote log with stone tools was comparable to that of quarrying a stone block of similar size.[63]

Bench

In Room 9 there is a low and broad rectangular platform or bench in the northwest corner (figs. 41, 69). This platform was constructed in the same fashion as the steps to the interior rooms; a border of squared facing blocks was set, the area within filled with lime and sascab mortar and limestone, and the whole platform covered with a thick coating of plaster. At Chichen Itza buildings often were plastered before the interior fittings were installed. At the Temple of the Chac Mool, for example, the walls were plastered white and the contours of a bench were traced in black lines on the wall before the bench was built.[64] A similar procedure seems to have been employed at the House of the Governor, for the low platform overlays the offset base of the rear wall of the room, indicating that the platform was installed only after the completion of the walls. This is the only masonry bench in the House of the Governor.

Fig. 69. House of the Governor, masonry bench in room 9.

Fig. 70. House of the Governor, beam hole and ventilator.

Wall Depressions and Openings

The exterior walls of the rooms are pierced with one or more small rectangular vents or air shafts (figs. 70–71). Exceptions to this are found in the walls of the interior rooms of the central building, and the west walls of Rooms 16 and 4, where the great thickness (ca. nine feet) of the exterior walls prevented the construction of vents.[65]

The air shafts are usually roughly centered when they occur in an end wall, and are placed near both ends of the side walls (figs. 70-71). They are positioned at a level one course below the vault spring on the interior and directly below the lowest course of the medial molding on the exterior. They are typically slightly higher than wide (ca. 9 inches high and 5 inches wide) and are formed either by leaving a space between two adjacent stones in a wall course, or by cutting out a rectangular section of a facing stone. The interior walls of the vents are merely roughly molded troughs left in the concrete core of the course in which they are constructed. In several rooms the vents are filled in with rough lime concrete. This was done in the 1950s by Ruz,

to prevent bats and swallows from living in the building.[66]

Cordholders

Cordholders are found flanking each doorway inside the rooms. They are devices from which some type of cord or rope could have been hung, or through which a thin pole could have been inserted to support a curtain door-covering. Cordholders are made of limestone cut in the form of a ring with an attached spigot or tenon for insertion in the wall (fig. 64). Two such cordholders are placed above and at either side of each doorway inserted in the wall just below the spring of the vault and spaced 2 feet 2 inches to 4 feet 6 inches from the edge of the door (fig. 71).

Partition Walls

In each room the transverse or end walls are constructed so that the facing stones abut the facing stones of the longitudinal walls (fig. 66).[67] From this

a.

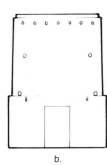

b.

c.

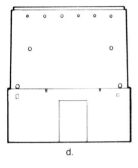

d.

Fig. 71. House of the Governor, diagram of beam, ventilator and cordholder arrangements: (a, b, c,) room 1; (d) room 3; (e) room 11; (f) room 10.

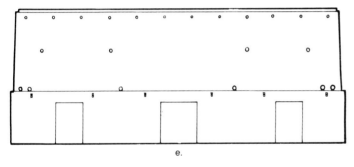

e.

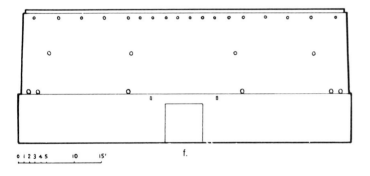

f.

nal wall.[68] According to the other possible method, the transverse walls could have been built across the rooms as each course of the main walls was raised, in which case the transverse walls would be structurally integrated with the rest of the building. If the latter technique was used, the builders nevertheless took pains to lay the main walls first and position them so that they were slightly overlaid by the facing stones of the partition walls.

Examples of both construction techniques are found elsewhere at Uxmal. The two walls blocking the passages of the transverse vaults of the House of the Governor were constructed using the first method (fig. 72). These are clearly partitions added as the result of a secondary building campaign. An example of the second method exists at the House of the Turtles, where it can be observed that the facing stones of the longitudinal walls do not continue completely behind the transverse walls, and that the concrete core is continuous within. This solid core construction was probably also used at the House of the Governor, for it is remarkably similar in masonry technique and architectural style to the House of the Turtles, suggesting that the two buildings were built close in time and probably by some of the same masons.

Vaults

After the lower walls had been capped and allowed to set,[69] work began on roofing the rooms with vaults. The lowest course of the vaults consists of a series of large, well-cut stones with a bevelled face and a long tapered tongue that tailed into the vault as much as half the width of the wall (figs. 64, 67). These stones were tenoned deeply into the wall to counterbalance and sustain the weight of the vault above. The height of this course is usually only about half that of the upper courses of the vault.[70] These stones were laid so that they project about four inches from the lower wall surface, forming a narrow offset or ledge that continues around all four sides of each room (figs. 64, 66).[71] A capping layer of smooth plaster was applied at the level of this course also, indicating that this vault foundation was permitted to dry thoroughly before construction progressed.

Once this course had set, the vault was continued upward and inward toward the midline of the room. The vaults, like the lower walls, were constructed one course at a time, permitting the concrete core of each course to set before adding addi-

a construction sequence of two different types can be postulated. One possibility is that the main walls could have been laid completely before the transverse walls were erected, with the facing stones continuing behind the transverse wall. In this case the transverse walls would have been simple partitions with no structural connection to the longitudi-

Fig. 72. House of the Governor, east side, north transverse vault, partition wall.

tional weight. Each course is composed of specially shaped facing stones which were used as forms to contain the concrete and rubble core packed behind. These vault stones are carved with a carefully squared and smoothed face that is bevelled to conform to the angle of the vault. In profile the stones taper downward from top front to bottom rear, so that they are often described as boot-shaped (figs. 64, 67). The tapering "toes" of these stones form long tenons that bind them tightly into the concrete core of the vault. The specialized shape of the tenon balances the stone at the rear and insures that once the concrete has been poured the vault stone will remain weighted in position while the core hardens. Because of their shape, the vault stones, like the wall stones, function principally as a facing and as forms to contain the concrete. Unlike earlier Maya vaults constructed of corbeled or cantilevered stone slabs that served some supportive function, those of the House of the Governor rely solely on the tenacity of the concrete core for sta-

bility, and the vault stones have no bearing surface whatever. Without the concrete core the vault would collapse.[72]

The vaults were carried up a course at a time and were narrowed progressively by setting each higher course inward so that the base of the face of the upper vault stones was flush with the top of the face of the lower vault stones (fig. 64). When the vaults reached a height where about two feet separated the two soffits, a low course of blocks was laid. These blocks have a low, well-cut rectangular face and taper in back to form a slablike tenon similar in form to that of the offset course of stones at the vault spring. These upper blocks project slightly inward from the plane of the vault, forming another offset around the four sides of the rooms (figs. 64, 73).[73]

To complete the vaults a row of capstones was laid across the one-and-a-half-foot gap separating the offset course. These capstones were cut from large slabs of limestone obtained from stratified de-

Fig. 73. House of the Governor, vault soffit showing off-set at peak of vault.

Fig. 74. House of the Governor, west side showing outer face of vault mass and cleavage plane.

posits where the limestone is naturally bedded in hard, straight courses.[74] The sides of these thick slabs were trimmed for a tight fit and the capstones were laid adjacent to one another to support the thick roof above the vaults.

Vault Beams

On the soffit of each vault there is an arrangement of holes that mark the position where wooden beams originally spanning the vault were embedded in the masonry (figs. 70–71, 73). These cross ties were laid in three registers, with large diameter beams near the bottom, middle-sized beams at the center, and small poles near the top.

Whether these cross beams served some structural purpose has been debated. W. H. Holmes suggested that the beams were used as braces to lessen

the possibility of collapse during construction.[75] E. H. Thompson, on the other hand, believed that the Maya arch was a stone representation of the lines of the roof structure of the typical Maya hut or *na*, and that the wooden cross beams are merely survivals of the cross ties of the framework supporting the thatched roof.[76] Lawrence Roys, however, believed that the vault beams served a structural purpose during the construction of the vault. According to Roys, vault spans, which are inherently unstable, could be widened substantially by reinforcing the vault with the end walls of the building, with the partition walls, and with the wooden beams laid across the vault. Roys argued that, when first applied, Maya cements were too weak and did not have enough tensile strength to prevent the overhanging vault masses from breaking away or sagging. Wooden struts were inserted at intervals to prevent this. These vault beams contributed to the strength of the vault in two ways. They prevented the vaults from collapsing inward, and also held the vault material from falling away near where the cross beams were embedded. Both of these functions were of great importance before the vault was capped and before the concrete had aged and set thoroughly.[77] Only the uppermost row of thin poles served no important structural purpose, though the Maya masons may have thought them necessary for the support of the capstones.[78]

Outer Faces of the Vaults

The vaults were laid one course at a time; unlike the lower walls, each layer of the vault was not extended completely to the outer façade, but rather was roughly finished at some distance behind the plane of the upper frieze (figs. 64, 74). As each course of the vaults was laid, the concrete core was roughly finished by laying a row of large, unshaped stones along the outer faces. The gaps between these rough stones were chinked with smaller wedges of limestone. The lowest course of this rough exterior face was set back about 2 to 3 feet from the edge of the lowest course of the medial molding. Each higher course was stepped back so that the completed outer face of the vault formed a roughly surfaced plane that was inclined inward slightly.[79]

Transverse Vaults

Transverse vaults were constructed with a method similar to that used to vault the interior rooms (figs. 75–78). Originally the transverse vaults passed entirely through the building, forming passageways whose floors were coterminous with that of Platform 3. At the southern edge of the east side of the north vault, where the vault face has fallen away, the inner construction is revealed as a mixture of large blocks and slabs bonded in lime aggregate concrete (fig. 76). Larger slabs and spalls are used to counterweight the tenons of the boot-shaped facing stones and to level the rear and bring the bevelled face of the vault stone to the desired angle. The vault soffits are composed of well-cut, squared, and smoothed stones which are well joined and coursed. As pointed out, the outer facing of the vault is of a whiter, finer limestone than are the inner soffits (fig. 49). It is possible that a rope was used to construct the soffits of these vaults. The

rope could have been fastened at the approximate height of the capstone by tying it to a beam resting on the completed vault mases of the buildings and spanning the passageway between. This construction method is discussed further in chapter 9.

The vaults as open corridors represent the first phase of construction at the House of the Governor (figs. 72, 76).[80] Later the passages were filled to the floor level of Platform 4. The basal molding of the House of the Governor was extended across the passage and the area within further raised to this height. The lower fill consists of large unshaped stones, smaller rocks, and lime mortar. Above this is a layer of smaller stones, pebbles and mortar about 4½ inches thick. The floor was finished with a capping layer of lime plaster about 3–4 mm. thick (fig. 72). After this new floor was built the vaulted passages were obstructed by a central wall.[81] The spaces on either side of this wall were converted into small rooms by walling each end of the vault to the height of the medial molding, which was then carried across the new doorways.[82] The floor plans of these rooms were squared up and the side walls brought into plumb by constructing vertically walled masonry abutments against the vault soffits. In front of these newly created rooms larger anterooms or porticoes with wide, two-columned doorways were constructed by extending the façade of the House of the Governor. Sculptured facing stones carrying featherwork designs found in the debris of the vaulted passageways suggest that these porticoes were roofed by a monumental representation of a Maya hut with a feathered roof (figs. 77–79). Close study of the transverse vaults indicates that the central walls were probably added to prevent slumping of the huge soffits. The added rooms and new decorative façade represent an attempt to put the best face on an architectural addition required to prevent possible structural failure.

Cleavage Plane and Upper Façade

On the west side of the central building a section of the façade above the medial molding has collapsed. Formerly a long section of the east façade of the central building had fallen in the same manner, as is recorded in the drawing by Catherwood and in early photographs (figs. 1, 18).[83] The collapse of these sections reveals that the vaults and upper sculptured façade were built as two separate sections rather than as a unified structural body (figs. 4, 64, 74).

The technique used for the construction of the

Fig. 75. House of the Governor, west side of north transverse vault.

Fig. 76. House of the Governor, east side of north transverse vault.

Fig. 77. House of the Governor, west side of south transverse vault.

Fig. 78. House of the Governor, east side of south transverse vault.

vaults and upper façade is visible at the fallen façade zone on the west side of the central building.
At the north and south ends of this zone there is a
distinct break or cleavage between the outer masonry face of the vaults and the concrete hearting of
the sculptured upper façade.[84] The cleavage is now
filled with cement to prevent the collapse of further
sections of the façade, but it is clearly visible as a
gap in earlier photographs and is still visible at the
southwest corner of the building. This cleavage
plane continues around the entire building, indicating that the sculptured mosaic façade was not applied until the outer face of the vaulting was completed and allowed to dry and set.

It is difficult to tell whether work progressed
on the upper façade the same way as on the walls
and vaults, that is one course at a time, or whether
the façade was constructed according to a sectional
technique. That the latter technique was used is
suggested by the compositional division of the
frieze into separate panels of frets, lattice, masks,
etc., and by the fact that the fallen section of
the west frieze collapsed leaving straight vertical
breaks.[85] To construct the frieze the various carved
stone mosaic elements were lined and set above the
medial molding, and backed with a concrete core
of lime plaster, sascab, and rough limestone. The
smaller pieces, such as the lattice Xs or the blocks
composing the steps of step-frets, are not tailed
deeply into the core (the depth of these blocks is
not much greater than the width of their faces),
while the stones that compose the frets taper in
back to form long tenons that are sunk deeply into
the concrete hearting. The frieze was erected to
the level of the lowest member of the cornice, or
perhaps to the top of the cornice, after which the
entire frieze was allowed to dry before the roof was
applied. The completed upper façade was in profile
a large triangular wedge of masonry resting at its
bottom corner on the medial molding and leaning
against the outer face of the vault.

This two-phased method of upper façade construction was widespread in northern Yucatan.
Roys documented the occurrence of this type of
upper façade on the House of the Deer at Chichen
Itza, where a clearly visible cleavage line separates
the inner unfinished sloping face of the vault from
an inverted wedge-shaped section of facing masonry which was applied subsequently.[86] A similar construction technique is found in the upper
temple of the Pyramid of the Magician at Uxmal,
and Morris noted the occurrence of this trait in
the Puuc-style Temple of the Three Lintels in Old

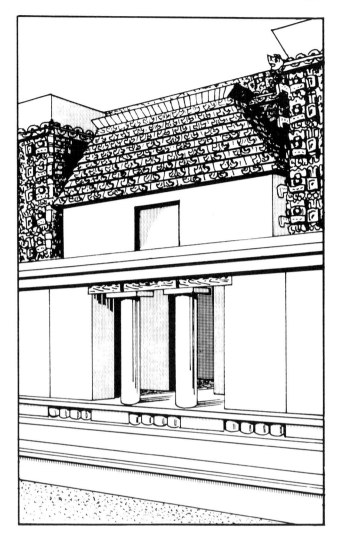

Fig. 79. *House of the Governor, reconstruction of south
transverse vault (redrawn after Ruz Lhuillier 1959:37
by Tid Kowalski).*

Chichen.[87] This method of upper façade construction also is found in various buildings at the Puuc
sites of Kabah, Sayil, and Xlapak. The two-stage
technique occurs with enough frequency in the
Puuc region to suggest that it was employed as
a standard procedure of accepted and traditional
building practice.[88]

Roof

When the upper façade was completed to the height
of the lower course of the cornice it was approach-
ing the top of the outer face of the vaults. The concrete core of the frieze was from this point extended across the entire upper surface of the vaults

Fig. 80.
Graffito from
House of the Governor
(after Seler
1917:abb. 125).

to form a thick roof.[89] A study of the roof in its present condition reveals that it is composed of a thick layer of lime plaster, sascab, and limestone (fig. 64). Large, rough stones mixed with many chinks and spalls form the lower part of this layer, while the upper part consists of a dense mixture of smaller stones in mortar. From many small fragments of crushed plaster that remain on the roof it is clear that the top of the building was given a thick final coating of lime plaster mixed with sascab. The roof was well smoothed and presumably was given a slightly convex surface to shed water, although the entire roof has settled slightly so that it is now irregular.[90] There is no trace of any upper story or superstructure such as a roof comb or flying façade, despite the fact that the rear wall of the building is some 9 feet thick.

Plaster Facing

The entire edifice of the House of the Governor was covered with a coating lime plaster, whose purpose was to cover the joints between the facing stones and to provide a surface for fresco painting. Patches of smooth plaster still adhere to many of the vaults, the inner walls, and the façade of the building.[91] The plaster, where observed today, is a creamy yellowish-white color, with no visible evidence of painting. Originally, however, many sections of the building may have been painted. Stephens, upon visiting the Nunnery Quadrangle in 1841, reported that all of the façades were painted originally and that traces of red paint were still visible in the lattice-work of the East Structure.[92] The plaster-covered capstones of several structures of the Nunnery were painted with hieroglyphic texts,[93] while a band of glyphs was also painted beneath the offset at the spring of the vault in the House of the Birds.[94] There is evidence that many of the other buildings at Uxmal and nearby Puuc centers were once painted.[95] At the House of the Governor itself there was originally a drawing of a Maya noble wearing a long-snouted headdress on the plaster wall of one of the small rooms built in the transverse vaults (fig. 80).[96]

CHAPTER 8

Plan and Massing

THE House of the Governor, although it is a unity in time and space, also represents the sum of many separate architectural forms that have been combined and skillfully adjusted by the architects of Uxmal. As well as being a unique edifice, the building is also intelligible as an outgrowth of an art historical tradition in which many separate strands of formal history have been woven into a complete and meaningful fabric. The study of the histories of the different classes of forms in a connected series permits us to discuss what Kubler has termed the art object's "durational meanings"—meanings which were not clear to the makers of the object, but which are revealed to the historian when the series is complete.[1]

The history of forms embodied in the House of the Governor stretches far back in time, and these long-lived formal solutions are in part responsible for the harmony and order seen in the building. George Andrews has commented on the way in which the historical aspect pervades Maya monumental buildings:

The smallest temple, including the platform which supports it, can be observed to be composed of a number of discrete parts, or elements, whose ordering appears to be dependent on a set of "rules" as explicit as those governing the Greek or Roman Orders. The temple proper, as seen in elevation, consists of a base, lower wall, upper wall, and roof comb, and each of these elements is carefully articulated by means of projecting cornices or moldings which divide the façade into a series of horizontal bands. Nothing is accidental in this composition, the details of which have been fully preconceived and the proportions and spacings of the doorways and moldings carefully adjusted to produce a visual harmony . . . Here is "classic" architecture with all its controls

and determinants, its pristine order designed to delight the eye and mind alike.[2]

Although Andrews gives us an appreciation of the traditions incorporated in each form of a Maya building, it is important to remember that in the case of a structure as large and complex as the House of the Governor, many of the separate forms may have separate heritages, different points of origin, and developmental sequences of varying duration. This composite nature of the work of art has been described by Kubler in his book *The Shape of Time,* and he recognized this polymorphic quality in the House of the Governor when he wrote "In it many scattered solutions were brought together to make up an edifice of striking harmony and repose."[3] In this and the following chapters we trace the sources and histories of the "scattered solutions" employed by the architects of Uxmal. Thus will we be able to understand the architecture of the House of the Governor in a way that the Maya, with their nearer perspective, were not able to perceive.

Plan

Like many Maya buildings of the Classic period, the House of the Governor has a plan that was determined in part by constructional considerations resulting from the use of the Maya vaulting system. This method of roofing favors longitudinal extension.[4] Because it is supported chiefly upon two longitudinal walls, the vault can be extended merely by lengthening the building. Turning corners presents greater difficulty, and Maya architects rarely attempted to do so.[5] Rooms are obtained by

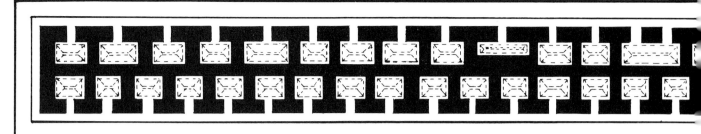

the addition of partition walls, which simultaneously serve to buttress the vault. In this system the simplest way to achieve greater depth is by adding another vaulted range parallel to the first.

The system of two parallel vaults serves to define the basic plan of the House of the Governor (figs. 41, 64). Within the basic system, however, are modifications and subtleties of room arrangement and size that contribute to the unique qualities of the edifice. Immediately apparent is the fact that the plan is interrupted; the structure has been divided into three bodies by means of two great transverse vaults. Study of the plan confirms that the two flanking buildings, although separated from the central structure, play an integral part in the plan of the House of the Governor as a whole. It is evident that the basic tripartite composition was designed from the beginning, and that, excepting the additions made to the transverse vaults, the building is the result of a unified building project. The interior spaces of the House of the Governor form a calculated hierarchy in which room areas increase progressively from the rear (NW and SW) corners toward the central chambers. In this plan the interrelatedness between the central building and the wings is shown by the fact that the plans of the flanking buildings attain symmetry and are intelligible only with reference to the central structure.

The graded succession of rooms suggests an accompanying rank according to function and prestige. During the Renaissance the size and exact proportions of rooms were determined by the assigned functions, the relationship often being expressed in terms of served and servant spaces.[6] The plan of the House of the Governor, while apparently lacking the harmonic proportions of the Renaissance villas and palaces, nevertheless seems kin to such buildings by virtue of its comprehensive symmetry and by the clarity of its spatial order. Servant spaces exist in the smaller end rooms, while served spaces are embodied by the spacious central

chambers, whose focal importance is confirmed by the placement of sculpture on the frieze above and by their relationship with the jaguar throne on the great terrace in front of the building (figs. 16, 54).

The long, multiroomed plan of the House of the Governor has its ancestry in the Maya lowlands rather than in other regions of Mesoamerica. In the southern Maya area, earlier versions of similar palace plans abound at sites such as Uaxactun, Tikal, or Nakum. Building L of Structure A-V at Uaxactun has a layout resembling that of the House of the Governor, being composed of two parallel vaulted ranges with a transverse room at each end.[7] Though it lacks the complexity of the House of the Governor, Building L appears to be one of the basic models for many later Maya palaces, including Building W of Structure A-V at Uaxactun and those of Uxmal. Basic similarities include the use of transverse end rooms, long parallel vaults and the internal division into a number of separate rooms. Room sizes in Building L vary enough to suggest a spatial hierarchy somewhat like that of the House of the Governor, where rooms increase in size progressively toward the center of the building. At Uaxactun there is a division between the south range, with its smaller rooms, and the north range, with its seemingly more public chamber.

At Tikal the tandem and the tandem/transverse buildings of the Central Acropolis are lengthy palaces with two or more parallel, corbeled ranges, sometimes with transverse rooms or wings attached at the ends (fig. 42).[8] The floor plans of some of these buildings, particularly those of the tandem/transverse class, closely resemble that of the House of the Governor, and it seems possible that such Tikal palaces belong to the same family.[9] Structure 5D-65, for example, is composed of two parallel, vaulted ranges, subdivided into rooms by partition walls. At each end is a transverse room that projects slightly to form a wing. The massing recalls that of the avant-corps apartments of the South Structure

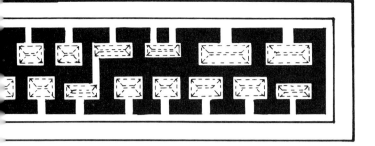

Fig. 81. Nakum, plan of Structure D (redrawn after Mar-quina 1964:lam. 171 by Tid Kowalski).

of the Nunnery at Uxmal, while the transverse room arrangement resembles that of the northern and southern end rooms of the House of the Governor. At Tikal the plans of the palaces composing the Group F Quandrangle also closely resemble that of the House of the Governor.[10]

In the Peten, the ultimate in such parallel-vaulted, many-chambered plans appears at Nakum in Structure D, a remarkably long and narrow building that forms the southern boundary of the Great Plaza (fig. 81).[11] The building is 412 feet long and contained about 44 rooms facing north and south.

The dominance of the vault construction system in determining the plan is indicated by the fact that many of the room partition walls are mere screens, built after the vaulted ranges were already complete. Variants of this plan appear in other structures at Nakum as well.[12] To the east, at Altun Ha, Belize, a layout reminiscent of that of the House of the Governor exists in the Early Classic Structure A-6B, composed of double ranges, each with thirteen doors.[13]

In the Rio Bec region, several examples of long, multiroomed palaces with transverse end chambers

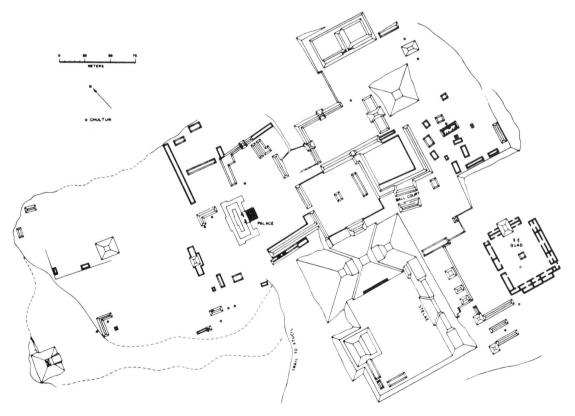

Fig. 82. Santa Rosa Xtampak, plan with Southeast Quadrangle (after Pollock 1970:fig. 56).

occur, as in the eastern building of the quadrangle at Pared de los Reyes, and Structures I and VI at Pechal.[14] In the Chenes area a variant of the extended palace form appears in Structure 1 at Dzibilnocac, where a long, central building is interrupted in the middle and terminated at both ends by raised dragon-mouth temples.[15] Long, parallel-vaulted buildings were linked at the corners to form the east, west, and south sides of the Southeast Quadrangle at Santa Rosa Xtampak as well (fig. 82).[16] Dzibilchaltun, on the northern plains, also featured a number of buildings of this type of both Early period and Florescent period date.[17]

Throughout the Puuc region proper many variants of the extended, multiroomed palace exist. A common plan, exemplified by the Adjacent Palace at Chunhuhub, consisted of three rooms in a line, all facing the same direction.[18] Related arrangements of four-roomed ranges occur in Structure 3C1 at Sayil,[19] the Half-Column Palace at Huntichmul,[20] and Structure 3 in Group 1 at Kiuic.[21] In larger multichambered buildings the rooms often were arranged in parallel lines, placed either as a series of connected inner and outer rooms, or with rooms facing in opposite directions. Puuc architects utilized variants of such plans to create several of their most imposing edifices, such as Structure 1A2 and the upper story of the Second Palace at Kabah (Structure 2C2).[22] The front of the Codz Poop (Structure 2C6) at Kabah also is based on a parallel ranges of rooms with transverse chambers at each end (fig. 158).[23]

At Uxmal the designers made use of this basic plan to create some of the most handsome buildings in the Maya area. An early version occurs in the Lower West Structure of the Pyramid of the Magician, where two parallel-vaulted ranges of five rooms each are terminated by transverse rooms (fig. 7). Although it was suggested that the associated radiocarbon date of 569 ± 50 may be too early, the building certainly predates the House of the Governor. Longer versions of parallel-vaulted, multiroomed plans occur in the Pigeons Group (fig. 98),[24] and the Nunnery Quadrangle (figs. 83, 85–87).

It is in the Nunnery buildings that resemblances to the House of the Governor become most pronounced. The North Structure shares an eleven-frontal entry plan and the use of paired transverse rooms at each end. Neither the South nor the North Structures have the same emphasis on hierarchical spaces seen in the House of the Governor. In the North Structure the transverse chambers are only

slightly shorter and the central chambers slightly longer than the other rooms.[25] In the East and West Structures the size differences separating the central from the flanking rooms are more pronounced. The East Structure has the most complex spatial design. Although it does not have a progressive increase in area toward the center, it does share with the House of the Governor a great differentiation in room size.[26]

From the above comparisons it is evident that the elongated, parallel-vaulted, multichambered plans had a wide distribution throughout the Maya area during the Classic period. Such buildings formed a long-lived tradition that supplied more distant and closer prototypes for the plan of the House of the Governor.

Massing

In architecture the notion of massing refers to the large-scale relationships produced by the dominant exterior masses of a building. The term is borrowed from discussions of European architecture, where it is known that such large-scale form relationships were designed and evaluated prior to construction by means of wax models.[27] The use of such preparatory mock-ups in Mesoamerica is unproven. Although small copies of architecture do exist, notably the stone models of Monte Alban-style temples,[28] their formality and durability suggest that they are ritualistic replicas rather than discardable working models. Nevertheless, it seems reasonable that the architects of a building as complex as the House of the Governor must have considered the disposition of the basic masses before the building was begun.

At the House of the Governor the plan initially generated the masses, but the plan itself was altered to create a dominant three-part massing. That is, the long, horizontal form of the House of the Governor was at first determined by the many-chambered, parallel-vaulted floor plan. However, the massive form and the division of the building into three structures by transverse vaults was based on considerations of external appearance.

Freestanding Block Design

Despite its tripartite division, the dominant impression conveyed by the House of the Governor is that of a stereometric block, a self-contained entity broken only at the insets of the portal vaults and by

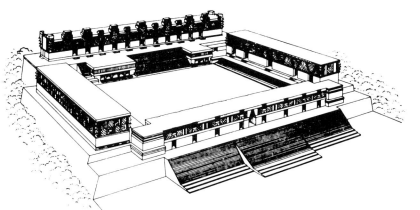

*Fig. 83.
Uxmal, Nunnery
Quadrangle, isometric view
and plan (after Kubler
1975:fig. 50).*

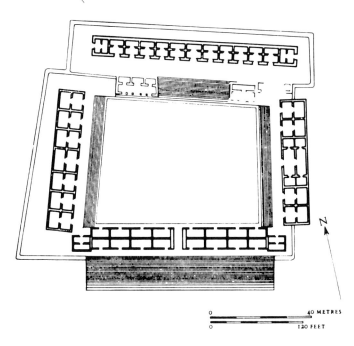

0   40 METRES
0   120 FEET

The most immediate predecessors of the House of the Governor were probably the freestanding block designs of the Nunnery Quadrangle. All of the Nunnery buildings feature a similar long, horizontal form, an insistent rectangularity and a prodigious bulk. Only in the North Structure are the clean outlines broken—its front façade serrated by a sequence of vestigial flying façades composed of tiered masks (fig. 85). The East and West Struc-

Fig. 84. Uxmal, view of House of the Governor from portal vault, South Structure of Nunnery.

the curling snouts of the corner masks. This compact quality is best appreciated when the building is seen at an angle, as through the portal vault of the South Structure of the Nunnery (fig. 84), or from the corner of Platform 2 (fig. 199). Kubler has aptly referred to the House of the Governor and the structures of the Nunnery Quadrangle as examples of freestanding block design (fig. 83).[29] In these structures roof combs and flying façades are abandoned, their vertical emphasis replaced by the horizontal lines of long flat roofs. In plan and shape there is a basic rectangularity. The haphazard addition of wings or stories seen in other buildings, such as the Main Palace at Labna, is avoided. Because of their self-contained quality, buildings like the House of the Governor will not easily tolerate extraneous additions without a loss of aesthetic power.

Fig. 85. Uxmal, North Structure of Nunnery. Building Y to right of stairway. 'Stela' 17 at center of stairway.

Fig. 86. Uxmal, East Structure of Nunnery, view along South Structure to Pyarmid of the Magician

Fig. 87. Uxmal, West Structure of Nunnery

tures seem most closely related to the House of the Governor in their general proportions (figs. 86–87). The resemblance is strengthened by specific correspondences in sculptural motifs and by a parallel interest in proportional harmonies. While an unbroken block sufficed for the shorter Nunnery buildings, however, the architect of the much longer House of the Governor was compelled to transform the monotonous blocklike mass into a more engaging three-in-one scheme.

Kubler, noting the exceptional quality of the open-cornered quadrangle design of the Nunnery at Uxmal, compared it with the architecture of the Mitla Palaces, and suggested close affinities between the two sites. Such resemblances certainly do exist, but whether they attest to a close contact between architects of the two regions is open to question.

At Mitla, the Arroyo, Church, and Column Groups are each composed of three quadrangles tied in a closely knit spatial scheme (fig. 88). In each case the northernmost quadrangle is a small patio, enclosed by rooms and accessible only through the rear wall of an adjacent palace building. Tombs were built beneath the palace platforms, a practice derived from Monte Alban. None of these traits, however, appear in the Nunnery Quadrangle. The Mitla and Uxmal architects also have different concepts of spatial design. In Kubler's words:

At Mitla the isolated edifices give the effect of suburban villas, jealous of their privacy, turning closed walls upon one another, walls which display wealth without inviting the spectator, without attempting to share a coherent space with the neighboring edifices.[30]

At the Nunnery Quadrangle, on the other hand, the buildings are ranked at different levels, so that from the highest north platform the East and West Structures extend to embrace a panorama of the southern section of Uxmal. The Nunnery also is firmly included in a larger planning scheme linking the axis of the Ball Court and the vaulted entrance through the South Structure (figs. 84, 99). Such fundamental differences of plan and spatial design suggest that the Mitla Palaces are not as closely related to the freestanding block buildings at Uxmal as has been supposed.

The fact that several open-corner and closed-corner quadrangles exist in the Maya area, built at the same time as or prior to the Nunnery, suggests that the Nunnery belongs to a wider Maya tradition. These other quadrangles include Group F at Tikal,[31] the Southeastern Quadrangle at Santa Rosa Xtampak (fig. 82),[32] and quadrangles at Dzehkabtun and Xcalumkin.[33] Landa describes a grand quadrangle at Tihoo (Mérida) that seems to have closely paralleled the Nunnery at Uxmal.[34]

In addition to these quadrangular groupings, several of which were composed of separate freestanding palace ranges, many other examples of freestanding block buildings exist in the northern Maya area. Early versions are found at Oxkintok and Dzibilchaltun. Oxkintok Structure 3C6, the build-

Fig. 90. Xpuhil, Structure 1 (after Proskouriakoff 1963a:53).

where three small buildings on a single platform define the eastern side of a plaza on whose western side is a large pyramid.[47] Outside of Uaxactun there are twelve sites where this assemblage occurs in almost pure form, and six where it is less clear. At Uaxactun the assemblage apparently had an astronomical significance,[48] but was later duplicated at other sites for ritual reasons.[49]

During the Late Classic period in the Rio Bec and Chenes areas architects created a number of new three-part arrangements. The most novel and original of these was the three-part façade, in which the moldings and decorative features of a single, unified building are treated so that they suggest three separate structures (fig. 90).

Structure III at Calakmul perhaps forms a link between the Rio Bec and Chenes designs and those of the Peten. It has twelve rooms which interlock to form a central roof-comb unit flanked by two pro-

jecting wings that also support roof combs. Kubler has suggested that this coalescence of temple and palace may have been a model for the towered structures of the Rio Bec region.[50] The placement of the roof combs and profiling of the rear façades suggest the three-temple arrangements of Uaxactun, here linked by rooms rather than isolated.[51]

The three-unit façade appears fully developed at Xpuhil in the Rio Bec area, where the eastern side of Structure 1 was divided into three parts by molding patterns and by recession of the central portion (fig. 90).[52] Structure 1 combines aspects of both palace and temple, consisting of twelve interlocking chambers, above which rise three steep towers with ornamental stairs and mock temple buildings.[53] The articulation of the eastern façade enhanced the division formed by the central recession, and created the impression of three adjacent buildings rather than a unified façade.

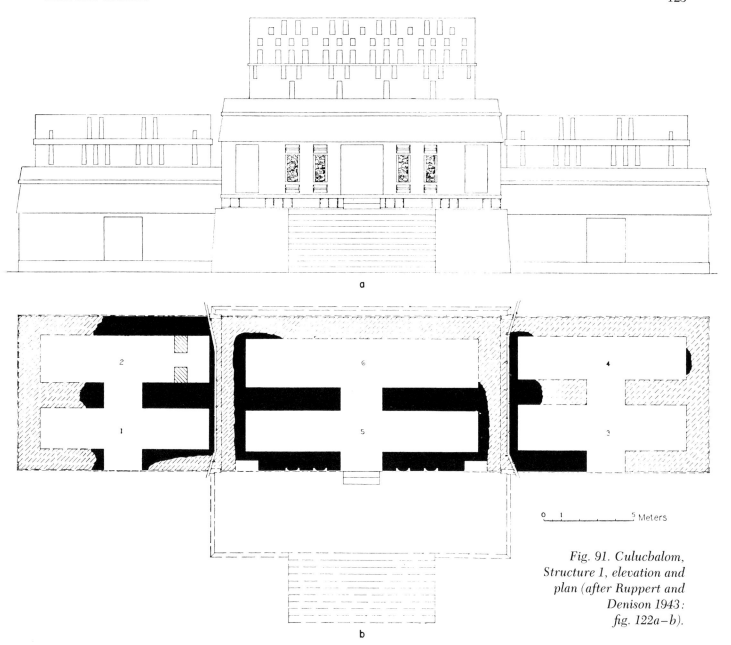

Fig. 91. Culucbalom,
Structure 1, elevation and
plan (after Ruppert and
Denison 1943:
fig. 122a–b).

At Channa, another Rio Bec region site, the north façade of Structure 1 is divided by a recessed central area that is separated from the two outset wings by engaged corner columns. As at Xpuhil, the impression of three separate structures was further emphasized by the discontinuous moldings of the frieze.[54] Structure 1 of Group IV at Rio Bec also features a three-part façade division by shallow insets.[55]

Structure 1 at Culucbalom presents another solution to the three-part composition (fig. 91). Unlike those suggesting three separate façades on a con-

tinuous structure, the Culucbalom edifice emphasizes the actual separation of the three buildings by placing the two wings on a lower level than the main structure, located on a pyramidal platform.[56] Although the central structure is richer in ornamentation, the ensemble is bound together by the rhythm of the three roof combs and shared upper profiling.[57]

At Pechal, Structure 1 has a tripartite façade division emphasized by vertical tiers of masks and projecting masonry panels in the form of miniature huts.[58] The central doorway was treated as a gigan-

Fig. 92. Hochob, Structure 2 (after Seler 1916:taf. VI).

tic reptilian mouth, so that the building conforms closely in iconography to Structure II at Chicanna, and to other buildings in the Chenes region.

Structure II at Chicanna is a particularly impressive example of a three-part façade.[59] The central door is enframed by a gigantic, conventionalized dragon-mouth motif. The two lateral façade units are treated visually as separate structures, projecting slightly from the main wall and differentiated from the central doorway mask by a varied articulation of base, lower wall, and frieze. The two doorways of the wings are framed by stylized versions of thatched roof huts. Ceramic associations and radiocarbon dates indicate that Structure II antedates the House of the Governor.[60]

Three-unit façades occur frequently in the Chenes region. A striking example is seen on Structure 2 at Hochob, where the central unit is recessed and elevated slightly above the level of the two flanking rooms (fig. 92).[61] This façade resembles that of Structure II at Chicanna, particularly in the use of

stylized huts as design elements. At Hochob Structure 2, however, the huts stand between and accentuate the separateness of the central façade and the wings. In this sense they function like the transverse vaults of the House of the Governor, breaching the façade as two vertical accents in a predominantly horizontal composition.

Structure 1 at Hochob is a less exuberant version of Structure 2. The three-part façade is divided into a central dragon-mouth unit flanked by two wings. Here the wings are more spare, and the stylized huts are lacking.[62] The Building with the Serpent Mouth façade at Santa Rosa Xtampak is like Hochob Structure 2,[63] as are similar buildings at Nohcacab and at Huntichmul near Labna.[64]

Many of the edifices featuring three-unit façades are the dragon-mouth type, but non-dragonmouth buildings such as Xpuhil Structure 1 or the Cuartel at Santa Rosa Xtampak also show the division of the façade into units simulating separate buildings (fig. 90).[65] A division recalling that of the Cuartel is also found on the Main Palace at Xkichmook, a long continuous range whose façade is interrupted by deep recesses between simulated buildings.[66]

All of the structures considered thus far, with the exception of that at Huntichmul, are located some distance from Uxmal. At Uxmal itself, however, there are three buildings in a style related to the Chenes and Rio Bec structures we have described, and which have similar three-unit façades. The best known of these is Structure 1 west of the House of the Governor (figs. 12, 15).[67] The center of the façade displays a stylized dragon-mouth mask executed in cut stone with final detail carried out in stucco.[68] The north building of Group 23 also may have been similar.[69] The two wings of Structure 1 had two plain lower walls and two-part medial moldings that stepped up over the doorways in a manner recalling the treatment at the Cuartel at Santa Rosa Xtampak. The upper façade carried corner mask panels and plain sections alternating with groups of split columns.[70]

Structure 1 is the most important example of the three-unit façade at Uxmal. It surely antedates the House of the Governor since it is partly covered by Platform 2.[71] Moreover, this building was still venerated and in use during the period when the House of the Governor was erected.[72] Structure 1 was thus well known to the architects of the House of the Governor and perhaps supplied them with a model for the bold tripartite division of the façade. That the Puuc architects of Uxmal were interested in reviving the forms of these earlier Chenes buildings is shown by the Puuc copy of a dragon-mouth entrance seen on the Upper West Temple of the Pyramid of the Magician.[73]

In Puuc architecture proper the three-part composition occurs in the Cemetery Group at Uxmal. There three adjacent buildings rest on a high platform and face east onto an enclosed amphitheater court (fig. 10).[74] The grouping consists of a longer central building flanked by two smaller structures separated by a narrow walkway. The central building is given greater stature by the addition of a perforated, flying façade and by a varied molding treatment. It seems probable that this group served as model for the House of the Governor. Chronologically, since it retains elements of Early Puuc style, it seems to predate the House of the Governor. The central building and two end apartments, though separated physically, are tightly linked compositionally, and the narrow walkways between suggest the vaulted passages between the buildings of the House of the Governor.[75]

George Kubler has suggested that the tripartite division of the House of the Governor may have been anticipated by the avant-corps end apartments of the South Structure of the Nunnery (figs. 83, 99).[76] This may be so, but it is difficult to prove because evidence indicates that both of these small flanking wings were added sometime after the main body of the South Structure was finished. The wings were built upon the platforms of the East and West Structures of the Nunnery, which in turn partly encase and are definitely later than the main body of the South Structure. Facing blocks on the wings have been cut to fit over the medial and cornice moldings of the central building, and the wings' own moldings are at different levels than those of the central structure. These inconsistencies suggest that the avant-corps buildings were added as afterthoughts, probably to obstruct the view at the corners.[77] The East and West Structures of the Nunnery are probably contemporary with the House of the Governor. We have no way of knowing whether the South Structure wings were built concurrently or slightly later. Perhaps these end apartments represent a response to the House of the Governor rather than a model. In any case, they also testify to the Uxmal architect's interest in traditional Maya three-part building schemes, which find one of their most perfect realizations in the House of the Governor.

Transverse Vaults

The two transverse vaults of the House of the Governor are pivotal elements in the massing of the building. The long horizontal mass of the edifice is severed at two points by these tall apertures, which provide a foil to the lateral extension of the building. The pointed contours direct our vision upward and accentuate the three-part division of the façade. Simultaneously, the vaults' sloping walls, bridged by a capstone, serve to bind the three structures together more effectively than would a mere void. The unique qualities of these vaults do not rest solely on their gigantic dimensions, but on the distinctive compositional role they fulfill. In this sense they occupy a singular position in the aesthetic development of the Maya vault.

A system of corbeled vaulting, relying on the structural properties of lime and rubble concrete, has long been recognized as a hallmark of Classic Maya civilization.[78] This vaulting system was developed by architects of the Proto-Classic period in the Peten region, at or near Tikal, where it served

Fig. 93. Kabah, Portal Vault (after Stephens 1963, 1:fig. 23).

first to roof tombs.[79] Above-ground corbeled-vault construction spread rapidly throughout most of the Maya area during the Early Classic period, so that nearly every Maya center of any prominence boasted several vaulted masonry structures.[80]

Throughout the Early Classic period, Maya architects lacked boldness in their employment of the vault, which was restricted mainly to the roofing of narrow interior spaces. During the Late Classic, however, the vault fulfilled new architectural functions, both in the composition of individual edifices and in the organization of larger civic spaces.

In its most striking innovation the vault was employed as an emphasized portal or passage. One early use of the vault as a portal occurs in the Twin-Pyramid Complexes of Tikal.[81] On the northern side of every Twin-Pyramid group there are a stela and altar enclosed within a small, walled precinct whose southern entry is formed by a vaulted doorway. The specialized contour of this doorway frames the stela within and confers distinction on the precinct's entrance, stressing its importance as a threshold between two different kinds of architectural space.[82]

The most striking vaulted portals were devel-

oped in the Chenes and Puuc regions of northern Yucatan. There two broad categories of portal vaults are found: freestanding gateways which resemble classical triumphal arches, and vaulted passageways which lead through palaces into enclosed courtyards.

The Chenes site of Santa Rosa Xtampak was apparently the place of gestation for the freestanding monumental gateway. At the head of the steep central stairway of the three-storied palace stands a solitary masonry portal or "pylon" that frames the entrance to a small third-story patio (fig. 82).[83] The stucco motif depicted on the portal was the dragon-mouth façade, a typical Chenes design that draws attention to a doorway by framing it with a gigantic monster mask.[84] This sculptural treatment thus emphasizes the pylon's function as a doorway or threshold rather than roof comb. Despite the fact that it was not vaulted, the pylon at Santa Rosa Xtampak apparently represents the first instance of a doorway given architectural prominence as a freestanding monumental structure.

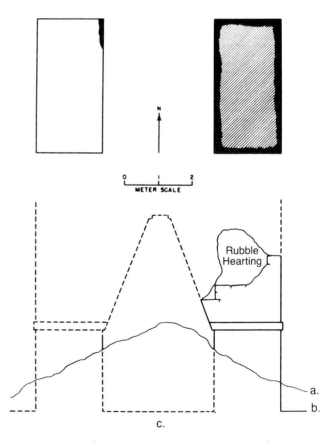

Fig. 94. Uxmal, Portal Vault (after Smith and Ruppert 1954:fig. 1).

Fig. 95. Labna, Portal Vault, east side.

The portal of Santa Rosa Xtampak perhaps served as a stimulus for the freestanding gateways which abound in the Puuc region.[85] Of the great Puuc gateways, those of Kabah and Uxmal resemble one another most closely in form and function (figs. 93–94). John Lloyd Stephens described the gateway at Kabah as a "lonely arch, . . . on a ruined mound, disconnected from every other structure, in solitary grandeur."[86] Catherwood pictures the portal as formed of two masonry piers, supporting a ruined Maya vault. The sole architectural articulation is a string-course dividing the lower wall from the upper at the level of the spring of the vault. A freestanding gateway virtually identical to that of Kabah also exists at Uxmal. The Uxmal gateway stands about three kilometers south of the House of the Governor.[87] The Uxmal portal consists of two thick masonry piers supporting a vault, and is unadorned but for a single string-course embracing the exterior at the level of the vault spring. The similar architectural style of the Uxmal and Kabah portals indicates that they were constructed at about the same time, undoubtedly to mark the ceremonial termini of the sacbe that linked the two cities.[88]

The handsome portal vault at Labna exhibits a complexity of plan and decoration that apparently represents an elaboration on the freestanding gateways of Uxmal and Kabah (figs. 95–96). The Labna portal defines the entrance to a small courtyard enclosed by palaces.[89] As Proskouriakoff observed, the Labna portal fuses the freestanding monumental gateway with the vaulted passageway that penetrates a palace building.[90] The Labna portal was conceived as an independent structure, yet it is fully integrated into the plan of the western courtyard.[91] Two small rooms facing the western court flank the vault. These habitable spaces evoke the idea of a palace, but the small rooms seem like caves carved from solid masonry piers like those of the Uxmal and Kabah gateways. The significance of this portal as a threshold is revealed by the different architectural treatment of its western and eastern sides. From the west it appears as a monumental gateway, with bold geometric ornament supported by seemingly solid piers. Passing through the vault one enters a secluded courtyard, an environmental change reflected by the opening of the piers with rooms and doorways, and by the placement of small replicas of huts on the frieze above.

The Maya portal vault attained its most complex and varied architectural development at Uxmal, where no fewer than ten portal vaults are known. Except for the freestanding gateway at the south

Fig. 96. Labna, Portal Vault, west side.

of the site, all are vaulted passageways that pass through palaces. They are found in the North Group, the House of the Pigeons complex, the Nunnery, the West Group, Structure No. 15, the structure north of the House of the Birds, and the House of the Governor.[92]

The earliest portal vaults at Uxmal are probably those of the North and Pigeons Groups (figs. 97–98).[93] The Pigeons complex is entered from the north, where a large quadrangle is formed by long, multichambered palaces on the east, south, and west, and by a long, low mound on the north.[94] A stairway abutting the façade of the southern palace provided access to a higher terrace, built up to the level of the southern palace roof and fronting the House of the Pigeons. The House of the Pigeons forms the northern edge of the central quadrangular court, which is bordered by range-type palaces. At the center of the House of the Pigeons is a portal vault or "arcade" passing through the building and providing the chief access to the central courtyard (fig. 98).[95]

Across the central courtyard to the south is a long palace built against a rubble terrace that forms the small courtyard in front of the south pyramid. A transverse portal vault, placed slightly east of the central axis of the portal vault of the House of the Pigeons, originally passed through this structure. Later, presumably when the south pyramid terrace was constructed, the southern and northern ends of this portal were walled.[96]

The two portal vaults of the Pigeons complex are important elements in a sequential and hierarchical system of architectural space.[97] Like the freestanding gateways of Uxmal and Kabah, they functioned as thresholds, both separating and linking two different spatial realms. Unlike the gateways, in which the separation is symbolic, however, the portals of the Pigeons Group formed passageways through imposing physical barriers and led to enclosed precincts. These portals are given prominence by participation in an axial architectural layout of directed movement along a pre-determined pathway, of which the portals form the clearest expression and focus.

The portal vault furnishing entrance to an enclosed courtyard finds its most lucid expression in the Nunnery Quadrangle at Uxmal (figs. 84, 99).[98] The principal access to the Nunnery is provided by a large portal vault that passes through the center of the southern palace. This portal vault dramatically ruptures the façade of the South Structure, cutting through the three-part medial molding and breaking the lowest course of the cornice.

Fig. 97. Uxmal, portal vault entrance to North Group. Pigeons Group visible in distance.

Fig. 98. Uxmal, Pigeons Group (after Proskouriakoff 1963a :31).

The importance of this portal vault is emphasized by a formal approach, defined by the Ball Court and a sequence of stairways. The Ball Court stands some 20 meters from the edge of a low esplanade south of the Nunnery. The longitudinal axis of the Ball Court has a deviation of 4–5° east of north, the same orientation as that of the transverse axis of the South Structure of the Nunnery (figs. 6, 99). Alberto Ruz Lhuillier noted that a line drawn perpendicular to the longitudinal axis of the South Structure from the center of the portal vault passes near the center of the Ball Court.[99] Horst Hartung also observed the intimate connection between the Ball Court and the portal vault, but noted that the central axis of the vaulted passageway, rather than passing along the center of the Ball Court playing field, actually passes 1.6 meters east of the midline. Since the portal vault is 3.25 meters wide, the midline of the Ball Court actually aligns with the west side of the portal.[100] These correspondences of orientation suggest that the portal vault and the Ball Court are contemporaneous, and that they were planned to accommodate processions moving along the alley of the court and through the portal vault into the Nunnery.

The long platforms bordering the playing field of the Ball Court create a strong perspective effect that focuses attention on the vaulted entrance (fig. 99). This channelling of space in depth is countered by the broad barrier formed by the South Structure of the Nunnery, whose doorways lead into small, shadowy rooms. Contrasting with the South Struc-

Fig. 99. Uxmal, view of portal vault of South Structure of Nunnery from centerline of Ball Court.

ture's mass and the darkened doors is the open central portal revealing the brightly illuminated quadrangle. From the Ball Court the portal vault perfectly frames a doorway of the North Structure of the Nunnery. Two crenellated mask towers of the North Structure project above and frame the portal.[101]

Through the central doorways of the north and south sides of the House of the Turtles, the portal vault of the South Structure of the Nunnery appears centered beneath the central doorway of the North Structure and points to it like a great arrow. Both from within and without the Nunnery the portal gains prominence from the "variable spacing of the doorways in both façades."[102] The intervals between the South Structure's doorways widen progressively toward the central portal vault, whose stature is enhanced by contrast with the two flanking doorways standing near the vault like humble attendants.

Passing from within the Nunnery Quadrangle into the city-space of Uxmal the portal vault again frames an impressive architectural composition (fig. 84). The Ball Court platforms again form a perspective vista leading toward the great platform of the House of the Governor, with the House of the

Turtles appearing just to the right of the central axis, and the House of the Governor itself seen in three-quarters view against the sky.[103]

Considered solely within the context of the Nunnery Quadrangle, the portal vault of the South Structure closely resembles those of the North Group and Pigeons complex, where vaults pass through extended palaces and conduct to enclosed courtyards. Judged within the framework of alignments that govern its position at Uxmal, however, the portal vault of the Nunnery gains new stature and becomes recognizable as a preeminent example of a Maya portal vault employed as a pivotal element in a unified site-planning scheme.

Other examples of portal vaults passing through palaces occur at Santa Rosa Xtampak, Dzehkabtun, and Oxkintok. Such portal vaults also formerly existed at Tihoo (Mérida). At Santa Rosa Xtampak a portal vault through the western palace formed the main entry to the Southeast Quadrangle (fig. 82).[104] The main palace at Dzehkabtun is composed of long palace buildings enclosing a large quadrangular courtyard whose principal entrance is provided by a portal vault passing through the north range.[105] The portal vault at Oxkintok passes through the center of a range-type palace, Structure 2B8, and links a western courtyard with an eastern quadrangle. The Oxkintok portal obviously played an important role in the affairs of the site, for it binds together a large, centrally located architectural complex.[106] The portal vaults at Tihoo were incorporated in a Puuc-style quadrangle that resembled the Nunnery Quadrangle at Uxmal.[107] The western range apparently had two transverse vaults that led through a building to an adjacent courtyard. Aside from the House of the Governor, this is the only building known to have had two portal vaults.

The new formal and symbolic usages of the vault were centered at or clustered around Uxmal, where they received their greatest systematic development. These varied manifestations define the precedents of the transverse vaults of the House of the Governor, and indicate an architectural tradition supportive of experimentation and supplying a large repertory of forms from which to draw inspiration.

The two transverse vaults of the House of the Governor are the masterpieces of the Maya portal vault, no longer used principally as gateways or passages, but functioning as key elements in the composition of an individual edifice (figs. 2, 75–78). These huge vaults originally passed entirely through the building,[108] and the floor of the vaulted passages was coterminous with that of the third platform. As originally planned, the transverse vaults of the House of the Governor are among the highest and boldest ever built by the Maya.[109] At a later date, however, the open vaults were filled to the floor level of the fourth platform, the passageways were walled to form small rooms, and colonnaded porticoes with upper sections in the form of huge feather-roofed huts were constructed in front of the vaults (fig. 79).[110]

Several factors indicate that these vaults were planned as an integral part of the building. Among these is the fact that the cornice molding of the third platform and the basal moldings of the three buildings of the House of the Governor do not continue along the sides of the passageways (fig. 63). If the three structures were originally isolated, without the connecting vaults, these moldings would have continued around all sides of the buildings. The transverse vaults also appear contemporaneous because they are firmly included in the formal composition of the House of the Governor. This integration was accomplished by the prolonging of the three-part molding across the face of the vaults and by continuing the guilloche cornice molding above. Tight bonds between the vaults and the three build-

ings also appear in the frieze, whose geometric ornament has been skillfully adapted to reflect the vault's outlines. At the gateway of Labna the sculptured panels of the frieze cease abruptly before reaching the vault (fig. 95). Similarly, at the South Structure of the Nunnery the flanking lattice panels terminate some distance from the vault (fig. 99). At the House of the Governor, however, the geometric step-fret and lattice designs and mask panels of the frieze were carried to the edge of the vaults in stepped panels which conform to the contours of the vaults.[111]

Though the transverse vaults of the House of the Governor were designed as an integral part of the edifice, the architects preserved a vestige of the vaults' earlier history. This was accomplished by recessing the vaults to stress their separateness, and by placing at the vault spring level a simple string-course molding that recalls the moldings on the monumental, freestanding gateways of Kabah and Uxmal (figs. 93–94). This string-course may have been employed intentionally as an evocation of architectural forbears and to symbolize the transverse vaults as two great gateways set between the three buildings of the House of the Governor.[112]

Despite the fact that they preserve elements of the freestanding gateway, as well as the portal vault that passes through a palace building, the transverse vaults of the House of the Governor are in one sense unique. Unlike all preceding portal vaults, the transverse vaults do not function chiefly as gateways or passages. Although they originally penetrated the building, the vaults led merely to a narrow walkway at the rear of the structure rather than conducting to a spacious courtyard or enclosed precinct. The compositional role fulfilled by the transverse vaults has been described by Kubler:

> The architect of the Governor's House . . . recessed the corbel-vaulted arch behind the façade, and exaggerated the vault overhangs, carrying them down in convexedly curved soffits like curtains down nearly to ground level, in order to accentuate the separation of the three pavilions by shadows and striking contours.[113]

The transverse vaults of the House of the Governor thus led nowhere because providing passage was not the prime architectural consideration. The architect's first requirement in the placement of the vaults rather was that they should contribute to the plan and massing of the building, where their bold outlines interrupt and enliven the freestanding block form and stress the three-part division of the façade.

CHAPTER 9

Visual and Proportional Effects

In this chapter we use the term "visual effects" to refer to those formal features contributing to the vivid aesthetic impression that the edifice evokes in the viewer. Such formal traits complement the building's basic three-part massing, insuring that the House of the Governor remains visually engaging not only at a distance, but also with close observation. Such features include the elaborate mosaic façade of the building, the outward lean or "negative batter," the sharply cut moldings, and the distinctive, recessed panels that frame the doorways. Proportional effects may be considered as a specialized category of visual effects, since they create subtle architectural rhythms in the House of the Governor, and contribute to its impression of symmetry and harmony.

Mosaic Façades

The upper façades of the House of the Governor support one of the most extraordinary examples of Maya architectural sculpture extant (figs. 2, 54, 58). More than fifteen thousand separate pieces of carved stone ornamented the frieze, covering it with successive and interpenetrating layers of complex geometric and figural sculptures. John Lloyd Stephens appropriately described such façades as "a species of sculptured mosaic," in which many separately carved stones are combined to form larger patterns and motifs.[1] Such sculptured mosaic façades are typical of Puuc architecture. Their pattern of use at the House of the Governor resembles that of many Puuc buildings, where the lower part of the façade is plain, and where the decorative elements are confined to the basal molding and to the

area between the cornice and three-part *atadura* medial molding.[2]

The basic elements of the architectural sculpture at the House of the Governor are colonnettes, serpent heads, guilloche, latticework, step-fret designs, mask panels, and human figures. The colonnettes appear in the basal molding while the guilloche, which resembles the caduceus, is used as the central member of the cornice (figs. 58, 173). Serpent heads project from some of the corners of the medial and cornice moldings and presumably originally were so placed at every corner (Figs. 100a–b).

As is common in Puuc architecture, the design elements were placed in planes so that some project from the walls more than others.[3] Ordinary lattice appears as the background (figs. 106–107, 112), while the step-frets form an intermediate plane (figs. 106–107, 173). Although the mask panels occupy the same plane as the step-frets, they may be considered as a third plane because they have the appearance of overlying the step-frets on the east façade and because they have long projecting snouts (figs. 152, 173). The outer plane is established by the human figures, which are carved in full round (figs. 106–129). As Kubler has noted, the multiplanar façade is superbly adapted to the strong sunlight of Yucatan, with the crisply cut mosaic elements forming "brilliant contrasts of light and shade."[4]

Such chiaroscuro effects were undoubtedly a consideration of Puuc architects. However, it is probable that their effect would have been weakened somewhat by the lavish use of color. Like Greek temples, parts of Puuc buildings frequently were painted.[5] Spinden suggests that color was used to make specific motifs and patterns clearer,[6]

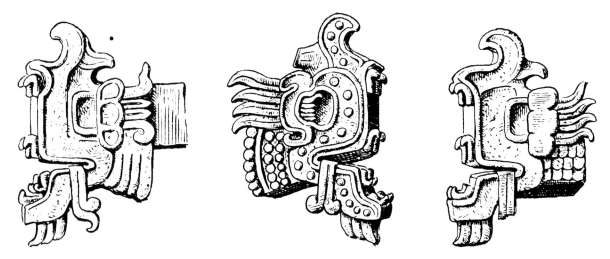

Fig. 100. House of the Governor: (left) serpent head at corner of medial molding; (above) serpent heads from corners of building (after Seler 1917: abb. 108–110).

and painting was used to endow motifs with a greater vitality. Patches of thin, smooth stucco still adhere to the House of the Governor, and although they are now devoid of color, it is possible that parts of the building were painted originally.[7]

The architectural sculpture of the House of the Governor differs in style and technique from that which preceded it in northern Yucatan and the southern Maya area. Naturalistic sculptures primarily executed in modeled stucco characterized previous architectural decoration (fig. 148), while the mosaic sculptures of the Puuc buildings are composed largely of pre-carved geometric elements (fig. 54). The sculptures of the southern cities are more independent of their architectural framework, whereas the sharpness of line of the Puuc mosaics permits a more complete interaction of structure and ornament and is better adapted to an architectural aesthetic.[8]

This difference in style and technique, however, need not mean that there was a complete rupture between the two traditions, although it sometimes has been so interpreted. Rosemary Sharp, for example, believes that the Puuc style, with its geometric rather than naturalistic emphasis, represents a fundamental change from the Classic Maya traditions.[9] Because of these differences Sharp has suggested that the basic culture and ethnic affiliation of the Puuc builders differed from that of the southern Maya, and that the Puuc people were in fact "Mexican" rather than Maya.[10]

A less radical view is taken by Kubler, who notes that Puuc decoration represents a "major morphological change in Maya sculpture," but concedes that the transition may have been gradual and the reasons poorly understood.[11] On the one hand he proposes that a cultural crisis or an ethnogeographic shift may account for the change in form, but he also suggests the possibility of autonomous stylistic renewal as an explanation.[12]

Marta Foncerrada de Molina interprets the geometric clarity of Puuc architecture and architectural sculpture as expressing a "will to form" that differs from that of the southern Maya partly due to differing environments. She relates Puuc sculpture more closely to that of the Classic Maya tradition, but sees the Puuc emphasis on certain motifs as dependent on local conditions. For example, the mask panel may have been stressed because of the lower rainfall in the north.[13]

For many years similarities have been pointed out between Puuc-style buildings, such as the House of the Governor, and the palaces at Mitla, Oaxaca (figs. 2, 88). The general resemblance of stone mosaic decoration was noticed early by W. H. Holmes and Marshall Saville.[14] More recently Kubler compared the northern Yucatecan use of mosaic decoration in the upper façades to the uses at Mitla.[15] Lee Parsons believed it was possible that architectural elements found in Mitla, such as stone mosaics and monolithic columns, diffused westward from the Puuc region during the early Post-Classic.[16]

Rosemary Sharp has made some of the most extensive studies of geometric sculpture used as architectural decoration. She reserves the term *greca* for such sculpture, and notes the architecture of the Valley of Oaxaca and northern Yucatan is characterized by unitary (i.e., composed of separate units), greca-decorated façades which contrast with the dominant unified and naturalistic forms of southern, lowland Maya architectural decoration.

Sharp further believes that these similarities in art form imply fundamental similarities in personality and society for people in northern Yucatan and Oaxaca. She proposes that the greca producers in Oaxaca were more closely related to those in Yucatan, than those of Yucatan were to the southern Maya. This leads her to conclude that "the producers of the Puuc style in Yucatan were not Maya, but were Mexican (used in its very broad sense) or Mexican-dominated."[17] Because of resemblances in construction, design and possible symbolic content between greca in Oaxaca, northern Yucatan, and El Tajin as well, Sharp believes that these three areas shared close inter-elite communications during what she terms a "greca horizon" or "international style" corresponding to the Epi-Classic period.[18]

How valid are Sharp's claims? Like others, she draws attention to the general similarities between the greca-decorated Nunnery Quadrangle at Uxmal and the Mitla palaces (figs. 85–88).[19] We have shown that the resemblances in quadrangular plan are broad and non-specific, but what about the greca designs and construction techniques? If the greca horizon is a reality we might expect them to match closely.

According to Oliver the buildings of the Hall of the Columns group at Mitla and the Palace at Yagul have a similar construction in which walls are composed of irregular rocks in a mud nucleus.[20] Cut stones were placed at some corners and base boards, and the entire wall was covered with a layer of smooth plaster over both mud and stone. Panels of stone mosaic are found both at Mitla and Yagul. Greca designs at Mitla are found both on the inside and outside walls of buildings,[21] whereas interior use is rare in the northern Maya area. Greca designs in Oaxaca are made of single, cut stones, flattened and triangular. Average dimensions are 6 inches long, 1¼-4 inches wide and 1¼ inch thick. The smallest elements (lattice Xs) at the House of the Governor, on the other hand, are about 8½ inches square by 9 inches deep and many other elements are much larger.[22]

At Mitla and Yagul the greca designs begin near the base of the buildings and cover most of the façade.[23] The Puuc designs, however, often decorated only the upper façade, leaving the high lower walls plain. This practice more closely resembles that seen in southern Maya architecture, where plain lower walls support richly sculptured friezes (fig. 135). The range of design elements used in the Puuc region is much greater than in Oaxaca. At Mitla and Yagul fairly simple elements were combined to form fields of fretwork or step-frets.[24] This contrasts with Uxmal, where Foncerrada lists the following important elements in the stone mosaic sculpture: masks, step-frets, lattices, columns, huts, serpents, owls, feathers, jaguars, and human figures.[25] At the House of the Governor we may add pieces with woven mat designs and guilloche elements.

Occasional similarities of form are found. For example, both the Yagul and Puuc sculptors used stones with an X carved on the face.[26] However, these stones were used for different purposes. In northern Yucatan they are always intended to form a unified lattice field in imitation of a woven material (see chapter 13), whereas in Oaxaca they stand alone and are read as a cross.[27]

Many of the motifs in Puuc architectural sculpture have antecedents in earlier Maya art rather than in Oaxaca. Mask panels are limited almost exclusively to the Maya area, and their evolution through space and time shows a gradual progression toward cut-stone mosaic forms (see chapter 11). The use of human figures as façade sculptures likewise has clear forerunners in the southern Maya area, whereas it is virtually nonexistent in Oaxaca.[28] Latticework also appears to derive from earlier examples in the Rio Bec and Chenes regions, where it is suggestive of a woven material (see chapter 13).

The most important mosaic element shared by the Puuc region and Oaxaca is the step-fret design, for which Sharp has demonstrated several important parallel uses.[29] This is a symbol of great antiquity in Mesoamerica, however, and it is difficult to prove it was popularized in northern Yucatan as the result of direct and frequent contact with Oaxaca (see chapter 12). Moreover, the step-frets on the House of the Governor have a two-planar form which has prototypes in the Rio Bec region rather than in Oaxaca.

At the time Sharp formulated her "greca horizon" theory, available archaeological evidence could still be interpreted to indicate that the geometric Puuc style did not develop out of the naturalistic Classic Maya style, because the chronological position of Rio Bec and Chenes architecture was imperfectly defined.[30] Sharp thus argued that the rectilinear Puuc style began suddenly in the north and later reached these intermediate areas in developed form. More recently, however, Potter has placed the Rio Bec and Chenes styles under the larger heading of Central Yucatan–style architecture, which the dates roughly from 9.6.0.0.0 (ca. A.D. 550) to 10.0.0.0.0 (ca. A.D. 830). Although the end of this style overlaps with the beginnings of Puuc, Potter feels that "the Puuc architectural style was largely subsequent to the Central Yucatan Style, and was for the most part a stylistic development from it."[31] Potter feels that the finely cut Puuc mosaic sculpture developed from the similar semi-mosaic sculpture found on Rio Bec and Chenes buildings (figs. 90, 92, 136, 182). He further points out that all of the mosaic designs of Puuc sculpture, such as long-snouted masks, applied columns, lattices, step-frets and T-forms or stepped designs, are also characteristic of the earlier Central Yucatan Style.[32] Thus, although some mosaic elements such as step-fret designs are shared by Puuc architecture and other

centers such as Mitla and El Tajin, and therefore suggest some contact, the bulk of these elements can be traced to earlier Maya Rio Bec and Chenes sources and probably represent a basically northern Maya elaboration of this tradition.

Negative Batter

A remarkable feature of the House of the Governor is the presence of a negative batter, a slight but perceptible outward lean in the façade (figs. 64, 101a–d). The negative batter at Uxmal was first described by Frans Blom in 1930.[33] Plumbline measurements were made of the façades of several of the principal structures at Uxmal, including the House of the Governor. According to Blom these measurements revealed that:

all the buildings at Uxmal which are of the Nunnery Type (i.e., the Nunnery, the House of the Turtles, the House of the Governor, the two upper temples of the Pyramid of the Magician, and probably also the lower temple, and the temple in group 22, and several other structures) have a negative batter [in] both wall and frieze.[34]

Such structures were also found at Kabah, Labna, Sabacche and Sayil.

At the House of the Governor we made four separate plumbline measurements in order to reconfirm the presence of the negative batter and to check the degree of outward lean. In each case the negative batter was observed both in the upper façade and the lower wall, although not to as pronounced a degree in the latter (fig. 101a–d). The first measurement, on the north building, showed an outward lean of 1 inch in the lower wall and about 5½ inches from the medial to cornice molding (fig. 101a). The second measurement, on the central building, showed an outward lean of almost 2 inches in the lower wall and about 7 inches from the medial to cornice molding (fig. 101b). The third measurement, on the central building, showed a lean of 2 inches in the lower wall and about 8 inches from the medial to cornice molding (fig. 101c). The fourth measurement, on the south building, showed an outward lean of about 1½ inches in the lower wall and about 2 inches from the medial to cornice molding (fig. 101d).

Blom attributed the presence of the negative batter to a collaboration between sculptor and architect, supposing that the outward lean was used by Puuc builders to "insure a more effective play of sunlight and shadow on the deeply undercut carv-

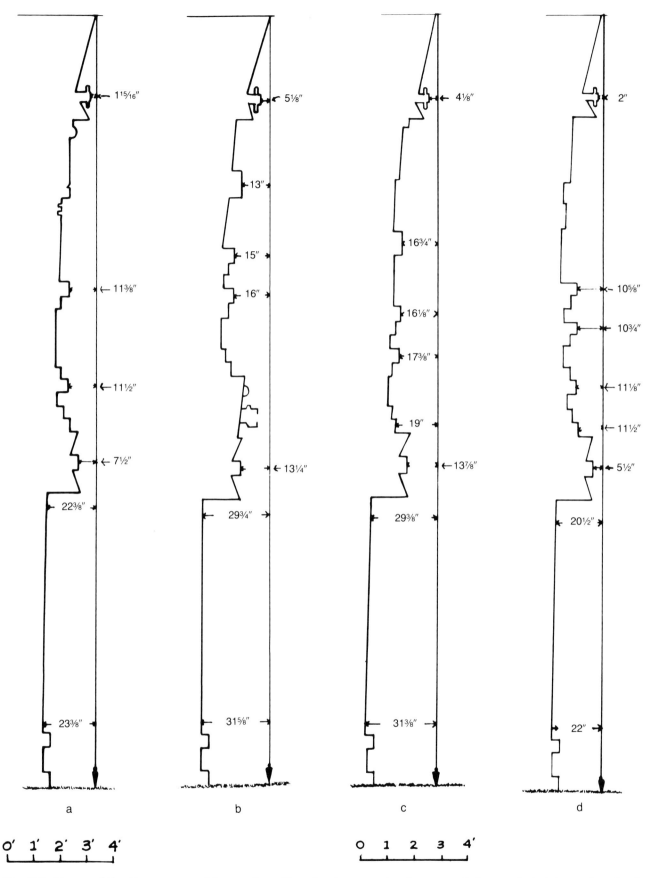

Fig. 101. House of the Governor, architectural profiles showing negative batter on (left to right): (a) east façade of north wing; (b) north end of east façade of central building; (c) south end of east façade of central building; (d) east façade of south wing.

ings."[35] Kubler, however, feels that the negative batter may be an optical refinement introduced for visual correction of the long horizontals in Puuc buildings.[36] Both of the above explanations seem plausible, but there are other possible reasons for the development of the negative batter. It is also possible that the architect incorporated a slight outward lean so that the façade would catch and reflect more of the incident light from the plastered flooring of the supporting terraces.[37]

Construction techniques used at the House of the Governor also may help account for the negative batter. As was mentioned, there is a cleavage plane between the inner vault mass and the outer facing of the frieze, which forms a wedge-shaped mass in cross-section (figs. 64, 74). It would have been simple to expand this mass outward slightly toward the top, thus creating the outward lean. Since this mass is monolithic, widening it would shift the center of gravity outward, concentrating the weight more directly on the wall rather than leaning it against the inner vault mass. This would create a more stable structure up to a point, but if the negative batter was too pronounced it would threaten the collapse of the frieze, since the outer mass is not effectively tied to the inner vault mass. Practically, the negative batter would also serve to protect the façade and the foundation of the building during the rainy season. The slight outward lean would help to keep runoff from the roof from damaging the plaster, and the overhang is great enough to keep drainage away from the foot of the building.

Kubler has pointed out a parallel usage of the negative batter at Mitla in Oaxaca (fig. 88).[38] As noted, Sharp argued that there were frequent and sustained contacts between elites of the Valley of Oaxaca and the Puuc region. If this was so, then the shared use of the negative batter presumably would again reflect this contact, but the evidence does not seem particularly convincing.

At Mitla the negative batter occurs in the two upper *tableros* of the Hall of the Columns. Horst Hartung comments on this phenomenon:

What distinguishes the upper ones is the outward slope of the rectangles at the corners of their frames. The outward slope is continued in the narrow sections of the outer and upper frames, and it is emphasized optically by displacing the vertical lines of the frame in the same direction.[39]

He assumes the slope at Mitla may have arisen to answer visual needs similar to those at Uxmal, al-

though he does not propose a direct contact between the two sites. In fact the dates of the Mitla palaces may well be too late to allow for any strong cross-fertilization with the Puuc region. A radiocarbon date from Building II of the Mitla fortress yielded a date of A.D. 1385 ± 85 years.[40] Sharp has written that Building II "is almost a duplicate in layout and dimensions of both Building 1-N at Yagul and the Hall of the Columns at Mitla."[41] The wall paintings at the Hall of the Columns also pertain to the Mixteca-Puebla codical style which dominated the region during the two or three hundred years preceding the conquest.[42]

One of the few earlier uses of the negative batter in Oaxaca occurs in the Tablero of the Cocijos at Lambityeco. Hartung noticed that the corner of the outer frame is inclined outward, and views this as a possible precedent for the negative batter of the Mitla palaces.[43] Lambityeco is an early Monte Albán IV site that has been dated between about A.D. 640 and 755,[44] and is thus a likelier candidate for connections with the northern Maya area. However, this example lacks a convincing sense of scale. At Lambityeco the negative batter is limited to the outer frame of a small altar. At Uxmal, on the other hand, it appears consistently as a design element of the finest late buildings, supporting the idea that it was developed independently by the architects of the Puuc region.

Moldings

The House of the Governor is divided into a series of vertical zones by means of sharply cut moldings. The basal molding is composed of two rectangular stringcourses which frame a recessed panel containing alternating plain zones and groups of four engaged colonnettes (figs. 58, 62). These colonnette groups mark an even rhythm across the base, and they themselves serve to express a supportive function. Above the plain lower wall projects a three-part medial molding, a form typical in Puuc architecture (figs. 58, 64). This binder molding, or atadura, consists of two outward-flaring courses separated by a stringcourse. Serpent heads were attached to the central course at the corners of the buildings, so that the molding forms a metaphorical serpent body (figs. 100a–b). Finally, the cornice molding surmounting the richly sculptured frieze is a variant of the three-part binder molding. It is composed of a flaring, lower course and a high-flaring, upper course that projects outward to form a strong overhanging cornice (figs. 64, 111–113). Between these flaring courses is a decorative member featuring a narrow stringcourse entwined by a serpent guilloche. Sculptured serpent heads again projected at the corners of the buildings, so that the undulating guilloche is intended to read as a serpent body. Although other types of decorated, binder moldings occur in the Puuc area, the cornice of the House of the Governor is unique.[45]

Virtually all Puuc buildings have base moldings of some sort.[46] The most common form is a simple course of dressed stone that projects slightly from the wall surface above. This type of molding is characteristic of Early Puuc architecture, but apparently continued to be used throughout the Puuc development.[47] Another common Puuc form is the three-member molding composed of rectangular upper and lower members separated by a row of colonnettes. Closely resembling the three-member molding with a continuous row of colonnettes is one with groups of colonnettes alternating with plain sections in the middle member. The groups may include three colonnettes,[48] four colonnettes, as at the House of the Governor, or occasionally five colonnettes, as at Sabacche Structure 5.[49] Within the Puuc region the various basal moldings with colonnettes are mostly restricted to the eastern sites, and were apparently used there somewhat later than the simple rectangular molding.[50]

The alternating colonnettes and plain-section basal molding of the House of the Governor probably has antecedents in the Chenes and Rio Bec regions to the south. In the Rio Bec area, three-member basal moldings of this type are found on the central building of Structure 1 at Culucbalom (fig. 91), as well as on Structure 1 of Group I and Structure 1 of Group III at Rio Bec.[51] The upper courtyard of Becan Structure IV has a base molding with a single group of three colonnettes framed by plain members,[52] while a variant at Xaxbil features plain panels alternating with two engaged colonnettes and panels containing step-fret and mat-weave designs (fig. 182).[53] Most of these buildings of the Rio Bec style apparently date between about A.D. 600 to 830, and thus predate the House of the Governor and the majority of Late Puuc buildings.[54]

In the Chenes area several buildings have three-part moldings like those of the House of the Governor. Moldings composed of two rectangular courses framing alternating plain panels and groups of three colonnettes appear on Structure 1 at El Tabasqueño[55] and on Structure 8 at Dzibilnocac.[56] Variants of such moldings with colonnettes are found at Santa Rosa Xtampak in the Cuartel[57] and the West

Range of the Southeastern Quadrangle.[58] At Uxmal the Chenes-style Structure 1 west of the House of the Governor has a three-member basal molding with groups of three colonnettes alternating with plain sections,[59] and the north building of Group 23 carries a similar molding.[60] The Santa Rosa Xtampak examples may date near to the site's 9.16.0.0.0 (A.D. 751) stelae.[61] Such moldings on the Chenes-style buildings undoubtedly precede those on later Puuc buildings, since Structure 1 underlies the great terrace of the House of the Governor.

Among the Puuc buildings at Uxmal examples of basal moldings with alternating panels and groups of colonnettes occur on the Lower West Structure of the Pyramid of the Magician (fig. 7),[62] and on the upper story of the Chimez.[63] The moldings of the East, West, and North Structures and Venus Temple of the Nunnery resemble that of the House of the Governor in having groups of four colonnettes (figs. 86–87).[64] Later examples of this four-colonnette molding appear on the upper building of the Pyramid of the Old Woman and on the unfinished building east-southeast of the same edifice (fig. 34).[65] The four-colonnette grouping again serves to connect the design of the Nunnery buildings closely with that of the House of the Governor.

The medial and cornice moldings of the House of the Governor are both variants of the three-part binder molding.[66] Earlier versions of the three-part molding feature three rectangular members and were popular in the western Puuc cities.[67] The most prevalent three-part molding is the atadura or binder molding, however, with a lower apron member, a middle rectangular member, and an upper reverse apron. Kubler has likened this form to "a girdle of tightly belted thatch flaring out both above and below the belt. . . ."[68] A similar idea was first expressed by E. H. Thompson, who compared the cornice binder moldings to the lines of the pachol-na, the "house-head wall" or thatch-roof binding and rain shield of the typical Maya hut or na.[69] He also suggested that the half columns of Puuc façades are derived from the wooden poles of Maya huts, the columns with atadura bands representing poles lashed together with vines. Robert Wauchope also points out resemblances between the profiles of heavily plastered hut walls of vertical poles with heavy stringers, and the profiles of several Puuc style buildings.[70]

Despite the resemblance between molding forms of Puuc architecture and the bindings found on Maya thatch huts, the former probably do not represent survivals in the strict sense of the word, since the buildings of the Early period in Yucatan lack the banded façade columns and feature only the simplest rectangular moldings. Rather, as Puuc architecture improved in quality the architects seem to have consciously adopted certain forms from the bush house because of their decorative or symbolic potential, transforming them into a cut-stone form that accords with the Puuc architectural aesthetic.[71]

Evidence that the northern Maya architects considered binder moldings to be stone versions of less durable forms of the Maya hut can be seen at several sites. At Hochob, for example, the two small huts on the façade of Structure 2 have two small ataduras resembling thatch, bound by cords flanking their simulated doorways (fig. 92).[72] Another early version of the binder molding occurs on the roof comb of the Mirador Temple at Sayil (fig. 30). The molding is composed of stone slabs supporting a thick coat of stucco, which was modeled to resemble bound thatch, or perhaps featherwork.[73] A similar molding also appears on the roof comb of Structure A at Mul-Chic.[74] The tops of several Puuc cylindrical altars also have atadura moldings which have been treated to resemble flexible natural materials.[75] Further support for the idea that the engaged colonnettes and atadura spindles of Puuc architecture were likened to wooden models is seen at Haltunchon. In the south room of the West Building of the Hilltop Group, a carved stone beam with an atadura spool was substituted for a more typical wooden vault beam.[76] Similar beams with binder moldings occur in the Five Story Palace at Tikal.[77]

Early versions of the atadura molding occur in the Rio Bec region at Channa and Culucbalom. Channa Structure 1 has column capitals of this form,[78] while at Culucbalom Structure 1 they form the capital and base of engaged colonnettes flanking the doorway (fig. 91). In the Chenes area, aside from its appearance at Hochob Structure 2 (fig. 92), the binder molding also occurs as a double-banded spool element at Nocuchich,[79] as the cornice of the Cuartel at Santa Rosa Xtampak,[80] and as a decorative element on the east doorjamb of the Three Story Palace at Santa Rosa Xtampak.[81] The Chenes style Structures 1 and 2 west of the House of the Governor also had binder cornice moldings (fig. 15).[82] These examples of the binder molding in the Chenes and Rio Bec region predate its use at the House of the Governor and the majority of Puuc buildings, although a few early versions occur on Early Puuc structures such as the Sayil Mirador or Structure A at Mul-Chic.

After apparently being adopted from the Chenes and Rio Bec areas, it was in the Puuc region, par-ticularly in the eastern Puuc, that the binder molding attained its greatest development. We have seen that it was used frequently as the spindles of engaged colonnettes and as a molding at the top of altars. In addition, it was often used as an articulation on doorway piers and columns,[83] and also as medial and cornice moldings, in which form it became a hallmark of the long horizontal buildings like the House of the Governor.

Recessed Doorways

Each of the doorways of the House of the Governor is articulated with a recessed panel that frames the door like an embrasure (figs. 2, 4, 54, 58). This optical refinement, which Pollock terms the pilaster variety doorjamb, is found only sporadically in other structures in Yucatan.[84] Optical and illumination considerations may account for its presence in part. The columned entrances of other Puuc buildings indicate a new interest in light interiors (fig. 31). By cutting back the thick supporting wall at the jambs, a greater amount of light would be admitted to the building, and those occupying it would obtain a broader field of vision through the doorway.

Such embrasures are employed primarily as an aesthetic refinement, however. Like the transverse vaults, the recessed frames of the doorways can best be attributed to a desire for architectural articulation and to provide additional stature to the doorways.

Early versions of such inset, framed doorways are found in the Chenes region, where they are associated with the dragon-mouth entrance. Examples include Structure 2 at Hochob (fig. 92), Structure 2 at Nohcacab, and Structure 1 west of the House of the Governor (fig. 15).[85] Such Chenes designs were imitated by Puuc builders in Structure 1A1 at Kabah and the Chenes Temple of the Pyramid of the Magician at Uxmal (fig. 8).[86] The interior doorway of the Lower Temple of the Pyramid of the Old Woman at Uxmal also has this treatment.[87]

Puuc architects may have found models for recessed doorways in Chenes practice, but they made them more emphatic design elements in their own right. Later and more polished versions of these framed doorways are found on the North, East, and West Structures of the Nunnery Quadrangle at Uxmal. The doors of the North Building have massive frames whose form arose from the cladding of the interior structure with a new façade (figs. 85, 141). The insets of the East and West Structures resemble those of the House of the Governor, forming graceful, shaded niches around the doorways (figs. 86–87, 140).

No later buildings in Yucatan continued the tradition of framed doorways. Although some of the pilasters of Chichen Itza bear some similarity to the inset doorways of the House of the Governor they differ in purpose.[88] The pilastered doors of the Chichen Itza buildings serve sculptural rather than architectural ends by enlarging the field available for figural relief on the jambs. In contrast, the inset doorways of the House of the Governor were calculated as a purely architectural refinement.

Proportion and Measurement

The House of the Governor conveys an impression of perfect symmetry, balance, and harmony (fig. 2). The two smaller wings flank the central structure symmetrically, with the three-part division of the building marked by majestic transverse vaults (figs. 75–78). The doorways are spaced in a rhythmic sequence, and the geometric elements of the frieze have a complex order on several planes (figs. 54, 58). Such consummately integrated architecture suggests that the architects of Uxmal had a strong interest in proportion and measurement.[89]

Doorways

This concern for symmetry and harmonious proportion appears clearly in the rhythmic placement of the doorways (figs. 2, 41). The doorways in the three buildings mark the grouping 2-7-2, while the central chambers yield another grouping of 2-2-3-2-2. The doorways are spaced in a hierarchical sequence that quickens toward the central portal. The central doorway is wider than its neighbors, its nearly square shape stressing the central axis of the building. This interest in variable width and spacing of doorways is part of a wider Maya architectural tradition, and is seen elsewhere in buildings at Palenque,[90] Becan,[91] Culucbalom (fig. 91),[92] and Uxmal,[93] particularly in the South, East, and West Structures of the Nunnery Quadrangle and in the House of the Turtles (figs. 85–87, 99, 14).[94] A progressive mastery of proportional effects is evident in the buildings of the Nunnery Quadrangle. The North Structure has a wider central doorway, but otherwise exhibits no interest in rhythmic spacing of doorways, perhaps because the architect had to conform to the plan of an earlier building (figs. 83, 85). At the South Structure the

apertures are variably spaced in both façades. The intervals between the doorways are small at the corners and widen progressively toward the central vaulted passageway, which is flanked by two doorways (figs. 83, 99). Kubler has likened this treatment to that found in Greek peripteral temples.[95] Similar refinement of doorway placement occurs tentatively in the East Structure and is well developed in the West Structure of the Nunnery (figs. 86–87). Both buildings also feature central doorways of nearly square proportions.[96]

Rope Measure

It is obvious that Maya architects were interested in and capable of incorporating sophisticated proportional effects in their buildings. The presence of such visual symmetries and ordered rhythms indicates skillful planning and implies the use of a measuring device of some sort, but the exact nature of Maya mensurational systems has been poorly understood. Pollock pointed out that no one has yet been able to demonstrate conclusively the presence of any standardized unit of measurement used throughout the Maya area. However, he notes that "It is . . . hard to think of them working without some unit of measurement, not necessarily standardized and in general use, but that leastwise would be held to during the construction of a single building."[97]

Evidence at the House of the Governor suggests that two different methods may have been used in planning the building: Long scale distances may have been determined accurately by the use of a rope, while the basic proportions of the plan may have been based on numerological considerations and determined by the use of a more or less standardized module.

First we will examine the evidence for the use of a rope measure. By measuring the lengths of wall between doorways in corresponding positions to the north and south of the central door, we found that the symmetry of the House of the Governor, although visually convincing, is somewhat inexact (table 4). Corresponding sections of wall are never exactly the same length, and vary from between 2 inches over a short distance, to as much as 7½ inches over a longer stretch. These differences are too great to have been tolerated, and could easily have been detected, had the Maya been using a solid measurement such as a "yardstick" or notched pole of some sort. On the other hand, the correspondence between sections is too close to suggest that the distances were simply paced off. It seems probable that some sort of flexible measure, such as a rope, was used.

Ropes were obviously well known to the Maya, as is attested by their ceremonial use on Lintels 17 and 24 at Yaxchilan, or by the many depictions of bound prisoners or slaves (fig. 168).[98] Green noted that the thorns attached to the rope on Lintel 24 seem to be spaced at more or less regular intervals, and proposed that a similar system could have been used for maintaining a desired length.[99] Knots also could have been tied to mark specific distance. The rope also is mentioned in the Chilam Balam of Chumayel, where it is said, "The rope shall descend, the cord shall descend from heaven. . . ."[100] An even more pertinent reference occurs in the *Popol Vuh*, where a measuring cord figures in the creation and quadripartite division of the world.[101]

Satterthwaite also believed that a rope measure was used to design the courtyards at Piedras Negras, where "Differential stretching of such cords might account for some of the discrepancies noted" among visually similar distances.[102]

At the House of the Governor we attempted to duplicate the measurements of the wall intervals of the eastern façade using a hand-held rope, and found that with only slight tightening or slackening each measurement could easily be matched. We used a heavy, one-inch hemp rope, which cannot be stretched too much. The Maya builders may have used a thinner cord with greater elasticity, which would account for discrepancies such as 7½ inches over 21 feet. Thus it seems fairly certain that many of the basic symmetries of the House of the Governor were laid out with the use of a rope measure.

Base

The House of the Governor rests upon a base formed by two plain, projecting, rectangular courses that frame a recessed band of alternating, smooth, masonry panels and groups of four engaged colonnettes (figs. 58, 62). These panels and colonnettes mark a measured rhythm around the entire edifice, broken only at each corner of the building, where the flat wall sections were shortened (fig. 59).[103]

Each of the alternating plain and colonnette sections of the base was measured to ascertain whether the Maya employed a standardized system in establishing the length of each section. At the corners of the three structures, the base invariably begins with smooth masonry panels that are shorter than the other sections. These corner sections average 2

Table 4. *Sections of Wall Between Doorways, House of the Governor*

Corresponding Wall Sections	Length
SE corner of south wing to Door 2	9'4"
NE corner of north wing to Door 12	9'1"
Door 2 to Door 3	18'9½"
Door 11 to Door 12	18'5"
NE corner of south wing to Door 3	9'6½"
SE corner of north wing to Door 11	9'3"
SE corner of central bldg. to Door 4	11'10"
NE corner of central bldg. to Door 10	11'6"
Door 4 to Door 5	21'7"
Door 9 to Door 10	21'2"
Door 5 to Door 6	19'1½"
Door 8 to Door 9	19'9"
Door 6 to Door 7	11'10"
Door 7 to Door 8	11'8"

feet 7 inches in length, varying no more than half an inch from the average. The blocks composing the corners vary in length, so that the uniform length of the sections cannot be attributed to the use of a certain number of identical blocks for each section.

The remainder of the alternating panels of smooth masonry and engaged colonnettes average about 3 feet 7½ inches long. The variation between the length of the sections is some 7⅞ inches, with the shortest section measuring 3 feet 3⅛ inches and the longest 3 feet 11 inches.[104] The similar length of the groups of colonnettes is easy to account for, since the colonnettes are all of approximately equal diameters of 8¼ inches. It would not be difficult to space them and set them by eye with reasonable accuracy. The sections of flat wall present greater problems in this respect. Once again, the stones of these panels vary in length, precluding the possibility of determining the length by counting a certain number of stones. The plain panels have a variation in length of some 5⅞ inches. Such a discrepancy seems to preclude the use of a solid measure, yet the regularity of the sections suggests that they were measured in some fashion. A stretchable measure such as a cord would better account for the discrepancies. Even so, a difference of almost six inches over three and a half feet seems excessive, even if some stretching is allowed. It therefore seems probable that a cord was used to mark off the basic divisions of the base, but that during the actual construction, the lengths were altered slightly because of the variable dimensions of the facing stones and engaged colonnettes. Thus, although some type of measurement was involved in the construction of the base, it seems that the architect was more interested in obtaining the effect of a regular rhythmic alternation of forms than in the intellectual knowledge that each panel exactly matched its neighbor.

Modular Planning and Numerological Considerations

Although the architect of the House of the Governor may not have been concerned with obtaining an exact correspondence among the sections of the base, there is evidence that he did take into consideration the number of sections composing each side of the three buildings, and that these numbers were chosen for symbolic purposes.

At the northern and southern ends of the House of the Governor the base consists of nine alternating panels of plain masonry and colonnettes, if the two shorter end sections are exempted (figs. 4, 57, 59).[105] The number nine had exceptional ritualistic importance for the ancient Maya. They conceived of the underworld as composed of nine layers or tiers, and ruled over by nine lords, the Bolon-ti-ku, who are probably referred to in glyphic texts as the nine "lords of the night."[106] The number nine commonly appears in Maya medicine and magic, and ritual caches often contain nine offerings.[107] Furthermore, several Maya deities have the number nine in their names, the most important of these being Bolon Dz'acab, identified as God K or the Manikin Scepter (figs. 160, 166).[108] Nine also appears to have had a sacred function in the architecture of Tikal, where the Twin-Pyramid Complexes have a southern building with nine doorways.[109]

The base of the longer sides of the two wings of the House of the Governor contains thirteen alternating panels of smooth masonry and colonnettes, again exempting the shorter end sections (fig. 2). Thirteen is another number of utmost ritualistic significance for the Maya, for they conceived of the heavens as divided into thirteen layers, in each of which separate gods resided. These gods were known collectively as the Oxlahun-ti-ku and they apparently ruled in succession over a period of thirteen days.[110] Like the number nine, the number thirteen appears frequently in ritualistic contexts. For example, at the beginning of the new year in the Tzeltal town of Oxchuc a venerated book is transferred from one clan to another in a ceremony lasting thirteen days, and in which the book is put

on a table accompanied by thirteen candles, thirteen rosaries, thirteen calabashes of lime mixed with tobacco, and thirteen vessels of atole.[111]

It is clear, then, that the Maya held the numbers nine and thirteen in particular veneration, and it is logical that the two numbers should be coupled frequently, as they are in many ceremonial contexts and ritualistic texts. It seems likely that their use, in the base of the wings of the House of the Governor, for example, was not haphazard, but was calculated and based on numerological considerations.

Numerology also may have played a role in fixing the length of the central building. Between the short sections of flat masonry at each end of the base there are forty-nine alternating panels of smooth masonry and colonnettes (figs. 2–3). The square root of forty-nine is seven, another number which was held sacred for various reasons. In this connection Thompson has pointed out that the 819-day cycle, which played an important augural and ritualistic role in the inscriptions, is composed of $7 \times 9 \times 13$.[112] He believed that there may have been a concept of a seven-layered earth presided over by seven terrestrial deities corresponding to the Bolon-ti-ku of the underworld and the Oxlahun-ti-ku of the skies.[113] In the creation account of the Chilam Balam of Chumayel, a god named Ah Uuc Cheknal, "he who fertilizes the maize seven times," is mentioned as coming from the seventh stratum of the earth.[114] A deity named Ah Uuc-ti-cab, "Lord Seven Earth," is also mentioned in the Ritual of the Bacabs.[115]

Pertinent to this discussion are several instances in Classic Maya art where the number seven, affixed to a specific glyph and associated with a long-snouted deity head, occurs in combination with the number nine, affixed to another glyph and associated with a deity.[116] Thompson identified the seven head with Ah Uuc-ti-cab (Lord Seven Earth), or possibly with Ah Uuc Cheknal.[117] Kubler is unwilling to accept Thompson's attributions of colonial period deity names to Classic glyphs, but nevertheless interpreted the seven head as a glyph of diurnal aspect, and contrasted it with the nocturnal nine head.[118] The *kan* cross (T281) that commonly appears in the headdress of the seven head also appears in the grotesque head from which a maize plant grows on the Tablet of the Foliated Cross at Palenque (fig. 102). The *kan* cross at Palenque is certainly associated with the earth, since it is the medium from which a maize plant arises.[119] A similar connection with the earth is suggested by the leafy sprigs (maize?) that are often attached to the

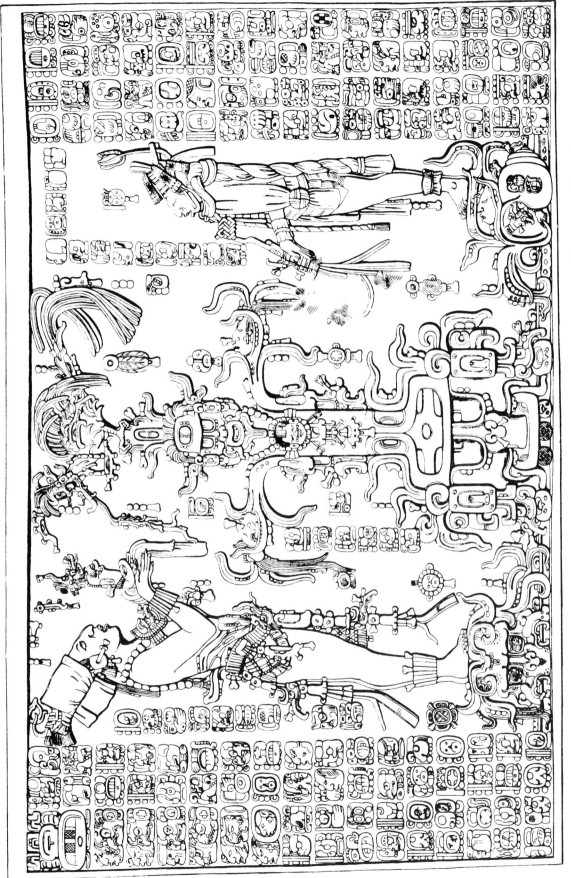

Fig. 102. Palenque, Tablet of the Temple of the Foliated Cross (after Maudslay 1889–1902, 4: Plate 76).

seven head, particularly as it appears on Yaxha Stela 2.[120]

The uses of the number seven described above indicate, then, that it was associated with the seven layers of the earth and with a grotesque head glyphic form with terrestrial associations. Its intimate connection with the numbers 9 and 13 is evident in the 819-day cycle formed of the multiples 13, 9, and 7. This strongly suggests that the forty-nine panels of the central building of the House of the Governor have numerological significance connected with their factor, the number seven.

Such numerological significance may not be limited solely to the base of the House of the Governor. Rosemary Sharp has pointed out that the building has thirteen doors leading to twenty vaulted chambers (fig. 41). It is well known that a cycle of thirteen numbers and twenty named days formed the pan-Mesoamerican sacred almanac, the Tonalpohualli or Tzolkin. Sharp has also pointed out that there are thirteen step-frets on each side of the central motif of the House of the Governor (fig. 54).[121]

Numerological considerations involving cosmological or calendrical coding similar to that proposed for the House of the Governor are known also in central Mexico, Veracruz, and elsewhere in northern Yucatan. The number of stone sculptures on the Temple of Quetzalcoatl at Teotihuacan, niches on the Pyramid of the Niches at El Tajin (fig. 180), and of steps on the Castillo at Chichen Itza all have been calculated as 365 or 366, the number of days in the solar year.[122] The Venus Platform at Chichen Itza has four staircases of thirteen steps each, or a total of 52 steps.[123] The Castillo has nine terraces decorated with 52 panels, the number of years in the native Mesoamerican Calendar Round cycle.[124] The incorporation of such calendrical data in other Mesoamerican buildings has long been recognized, and supports the idea that such numerological symbolism was purposeful in the House of the Governor.[125]

Aside from these recognized uses of sacred numbers in other Mesoamerican buildings, there is also an indication in the Chilam Balam of Chumayel that the Maya were accustomed to incorporating cosmologically significant proportions into their buildings. In Chapter XVI it is written that:

13 Cheneb (Chen or Eb?) was when they measured off the paces of the cathedral, the dark house of instruction, the cathedral in heaven. Thus it was also measured off by paces here (on earth). Thirteen Katuns was the total count, (that is thir)teen feet in heaven. Four feet, and

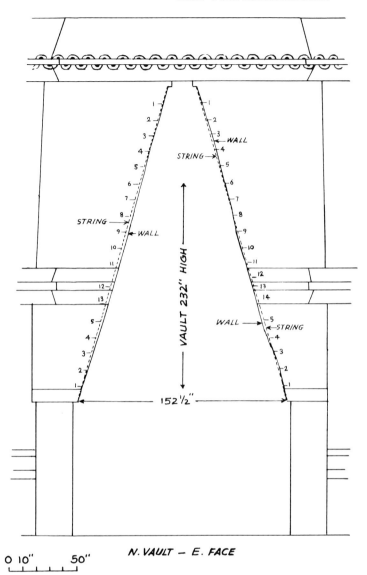

Fig. 103. House of the Governor, east face of north transverse vault.

from there nine feet, the total count of its extent in heaven. Then it is measured off by feet from the face of the earth.[126]

Roys has suggested that the central idea of this passage is that "any sacred thing on earth must previously exist in heaven."[127] If this is true, then to understand the significance of the 7, 9, and 13 proportions embodied in the plan of the House of the Governor, one must interpret them as references to the basic vertical structure of the Maya universe. Just as the neo-platonic, inspired architects of the Italian Renaissance used proportion to suggest the order and perfection of God,[128] so the architect of

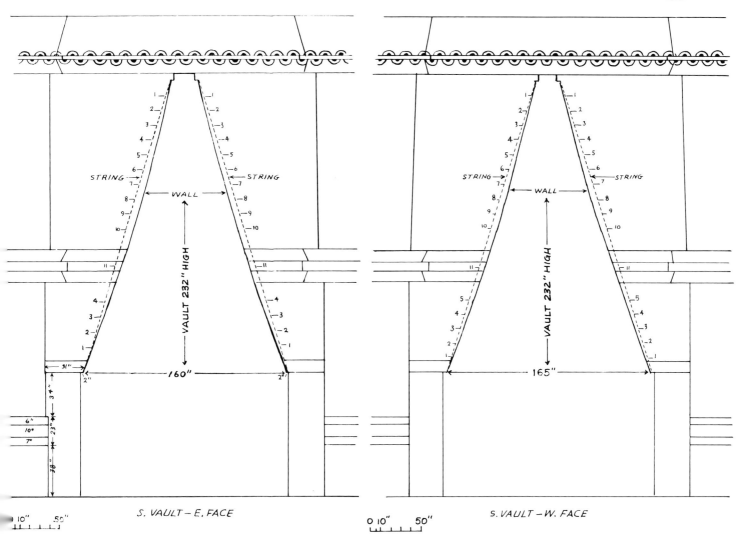

Fig. 104. House of the Governor, east face of south transverse vault.

Fig. 105. House of the Governor, west face of south transverse vault.

the House of the Governor incorporated sacred, numerological proportions to insure that the building would participate in a higher order of existence. The ruler of Uxmal, whose portrait appeared above the central doorway, thus governed from an edifice whose very structure symbolized and confirmed his central authority in the cosmos.

Curvature of the Transverse Vaults

An exceptional feature of the transverse vaults of the House of the Governor is the gentle, convex curvature of some of the vault soffits (figs. 75–78).

Kubler likens this delicate convexity to the slight sway of a hung curtain. Such catenary curves give these vaults a buoyancy and grace that is lacking in all other portal vaults. Such refinements recall the entasis employed in Greek peripteral temples, where varying curvatures were used for optical corrections and to impart qualities of resiliency and suppleness to the structure. Measurements taken at the House of the Governor, however, indicate that the curving soffits of the transverse vaults are not regular, and may well be accidental rather than the result of deliberate design (table 5, figs. 103–105).[129] The south vault does have fairly regular cat-

Table 5. *Measurements of Curvature in Transverse Vaults, House of the Governor, showing deviations from Chord.*

S.V./wf/rs (Fig. 144)	S.V./ef/ls (Fig. 145)	S.V./ef/rs	N.V./ef/ls (Fig. 146)	N.V./ef/rs
MEASURED DOWN FROM TOP				
1. 1-1/2″	1. 1-1/4″	1. 3/4″	1. −1/8″	1. 0″
2. 2-1/2″	2. 2-3/8″	2. 1″	2. 0″	2. −5/8″
3. 3-1/4″	3. 3-1/8″	3. 1-9/16″	3. 0″	3. −3/4″
4. 4-3/16″	4. 3-15/16″	4. 2″	4. 0″	4. −11/16″
5. 4-7/8″	5. 4-1/2″	5. 2-3/8″	5. 1/4″	5. −1/4″
6. 4-3/4″	6. 4-7/8″	6. 2-7/8″	6. 1/4″	6. 0″
7. 4-1/2″	7. 5-3/16″	7. 3-1/4″	7. 1/2″	7. 1/4″
8. 4-1/2″	8. 5-1/4″	8. 3-9/16″	8. 1/16″	8. 0″
9. 4-1/4″	9. 5-3/16″	9. 3-15/16″	9. 1″	9. 0″
10. 3-3/4″	10. 4-1/2″	10. 4-1/4″	10. 1-5/16″	10. 0″
11. 3″	11. 5-1/8″	11. 4-1/8″	11. 1-1/2″	11. 0″
			12. 1-3/4″	12. 1/8″
			13. 2-1/2″	13. 3/8″
				14. 1″
MEASURED UP FROM BOTTOM				
5. 2″			5. 1-7/8″	5. 1/2″
4. 1-7/8″	4. 3-3/4″	4. 2-13/16″	4. 1-3/8″	4. 11/16″
3. 1-3/8″	3. 2-5/8″	3. 2-1/8″	3. 7/8″	3. −3/16″
2. 1″	2. 1-1/2″	2. 1-1/4″	2. 0″	2. −3/16″
1. 3/4″	1. 3/4″	1. 5/8″	1. −1/4″	1. −1/8″

KEY: S.V.: south vault, wf: west face, rs: right side.
N.V.: north vault, ef: east face, ls: left side.

enary curves in both soffits. The curvature of the south soffit is more pronounced, however, projecting beyond the chord 5³⁄₁₆ inches at the widest point, while the north soffit projects only 4¼ inches. The north vault is completely different, showing either a very slight curvature or none at all. The south soffit has a slight convexity, but nowhere projects more than 2¼ inches beyond the chord. The north soffit is straight for practical purposes, nowhere varying more than an inch beyond the chord.

The fact that the north soffit of the north vault is virtually straight strongly suggests that the curvature in the other vaults was not planned by the architects. The interior rooms of the House of the Governor have high vaults with exceptionally straight soffits (figs. 64, 66), and this was probably the intention in the transverse vaults as well. The curvature may be the result of the building technique. It is possible that during the construction the soffit was determined by stretching a rope from the spring of the vault to the height of a capstone. The rope could have been secured by tying it to a pole laid across the top of the passageway between the two buildings. As mentioned, rope was used by the Maya as a measuring tool and this further use seems reasonable. If the rope were drawn tautly it would produce a straight edge, while a slight amount of stretching would produce the gentle curves of the vault.[130] Since the transverse vaults lack vault beams, it also seems likely that some subsidence of the vault mass contributed to the uneven curvature of the vaults.[131] This would account for the later blocking of the vaults and the construction of the small rooms and porticoes. It is difficult to explain such additions unless there was a perceived threat to the stability of the original open vaults, the aesthetic power of which was compromised by later renovations.

PART THREE

Architectural Sculpture

CHAPTER 10

Human Figural Sculpture

ACROSS the east façade of the House of the Governor is a series of sculptured, full-round, human figures sitting on thrones or cushions and wearing splendid feather headdresses (Figs. 2, 106–109, 111–129).[1] These figures are distributed rhythmically and symmetrically across the frieze and are well-integrated with the overall arrangement of mask panels and geometric ornament, indicating that they represent a part of the original sculptural program of the House of the Governor. This is particularly clear at the centers of the main building and north and south wings, where the principal figures serve as the foundations for the geometric arrangements of frets and masks emanating from them (figs. 54, 106–108, 111, 113).

Unfortunately, many of the human figures formerly attached to the façade no longer appear, perhaps having fallen before the explorations of Stephens and Catherwood. Possibly they were removed from the debris of the House of the Governor, either by Spanish prelates seeking to stamp out any vestige of idolatry, or by later local inhabitants near Uxmal who used the ready-cut stones of ancient edifices for modern buildings. Nevertheless, enough sculptures remain to form a sound idea of how the figures were placed, what constituted their

basic elements of costume, to what stylistic tradition they pertain, and the nature of their iconographic significance.

South Wing Figures

At the center of the east frieze of the South Wing was a human figure who sat on a cushion-type throne supported by the upturned mouth of a stylized serpent head (fig. 108). Today only the left half of the figure's headdress and the serpent-head podium remain. The headdress consists of a tall framework from which issues a row of horizontal plumes. This plumage forms overlapping planes near the outer edge, with the tips of the feathers curving outward slightly. Set outward from this wide featherwork is a cascade of overlapping, bell-shaped plumage with feathers tipped with small disks.

The serpent head podium upon which the figure rested has its jaws open at a 180° angle. Sharp, crescentic fangs line the upper edge of the jaws, which are treated as long, narrow bands, bordered with raised edges and decorated with a row of raised dots. The creature faces north, so that below the

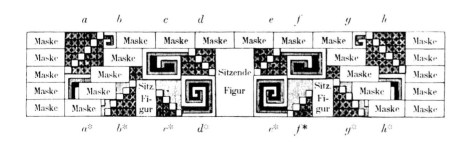

Fig. 106. Diagram of east façade of south wing of House of the Governor (after Seler 1917:abb. 113).

149

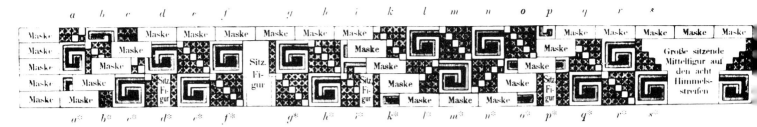

Fig. 107. Diagram of east façade of central building, House of the Governor (after Seler 1917: abb. 114).

jaws on the right is a nose scroll, from which emanates a feathered scroll. From the left jaw hang two other scroll ornaments. The eye is treated as a sunken rectangle with an inscribed pupil, and below the eye is a superorbital plate with scrolls at either end.

Flanking the central figure of the frieze of the south wing were two smaller figures, neither as large nor as sumptuous as the central personage. Nothing whatever remains of the figure north of

center. The headdress of the southern figure is intact and a small piece of the serpent podium remains (fig. 109). The headdress is less imposing than that of the central figure. It rises only to slightly over half the height of the row of mask panels beneath the cornice, and is much narrower. The headdress is composed of two stone sections tenoned into the concrete hearting of the façade. The lower section is an H-shaped block carved with featherwork. In the upper bracket of the H is a

Fig. 108. House of the Governor, south wing, central human figure.

Fig. 109. House of the Governor, south wing, figure above door 2.

Fig. 110. House of the Governor, lower half of human figure from façade.

stone piece consisting of a long-snouted reptilian head with scroll eyebrows. Surmounting this head is a feather panache, ornamented with disks and flowing symmetrically from a human skull centerpiece. Above the skull is the broken tenon of another headdress element which, to judge from the corresponding figure of the north wing, was an outward-curved bunch of plumes. The open-jawed serpent podium placed beneath the figure originally was located so the serpent head faced away from center, according to the position of similar elements on other intact serpent heads.[2] Though the figure is now gone, it was probably somewhat smaller than the figure at the center of the building. These smaller figures are represented by a sculptured figure found within the House of the Governor (fig. 110). This sculpture represents the lower half of a figure seated crosslegged, wearing a belt and loincloth. The trunk and legs are considerably smaller than those of the major figures of the façade.

North Wing Figures

The figural sculpture of the north wing corresponds closely to that of the south. At the center was a human figure with a tall, plumed headdress re-

sembling that of the southern wing in general form, but with slightly more delicate and ornate featherwork (fig. 111).[3] A similar projecting, vertical cascade of feathers was originally present with its elements tenoned into the three round holes now visible on either side of the headdress. The figure rested on an open-mouthed serpent head closely resembling that of the south wing, but with a slightly different treatment of the central teeth. Above the serpent is a low, cylindrical cushion or throne, bordered at the top with a guilloche pattern and decorated on the side with panels containing mat-weave motifs.

As on the south wing, two smaller figures flanked the central personage. Nothing remains of the figure to the south of center. A headdress much like that of the corresponding figure on the south wing remains to the north (fig. 112). At the base of the headdress was an H-shaped framework with carved featherwork. Above this is a long-snouted reptilian

Fig. 111. House of the Governor, north wing, central human figure.

Fig. 112. House of the Governor, north wing, headdress of human figure above door 12.

Fig. 113. House of the Governor,
central building, central human
figural motif (photo courtesy of
American Museum of Natural
History, New York, neg. 122257).

Fig. 114. House of the Governor, central building, arrangement of hieroglyphic serpent bars of central motif (after Seler 1917: abb. 120a).

head, over which is a spray of feathers decorated with disks. These feathers emanate from a small central medallion carved with a bat. Surmounting the headdress is a vertical, outward-curving panache of feathers.

Central Building Figures

At the House of the Governor the largest single figural motif on the entire east frieze is placed above the central doorway of the large, middle chamber (figs. 54, 113–115).[4] A frontal human figure sits at the center of a tiered arrangement of eight bars terminating in serpent heads (figs. 113–114). Within the bars are hieroglyphic inscriptions, some of which pertain to astronomical phenomena and some of which are grotesque reptilian heads (fig. 114). Recognizable astronomical symbols include the *kin* glyph (sun), the crossed bands (a possible sky symbol), a moon sign, and a possible venus symbol.[5]

The central personage of the design sits on a semicircular pedestal ornamented with disks (fig. 115). The sculpture's head and arms are missing, but we can presume from an extant sculptured head taken from elsewhere on the frieze that the visage was human (fig. 19).[6] The individual's shoulders are covered by a broad cape, at whose center is a plaited mat-weave medallion (fig. 115). He wears a belt decorated in front with an inverted, miniature human head and with step-frets, mat-weave de-

Fig. 115. House of the Governor, central building, human figure of central motif.

Fig. 116. *House of the Governor, belt of human figure of central motif, south side.*

Fig. 117. *House of the Governor, belt of human figure of central motif, north side.*

sign, and serrated bands on the sides (figs. 116–17). The figure supports a huge feather headdress whose plumes are attached to a tall central frame, only the armature of which exists today.

Next in stature and importance on this façade are the two human figures centered beneath the flanking mask canopies. These figures are placed between doors 4 and 5, and doors 9 and 10, of the central building (figs. 118–24). They correspond in size and general arrangement with the two central figures of the north and south wings, but there are minor differences in their headdresses and in the podia beneath the figures. With the exception of the central motif, the best preserved sculpture of the frieze is the southern figure, whose trunk, belt and upper legs remain (figs. 118–19). The head is missing and the arms and lower legs have been broken off. The figure wears a cape composed of large mosaic beads and trimmed with feathers (fig. 120). At the front is a large knotted breast ornament. The wide belt is trimmed with plaited designs and contains panels decorated with complex mat-weave motifs (fig. 121). The figure sits on a throne with a plaited upper edge and with mat-weave designs on the sides (fig. 122), and wears a lofty headdress that reaches to the height of the masks beneath the cornice. The tall, central framework consists of long-snouted heads with spiral-pupilled eyes. Spreading at either side are long plumes that fall to shoulder level. Two smaller symmetrical sprays of feathers replace the vertical cascade seen on the figures on the wings. The open-mouthed serpent podium has a carved relief similar to that of the wings, but its form differs slightly. Here the jaws turn downward at the end and the nose scroll has a tubular noseplug. The serpent head faces away from the central motif.

Less of the northern figure remains intact, but it was apparently similar to the southern (fig. 123). The figure sits crosslegged with right leg supported on the left knee (fig. 124). He wears a short kilt decorated with a series of overlapping, serrated devices and large circles, and a cloth or rope is knotted below the left knee. Beneath the figure is an open-mouthed, serpent-head podium closely resembling that beneath the southern figure, and a cylindrical throne whose sides are adorned with crossed bands and serrated designs and whose upper border is an interwoven mat-weave motif. The headdress, only part of which remains, consisted of a tall central column of long-snouted masks, from which spreads a broad spray of feathers.

Flanking the central motif, and each of the two

Fig. 118. *House of the Governor, central building, human figure above and between doors 4 and 5.*

Fig. 119. *House of the Governor, central building, human figure above and between doors 4 and 5.*

Fig. 120. *House of the Governor, central building, collar of figure above and between doors 4 and 5.*

Fig. 121. *House of the Governor, central building, belt of figure above and between doors 4 and 5.*

Fig. 122. House of the Governor, central building, seat of figure above and between doors 4 and 5.

Fig. 123. House of the Governor, central building, human figure above and between doors 9 and 10, from south.

Fig. 124. House of the Governor, central building, figure above and between doors 9 and 10, from north.

larger figures of the central building, were two smaller figures, placed so that they appear above the three northern and three southern doors (doors 4, 5, 6, 8, 9, 10). All of these figures sat upon upturned serpent-head podia and all wore feather headdresses that resemble those of the larger figures, but which are shorter and narrower. Of the figure that originally sat above doorway 4 only an eye section of the upturned serpent seat and a section of the feathered headdress survive (fig. 125). Of the figure above doorway 5 the larger portion of the headdress survives, showing it to have consisted of a central long-snouted head on a tall, vertical framework to which plumes were attached (fig. 126). Two sections of the serpent-head podium remain. Above door 6, two sections of the podium and a section of the headdress remain (fig. 127). Above door 8, only three sections of the serpent-

Fig. 125. House of the Governor, central building, figure above door 4.

Fig. 126. House of the Governor, central building, figure above door 5.

head base survive (fig. 128). The remaining sections of this and the two subsequent figures were found in the rubble of this section of the façade, which collapsed in 1825. They and other portions of the northern half of the façade have been reconstructed on the basis of the surviving southern section. Only an eye section of the serpent-head podium is in place above door 9. Above door 10 there are three sections of the serpent podium (fig. 129).

Inside one of the rooms of the House of the Governor there are several pieces and fragments of human figural sculpture from the façade which were collected from the debris in front of the building during consolidation and reconstruction. Since their former position on the façade is not known they have not been replaced. Among these fragments there are three human torsos, the lower

trunk and legs of a seated figure, the midriff of what may have been a standing figure, and four long-snouted heads that form the central columns of figures' headdresses (figs. 130–134).[7]

Our best evidence of the sculptural style of the human figures of the House of the Governor is provided by a sculpture from the frieze now in the American Museum of Natural History in New York (fig. 19). This piece, along with other sections of plumes and panaches of headdresses (figs. 20–21), and the decoration representing a bird taken from the East Structure of the Nunnery, was removed from Uxmal by John Lloyd Stephens and subsequently shipped to the United States.[8]

The New York sculpture is important because it is the only extant piece with a head accompanying the torso. The figure's trunk is roughly cylindrical, and he wears a broad cape with a central mat-weave

Fig. 127. House of the Governor, central building, figure above door 6.

medallion much like that of the figure of the central motif. The headdress is also cylindrical and bound by three horizontal bands knotted in front. The individual seems to have shoulder-length hair, and the face is flanked by two large, disk-shaped earplugs. The face is broad and relatively flat with high cheekbones. Each eye is treated as an almost almond shape, defined by slightly raised ridges at top and bottom. The nose has been broken but appears to have been fairly broad.[9]

Human Figural Traditions in Maya Architectural Sculpture

In her analysis of the architectural sculpture of Uxmal, Marta Foncerrada distinguished two separate strains of human figural representations: (1) images that can be considered essentially Maya because they form part of the original decoration of the Florescent Puuc buildings; and (2) images executed in a non-Maya style and showing the influence of foreign groups or ideas in Yucatan, principally Toltec or Huastec.[10]

Foncerrada classes the human figures of the House of the Governor among the Maya-style sculptures. She refers to the central figure as a "sacerdotal image" and compares it on the basis of cos-

Fig. 128. House of the Governor, central building, figure above door 8.

Fig. 129. House of the Governor, central building, figure above door 10.

Fig. 130. House of the Governor, sculpture of human torso from façade.

tume elements with figures appearing in the reliefs and stelae of the central Maya area.[11]

The scheme of human figures of the House of the Governor should also be viewed as belonging to a basically Maya tradition because it is only in the Maya area that other structures are found with similar arrangements of figural sculpture. Aside from two portraitlike stucco sculptures at Lambityeco, Oaxaca, nothing comparable to the high-relief and full-round human figural sculpture seen on Maya buildings occurs elsewhere in Mesoamerica.[12] On the other hand, several buildings with human figural sculpture occur in the southern Maya area. Most of these predate and provide precedents for and parallels to the façade of the House of the Governor.

Structure 33 at Yaxchilan is an example of an earlier building supporting a similar arrangement of human figures (fig. 135).[13] The front frieze is interrupted by three niches centered above the middle doorway and placed slightly outside of the centers of the two flanking doorways. These niches contain remnants of stone and stucco human figures seated

Fig. 131. House of the Governor, sculpture of human torso from façade.

Fig. 132. House of the Governor, sculpture of human torso from façade.

Fig. 133. House of the Governor, sculpture of human figure trunk and legs from façade.

crosslegged.[14] The figures sit on simplified, geometric, serpent mask panels with square eyes and rectangular mouths.

The remainder of the frieze contains an arrangement of smaller, stepped niches framed in a system of vertical and horizontal crossed bands. The smaller niches also bear traces of small stucco figures or ornaments. This arrangement was apparently continued around the sides and rear of the building.[15]

At the center of the roof comb is a solid masonry panel, the bottom of which forms a three-legged bench or throne. Upon the throne is a stone and stucco armature of a human figure, seated with legs hanging over the front of the throne and with arms upraised, and wearing "an animal mask with cruciform headdress."[16]

Like Structure 33, Structure 40 at Yaxchilan also has an arrangement of human figural sculptures on its upper façade.[17] Above the central doorway is a niche housing a seated stone and stucco figure, from which the exterior layer of stucco has eroded but the framework of which still exists. Four small niches, containing evidence of figures, are placed along the bottom of the frieze above the medial molding. Flanking the large central niche, and in the center of each of the remaining frieze surfaces

Fig. 134. House of the Governor, three long-snouted heads from headdresses of façade.

Fig. 135. Yaxchilan, Structure 33 (after Maler 1903: Plate XLII-2).

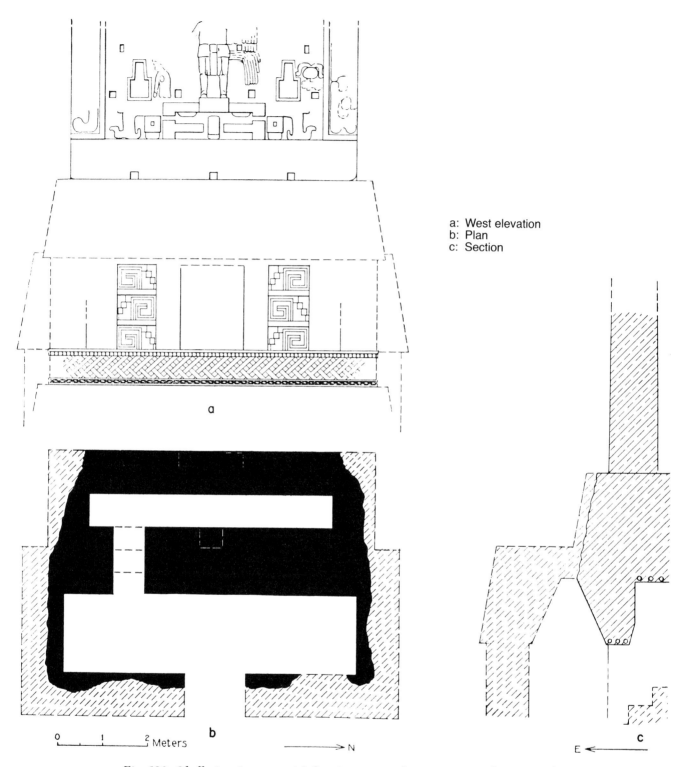

a: West elevation
b: Plan
c: Section

0   1   2 Meters

N

E

Fig. 136. Okolhuitz, Structure 1 (after Ruppert and Denison 1943: fig. 103a–c).

are geometric designs composed of a square intersected by a cross.[18]

Structure 1 at Bonampak, which contains the famous wall paintings, has an arrangement of human figural sculpture resembling that of the Yaxchilan buildings.[19] Above each doorway, and on each end of Structure 1, is a niche containing the remains of a stucco figure, seated crosslegged on an "elaborate stucco mask" and wearing a headdress.[20] On the frieze between the middle and west doorways are the remains of a stucco figure, standing in profile and surrounded by flamboyant scrollwork.

To the northeast, in the northern Peten district or in the Rio Bec and Chenes regions, other buildings have human figural sculptures that resemble those of the House of the Governor adorning their façades. At Pared de los Reyes, for example, the roof comb of the West Building had nine panels, each of which apparently carried a stucco sculpture depicting an individual seated crosslegged on a projecting stone above a mask panel.[21] The figures wear large feather headdresses with plumes falling symmetrically at each side.

At Okolhuitz Structure 1, a human figure standing on a geometric mask panel appears at the center of the rear face of the roof comb (fig. 136). Only the lower part of the figure survives, showing that he wore a thick belt, narrow loin cloth apron, and perhaps a short kilt. A spray of feathers is attached to the belt, and traces remain of another that formed part of the headdress.[22]

At the Chenes site of Hochob, full-length, standing stucco figures occupy the vertical masonry columns of the perforated, flying façade of the Dragon-Mouth Structure 2 (fig. 92).[23]

Both the Rio Bec and Chenes structures pertain to the same general Maya tradition of figure sculpture as seen as at Yaxchilan and Bonampak, in which ornately costumed individuals are placed in the upper zones of buildings. As we have seen, these edifices were already extant by the time the House of the Governor was constructed, and so may have supplied distant prototypes. It seems unlikely, however, that the Uxmal architects had firsthand knowledge of these buildings. More likely the figural tradition they represent was first emulated in earlier Puuc architecture, which then supplied closer models for the designer of the House of the Governor.

In the Puuc region there are a number of buildings whose façades were decorated with human figures. In many cases either these figural sculptures, or their methods of arrangement on the façade, provide parallels to those at the House of the Governor. Although it is difficult to be certain that these buildings precede the House of the Governor, the recognized date of the latter makes it clear that few postdate it. Thus one or several of such Puuc buildings may have supplied the model for the House of the Governor.

At Labna, human figures executed in stucco adorned the façade and the perforated, flying façade of the Mirador Temple.[24] Today the lower half of a figure wearing a loincloth apron stands on the southwest corner, while the lower half of a human figure with legs spread is seen on the east side. The figures on the Labna flying façade seem to belong to the same tradition as those on Structure 2 at Hochob.[25]

Also included in this tradition of stucco figures on upper façades and roof combs is the Temple of the Old Woman at Uxmal, whose single-wall, perforated roof comb is studded with a series of stone tenons (fig. 33).[26] Traces of modeled stucco still adhere beneath one of these tenons on the south side of the roof comb. Not enough of these sculptures remains to be certain they were human figures, but the idea is supported by their appearance on similar combs at Pared de los Reyes, Hochob, Labna, and Sabacche. Stucco sculptures also originally were modeled over the two projecting tenons found in the upper west façade of this temple. As mentioned, the Temple of the Old Woman has several traits of Early Puuc architecture and surely antedates the House of the Governor.

There is also evidence that the nine-gabled roof comb of the House of the Pigeons at Uxmal formerly supported an extensive program of stucco figural sculpture.[27] These stucco motifs were modeled over the surface of the masonry and attached to tenons that are placed at intervals across the face of the roof comb.[28] The presence of featherwork sprays from headdresses indicates that human figures formed part of the program. There is general agreement that the House of the Pigeons precedes the House of the Governor at Uxmal, so that it was available as a model.

Stucco human figures probably also once adorned the frieze and flying façade of the Cemetery Temple at Uxmal (fig. 10). Tiers of stone tenons are placed in the upper façade near each end of the building and above the central doorway. Smaller tenons are set into each of the struts, suggesting that smaller stucco sculptures were placed between the larger compositions below. This symmetrical and hierarchical sculptural scheme recalls that of Structure 33 at Yaxchilan (fig. 135). Assuming that the stuccos were human figures, this arrangement closely resembles, and probably served as, another model for that of the House of the Governor.

This tradition of stucco modeling also is found at the Palace by the water works at Ichpich.[29] The frieze of the building has an upper and lower row of projecting stones which undoubtedly supported figures formerly. At Almuchil, a two-roomed building had the remains of a seated human figure modeled in stucco above the doorway.[30]

Although stucco sculpture is characteristic of Early Puuc architecture, the presence of stucco figures apparently is not limited only to Early Puuc buildings. Both the structures from Ichpich and Almuchil have better cut masonry and more complicated moldings associated with the mature Puuc tradition. Likewise, at Labna, stucco figures appeared on the façade of the Portal Vault, a clear example of later Puuc architecture (fig. 96).[31] Within the doorways of the miniature huts on the west side are projecting tenons and traces of a blue-green featherwork headdress executed in stucco, indicating that the space was originally occupied by seated human figures.[32]

At Sayil the Late Puuc third story of the Palace has tiers of tenons that formerly supported stucco sculptures above each doorway (fig. 31).[33] Proskouriakoff believes this arrangement of tenons once supported human figures, and that the design projected above the roof level to break its horizontal silhouette.[34] The rhythmical placement of figures in the façade parallels the arrangement of the House of the Governor, but lacks the more complex hierarchical aspect.

Stucco sculptures of human figures also formerly adorned the façade of the Palace at Chacbolai,[35] and apparently appeared on the Adjacent Palace at Chunhuhub, where a plain masonry panel with the remains of a seated human figure is placed above the central doorway. Two colonnettes and a large step-fret flank the figure on each side. Above the two flanking doorways of this palace there are similar panels containing human figures framed by angular frets.[36] The symmetrical composition, with the figures forming nodes for fret designs, is like a condensed version of the arrangement at the House of the Governor.

In general, Early Puuc architects preferred to use stucco sculpture for the decoration of façades. In some instances this usage persisted into the mature Puuc style as well. However, many later Puuc buildings utilized cut stone rather than stucco as a medium for figural sculpture. The House of the Governor belongs to this later tradition, which is found at several other Puuc sites as well as at Chichen Itza.

An arrangement of stone figures resembling that of the House of the Governor occurs at the Figure Palace at Chunhuhub, where the frieze was originally set with twelve stylized figures, seated cross-legged in recessed panels.[37] The panels are placed between groups of colonnettes and angular frets. Unlike the human-faced figures of the House of the Governor, these figures wore a birdlike costume consisting of a beaked mask and wings.[38]

Seated stone figures like those of the House of the Governor also appear at Chacmultun.[39] On the south front and west end of Structure 1 each doorway was surmounted by a model Maya hut. The hut doorways contined small, stone human figures, about one-half life size, seated crosslegged and wearing elaborate costume.[40]

A parallel to the central motif of the House of the Governor also occurs at the East Wing of the Monjas at Chichen Itza (fig. 137).[41] Above the eastern doorway is a small figure seated crosslegged within an oval nimbus bordered with feathers. This figure sits upon a "constellation band" composed of twenty-four glyph blocks containing astronomical signs such as crossed bands, venus or star symbols, and other glyphs.[42] This recalls the hieroglyphic bands that flank the central figure of the House of the Governor and the door of the Chenes-style Temple of the Pyramid of the Magician at Uxmal (figs. 8, 114).[43]

The Monjas figure is seated frontally and is flanked by two feather panels. He wears an elaborate feather headdress and a broad mosaic collar that covers his shoulders, as well as a belt and kilt or loincloth.[44] This costume resembles that worn by the figures on the House of the Governor. However, the figure's facial features are highly stylized, resembling the small faces above the snouts of the masks of the upper façade of the Monjas.[45] The better preserved of these small faces appear to be versions of the figure with a cruller ornament above his nose, who is known as the Jaguar Lord of the Underworld.[46]

The sculptural style and facial treatment of the Monjas figure closely resemble those of two sculptures found during excavations of the base of the Pyramid of the Magician at Uxmal. One sculptured head, which probably came from the façade of the Lower West Structure of the Magician Pyramid, has Jaguar Lord of the Underworld features like

Fig. 137. Chichen Itza, eastern façade of East Wing of the Monjas (after Bolles 1977:115).

those of the Chichen Itza figure.[47] These sculptured heads from Uxmal are contained within the gaping jaws of serpent heads.

The serpent heads are carved in the same style as that of the well-known sculpture, the "Reina de Uxmal" (Queen of Uxmal) (fig. 138).[48] The "Reina de Uxmal" probably represents a man rather than a woman, and depicts a handsome, naturalistic human face within the distended mouth of a fantastic serpent with noseplugs and feathered eyelids. The human face has a compelling portraitlike quality, with its individuality marked by scrollwork scarification patterns of raised dots on the cheeks. The close formal analogy between this figure and the others discovered at the Pyramid of the Magician suggest that the latter may also represent living rulers donning supernatural disguises.

A wide variety of human figures ornament the façade of the North Structure of the Nunnery at Uxmal (fig. 85). Several full-round figures are attached to the rear frieze of the building. Near the eastern end is a standing, nude male figure, with penis displayed and hanging downward, and with ropes around the upper arms, suggesting this is a captive.[49] A second figure also is naked with hanging penis and has his arms crossed with the right arm extended and resting on the opposite shoulder in a gesture of submission or fealty.[50]

On the principal façade of the North Structure are a number of human figures, some of which are still in place and some of which have fallen and are now found in the interior rooms of the building. One figure located above doors 4 and 5 (counting from the west) shows a seated male captive, again with exposed penis, and with hands bound at the wrist (fig. 139).[51] Two other figures are still in place on the frieze between the southeast mask tower and the first mask tower to the west. The westernmost of these figures is headless and apparently holds a feathered rattle in his upraised hand while pressing a cylindrical wooden drum to his body.[52] The second figure is only partly human, and has

Fig. 139. Sculpture from south façade of North Structure of Nunnery (after Seler 1917:abb. 52).

Fig. 138. "Reina de Uxmal" (Queen of Uxmal) (after Seler 1917:abb. 84a).

been identified as an eagle with a human head and feather crest.[53]

Because of the emphasis on nudity and warfare in these sculptures, Foncerrada interpreted them as additions made to the original Puuc decorative program during the final phase of culture in the area, when the religious emphasis of the Maya was being replaced by a new secular and militaristic spirit that culminated in the monuments of Post-Classic Chichen Itza.[54] It is possible that these figures are part of the original sculptural program, however, since such militaristic themes and "Mexican" influences appear even earlier in the Puuc region. Scenes of warfare occur in the Mul-Chic murals (fig. 29), dated about A.D. 800–820, while images of bound and naked captives appear on Stela 14 at

Uxmal (fig. 27). The inclusion of such themes in Uxmal's sculpture suggests that the human figures on the North Structure of the Nunnery are not later additions, but original parts of the design.

The North Structure sculptures differ from those of the House of the Governor. At the North Structure the captive figure, normally of secondary importance in Maya art, is made a dominant feature of the program. At the House of the Governor, on the other hand, the arrangement and costume of the figures resembles that of earlier figural façades in the southern Maya area (fig. 135), where the authority of the ruler is asserted by a thoroughgoing symmetrical and hierarchical composition (fig. 2).

It is clear that the arrangement of human figures on the façade of the House of the Governor has parallels in the southern area and is the outgrowth of a basically Maya tradition. Nevertheless, there are localized, non–Classic Maya traits evident in the figural sculpture. For example, the face of the American Museum of Natural History sculpture differs from the standard Classic Maya representations (fig. 19).[55] The forehead is broad and lacks the pronounced backward slope of Classic Maya sculptures (fig. 148), while the eyes are more horizontal and less heavy-lidded. Closer resemblances may be found with the "Maya" figures from the Temple of the Chac Mool at Chichen Itza, Stela 21 at Oxkintok (possibly dating to 10.1.10.0.0),[56] or a jamb from Halal.[57] Also reminiscent is the face of the lower left figure on Oxkintok Stela 19.[58] These resemblances extend to costume as well. The Uxmal figure wears a cylindrical headdress secured with three parallel knotted bands. A similar, complicated knotted costume appears in the girdle and wristlets of the figure on Oxkintok Stela 21.[59] On Oxkintok Stela 9, the figure in the upper panel has elaborate ties just below the knees resembling the hose on the human figure located between doors 4 and 5 of the House of the Governor.[60]

Iconography of Human Figural Sculpture

The human figural sculpture of the east frieze is of fundamental importance for a study of the iconography of House of the Governor. These human figures form the highest plane of relief sculpture on the building's façade, and are also the most vividly realistic in conception. Their conspicuous position, coupled with their magnificent costume, suggests that they provide keys to unlock meaning the building possessed for the Maya of Uxmal. Among these figures, the one at the middle of the building is nodal, forming the compositional center from which many of the geometric designs seem to take root and to which all other figures appear subordinate. If the figures generally furnish keys to our knowledge, then the central figural motif, by its superior stature and focal position, must be the masterkey.

Central Motif

The central motif of the House of the Governor has obvious symbolic importance. It is the largest single figural motif on the entire east frieze, and is placed above the central doorway of the spacious middle chamber (figs. 54, 113).[61] As we have seen, the central personage sits on a semi-circular pedestal terminating in serpent heads (fig. 115). His shoulders are covered by a broad collar with a central mat-weave medallion, and he wears a belt adorned with an inverted miniature human head and with step-frets, mat-weave design and serrated bands on the sides. Above the individual towers a huge feather headdress whose plumes stream from a tall central frame. The sculpture's head is now missing, but the face was probably human.[62] The frontal human figure sits at the center of a tiered arrangement of eight bars bound by raised stone courses and terminating in serpent heads (fig. 114). Within the bars are hieroglyphic inscriptions[63] that pertain to the astronomical phenomena described in chapter 10.

The arrangement of serpent-head hieroglyphic bands is an element of the central motif that can be related to other aspects of Maya art. If the hieroglyphic bands are interpreted as continuing behind the figure and his headdress, then they form bicephalic serpents, a motif seen elsewhere at Uxmal and appearing frequently in Maya art.

Fig. 140. East Structure of Nunnery, detail of door and tiered arrangement of serpent bars on upper façade.

At Uxmal, bicephalic serpents resembling those of the House of the Governor are found on the East Structure of the Nunnery (figs. 86, 140). There the serpent heads occur at the ends of eight bands disposed in an analogous, tiered trapezoidal scheme. On the East Structure, however, the bands lack the interior hieroglyphs seen on those of the House of the Governor, and the central human figure is replaced by small, grotesque masks wearing circular, feather headdresses. Naturalistic and more schematized versions of bicephalic serpents occur on the North Structure of the Nunnery, where they surmount the roofs of the miniature huts which appear above several of the doorways (fig. 141). The bicephalic serpent is an important leitmotif that relates several structures at Uxmal.

The two-headed serpent bands of the House of the Governor are conceptually and formally related to the ceremonial bar, one of the most typical ritual

Fig. 143a–b. (a) Piedras Negras, Stela 25 (after Maler 1901:Plate XXII). (b) Piedras Negras, Stela 25, drawing of framing elements (after Spinden (1913:fig. 57d).

is striated to represent mosaic. In one instance the supporting pedestal rests on a bench-type throne, providing the clearest link with the Jonuta throne figurine group.[83] This example also differs from others in the Jaina Group O in that the central pedestal is flanked by two serpents in profile, portrayed in a style closely resembling serpent heads found on a more elaborate pedestal figurine said to have come either from Isla del Carmen or Jaina (fig. 145).[84]

It is this more elaborate figurine that possesses the most pronounced formal and thematic resemblances to the Piedras Negras accessional stelae (fig. 145). It depicts a person seated in a raised niche or doorway reached by a diminutive stairway. The individual wears a profile serpent headdress

with inverted T-shaped plumage. At each side of the niche is an arrangement of tiered bars, and above is a head with Tlaloc characteristics flanked by serpent heads and surmounted by a bird.[85]

Several variants of these elaborate pedestal and niche figurines are known. Another such figurine from Jaina conforms generally to the previous example, but lacks the Tlaloc above the central figure and the tiered bars flanking the niche.[86] A related example shows an individual seated crosslegged in a niche and resting on a recumbent jaguar (fig. 146).[87] The figure wears a beaded necklace, mosaic wristlets, a loincloth, and a feather headdress with a central mask composed of profile serpents. The niche is flanked by an arrangement of tiered bars and is spanned above by a bicephalic serpent, while

Fig. 144. Jonuta-style throne figurine from Jaina, Campeche (after Corson 1976:fig. 24a).

Fig. 145. Pedestal Niche Figurine, Jaina? or Isla del Carmen? (redrawn after Piña Chan 1968:lam. 21 by Tid Kowalski).

a Tlaloc face again surmounts the composition. Another variant shows a figure seated within a niche on a trough-shaped throne.[88] Rectangular flanges project from the sides of the niche. Appearing above instead of Tlaloc is a human head wearing a profile serpent headdress. On another pedestal figurine from a private collection in Mexico the figure wears a profile serpent headdress and sits in a niche on a recumbent jaguar. Flanking the niche are projecting trapezoidal flanges that slant inward toward the bottom.[89]

These elaborate pedestal and niche figurines are allied, formally and iconographically, with the central motif of the House of the Governor. Among the resemblances are the frontal seated postures of the centralized human figures, and their treatment as men of high rank wearing splendid feather headdresses. However, the most telling resemblance is the use, both in the pedestal figurines and at the House of the Governor, of an arrangement of tiered bars that frames the figure. At the House of the Governor each of these bars concludes in a serpent head (figs. 113–14). Among the Jaina pedestal figu-

172

PART THREE: ARCHITECTURAL SCULPTURE

Fig. 146. Pedestal Niche Figurine, Jaina, Campeche (after Groth-Kimball 1961: Plate 44).

rines the bars do not form serpents, but bicephalic serpents span the niche above the figures, and in several examples, the style of these serpent heads closely recalls that of Uxmal. Furthermore, a Jaina figurine now in the Gilcrease Collection features a woman standing beneath an overarching two-headed serpent whose body is marked with astronomical symbols like those on the tiered serpents of the House of the Governor.[90]

The Tlaloc faces, jaguar thrones, and birds at the top of the compositions on the pedestal figurines are not found in the central motif of the House of the Governor, but do occur elsewhere at Uxmal. Tlaloc imagery is seen on the mask towers of the North Structure of the Nunnery and on the Lower West Structure of the Pyramid of the Magician (fig. 141).[91] The jaguar throne is found in bicephalic form on the terrace directly in front of the House of the

Governor (fig. 16).[92] A bird identified as an owl occurs as the centerpiece of the tiered arrangement of bars found on the East Structure of the Nunnery (fig. 140).[93]

We have seen that a two-headed reptilian monster appears at Piedras Negras on Stelae 25, 6, 11, and 14 in a composition related formally to that of the central motif of the House of the Governor. The series of figurines from Jonuta, Isla del Carmen, and Jaina helps account for the transmission of this iconographic theme from Piedras Negras to Uxmal. The continued use of this motif implies the conservation of much of its original symbolism, the essential nature of which has been defined by Tatiana Proskouriakoff. By studying patterns of the hieroglyphic inscriptions and iconographic motifs which appear on the stelae at Piedras Negras, she has shown that the human figures carved on the monuments are historical rulers of the Maya area.[94] At Piedras Negras the monuments cluster in distinct chronological and spatial groupings. Each group begins with the specialized symbolic design portrayed on Stelae 25, 6, 11, and 14 (fig. 143). These initial stelae are carved with what has been termed the "niche motif" or the "ascension motif,"[95] in which a person garbed in rich attire is seated on a cushion in a small elevated niche or doorway. We have seen that the niche is framed with a glyphic "sky band" of astronomical signs, terminating below in the two-headed reptilian monster, and with a grotesque bird placed above in the center (fig. 143).[96]

The dates recorded on the niche stelae that immediately precede the dedicatory date of the monument are always followed by a particular hieroglyph, T684, known as the "toothache glyph."[97] Proskouriakoff interpreted this glyph and the dates which precede it as marking the accession to power of a new ruler at Piedras Negras. The stelae that portray the niche figure depict a dynastic ritual associated with formal ascension to power, comparable to the seating of the ruler in the "house on high" mentioned in the *Chilam Balam of Chumayel*.[98]

The correspondence between the hieroglyphic serpent bars, both flanking the human figure in the central motif of the House of the Governor and forming the "cosmic motif" of the accessional stelae of Piedras Negras, suggests that the design at Uxmal manifests rulership and authority. From its inception at Piedras Negras, through its adaptation in the figurine types of Jonuta, Isla del Carmen, and Jaina, to its culmination at Uxmal, this iconographic

Fig. 147. Palenque,
Oval Relief Tablet
in House E of the Palace
(after Proskouriakoff
1950:fig. 54b).

theme retained a basic continuity that emphasized a dynastic ideal and the overarching power of the Maya lord. The seated personages of the stelae are recognized as historical figures. Their counterpart exists in the magnificently garbed individual sitting at the center of the House of the Governor, who we can assume was a ruler of Uxmal (figs. 113–15). The hieroglyphic serpent-headed bars that flank the figure establish a supernatural locus exalting the ruler above the remainder of society, while the astronomical symbols on the serpents' bodies signify his divine or heavenly nature.

The House of the Governor is not the only Maya building to feature the "cosmic motif" and the accessional symbolism found on the niche stelae at Piedras Negras. The two-headed monster with hieroglyphic body also occurs at Palenque, where it spans the northern doorway of House E of the Palace.[99] The heads of the monster, one reptilian and

one with *kin* glyph and tripartite badge, resemble those of the Piedras Negras monuments. The two-headed monster also is found above the inner doorway of Copan Temple 22.[100] In this case the heads are connected not by a hieroglyphic band, but by a series of S-scrolls. At Uxmal, hieroglyphic bands that resemble the body of the two-headed monster, but which lack heads, flank the doorway of the Chenes-style Temple of the Pyramid of the Magician (figs. 7–8). Foncerrada believes that the Chenes-style Temple is contemporary with both the House of the Governor and the Nunnery Quadrangle.[101] Although its façade is treated as a gigantic mask, like those of the earlier structures of the Chenes region to the south, the stone mosaic and construction technique are pure Puuc.[102]

On the basis of the presence of the "cosmic motif," Kubler has suggested that both House E at Palenque and Temple 22 at Copan may have been buildings in which dynastic accession rituals were actually performed.[103] Supporting his hypothesis is the oval stone relief at House E, on the medial wall facing west onto the tower court, and showing a woman proffering a mosaic crown to the ruler Pacal seated on a bicephalic jaguar throne (fig. 147).

The structure which corresponds most fully to the ascensional idea at Uxmal is the Chenes-style Temple of the Pyramid of the Magician (figs. 7–8). The treatment of its façade as a gigantic mask with the doorway as mouth resembles that of the exterior doorway of Copan Temple 22, another possible physical center of accession. Long "sky bands" flank the doorway, relating the façade to the "cosmic motif" depicted on the stelae of Piedras Negras. Whereas the bands at Piedras Negras terminate in two heads, one celestial (venus symbols) and the other terrestrial (fleshless lower jaw and tripartite badge), those of the Chenes-style Temple are headless. The dualism expressed at Piedras Negras may occur, however, in the large doorway mask where venus symbols, plaited mat motifs and crossed bands are found in the superorbital plates, while death motifs such as crossed bones and *cimi* "percentage signs" are found in the suborbital plates.[104] Indicating the royal nature of the structure is the fact that between the eyes of the large doorway mask there is a large sculpture of a feather headdress, belonging to a ruler figure supported on the backs of kneeling captive figures that remain below. The ascensional idea is also fulfilled by the steep western stairway leading to the temple and providing for the seating of the lord in the "house on high." This staircase culminates in a large central mask that forms a pedestal or throne.[105]

Whether the hieroglyphic bands of the House of the Governor mark it as an ascensional center is uncertain, for the Chenes-style Temple seems better adapted to such a ritualistic seating of a lord. Rather, the use of the bicephalic serpent bars at the House of the Governor seems to mark it as a royal house, the principal residence and administrative center of the ruler of Uxmal and members of the local Maya elite.

At the heart of the central motif of the House of the Governor, framed by the hieroglyphic serpent bands discussed above, are the remains of a seated figure wearing a grandiose headdress (fig. 115). Having interpreted the hieroglyphic bands as a regal symbol related to the "cosmic motif" that surrounds portraits of historical rulers at Piedras Negras, it is tempting to think that the figure at the House of the Governor was a portrait of an actual

ruler of Uxmal. The figure's head has been destroyed, but other extant sculpture from the façade indicates the face was human. To demonstrate that this is a portrait of an Uxmal ruler we will first consider whether portraiture was practiced in Maya art, and in what contexts. We will then demonstrate the evidence at Uxmal supporting the idea that this figure represents a specific person.

Portraiture in Maya Art

Whether true schools of portraiture existed in Maya art is a question that has been posed many times. Varying responses have been offered, according to when the authors wrote, and depending upon their special interests in the field.

Several early explorers were willing to consider the possibility that historical individuals were depicted in Maya art. John Lloyd Stephens, writing in 1843 on the central sculptural motif of the House of the Governor, and of the other figural sculptures applied to the façade, believed that "each figure was perhaps the portrait of some cacique, prophet, warrior, or priest, distinguished in the history of this unknown people."[106] Alfred P. Maudslay remained uncertain whether the personages portrayed on the stelae of Copan were specific rulers or priests, or idealized representations of gods and mythical heroes, but noted that the "strong individuality of many of the figures supported the idea of portraiture."[107] Teobert Maler, faced with the same conundrum as Maudslay, identified some of the figures on stelae at Piedras Negras as gods, and others as warrior chieftains.[108]

By the middle of the twentieth century most of the calendrical material in the Maya writing system had been identified, and was yielding important information on Maya chronology and culture history. The non-calendrical glyphs, however, obstinately refused to submit to any hurried interpretation. As a result they were largely neglected by the two great students of Maya writing, S. G. Morley and J. E. S. Thompson. This attitude was summarized by Thompson, who wrote in his *Maya Hieroglyphic Writing: an Introduction* [1950], "I do not believe that historical events are recorded on the monuments."[109] His idea that the monuments were erected primarily to commemorate a sacred chronology led him to posit that even such seemingly obvious secular scenes, such as those depicting warriors and conquest, were really subtle references to calendrical ceremonies or astronomical events.[110]

Although Thompson's ideas concerning the basic

calendrical-astronomical content of Maya writing and art had great influence from the 1920s until the 1950s, others continued to suggest that history was recorded. As early as 1916 Herbert J. Spinden questioned the theory that Maya monuments were erected primarily as ritualistic markers of time.[111] Anticipating by more than forty years the later, epigraphic discoveries of Heinrich Berlin and Tatiana Proskouriakoff, Spinden predicted that true historical material was contained among the bellicose scenes on the monuments of Usumacinta River sites such as Piedras Negras and Yaxchilan. He believed that Stela 12 of Piedras Negras "doubtless memorializes a conquest of importance" in which a "war-chief" haughtily surveys a group of huddled and bound prisoners. He also pointed out that both the victors and victims were identified by short inscriptions near their heads or on their bodies, and properly suggested that "names of both persons and places are recorded."[112] With uncanny prescience, Spinden also predicted that the niche Stelae 25, 6, 11, and 14 at Piedras Negras were historically significant, and that they might represent "the ascension to the seat of theocratic power of the person portrayed" (fig. 143).[113] In addition to Spinden, in 1918 George Byron Gordon outlined some possible examples of Maya portraiture at Copan, Piedras Negras, and Yaxchilan.[114]

One of the few Maya scholars of the 1930s to study Maya portraiture in detail was Mary Butler.[115] She sought to determine the character of the figures by a study of the contexts in which they appear, assuming that a figure's position might mark it as either divine or human. Butler identified some of the solitary figures as gods or deities—as in the case of the aged, cigar-smoking figure from the Temple of the Cross at Palenque—or viewed them as god-impersonators—exemplified by the masked figures on Stelae P and I at Copan, Stelae A and C at Quirigua, and Stela 11 at Seibal. The majority, however, she interpreted as actual portraits of priests, rulers, or warriors, as expressed by the countless depictions of individuals with naturalistic features holding insignia such as ceremonial bars, Manikin Scepters, or shields and spears. Butler's argument was supported by a study of Maya costume and accoutrements; she drew attention to two instances at Piedras Negras where figures garbed in identical costume appear on monuments erected within a few years of one another, suggesting that they are portraits of the same person.[116]

Tatiana Proskouriakoff initiated a new era in the study of Maya portraiture in 1960 with her study of

the inscriptions at Piedras Negras. As we have seen, she was able to demonstrate convincingly that several "ascension" scenes showing a person seated in a niche and doorway surrounded by a cosmic monster are portraits of individual rulers and their families, and were erected to commemorate their accession to power. Later she was able to identify many significant events in the lives of four rulers at Yaxchilan, the two most prominent of whom she identified by their glyphic names as Shield Jaguar and Bird Jaguar.[117]

David Kelley extended Proskouriakoff's dynastic hypothesis to the southeastern Maya sites of Copan and Quirigua, identifying birth and inaugural glyphs at both sites, and defining a cluster of shared names and titles linking the two centers politically. Kelley's interpretation of the epigraphic evidence supported and clarified the close ties that had already been noticed between these two centers in the realm of art and architecture.[118]

George Kubler carried Kelley's textual evidence to the visual domain, seeking to make a case for portraiture among the carved monuments of Quirigua. In a convincing argument, he showed that the series of Stelae S, H, J, F, D, E, A, and C, which were carved over a period of about thirty-five years, and which commemorate hotun endings beginning with the Long Count date 9.15.15.0.0 (A.D. 746) and reaching to 9.17.10.0.0 (A.D. 781), portray a succession of figures with facial features retaining enough shared physiognomic traits to be considered versions of the same person, while varying enough over time to suggest the physical effects of aging.[119]

Further evidence of portraiture in Maya art is found at the site of Seibal, where striking resemblances occur between two pairs of stelae: nos. 5 and 7, and nos. 10 and 11 (fig. 142). These correspondences have been remarked upon by Maler, Morley, and John Graham. Spinden noted that Stelae 8 through 11, erected on four sides of the temple platform A-3 at Seibal,[120] all carry the same Calendar Round date of 5 Ahau 3 Kayab, fixed in the Long Count at 10.1.0.0.0 on Stela 11. The "compelling individuality" of the separate faces convinced Spinden that they were portraits in which characterization was achieved by variation of forehead, nose, and chin profiles, by the shape and size of the lips and eyes, and by the presence of facial hair.[121]

The most remarkable resemblance occurs between Stelae 10 and 11, which John Graham believes may represent the same individual in differ-

Fig. 148. Palenque, stucco portrait head, probably of Pacal (after Griffin 1976:fig. 10).

ent dress (fig. 142). Rice paper rubbings of the two monuments were measured by Frank J. Sanders, who obtained close enough correspondence to convince him that patterns or templates were employed in the carving. Apart from the possibility that templates played a role in the design of these two stelae, it is obvious that they were carved by the same hand, and that they surely represent the same mustachioed ruler of Seibal.[122]

Outlined above are some of the more convincing arguments for the application of a historical approach to the study of Maya carved monuments. Specifically it has been illustrated that many of the figural representations can be viewed as portraits of prominent Maya lords and rulers, whose deeds and exploits are commemorated in the glyphic texts and recorded visually in the sculpture.

It is becoming increasingly clear that the histori-

cal approach should not be limited merely to free-standing monumental sculpture carrying glyphic texts, but that it can provide a fruitful method for the interpretation of Maya architectural sculpture as well. Peter D. Harrison has recognized the importance of architectural sculptures applied to the buildings of the Central Acropolis at Tikal and has remarked that "the monumental art decorating them could have emblematic or heraldic significance associated with an expanding dynastic family or families."[123]

Also writing of Tikal, and confirming Harrison's ideas as to the dynastic importance of architectural sculpture, Arthur Miller has pointed out similarities of costume and insignia between the roof-comb sculptures of Temples I and IV and the various sculptures on the carved wooden lintels found within the temples themselves. These correspondences led Miller to conclude that the sculpture and the associated lintels of Temple I depict the same individual, a ruler whom Kubler has designated as "Sky-Rain" (fig. 191).[124] On the first tier of the roof comb of Temple IV is a large human figure seated crosslegged, holding a ceremonial bar, and wearing a feather headdress, only fragments of which remain. Miller believes that this figure is a "royal personage seated on a throne holding the symbol of his authority."[125] He suggests that this is the same individual ruler depicted on both of the interior lintels, the lord named "Sun-Sky-Rain" by Kubler (fig. 168). Miller further compared the roof-comb sculptures of Temple IV with figural sculpture applied to the façade of Structure 5D-141 of the Central Acropolis, believing that they may portray the same individual.[126]

Some of the most startlingly vivid and naturalistic portraiture in Precolumbian America was produced at the Maya site of Palenque. Much of this portraiture was executed in the form of splendidly modeled heads of stucco originally used in various architectural contexts. Accompanying the deceased ruler Pacal, or "Lord Shield," in his magnificent tomb beneath the Temple of the Inscriptions was a stucco head, wrested from some architectural setting and presumably a portrait of the lord (fig. 148).[127] This and other stucco heads from the tomb are modeled with a delicate and sure touch, but, as Gillett Griffin has noted, despite their great realism, they remain tied to an idealized, courtly tradition.

True portraiture was developed most fully at Palenque during the reign of Pacal's successor, Chan Bahlum, who ruled A.D. 684–702. Exceptionally naturalistic portraits of him, depicted with a large nose, drooping lower lips, and heavy lids, were carved on large, limestone relief tablets set into the walls of the temples erected during his reign (figs. 102, 192). Also among the finest portraits of Chan Bahlum are various stucco modeled heads that were probably removed from some building. These strongly individualized stuccos show that portraiture played a major role in the architectural sculpture of Palenque, and that the rulers were proud and confident enough of their accomplishments to want to display themselves to their own populace and to posterity.[128]

Other examples of convincing naturalism in architectural sculpture occur at Seibal, where several examples of life-size, and larger than life-size, stucco, portrait heads were discovered in the debris of Structure A-3. One of these heads has specific facial features, such as a mustache and small goatee, which permit it to be identified as the same ruler portrayed on Stelae 10 and 11 associated with the building.[129]

The façades of several structures at Yaxchilan and Bonampak also provide an important avenue for the interpretation of Maya architectural sculpture, and offer a further confirmation of Harrison's ideas about the dynastic significance of such sculpture. Structures 33 and 40 at Yaxchilan, and Structure 1 at Bonampak, yield readily to such a study of Maya architectural sculpture because they retain substantial portions of their sculptural programs and because epigraphic researches have provided a framework of dates for these buildings and a dynastic history with clues to their use.[130]

We have already described Structure 33 at Yaxchilan, and noted that its hierarchical and symmetrical arrangement of human figural sculpture resembles the scheme at the House of the Governor (fig. 135). Important for a discussion of the meaning of Structure 33's architectural sculpture is a seated stone statue found within a niche on a low platform within the Yaxchilan temple (fig. 149).[131] This statue seems related to the figures on the façade of Structure 33 by costume and posture. The figure sits crosslegged with hands resting on the knees, and wears a jaguar-head headdress surrounded by a fan-shaped panache of feathers.[132] He wears a large mosaic collar, presumably of jade or shell.[133] At the center of this collar, and over each shoulder, are small, human maskette medallions. At the base of the jade collar is a tubular chest ornament with fringed or beaded ends. The figure also wears a wide belt, with a human maskette attached to the front. Below the maskette a loincloth or sash falls

Fig. 149. Yaxchilan, seated stone figure, Bird-Jaguar, from Structure 33 (after Morley (1937–1938, 5–Plate 107a).

over the front of the figure's crossed legs. The figure wears wristlets composed of rectangular plates with a beaded upper border, and in each hand he holds a small feather fan with a pendant ornamental chain.[134]

The determination of the proper identity of this seated statue would provide an important key toward unlocking the meaning of the similarly posed figures on the frieze of Structure 33. Teobert Maler believed that the figure was a representation of Quetzalcoatl-Kukulcan,[135] while Desiré Charnay in-

Fig. 150.
Yaxchilan,
Lintel 6 from Structure 1
(after Maler
1903:Plate L).

terpreted the figure as an idol known as the canal-uinic ("Man from above" or "Man from heaven") and worshipped by the Lacandon Maya of the region.[136] Both of these identifications seem implausible. The Quetzalcoatl-Kukulcan cult did not take firm hold in the Maya area until about A.D. 900–1000,[137] while Structure 33 dates to about A.D. 756. The Lacandon's worship of the statue as an idol tells us little of its original identity, since those people probably moved into the area after the abandonment of Yaxchilan.[138]

Rather than representing a supernatural being or an idol, the sumptuously attired figure is apparently a human being, albeit a highly venerated personage. Several strands of evidence indicate that this figure is a portrait of the great ruler of Yaxchilan, Bird Jaguar.[139]

The first line of evidence concerns the dedi-

catory date and the dedicatory nature of Structure 33. Lintels 1, 2, and 3 of this structure record the dates 9.16.1.0.0 (A.D. 752), 9.16.6.0.0 (A.D. 756), and 9.16.5.0.0 (A.D. 755) respectively. These dates all fall within the period of Bird Jaguar's reign at Yaxchilan. The date on Lintel 1, 9.16.0.0.0 11 Ahau 8 Tzec, commemorates Bird Jaguar's accession to power,[140] while the 9.16.6.0.0 date on Lintel 2 celebrates the fifth Tun anniversary of that accession.[141] The seated, stone figure thus occupies a commanding position in Structure 33, which was dedicated on the fifth Tun anniversary of Bird Jaguar's inauguration to power, and the lintels of which all bear portraits of Bird Jaguar accompanied by other individuals.

The next line of evidence concerns the costume of the seated figure, which resembles that of the sculptured portrayals of Bird Jaguar. His clothing on Lintel 1, for example, shows the following similarities with that of the statue; a mosaic collar with three circular maskette medallions, a tubular chest ornament with fringed ends, wrist cuffs, and a loincloth apron with two roundels.[142] Similar costume is worn by Bird Jaguar on Lintels 2, 3, and 54.[143] Although no single depiction of Bird Jaguar on these lintels exactly matches the costume of the seated stone figure, each of the individual costume elements, except the jaguar helmet, is accounted for. Bird Jaguar (name glyph at A7), however, does appear in a jaguar helmet on Lintel 6 of Structure 1 (fig. 150),[144] which falls within the period of time covered by Lintels 1, 2, and 3 of Structure 33.[145]

Taken alone the costume correspondences between Bird Jaguar and the seated, stone figure would not prove its identity conclusively, for such costume elements also occur in representations of two other rulers of Yaxchilan, Shield Jaguar and Shield Jaguar's descendant.[146] Because the dedicatory date of Structure 33 falls within Bird Jaguar's reign, however, and since the lintels all portray him, it is reasonable to assume that the costume elements are those of Bird Jaguar.

Epigraphic evidence also supports the identification of this figure as Bird Jaguar. There is a partly effaced inscription on the back of the statue which was probably originally composed of four vertical columns of glyphs. Of these, only parts of columns C and D remain.[147] The glyph at D5 consists of the lunar sign (T683a) combined with a T12 superfix and a T104 subfix. This glyphic compound is found as a title or epithet of Bird Jaguar's name glyph in several instances.[148] Significantly, the compound appears as an epithet of Bird Jaguar's name on Lintels 1, 2, and 3 of Structure 33 (Lintel 1 at A5–A6, with T229 for T12; Lintel 2 at M1–N1; Lintel 3 at E1–E2). The T12:683a:109 compound surely forms part of Bird Jaguar's name on the seated statue, for preceding it at D5a there is a jaguar head (T751a) with an elongated superfix which was probably a bird (T236).[149] Considering this fact, along with the date of Structure 33 and the costume resemblances outlined above, the anthropomorphic statue must be considered a full-round portrait of Bird Jaguar.[150]

The determination of the identity of this stone, portrait-statue makes possible an interpretation of the architectural sculpture of Structure 33, since its posture closely resembles that of the stone and stucco figures in the large niches above the doorways (fig. 135). These niche figures are seated crosslegged and frontally portrayed. The strict frontal presentation of both the niche figures and the seated statue is an important indication of high rank.[151] Moreover, the costume elements were apparently similar. Depressions in the chests of the niche figures suggests that they may have worn chest ornaments like those of Bird Jaguar. Remnants of tall feathered headdresses remain on the figures in both of the smaller, stepped niches above the medial molding, and on the large, seated figure in the center of the roof comb, and presumably were present originally on the large niche figures. These headdresses correspond to those worn by the seated portrait of Bird Jaguar, as well as to other depictions of the elite at Yaxchilan. Both the large niche figures and the roof-comb figure are seated on symbols of rulership. The niche figures sit on dragon-head podia, which are commonly found as the bases upon which rulers stand,[152] or as their seats.[153] A three-legged bench or throne supports the roof-comb figure. The bench is a symbol of rulership in the *Popol Vuh*,[154] and depictions of similar benches with seated rulers are found at nearby Piedras Negras.[155] These symbols of rulership, and the resemblances of costume and posture betwen the façade figures and the portrait of Bird Jaguar, suggest that the architectural figures were modeled after men, not gods, and were perhaps representations of the Maya ruler in power at the time of the dedication of Structure 33.

The theme of a human figure seated in a niche relates Structure 40 to Structure 33. Like the large niche figures and the seated portrait of Bird Jaguar of Structure 33, that at the center of Structure 40 is seated crosslegged and frontally. Costume resemblances include what appears to have been a mosaic collar and perhaps a chest ornament. The date 9.16.1.0.0 11 Ahau 8 Tzec, found on Stelae 11 and 12, and Altar 14 associated with the building, marks the accession of Bird Jaguar.[156] There are also references to and portrayals of Bird Jaguar's predecessor Shield Jaguar on Stelae 11, 12, and 13.[157] These references to Shield Jaguar on stelae commemorating the accession of Bird Jaguar, and the placement of Structure 40 next to Structure 41, a building that memorialized Shield Jaguar's conquests, suggest that Bird Jaguar sought to make clear his position as the legitimate successor of Shield Jaguar and the lawful lord of Yaxchilan.[158] The treatment of the façade sculpture on Structure 40 emphasizes the regal nature of the building, for the posture and costume of the figure identify it as a ruler. Seated in its enclosure above the doorway it resembles the portrayals of the Maya lords on the accessional stelae at

Piedras Negras. The niche figure of Structure 40 probably sat on a dragon mask resembling those of Structure 33. A similar dragon mask serves as the seat of a niche figure on Stela I of Quirigua, which Kubler has interpreted as an accessional monument.[159] The absence of the "niche motif" on the monuments of Yaxchilan suggests its possible transferral to an architectural setting.[160] By this hypothesis Structure 40 may be interpreted as a great commemorative edifice, with its niche figure symbolizing the accession to power of Bird Jaguar.

At Bonampak the mural paintings of room 2 of Structure 1 depict a pitched battle and an arraignment scene,[161] while the building's lintels feature the capture of prisoners. This emphasis on violence suggests that the building itself may have been erected to commemorate a military victory of the lords of Bonampak, or of the Yaxchilan area.[162] The figures seated in the niches on the frieze of Structure 1 can be interpreted as representations of the ruler of Bonampak, and perhaps his captains or secondary chiefs. The rigid frontality of the façade figures suggests that they are important personages, for it is the frontal pose which is reserved for the head chief and his wife in the arraignment scene. These niche figures at Bonampak again serve to identify the lordly nature of Structure 1 and the importance of the events depicted in the murals for the ruling family of the site. Unlike the paintings, however, they do not provide us with specifics or a narrative. The seated figures are like dynastic icons, portraying the ruler in majesty and signifying the royal import of the structure, but conveying no more exact information.[163]

Patronage and Portraiture of the House of the Governor

We have now seen that an important tradition of portraiture flourished in Maya art. Moreover, the custom of creating likenesses of rulers was not restricted to the monuments, but existed in architectural sculpture as well, as has been demonstrated at Tikal, Palenque, Seibal, Yaxchilan, and Bonampak. With this in mind, we can now affirm that the human figure at the center of the House of the Governor is a portrait of a human ruler. Furthermore, the epigraphic evidence presented in chapter 5 provides a basis for identifying the name of this lord.

When examined in conjunction with other data, the hieroglyphic inscriptions of Uxmal strongly suggest the House of the Governor was constructed during the reign of Lord Chac. The evidence for such a conclusion is as follows. First, the

name glyph of Lord Chac certainly appears on Stela 14 at Uxmal (figs. 27, 38). Stela 14 is thought to be a late monument at Uxmal, in which aspects of the Classic Maya style are combined with non-Maya "Mexican" traits.[164] One such feature is the presence of two small figures at the lower left who wear long-lipped masks reminiscent of the Mexican deity Ehecatl. Somewhat similar Ehecatl masks are found on Seibal Stela 3, which Graham has dated to 10.2.5.3.10 (A.D. 874).[165] In addition, Proskouriakoff has pointed out that the principal figure on Uxmal Stela 14 wears "Toltec" style sandals.[166] Related non-Classic slipperlike sandals are worn by the figure on Seibal Stela 14, dated about A.D. 870.[167] These details might serve to place Uxmal Stela 14 somewhere in the first half of Cycle 10. More precisely, we have seen that Lord Chac's name glyph also occurs on the painted capstone in Building Y of the Nunnery (fig. 25), where it is associated with a probable date of 10.3.18.9.12 4 Eb 5 Ceh (A.D. 907). This suggests that Stela 14 was carved near that time. By the same token, the House of the Governor is generally acknowledged to be one of the last major buildings of Uxmal, certainly constructed at about the same time as, or perhaps a little later than, the Nunnery Quadrangle.[168]

The most convincing connection between Stela 14 and the House of the Governor is the association with both of a bicephalic jaguar throne. On the platform directly in front of the House of the Governor a two-headed jaguar throne stands on a small, radially symmetrical platform (figs. 16, 46). The alignment of the throne with the center doorway of the building suggests that the two were planned as a unified complex, with the royal symbolism of the jaguar throne complementing that of the House of the Governor. On Stela 14 the magnificently garbed ruler Lord Chac stands upon a bicephalic jaguar throne whose basic form resembles the one at the House of the Governor. It seems probable that the jaguar throne of the stela was intended to depict the actual sculpture at the House of the Governor, in which case we may suppose that it was at one time used as a royal seat by Lord Chac.[169]

The date 10.3.18.9.12 associated with Lord Chac's name glyph falls less than a year after another date, 10.3.17.12.1 5 Imix 18 Kankin, on a similar painted capstone from the East Structure of the Nunnery (fig. 25).[170] Although the name Lord Chac does not appear in the earlier text from the East Structure, we might nevertheless suppose that he was in power at the time. Like the House of the Governor, the East Structure of the Nunnery is generally conceded to be a late building at Uxmal.[171] Moreover, it shares several distinctive architectural features with the House of the Governor. Both buildings have extremely fine facing masonry, and both have recessed panels framing the doorways (figs. 58, 140). The most striking parallel between the two structures occurs in the upper façades. At the East Structure of the Nunnery, six tiered, trapezoidal arrangements of two-headed serpent bars adorn the frieze (fig. 140). These serpent bar schemes almost exactly duplicate the arrangement of tiered, two-headed serpent bars with hieroglyphic bodies at the center of the House of the Governor (fig. 113). These architectural correspondences between the East Structure of the Nunnery and the House of the Governor indicate that the buildings were erected very close in time. Thus, Lord Chac, who we know to have been in power when the Nunnery capstones were painted, was quite likely the ruler of Uxmal when the House of the Governor was constructed. From this, coupled with the fact that Lord Chac appears on Stela 14 standing on a jaguar throne like that in front of the House of the Governor, we may suppose the entire edifice was commissioned by and dedicated to this ruler, and that the headless, nameless figure of the central motif originally portrayed Lord Chac of Uxmal. It now seems doubly unfortunate that the sculptured wooden lintel from the House of the Governor perished in flames,[172] for its hieroglyphic text might have explained more fully the nature of the House of the Governor and its connection with this ruler.

If, as seems likely, the central figure represents Lord Chac, then who do the other figures represent? Possibly they are simply reduplicated images of the same ruler, spread across the façade as generalized symbols of power. More likely, however, they represent other individuals who held positions of authority at Uxmal. Despite generalized resemblances, each of the surviving figures shows distinctive costume elements, and clothing is often used to specify identity in Maya art. Moreover, only the central figure, whom we suppose to be Lord Chac himself, is glorified by being surrounded by hieroglyphic serpent bands. If the other figures do represent secondary nobles, their symmetrical and hierarchical disposition can be understood as an architectural counterpart of Maya sociopolitical structure. At the time of the conquest, Maya society was distinctly aristocratic, with power centered in the head chief or Halach Uinic, who in turn delegated authority to lesser officials.[173] A similar pattern seems to hold true for Classic times as well, since epigraphic research has demonstrated the existence of dynastic organizations with power centered in successive rulers who were usually members of the same lineage. The flanking figures on the façade of the House of the Governor may thus be interpreted as the deputies of Lord Chac, acknowledging his superior status by their subsidiary placement.

It was an achievement of the architect of the House of the Governor to retain the essential meaning of the accession motif of the southern monuments while adapting it to an architectural aesthetic. The static composition of Piedras Negras became dynamic at Uxmal, with the slope of the tiered serpent bars echoed by the rhythmic diagonals of the great step-frets which adorn the frieze (figs. 54, 107). As the central motif determines the organization of the upper façade, so the House of the Governor, with a manifest symbol of the dynastic power of Lord Chac at its center, must have played a dominant role in the political and cultural life of Uxmal and the surrounding region.

CHAPTER 11

Mask Panels

Among the most distinctive elements of the sculptured frieze of the House of the Governor are the long-snouted mask panels (figs. 151–153). These are conventionalized depictions of grotesque, frontal faces with features adapted to a rectangular space. The masks are constructed according to a technique whereby individual facial parts are carved on separate stones and later combined on the façade to form the entire face. Each piece is carved in a low-relief style of great precision and finish, with facial features clarified by raised borders of more or less uniform width. Scroll patterns are used for anatomical and decorative detail. The scrolls strike a balance between curvilinearity and rectilinearity, while conforming to the dominant, rectangular composition. Mosaic masks resembling those of the House of the Governor are encountered frequently on other Puuc structures. They normally share a number of major features, the most striking of which is an elongated snout which curves upward or downward (fig. 141).[1]

On the foreheads of the masks at the House of the Governor is a headband or wreath of overlapping segments, probably representing featherwork ping segments, probably representing featherwork (fig. 151). At the center of the headband is a rosette. The eye sockets are somewhat squared, with the upper brow arching over a tabular "eyelid" and the suborbital plate a U-shaped bracket around the bottom and sides of the eyeball. The eyeballs are semi-spherical with inscribed spiral pupils. The supraorbital plate (brow) has a scroll design with three (or occasionally two) large circles inside and two pairs of small disks set along the upper edge. On the suborbital plate is a star symbol or hieroglyph for the planet Venus, consisting of two disks separated by a curvilinear band.[2] The mouth has only an upper jaw filled with teeth. At the center are two vertical incisors and adjacent are two scrolllike fangs. Two other fangs appear beneath each suborbital plate. At the corners of the mouth are forked scrolls which Seler interpreted as molars.[3] The inner scroll, thinner and lacking an incised border, possibly is related to the tongues that protrude from other versions of these masks. Above the mouth is a protruding, downcurving snout, bordered on each side by a raised band and ornamented with a line of disks (figs. 152–153). On

Fig. 151.
House of the Governor,
drawing of typical mask
panel (after Seler
1917:abb. 115).

Fig. 152. *House of the Governor, side view of masks on west façade.*

Fig. 153. *House of the Governor, masks at northwest corner of south wing.*

top of the snout is a nasal scroll, above which is a bundlelike ornament.[4] Flanking the face are square earplugs with a striated border. Above these are feathered ear scrolls, and below are pendant scrolls. At each side is a low-relief panel bearing a stylized and condensed version of a serpent head. All of the masks on the building replicate one another in their principal features, with only slight variations, suggesting that all were carved for a single building campaign.[5]

At the House of the Governor columns of five-mask panels are placed at the corners of the frieze on each structure (figs. 58, 63, 153). Five-mask tiers are also situated in the middle of the friezes of the north and south wings, as well as spaced along the west frieze of the building (figs. 3–4, 57). The masks of the east frieze form a more compelling integrative device. They are arranged in pyramidal

fashion to form a zigzag rhythm winding across the entire façade, a unique usage of masks in the Puuc region (figs. 54, 106–107). These diagonal stairstep patterns also form trapezoidal canopies that frame the naturalistic human figures on the façade. The rhythmic repetition of the stepped canopies firmly allies the composition of the wings with that of the central building.[6]

Origins

Herbert Spinden applied the general term "mask panel" to long-snouted masks like those of the House of the Governor,[7] while Proskouriakoff grouped the Puuc masks in a class of stylizations characteristic of Classic Maya art which she termed "grotesques."[8]

The use of such grotesque architectural masks is not restricted solely to the Puuc region, but also occurs from very early times in the southern Maya cities, in the Rio Bec and Chenes areas, as well as at Chichen Itza. Although the forms and construction techniques of the southern Maya masks differ, the basic concept of adorning buildings with long-snouted reptilian or ophidian masks is shared, suggesting some continuity of tradition and meaning between the southern Maya masks and those of the Puuc area. This shared emphasis on masks in architecture serves to distinguish Maya buildings from those of Mesoamerican neighbors, where few comparable architectural masks exist.[9]

The roots of the masking tradition are firmly embedded in the Maya region and extend far back in time. At Uaxactun the late Pre-Classic pyramid E-VII-Sub had eighteen large masks flanking the stairways.[10] At each stairway a triple-ramped composition was formed by four masks on heavy, projecting masonry blocks. The two lower blocks bore serpent-form masks, while the upper had large anthropomorphic faces with squarish eyes and filed frontal teeth like those of the Sun God of later Maya art. Two more masks embraced the small stairway leading to the temple. They were constructed of an armature of roughly cut stones supporting a thick coat of modeled plaster.

The masks at Uaxactun are not a unique example of this tradition in the Pre-Classic period. Structure 5-D-Sub-1-1° at Tikal was built shortly before the time of Christ and shares with E-VII-Sub at Uaxactun the concept of setting the main stairway into the body of the pyramid and the tripartite division of the stair by imposing masonry blocks. Two large masks of stucco over stone flanked the entrance to the crowning temple.[11]

Two Pre-Classic structures, 6B and 5C-second, at Cerros, Belize, also are decorated with large, grotesque, full-face masks. They are made of modeled plaster over masonry armatures and have additional details in polychrome fresco painting. Freidel believes they correspond in date to Structure 5D-Sub-1-1° at Tikal.[12]

Early Classic versions of stucco-modeled mask panels occur at Holmul in the Peten. The east face of the platform of Building A of Group II, which dates earlier than 9.5.0.0.0 (A.D. 535), was a huge serpent mask built of recessed planes of masonry covered with stucco. Two smaller mask panels adorned the south corner façade.[13]

Although the style varied through time, the use of architectural masks persisted through the Late Classic period in the Peten and Usumacinta River areas. At Late Classic Nakum, masks were com-

posed of a rough framework of projecting stones covered with thick stucco to which the final modeling and detail is administered.[14] The Nakum masks are simpler than those of northern Yucatan. They share several basic features such as spiral-pupiled eyes, scroll-shaped fangs in the mouth, and ornamented earplugs, but lack many of the characteristic Puuc elements such as rosettes, bundle elements, and complicated linear and dotted designs.[15]

Variations of such stucco-modeled mask panels also occur at Piedras Negras, Yaxchilan, and Palenque. At Piedras Negras eight large masks on projecting masonry blocks flanked the stairway of Structure 5-K-1st.[16] The masks are adapted to a rectangular area, but are modeled in a more curvilinear and organically integrated style than those of Yucatan. Similar stucco masks occur at Yaxchilan on Structure 33, where a series of human figures sit on serpent mask panels with squared eyes and rectangular mouths (fig. 135).[17] Stucco masks on rough stone armatures were also applied to the façades of several buildings at Palenque.[18]

Long-snouted masks like those of the Puuc region also adorned some of the buildings at Palenque.[19] The exact setting of the fragments of these masks is undetermined, but they are interesting because, like the long-snouted masks on Temple 22 at Copan (fig. 155), they suggest a certain continuity of form between the northern and southern Maya areas, even though the stylistic expression of that form may vary considerably.

The technique of adorning buildings with stucco masks was also employed during the Early Period in northern Yucatan. Each stairway of the top terrace of the radially symmetrical pyramid at Acanceh was flanked by two large masks modeled in stucco. These were basically anthropomorphic and surrounded by scrolls.[20] Stylistic connections with Early Classic Peten structures suggest a similar date for the Acanceh Pyramid,[21] but recently Andrews V has suggested that the possibly contemporary Stucco Temple at Acanceh, with its "Mexican" influenced façade, was constructed during Tepeu 2 times, or about A.D. 700.[22]

Early versions of architectural masks also appear at Dzibilchaltun on the Temple of the Seven Dolls, which was probably built near the beginning of the eighth century A.D. (fig. 154).[23] The upper façades of the Temple of the Seven Dolls were covered with elaborate carved stucco motifs, including large masks above the doorways and at the corners.[24]

The architectural masks of the House of the Governor also may be compared with those of Temple

Fig. 154. Dzibilchaltun, Temple of the Seven Dolls.

22 at Copan (fig. 155).[25] At each corner of this structure are two identical, superimposed masks with large rectangular eyes, bordered above by scroll type supraorbital plates, and below by a thin strip and small scroll. The eyes are partly covered by an incised, featherlike eyelid. The mouth contains molar-type teeth, and scrolls protrude from the corners. The creature depicted has a long recurved snout like those of the Uxmal masks. The most salient symbolic motif that appears on these Copan masks is a triangular grouping of disks, found on the upper surface of the snout and within each supraorbital plate. This motif is commonly found in the glyph cauac, the nineteenth day of the Maya calendar.[26] The long-snouted heads containing these markings have been referred to as cauac heads or the cauac monster.[27]

At the foot of the platform of Structure 22 were found fragments of masks that resemble those set at the corners. They are long-snouted cauac masks with scrolls at the corners of the mouth. Maize vegetation sprouts above the earplugs. This may be cognate to the more schematized scrolls that flank the masks of the House of the Governor (fig. 151).

A number of these masks were probably situated in the upper zone on all four sides of Structure 22.[28] This repetitive use of masks is reminiscent of the Puuc examples.

The architectural masks from southern Maya sites all share enough basic features with those of the House of the Governor to form a common tradition. As Kubler has pointed out, however, such earlier versions all share a more or less naturalistic and curvilinear approach to form, and seem encrusted on buildings or terraces so that there is an incomplete interaction between the masks and the structures they adorn.[29] In the Puuc area such masks were redesigned as mosaic assemblages of separable carved stone elements whose sharply cut designs and geometric forms were adapted to an architectural aesthetic.

Intermediate in time and space between the modeled stucco façades of the south and the geometric Puuc masks are the forms found on Rio Bec and Chenes buildings, where many masks show a mixture of cut-stone and modeled stucco techniques. Kubler defined two different types of architectural sculpture in these sites, one curvilinear and one

Fig. 155. Copan, Structure 22, west corner mask (after Trik 1939: Plate 11a).

like those on the upper courtyard of Structure IV at Becan,[32] as well as stepped *tau* designs in the medial molding. This combination of curvilinear and rectilinear ornament suggests that the two approaches were not mutually exclusive.[33]

Some of the earliest masks at Uxmal are those on Structure 1 west of the House of the Governor (fig. 156). The upper façade of Structure 1 carried long-snouted corner masks. The snouts lack the raised borders or interior designs found on the masks of the House of the Governor. Like Kubler's Rio Bec rectilinear masks, these are composed of stone elements cut before setting and assembled on the façade.[34] The individual elements have deep grooving to indicate the main detail on features such as the earplugs or orbital plates, but the incision is rather irregular, suggesting that the later detail was executed in stucco. The final effect of these masks probably resembled that of the corner masks of Structure 2 at Hochob (fig. 92). There the masks are more complete, and the working method clearly involved cutting most of the stone elements before assembling them on the façade and subsequently using stucco to create fine detail.[35]

The masks on Structure 1 at Uxmal are probably among the earliest masks in the Puuc area. The building they decorate is of Chenes design and construction and was undoubtedly built during the period of architectural activity in the Chenes area to the south, between about 600 and 830. More specifically, Ruz found a vessel of Dzibilchaltun Fine Orangeware during excavations in this structure. Andrews V believes this ware probably dates from

rectilinear, and supposed that the rectilinear versions occurred later because of their resemblance to Puuc architecture. According to this scheme, examples of the curvilinear masks occur on the mask towers at Hormiguero, Payan, and Xpuhil (fig. 90),[30] while the rectilinear approach occurs at Becan, Xaxbil, and Okolhuitz (fig. 136).

Kubler's suggestion of movement from curvilinear toward rectilinear forms through time is probably basically correct, but the difficulty of maintaining a rigid distinction is illustrated at Chicanna Structure 1. Structure 1 was built during the Bejuco phase, perhaps about A.D. 600–700.[31] Panels on the front façade held stacked masks, only fragments of which survive, but which show that the designs were basically curvilinear with all final detail realized in stucco. Nevertheless, a recessed panel on the north end of the building contain countersunk cross motifs

Fig. 156. Uxmal, Structure 1 west of House of the Governor, masks on northeast corner of upper façade (after Pollock 1970: fig. 95a).

the first half of Tepeu 2, or about A.D. 700–750.[36] This indicates that the idea of using mosaic mask panels probably came to the Puuc area from the Rio Bec and Chenes regions to the south. This is further supported by the fact that although the western Puuc sites have many architectural traits which seem to be forerunners of the eastern Puuc, mosaic masks are extremely rare in the west.[37]

The masks of the Great Pyramid mark an intermediate step from the relatively simple masks of Structure 1 to the complex masks of the House of the Governor (fig. 157). The corner masks of the central façade have more detailing on the individual stone pieces than those of Structure 1. Unlike the masks of the House of the Governor, however, the separate blocks are carved in the shape of the motif they depict, so that there is a good deal of space left between each element. This space was undoubtedly filled with plaster, suggesting that the final effect still relied on stucco modeling to some extent. The same can be said for the masks on the northwest corner of the upper structure (fig. 157). Here the orbital plates are large, rounded forms with imprecise and lightly carved interior detail. This contrasts with the deeply cut detail on the corresponding pieces of the House of the Governor (figs. 112, 153).

We have previously shown that the East and West Structures of the Nunnery and the House of the Governor are among the last major edifices built at Uxmal. Their architectural sculpture thus defines the style of Late Puuc mask panels (fig. 186). Although these masks vary in appearance, they do share important formal features. For example, they are carved of clearly defined, separable, stone pieces assembled on the façade to form the image.[38] Each of these mosaic pieces has a basically rectangular outline, into which the separate carved motifs are fitted. The carving of the designs on squared blocks allows a close fit between the mask pieces and permits the entire mask to fit into a rectangular area on the façade. Within the masks themselves the lines tend to echo this rectangularity, and the curved forms tend to be tightly coiled or bent at right angles so as to fit neatly within the block. Such style traits indicate an attempt to harmonize the lines of the masks with those of the buildings. Late Puuc masks also resemble the structures they adorn by the sharpness with which their forms are cut. Bands, disks, feathers, rosettes, and other motifs are defined clearly and must have relied on plaster only for added color, not for final sculptural detail. As with other forms in Puuc architecture,

Fig. 157. Uxmal, Great Pyramid, west section of north façade, masks at northwest corner.

the geometric elements of the late masks enhance the chiaroscuro effects produced by the strong sunlight of Yucatan.

Iconography

Long-snouted masks are among the most typical and distinctive architectural sculptures on the buildings of the Puuc region. As we have seen, mask panels have a long history in Maya architecture, and masks of various forms often were used to embellish platform terraces, doorways, upper and lower façades, and roof combs. In the Puuc area this mask cult reached a peak development, with masks proliferating on the façades of cut-stone buildings, and in many instances forming the chief element of architectural sculpture. At the Codz Poop of Kabah,

Fig. 158. Kabah, Codz Poop (Structure 2C6), section of west façade. Hieroglyphic platform in foreground.

for example, almost every square inch of the façade is blanketed by long-snouted visages (fig. 158). At the House of the Governor, masks in columns adorn the corners of the building and are set at intervals along the north, west, and south frieze, while a unique sequence of stepped mask canopies graces the principal façade. From their distinctive long-snouted form, as well as from their integral role in architectural composition, it is clear that the Puuc mosaic masks function as elements of a symbolic system that was of great importance to their creators. A study of their meaning will undoubtedly tell us much about the House of the Governor.

Unfortunately, our investigation is hampered by the fact that no interpretation of the masks is given in native Maya sources. Early descriptions of Yucatecan façades by the Spanish conquerors are often brief and sketchy, paying scant attention to an analysis of meaning. Bernal Díaz del Castillo provides such an early view of Maya architecture in his

1517 description of the Maya town of Ah Kin Pech (Campeche):

They led us to some large houses very well built of masonry which were the Temples of their Idols, and on the walls were figured the bodies of many great serpents and other pictures of evil-looking Idols. These walls surrounded a sort of Altar covered with clotted blood. On the other side of the Idols were symbols like crosses, and all were colored.[39]

Early Spanish accounts of the House of the Governor, such as those of Ciudad Real or Cogolludo, praise the artistry of its builders, but neither describe nor suggest any interpretation of the meaning of the mask panels.[40]

The first interpretation of meaning was provided by Jean Frederic M. de Waldeck in 1838. Believing that there was strong Asiatic influence in Maya art, he interpreted the masks, with their long, curving snouts, as elephant heads with curling trunks (fig.

152). The side fangs of the masks were taken to be tusks.[41] Since Waldeck's time it has been demonstrated that elephants had been extinct in the New World for thousands of years at the time when Uxmal and other Puuc cities were built. Despite the farfetched quality of Waldeck's theory, it still strikes a responsive chord in romantic souls.

Various other scholars have attempted to elucidate the meaning of the Puuc masks by determining their origins. Most of these theories have tried to trace the Maya mask back to some original prototype, either in nature or in art, and then have charted the sequential steps in its development.

According to Miguel Covarrubias the Puuc mask panels, which he interpreted as representations of the Yucatec rain god Chac, stem originally from an Olmec prototype. He believed the "werejaguar" of the Olmec—whom he regarded as the "cultura madre" of all Mesoamerica—provided the basis for all the later raingods of Mesoamerica: Tlaloc, Tajin, Cocijo, and Chac.[42] Alfonso Caso, another great champion of Olmec priority in Mesoamerica, expressed a similar idea.[43]

Covarrubias's theory may now strike many scholars as too sketchy, but he was probably correct in interpreting the Olmec werejaguars as distant ancestors of the Maya masks. At the time he wrote, however, the chronological position and stylistic character of Izapan art had not been fully defined, and so he overlooked the link it provided between Olmec and Maya art and culture. Late Pre-Classic sites such as Izapa, Chiapa de Corzo, Kaminaljuyu, El Baul, and Abaj Takalik are now recognized as heirs to and bearers of important traits of Olmec civilization, as well as innovative formulators of several key traits of later Maya civilization such as the stela and altar complex and the Long Count dating system.[44] In addition, prototypes of the long-snouted supernaturals of Maya art are found in the long-lipped figures that are a diagnostic element of Izapan-style art. The Izapan long-lipped heads probably derive from certain of the thick-lipped Olmec werejaguar figures, but take on a greater reptilian aspect that was then continued among the Classic Maya.

Writing earlier than Covarrubias, Spinden believed that the dominant model for many of the long-snouted creatures in Maya art was the serpent, whose conventionalized form was exaggerated, elaborated and to a certain degree anthropomorphized by the Maya artists.[45] The geometric masks of northern Yucatan were interpreted as serpent faces, with the long, downward or upward curving snouts representing the extended upper lip of the serpent as it is often depicted in Maya art. Spinden further inclined to the belief that the majority of the masks were conventionalizations of the feathered serpent (Kukulcan), although he considered it possible that the masks might be representations of the Maya Long-Nosed God (i.e., God B or God K).[46]

As noted earlier, when Spinden wrote of the masks in 1913, the Puuc buildings were thought to be remains of the Maya "New Empire" that flourished after the abandonment of the southern cities during a period when northern Yucatan was subjected to heavy highland Mexican influences. Thus, he found it logical to suppose that the masks, with their "feathered eyelids," depicted the feathered serpent, a deity linked with the religious cults of central Mexico.

Spinden's identification no longer seems tenable in light of present evidence. Foncerrada notes that his hypothesis does not square with archaeological facts. The Puuc ruins have been shown to be of greater antiquity than Spinden supposed, overlapping in time with the Late Classic period in the south and substantially abandoned at or shortly after the time of the major Toltec occupation of Chichen Itza. In at least one instance where masks are shown with serpent bodies, the serpents clearly are not feathered (fig. 163). Foncerrada also notes that the mask is an iconographic form common to the entire Maya area, which would preclude its use as a feathered-serpent symbol. She believes that it is:

difficult to trace the natural prototype from which it [the mask panel] originated. I am inclined to think that the physiognomic traits that characterize it resulted from the fusion of feline, ophidian and human elements, which, from very remote times, stimulated the Maya imagination to create a religious image that was simultaneously animal, monster and human being.[47]

In addition, it should be noted that the masks' feathered eyelids, which Spinden took as a symbol of the feathered serpent, are often found on representations of the cauac monster during the Classic period. This is evident at Copan Temple 22, where we have seen that long-snouted masks with cauac markings adorn the corners of the building (fig. 155).

Foncerrada has criticized the approaches of both Spinden and Covarrubias because they seek to trace the basic imagery of an art style to a single natural source, thereby placing undue emphasis on iconog-

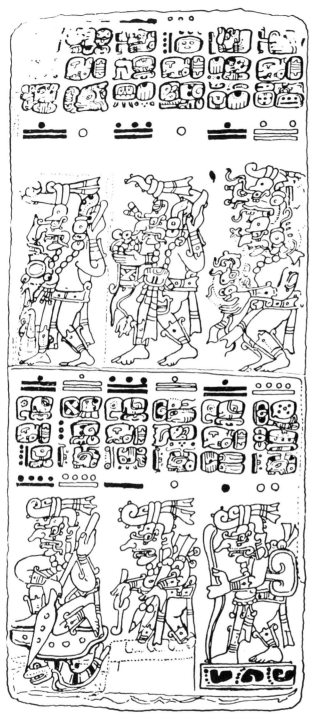

Fig. 159. Representations of God B on page 65 of the Dresden Codex (after Villacorta and Villacorta 1930:140).

Fig. 160. God K as regent of the Ben years on page 25 of the Dresden Codex (after Villacorta and Villacorta 1930:60).

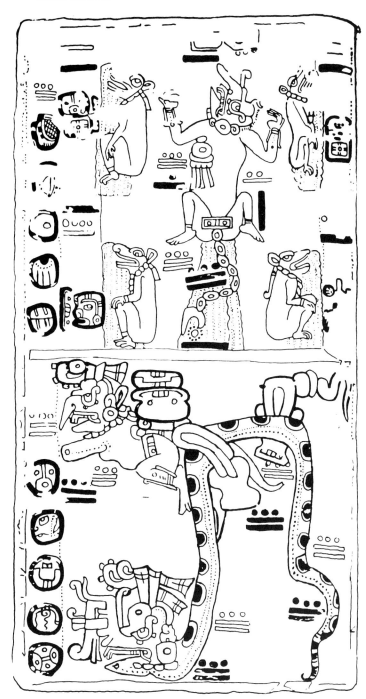

Fig. 162. Chichen Itza, Temple of the Chac Mool, seated figure from fresco on south bench (after Roys 1967:fig. 2, with additions supplied by author).

Fig. 161. God B riding God K (in serpent form) on page 31 of the Madrid Codex (after Villacorta and Villacorta 1930:286).

raphy rather than style. While recognizing the important role that the jaguar and serpent have played as religious symbols in Maya art, she points out that manifestations of these two animals appear in most other Mesoamerican art styles as well. Thus, for Foncerrada:

> The iconographic analysis serves to trace the origin and the antiquity of the cult of these animals, but in a certain sense, it is incapable of defining the "will to art" or the essential motivation that determines the particular form in which each culture resolves the problem of style.[48]

Seler, in his 1917 study of Uxmal, suggested that the Puuc mask panels, with their upward or downward curling snouts, represent the two Gods K and B who appear in the Maya codices (figs. 159–162).[49] Although these deities appear with varying costume and headdress in the manuscripts, their fundamental facial attributes, such as the long, proboscislike snout of God B or the foliated snout of God K, remain constant and can be equated with the downturned or upturned snouts of the masks. Likewise, God B and God K always have a thin ribbon passing beneath the eye and curling downward at each end, often with small dots attached. This same feature can be recognized on the suborbital plates of many of the masks, including those of the House of the Governor (fig. 151). The masks of the House of the Governor also have hooks inscribed on their large, round eyes. Similar hooks often appear in the large eyes of God B or God K in the codices, where they have been interpreted by Thompson as signifying the animal nature, in this case ophidian or reptilian, of the gods.[50]

Seler's study of the masks remains convincing in broad terms, and various other scholars have supported the identification of the masks with God B or God K. Seler points out that God B is represented differently in the codices according to directional and color associations, and is shown in different contexts "girding himself with the serpent, carrying the torch in his hand, and revealing himself in rain."[51] He identifies God B with Chac, or the Chacs, who were the great gods of rain and agricultural fertility in northern Yucatan.[52] Their cult has persisted until modern times but is apparently quite ancient, to judge from the depictions of long-snouted creatures identified as rain gods in the art of the Classic Maya and in the Post-Classic Maya codices. Landa furnishes the first reference to the Chacs, whom he calls the gods of the cornfields and the grains. He also associates them with a ceremony for rain, confirming their function as raingods.[53] In his description of the Maya new year's rites Landa mentions four Chacs, each associated with a different world direction and color. These four gods bore the names Chac-xib-chac (red rain god of the east), Zac-xib-chac (white rain god of the north), Ek-xib-chac (black rain god of the west), and Kan-xib-chac (yellow rain god of the south).[54]

The *Diccionario de Motul* suggests that aside from his role as a rain god, Chac, was also considered a Promethean figure and a great civilizer, the god of bread, water (in the form of rain), thunder, and lightning. The entry reads:

Chaac—fue un homre assi grande que enseno la agricultura al kual tuvieron despues por dios de los panes, del agua, de los truenos y relampagos.[55]

The Motul also glosses the word chac as follows:

Chac—significa agua en algunos maneras de dezir.[56]

According to Thompson, Chac probably became the god of the milpas and agriculture because in northern Yucatan the life of the maize is directly dependent on abundant and regular rains.[57]

Most Maya scholars accept the identification of the Chacs with God B of the codices, a figure with a long, pendulous nose or snout, a large eye with spiral or volute pupil, and a mouth that normally contains a thin ribbonlike strand, probably a flickering serpent tongue, dangling from the upper lip (fig. 159).[58] Seler connected God B with the Mexican rain and storm deity Tlaloc. Various attributes associated with God B in the codices that were linked to those of Tlaloc include the serpent (cloud serpent, or lightning serpent, well known attributes of Tlaloc and of the Tlaloque, the storm gods), the axe, spear, arrow, and shield (representing the "rain gods striking where they will with the lightning").[59] Seler's identification of the axes held by God B as thunder axes is further supported by modern ethnography. The Mopan Maya of southern British Honduras called the polished stone celts that they find in their milpas baatchac, "Chac's axes," believing that they are the thunderbolts hurled by the rain god.[60] It was in part because of these resemblances to Tlaloc that Seler suggested that God B could be equated with the Yucatec Maya god Chac, or the Chacs, who were invoked by the people to obtain an abundance of rain.

Several scenes in the codices show God B pouring water from inverted vases or bowls (Codex Dresden 36c, 39b, 67a, 74; Codex Madrid 9b, 13a, 14b), just as the Tlalocs are depicted in Mexican manuscripts.[61] This clear reference to the gods as providers of water confirms their identification as Chac. In the Maya codices God B is associated with world directions and colors that correspond to those reported by Landa, also strengthening their identification as Chacs.[62] According to Thompson, modern-day Maya recognize four major Chacs, known as Nucuch Chacob, "The Great Chacs," with the same color and directional associations. There are many other minor Chacs as well.[63] A few of the Chacs have titles such as "Vulture Sky Chacs" or "Chacs of little profit," which suggest that the rain gods could occasionally be harmful. But by far the majority of their appellatives suggest that they were considered generally beneficent, and with proper supplication they could be counted on to supply fructifying rains.[64]

Since Seler's time several other scholars, including Morley, Foncerrada, and Ruz,[65] have interpreted the Puuc mosaic masks as images of the rain god Chac. Commenting specifically on the House of the Governor at Uxmal, Ruz writes that "the principal motif on the frieze is a mask of the Rain-god, which is repeated and combined in a most harmonious fashion."[66]

Thompson several times has identified the Puuc masks, including those of Uxmal, as "rain dragons," a term that he also applies to Itzamna.[67] Elsewhere he describes the masks on the Temple of the Warriors at Chichen Itza as "rain gods",[68] with the implication that they represent the Yucatec deity Chac. This reflects ambivalence on Thompson's part, for he writes that:

the Chacs, like the Itzamnas, are rain-gods, and have ophidian attributes. It is possible that they merely represent a different manifestation of the Itzamnas, but it is, perhaps, a shade more probable that they are elements of a simpler and older religion which survived, particularly among the peasants, in a rivalry with the more occult deities, such as the Itzamnas, favored by the hierarchy.[69]

The most compelling reason for accepting Puuc masks with down-curved snouts, like those of the House of the Governor, as representations of Chac is their resemblance to God B of the codices. God B's most salient characteristic is his elongated, recurved snout which resembles those of the masks (figs. 152, 159, 161).

Various theories have been proposed to account for the strange, pendulous snout of God B, and by extension those of the masks. Seler believed that the tapir provided the model for the snout, noting the fact that in Yucatan the name of the rain god is found in connection with that of the tapir, Tzimin, as in Tzimin-Chac.[70]

Seler's identification of the mask snouts as modeled on the tapir's trunk is probably incorrect. Although it is true that the word Tzimin is sometimes coupled with the name of the rain god, this association probably dates from post-conquest times and can be traced to a bizarre episode involving the Itza of Tayasal and Cortes's horse. During the march through Guatemala in 1525, Cortes's mount became lame and he left it with Canek, the Itza ruler at Tayasal.[71] After Cortes departed the Itza treated the horse as a god, feeding it chicken and offering it flowers, and the beast soon starved. Many years later, in 1618, when Fray Fuensalida and Fray Orbita visited Tayasal they encountered an idol of the horse made of lime and stone, which the Itza worshipped as a rain and thunder god named Tzimin-Chac, meaning "thunder-horse."[72] The word tzimin can now refer either to a horse or to a tapir, but it is certain that the term was applied to the horse because the horse was the only animal that resembled a tapir in the Maya area. The coupling of the term with Chac probably arose not because of any innate affinity between a tapir and the rain god, but rather because the Itza saw that the Spaniards shot arquebuses from astride a horse. Associating the horse

with the bullet blast, they viewed it as a counterpart of Chac, who produced similar blasts of thunder with his hafted axe. Moreover, in pre-conquest Maya codices Chac does not appear with the tapir, but with the serpent, which often provides his sinuous steed (fig. 161).[73] Thus, the model for the masks is more likely to be ophidian or reptilian. As noted, Spinden equated the long curved snouts with the extended upper lip of the serpent or dragon as it is often shown in Maya art (fig. 142). This identification is also supported by the fact that in the Maya codices Chacs are often depicted with serpent bodies.[74]

Decorating the sides of the snouts is a series of disks or roundels, such as occur on many mosaic masks in the Puuc region. Karin Hissink compared these disks with a representation of God B on page 12 of the codex Madrid, where a naked Chac is pictured in the form of a toad. She writes:

This figure is competely covered over the whole body and the snout with small disks; these apparently correspond to the round disks in the masks. It remains an open question whether these circles represent rain drops or spots, undoubtedly the warts of the toad. In any case, the same marking also appears on a water toad, which brings the rain, on leaf 12 of the same Codex.[75]

This association of toads and the rain god is well known, since toads are still regarded in Yucatan as the "musicians" of the Chacs.[76] On the other hand, it seems possible these roundels may mark the serpentine nature of Chac, since circular patterns adorn the bodies of serpents in the codices. The disks also might have been intended to portray roundels of jade, representing preciousness, and by extension the life-giving quality of water and rain. Green jade jewels, Chalchihuitls, were attributes of the rain and water gods of the Aztec.[77] These interpretations need not be mutually exclusive.

Why were these long-snouted masks, thought to represent Chac, used in such abundance on the façade of the House of the Governor and other Puuc buildings? Seler interpreted their proliferation as a type of sympathetic magic intended to insure an ample supply of rain for the agriculturally oriented Maya of the region.[78] Foncerrada concurred with this idea, pointing out that the Puuc district is particularly suited ecologically to a blossoming of the rain god cult.[79] The Puuc region, despite the fact that its soils are much more fertile than those of the northern plains, is singularly poor in water resources. No cenotes, which supply a continuous source of water in many other regions of northern

Yucatan, are found in the Puuc area, nor are there any permanent lakes or streams. In some areas, low-lying basins known as aguadas were lined to catch rain, but this still water was not good for drinking, nor could it be used effectively for agriculture. Drinking water was furnished largely by the artificial cisterns or chultunes. For the germination and ripening of the precious maize crop the Puuc Maya had to rely solely on the annual rains. Normally the rainy season begins in March or April and lasts to November, but some years the rains come late or have a false start—in which case the sprouts die—or the rains may be scant, causing droughts that could lead to general famines. Famine was a dreadful calamity in northern Yucatan, and apparently occurred with enough frequency that the Maya regularly sought to petition the gods to avert its ill effects.[80]

The great importance of the rain god in the affairs of the Maya of northern Yucatan can be gauged from the fact that his name glyph, T668, appears frequently in the inscriptions of Uxmal, Kabah, and Chichen Itza, but scarcely ever at any other Classic Maya site.[81] At Uxmal, for example, Chac's glyph appears on Uxmal Altar 10 (figs. 36–37, 39), Stela 14 (figs. 27, 38), the painted capstone from Building Y of the Nunnery (fig. 25), and on the Ball Court rings (fig. 26). As is discussed in chapter 5, there is good reason to interpret these rain god glyphs as the name or title of a human ruler of Uxmal who has, for convenience, been nicknamed Lord Chac.

Despite the fact that the cult of the Chacs was one of the few to continue to thrive among the Maya peasantry after the Spanish Conquest, this need not mean that the nobility did not also participate in the cult, or that it was merely a folk religion. As Thompson suggests "Priest, noble, and peasant unite in worship of the Chacs, an understandable convergence of beliefs since drought was a constant anxiety of both the peasant and his parasites."[82]

To conciliate the peasant farmers, whose labor and crops supported society,[83] the rulers may not only have sought to placate the rain gods, but also to establish themselves either as mediators for or direct representatives of the rain gods on earth. This is strongly suggested by the murals of the south bench in the Temple of the Chac Mool at Chichen Itza, where a group of Maya lords wear masks with curving snouts resembling those of the House of the Governor (fig. 162). Roys has commented on these figures:

Chac-xib-chac, a governor or head chief of Chichen Itza, may have taken his name from the red rain god of the east, mentioned by Landa. If this is so he may have figured as a representation of the god. . . . In the Temple of the Chac Mool was found a fresco representing five men wearing the mask and headdress of God B. These may be impersonators of the rain god.[84]

Further confirming this connection between human rulers and the rain deities is the fact that one of the Xiu lords of Uxmal, Hun Uitzil Chac, bore the name of the rain god.

Evidence that northern Maya rulers were considered mediators between the rain gods and their people also is found in the Xiu Family Chronicles and several other native Maya sources. In 1536 to alleviate a severe drought plaguing his people, the Xiu ruler of Mani, Ah Dzun Xiu or Napot Xiu, and his court embarked on a pilgrimage to Chichen Itza to offer sacrifice to the rain gods thought to dwell in its cenote's depths. However, before the Xiu reached Chichen Itza, they were treacherously murdered by the Cocom rulers of the province of Sotuta in a town called Otzmal.[85] The episode is described in the Xiu Family papers as follows:

1537. 8 Cauac on the first day of pop when there died the "rain-bringers" at Otzmal, namely ah Ɔun tutul xiu and ah ciya. . . . napuc chi and namay che and namay tun and the priest euan . . . , men at Mani they were, "rain-bringers" at Chichen ytza then; and there escaped it took place, in 12 Ahau it was, the tun on 2 yaxkin it was, that it may be remembered.[86]

In this document the slain nobles from Mani are referred to as rain-bringers (Maya *ahpulhaob*), a designation that also appears in a number of later accounts of this same incident.[87] The fact that the Xiu nobles undertook a special pilgrimage to the Sacred Cenote at Chichen Itza, where sacrifices were to be made to alleviate drought, and the reference to the lords as rain-bringers suggests that the rulers were considered to have particularly close ties with the rain gods and to be able to intercede with them on behalf of their people.

Both the use of God B masks as royal headgear and the occurrence of the name of the rain god as a lineage name or title of the Yucatec Maya lords suggests that Chac formerly was conceived of not only as a rain god, but also as a supernatural legitimizer of royal authority. The ruler donned the disguise of the spirit and appropriated his name in order to become his earthly agent. Consequently, since the masks of the House of the Governor are related to

God B, they also convey this regal aspect. They are a symbol that the house of the ruler Lord Chac is an earthly extension of the house of the rain gods.

How far can one interpret the arrangement of masks on Puuc buildings as reflecting the world directional symbolism attributed to the Chacs by Landa and exhibited in the Maya codices? Many buildings have the masks placed at their four corners or on all four fronts of the building, suggestive of directional symbolism, but many others have masks only on one face of the structure, or a single mask above a central doorway. Because remaining paint traces are so faint it has not been shown that different masks were different colors—red, white, black, or yellow—which would connect them with specific cardinal points.[88] At the House of the Governor we have seen that mask columns adorn the corners of each of the three buildings. Such columns are also set at intervals along the north, west, south façades. Although difficult to prove, it seems reasonable to suppose that when masks do appear on all four corners of a building the Maya would have recognized their directional significance. It seems possible that the masks of the House of the Governor, aside from providing an accent at each corner, were applied to lend a sense of completeness to the edifice and to set it firmly in an ordered and cardinally oriented cosmos.

In addition of the corner mask columns, the House of the Governor is also distinguished by the unique tiered-mask canopies on the east façade (figs. 54, 106–107). The stepped arrangement of these masks recalls the terraced composition of the Maya heavens as described by Thompson:

There were thirteen "layers" of heaven and nine of the underworld. Although the Maya spoke of the thirteen *taz* ('layers') of the heavens, *taz* covering such things as blankets spread out one above the other, in fact, the thirteen celestial layers were arranged as six steps ascending from the eastern horizon to the seventh, the zenith, whence six more steps led down to the western horizon.[89]

While the corner masks suggest the horizontal arrangement of the Maya world, the mask canopies generally recall the vertical structure of the heavens. However, the mask terraces also form a distinctive undulating pattern, which may have been incorporated as a serpent symbol.

Although it is likely that many of the Puuc masks represent Chac, another figure who may have been a model for some masks is God K (figs. 160–61), a figure appearing on Classic period monuments as

Fig. 163. Uxmal, Chenes-style Temple of Pyramid of the Magician, southwest corner.

the Manikin Scepter (fig. 166). Paul Schellhas was one of the first scholars to suggest that the architectural masks of Puuc region portray God K, writing:

In the head of god K we recognize the ornament so common in the temple ruins of Central America—the so-called "elephant trunk." The peculiar, conventionalized face, with the proboscis-shaped nose, which is applied to the corners of temple walls, displays unquestionably the features of god K.[90]

Seler also related the masks with upward curving snouts to God K, the "god with the branching nose" of the codices. He mentioned several examples at Uxmal, such as the masks of the East Structure of the Nunnery (fig. 86),[91] and the corner masks of the Chenes Temple of the Pyramid of the Magician (fig. 163). The latter masks have serpent bodies,

Fig. 164.
Dzibilnocac,
Structure 1,
God K on a
painted capstone
from the west room
(after Seler
1916:abb. 49).

Fig. 165. Minor sculpture from Copan depicting the
Manikin figure (God K) with Tlaloc features (after Pros-
kouriakoff 1950:fig. 351).

which Seler compares to the serpentine depiction of God K in the Madrid Codex (fig. 161).[92] Karen Hissink, following Seler, also interpreted the masks with upturned snouts as God K.[93]

On page 25 of the Dresden Codex, God K is depicted seated in a temple as regent of the *Ben* years (fig. 160). Although the day-signs listed as year-bearers in the Dresden Codex differ from those named by Landa, Seler was able to correlate the four deities pictured in the central sections of Dresden 25–28 with those named by Landa as regents of the years. Thus God K was equated with the Yucatec deity Bolon Dz'acab, who ruled over the *Kan* years of good omen and agricultural abundance.[94]

There is fairly good evidence that God B and God K are closely related, not only in form but in function. In the codices the augural texts connected with God K often contain the "good glyph,"[95] and he is often contrasted with clearly malevolent deities,[96] indicating conversely that he is a god of life. Several times in the codices, God K's glyph is coupled with that of God E, the maize god, suggesting that he is concerned with agricultural fertility.[97] As noted above, his role as a provider of agricultural bounty is further supported by his appearance in the New

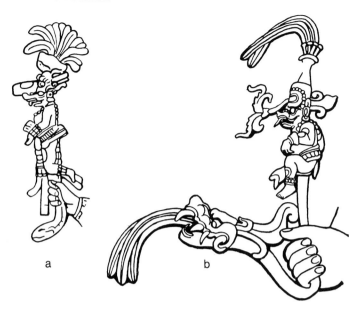

Fig. 166. Manikin Scepters: (a) Yaxchilan; (b) Quirigua
(after Spinden 1913:fig. 47).

Fig. 167. Sayil, Structure 4B1, central lintel (after Proskouriakoff 1950:fig. 102b).

Years' pages of the Dresden Codex (fig. 160). A cor-
nucopialike representation of God K on a painted
capstone at Dzibilnocac also implies an intimate
connection with maize and fertility (fig. 164).[98]

Parallels between the Venus tables of the Dresden Codex and certain central Mexican manuscripts suggest that God K may be analogous with
Chalchiuhtlicue, a water goddess (and intimate of
Tlaloc).[99] A representation at Copan of the manikin
figure (God K) as Tlaloc also supports this identification of God K as a rain or water god (fig. 165).[100]
God K is closely associated with God B both in the
codices and in parallels between the 819-day and
codical texts. This again seems to indicate that he is
a rain deity, for God B is generally acknowledged to
be Chac, the Yucatec rain god. There is also linguistic evidence connecting God K with the word
canhel, and tying Maya rain gods (Chaac, Chauc)
with the cognate words *Cangel* and *Anhel*, providing more evidence of God K's relationship to storm
and rain.[102]

Several representations suggest the masks of the
House of the Governor might be related to the
long-snouted, serpent-footed version of God K who
frequently appears in Classic Maya art as the Manikin Scepter[103] (fig. 166). In its most typical form the
Manikin Scepter is pictured as a short staff, carved
to represent a grotesque figure, and held in the
hands of rulers as a badge of power and authority.
The Manikin's face is a blend of human and reptilian
features. The snout is characteristically the long,
upward-curling variety by which the Maya symbolized the reptilian nature of the figure.[104] The forehead is distinguished by a projecting smoke tube,
celt, or torchlike bundle, from which issue long
curling flares of smoke or flame.[105]

As we have seen, in the Maya codices God K is
easily recognized by his large branching and up-

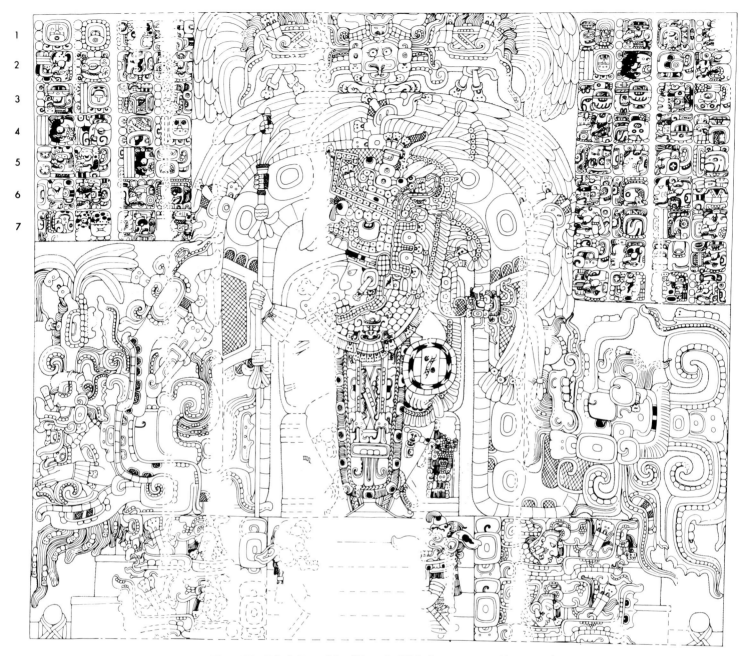

Fig. 168. Tikal, Lintel 3 of Temple IV (after Jones 1977: Fig. 11).

turned snout (figs. 160–161). That the Manikin figure is the ancestor of the God K of the manuscripts is made clear by the latter's name glyph, which features a tubelike or axe-shaped element projecting from the forehead of an anthropomorphic reptilian head. Issuing from the tube is a double volute of smoke or flame.[106]

Comparable features of the Puuc masks and the Manikin figure include the general grotesque, reptilian quality of the face and the elongated snout.

The facial features of the masks of the House of the Governor are related to those of full-figure representations of the Manikin figure on the east, center, and west lintels of Sayil Structure 4B1 (fig. 167).[107] The Sayil Manikin figures have large, bracketed eyes, with pupils indicated by spirals in two examples. The snouts are recurved at the tip in a manner similar to those of the House of the Governor. The ruler depicted on Sayil Stela 5, an early Cycle 10 monument,[108] holds a Manikin Scepter

Fig. 169. Copan, Stela B, side (after Maudslay 1889–1902, 1:Plate 33).

Fig. 170. Copan, Stela B, back (after Maudslay 1889–1902, 1:Plate 36b).

that also appears to have a long, downcurved snout resembling those of the masks of the House of the Governor. Another possible relation between the masks and the Manikin occurs on a sculptured lintel from Xculoc, where a figure wears a God K head-dress with a long curved snout.[109]

Kubler has written of possible functions of both the ceremonial bar and the Manikin Scepter:

The personages (depicted on stelae) possibly represent a succession of priest-rulers, whose rank is marked by the ornate serpent bar surrounding the figure, or carried in both hands. By this hypothesis, the bar symbolized the sky, and it conferred the status of "sky-bearer," or temporal governor, upon its possessor; after the fifth century its use was less common, and an effigy scepter replaced the bar, concurrently with the appearance of armed warrior figures in greater numbers than in early Classic art.[110]

The close relationship between the ceremonial

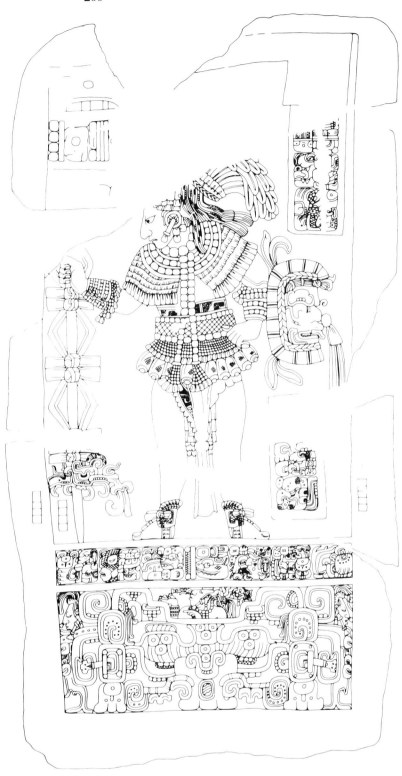

Fig. 171. Bonampak, Stela 1 (after Mathews 1980:fig. 3).

bar and the Manikin Scepter is illustrated by the frequent placement of the Manikin figure in the jaws of the serpent heads of the bar.[111]

It is apparent that the Manikin Scepter, as depicted on the Classic Maya stelae, is a symbol of authority and rulership. There is also linguistic and historical evidence indicating that it functioned as a token of royal power. In the *Chilam Balam of Chumayel*, chapter II (the rise of Hunac Ceel to Power), a battle is described in which several Maya lords are defeated. It reads, "Then Chac-Xib-Chac was despoiled of his insignia. Zac-Xib-Chac and Ek-Yuuan-Chac were also despoiled of their insignia."[112] The "insignia" despoiled is referred to by the Yucatec Maya word *canhel*, which Beltran defines as "dragon."[113] In the Pio Perez Dictionary the word canhel is glossed "dragon, serpiente."[114] This canhel is probably the Manikin Scepter; it is the most common type of portable insignia pictured in Maya art, and its grotesque reptilian head could easily be described as a dragon or serpent.[115]

The artistic and linguistic evidence indicates that the Manikin Scepter was a symbol of royal authority. If the masks of the House of the Governor are to some extent related to the reptilian, long-snouted head of the manikin they undoubtedly fulfill a similar function. Just as the rulers carry their insignia of power, so the House of the Governor carries the masks on its frieze as visible tokens of its exalted and regal nature.

Earlier in this chapter the masks on the House of the Governor were compared to those on the corners of Copan Temple 22 (fig. 155). As noted, the Copan masks are cauac monsters, marked with elements found in the hieroglyphs for the day-sign cauac, which has the meaning of "thunder, storm, or rain" in almost all Maya dialects.[116] Such cauac heads are apparently connected with fertility and vegetation. Linda Schele has pointed out a correspondence between the cauac mask on the back of Stela B at Copan and the tri-headed mask which serves as a base for Pacal on the tablet of the Temple of the Foliated Cross at Palenque (figs. 102, 169–70). She calls this mask motif the "Foliated God" due to the abundant vegetation that sprouts from the mask's head. Other occurrences of the Foliated God (cauac heads) appear on Lintel 3 of Temple IV at Tikal (fig. 168), the altar of Stela D at Copan, on the south substructure of the Palace at Palenque, and on the base of Stela 1 of Bonampak (fig. 171).[117]

The symbols which are the common denominator of the cauac monster or Foliated God, as well as the abundance of vegetation which often sprouts from its head, suggests that it may have been a beneficent spirit, associated with rain and agricultural fertility. These supernaturals probably are related to the present-day Tzotzil Maya rain deities, which are known as Chauc or Anhel. The word Chauc is defined as "thunder," "lightning," and "thunderbolt," and corresponds to the previously mentioned nineteenth day of the Yucatec Maya calendar, cauac.[118] Thompson has suggested that these highland Chauc are conceptually related to the Chacs of Yucatan.[119] Both control the rains, thunder and lightning; both are associated with serpents; and both were probably originally associated with world directions. Bolstering the connections between cauac heads and the chacs is the fact the the Yucatec Maya word chac represents a linguistic borrowing from the Chol Maya word *chajk*, or from the Chorti Maya word *chajac*.[120] Both the Chol and Chorti words are glossed as "thunder" or "lightning" and also correspond to the Yucatec day cauac.[121]

Cauac heads flank and surmount a lord on Stela B at Copan (fig. 169). The rear face of the stela is also a gigantic cauac mask (fig. 170).[122] This surrounding of the ruler with cauac monsters, creatures associated with water and rain, may symbolize the ruler's intimate connection with, and perhaps control over, these forces of nature. By the same token, the heads may be seen as tutelary divinities of the ruler, legitimizing his claims of authority. The gigantic cauac mask on the back of the stela establishes a supernatural locus for the figure,[123] setting him apart from profane levels of everyday existence.

Another cauac head forming a similar supernatural abode is seen on Stela 5 of Piedras Negras (fig. 196). Here the head is gigantic and of architectural proportions, with its upper jaw enclosing a ruler seated on a throne. This theme is reminiscent of the looming, protective figures above the rulers on the wooden lintels of Tikal (fig. 191).[124] Other examples of cauac heads are also known surrounding or associated with lordly individuals, establishing supernatural frames which serve to separate the actions of the Maya elite from those of the lower classes.[125] Because of such associations, Linda Schele has suggested that the Foliated God or cauac monster is connected with the power of office of each of the individuals with whom it is represented.[126]

Cauac heads have been compared to the the masks of the House of the Governor because of morphological resemblances and because they occur in architectural settings (Copan Temple 22). The relationship shown to exist between cauac heads and concepts of rulership also existed for the

Fig. 172. Stela from Hacienda Tabi (Pich Corralche), Yucatan (photo of plaster cast in the Peabody Museum of Archaeology and Ethnology, Harvard University).

masks of the House of the Governor, where canopies of long-snouted supernaturals frame rulers seated on the façade.

Various long-snouted figures appearing as elements of Maya headdresses also may relate to the masks of the House of the Governor. Large and elaborate headgear is worn by persons depicted on Maya stelae at various sites. Early Classic headdresses are composed of single, large, grotesque creatures and most often include a lower jaw which frames the face of the personage wearing the head-dress.[127] During the Late Classic period the lower jaw of the creature is eliminated and the masks become smaller. Occasionally the headdresses are composed of several smaller masks arranged in a vertical stack.

Examples of stacked headdresses are found throughout the Maya area. At Quirigua they appear above the rulers depicted on Stelae D, E, F, J, and K.[128] Stacked grotesque masks are also found on the east side of Copan Stela C,[129] as well as on Bonampak Stela 2.[130] The latter masks have recurved snouts which recall those of the House of the Governor. Long-snouted masks also comprise the frame of the headdress worn by a figure on a stone panel probably from Yaxchilan.[131]

The stacked, long-snouted masks described above relate formally to the masks columns of the House of the Governor. Also similar in form, though not stacked, is a mask with recurved snout on a relief panel from Hacienda Tabi (Pich Corralche), Yucatan (fig. 172).[132]

It is now recognized that the principal figures depicted on Maya stelae, lintels, and wall panels are historical personages, the rulers of the cities in which such stone monuments are erected. The function of the headdress thus is clearly related to concepts of rulership and the identification of the Maya elite classes. As Kubler has noted:

The chief purpose of the stelae was to represent standing or seated human figures, richly dressed and burdened by serpent symbols [i.e., reptilian long-snouted masks]. . . . The meaning of this symbolic system is far from sure, but its proliferent serpent-head elements suggest that the figures garbed in them have transcendental meaning; that they are god-impersonators wearing the shreds of the space of upper and nether worlds, represented by serpent mouths, eyes, and fangs.[133]

The formal correspondences between the headdress masks and those of the House of the Governor suggest a concommitant conceptual relationship. If the personages wearing the headdresses are "god-impersonators" then the masks of the House of the Governor identify it as a sacred space, the domain of rulers whose contact with the supernatural was greater than that of other men.

The inclusion of Venus symbols on the suborbital plates of the masks of the House of the Governor suggests that they are possibly related to other figures in Maya art. Venus symbols are found frequently in one of the heads of the two-headed monster.[134] The rear head is usually a long-snouted creature with a fleshless lower jaw and a tripartite badge headdress, while the frontal head is crocodilian. Venus symbols are often found in the crocodilian heads, such as those of the two-headed monsters whose bodies frame the rulers seated in niches on Piedras Negras Stelae 6, 11, and 14 (fig. 143).[135] At Palenque the Venus symbol is found in the crocodilian head of the great stucco decoration of the northern door of the eastern corridor of House E, while at Copan Venus symbols appear at both ends of the two-headed monster which spans the interior doorway of Temple 22.[136]

At Piedras Negras the two-headed monster forms a cosmic frame for seated figures who have been shown to be historical rulers.[137] The two-headed monster above the doorway in House E of the Palace at Palenque has been interpreted as a royal symbol associated with rituals of investiture.[138] The relationship of the Venus symbol on the masks of the House of the Governor with those on the two-headed monsters again suggests that the Uxmal masks are symbols of royal authority. Aside from this possible general significance, however, it is probable that the Venus glyphs were included in the masks of the House of the Governor for more specific astronomical reasons, since Aveni has demonstrated that the building faces a significant Venus-rise position above the mound on the horizon at the site of Nohpat.[139]

It should be reiterated that there is compelling evidence that the principal model for the masks of the House of the Governor, with their pendulous, downcurving snouts, is long-snouted God B of the codices, or the Yucatec rain god Chac. Although the masks seem to basically represent Chac, however, it is possible that aspects of other figures in Maya art, such as God K, the cauac monster, or the two-headed monster, were incorporated as well. This is possible since the functions and iconography of Chac and these other figures seem to be closely related and to interpenetrate to some degree.

The more generalized message of the masks of the House of the Governor is clear regardless of their exact identity. They are images of supernatural power, symbolizing to the people that the authority of the Maya lord who lived within was divinely granted. The ruler was their intercessor and benefactor acting as a divine agent. Just as the monumental representations of Maya lords show them bedecked with a multitude of long-snouted creatures which distinguish them from ordinary mortals, so the House of the Governor is laden with countless masks of like supernaturals, whose distinctive appearance serves to identify the royal nature of the structure from great distances.

CHAPTER 12

Step-Frets

ONE of the most important elements in the geometric mosaic sculpture of the House of the Governor is the step-fret (fig. 173), a design composed of
a large angular fret or meander and a connected
stairstep pattern.[1] At the House of the Governor
the angular frets occupy two planes, consisting of
a salient outer fret and a recessed inner fret. The
steps are composed of projecting rows of six square
stones set diagonally across quadrants of latticework. The projecting stones were carved either
with a low-relief design consisting of a raised
border and two interlocking triangles (the *pop* or
mat-weave motif) or a series of concentric squares
(figs. 153, 173–74).

Various organizational schemes determine the
placement of the step-frets on the frieze.[2] On the
narrow ends of the north and south wings the pattern is in both cases identical to the viewer (figs. 4,
57, 175), but deviates in symmetry with respect to
the main façade. Each of the end friezes is framed
at the outer edges and divided centrally by mask
tiers. Between the tiers the frieze is divided into
six quadrants, in two vertical registers of three
each. All the quadrants of the upper register contain frets, while the lower register contains frets
separated by a quadrant. This quadrant is comprised of a lattice-ground with two projecting rows
of six square stones set diagonally to form the steps
of two interpenetrating step-frets. The square projecting stones carry the mat-weave motif. Each fret
joins the diagonal at the upper corner and turns
outward. The lower register is thus symmetrical
with reference to the central lattice quadrant. As
noted, the upper registers contain three fret quadrants. On both the north and south frieze the left
and central frets turn clockwise while the right fret
turns counterclockwise.

On the rear walls of the two wings the friezes are
divided centrally by a mask tier (fig. 3). Each of the
resulting two halves contains eight quadrants of
meander and lattice-step panels arranged according
to the pattern presented in fig. 176. The two halves
are symmetrical with respect to the central mask
tier. Subdividing the field into eight quadrants permitted the architect to incorporate two interlocking
step-frets into his design, while avoiding the neces-
sity of placing two frets turning the same direction
next to one another. The diagonally placed lattice-
step quadrants form a trapezoidal area which resembles the organization of the façade on the front
of each of the wings. Most of the square stones
which form the interlocking steps of the step-fret
carry a design formed by three concentric squares
(fig. 174).

A large portion of the rear frieze of the central
building had collapsed before the time of its earliest
exploration and description. Enough of the frieze
remains preserved, however, to suggest the main
compositional outlines (fig. 3). The length of the
extant frieze sections and the position of the one
extant mask tier indicate that the entire frieze was
divided by three mask columns into four fields of
sixteen quadrants each (fig. 177). These quadrants
again contain a series of frets and lattice-step panels
which combine to form interlocked step-frets.

In the preserved sections of the frieze there is
a noticeable deviation from symmetry between the
northern and southern sections (figs. 3, 177). The
first two frets of the north end of the central frieze
are symmetrical to the southern end of the frieze of
the north wing, from which they are separated by
the recess of the transverse vault. However, the
frets at the south end of the central frieze correspond to, rather than reflect, the frets of the north

Fig. 173 (left). House of the Governor, step-frets on west façade.

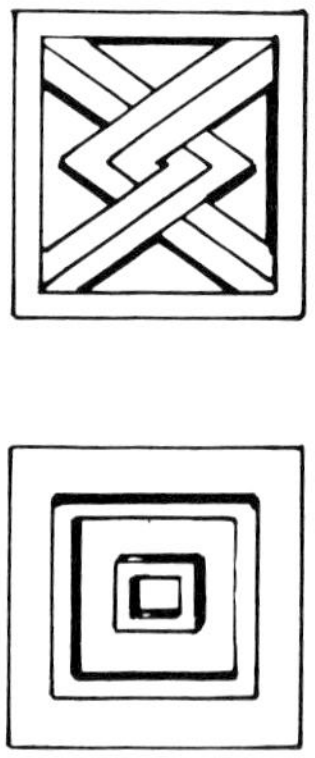

Fig. 174 (right). House of the Governor, designs on square stones that form the steps of step-frets (after Seler 1917:abb. 112a−b).

clockwise turning fret	clockwise turning fret	counter-clockwise fret
counter-clockwise fret	step and lattice	clockwise turning fret

Fig. 175 (above). House of the Governor, step-fret scheme on either side of central mask column of north and south façades (adapted from Seler 1917:schema 1).

a

clockwise turning fret	counter-clockwise fret	step and lattice	clockwise turning fret
counter-clockwise fret	step and lattice	clockwise turning fret	counter-clockwise fret

b

counter-clockwise fret	step and lattice	clockwise turning fret	counter-clockwise fret
clockwise turning fret	counter-clockwise fret	step and lattice	clockwise turning fret

Fig. 176. House of the Governor, step-fret scheme on west façade of north and south wings (adapted from Seler 1917:schema 2).

a

clockwise turning fret	clockwise turning fret	counter-clockwise fret	step and lattice	clockwise turning fret	counter-clockwise fret		
counter-clockwise fret	step and lattice	clockwise turning fret	counter-clockwise fret	step and lattice	clockwise turning fret		

b

end of the south wing. The placement of the lattice-step quadrants of the north and south sections is symmetrical, as are many of the frets.

This conspicuous deviation from symmetry in a structure so meticulously crafted and organized is difficult to explain. Possibly the façade was first applied in the north, with the direction of the first two frets determined by turning them opposite to the final two frets of the north wing. This committed the next quadrant in the lower register to a lattice-step panel. Above this lattice-step panel the second fret of the upper register turns clockwise as does its left neighbor. The third upper fret turns counterclockwise, and is connected to the central step-fret of the upper register. Why the architect employed a fret in the third quadrant from the north of the upper register is puzzling, since a lattice panel placed here would achieve a greater vitality and integration of the façade. The design actually employed may have resulted from transcribing the design of the ends of the buildings to this section of the frieze. The architect may have chosen not to use the lattice panel because the dominant diagonals created by the step-fret quadrants then would have sloped downward with regard to the mask columns.

This problem of downward-sloping diagonals was overcome in the design of the southern portion of the frieze (fig. 177). The more systematic and tightly knit design of this section suggests that it was applied after the northern section. Here the architect managed to incorporate five, rather than four, lattice-step quadrants while still managing not to place one directly above another. Moreover, as with the rear friezes of the wings, no fret repeats the direction of its neighbor. In the resulting composition the steps of the lattice-step panels form

three prolonged diagonals. The two diagonals nearest the mask columns rise toward the column. This mirrors the arrangement of the two wings. The central diagonal, though slightly nearer to the outer mask column, parallels and visually strengthens the upward-sloping inner diagonal. This composition seems superior to that of the north, save that it fails to relate symmetrically to the wings.[3]

The eastern façades of the two wings and central building of the House of the Governor are also governed by an underlying division of the frieze provided by an alternating pattern of lattice-step and meander patterns. Unlike the ends and rear of the building, however—where these elements dominate—on the eastern façade, they form a ground for new elements added to the frieze such as the stepped and tiered arrangement of masks and the human figural sculptures. The secondary role played by the geometric ornaments on the eastern frieze is indicated by the distortion and compression they undergo to accommodate the additional pattern of masks and figures.

Seler analyzed the underlying logic of the arrangement of meanders and lattice-steps on the east frieze of the north and south wings (fig. 178). The lattice-step panels of the east frieze, unlike those of the rear and ends of the building, contain only one diagonal row of stepped squares, each of which connects with a meander quadrant to form a step-fret. This arrangement provides a more systematically varied alternation of lattice and meanders, while still forming eight step-frets; the same number found on the rear friezes of the same buildings.

The ideal configuration of fret and lattice posited by Seler was altered by the introduction of a new organizational scheme for the masks panels. From the lowest masks of the corner-mask tiers, two

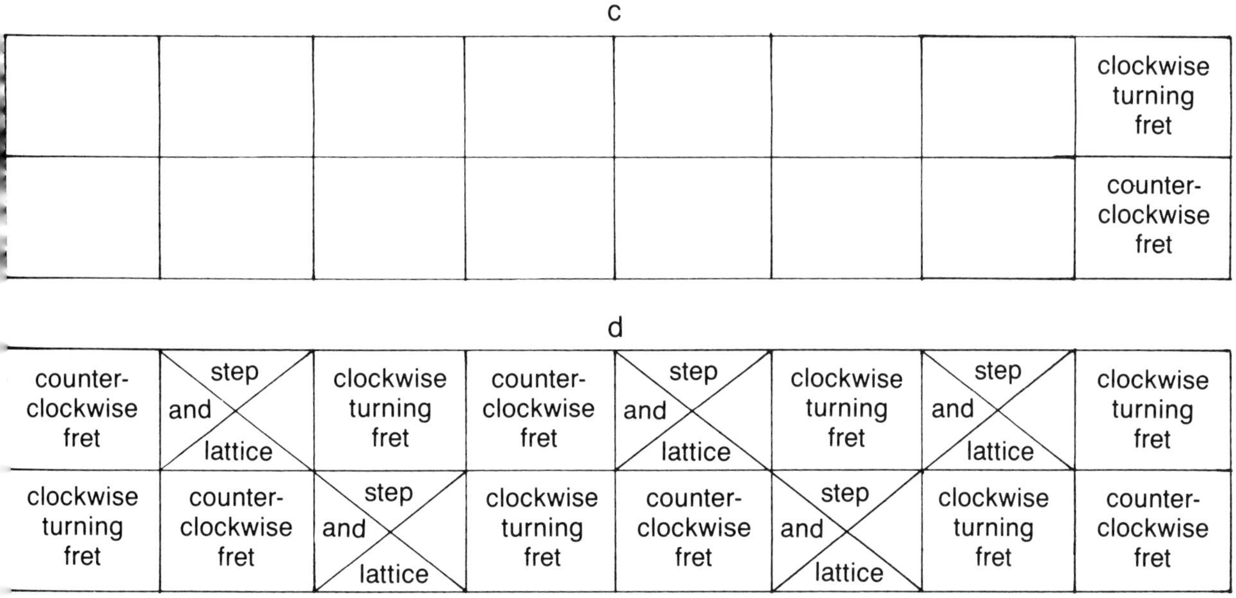

Fig. 177. House of the Governor, step-fret scheme on west façade of central building (adapted from Seler 1917: schema 3).

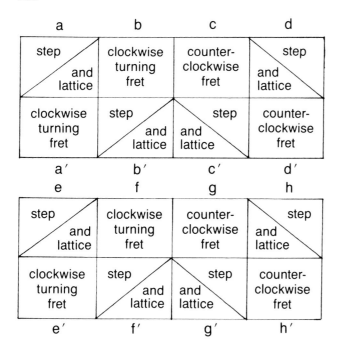

stepped rows of five masks rise diagonally, inclining toward the center to the height of the lower member of the cornice. Between the upper masks of the diagonal rows there are four more masks running beneath the cornice. This arrangement of masks marks a dominant trapezoidal field in the frieze, and forms a canopy for the sculpture of a human figure with a splendid headdress centered beneath.

The additions to the frieze forced the following changes in the fret and lattice-step quadrants (fig. 106). Quadrants *a* and *h* were left virtually intact, while their accompanying meanders, quadrants *b* and *g*, were reduced to miniature frets adjacent to the two uppermost masks of the diagonal rows. Quadrants *c*, *d*, *e*, and *f* are compressed in height by the file of masks below the cornice. The frets penetrate the lattice panels in order to connect directly with the step. In the lower register the fret quadrants *a** and *h** were largely covered by the first, second, and third masks from the bottom of

Fig. 178 (above). House of the Governor, step-fret scheme on east façade of north and south wings (after Seler 1917: schema 4).

Fig. 179 (right). House of the Governor, step-fret scheme on east façade of central building (after Seler 1917: schema 5).

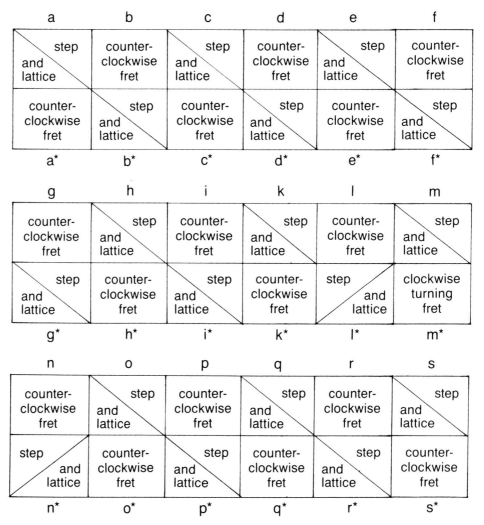

the diagonal rows. Lattice panels *b** and *g** lost their upper halves. Quadrants *c**, *d**, *e**, and *f** underwent slight lateral compression, but none vertically. Thus, the two most complete step-frets are those flanking and framing the central human figure, which forms the axis of a symmetrical and hierarchical composition.

The basic formula governing the arrangement of the lattice-step and fret quadrants on the southern frieze of the central building is given in figure 179. Lattice-steps and frets again alternate regularly in a checkerboard fashion, but the rhythm is more systematic, with the meander of each step-fret turning counterclockwise and connected to a step which ascends to the left. The lower right corners of the lattice-steps of the upper register form a series of parallel diagonals reflecting the diagonal of the trapezoidal tier of bicephalic serpents framing the central figure of the frieze (fig. 54).

One major break occurs in the uniformity of this pattern of lattice-steps and frets. Quadrant *m** contains a meander that turns clockwise rather than counterclockwise. As a consequence the step of lattice quadrant *l** ascends to the right upper corner, where it connects to form a step-fret. The stepped diagonal of quadrant *n** parallels that of *l**. Seler attributes this deviation from regularity to the fact that the fret marks the approximate center of the southern half of the east frieze of the central building.[4] This assumes that the deviation is intentional and expressive.

The general significance of the variation is clear, but Seler's reasoning seems incorrect. If the architect's purpose was to mark the center of the southern half of the frieze, then why choose a fret so obviously off center? The approximate center of the frieze is actually marked by the smaller human figure to the right of the large southern figure (figs. 107, 126). However, the large figure, placed centrally beneath one of the three mask canopies that cover the frieze, forms a more insistent visual center for the southern "half" of the frieze than do either of the other motifs (figs. 107, 118–119). The aberrant placement of this fret can be better explained as a conciliation made to the divisions of the lower façade and the groupings of the doorways of the House of the Governor. This change of direction occurs directly above the section of wall that divides the group of three doorways of the central room from the doorways of the two flanking rooms (fig. 54).

The pattern of masks applied to the frieze of the central building is basically a triple replication of

that applied to the wings. From the lowest mask of the tier at the southeast corner, a row of five masks rises diagonally to the level of the cornice. A row of five masks also rises diagonally to the height of the cornice from the left side of a masks beneath quadrant *m**. Between these diagonal rows a line of four masks runs beneath the cornice. This arrangement is repeated on the north of the frieze.[5] To the right of the mask beneath quadrant *m**, another diagonal row of five masks rises to below the cornice. This diagonal had its counterpart on the north half of the frieze. The space between the uppermost masks of these diagonals contained a file of five masks running below the cornice and above the central motif of the House of the Governor.

The introduction of extra masks and figures to the frieze caused the basic pattern of lattice and fret quadrants to undergo considerable distortion (fig. 107). The quadrants *d, e, f, g, h, (i)* and *c**, *e**, *f**, *g**, *h**, *i** are forced downward and reduced in height by the file of masks above. This also occurs at quadrants *q, r, s,* and *q**, *r**, *s**. Quadrants *k, l, m, n, o,* and *l**, *m**, *n**, are forced upward and reduced in height by the line of masks below. Quadrants *a**, *b**, *c**, *d**, *i, i**, *k**, *o**, *p, p** are largely obliterated by either mask panels or human figures. Meander quadrant *p* has been reduced to a miniature fret adjacent to the mask on its right. Irregular spaces in the frieze are covered either with small frets (*k**, *o**, *p**) or lattice patterns (*c*). With the exception of the change in direction of the fret at quadrant *m**, the greatest irregularity occurs at the southern end, where quadrants *a* and *b* reverse the regular pattern of fret and lattice alternation. Quadrant *a*, which logically should be a lattice panel, is here a fret and *b* is a lattice. This was done because the smaller pieces of the lattice could be accommodated to the irregular shape of quadrant *b*, limited by the diagonal row of masks, better than could a fret. The fret is thus fully preserved in quadrant *a*, with enough lattice-step accompanying it to create a legible step-fret. The height of quadrants *a* and *b* conforms to that of the upper register composed of quadrants *d, e, f, g, h,* and *i* to the north. The narrow space above them contains a third compressed tier of alternating fret and lattice panels.

Origins

The widespread use of the step-fret in Mesoamerican art has made it difficult for past investigators to trace its origins with precision. Rosemary Sharp has provided a recent study of the origins, distribution, and significance in her dissertation on greca, the distinctive geometric mosaic architectural sculpture found in Oaxaca and northern Yucatan.[6] The earliest step-frets known in Mesoamerica occur on Monte Alban II Period pottery from the valley of Oaxaca.[7] Radiocarbon dates for the Monte Alban II period range from 273 B.C. ± 145 years to A.D. 190 ± 95 years,[8] but Paddock believes that the Monte Alban II culture may have had its floruit from about 300 to 100 B.C.[9]

Step-fret motifs also appear quite early in the northern Maya area on Early Regional Dichrome jar sherds from Balankanche cave near Chichen Itza.[10] This ware was placed in the Early Regional Stage (Andrews IV's Early Period) by Brainerd, while Andrews IV believed that the Incised Dichrome Complex is transitional between the Formative and Early periods and was produced sometime between 100 B.C. and the time of Christ.[11]

Sharp has compared the Early Regional Dichrome pottery of Yucatan with the Red-on-Orange Dichrome type of Monte Alban II period date in Oaxaca. The two wares were both produced during the late Pre-Classic period, although Sharp feels that the Oaxaca wares may have been produced slightly earlier than those of Yucatan. She believes that the shared decorative techniques and a common cluster of design elements, including the step-fret, indicate that some relationship may have existed between Oaxaca and Yucatan even at this early date.[12]

Distribution in Mesoamerica

Following its introduction in the pottery of Pre-Classic Oaxaca the step-fret was spread throughout most of Mesoamerica, and was used frequently during the Classic and Post-Classic periods as a motif on a variety of media. The following section is not intended to serve as a comprehensive survey, but rather to illustrate the importance and durability of the motif in the history of Mesoamerican art.

In Oaxaca the step-fret continues to appear after Monte Alban II times on pottery and other objects.[13] Curiously, the motif does not appear on the well-known figural urns of Monte Alban IIIa–IIIb date, although it does occur on an effigy urn from the Nuiñe or Mixteca Baja region of western Oaxaca.[14] In the Post-Classic Mixtec screen-fold manuscripts, step-frets often appear in architectural con-

texts, serving to decorate the friezes of palaces, temples, platforms, and pedestals.[15] Many formal variants also appear on examples of Mixtec polychrome pottery and jewelry.[16]

Step-frets occur frequently on Classic period pottery figurines from Veracruz.[17] For example, the motif occasionally appears on the headdresses of the well-known Nopiloa smiling figures.[18]

During the Classic period at Teotihuacan, step-frets and embellished pottery are also found in several of the painted murals.[19] Boldly scaled step-frets adorn the sides of a bench in the Patio of the Columns in the Palace of the Quetzal-Butterfly (Quetzalpapalotl), probably dating to late Xolalpan times (c. A.D. 550–650).[20] At Tetitla palace, thought to date the Xolalpan phase, a large blue and green step-fret adorns a vertical object that is placed before a hand offering.[21] One of the most striking uses at Teotihuacan occurs in Murals 1 and 2 of Zone 5-A (Palace of the Sun). Here step-frets were employed to decorate the dorsal area of a stylized rattlesnake, while a border above the serpent representation consists of a series of step-frets and a zigzag pattern.[22]

Among the Mexica-Aztec the step-fret continued to be employed as a ceramic decoration and symbolic device in costume. Running bands often served to enliven the surfaces of typical Aztec Black-on-Orange pottery.[23] An audacious use of the motif occurs on featherwork garments and arms of the nobility, as on the resplendent, brightly hued featherwork shield now in Stuttgart.[24]

As noted, in the Maya region step-frets are known to occur as early as the Pre-Classic period.[25] During the Classic period in the southern Maya area they occasionally decorate the garments worn by elite personages, or embellish ritual objects and paraphernalia. At Bonampak a single, large one adorns the cloak of a noble or priest in the mural painting in Room 2 of Structure 1,[26] while the waistband of the haughty ruler on Stela 1 also bears a series of step-frets (fig. 171).[27] The belt of a male figure on a tablet from Temple 21 at Palenque is similarly decorated, and the motif also appears on a basket containing blood-spattered, sacrificial, bark-paper strips at the feet of a noble woman on Lintel 24 of Structure 23 at Yaxchilan.[28] A step-fret design also appears on Stela 14 from Piedras Negras, where it borders the hem of a robe worn by a woman standing below the enthroned ruler.[29]

Appearances of the step-fret are rare in southern Maya architecture. The most important example occurs at Palenque, where one that is bilaterally

Fig. 180. El Tajin, Pyramid of the Niches.

symmetrical and opposed adorns the rear wall of the southeast room in Structure B of the Palace. They also appear on the basement of a construction of the lower east gallery of the Palace.[30] At Bonampak, large red-painted step-frets embellish the sides of the large benches in Structure 1.[31]

The step-fret apparently was not employed as a decorative element in either the architecture or the sculpture of the central Peten district of Guatemala. They do occur, however, with some frequency as designs on polychrome ceramics produced at Uaxactun and other Peten sites during both the Tzakol and Tepeu phases.[32] According to Smith, they also occur during the Early Classic period on the pottery of Holmul and Kaminaljuyu.[33]

Antecedents

It is obvious from the foregoing chronological and areal survey that the step-frets on the House of the Governor at Uxmal represent a motif of long-lasting and widespread importance in Mesoamerican art. It is also evident, however, that those of our building show closer connections with the forms used in certain regions of Mesoamerica than in others, suggesting that these regions had a particularly strong influence on the architects of Uxmal. The architecture of Late and Epi-Classic Oaxaca, Veracruz, and northern Yucatan share an emphatic use of the motif. This fact has suggested to several scholars that these regions had important contacts with one another during this time. We will now examine these areas in order to define several possible direct antecedents of the step-fret at the House of the Governor.

El Tajin was one site where the step-fret was often employed in architecture. It is therefore a likely candidate for providing models for the Puuc architects of Uxmal. Numerous examples of single or bilaterally symmetrical, opposed step-frets exist at the site, where they were normally used to en-

Fig. 181. Atzompa, detail of a greca panel from a patio (after Sharp 1970:fig. 3).

liven the many countersunk and coffered niches that are the hallmark of Tajin architecture.[34] A singular usage of the motif occurs at the Pyramid of the Niches, where boldly scaled ones adorn the balustrades of the stairway (fig. 180).[35] The richest ensemble of step-frets and related meander designs at El Tajin occurs on Edifice A. A sham stairway on the supporting platform of this building is flanked by panels of large step-frets that resemble those on the Pyramid of the Niches,[36] while a horizontal series encircles the pedestal in a narrow frieze beneath a flaring cornice.[37]

Foncerrada believes that the Maya of the Puuc region originally may have adopted the design as a result of trade and contact with the people of El Tajin. She posits that a coastal trade route, similar to that maintained by the Chontal during the Post-Classic period, also existed during Classic times and would have provided channels of communication and trade between northern Veracruz and northern Yucatan.[38] According to Foncerrada, contact is indicated because the architects of Uxmal and El Tajin preferred to emphasize the step-fret in the decoration of their buildings, and also because they employed the motif with the same "formal intention" or "will to form."[39]

Several other indications of connections between the two areas exist. For example, striking Mayalike elements occur in the architecture of Edifice A at Tajin Chico. These include the use of a corbeled vault to cover the recessed stairway, and the treatment of the façade as a false stairway like the stairways of the Rio Bec region's sham temples. The architectural profiles of both regions also share some traits in common. The architecture of El Tajin is distinguished by its prominent flaring cornices, whose sharp contours animate the platforms and terraces. Many northern Maya buildings likewise have the topmost members of their cornices in-

clined strongly outward. The flaring cornices of El Tajin and northern Maya architecture contrast with the simpler cornice moldings of the southern Maya region.

Despite the evidence of some connections between El Tajin and northern Yucatan, however, forms of the step-frets at El Tajin do not match most closely those of the House of the Governor. El Tajin step-frets are invariably simple and single-plane versions, unlike the complicated motifs at Uxmal with their steps of squared stones and two-plane frets. Thus it seems that El Tajin, while it must have participated in an important architectural interchange with the Puuc region, did not supply the immediate forerunners of the step-frets of the House of the Governor.

Resemblances between the architecture of Oaxaca and northern Yucatan have long been recognized. As early as 1909 Marshall Saville remarked on the striking similarities of construction and decorative motifs between the mosaic façades of Uxmal and Mitla (fig. 88).[40] In 1962 Kubler also pointed out several strong affinities between the architecture of Uxmal and that of Mitla, including their common use of open-cornered quadrangles, and their distinctive use of mosaic sculpture on the façades.[41] Within this sculptural system the step-fret is the most prominent shared design.

Early examples of this motif in Oaxaca architecture occur at Atzompa, where simple bilaterally symmetrical step-frets were recessed within the tableros of building platforms (fig. 181). Sharp has termed the field stone and stucco construction style "proto-greca," and suggests that it dates to the Monte Alban III-B period (c. A.D. 300–700).[42]

Later versions of the step-fret become more complex and elaborate. On Tomb 11 at Yagul the Atzompa design is enlarged and subdivided into a central T-shaped form and two linked, opposing step-frets.[43] The form is further complicated on the façade of Tomb 15 at Yagul and on the wall of a tomb at Tlalistac by the insertion of an additional stepped form between the T-shape and the opposing step-frets.[44]

At Lambityeco, an early Monte Alban IV site dated at about A.D. 700, sequences of step-frets flank a stairway of Mound 195. Bilaterally symmetrical step-frets also appear on panels of the south wall of a house group buried beneath Mound 195.[45] These designs were composed of sherds and small bits of stone heavily plastered over, in contrast to the earlier field stone construction at Atzompa and the later volcanic cut-stone façades of Mitla.

Sharp believes that the final versions of the step-fret design in Oaxaca are those displaying quadrilateral symmetry. Such designs occur at Yagul on the façades of Tomb 13 and on the rear wall of Building 1-N.[46] A similar pattern appears on the interior of the cruciform tomb at Xaaga and at Mitla on one of the palaces.[47]

There is reasonably good evidence that the more complicated patterns at Mitla and Yagul date from the final two or three centuries preceding the Spanish conquest. A radiocarbon date of A.D. 1385 ± 85 years is associated with a building on the hilltop fortress near Mitla, and Sharp has pointed out that this building corresponds closely in plan and dimensions with Building 1-N at Yagul and the Hall of the Columns at Mitla (fig. 88).[48]

As we have seen, Sharp has proposed that a strong relationship existed between Oaxaca and Yucatan, contrasting the unitary and geometric character of the cut-stone façades of these two regions with the more naturalistic and organically unified architectural sculpture of the southern Maya lowlands. On the basis of this comparison she believes that the ruling elites of Oaxaca were more closely related to those of northern Yucatan than the northern Yucatan group was to that of the southern Maya.[49]

It seems almost certain, as Sharp suggests, that some connection existed between the Valley of Oaxaca and the northern Maya region during the Late and Epi-Classic periods. This relationship is supported by the strong formal parallels between step-fret patterns such as those of Atzompa, or on Tomb 11 at Yagul and the Portal Vault at Labna (figs. 181, 95), on Tomb 15 at Yagul and the design above the doorway at Rancho Perez (fig. 184), and on the platform of Building 1-N at Yagul and the second story of the Monjas at Chichen Itza (fig. 185). The appearance of such similar step-fret compositions, executed in a related mosaic stonework technique, in both regions at roughly the same time surely indicates some interconnection.

On the other hand, this evidence of contact between Oaxaca and the Puuc region does not necessarily imply, as Sharp believes, that the inhabitants of the Puuc district were Mexican rather than Maya, or that they owed more culturally and artistically to Oaxaca than to the southern Maya lowlands. We have seen that many traits of Puuc architecture and art are closely related to and probably derive from that of the southern Maya. Range-type palace plans, the corbeled vault, the use of masks panels, and the tendency to clearly mark the level of the vault im-

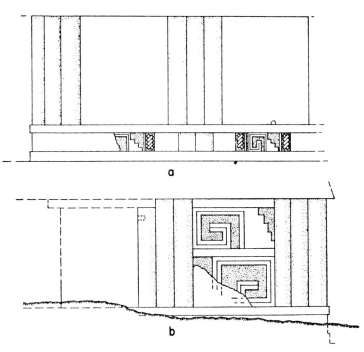

Fig. 182. Xaxbil, (a) south elevation, (b) west elevation (after Ruppert and Denison 1943:fig. 102a–b).

post on the outer façade with a medial molding might all be mentioned as elements of this type. Despite some differences in style, the stela and altar complex and attendant hieroglyphic writing of the Puuc sites seems to stem from that originally developed in the south. At the House of the Governor itself we have seen that the central figural motif is closely related to the niche motif of the accessional stelae of Piedras Negras. All of these traits testify to a Puuc population whose basic cultural orientation was Maya, in the sense of being closely related to the southern Maya, rather than Mexican.

In affirming the basic Maya quality of Puuc culture, however, we should not lose sight of the fact that it manifests many non-Classic or "Mexican" features as noted. Evidence of such Mexican influence at Uxmal is seen in the feathered serpent imagery on the Ball Court and the West Structure of the Nunnery, and perhaps in the tzompantlilike platforms of the Cemetery Group, and in the Tlaloc representations on the North Structure of the Nunnery and the Lower West Structure of the Pyramid of the Magician. Thus the Puuc region seems to have had an art style willing to incorporate foreign elements. It offered fertile ground for the possible introduction of step-fret designs from Oaxaca. On the other hand, it is not likely that such influences flowed only one way, nor were the Puuc architects slavish imitators of Oaxaca greca compositions.[50] As at El Tajin, the step-fret in Oaxaca was kept to single-plane presentations; nothing like the two-plane frets of Yucatan occurs.[51] This suggests that the step-frets of Oaxaca are at best distant relatives of those of the House of the Governor. For closer parallels we must look to the architectural styles of central and northern Yucatan.

The Rio Bec region contains several possible forerunners for the step-frets of the House of the Governor. At Rio Bec itself, for example, large ones were used as framing elements for the doorway of Structure V of Group 1.[52] Step-frets also occur at Xaxbil on the standing walls of the east range of a small quadrangle (fig. 182).[53] Here the basal molding is ornamented with step-frets that are flanked by small *pop* or mat-weave designs, and the southern half of the lower zone of the west façade had a panel containing both a step-fret and a simple angular fret. In the Xaxbil examples the step sections are solid, while the angular frets are divided into two parallel sections by a groove. Apparently the inner portion of the fret was recessed slightly.

On Okolhuitz Structure 1, step-frets are arranged in two vertical columns (fig. 136).[54] These bear a closer resemblance to those of Uxmal than do any from either El Tajin or Oaxaca. At Okolhuitz the step section is treated as a diagonal row of four square stones projecting from the façade, a formal selection that seems to anticipate the one seen at the House of the Governor. As at Xaxbil, the Okolhuitz architects enlivened the fret by breaking it into two parallel planes. This trait probably originated in the Rio Bec region, since the division of the fret has a tentative, linear look, contrasting with the more fully sculptural two-plane frets of Puuc architecture (fig. 173). Such Rio Bec step-frets undoubtedly served as prototypes for those of the Puuc region. The Rio Bec style buildings they adorn surely predate the House of the Governor, which was constructed near the end of the Puuc sequence.[55]

Step-frets associated with architecture are rarer in the Chenes region than they are in either the Rio Bec or Puuc areas. The temple at Dzibiltun had its principal (south) façade adorned with them in a sunken panel on the lower wall.[56] Panels containing step-frets also decorated the ends of the wings of the Palace.[57] Although Dzibiltun is located within the Chenes region its architecture has some Puuc characteristics.[58]

In the Puuc region proper, the number of step-frets resembling those of the House of the Governor proliferates dramatically. It is likely that at least some of these provided direct inspiration for those at Uxmal. In the Puuc area, however, chronology becomes a problem, and it is difficult to be sure whether the step-frets of a certain building were the forerunners, contemporaries, or descendants of those of the House of the Governor.

Judging from the extant portion of its façade, Structure 5 at Xkichmook must have featured step-frets as a major element of architectural sculpture (fig. 183).[59] Here each has a terraced section of three staggered squares and an angular fret on two planes. The step-fret panels are coupled with stepped-pyramid borders, recalling the treatment at Rio Bec Structure V, while the framing of the panels with heavy columns resembles the treatment at Xaxbil and on the Temple at Dzibiltun (fig. 182).

As was mentioned, the architecture of Xkichmook is a blend of Puuc and Chenes styles. The greater use of stucco and less sharply cut stonework of the façades at Xkichmook suggest that its buildings predate later Puuc structures like the House of the Governor. Certainly the step-frets of Structure 5 seem transitional between those of the Rio Bec and Puuc regions. At Xkichmook the two-plane treatment of the fret is sharper and more pronounced than at Okolhuitz, but not so emphatic as that of the frets of the House of the Governor.

Step-frets that closely mirror those of the House of the Governor appear in the Puuc area at Yaxche, Sabacche, Chunhuhub, Xkalupococh, Xlapak, and Labna.[60] At Chunhuhub several large, angular frets appear on the west façade of the Figure Palace. Here the frets are constructed on two planes and flank small human figures placed above the doorways.[61] This framing of figural sculptures with frets resembles the scheme employed at the House of the Governor. Both simple, large frets and step-frets were combined with figural sculptures in similar arrangements on the façade of the Adjacent Palace at Chunhuhub.[62] Among the most impressive step-frets at Labna are those adorning the outer façade of the Portal Vault (fig. 95). There two bilaterally symmetrical, opposed step-frets were placed in the upper façade framing the portal. The terraced sections were built of diagonal rows of square stones overlying a field of engaged colonnettes. The frets branching from this central field consist of two planes set against a smooth ground.[63] At Xlapak, a small ruin lying between Labna and Sayil, the step-frets on the upper façade of a small palace closely resemble those of the Labna Portal Vault.[64] Step-frets were also one of the key elements on the

Fig. 183. Xkichmook, Structure 5, step frets on façade.

Fig. 184. Façade of building at Rancho Perez, Yucatan.

Fig. 185. Chichen Itza, Second Story of the Monjas.

richly decorated façade of a small combined temple-palace building at the site of Rancho Perez (fig. 184). Above the doorway is a complicated version of the step-fret arrangement seen on the Portal Vault of Labna and the palace at Xlapak, while other step-frets appear elsewhere on the façade.[65]

Outside of the Puuc region proper, at Chichen Itza, step-frets embellished the façades of several structures whose mosaic sculptural programs are closely related to those of Puuc architecture. On the Iglesia, for example, the central band of the medial molding contains a series of simple step-frets, while a second sequence forms the base of the roof comb. In both cases the terraced sections are on one plane.[66]

One of the most complex step-fret compositions in northern Yucatan occurs on the second story of the Monjas at Chichen Itza (fig. 185). The lower façades on the north and south sides are covered with large geometric mosaic panels, each of which displays four step-frets in a quadrilaterally symmetrical scheme resembling compositions on Building

1-N at Yagul and on one of the palaces at Mitla.[67] The terraced sections of the step-frets at the Monjas are formed of diagonal rows of square stones that project above a background of colonnettes and spools. The frets are constructed on two planes, like those of the Puuc region.

At Uxmal various forms of geometric fretwork designs occur on structures other than the House of the Governor.[68] Several structures boast simple angular frets alone. These forms are like the meander of a step-fret, but with the terraced section eliminated. Foncerrada believes that the simple angular fret and the related step-fret were probably considered indistinguishable in the decorative art of Mesoamerica.[69] This seems to be particularly true in the context of Puuc architectural sculpture. In addition to isolated frets, true step-frets are also found on some structures.

Normally at Uxmal these framework designs are composed of two parallel rows of sharply cut stones, establishing the pattern on two planes. Each fret consists of a recessed inner course and a projecting outer course. This multiplanar, high-relief design is characteristic of Puuc façades. Under the strong sunlight of Yucatan this technique enlivened Puuc buildings by contrasting areas of brilliantly lit façades with deep, shaded hollows (figs. 141, 186).

At the Nunnery Quadrangle large angular frets alternate with panels of serrated latticework on both the North and West Structures. On the North Structure these frets and lattice panels occur in the upper façade, where they were used between the miniature huts and tall mask columns that mark the doorways (fig. 141). The fretwork composition of the North Structure seems somewhat hesitant and indecisive. In some instances the two frets oppose one another in opposite upper and lower quadrants, but are linked at the center, resulting in an imperfect, reverse-mirror symmetry. Other frets on this same façade occupy upper and lower corners, but are not similarly linked.

The frets of the West Structure of the Nunnery also alternate with panels of serrated lattice, but the compositional problem evident on the earlier North Structure façade seems to have been resolved (fig. 186). On the West Structure the frets are once again linked and placed in opposite corners, but there is a regularity here that is missing in the North Structure, where the architect seemed unable to bridge the juncture between the two frets effectively. This area is problematical since the raised outer edge of one fret must merge with the recessed inner edge of the opposite fret at this point. On the North Structure, because the frets are aligned horizontally, the architect sacrificed some effect regardless of what approach he took. If he prolonged the band of one fret to continue its strong shadow across the entire panel, he faced an awkward passage at the turn of the opposite fret. On the other hand, if he respected the integrity of each fret, an abrupt break in the shadows cast by the forms was produced at their juncture. The architect of the West Structure of the Nunnery was largely able to avoid this problem by shifting the axis of the juncture from the horizontal to the vertical. Thus, although the integrity of each fret was maintained, the shadow cast where the projecting fret abutted the recessed fret was so slight the juncture was unnoticeable. Writing of the West Structure, Kubler noted that the "big key frets scaled to the changing intervals of the doorways mark a broad rhythm across the entire length of the frieze."[70] Because it exhibits such proportional advances, he believes that the West Structure was constructed after the North Structure. The more

Fig. 186. West Structure of Nunnery, fret pattern at south end of east façade.

consistent and successful treatment of the fretwork designs on the façade of the West Structure supports Kubler's placement.

Formal solutions of the House of the Governor apparently represent a final development of the step-fret design in Puuc architecture (fig. 173). New complications and subtleties are introduced in the architectural sculpture of this edifice. On the north, south, and west façades the step-frets have a novel and sophisticated interpenetrating design (figs. 3–4, 57), while those on the east façade focus attention on the principal human figural sculptures, and their diagonal terraces are arranged to echo the tiered arrangement of serpent bars of the central motif (fig. 56).

Iconography

At the House of the Governor, step-frets provide a unifying theme for the entire façade. They form the basic, modular grid division of the frieze and utilize rhythmic changes in direction to focus attention on key points in the ensemble of architectural sculpture (figs. 56, 106–107). Aside from its role in architectural composition, however, it is possible that the step-fret itself may have had some independent symbolic significance to the Maya of Uxmal.

The step-fret is a design that appears so frequently and in such varied contexts in the arts of Precolumbian America that it might be said to characterize the cultures of these regions symbolically, in much the same manner that the ankh epitomized those of Egypt or the cross the Christian cultures of Europe. Unfortunately, it is this very ubiquitousness and depth in time that make the step-fret's significance all the more difficult to interpret.[71]

One of the basic questions investigators have posed is whether the step-fret design represents the final stage in a long process of simplification and abstraction deriving from some important model in nature, or whether the motif is essentially decorative, representing the outgrowth of some craft design. Another problem is whether it should be considered a purely religious symbol, or whether it may be interpreted primarily in aesthetic terms, "as one of the geometric-abstract forms which the artistic sensibility of man has created to enrich, and simultaneously to order, his visual experience."[72]

Among the studies that have sought to demonstrate the naturalistic origins of the step-fret the most important is that of George Byron Gordon. In *The Serpent Motive in the Ancient Art of Central America and Mexico* of 1905 he attempted to demonstrate that the serpent formed the basis of several of the most important art forms of Mesoamerica, including the step-fret.[73] Gordon believed that the rectilinear meander of the step-fret was an extremely rigorous abstraction of the mouth of a serpent viewed in profile. He illustrated his ideas in a diagram purporting to show the progressive evolution of the form from its naturalistic beginning to its abstract culmination. For Gordon the stairstep of the step-fret was merely a stylization of the serpent's fanged mouth.[74]

Herbert Spinden recognized the tremendous role that stylization and abstraction played in the development of Maya art, but he was reluctant to accept Gordon's hypothesis. He believed that geometric motifs such as the step-fret and the guilloche attained their long-lived popularity as a result of their formal appeal, rather than because of arcane symbolism.[75]

In 1924 Hermann Beyer published a study of the step-fret in which he summarized the opinions of several other scholars regarding its derivation and meaning. Thus he referred to Gordon's theories, as well as citing those of Preuss, who believed that it represented a marine shell; Saville, who thought the design depicted a cutaway view of a gourd or calabash; and W. H. Holmes, who interpreted certain forms as symbols of wind or waves.[76]

Beyer himself stressed the powerful formal appeal. Though he pointed out the various natural models proposed by other authors, he also considered the possibility that the step-fret may have originated as a purely formal ornament. Noting the success with which it was employed as a decorative design in many media, Beyer favored this strictly formal interpretation.[77]

More recently Paul Westheim has interpreted the step-fret as a symbol of lightning, a motif that seems appropriately coupled with the countless masks of the rain god that adorn northern Maya temples and palaces.[78]

Marta Foncerrada de Molina has criticized all of the above interpretations, with the exception of Beyer's, because they "imprison the creative process and the creative form within a strictly morphogenetic scheme."[79] She argues that such interpretations fail to appreciate the essential character of the step-fret because all seek to understand the final form solely by reference to a prototype in nature. They view the step-fret as the product of a long process of abstraction in which the image becomes further removed from reality at each step. The process is conceived more as a degeneration from a sacred original than as a progression toward a final formal goal.

Foncerrada, who was influenced by the opinions of Wilhelm Worringer, concedes that the step-fret may be rooted in some natural form, but that this alone is not sufficient to explain the birth of this new symbol. She attributes the creation of the symbol to a positive attempt to create an abstract-geometric aesthetic order that transcends the transient appearances of organic nature. Foncerrada thus believes that the step-fret is a symbol whose extraordinary longevity in Mesoamerica can best be explained by the power of its visual form rather than by an arcane knowledge of its prototype.[80] Despite her desire to interpret the step-fret primarily in aesthetic terms, Foncerrada tentatively proposed that it might also be a stylized lightning bolt, a symbol of rain and rain gods.[81]

Rosemary Sharp, in her new studies of the step-fret, admits that the many contexts in which it appears often render its exact meaning ambiguous, but she nevertheless believes that "without question, the closest association was with the serpent, and very often, with a serpent with rattles and feathers."[82] As evidence for this relationship Sharp mentions the step-fret and serpent connection in the Serpent Mural from the Palace of the Sun at Teotihuacan.[83] Step-frets also adorn a pair of serpents (or a two-headed serpent) on one side of a stone from Placeres del Oro, Guerrero.[84] Sharp has also pointed out a monument from Cholula, a stone carving of a serpent head, in which a step-fret form seems to be blended with the creature's upper jaw and mouth.[85]

If Sharp is correct, then what is the meaning of this profusion of geometric imagery for the Maya of Uxmal? As noted, George Kubler associated the proliferant serpent symbols in Classic Maya art with the supernatural ties of the nobility, identifying them as "god-impersonators wearing shreds of the space of upper and nether worlds. . . ."[86] In a similar fashion, Sharp sees the serpent and serpent-derived designs, such as the step-fret, as potent symbols of power used by Mesoamerican elites. As support for this theory she cites an interesting cross-cultural study of serpent symbolism made by Ting-jui Ho. He has demonstrated that many common geometric designs such as triangles, lozenges, crosses, and zigzags, incorporated in weaving, embroidery, painting, carving, inlaying, tatooing, and pottery of the Paiwan of central Formosa can be traced to the skin markings of the extremely venomous Vorang snake, which is associated with the primal ancestors of the chief family of the village. As a result, all motifs derived from the Vorang's markings have become the sacred symbols of the principal family and commoners are prohibited from using them.[87]

According to Ho, the use of such snake-derived motifs should not be interpreted merely as an aesthetic choice, but is based on the symbolic importance people have traditionally attached to serpents.[88] Extrapolating from Ho's arguments, Sharp believes that the rattlesnake and the fer-de-lance formed the principal serpent images used by the peoples of central Mexico and the Maya region, respectively. She suggests that "These two species of snake were used as possible elite symbols or insignias in Mexican and Maya art,"[89] and that:

Although the interpretation of this symbol may have varied slightly for different groups of people at different times in different places within Mesoamerica, some continuity in meaning very probably existed. This conti-

nuity was most likely associated with the feature though which elites maintain control, that is, the "great and potent power" which both deadly serpents and elites have despite their size. The need for and value placed on power by such elites was expressed through the symbol which represented a deadly snake.[90]

A proper understanding of the step-fret's meaning must accommodate aspects of both Foncerrada's and Sharp's views of its significance. Foncerrada points up the value of interpreting formal systems on their own terms, attributing the peculiar efficacy of the step-fret to its purely abstract design rather than viewing it only as a much-stylized form from nature. In the study of Mesoamerican art it is often tempting to rely on texts to explain images, ignoring the fact that artistic form may convey powerful meanings without recourse to words, and in modes that are peculiarly suited to the senses rather than to the intellect. This notion of symbolic form has been explored by Kubler in his article on architectural profiles at Teotihuacan. Noting the omnipresence of the specialized talud-tablero (slope and panel) profile in the art and architecture of Teotihuacan, Kubler writes:

. . . The tablero and its base may have had a meaning like "sacred architecture." . . . In this case we may suppose that the architectural profile is, in itself and of itself, a major indicator of meaning, specifying both the function of the building and the ethnic identity of the builders.[91]

The step-fret may also have been a motif whose visual form carried its primary meaning. Certainly in many appearances in northern Maya architecture, it may be said to have played an overriding architectural-compositional role. The motif's strong, abstract form accorded particularly well with the Puuc architect's preference for crisp, geometric ornament. That these architects had an interest in the step-fret's purely formal possibilities is demonstrated by their creation of the two-plane fret, whose varied relief enriched the façades with lively patterns of light and shadow.

Sharp's arguments concerning the step-fret's elite significance in Mesoamerica are convincing in broad outline, although some specific interpretations are doubtful. For example, the step-fret is not necessarily always representative of or connected with feathered serpents. The fact that the motif occurs in Oaxaca and northern Yucatan during the Pre-Classic period, a time when the feathered serpent concept does not yet seem to have been fully synthesized in Mesoamerica, should provide a caution against connecting the two symbols.[92] Further-more, many examples from the Classic or Post-Classic periods demonstrate no clear connection with feathered serpent symbolism.[93]

Sharp's arguments regarding the generalized ser-pent symbolism of the step-frets seem more plausi-ble. Their appearance on the body of a serpent in the mural of the Palace of the Sun at Teotihuacan, as well as adorning snakes on the stone from Placeres del Oro, Guerrero, certainly suggests a strong association between the serpent and the step-fret motif. On the other hand, there are many other instances of step-frets, including those on northern Maya architecture, that exhibit no ob-vious serpent associations. The significance of this can be explained, however, in terms of Sharp's broader theory, namely that the step-fret motif was closely connected with and served as a potent sym-bol of power for Mesoamerican elites.

That the step-fret was intimately associated with the elite in the Maya area is demonstrated by the contexts in which it regularly appears. As we have seen, many in the southern Maya region occur on items of apparel or on ritual objects used by histori-cal rulers, their retainers, and their families. Thus on Lintel 24 of Yaxchilan the step-fret motif adorns a sacrificial basket placed before a richly garbed noblewoman who performs an auto-sacrifice before the ruler Shield Jaguar.[93] On Lintel 26 of Yaxchilan, step-frets decorate Shield Jaguar's jerkin,[94] and in a similar vein thay appear on the belt of the ruler Chan-Muan depicted on Bonampak Stela 1 (fig. 171). The appearance of step-frets on the benches in Structure 1 at Bonampak also suggests a connection with elites, since a principal function of this build-ing and its murals seems to have been to commem-orate the battle prowess and courtly pomp of this lord, his family, and his three secondary chiefs.

It seems probable that the step-fret has similar elite connotations in northern Maya architecture. The motif appears on masonry buildings whose use undoubtedly was reserved largely to members of the native nobility. The imposing stone edifices form the nucleii of these sites and contrast with the numerous smaller, undecorated buildings, many of perishable pole and thatch, that housed the bulk of the population. Aside from this general elite con-text, in several instances, step-frets on northern

Maya buildings appear intimately associated with human figural sculptures on the façades. These hu-man figures, as we have demonstrated at the House of the Governor, are expressive of dynastic themes and may have been considered portraits of the rul-ers of the sites where the buildings were erected. One such association of step-frets and a regal hu-man figure occurs at Okolhuitz in the Rio Bec area. There the step-frets of Structure 1 frame a false door on a temple whose roof comb bears a stucco sculpture of a ruler standing frontally above a mask panel (fig. 136).[95] In the Puuc region at Chunhu-hub, the Figure-Palace used large angular frets to frame human figures on the upper façade in a man-ner resembling that at the House of the Governor. Also at Chunhuhub, the Adjacent Palace has three figural panels above the doorways.[96] The central panel was flanked by colonnettes and step-frets, while the side panels were framed by angular frets. Although not as obviously, the great step-frets of the Portal Vault at Labna are also associated with this type of dynastic figural sculpture, since small stucco human figures occupied the nichelike door-ways of the miniature huts that adorn the opposite façade (figs. 95–96).

The best example of the connection between the step-fret and northern Maya rulers is seen at Uxmal at the House of the Governor itself. Pertinent in this respect is the graffito drawing that Seler illus-trates from one of the walls of the transverse vaults of the building. It depicts a lord of Uxmal wearing a lofty headdress decorated with a long-snouted mask and sprays of plumage. Attached to the rear of the headdress is a train, a long rectangular strip carry-ing a series of step-fret designs.[97] Another clear ex-ample is seen on the central motif of the House of the Governor. Step-frets similarly adorn "Lord Chac's" belt and the belt worn by the ruler Chan-Muan on Bonampak Stela 1 (figs. 116–17, 171). This incorporation of the motif into the attire of the lords of Uxmal is the surest indication of the regal importance the Maya attached to the step-fret. As these smaller step-frets were featured in the dress of Uxmal's rulers, so the great ones of the House of the Governor were designed to impress on the viewer the lordly and majestic quality of the build-ing, and to signal its importance as a seat of dynastic authority at Uxmal.

CHAPTER 13

Latticework

THE complex geometric and figural sculpture of the House of the Governor occupies several planes. Forming the background is a geometric pattern resembling a latticework or trellis of interwoven, crossed members made of many individual cut-stone elements, each cut roughly square on the visible surface, and each bearing an X-shaped design (figs. 56, 112, 153). These stones are set adjacent to one another with the ends of the crossbars of the Xs touching so that when viewed in the aggregate they assume the lattice form. The design formed by the individual stones is intended to be read as a unified sculptural field, not simply as a collection of separate X motifs repeated on the façade.[1] The original integrity and coherence of the lattice field would have been enhanced further by the finish coat of stucco that once covered the individual X stones and concealed the joints between them. Portions of such stucco covering survive at the East Structure of the Nunnery, where the gaps between the lattice strips are painted a dark red. A similar treatment was perhaps used at the House of the Governor.

Foncerrada distinguishes two principal variants of latticework at Uxmal: simple and compound. The simple form of lattice consists of panels of plain, diagonally crossing bands. This is the type found at the House of the Governor. The compound type of lattice is composed of panels of wide, dentate or serrated diagonal bands that form rhomboids whose interiors are decorated with various motifs such as flowers, rosettes, or concentric sqares.[2] Examples of compound lattices occur on the North and West Structures of the Nunnery at Uxmal. (Figs. 141, 186).

At the House of the Governor the latticework forms the background for the quadrants of the frieze containing the terraced sections of the large stepped-fret designs (figs. 56, 153, 173).[3] Diagonal strips of the lattice echo the diagonal rows of square stones that form the steps. The lattice elements are also used to fill the irregular spaces that result from the introduction of the diagonally tiered arrangement of mask panels and figural sculptures to the east frieze.

The latticework of the House of the Governor lends opulence and grace to the façade. It serves to lighten the frieze visually, seeming to pierce its mass with a subtle pattern of light and shadow (figs. 16, 56, 153). Its intricate and delicate surfaces form an open-weave texture that contrasts vividly with the dense, compact surface of the lower wall. This contrast between a richly decorated frieze and a spare lower wall appears in many Puuc buildings, and was a consciously sought-after effect at the House of the Governor, where the height of the frieze is about one and one third times that of the lower wall.[4] The openwork appearance of the lattice thus lessens the visual weight of the building, alleviating what threatened to become a ponderously top-heavy feeling.

Origins

Foncerrada suggests that the generative impulse for the latticework of Uxmal may have been produced by cultural and artistic interaction between Uxmal and El Tajin, the Classic Veracruz center. She points out that the Classic Veracruz art style found in El Tajin is motivated by "fantastic designs" based on complex, interlaced scrollwork that may

Fig. 187.
El Tajin,
Structure D
(redrawn after Marquina
1964:fot. 199 by
Tid Kowalski).

be related to the interwoven lattice panels of the Puuc region.[5] She also notes that Structure D in Tajin Chico is decorated with "flat and narrow bands which form interlaced rhombuses" (fig. 187).[6] This interlace pattern on the base of Structure D is the closest formal equivalent to the Puuc-style latticework outside of the Maya area. Unfortunately, its relationship to the Maya designs is difficult to clarify chronologically. Structure D at Tajin Chico has been dated to about A.D. 1100 by Garcia Payon, however, which suggests that it may have received architectural influences from the Puuc region rather than itself influencing the northern Maya buildings.[7]

Closer and more convincing formal parallels to the Puuc-style latticework occur within various contexts in the art and architecture of the Maya area, and it is in this region that we should look for the ancestry of the form and search for clues to its meaning. According to Marta Foncerrada the lattice motif is restricted almost exclusively to the architecture of the Puuc region.[8] There is evidence that earlier forms of the lattice originated elsewhere, however, and that the lattice subsequently attained its most characteristic architectural expression in the Puuc area. Such a probable early form of the lattice is found in the Rio Bec region at Okolhuitz, where Structure 1 possesses a latticework band that serves as a podium on the west side (fig. 136). It appears that the latticework was executed primarily in stucco applied to a framework of stone slabs, rather than composed of individual carved stones as in the Puuc area. At Okolhuitz the lattice is clearly revealed as an interwoven or plaited design, reminiscent of the typical Maya mat-weave pattern. Two crossed bands designs which resemble the X-shaped stones of the Puuc latticework are also found on a

palace-type structure at Payan in the Rio Bec region.[9] Reasonably good evidence exists that these Rio Bec-style buildings at Okolhuitz and Payan were constructed before the House of the Governor, since Potter has placed the major architectural activity in the Rio Bec region between 9.8.0.0.0 and 10.0.0.0.0 in the Long Count, or about A.D. 600–830.[10] Furthermore, the mat-weave, latticework podium of Structure 1 at Okolhuitz seems to precede the Puuc lattice technically, having a finished appearance that relies heavily on stucco rather than on the precisely cut X-shaped stones of the Puuc buildings.

Latticework also occurs outside the Puuc area at the Chenes site of Hochob. Hochob Structure 2 has two stylized representations of Maya huts flanking the central dragon-mouth doorway (fig. 92).[11] The high, nichelike doorways of these huts contain crossed bands which form a latticework. These crossed bands are interwoven, thus representing another mat-weave motif. The use of the mat-weave design in the doorways of these stylized huts has a parallel among the doorway types of modern Yucatec Maya houses, where doors known as (x) mak ak (mak, close, door; ak, vine) are often constructed with a twined network of uprights and vines.[12] It is reasonably certain that Structure 2 at Hochob predates the House of the Governor, since a similar Chenes-style dragon-mouth building, Structure 1, is partly covered by the main platform of the House of the Governor at Uxmal.[13] Potter has also suggested that the Chenes dragon-mouth structures be included in his Central Yucatan Style of architecture (incorporating both Chenes and Rio Bec manifestations), which he dates between A.D. 600 and 830.[14]

Within the Puuc region proper, and at Chichen

Fig. 188. Xcalumkin, Palace of the Inscriptions, Initial Series Building (after Pollock 1980:fig. 707).

Itza, certain tentative and crude examples of simple latticework appear to be earlier than the latticework of the House of the Governor. One such simpler and earlier form occurs on the upper façade of the Palace of the Inscriptions at Xcalumkin (fig. 188).[15] Here the latticework differs from that of the House of the Governor in that each of the arms of the **X**s is formed of a separate piece of stone, rather than carved on a single mosaic element. The Initial Series inscription associated with the Xcalumkin building indicates it was constructed about A.D. 744,[16] probably some 150 years before the House of the Governor. This is the clearest evidence that this crude lattice is earlier than the type used on Late-Puuc buildings.

Crude latticework also occurs at Uxmal on the south frieze of the structure that surmounts the Great Pyramid (fig. 189). Here the lattice alternates with large fretwork designs. Neither the pieces composing the arms of the lattice nor the frets are well cut. The finished effect of the pattern relied on a thick coat of stucco that is still visible in the gaps of the lattice.[17] However, there are one-piece lattice **X** elements used elsewhere on this building, indicating that the earlier form may have continued to be used during a later period.

Another version of the large-scale, separate-block lattice was applied to the rear face of the flying façade of the Iglesia at Chichen Itza.[18] The separate blocks of stone that form the lattice are cut on a bias at the ends, permitting a tighter fit at their juncture than at Xcalumkin or at Uxmal. Radiocarbon dates of A.D. 600 ± 70 and A.D. 780 ± 70 are

Fig. 189. Uxmal, Great Pyramid, lattice and frets on south façade.

associated with the Iglesia,[19] while the hieroglyphic date of A.D. 880 occurs on the adjacent Monjas. Again, at the Iglesia it seems likely that the cruder lattice represents the continued use of an earlier form in a later building.

The earlier examples of latticework from the Rio Bec and Chenes regions, as well as from Xcalumkin in the Puuc area, are the antecedents of the simple lattice type seen at the House of the Governor. In Late-Puuc buildings, such as the East Structure of the Nunnery or the House of the Governor, however, the lattice became a sharper and more precise, formed of one-piece Xs set adjacent to one another to form an interwoven design (figs. 140, 153, 173).

Iconography

The latticework of the House of the Governor, as was noted, enhances the appearance of the building. Yet, like most Maya architectural sculpture, it is doubtful that it was used solely for aesthetic purposes. Earlier writers' speculations on the origins and symbolic meanings of latticework designs have centered on two possibilities: (1) that the lattice is the geometric form of intertwined serpent bodies, or representation of serpent-scale patterns; or (2) that the lattice either derives from, or is a copy of, the original wooden and fibrous materials used to construct the perishable Maya house.

Eduard Seler did not attempt to decipher the meaning of the simple latticework like that of the House of the Governor. He did propose, however, that the serrated lattice, like that of the North and West Structures of the Nunnery, was a geometric stylization of the body of the central Mexican deity Itzcoatl, the odsidian serpent.[20] Manuel Cirerol Sansores likened the lattices to the interlaced bodies of serpents, which he considered symbolic of phallic, generative, and life-giving forces.[21]

J. E. S. Thompson described the decoration on the East Structure of the Nunnery at Uxmal as "a lattice pattern derived from the scales of a serpent" (figs. 86, 140).[22] He also interpreted the latticework's meaning on the basis of its appearance at the Temple of the Three Lintels at Chichen Itza, where he suggested that "The lattice-work represents the scales of the half-snake, half-crocodile bodies of the celestial monsters, and the masks at each corner accordingly represent the heads attached to these bodies."[23]

Thompson later restated this serpent-scale hypothesis in expanded form, modifying Cirerol's the-

ory that the lattice represents the interlaced bodies of serpents to accord with his own notions regarding the paramount importance of the deity Itzam Na in Maya religion. For Thompson the grotesque masks which were applied to the Puuc structures:

represent the heads of Itzams, four of which set at the four sides of the world and the heavens form a house, *na* in Yucatec, which encloses our world, hence Itzam Na, House of the Itzam (Itzam being an iguana); and that the latticework represents their scaled bodies.[24]

Recently Rosemary Sharp again has suggested that the X-motifs, and the latticework panels composed of them, are connected with serpent symbolism. She notes that masks often are found in association with the lattices at Puuc sites, suggesting that the lattice represents the reticulated patterns of snakeskin. Sharp also acknowledges the possibility that the latticework might represent the pole and thatch construction of a Maya house. She believes that the two seemingly opposed interpretations might actually be complementary.[25]

There are ample grounds for rejecting the arguments that seek to support the serpentine derivation of the simple lattice. The notion that the latticework represents snake bodies, or their scale patterns, and that the mask panels represent the heads of these serpents is refuted by several facts. First, no real organic connection is ever established between the latticework and the mask panels it occasionally abuts. The actual relationship is usually one of figure (mask) and ground (lattice), rather than of head and connected body. Second, in the rare instances where the mask panels possess well-defined bodies, they are shown to be much more realistic serpent bodies. Such examples occur on the Chenes-style Temple of the Pyramid of the Magician at Uxmal, where guilloche-patterned rattlesnake bodies are attached to columns of corner masks (fig. 163). These naturalistic serpent bodies partly overlap a simple latticework background, thus precluding the identification of the lattice as the bodies or scale patterns of the corner masks.[26] Finally, the interpretation of the interwoven latticework as the intertwined bodies of serpents, or their scale patterns, fails to explain the lattices' form as effectively as the idea that it is the copy of fibrous material, specifically of the woven mat-motif.

Frederick Catherwood was the first to express the viewpoint that the latticework pattern originated from a prototype in wood and thatch. He advocated the Vitruvian theory that derived many of the characteristic forms of Greek temple architecture from original timber construction, and he believed that this theory was applicable to Maya architecture as well.[27]

Eugène Viollet-le-Duc likewise interpreted much of the stone sculpture applied to the Yucatecan façades as a recollection of forms first perfected in the primitive wooden houses of the Maya.[28] He accounted for the features of the East Structure of the Nunnery, where latticework forms the background for tiered, trapezoidal arrangements of two-headed serpent bars, as deriving from a roofing system based on corbeled log cribbing, which was accompanied by a screen or grating of trelliswork (figs. 86, 140).[29]

Herbert Spinden objected to Viollet-le-Duc's theory because latticework and other features, taken to have derived from wooden prototypes, are restricted to the northern Maya area, where they occur only on buildings that stand late in the chronological development of Maya architecture.[30] Nevertheless, in a later work, Spinden suggested that the Florescent period houses in Yucatan actually may have incorporated features such as columns and latticework, and thus may have provided models for the Puuc style buildings.[31]

Robert Wauchope, in his study of Maya houses, interpreted the Puuc architectural elements such as half-columns or latticework not as survivals or vestiges of wooden prototypes, but rather as deliberate copies of features found in the construction of the Maya bush house whose form pleased the Maya architects.[32] His theory that such forms result from conscious copying rather than as unconscious holdovers eliminates Spinden's chronological objections to deriving such forms from the Maya hut.

Of the two sets of theories regarding the model for and meaning of the latticework, the second group is the most convincing, namely that the lattices on Puuc buildings are derived from or are a copy of forms in the perishable pole-and-thatch construction of the Maya hut. Nevertheless, there are actually few forms in a Maya house closely resembling the form of the Puuc latticework. The closest parallel is the twined vine doorway, or *(x) mak ak*, of the Yucatec houses illustrated by Wauchope.[33] This doorway has a plaited, strand-over-strand construction resembling the interwoven structure of the latticework, and there is the further suggestion that such door construction is related to the lattice since it appears in the doorways of the miniature huts on the Dragon-Mouth building (Structure 2) at Hochob (fig. 92).

That the latticework of the House of the Governor and other Puuc buildings was intended to represent a background of woven fibers is also suggested by several representations of buildings in the Maya codices. In these manuscripts temples are surmounted by strips that contain repeating, plaited or chevron patterns used to represent mat-weave designs on pedestals and thrones depicted elsewhere in the codices. The chevron design employed in this context may represent thatch, the material used to roof Maya huts and other buildings not covered with a corbeled vault.[34]

The correspondence between the Puuc latticework and these interwoven strips of thatching seen atop temples in the manuscripts is further demonstrated at Chacmultun, a site southeast of Uxmal. On Structure 1, small replicas of Maya huts were placed above the doorways of the principal façade. The upper section of the roofline of these huts is adorned with a strip of interwoven latticework.[35] A strip of lattice also occurs as the medial member of the cornice of the Main Palace at Dzibiltun, where it alternates with sections of colonnettes. Here the lattice again suggests the thatched roofs of the temples in the codices.[36]

On two small temples depicted on pages 66b and 68a in the Madrid Codex the roof is formed not only of a tightly woven matting strip at the top, but also of a lower section whose construction is of loose, open-weave matting that closely resembles the latticework of the House of the Governor (fig. 190).[37] These lower sections of temple roofs in the Madrid Codex suggest that the latticework of Puuc buildings was intended to simulate a woven mat. This correspondence is further supported by appearances in Maya art of several mat-weave designs whose structure closely matches that of the lattices. For example, matting with an over-and-under construction like that on the House of the Governor occurs on the side of Altar 17 at Tikal.[38] A similar loosely woven matting appears in the headdress of an effigy censer from Chimuxan, Alta Verapaz.[39] Another mat-weave pattern resembling the lattice of the House of the Governor is found on the basket-like objects that surmount staffs on Lintels 6 and 43 at Yaxchilan (fig. 150). Finally, Stela J at Copan has the hieroglyphic text on its rear face arranged in the pattern of a plaited mat whose structure generally resembles that of the Puuc latticework, but with the strands of fiber interwoven less regularly.[40] As noted, the latticework podium of Okolhuitz Structure 1 clearly represents a plaited, mat-weave pattern.

If the Maya of Uxmal viewed the latticework of their palaces and temples as a type of interwoven mat-weave pattern, then it is likely that the pattern had more than the merely decorative value sug-

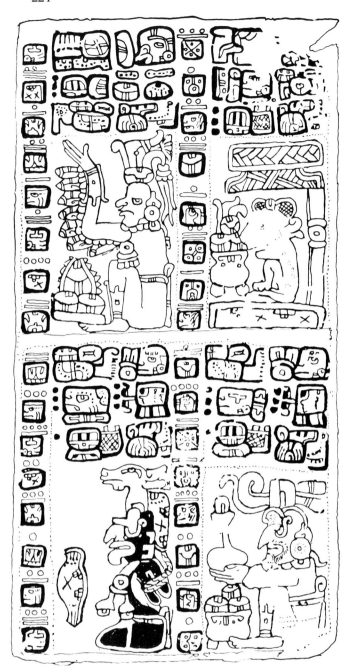

Fib. 190. Madrid Codex, page 68a (after Villacorta and Villacorta 1930:360).

gested by Wauchope. It is probable that the mat-weave lattice symbolized rulership, for Maya literature contains abundant references to the mat as a seat of royal power and authority.

In the *Chilam Balam of Chumayel* the term mat (*pop*) was in some instances clearly considered synonomous with a royal throne. For example, in an account of the creation of the world we are told, about

various miseries accompanying the god Bolon-ti-ku to power, that, "it came during his reign, when he arrived to sit upon the mat. . . ."[41]

Elsewhere in the Chumayel manuscript there are references to the mat as an item that regularly accompanies the royal seat. In a passage describing the flight of the Itza upon the introduction of Christianity we are told:

Complete was the month; complete, the year; complete, the day; complete, the night; complete, the breath of life as it passed also; complete, the blood, when they arrived at their beds, their mats, their thrones.[42]

Those who aspired to public office in northern Yucatan at the time of the conquest were required to verify their claim to rule by a stringent test of their nobility. A series of arcane riddles, known as the "language of Zuyua," were posed to them, with the answers known only to lords and their progeny. Of those who passed this test it was said, "But those who are of the lineage shall come forth before their lord on bended knees in order that their wisdom may be made known. Then their mat is delivered to them and their throne as well."[43]

A young man who thus demonstrated his knowledge and confirmed his nobility was addressed as follows: "Oh my fellow headchief, I will deliver your mat and your throne and your authority to you, son, yours is the government, yours is the authority. . . ."[44]

The Maya believed that not only temporal rulers, but the very gods, were seated on mats. The *Chilam Balam of Chumayel*, again in the account of the creation of the world, mentions that the four gods who presided over the cardinal points were exalted on mat-covered thrones.[45] In addition, the deities who governed and determined the fortunes of the thirteen Katuns also occupied mat-covered thrones.[46]

It is clear that among the Maya the mat could represent the throne or royal seat, but the mat's meaning could be extended metaphorically to symbolize the seat of government as well. For example, in the *Chilam Balam of Chumayel* the settlement of the Maya city of Ichcanziho (Tihoo: modern Mérida) is described as follows:

Then they established the land: then they established the country. Then they settled at Ichcanziho. Then came the people of Holtun-Ake, then came the people of Zabacna. Then the rulers came, all together. The man of Zabacna was the first of the men of the na family. Then they assembled at Ichcanziho, where the official mat was, during the reign of Holtun/Balam, . . .[47]

In this passage the phrase *Ix pop ti balam* is used to designate the mat at Ichcanziho. Although, as previously noted, one meaning of the word *balam* is jaguar, Roys states that it can also mean priest, priesthood, or town officials generally, and that the term "official mat" as used here probably refers to Ichcanziho as the official seat of government.[48]

Another indication of the strong link between the mat and rulership is found in the *Popol Vuh*, in which the Quiché ruler is referred to as the Ahau Ahpop, or "Lord of the Mat," while his oldest son, who normally succeeded him in office, is called the Ahpop Camha.[49] Both the *Popol Vuh* and the *Titles of the Lords of Totonicapan* tell us that the right to bear such titles and to display attendant emblems of rulership had been granted to three Quiché men— Qocaib, Qoacutec, and Qoahan—by the great lord Quetzalcoatl (Nacxit) of Chichen Itza.[50]

The Quiché were not only highlanders for whom the mat was a symbol of government and a title of rulership. According to Recinos, the bat (*zotz*) was the symbol of the Cakchiquel Maya, whose totemic name was Zotzil. The ruler of the Cakchiquel nation thus bore the title Ahpop-Zotzil, which means lord of the mat, or chief, of the Zotzils.[51] The royal connotations of the mat were also recognized by the Pokomchi Maya, among whom the chief was referred to as "Ah Pop" (he of the mat), while the phrase *Im pop im camha* meant "I am chief."[52]

In addition to the foregoing literary references to matting as a substitute for or closely allied with the royal throne, or the designations of important Maya lords as "he of the mat," there exist in Maya art a number of representations of rulers seated on thrones that were actually constructed of or decorated with interwoven caning or rushes. Such thrones occur, for example, in a painting from the south bench of the Temple of the Chac Mool at Chichen Itza, where god-impersonators are shown on seats upholstered with jaguar skin secured by a mat-weave motif appearing as a band of chevrons (fig. 162).[53]

Late Classic Tikal offers the most sumptuous versions of these elaborate, mat-weave–decorated thrones. On Lintel 3 of Temple 1, Ruler A (Kubler's "Sky-Rain," inaugurated 9.12.9.12.16 or A.D. 682) appears on a cushioned throne decorated with a jaguar skin (fig. 191). Two interwoven mat symbols and a small human head of jade are fastened to the sides of the throne, while strips of matting secure the cushion atop the seat and the fringe at its base.[54] Cushioned thrones resembling that on Lintel 3 of Temple I appear on Lintel 2 from Temple III, and on Lintel 2 from Temple IV as well.[55] Similar thrones, adorned with mat-weave symbols, also appear on Naranjo Stela 33 and Piedras Negras Stela 22,[56] and can be seen on pottery and jades as well.[57]

In addition to portrayals of enthroned rulers, depictions of gods seated on mats also occur in Classic Maya art. On the tablet of the Temple of the Sun at Palenque, the ruler Pacal, clothed in elaborately knotted garments, bears aloft a small effigy of the "jester god" seated on a mat-weave throne (fig. 192).[58] On Lintels 6 and 43 of Yaxchilan the ruler Bird-Jaguar is shown holding a tall staff or standard (fig. 150), the top of which is a peculiar woven object that resembles an inverted basket.[59] Seated atop this basketry pedestal is an effigy of the flare god (God K), who often appears in Classic Maya art as the Manikin Scepter. Morley believed that the woven object on these staffs "may be a mat of some kind, always an emblem of authority among the ancient Maya, and here used as a throne for the Long Nosed God [God K]."[60]

Scenes of deities seated on mats, probably corresponding with the mention of the gods' mats and thrones in the *Chilam Balam of Chumayel*, abound in the codices. For example, on page 7 of the Dresden Codex God D (Itzamna) appears seated on a low pedestal covered with matting, while a similar seat appears on page 20 beneath another god.[61] A good example of gods seated on mats also occurs in the Madrid Codex on page 91, where God C and the young Maize God are shown. Each of the gods holds a *kan* (ripe maize) glyph while seated on a mat-weave pedestal.[62]

Because of its substitution for and close association with the royal throne, the mat symbol eventually became an independent motif among the Maya, signifying the power and prestige of lordship. As such, variants of mat-weave motifs often appear in the attire of or decorating the ritual objects used by Maya rulers. On the stone monuments they are proudly displayed as badges of honor and title (recalling the Quiché titles of Ahau Ahpop and Ahpop Camha) and serving as emblems of dynastic authority. Items of costume adorned with mat-weave patterns included headdresses (fig. 142),[63] belts, and loincloths (fig. 142).[64] Belts were frequently adorned with miniature masks of jade coupled with mat motifs that appear in the position of a collar or necklace.[65] It is possible that these maskettes, depicting a youthful human face, represent a lord (ahau).[66] The combination of the mat design with the masks thus identifies the wearer as a "lord of the mat" (Ahau Ahpop).

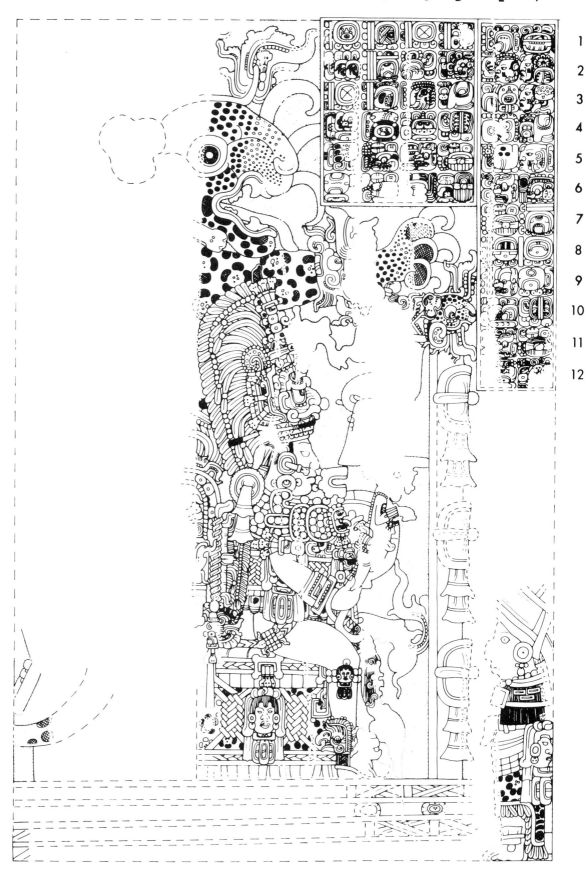

Fig. 191.
Tikal, Lintel 3
of Temple I
(after Jones
1977: fig. 1).

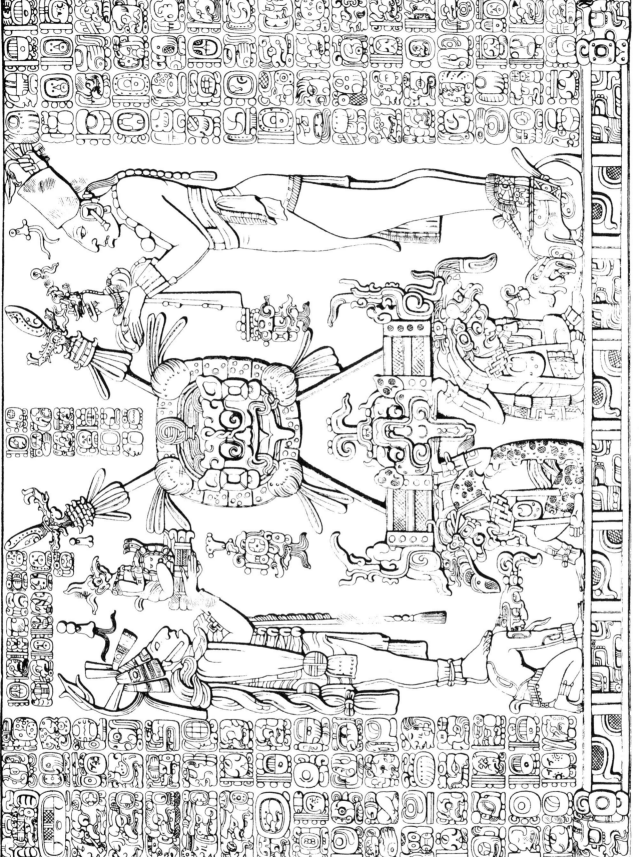

Fig. 192. Palenque, Tablet of the Temple of the Sun (after Maudslay 1889–1902, 4: Plate 76).

Maya rulers also attached the mat motif to neck-laces and collars, where its prime function was to advertise the lord's connection with the mat as a symbol of dynastic power. Such mat symbols pen-dants occur on Yaxha Stela 4, Tikal Stela 9, Piedras Negras Stela 8, and at Palenque on the tablets in the Temple of the Sun and the Temple of the Cross.[67] This type of mat-weave medallion is worn by Lord Pacal (A.D. 603–683) and by two underworld super-naturals who support the thone of the central jag-uar shield in the Temple of the Sun (fig. 192).[68]

The mat symbol apparently was as much valued as a token of eminence and prestige by the rulers of Uxmal as by those of the southern Maya region; a mat-weave ornament forms the centerpiece of the medallion worn by the seated ruler on the central motif of the House of the Governor (figs. 113, 115). An interwoven design that is a variant of the mat symbol also adorns this figure's belt (fig. 116).[69] Mat symbols also embellish the belts and thrones of sev-eral other human figures on the east frieze of the House of the Governor. For example, the figure seated between and above doors 4 and 5 wears a waistband marked with a complex curvilinear vari-ant of the mat motif (figs. 119, 121). This figure sits on a pedestal throne whose sides are adorned with angular mat-weave patterns and whose upper edge is bound by a strip of matting resembling those atop the thrones in the murals of the Chac Mool Temple at Chichen Itza and on the lintels of Tikal (figs. 122, 162). The form of the mat motifs on the waistband and the throne is significant because both have an open-weave, strand-over-strand composition that closely resembles that of the Puuc latticework. Somewhat simpler mat symbols adorn the sides of the thrones of two other human figures on the fa-çade, one appearing between and above doors 9 and 10 (figs. 123–124), and the other set at the cen-ter of the northern wing. These examples of plaited designs appearing on thrones, as well as in the at-tire of figures who sit upon such royal seats, con-firm that the mat was as important a symbol of rulership and authority at Uxmal as it was else-where in the Maya area. It seems certain that for the Maya of Uxmal the latticework, with its obvious structural similarity to a woven mat, would have as-sumed the mat's regal symbolism. Thus the lattice-work probably serves to identify the House of the Governor as an edifice fit for the Lord of the Mat, who himself appears with his mat-weave medallion insign seated in majesty at the center of the build-ing (figs. 54, 113).

CHAPTER 14

Bicephalic Jaguar Throne

A HANDSOME SCULPTURE of a bicephalic jaguar occupies a conspicuous centralized position on the broad second terrace of the House of the Governor (figs. 12—Feature A, 16, 46). This jaguar sculpture is a limestone monolith, some three feet, two inches long and two feet high.[1] The sculptural form of the monument is massive and powerful, with no deeply undercut or pierced areas detracting from the essential blocklike quality (fig. 16). The conception is heraldic, with two jaguars facing away from one another and joined at midsection. The juncture is marked by the animals' tails, which rise up the sides and merge in a tight curl at the top of the back. The northern jaguar's head is slightly larger than that of its counterpart, breaking the symmetry of the heraldic scheme and endowing the sculpture with a more lifelike quality.

The double-headed jaguar sculpture was discovered in 1841 by John Lloyd Stephens in a "rude, circular mound, about six feet high," some 140 feet east of the foot of the stairway of the House of the Governor. Stephens excavated the mound to a depth of three or four feet, where the jaguar sculpture was found standing upright (figs. 1,16).[2] The mound supporting the sculpture has been reconstructed as a quadrangular platform, faced with limestone, and measuring 15 feet 11 inches per side and 4 feet high. Access is provided by stairways on each side of the platform (fig. 2).[3]

Donald Robertson has called attention to the marked architectural character of the many stone monuments erected in the public space of Maya centers, where:

Set in large plazas before temples, they were essentially markers of architectural space. So closely did they adhere to their architectural role that they were in the strict sense of the phrase, architectural sculpture rather than mere sculptural monuments.[4]

This intimate connection between building and sculpture is particularly evident at the House of the Governor, where both the Picote monument and the bicephalic jaguar sculpture are located on a line passing through the center of the House of the Governor perpendicular to the façade.[5] East of the central doorway of the House of the Governor a large mound of the neighboring ruin of Nohpat is visible on the horizon, where it rises directly above the jaguar sculpture (fig. 46).[6] A pronounced complementary and reciprocal relationship exists between the jaguar sculpture and the House of the Governor, which itself looks toward Nohpat and the sites of Kabah, Sayil, and Labna beyond. In the connection thus established among the House of the Governor, the ruin of Nohpat, and the bicephalic jaguar sculpture, the latter plays an intermediary role, suggesting that a determination of its function will further illuminate the significance of the House of the Governor and help define the part it played in the cultural history of Uxmal and the surrounding region.

Jaguar imagery and symbolism pervade the art and iconography of the Maya and of Mesoamerica. Some of the contexts in which jaguars appear are here examined in order to understand the animal's special significance and to explain its function at the House of the Governor. Jaguar symbolism in Olmec art is discussed briefly as an antecedent and foundation for later Maya developments. In Maya art the jaguar is considered as a possible war symbol, and as a pervasive symbol of royal lineage and dynastic power. Maya historical references and monuments support the identification of the Uxmal sculpture as a jaguar throne, an important seat of authority for Maya rulers.

Jaguar and the Olmec

The jaguar is the largest, most powerful and most distinctively pelted wildcat of the Americas.[7] This awesome animal played a prominent role in the religious and political symbolism of Mesoamerica from the earliest civilized times. Among the Olmec, who created a complex civilization between about 1200 to 600 B.C. on the gulf coast plain of Veracruz and Tabasco, the jaguar held an important position in the religious pantheon and art style.[8] Among the most common forms of Olmec portable sculpture are axelike implements carved to represent an admixture of human and feline features.[9] These supernatural creatures, termed werejaguar babies, usually have cleft heads, a form perhaps deriving from the furrowed skin at the top of a jaguar's head.[10] Other possible jaguar characteristics include downturned, snarling mouths and a blunt nose. These features are combined with other human, animal, and avian traits to form recurrent patterns or complexes. Kubler has likened these to an interchangeable system of symbols descriptive of natural forces and phenomena, while others like Coe and Joralemon prefer to view them as the gods of the Olmec people.[11]

An important aspect of the werejaguar is its function as a symbolic object. Werejaguars appear as elements of headdress, or as frames for niches from which seated figures emerge. The human figures, whose realistic visages surely identify them as portraits of Olmec rulers, occasionally hold supernatural werejaguar babies on their laps, as on Altars 2 and 5 at La Venta, Monument 12 from San Lorezo, and Los Idolos Monument 2.[12] The jaguar figures serve as symbols manifesting the power of the person who holds them, and perhaps represent various supernatural clan or lineage patrons. In this fashion werejaguar images were often incised on sculptured figures and masks, where, as Benson suggests, they functioned as "a glyphic text of attributes, power, dynasty, or totems added to representations."[13]

Coe has proposed that there existed an equivalence between the Olmec rulers and the jaguar, and that the many depictions of feline supernaturals in Olmec art were calculated to validate the authority of the royal dynasty.[14] Supporting this idea is the Juxtlahuaca cave painting that depicts a standing, bearded Olmec ruler wearing jaguar paws as arm and leg coverings, and a long jaguar tail hanging between his legs.[15] An even stronger link between jaguar and human occurs at Oxtotitlan Cave in Guerrero, where an ithyphallic human figure stands with a rampant jaguar emanating menacingly from his testicles.[16] The scene has been interpreted as symbolizing royal lineage and power.[17] It is reminiscent of Late-Classic Maya scenes in which gigantic jaguars serve as animal protectors for human rulers (fig. 191).[18]

Jaguar and the Maya

The jaguar apparently had a variety of meanings for the Maya. Prominent among these are its functions as a war symbol and as a symbol of royal authority and power. According to Landa, the late Post-Classic Maya nobility of northern Yucatan engaged in warfare decked with pelts of "tigers and lions."[19] Landa's "tiger" is surely a reference to the jaguar, for the common term for the animal in Mexico and Central America remains "tigre" to this day. Both Tozzer and Roys believed the practice of wearing jaguar skins in war may have represented Central Mexican influence in the form of organized military orders.[20] Roys also notes that according to the Tizimin Manuscript the spreading of a jaguar skin in the marketplace was a symbol of war, famine, and pestilence.[21]

Despite Tozzer's and Roy's belief that the use of jaguar warrior insignia derives from Central Mexico, there is some evidence that Landa's observations can be extended into the Late Classic period as well, and that the jaguar occasionally symbolized war in the southern Maya region. In the murals of Room 2 of Structure 1 at Bonampak, for example, is portrayed a pitched battle in which several principal figures clad in jaguar pelts, and their cohorts, subdue a small band of naked, long-haired antagonists.[22] This battle scene has been interpreted as either a punitive expedition or a small-scale raid for prisoners on a neighboring village.[23] For our purposes it is important merely to note that the leading warriors or war captains are identified by their elaborate jaguar regalia.

The jaguar also appears in an iconic symbol of warfare at Palenque. The wall panel of the Temple of the Sun depicts a frontal half-human, half-jaguar visage emblazoning a shield placed at the center of two crossed spears (fig. 192). David Kelley interpreted this shield and crossed spears as a war symbol, believing that the Temple of the Sun was dedicated to a war deity with the calendar name "13 Death."[24] Kubler objected to this argument because the primary topics in the inscription are dynastic and historical in nature, and make reference to an individual Palenque ruler whom Kubler called "Sun Shield" after his appellative glyph. He believed that the sun shield panoply might represent the personal insignia of this ruler.[25] Kubler's identification of the ruler Sun Shield has been amply confirmed by Schele, Mathews and Lounsbury, who have outlined the dynastic history of Palenque and designated this ruler as Pacal.[26] Schele has further determined that the Temple of the Sun inscription records the accession of Chan Bahlum, Pacal's successor at Palenque.[27] The possibility remains that Kelley was correct in his interpretation of the jaguar motif as a symbol of war; it may represent the military prowess of the Maya lord Chan Bahlum, who is shown presenting a Manikin figure to the shield panoply. The same jaguar visage that appears on this shield also appears as an insignia on many of the small, round shields held by Maya warriors and lords during the Late-Classic period (fig. 171).[28] These anthropomorphic jaguar faces are distinguished by a cord that passes beneath the eyes and loops in a figure eight or "cruller" above the nose. Also typical are the large squared eyes and the T-shaped, filed frontal incisors. Thompson identifies this figure as the god of the number 7, and as an underworld deity merged with the night sun.[29] This identification may explain the figure's connection with war, for among the Post-Classic peoples of the Mexican plateau it was thought that the sun, aided by gifts of human sacrifices obtained in sacred warfare, fought a perpetual nightly struggle for existence in its passage through the underworld.[30]

The jaguar, as noted earlier, also was a prime symbol of power and rulership among the Maya. Jaguar hides and other parts of the animal's body were often used in the sumptuous costumes of the rulers portrayed on the monuments.[31] Jaguar-head helmets are worn by the ruler Bird Jaguar on Lintels 6 and 43 of Yaxchilan (fig. 150). On Lintel 6, both Bird Jaguar and his companion carry jaguar forepaws as emblems of their authority. Jaguar headgear is also worn by Shield Jaguar on Yaxchilan Stela 20.[32] Similar headdress is found on the ruler surmounting the composition on Stela 12 at Piedras Negras, and on Stela 33 at the same site.[33] Jaguar-head helmets also are featured on several warriors in the battle scene at Bonampak mentioned above,

are worn by the central figure seated on the throne on the Initial Series Vase from Uaxactun, and by the Tikal ruler clothed in jaguar skin on Lintel 2 of Temple III.[34] Jaguar pelts were utilized in items of clothing such as kilts or loincloths, tunics, capes, and sandals.

The use of jaguar hides as a symbol of nobility and high office persisted down to the time of the conquest. Landa, in the passage on warfare mentioned previously, states that the "nobles, such as the lords and captains, . . . went to war clothed with feathers and the skin of tigers and lions. . . ."[35] The use of such skins was an important prerogative of the aristocracy, for the common soldiers were armored only with quilted cotton.[36] According to the *Title of the Lords of Totonicapan*, Quiché Maya ambassadors were sent to lord Nacxit (Quetzalcoatl) in Yucatan and subsequently returned to the Guatemala highlands bearing titles of nobility (including the title Ahpop). The insignia listed as proper to these offices "were the claws of the jaguars and eagles, skins of other animals, and also stones, sticks, and so on."[37] Also reflecting the relationship between jaguars and authority is the previously mentioned fact that in Yucatan the word for jaguar, balam, was an honorific term also applied to the native priests and town officials.[38]

During the Late-Classic period, jaguar glyphs occur with some frequency as the names or appellatives of Maya rulers. At Yaxchilan the two most prominent leaders of the site, Bird Jaguar and Shield Jaguar, both have a jaguar main sign in their appellatives. At Palenque the important ruler Chan Bahlum (Snake-Jaguar) has a glyphic name with mixed serpent and jaguar features.[39]

Stela 8 at Seibal depicts a ruler wearing both mittens and boots fashioned from jaguar paws.[40] He appears as an impersonator of the Jaguar Lord of the Underworld, the visage that appears on the shield in the Temple of the Sun at Palenque (fig. 192). A similar portrayal is found on Altar 1 at Hatzcap Ceel,[41] and human impersonators of jaguars also occur on Stela A at Quirigua and on Stela 10 at Piedras Negras (fig. 193).[42]

La Amelia Stelae 1 and 2 feature recumbent, naturalistic jaguars which are confined to separate panels at the bottoms of the monuments.[43] The jaguars are placed below the feet of dominant human figures. Division of the stelae into separate registers may signal that two different planes of existence are depicted, with the realistic level of the human ruler sustained by the symbolic presence of the feline. The exact meaning of these jaguars re-

Fig. 193. Piedras Negras, Stela 10 (after Maler 1901: Plate XIX).

lower leg of the jaguar figure remains (fig. 193).[46] The jaguar-as-protector theme also occurs in Maya ceramics, as in the example from Jaina illustrated by Spinden.[47] Whether these gigantic jaguars represent dynastic lineage symbols, or whether they are merely emblematic of the unassailable power of the ruler is unclear, but their intimate relationship to royal authority is certain.

Having established that the jaguar occupied various positions of importance in the life of the Maya nobility, we will now return to the bicephalic jaguar throne of the House of the Governor. There is abundant evidence that the two-headed jaguar at Uxmal functioned as a throne, one of the most obvious and universal symbols of royal authority. Part of this evidence is linguistic and historical in nature, for firm links exist between the concepts of the mat or throne and the jaguar. Other proofs are derived from monuments that portray Maya rulers seated on jaguar cushions and effigy thrones resembling the one at the House of the Governor.

In the *Chilam Balam of Chumayel* it is stated that Ah Canul occupied the jaguar mat.[48] We have seen that the Mexican allies of the Cocom rulers of Mayapan were called the Ah Canuls;[49] this provides an instance of the close relationship between the jaguar mat and a position of rulership. The connection between the jaguar and matting is also found in the Classic period inscriptions, where the jaguar as an Initial Series Variable Element functioned as patron of the month *pop*, the symbol of which, we noted, is the woven mat.[50] Jaguar cushions of mats were also used as a main sign in the Maya inscriptions. At Palenque, in the Tablet of the 96 Glyphs, a jaguar mat glyph was used in a phrase commemorating the first Katun anniversary of the accession date of the ruler known as Lord Kuk (quetzal).[51] The jaguar mat glyph is coupled with the "seating" glyph, so that the entire accessional phrase probably means something like "his (Lord Kuk's) seating on the jaguar mat."[52]

An archaeological parallel to the references to the jaguar mat in the book of *Chilam Balam of Chumayel* and in the Tablet of the 96 Glyphs at Palenque occurs in a mural painting from the Temple of the Chac Mool at Chichen Itza, where a series of god-impersonators sit on small cushions covered with jaguar pelts (fig. 162). As we have seen, some of these cushions are bordered with mat-weave designs. The figures wear rich costumes and carry staffs that have been identified as late forms of the Manikin Scepter. These, then, are men of high rank.[53]

mains unclear. It has further been suggested that they are a badge of office or symbolize a military order, that they are the lineage totem of a local jaguar dynasty, or that they represent the underworld and indicate that the figure depicted on the monument is dead.[44]

Another important role played by the jaguar in the life of the Maya aristocracy was that of animal protector or guardian. Lintel 3 of Temple I at Tikal depicts a seated ruler with a huge jaguar standing behind him (fig. 191). The menacing claws of the jaguar are stretched over the ruler as if to ward off harm.[45] A similar theme is found on Stela 10 at Piedras Negras, though in this instance only the

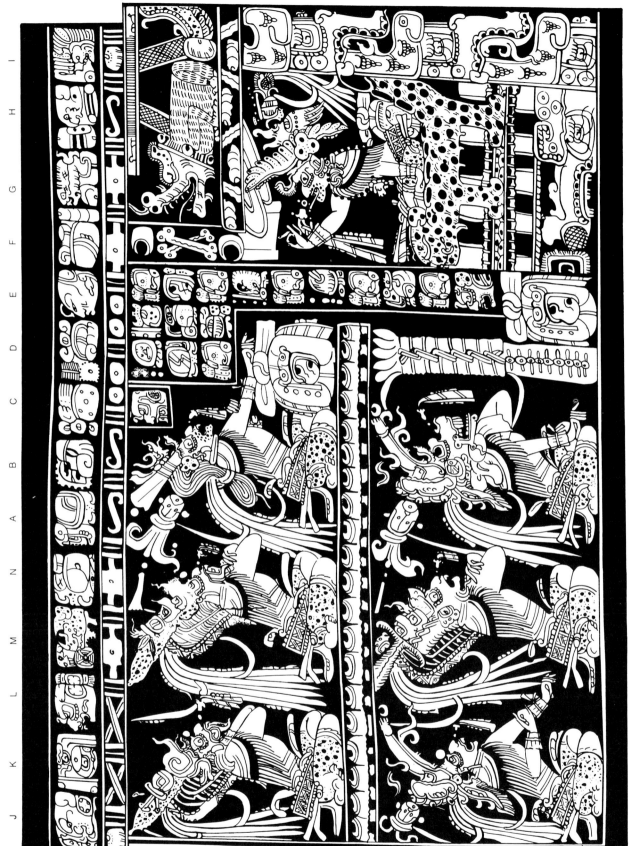

Fig. 194. Roll-out drawing of the Vase of the Seven Gods (after M.D. Coe 1973:vase no. 49).

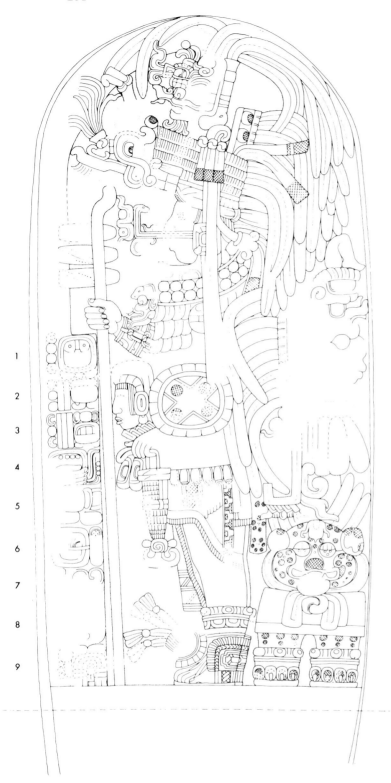

1
2
3
4
5
6
7
8
9

Fig. 195. Tikal, Stela 20 (after Jones 1977:fig. 15).

Fig. 196. Piedras Negras, Stela 5 (after Maler 1901:Plate XV–2).

Such jaguar-skin cushions abound in Late Classic Maya art. A well-known representation is found on Wall Panel ('Lintel') 3 from Piedras Negras, where the central ruler leans forward on an elaborate throne, against the back of which is a large cushion covered with jaguar skin.[54] Similar jaguar-pelted seats occur on Stela 22 at Naranjo and on Stela 25 from Piedras Negras (fig. 143).[55] Many such cushions appear on Maya painted ceramics as well.[56]

During the Late Classic period the Maya devel-

Fig. 197. Chichen Itza, Temple of the Chac Mool, fresco showing Mexicanized warrior occupying a jaguar-seat (after Roys 1967:fig. 3).

Fig. 198. Waldeck's painting of stucco relief in the Temple of the Beau Relief at Palenque (after Graham 1971:fig. 38).

oped and elaborated the concept of the jaguar mat to the ultimate stage, creating veritable thrones carved as single- or double-headed jaguar effigies. A large, single-headed jaguar throne is found at the entrance to the Eastern Court at Copan,[57] and another may have existed in front of the round pyramid at Seibal.[58] A single-headed jaguar effigy throne also occurs in the so-called Vase of the Seven Gods in a scene Coe interprets as a convocation of the prime underworld deities of the Maya, with the ruler of the infernal regions, God L, seated on the throne (fig. 194).[59] A single-headed jaguar throne also appears beneath the ruler on a niche-figurine from Jaina that has been linked iconographically with the ascension motif at Piedras Negras (fig. 146).[60]

On Tikal Stela 20 a jaguar throne is depicted frontally at the lower right, where it is placed behind a sumptuously attired ruler who holds a staff and a small round shield (fig. 195). The jaguar has a fabric knotted around its neck and draped over its shoulders. The frontal representation makes it impossible to determine whether the jaguar is bicephalic.[61]

Stela 5 of Piedras Negras depicts a young man

confronting a ruler seated on a jaguar throne surrounded by a gigantic cauac head (fig. 196). Proskouriakoff interprets this scene as possibly recording a ruler appointing a successor.[62] Here it is again impossible to say whether the jaguar seat is one- or two-headed.

Single-headed jaguars occur frequently in the Post-Classic period painting and sculpture of Chichen Itza. In the Temple of the Chac Mool murals, Mexican warriors are depicted occupying jaguar seats (fig. 197).[63] Actual sculptured versions of these jaguar thrones were found in the Inner Castillo Temple, in a small mound west of the Ball Court, in the Lower Temple of the Jaguars, and in front of the Monjas.[64] Because they occur with such frequency in the Mexican sector of the site, and because other jaguar imagery at Chichen is probably derived from prototypes at Tula, Hidalgo, these jaguar thrones were viewed as among the intrusive Mexican or "Toltec" elements in Chichen Itza's art.[65]

Alberto Ruz Lhuillier, who supervised the excavation and reconstruction of the platform of the jaguar throne at Uxmal, related the Uxmal throne to the single-headed thrones at Chichen Itza. He did not deduce from this connection that the Uxmal example demonstrated a Central Mexican or "Toltec" presence at the site, but rather viewed the Post-Classic versions of the jaguar throne at Chichen Itza as continuations of an essentially Maya theme. Ruz related the bicephalic jaguar throne of Uxmal to examples at Palenque, the type-site for the two-headed jaguar throne and the only site where it occurs aside from Uxmal.[66] In the Temple of the Beau Relief at Palenque, a stucco panel formerly depicted a ruler sitting on a large cushion atop a splendid bicephalic jaguar throne (fig. 198). The jaguar heads have textile collars recalling that worn by the jaguar on Tikal Stela 20.[67]

The Oval Relief Panel in House E of the Palace at Palenque shows a woman kneeling and offering a mosaic crown to the ruler Pacal (fig. 147). Pacal, seated crosslegged, regards the woman from atop a naturalistic double-headed jaguar throne. According to Kubler, House E may have functioned as a physical center for the accessional rituals of Palenque rulers.[68] The symbolism of the bicephalic jaguar throne thus complements and reinforces the royal theme.

The bicephalic jaguar at the House of the Governor evidently derives from the earlier models at Palenque. At Uxmal, two-headed or double jaguars became an important motif, repeated twice elsewhere in the art of the site. On the south façade of the North Structure of the Nunnery is found a small relief sculpture of two jaguars with intertwined tails.[69] These doubled jaguars are placed like a heraldic device below the doorways of miniature huts that were centered above several of the doorways of the North Structure (fig. 141). At other sites in the Puuc region, doorways of these miniature huts are known to have contained small human figural sculptures.[70] Such figures probably were placed originally in the huts' doors at the Nunnery, with the result that the two jaguars beneath would have formed a throne.[71]

The theme of the bicephalic jaguar also occurs on Stela 14 at Uxmal (fig. 27). As we have seen, this stela depicts a dominant figure who is identified in the accompanying text as Lord Chac. His attire indicates that he is a powerful ruler, for he wears an enormous feather headdress, a beaded cape, and an elaborate belt set with miniature human heads. Lord Chac stands on the back of a bicephalic jaguar, in whose maws appear two small human faces. In this case we may interpret the two-headed jaguar both as a throne and as a pedestal of rank. If we discount the two human faces in the jaguars' mouths as dramatic or symbolic embellishments, then this two-headed jaguar is likely to be a portrayal of the actual sculptured throne in front of the House of the Governor (fig. 16).

The placement of the bicephalic jaguar throne at the center of the second platform, and its alignment with the central doorway of the House of the Governor, further confirm the royal nature of the building. This regal quality is clearly expressed in the reciprocal relationship between the jaguar throne and the central sculptural motif, where the focal portrait of Lord Chac surrounded by bicephalic serpents is a symbol of dynastic power derived from the accessional stelae of Piedras Negras (fig. 113). The fact that the entire edifice, as mentioned, looks eastward toward the ruins of Kabah, Sayil, Labna, and to the great mound at Nohpat, seen on the horizon directly above the jaguar throne from the central doorway of the House of the Governor, confirms that the entire complex was the chief administrative center not only of Uxmal, but for much of the surrounding Puuc region as well.

CHAPTER 15

Epilogue

THE House of the Governor at Uxmal marks a pivotal moment in the history of Maya architecture (figs. 2, 199). The time of its construction, in the late ninth or early tenth century A.D., was a period of dramatic change and fermentation in the social, religious, and artistic spheres in northern Yucatan. The rapid rise of the Puuc cities attests to the large-scale cultural transformations that were occurring.

Although the beginnings of the Puuc architectural tradition may be placed perhaps as early as A.D. 600 to 750 at sites such as Edzna, Mul-Chic, or Xcalumkin, current evidence indicates that the majority of Late or Classic Puuc buildings were constructed from between about A.D. 770 to 925. During roughly the same period, the major centers of Maya civilization in the south were being abandoned, their ruling elites no longer able to command authority effectively.[1] The simultaneous rise of the north and fall of the south can be attributed in part to a major shift in trading routes, fostered by the growing power of the Chontal or Putun Itza Maya. As J. E. S. Thompson has pointed out, the major traders in southeastern Mesoamerica at the time of the conquest were the Putun or Chontal, who occupied a region stretching from Tabasco almost as far north as Champoton on the west coast of Campeche.[2] The Chontal maintained and controlled a regular sea-trade, skirting the coast of Yucatan, acting as middlemen for the Culhua-Mexica pochteca merchants.[3] Thompson believes that this Putun trade and expansion began as early as the Late and Terminal Classic periods, when from a position peripheral to the Maya lowlands, the Chontal began to penetrate up the Usumacinta, Pasion, and Chixoy Rivers, where they were responsible for the introduction of foreign "Mexican" traits at sites such as

Altar de Sacrificios and Seibal.[4] Gordon Willey has further suggested that the causes of the Classic Maya decline and collapse are involved with the rise of the Chontal, who effectively cut off major trade routes to the west and north of the southern Maya centers. According to Willey:

Some few sites, such as Seibal, were given a brief, late lease on life by Putun alliances; but as the Postclassic Period continued, such sites were bound to be too far from the coast and from the main trade routes to be maintained as profitable concerns.[5]

As the Chontal expanded their power, the centers of northern Yucatan became beneficiaries of the new trade routes. At the time of the conquest Yucatan was known as an exporter of cotton cloth, slaves, and salt.[6] It is likely that these commodities were supplied during earlier times as well. Thus, the Puuc cities, and other centers such as Dzibilchaltun and Chichen Itza, were located strategically to serve as trading centers, supplying the Chontal traders with goods that could be transported to highland Mexico. At first this trade seems to have involved centers such as Xochicalco, El Tajin and Cacaxtla.[7] Later, probably after A.D. 850, this trade was aimed at the Toltecs of Tula, who were rapidly rising as a political power in central Mexico.[8]

Chontal trade produced a dramatic increase in the wealth of the Puuc centers and in the political power of their rulers. Their location in a "breadbasket" area characterized by good, deep soils and high crop yields also contributed to the wealth of Uxmal and the other Puuc centers.[9] Thus they may have prospered both through trade and through effective use of the land, perhaps with agricultural

Fig. 199. House of the Governor from northeast corner of Platform 2.

products and cotton exchanged for the luxury goods necessary to maintain the elite.

Connections with the Chontal traders help explain the introduction of foreign-looking or "Mexican" features in Puuc art and architecture—prior to the traditional date of A.D. 987 associated with the Toltec conquest of or intrusion at Chichen Itza. At Uxmal such features include the feathered-serpent sculptures on the West Structure of the Nunnery and the Ball Court, the skull and bones motifs on the platforms of the Cemetery Group, and certain elements on Stela 14 (figs. 186, 11, 27). Stela 14 also may document such trading contacts with foreign peoples, since Lord Chac confronts two smaller emissaries who wear Ehecatllike masks. "Mexican" influences may have come about not solely through trading contacts, but also by actual imposition of Chontal rulers' power at certain sites such as Chichen Itza. Thompson proposed that the first wave of the Itzas, who were a subdivision of the Chontal, invaded Chichen Itza about A.D. 918.[10] More recently, however, it has become evident that the Itza, led by a figure named Kakupacal, had assumed power at Chichen Itza by about A.D. 866 or 869.[11]

During the ninth century, Chichen Itza and the various Puuc centers probably were competing with one another economically and politically.[12] This competition could turn violent. Warfare seems to have been occurring sporadically at the time the House of the Governor was built. Uxmal's cere-

monial district was surrounded by a defensive wall, and several sculptures on the North Structure of the Nunnery depict captives with bound hands and exposed genitals. Interregional conflicts eventually must have damaged the ability of the Chontal traders to conduct business effectively in northern Yucatan, preventing commodities from reaching their Toltec sponsors in central Mexico. As a result, it finally became necessary to consolidate northern Yucatan politically by establishing a centralized capital at Chichen Itza, already controlled by a division of the Itza.[13] Thus the Toltecs of Tula, or perhaps a more highly Mexicanized group of Chontal Maya who were associated with the Toltecs, sent a contingent of warriors to impose order over the various factions. The Toltecs (or Mexicanized Chontal) may have entered Yucatan on their own initiative or might have been responding to an invitation from the already present and closely allied Itza. This new group arrived either during the traditional Katun 4 Ahau from A.D. 968 to 987, or perhaps as early as about A.D. 900.[14] The abandonment of the Puuc cities was probably a direct result of this new political consolidation. Some centers may have resisted and were depopulated forcibly, while others, realizing that the political situation was shifting radically, may have collaborated with the new rulers of Chichen Itza.[15]

It is against this historical background that the House of the Governor must be viewed. The competition among the various Puuc centers and Chichen Itza seems to have been carried out in peaceful as well as warlike ways. For example, during the reign of Lord Chac, there were evidently close dynastic ties between Kabah and Uxmal. Nohpat, which is located on the sacbe system that links Uxmal with Kabah, was probably included in this relationship as well. It may be that the rulers of these three cities were collaborating to forge a more powerful political force, capable of dominating trade from the entire Puuc region. As a result of such trade a great deal of wealth was flowing into the hands of the rulers of these cities. Much of this wealth was invested in the creation of civic projects and large masonry buildings, such as the House of the Governor. Architecture played an important social role, serving to display the economic power and political authority of the ruler in noble edifices.

The increase of wealth through trade may have been the catalyst that stimulated the rulers to commission buildings of the size and magnificence of the House of the Governor. It also helps account for the constructional improvements made at this time. The House of the Governor has superlatively finished masonry. The wall facing-stones and boot-shaped vault stones are all expertly cut, pecked, and ground smooth, while the cut-stone mosaic façade elements possess a sharpness of detail not found in earlier Maya architecture. The facing stones and vault stones are all designed to be used as forms to contain a lime concrete core (fig. 64). Such concrete construction is typical of the Puuc region, and it enabled the architects of the House of the Governor to increase the width of the building's rooms beyond that common previously, providing more commodious living arrangements for the upper class. As noted, several lines of evidence indicate that the House of the Governor functioned as an elite residence and administrative center, and also possessed an important astronomical alignment connected with the planet Venus.

In the House of the Governor the ruler of Uxmal sought to obtain not only a building of great luxury and superlative technical finish, but also to create a symbolic form that defines an image of the exalted position he occupied in northern Maya society. We are uncertain whether the lords of the Puuc cities were drawn from local dynasties or whether some may have been people from the southwest who imposed their authority over the local inhabitants by force.[16] It is interesting to note, however, that many of the forms they incorporated in their buildings are derived from the earlier Classic Maya tradition

of the southern lowlands, or from the traditions of Central Yucatan, although these were modified to suit local tastes and transformed to accord with Puuc technical practice. Many of the basic principles of Maya architecture were already long-established when the House of the Governor was built. The architect drew on these earlier models in formulating his own design, in some instances with personal knowledge of his models, but probably more often absorbing these influences at second-hand, as they had become standard canons of good design. The long, parallel-vaulted, multi-chambered plan of the House of the Governor has many antecedents in the southern Maya area, occurring at Uaxactun, Tikal, Nakum, and Altun Ha (figs. 41–42, 81). Earlier variants of these elongated plans also occur in the Rio Bec and Chenes regions, and such ranges of adjacent rooms then became a common plan in the Puuc area. Both the House of the Governor and the buildings of the Nunnery Quadrangle at Uxmal have a freestanding block form that emphasizes the self-contained character of the edifices (figs. 2, 199, 83–87). Although the Uxmal structures possess an exceptional purity of stereometric form, precedents for the Nunnery Quadrangle and its freestanding block buildings are found at Tikal or Santa Rosa Xtampak, while a close parallel existed at Tihoo.

One of the most striking features of the massing of the House of the Governor is the bold tripartite division of the façade (figs. 2, 54). Such three-part architectural arrangements have a long heritage in the Maya area. Three temples were arranged hierarchically around a courtyard in Group A-V at Uaxactun, while in the Rio Bec and Chenes regions, such three temple groupings were combined with palaces. Perhaps from these palace-temple groupings the architects of the Rio Bec and Chenes regions developed the three-unit façade, where massing and articulation create the impression of three separate buildings on a separate structure (figs. 90–92). At Uxmal, this three-unit design appears on the early Chenes Structure 1 west of the House of the Governor, while a grouping of three separate structures slightly predating the House of the Governor occurs on the west side of the Cemetery Group (fig. 10). Maya architects may have favored this three-part composition because of its clear hierarchical quality, which conforms to the structure of dynastic society.

The connections with the southern Maya area found in the plan and massing of the House of the Governor are evident in its architectural sculptures as well. The latticework of the building seems to imitate the interwoven structure of the Maya mat-weave design, although the design was translated from small-scale contexts and applied in ample architectural settings by Puuc architects (fig. 173). Earlier versions of the latticework exist in the Rio Bec region at Xaxbil, Payan and Okolhuitz, where the lattice is clearly based on a plaited mat (fig. 136). Hochob Structure 2 also has interwoven lattice designs reminiscent of flexible, plaited materials (fig. 92). The lattice of the House of the Governor resembles the mat-motifs on Altar 17 at Tikal, and on Lintels 6 and 43 from Yaxchilan (fig. 150). The correspondence between the lattice and the mat-motif suggests that it was used on the façade of the House of the Governor and other stone edifices in the Puuc area as a symbol of dynastic authority. Many references in Maya art and literature indicate that the mat-motif was an emblem of lordly power. The latticework thus served to mark the House of the Governor as a palace and administrative seat worthy of the Lord of the Mat.

The bicephalic jaguar throne in front of the House of the Governor also appears to be a fundamentally Maya sculptural type (fig. 16). It corresponds in function to the many jaguar mats and cushions that form the seats of Maya lords, and resembles the several single- or double-headed jaguar effigy thrones found in Maya art. A single-headed jaguar throne is found at Copan, as well as on the Vase of the Seven Gods and a pedestal-niche figurine from Jaina (figs. 194, 146). Sculptured representations of jaguar seats occur on Tikal Stela 20 and Piedras Negras Stela 5. (Figs. 195–96). The bicephalic-jaguar throne concept may have originated at Palenque, where it appears in the Temple of the Beau Relief and on the Oval Relief Tablet in House E of the Palace (figs. 147, 198). At Uxmal, Stela 14 shows the ruler Lord Chac surmounting a bicephalic jaguar throne like that at the House of the Governor (fig. 27). Literary references indicate that the Maya considered the jaguar mat to be a seat of royal authority. The Maya of Uxmal thus seem to have placed the jaguar throne at the House of the Governor because of the motif's traditional connections with Classic Maya concepts of rulership and dynastic power.

The long-snouted mask panels of the House of the Governor are other elements of the architectural sculpture that have a basic Maya heritage (figs. 151–53). Stucco masks appear as early as the Pre-Classic period on buildings at Uaxactun, Tikal, and Cerros, Belize. This stuccowork masking tradition was maintained during the Early- and Late-Classic periods at Holmul, Nakum, Piedras Negras, Palen-

que, Yaxchilan, and other sites, while carved stone masks resembling those of the north are found on Copan Temple 22 (figs. 135, 155). Transitional between the Puuc masks and these southern examples are those of the Rio Bec and Chenes regions, where greater use was made of pre-carved stone elements, but where the final effect still relied heavily on stucco modeling (figs. 90, 92, 136). In later Puuc buildings, like the House of the Governor, the masks were redesigned as assemblages of cut-stone pieces that fit together precisely to form the image.

It is possible to relate different features of the masks to the following figures in Maya art: the Yucatec rain god Chac, the God B of the codices; God K of the codices, the Manikin Scepter of the Classic monuments; the Cauac monster; long-snouted masks in Maya headdresses; and the "frontal" head of the two-headed monster.

The principal model for the masks of the House of the Governor was apparently the rain god Chac, who appears as the pendulous-snouted God B in the manuscripts (fig. 159). However, aspects of the other figures, particularly God K, also may have been incorporated (figs. 160–161, 166–167). Linking all of these supernatural figures is their function as symbols of dynastic authority. The display of masks on Puuc buildings visibly demonstrated the connections between such supernaturals and the Maya elite, whose members served as earthly representatives of these deities.

The human figural sculpture also belongs to a wider Maya tradition, since it is only in the Maya area that other buildings are found with compositions of human figures like those at the House of the Governor (figs. 2, 54, 106–133). Similar symmetrical and hierarchical schemes occur in the southern area on Structures 33 and 40 at Yaxchilan and Structure 1 at Bonampak (fig. 135). Human figures also adorned the façades at Palenque, Tikal, Pared de los Reyes, and undoubtedly many other Maya sites as well. The Rio Bec building at Okolhuitz and the Chenes Structure 2 at Hochob also have human figures on their façades (figs. 92, 136). Puuc architecture shows two traditions of figural sculpture. Stucco figures tend to be earlier and are found on structures at Labna, Sabacche, Ichpich, Almuchil, and Uxmal. Some later Puuc buildings at Sayil, Chacbolai, and Chunhuhub also used stucco for figural sculptures. Consonant with general architectural trends, however, Late-Puuc buildings tended to use cut-stone rather than stucco for figural sculpture, as at Chunhuhub, Chacmultun, Chichen Itza, and Uxmal.

Human figures at the House of the Governor

share not only the compositional formats, but also the dynastic symbolism of the southern buildings and monuments. For example, the central motif, with its richly garbed ruler surrounded by tiered serpent bars, resembles the ascensional motifs on Stelae 25, 6, 11, and 14 at Piedras Negras (figs. 113–15, 143). These stelae name specific Maya rulers and depict a dynastic ritual associated with their accession to power. Similar dynastic subjects were depicted in the architectural sculpture on buildings at sites such as Tikal, Yaxchilan, Bonampak, Palenque, and Seibal (figs. 148–49). The human figural sculptures of the House of the Governor thus portray and demonstrate the power of a series of exalted individuals. The central human figure seated within the tiered serpent bars was probably a portrait of Lord Chac, who sits within a cosmic frame that asserts his supernatural legitimacy as the lord of Uxmal and surrounding Puuc centers.

The continued use of so many forms and motifs derived from Classic Maya art suggests that the rulers of Uxmal sought to define themselves as inheritors of and bearers of Classic Maya culture. Despite the fact that the Puuc centers seem to have been competing successfully with the southern cities economically, and were in fact rising in power as the southern centers declined, the Puuc rulers were loath to abandon the symbols of religious and political authority that had endured for several hundred years. The situation is reminiscent of that at Seibal, where John Graham has defined two groups of foreigners in the monumental sculpture. The first group, called the Facies A people, are associated with monuments dating from 10.1.0.0.0 (A.D. 849) to 10.3.0.0.0 (A.D. 889) (fig. 142).[17] Although they are usurpers at Seibal, they adhere fairly closely to Classic Maya traditions in costume. Standard dynastic imagery and lengthy hieroglyphic texts are still used to express authority. The later group, called the Facies B people, seems to have mixed with and then supplanted the earlier after about 10.2.5.3.10 (A.D. 874).[18] At this time the monuments change dramatically, with the introduction of many more non-Classic and "Mexican" motifs, such as long-haired figures in foreign costume, Ehecatl figures, Tlalocs, and Mexicanlike glyphs. Graham suggests that these people may have been located on the gulf coast between western Yucatan and southern Veracruz.[19] At Seibal the replacement of an earlier, more Classic Mayalike elite with one more foreign, suggests that the older dynastic organization no longer had the power to compete effectively against the rising power of peoples located on the periphery of the Maya area.

The situation of the rulers of the Puuc cities such as Uxmal seems to correspond roughly to that of the Facies A people at Seibal.[20] Like them, the Puuc lords reach the height of their power during the waning years and shortly after the time of abandonment of the southern cities, and also like them, they prefer to maintain a basically Maya cultural and artistic orientation. The Puuc rulers were aware of other artistic trends and political realities, however, as is indicated by their use of many non-Classic motifs in their art and architecture, such as feathered-serpent imagery, tzompantlilike platforms, Tlalocs, and possible Ehecatl figures. Some of the finest buildings at Uxmal, such as the West Structure of the Nunnery and the Ball Court, suggest attempts to work out a new synthesis of Maya and Mexican forms and symbols (figs. 87, 186).

The prominent use of the step-fret in the façade of the House of the Governor and other Puuc buildings also suggests the importance of foreign influences in the formation of the Puuc style—although because of the design's deep roots in time and broad extension in space it is difficult to be certain where such influences originate, or in which direction they travel (fig. 173). Architecturally, the closest formal counterparts to the step-frets of the House of the Governor are found on earlier edifices in the Rio Bec and Chenes regions to the south (figs. 182–83). Other close parallels exist on buildings in the Valley of Oaxaca and at El Tajin, Veracruz, both of which areas may have had long-distance trading contacts with the Puuc rulers (figs. 88, 180–81).

Ultimately, of course, the Puuc architecture must be viewed as an integral style characteristic of northern Yucatan, not merely as a blend of Classic Maya and foreign influences. Puuc architecture displays strongly defined regional features, such as the fine cut-stone facing, a general sharpness of line, an emphasis on horizontality, a use of cut-stone mosaic sculptures intended to produce bold chiaroscuro effects, and a more complete interaction of sculpture and architecture (figs. 2, 54, 199). The ruling elites of the Puuc area were sensitive patrons, who supported gifted architects capable of forging a new regional style. Nevertheless, the House of the Governor, with its ascensional symbolism, its profusion of masks, and its elongated palace form, also must be viewed as an outgrowth and final expression of the Classic Maya tradition in architecture and architectural sculpture. In this sense it is a grand culmination rather than a beginning. The future of Maya architecture lay not in the Puuc region, but on the northern plains. Shortly after, or perhaps even as the architects of the House of the Governor were giving a final grandiose and powerful expression to the forms of the old Maya world, a new Toltec-Maya culture, art and architecture were being born at Chichen Itza.

Interpreting the House of the Governor as a product of specific historical conditions and separate stylistic strains is essential for a complete appreciation of the building. It is equally important, however, to realize that the House of the Governor was conceived and continues to exist as an integrated aesthetic object, a work of architecture of surpassing symmetry and grace. Features such as the tripartite division of the façade, innovative use of the transverse vaults, incorporation of the negative batter, subtle spacing of the shadow-framed doorways, and the unique staggered composition of the mask canopies mark the building as the work of an architect of exceptional talent and creativity.

Today many of the more complex questions of iconography no longer have the power to move us as they did the Maya nobles, priests, and people of Uxmal. The rain, sun, and corn are no longer the domain of gods such as Chac, Kinich Ahau or Uaxac Yol Kauil, but are viewed as elements in a world governed by natural law. The House of the Governor, however, marks a moment when such phenomena were endowed with vital personality and sacredness. Neither do the political connotations of the building carry as much weight today. We have our own social concerns and political problems, and it is difficult to feel awe before the power of a long-forgotten lord. Yet this lord and his architect brought into existence a building which, like all great works of art, possesses aesthetic qualities transcending these limitations of time and place. Through its masterful technique and harmonious design the House of the Governor may move us still, and it is this inherent expressiveness that assures it a place of honor in the artistic patrimony of mankind.

Mexican Archaeological Activities and Reconstruction at Uxmal and the House of the Governor

MUCH important information about Uxmal and the House of the Governor has come to light as the result of excavations and reconstructions undertaken by Mexican archaeologists and sponsored by the Mexican government. The first official inspection of Uxmal was made in 1913 by Juan Martínez Hernández at the behest of the Mexican Museo Nacional. On the large platform of the House of the Governor he noted that the House of the Turtles was much destroyed. His photographs of the House of the Governor permit a description of the condition of the building. On the west side of the central structure a great portion of the wall and frieze, beginning at the fifth fret from the northwest corner, had collapsed (fig. 3). The lintel of the north doorway and masonry above it had fallen. On the east façade, the jambs, lintels, and parts of the frieze above each door had fallen. A long section of the upper façade of the central structure, beginning north of the central motif and continuing to the northeast corner, had collapsed completely (figs. 1, 18). Martínez concluded, however, that not much damage had occurred to the House of the Governor since the reported collapse of the section of the east façade in 1825.[1] He cleared the large platform of the House of the Governor in 1914 and again in 1917.[2]

In 1922 the archaeologist Eduardo Noguera made an inspection of Uxmal and filed a report that included descriptions and measurements of the House of the Governor.[3]

During 1926 the archaeologist Eduardo Martínez Cantón, accompanied by José Erosa Peniche, inspected Uxmal, with the intention of giving a detailed description of damage that had occurred at the House of the Governor, to see what measures could be taken to shore up falling masonry and to replace fallen sculpture. On the west side of the north structure a section of the upper façade 28 feet 3 inches long was intact, but south of this a section 23 feet 8 inches had collapsed. This had occurred since Martínez's visits twelve to thirteen years earlier.

Several other sections of the upper façades of the north and central structures were separated from the interior vault mass by large cleavages. (See chapter 7.) On the north building, masonry around and above the interior and exterior doors (door 13) had collapsed. On the east side, sections above and around doors 12 and 11 had also fallen. A figural sculpture remained in the center of the east façade. On the east side of the central structure the entire upper façade above the first three doorways (doors 10, 9, 8) had collapsed (fig. 18). This fallen section stretched from the northeast corner to the northern edge of the central figural sculpture, which was still well preserved. The three southernmost doors (doors 6, 5, 4) were damaged above the lintels, but the upper façade south of the central motif was basically intact. Much of the facing of the lower wall had fallen, but impressions of the stones were still visible. On the south building, a section of masonry above door 1 had collapsed and the facing east of the jamb had fallen. The entire southwest corner had collapsed, and sections above and around doors 2 and 3 of the east side of the building had fallen.[4]

In 1927 Martínez Cantón initiated reconstruction operations at the House of the Governor. At the fallen southern section of the west façade of the northern building, rubble was cleared from the base and sculpture was arranged for replacement on the frieze. The lower wall-facing was replaced, the southwest corner was reconstructed, and the medial molding was reset. The lower cornice stone of the southwest corner had broken and was doweled together with steel bars and tenoned into the hearting. Following the resetting of the medial molding, scaffolding was erected and the fallen sculpture was reconstructed.[5]

Reconstruction continued during 1928. Because of the cleavage between the façade and the hearting, the northern section of the west side of the north building was dismantled and replaced to the height of four masks at the central-mask column and three masks at the northwest corner. Pieces were marked, and photos of the façade were taken to insure accurate reproduction. The lower wall and the medial molding were then reconstructed. Because the original cornerstone was broken, a concrete duplicate was used for the lower member of the medial molding at the northwest corner.[6]

In 1936 restoration was resumed at the House of the Governor under the supervision of the archaeologist Manuel Cirerol Sansores. A reconnaissance of the west façade was made, and sculptured stones were marked with a numerical–alphabetical system to facilitate removal and replacement.[7]

During 1937 a section of the frieze of the west façade, south of the northern transverse vault, was dismantled until no further cleavage existed between the frieze and hearting. Below this the lower wall was refaced and the medial molding was reset.[8] By July of 1937 the west side of the central structure had been reconstructed to the height of the medial molding.[9]

In 1939 Cirerol published an article entitled "La Realidad de las Fachadas Mayas" as a result of his work at Uxmal.[10] His interpretation of latticework panels as interlaced serpent bodies is discussed in chapter 13.

In 1952 Cirerol published a monographic guidebook on Uxmal, in which he described the major structures, outlined several of the archaeological discoveries made during his period as director of excavations, and espoused rather idiosyncratic theories concerning the agricultural–fertility–phallic component he saw in the architectural sculpture of the site.[11] His description of the House of the Governor devotes attention to the transverse vaults. Noticing the convex curvature of the vaults, he attributed such a "bold innovation" to the desire on the part of the architects to "imitate the gentle lines of an artistic canopy or draped curtain."[12] Cirerol believed that because of their exaggerated convexity the vaults began to weaken, for which reason

they were later buttressed by the addition of partition walls.[13] We examine this question in chapter 8.

In 1945 José Erosa Peniche, who was now in charge of reconstruction at Uxmal, began repairing the faces of the fourth platform of the House of the Governor. In addition, on the east side of the fourth platform, rubble was arranged for replacement on the façade, and reconstruction was begun at the north and south corners of the central building.[14] During this season the north and south corners were completed, and the jambs and lintels of doors 4, 5, 6, 7, 8, 9, and 10 were reconstructed.[15] As each doorway of the central structure was completed, any fallen facing stones inside the chambers were replaced simultaneously. Replacement of the large, collapsed section of frieze north of the central motif was begun also, with metal tie rods bonding facing to hearting.

By the end of the 1945 season the medial molding was completed to the northeast corner of the central building, and a substantial section of the upper frieze had been replaced. At this time the large excavation made by Stephens in the rear of the central chamber was filled and the wall reconstructed.[16]

During 1946 reconstruction of the entire eastern façade of the central building was completed. The monumental stairway was reconstructed to the height of the fourth step.[17]

During the 1947 season the small stairway from the third to the fourth platform of the House of the Governor was cleared and reconstructed. The terrace walls north and south of the stairway were also restored.[18] Seven more steps of the monumental stairway were reconstructed, and an exploratory trench was dug in the center of the stairway, revealing that it abuts a basal platform of four terraces supporting the House of the Governor.[19] An excavation was also made at the center of the third platform, where a stone-lined cist was found containing a cache. The contents of this cache are discussed in chapter 6. During 1947 the cornice of the central structure was also reconstructed and a portion of the roof was restored. On the north wing, the base of the east façade was reconstructed, jambs and lintels were replaced in the door 11, work was begun on door 12, and the northeast corner was refaced.[20]

In 1947 Erosa wrote an official Instituto Nacional de Antropología e Historia (I.N.A.H.) guidebook for Uxmal.[21] His most interesting observations regard Uxmal's water supply. Erosa doubted that the chultunes could have provided sufficient water for constructional purposes as well as for drinking water. For this reason the local inhabitants covered natural depressions (aguadas) with layers of clay to make watertight basins. One of the most important of these aguadas is that known as "Chenchan," located to the west of the city. Explorations in 1936 revealed its artificial construction.[22] The third edition of the guidebook contains a detailed drawing of the east façade of the House of the Governor by Roman Piña Chan.

During 1947 Alberto Ruz Lhuillier explored and excavated Structure 1, the Chenes-style building west of the House of the Governor, partly covered by the second platform. This building has implications for the dating of the House of the Governor and is discussed in chapter 3.[23] During 1948 Ruz conducted further excavations at Uxmal, concentrating on the Ball Court. The results of this work were published as "El Juego de Pelota de Uxmal."[24]

In 1948 further reconstruction at the House of the Governor was accomplished by Erosa Peniche. The mask column of the northeast corner of the north building was rebuilt, as well as the cornice of this wing.[25] Reconstruction of the monumental stairway also was completed this year.[26]

During 1950 Ruz continued reconstruction at the House of the Governor. The monumental stairway was cleared, cracks were filled with gravel and sascab, and the surface was covered with white mortar and cement.[27] Door 3 of the south wing was reconstructed, as well as sections of the medial molding and frieze above the door, and the interior facing of the vault and flanking walls.[28]

In 1951–52 Ruz headed extensive explorations and reconstructions at Uxmal, including work at the Pyramid of the Magician, the Nunnery, and the House of the Governor. The results of this season's work were published as "Uxmal: Temporada de Trabajos 1951–1952."[29] During this season fallen facing-stones on the south façade of the south wing were replaced and door 1 was reconstructed. The south frieze, separated from the hearting by a 10-cm. crack, was removed and replaced with stone spigots to anchor it.[30] The lowest mask of the southwest corner was also reconstructed.

On the east façade, door 2 was reconstructed, along with adjacent sections of wall and frieze. At this time the excavation at the center of the third platform made by Erosa was refilled. To prevent heavy use of the building by bats and swallows, several of the vents and beam holes were filled with concrete. On the north wing, door 13 was reconstructed, and missing stones from the adjacent interior and exterior walls and frieze were replaced.[31] Ruz also investigated and excavated the two trans-

verse vaults, permitting a more thorough understanding of their building sequence and of the form of the columned porticoes added later.[32] He explored the Picote platform and established its outlines. His examination of the monument led him to reject the claim that it was a phallus, interpreting it rather as "a type of column that is found at the center of the adoratorio and whose upper part is plain. . . ."[33] The small platform of the bicephalic jaguar also was excavated and reconstructed during this season, and the jaguar sculpture was returned to its former position.

In 1953 Ruz delegated reconstruction work at the House of the Governor to the archaeologist César Sáenz. At the south wing several missing elements of the east frieze were replaced and missing sections of the cornice were reconstructed.[34] The low extensions south of the stairway of the fourth platform were also restored at this time, along with several small areas of fallen masonry on the central and northern structures.[35] A mask partly covered at the base of the northeast corner of the fourth platform also was unearthed at this time. The Picote platform was reconstructed, and a small cache was unearthed during the excavations.[36]

A new official I.N.A.H. guidebook for Uxmal, written by Ruz, was published in 1959.[37]

In 1969 Sáenz directed further reconstruction work at the House of the Governor. Sections of the west frieze were restored and tied to the hearting with concrete tenons. The northeast corner of the central building was rebuilt in concrete, and several facing-stones from the lower walls were replaced.[38]

During 1973–74 Pablo Mayer Guala and Barbara Konieczna directed archaeological studies at Uxmal, made necessary by the trenching of the site for the installation of a sound and light show. Only superficial reconnaissance was carried out at the House of the Governor, but a great quantity of painted stucco fragments was discovered in a trench near the western side of the base of the second platform. Among these was a painted Tlaloc head.[39]

Recently the Centro Regional del Sureste of I.N.A.H. has been investigating settlement patterns in the Uxmal region. These investigations, directed by Norberto González Crespo and headed in the field by Alfredo Barrera Rubio, have resulted in the rediscovery of a wall surrounding the site, and have studied a residential sector north of the main site.[40]

While mapping the civic-ceremonial center of Uxmal, Barrera's team relocated the wall around the central part of the site that had formerly been partly mapped by Stephens and Catherwood.[41] This wall has now been mapped with the aid of 1:20,000 scale airphotos of Uxmal. It has an irregular, elliptical plan with a north–south axis of approximately one kilometer and an east–west axis of about 600 meters. Most of the larger masonry buildings, including the House of the Governor, are located within the wall. Test pitting suggests that the wall dates to the Pure Florescent period (ca. A.D. 800–1000).[42]

Mapping and excavations in residential sites north of the civic-ceremonial center of Uxmal revealed considerable diversity in house size and construction. Several of these house types are discussed in chapter 6. These excavations have produced some ceramics dating to the Formative period. The primary period of occupation seems to have been Pure Florescent, however, since the bulk of the pottery belongs to the Cehpech complex.[43]

Notes

Introduction

1. Tozzer (1941:170–71).
2. Stephens (1841, 2:429–30).
3. Recent surveys of Maya civilization include M. D. Coe (1980), Hammond (1982), Henderson (1981), and Morley, Brainerd, and Sharer (1983).
4. For a more detailed consideration of the relationship between northern Maya culture history and the House of the Governor, see chapter 15.
5. More extended coverage of the House of the Governor is provided by Seler (1917:121–46) and Foncerrada (1965). These studies, however, deal with Uxmal as a whole and not specifically with the House of the Governor.
6. de la Croix and Tansey (1970:2).

Chapter 1

1. Kubler (1975:157); Ruz Lhuillier (1959:8).
2. Barrera Rubio (1978:4); Kurjack, Garza T. and Lucas (1979:39).
3. Kubler (1975:158–59); Hartung (1971:52–53).
4. Ruz Lhuillier (1958a). See chap. 5.
5. Kubler (1975:158).
6. Proskouriakoff (1963a:79–80); G. Andrews (1975:65–71).
7. Pollock (1980:257–62). Ruz Lhuillier (1959:50–51).
8. Smith and Ruppert (1954); Kurjack, Garza T., and Lucas (1979:40).
9. Hartung (1971:51), Aveni (1975:184).
10. Pollock (1970:66–75, 80–85).
11. Pollock (1970:75–78).
12. The presence of this stairway was first noticed by Brasseur de Bourbourg (1867c:281).
13. The building was poorly preserved when visited by Stephens (1963, 1:106–108), but has been restored subsequently (Sáenz 1969:5; 1972:34–35).
14. Ruz Lhiullier (1958a:653).
15. See chap. 14.
16. Stephens (1963, 1:104).
17. Ruz Lhuillier (1955b:10–11); Morley (1970). It is possible that the Picote column is related to the large columnar stone

monument worshiped as the Yaxcheel Cab (Green Tree of Abundance) by the Itza of Lake Tayasal (Roys 1967:102).
18. The extensions are 10½ inches high, while the platform is 1 foot 2 inches high.
19. Stephens (1963, 1:106). The present whereabouts of these sculptures are unknown.
20. Pollock (1980:243).
21. Ruppert and Smith (1957:582).
22. Stephens (1963, 1:104).
23. Pollock (1980:242, 274–75) places the hieroglyphic columnar Altar 4 north of the jaguar throne, perhaps on our Feature G, but states that he is relying on memory rather than field notes. Feature F seems to be designed as a monument platform, however, rather than as a building platform.

Chapter 2

1. Roys (1943:175).
2. Roys (1943:178).
3. Stephens (1963, 2:170–74, pl. XXV); Roys (1943:178).
4. Stephens (1963, 2:173–74).
5. Stephens (1963, 2:175) believed that Uxmal was a thriving and populous town at the time of the conquest. However, this is contradicted by archaeological and documentary evidence (Ciudad Real 1875:455–61; Roys 1967:145).
6. Roys ([1941]:621–31; 1943:129–30, 179, 187–88, Map 5, figs. 19–20).
7. Roys (1943:179, 185–92, Map 6, fig. 18); Gropp (1933:260–62).
8. Relaciones de Yucatan (1898–1900, 1:287).
9. Ciudad Real (1875:455–61). See Spinden (1913:5).
10. Ciudad Real (1875:455–61), quoted in Saville (1921:76–78).
11. Roys (1967:71, 78).
12. Sanchez de Aguilar (1937:140).
13. Stephens (1963, 1:197).
14. Cogolludo (1971:231). Cogolludo's history was first published in Madrid in 1688. See Saville (1921:84:86).
15. Ciudad Real (1875:455–61), quoted in Spinden (1913:6).
16. Another early account of Uxmal is that of Father Thomas

De Soza, a Franciscan friar in the monastery of Mérida (Del Rio, in Cabrera 1822:6–7; Warden 1825:176–77). Foncerrada (1965:17–18), however, believes that de Soza probably did not have firsthand knowledge of the site.

17. Among the earliest nineteenth-century reports is that of Lorenzo de Zavala (1834:33–35), in a volume describing the expeditions of Captain Dupaix in Mexico.

18. Waldeck (1838:67–74, 93–104, pls. VII–XVII). Waldeck was inspired to visit Uxmal by a mention of the site in Buchon's (1825) historical atlas of the Americas. His plans are sketchy and inaccurate, while his detailed drawings are somewhat more reliable, but distorted by a tendency toward neoclassical idealism.

19. Waldeck (1838:pl. VII).

20. Waldeck (1838:71).

21. Friedrichstall (1841:291–314).

22. Friedrichstall (1841:307–309).

23. Stephens (1841, 2:428).

24. Stephens (1841, 2:428–29). The plan published by Stephens was good for its day, but is inaccurate in several particulars. Catherwood's drawing is sketchy and not up to his usual standard.

25. Stephens (1841, 2:428, 432–33). Stephens' arranged for the removal and safekeeping, for shipment to him later, of a sculptured death's head from the headdress of one of the figures on the facade. The sculpture is now in the collection of the American Museum of Natural History, New York. (Fig. 21)

26. Stephens (1963).

27. Stephens (1963, 1:95, 99, 101).

28. Stephens (1963, 1:101–102).

29. Stephens (1963, 1:102–103).

30. Stephens (1963, 1:97, 104–105).

31. Catherwood (1844:7–8, 15–17, pls. VIII–XV).

32. Norman (1843:154–67, 199); Heller (1853, 2:258–59); Brasseur de Bourbourg (1858, 2:22–23); José Fernando Ramírez (1926:31–60) visited Uxmal in 1865, in which year the first edition of his work was published.

33. Viollet-le-Duc (1863:1–104).

34. Viollet-le-Duc (1863:64–66, 69–70).

35. Charnay (1863:361–74).

36. These appear in a photographic folio accompanying *Cités et Ruines Americaines*. Photographs of Uxmal appear in plates 35–49, with the House of the Governor in plates 45–49.

37. Brasseur de Bourbourg (1867a:457–60). In one article Brasseur (1867b:39) illustrates a sculptured stone head from an edifice at Uxmal.

38. Brasseur de Bourbourg (1867c:277).

39. Brasseur de Bourbourg (1867c:281). Brasseur's report is also notable for his descriptions of the transverse vaults of the House of the Governor, and the aguadas, chultunes, and water supply of Uxmal.

40. Ober (1884:56–81; 1888:62–65); Alice D. Le Plongeon (1885:376–81); Chavero (1887, 1:424–33, 436–56); Charnay (1887:331–49); Brine (1894:xv–xvi, 336–59). "Neue Forschungen in den Ruinen von Uxmal (Yukatan)," *Globus*, Bd. 71, no. 14, April 3, 1897:220–24.

41. Bancroft (1875:149–200); Holmes (1895–1897:80–94). During this period Lewis Henry Morgan (1880; 1881) attempted to demonstrate that multiroomed palace buildings such as the House of the Governor at Uxmal were joint-tenement houses similar to pueblo architecture of the American southwest. His appraisal of the palaces' communal character was based on an erroneous view of Mesoamerican civilizations as egalitarian

tribal democracies. The function of the House of the Governor is considered further in chap. 6.

42. Holmes (1895–1897:90).

43. Holmes (1895–1897:94).

44. Seler (1906:414–22; 1913:220–35).

45. Seler (1917:121–46).

46. Gordon (1905:144, 147, 153–154, 159, pls. VIIb–VIII).

47. Saville (1909:188, pl. XIII).

48. Morley (1910).

49. Rickards (1910, 1). The House of the Governor and related monuments are shown in plates opposite pp. 32–34.

50. Case (1911). Views of the House of the Governor are opposite pp. 124, 128, 132, 152, and 154.

51. Morley (1911:627–42).

52. Spinden (1913:109, 115).

53. Spinden (1920).

54. Gann (1918:47, 140–42).

55. Saville (1921); Totten (1926:176–217, pls. LXXXIV, LXXXVII) included a discussion of Uxmal and the House of the Governor, but adds little to previous descriptions. Several conjectural color reproductions of the House of the Governor are of interest.

56. Blom (1930, 1931, 1934).

57. The main objectives of the expedition were to map, measure, draw, photograph, and take plaster casts of the buildings of the Nunnery Quadrangle, in order to reproduce and reconstruct the edifice at the 1933 Chicago World's Fair. See Blom (1934:55).

58. Blom (1930:201, 206). A plan of the Nunnery Quadrangle, surveyed by Robert H. Merrill, was published in this article. See also Blom (1934:56).

59. Blom (1932:557–66; 1934:56; 1930:207).

60. Blom (1934:57–58; 1930:209).

61. Morley (1946:330). In 1941 Morley (1942:250–53) also conducted preliminary and exploratory excavations at the Great Pyramid southwest of the House of the Governor.

62. Morley (1946:86–93, 95–97, 107, 109, 113, 165–68, 329, 341, 400). A more detailed study of the Xiu is contained in Morley ([1941]).

63. Morley (1946:167, 330–31). The dominance of Morley's Old Empire-New Empire paradigm is reflected in the work of two art historians who wrote on Uxmal, Salvador Toscano (1970) and Paul Westheim (1962).

64. Kubler (1962:147–50, 163–64).

65. Kubler (1962:149).

66. Foncerrada (1965). Quirarte (1968) contributed a study of architectural differences between Uxmal and Chichen Itza that includes a short description of the House of the Governor.

67. Hartung (1971:51). Teobert Maler's (1971:55, Plan 1, fig. 6) plan of the House of the Governor was published in 1971. No description of the building is included, but Maler's photographs were used by Seler (1917) to illustrate his monograph on Uxmal.

68. G. Andrews (1975:289).

69. G. Andrews (1975:290–91). Andrews's description of the House of the Governor contains a few inaccuracies. He gives the length of the building as "nearly 340 feet" (p. 293) and says that the monumental stairway is nearly 150 feet wide. The building is actually closer to 324 feet long, and the stairway is closer to 135 feet wide.

70. Pollock (1980:242–43). Another brief description and analysis of the House of the Governor has been provided recently by Stierlin (1981:145–48).

Chapter 3

1. Masonry buildings of the Early Period II (c. A.D. 600–800) have walls composed of stone blocks normally extending some distance into the lime concrete core and providing a functional load-bearing surface. Vaults utilize a true corbeling formed of rough slabs tenoned into the mass of the vault. Interior and exterior stonework was rough, with considerable spalling used for stress contact. A thick coat of plaster concealed imperfections and provided a smooth finish. Moldings are normally simple, heavy and rectangular. Decoration was of modeled, painted stucco, which tended to be naturalistic and curvilinear. See Andrews IV (1965a:301–02, figs. 10, 12–13) and Andrews V (1979:1). Differences between Early Period and Puuc architecture are clear at Oxkintok, where two stylistically and chronologically distinct types of building remains are found. Structure 3C6, a building of early style, has an Initial Series Lintel dated 9.2.0.0.0 (A.D. 475). Later buildings are in the pure Puuc style. See Shook (1940).

2. According to Andrews V (1979:3), this new vaulting technique permitted the Maya to build slightly wider rooms.

3. Kubler (1975:153).

4. Pollock (1965:fig. 21).

5. Foncerrada (1965:96); Andrews IV (1965a:309).

6. Foncerrada (1965:41) provides a list of traits characteristic of Puuc architecture.

7. Freidel and Leventhal (1975:fig. 9). A. Miller (1982:38–40) notes Puuclike traits in several possible Terminal Classic/Early Post-Classic structures at Tancah and Xelha, Quintana Roo.

8. Other sites, such as Xkichmook, have architecture that seems to be a blend of both styles. Andrews V (1979:1) and Pollock (1970:82–83).

9. Morley (1946:73).

10. Morley (1946:89–90).

11. J. E. S. Thompson (1945:2).

12. J. E. S. Thompson (1945:4).

13. J. E. S. Thompson (1945:8–9).

14. Foncerrada (1965:36); Andrews V (1979:1).

15. J. E. S. Thompson (1945:8).

16. Andrews IV (1960, 1961, 1965a, 1965b, 1968, 1973).

17. Andrews IV (1965a:298).

18. Parenthetical dates give the duration of the Early period phases in the Goodman-Martínez-Thompson correlation of the Maya and Christian calendars. This is the correlation preferred by the author. Andrews IV, however, preferred the Spinden correlation, which places all Initial Series dates about 256 1/2 years earlier than the Goodman-Martínez-Thompson correlation. Andrews IV's views are considered in this chapter's section on radiocarbon dates.

19. Andrews IV (1965a:298–99; 1965b:51).

20. Andrews IV (1965a:300).

21. See the chronological charts in Andrews IV (1965a:table 1; 1965b:table 4).

22. Andrews IV (1968:42–44).

23. Andrews IV (1965a:310).

24. Andrews IV (1965a:311–13).

25. Andrews IV (1965a:316).

26. Proskouriakoff (1950:170); Kubler (1975:202–13).

27. Andrews IV (1965a:317–18).

28. Andrews IV (1965a:318).

29. Andrews IV (1965a:330).

30. Kubler (1962:142–44).

31. Kubler (1962:143–44).

32. Kubler (1975:152).

33. Deevey, Gralenski, and Hoffren (1959:165); Foncerrada (1965:57).

34. Foncerrada (1965:158–59).

35. Brainerd (1958:3–4).

36. Brainerd (1958:26).

37. Brainerd (1958:27).

38. Brainerd (1958:28) characterized predominant Puuc pottery types as medium and thin slatewares and redwares, as well as tradewares such as Z-fine orange (see Brainerd 1941), and scattered examples of polychrome, suggesting trade with the Motagua Valley, the Campeche-Chiapas area, and more rarely the Peten. X-Fine Orangeware and Plumbate pottery characteristic of the Early Mexican substage at Chichen Itza are either absent or scarce in Puuc collections.

39. Brainerd (1958:28).

40. R. E. Smith (1971:168).

41. R. E. Smith (1971:144).

42. R. E. Smith (1971:162). These two Fine Orange groups influenced northern Yucatan ceramics, particularly Fine State and Puuc Red wares, in terms of vessel forms and decorative techniques. For a close correspondence between a modeled-carved Puuc Red bowl from Uxmal and an Altar Fine Orange pedestal vase from Seibal see Smith (1971:fig. 8m) and Sabloff (1975:figs. 384, 386).

43. R. E. Smith (1971:144).

44. Ruz Lhuillier ([1947]).

45. Ruz Lhuillier (1958a:652, 655).

46. Sáenz (1969a:12).

47. Sáenz (1976:183).

48. Sáenz (1976:186).

49. Ball and Andrews V (1975:239, 243). Dzibilchaltun Structure 57, the "Standing Temple," was constructed during late Early period II. Associated Sayan Red-on-Cream pottery, mixed with Late Copo I ceramics, indicate that this building was constructed no earlier than the second half of Tepeu 2 (c. 9.15.0.0.0 or 9.16.0.0.0 to 10.0.0.0.0), probably around A.D. 800.

50. Ball and Andrews V (1975:243).

51. Andrews IV (1965b:54).

52. Ball and Andrews V (1975:243, note 4).

53. R. E. Smith (1971:144).

54. Ball and Andrews V (1975:44).

55. Andrews V (1979:9) has remarked on this evidence: "It might be argued that if the Cehpech and Sotuta ceramic spheres were contemporary but geographically isolated, then one would not expect to find Sotuta sherds at the Puuc sites. A problem with this argument, however, is that many of the diagnostics of the Sotuta complex, such as Plumbate and X-Fine Orange, are very widespread during Toltec times and could be expected to appear at most, or perhaps all, major sites in the northern lowlands still occupied during the Toltec period. That they do not appear at the Puuc sites must have chronological significance."

56. Traits of Early versus Late-Puuc architecture are considered later in this chapter.

57. Ruz Lhuillier (1945:59–61); Andrews V (1979:6–7).

58. Pollock (1936:123); Kubler (1975:153); G. Andrews (1975:246–70, figs. 163–66, 177); Piña Chan (n.d.:15–18, 23).

59. Proskouriakoff (1950:138, 158–59; 1951:111).

60. Pollock (1980:422–27, fig. 707); Maler (1902:202–204, abb. 4).

61. J. E. S. Thompson (1937:189).

62. J. E. S. Thompson (1937:186; 1950:199); Kelley (1982: 11–15, table 1).

63. Kelley (1982:13).

64. Kelley (1982:11–12); J. E. S. Thompson (1937:185–86).

65. J. E. S. Thompson (1937:196) demonstrated that at a number of Yucatecan sites, including Chichen Itza, Calendar Round dates were accurately placed in the Long Count by accompanying them with a so-called "Tun-Ahau" statement. This places the CR date in a current, numbered Tun of a current Katun ending on a numbered Ahau. As Thompson noted, "Such a combination of Calendar Round date, Tun, and ending day of a Katun can occur only once (18,980 years) in the course of Maya history. Accordingly, this system is as definitive as the Initial Series."

66. Andrews V (1979:7).

67. Morley (1920:358); Beyer (1934:9–13).

68. Pollock (1980:fig. 475).

69. Blom (1934:figs. 3–4).

70. Morley (1920:511).

71. Blom (1934:fig. 3).

72. Spinden (1920:379, 382).

73. Kelley (1982:16).

74. J. E. S. Thompson (1941:106–108; 1973a:61–62).

75. Beyer (1941:337).

76. J. E. S. Thompson (1973a:62).

77. In an earlier paper Thompson (1937) refers to the month position as 19 Kankin. Later (1973a) he switched to calling the month position either 18 or 19 Kankin. The actual numerical coefficient apparently is flaked here and does not permit a final determination of this point. Thompson emended the month position to correspond with the standard Yucatec (Puuc Style) month position for the day Imix. See J. E. S. Thompson (1960:124).

78. Blom (1934:fig. 4). See also Thompson (1973a:fig. 4).

79. The precise placement of this Calendar Round date has been questioned by Kelley (1982:16), who believes that it is inappropriate to place the dates at 10.3.18.9.12 4 Eb 5 Ceh, or at 10.3.8.7.12 4 Eb 15 Ceh, simply because they are nearest in time to his reading of the other Nunnery date. Kelley also questions Thompson's date of 10.3.17.12.1 for the capstone from the East Structure of the Nunnery. These objections will be considered further in chap. 5, where evidence will be presented to support Thompson's readings.

80. Ian Graham (personal communication, 1984). Pollock (1980:274).

81. Ruz Lhuillier (1958a:650). A more detailed discussion of the Uxmal Ball Court Rings occurs in chap. 5.

82. Kelley (1982:15); Ruz Lhuillier (1958a:655).

83. A date from the Chenes region provides some support for the late placement of the House of the Governor. Beneath the second platform of the House of the Governor is the Chenes-style building, Structure 1, whose façade has a dragon-mouth doorway (Pollock 1970:66–75; Seler 1917:17–19. An eighth-century date (9.16.0.0.0, A.D. 751) from the Chenes site Santa Rosa Xtampak may place Structure 1 roughly in time (Pollock 1970:47), and we can assume that some time elapsed between the building of the Structure 1 and the construction of the House of the Governor.

84. Pollock (1980:fig. 472).

85. Morley (1970); Proskouriakoff (1950:163).

86. Kubler (1975:152).

87. Proskouriakoff (1950:162–163, fig. 91a).

88. Morley (1970:169), however, read the day sign as Muluc.

89. Proskouriakoff (1950:figs. 91b, 80d).

90. Proskouriakoff (1950:163–64).

91. Proskouriakoff (1950:fig. 92a–b).

92. Proskouriakoff (1950:164).

93. Proskouriakoff (1950:164).

94. Proskouriakoff (1950:164, fig. 75b).

95. Ruppert, Thompson, and Proskouriakoff (1955:37, 45, fig. 28).

96. Proskouriakoff (1950:163–64).

97. Greene, Rands, and Graham (1972:pl. 148).

98. Graham (1974–216); Greene, Rands, and Graham (1972: pls. 103, 112).

99. Andrews V (1979:5). A more comprehensive discussion and expanded table of dates appears in Andrews IV and Andrews V (1980:281–85).

100. Andrews V (1979:5).

101. Damon, et al. (1974); Pollock (1980:562).

102. Tamers (1969:411).

103. Pollock (1980:211).

104. Deevey, Gralenski, and Hoffren (1959:165).

105. Andrews V (1979:4).

106. Pollock (1980:211).

107. Pollock (1980:211).

108. Tamers (1969–411).

109. Pollock (1980:211).

110. De Vries, Barendson and Waterbolk (1958:136); Vogel and Waterbolk (1963:163–67). According to Kubler (1975:159), a radiocarbon date from a lintel in the North Structure yielded A.D. 893±100. Andrews IV (1965b:64) gives the C-14 date from the same source as A.D. 885±100 (GRO-613). However, Foncerrada (1965:57), citing De Vries (1958:1551), states that the same sample produced a date of A.D. 653±100. Andrews IV's date of A.D. 885±100 is apparently the latest reference to this sample. One would like to know the exact provenance of the lintel beams used for this sample. The North Structure of the Nunnery was built in a two-stage campaign, with an inner structure covered by the now visible outer façade. The sample might thus refer either to the earlier, inner building or to the later, outer structure.

111. Andrews V (1979:5).

112. Andrews IV (1960:263).

113. Andrews IV (1960:264; 1965b:60).

114. Andrews IV (1960:264; 1965b:53–54).

115. Andrews IV (1960:264–65).

116. Andrews IV (1965b:64).

117. See Willey and Shimkin (1973:41).

118. Andrews V (1979); Ball and Andrews V (1975); Andrews IV and Andrews V (1980:281–85).

119. Ball and Andrews V (1975:243).

120. Ball and Andrews V (1975:244); Andrews V (1979:3).

121. Andrews V (1979:5).

122. Foncerrada (1964).

123. Ralph (1965:424–25).

124. Andrews V (1979:5).

125. Pollock (1936, 1940, 1965, 1980); Kubler (1962, 1975); G. Andrews (1975); Andrews V (1979).

126. Pollock (1936:122, 1940:266; 1980).

127. Pollock (1936:123–24).

128. Kubler (1975:153); G. Andrews (1975:246–70).

129. Pollock (1965:431).

130. Proskouriakoff (1963a:56).

131. Proskouriakoff (1963a:56). Shook and Proskouriakoff (1951:238) also reported on two sites called Tohkok and Kayal along the road from Hopelchen to Campeche. Kayal was iden-

tified as an early Puuc site, with veneer masonry walls and slab vaults.

132. G. Andrews ([1979]:7).

133. Piña Chan (1963:101, lams. I–III).

134. Piña Chan (1963:115); Pollock (1980:585, fig. 934).

135. Piña Chan (1963:105, lams. IX, XI).

136. Piña Chan (1963:111–13, lam. XII; 1964:64, lam. 1).

137. Piña Chan (1963:113, lam. XIII; 1964; 67, lam. 3).

138. Ruppert, Thompson, and Proskouriakoff (1955:37, 45).

139. Proskouriakoff (1950:fig. 70c). Headdresses resembling that of the Mul-Chic figure appear on Oxkintok Stela 21, a monument possibly dating to about 10.1.0.0.0 (A.D. 849) according to Proskouriakoff (1950:161), and on El Caribe Stela 2, which is given a style date of 9.17.10.0.0 ± 2 Katuns (Proskouriakoff 1950:145).

140. Proskouriakoff (1950:fig. 75b).

141. G. Andrews ([1979]:9).

142. G. Andrews ([1979]:10, 12, 42–50).

143. G. Andrews ([1979]:fig. 42).

144. G. Andrews ([1979]:12–15); Pollock (1965:431); Stephens (1963, 2:12). Also included in the group of Early Puuc buildings is the temple known as the Mirador at Labna (Pollock 1965:431; G. Andrews [1979]:19–21).

145. Pollock (1965:431).

146. G. Andrews ([1979]:17).

147. G. Andrews ([1979]:42); Pollock (1980:216, fig. 397).

148. Seler (1917:16, abb. 3). See also G. Andrews ([1979]:93).

149. Pollock (1980:216).

150. G. Andrews ([1979]:46).

151. G. Andrews ([1979]:48–50); Pollock (1980:220–22).

152. A woman designated "Lady Kuk" is named on one of the Cemetery Platforms. The same woman is named on several of the monuments dating from the third Katun of Cycle 10 (A.D. 869–889) at Chichen Itza (Kelley 1982:6).

153. Small pieces of these sculptures remain, and traces of red-orange paint are still visible.

154. G. Andrews ([1979]:48).

155. Pollock (1980:585, fig. 934).

156. Pollock (1965:431, note 78; 1980:257).

157. Kubler (1975:158).

158. Kubler (1975:158).

159. Kubler (1975:158).

160. Foncerrada (1965:48).

161. Pollock (1980:179, 188, 241, fig. 349, 366).

162. Bolles (1977:266).

163. Kubler (1975:158).

164. Andrews V (1979:3).

165. Kubler (1975:159).

166. Kubler (1975:159).

167. Seler (1917:abb. 44).

168. Kubler (1975:361, note 43).

169. Kubler (1975:159).

170. Ball (1974, 1979a, 1979b); Ball and Andrews V (1975); Andrews V (1972, 1979); Andrews IV and Andrews V (1980).

171. Andrews V (1979:3); Andrews IV and Andrews V (1980:274–78).

172. Ball (1979b:47); Ball (1977:173–75).

173. Pollock (1980:fig. 934). Andrews V (Andrews IV and Andrews V 1980:274) recently has suggested that "the less elaborate but nevertheless recognizably Puuc architecture of the Western Puuc zone in Campeche is almost certainly earlier [than Classic Puuc] . ., perhaps dating back to 9.16.0.0.0 or 9.17.0.0.0 (ca. A.D. 750–770)."

174. Ball (1979a:33). Ball also has suggested an alternative "total overlap" model, in which the Cehpech and Sotuta ceramic complexes are seen as largely contemporaneous. More recently Charles E. Lincoln, a Harvard graduate student, has argued for a complete overlap of the Pure and Modified Florescent traditions. This view holds that all of the Toltec-style sculptures and buildings at Chichen Itza are basically contemporaneous with the latest Puuc structures at centers such as Uxmal (Lincoln [1982]). Andrews V (Andrews IV and Andrews V 1980:279–80) has argued for the "partial overlap" position, pointing out that "an increasingly accepted argument is that Mexican influence was present in Yucatan considerably before the collapse of the Puuc cities, quite possibly before A.D. 900, and that Puuc and 'Toltec' Chichen Itza coexisted in northern Yucatan for a century or more." However, Andrews V and Sabloff (n.d.:18) have also suggested that it is possible to see "varying amounts of overlap among the different components of the Puuc and Toltec traditions." Thus, while the overlap between ceramic complexes was substantial, the overlap between architectural traditions may have been shorter "even if Toltec buildings are as early as 10.3.0.0.0, because we have so far almost no evidence of major Puuc construction much beyond this time anywhere in the lowlands. This may mean that the construction of buildings in the Puuc and Toltec styles overlapped less than 50 years." I feel the last-mentioned version of the "partial overlap" scheme provides the best interpretation of the data at this point.

175. Ball (1979a:33).

176. Ball (1979b:50). For recent discussions of Chichen Itza inscriptions and discussions of Kakupacal see Kelley (1982), Davoust (1980), and Kowalski (1986b).

177. Ball (1979a:33); Adams (1971:106).

178. Excavations by Ruben Maldonado Cardenas, reported by Lincoln ([1982]:30) and Andrews V and Sabloff (n.d.:10). Ball (1978:139) has suggested that Silho Fine Orangeware was produced in the Canbalam region of western Campeche-Yucatan by at least A.D. 900, "in which case it would have been at least a partial contemporary of the Balancan/Altar group, believed to have been produced further south."

179. Ball (1979a:33).

180. Lee (1973:82–83).

181. Ball (1979a:33).

182. Andrews V (1979:8).

183. Andrews V (1979:9).

184. Andrews V and Sabloff (n.d.:8).

185. Foncerrada (1965:40).

186. Andrews IV (1965a:fig. 17); Proskouriakoff (1950:169).

187. Proskouriakoff (1950, 1951).

188. Proskouriakoff (1970:462–65, figs. 15–17).

189. Ruppert (1952:fig. 151); Kelley (1982:12–13).

190. Andrews V and Sabloff (n.d.:16) recently have suggested that "the inception of Toltec architecture at Chichen Itza cannot yet be firmly placed, but we think that it began shortly after the end of the Cycle 10 inscriptions, perhaps by A.D. 890." Ball (1979b:48–51), on the other hand, has argued for the development of the Puuc style at Chichen Itza from A.D. 866 until A.D. 987, at which point "emphatically Toltec traits" were introduced.

191. Andrews V and Sabloff (n.d.:16) have suggested that the Puuc sites might have been occupied until about A.D. 1000, but admit that the end of the Puuc tradition is difficult to place. Ball (1979b:48), on the basis of ceramic studies, suggested a possible occupation until A.D. 1050 or 1100. In an attempt to resolve this problem, Andrews V and Sabloff (n.d.:16) have

also suggested that "one very real possibility is that the Puuc architectural tradition in northern Yucatan met its demise not too many years after A.D. 900, especially if Chichen Itza was directly involved in this collapse, but that in other parts of Yucatan, and perhaps here as well, the Puuc ceramic tradition continued to exist with little modification, sometimes mixed with Sotuta types, for years afterwards."

Chapter 4

1. Morley (1946:90, pl. 25).
2. Davies (1977–4:5).
3. For example, the surveys of Ball (1974) and Andrews IV (1965a).
4. The *Relaciones de Yucatan* (1898–1900) are fifty reports, dated from 1579 to 1581, made by the encomenderos of Yucatan to the Council of the Indies in response to a questionnaire sent from Spain in 1577. Several of the relaciones from towns in western Yucatan either were written or inspired by Gaspar Antonio Chi, a Xiu on his mother's side. These accounts tend to exaggerate the importance of the Xiu (Tozzer 1957:21).
5. Roys ([1941]); Morley ([1941]).
6. The Katun is a period of 7200 days. The final day of the Katun is always an Ahau, to which the numbers 1 through 13 are assigned. In a full Katun round (a period of 13 Katuns), the numbered Ahaus would run as follows: 1 Ahau, 12 Ahau, 10 Ahau, 8 Ahau, 6 Ahau, 4 Ahau, 2 Ahau, 13 Ahau, 11 Ahau, 9 Ahau, 7 Ahau, 5 Ahau, 3 Ahau, at which point the cycle recommences. A Katun designated by the same numbered Ahau will recur every 256 years and 160 days.
7. J. E. S. Thompson (1937:187–88).
8. Barrera Vasquez and Morley (1949:13–19). On the Codex Perez see Roys (1949a).
9. Tozzer (1957:20). The ancient histories and prophecies of the Maya of Yucatan were copied down and became known collectively as the Books of Chilam Balam, after a priest (Chilam) Balam of the town of Mani who was said to have predicted the advent of a new religion and the coming of the Spanish (bearded white men) a few years before their arrival (Barrera Vasquez and Morley 1949:12–13; Roys 1949b:157). One of the most thorough attempts to correlate and synthesize the historical material in the Chilam Balam Books has been made by Barrera Vasquez and Morley (1949). Barrera Vasquez has translated and annotated the historical sections of the Codex Perez (Chronicle I), Tizimin (Chronicle II), and Chumayel (Chronicle III). He points out that Chronicles I, II, and III are in reality a single chronicle, except that "Chronicle III lacks the first thirty-nine lines in the other two." These missing lines in the Chumayel deal with the early history of the Xiu, which is covered most fully in the first thirty-six lines of Chronicle I (Codex Perez, Mani Manuscript). On the Chilam Balam of Mani or Codex Perez see Barrera Vasquez and Morley (1949:14). For the Chilam Balam of Chumayel see Barrera Vasquez and Morley (1949:16–18), Roys (1933, 1967), and Mediz Bolio (1930). The Chilam Balam of Tizimin is described by Barrera Vasquez and Morley (18–19), and a recent transcription is provided by Edmonson (1982).
10. Roys (1949b:157); Tozzer (1957, XI:20–21).
11. Roys (1933:145).
12. See chap. 2, notes 9–10.
13. Scholes and Roys (1948:74).
14. Barrera Vasquez and Morley (1949:26).
15. Tozzer (1941:43, note 128); Barrera Vasquez and Morley (1949:26, note 2).
16. Tozzer (1941:43, note 128).
17. Sahagún, Book 10, Chapter XXIX. See Anderson and Dibble (1961:197).
18. Seler (1960, 2:1040).
19. Seler (1960, 2:1041).
20. Lehmann (1941:13).
21. Jimenez Moreno (1942:136–37).
22. Ruz Lhuillier (1953:458).
23. Davies (1977:164–65).
24. Davies (1977:165).
25. Davies (1977:165).
26. Tozzer (1941:29–31).
27. J. E. S. Thompson (1970:47).
28. Tozzer (1941:29, note 159).
29. Barrera Vasquez and Morley (1949:26); Brinton (1882:95, 100).
30. Seler (1960, 3:576).
31. Davies (1977:36).
32. Davies (1977:36–37).
33. J. E. S. Thompson (1970:23).
34. J. E. S. Thompson (1970:23).
35. Seler (1960, 3:576).
36. Barrera Vasquez and Morley (1949:27, note 5).
37. Krickeberg (1933:135); Recinos and Goetz (1953:51–59).
38. Barrera Vasquez and Morley (1949:27, note 5).
39. Barrera Vasquez and Morley (1949:27, note 7).
40. Lehmann (1941:14); Davies (1977:36).
41. Recinos (1950:174).
42. Brinton (1882:110); Davies (1977:35); Carmack (1973:273, 287).
43. Tozzer (1941:29–31). See also Landa (1978:15–16).
44. Tozzer (1941:215).
45. *Relaciones de Yucatan* (1898, 1:287).
46. *Relaciones de Yucatan* (1898, 1:288).
47. *Relaciones de Yucatan* (1898, 1:161).
48. Sanchez de Aguilar (1937:140).
49. Tozzer (1941:31–32).
50. Roys (1933:193); Morley ([1941]:18–19).
51. Morley ([1941]:19).
52. Tozzer (1941:30, note 159).
53. Brinton (1882:109).
54. Roys (1940:36).
55. Morley ([1941]:17).
56. *Relaciones de Yucatan* (1898, 1:287).
57. Morley ([1941]:17).
58. J. E. S. Thompson (1970:5).
59. Foncerrada (1965:66).
60. Barrera Vasquez and Morley (1949:26–28).
61. Barrera Vasquez and Morley (1949:33–34).
62. Barrara Vasquez and Morley (1949:29, note 15).
63. Barrera Vasquez and Morley (1949:26–28, 73–74).
64. The name of the Xiu leader in both sources is Ah Mekat (Mani) or Mekat (Tizimin). According to Morley ([1941]:22), this is clearly a title, since the word *mekat* means, "chieftain, leader or captain" (Brinton 1882:124), and *ah* is the masculine prefix. Barrera Vasquez (Barrera Vasquez and Morley 1949:29, note 19), however, has also suggested the possibility that mekat may be related to *mecatl*, from which the Mexican word mecate for "cord, stringer or thread" is derived. In Nahuatl the word, in addition to meaning thread also means "lineage." It is

thus possible that *Ah Mekat Tutul Xiu* may mean "he of the lineage of the Tutul Xiu."

65. Roys (1962:71, 73). Edmonson (1982:4–5) considers the arrival in Yucatan by Mekat Tutul Xiu (the chief of the Tutul Xiu) to have occurred in an earlier Katun 2 Ahau corresponding to A.D. 731–751. Chac-na-Bi-Ton (The East priest Bi Ton) is interpreted as the name of this ruler rather than a place name.

66. Brinton (1882:102).

67. Barrera Vasquez and Morley (1949:33–34).

68. Juan Pío Perez (1866–1877:125).

69. Diccionario de San Francisco (1976:138).

70. According to Barrera Vasquez (Barrera Vasquez and Morley 1949:33, note 37), the name Suytok probably means something like "living flint." He writes, "I have adopted the form *Suytok*, which appears in line 115 of the Tizimin text, because *çuytun* means the "living rock" (tun meaning "stone"); *tok* means "flint." On the other hand, it is probable that in the original text from which the Mani version was copied, this word must have been written as *çuitok*, with the cedilla which has later been lost, leaving simply cuitok."

71. Codex Perez:111, quoted in Morley ([1941]:24–25).

72. Codex Perez:114, quoted in Morley ([1941]:25).

73. Chilam Balam of Tizimin, folios 6r., 7r., quoted in Morley ([1941]:25).

74. The coefficient coupled with the Ahau is partly missing and was originally read by Gates (1937:123) as three, corresponding to the Katun 3 Ahau ending in 1382. Morley ([1941]:29–30), however, noting the presence of the name of Hun Uitzil Chac, suggests that 2 Ahau is the preferred restoration of the dots. Considering the evidence which will be presented in this chapter that suggests that Hun Uitzil Chac was alive near the time of the abandonment of Mayapan, Gates' original reading now seems preferable.

75. On the identification of the figure at the base of the tree as Hun Uitzil Chac see Morley ([1941]:29–30).

76. Morley ([1941]:27); Barrera Vasquez and Morley (1949:74). On Maya naming practices see Roys (1940:35). Edmonson (1982:21, 70, 103) recently has identified Hun Uitzil Chac as the rain priest of Uxmal in a Katun 5 Ahau ending in 1598. However, this ignores the fact that Hun Uitzil Chac is named by Juan Bote as the first lord of Uxmal and pictured on the Xiu family tree as the founder of the Xiu lineage.

77. Barrera Vasquez and Morley (1949:33–74).

78. Gates (1937:15–16); Tozzer (1941:31).

79. Brinton (1882:140, 146).

80. Barrera Vasquez and Morley (1949:33).

81. Barrera Vasquez and Morley (1949:34).

82. Morley ([1941]:23).

83. Foncerrada (1965:62).

84. Brinton (1882:96, 102). See also Barrera Vasquez and Morley (1949:33–34).

85. Brinton (1882:88).

86. Barrera Vasquez and Morley (1949:75–76).

87. Roys (1949a:91–92; 1962:68–78). Tozzer (1957, 11:51) quotes Roys as writing: "It is very difficult, if not impossible, to reconcile this historical material with an often-published belief that there was a league of Mayapan, Uxmal, and Chichen Itza in the 11th and 12th centuries. I do not doubt that such a league did exist at a much later time. Also, it could have included the three cities in question. But, if so, I would suggest that it consisted of the walled city of Mayapan as the dominant member, along with a small but important and aggressive group of Xiu camping out among the magnificent ruins of Uxmal, and another warlike aggressive group living in the post-hegemonic Chichen Itza, which continued to be an important center of pilgrimage, in spite of its loss of military supremacy."

88. Pollock, Roys, Proskouriakoff, and Smith (1962:6).

89. Roys (1933:177–81).

90. Roys (1962:47).

91. Brinton (1882:102); Barrera Vasquez and Morley (1949:34–38).

92. Barrera Vasquez and Morley (1949:34–36).

93. Roys (1933:204, appendix H).

94. Morley ([1941]:51); Barrera Vasquez and Morley (1949:76–77).

95. J. E. S. Thompson (1937:188:89).

96. J. E. S. Thompson (1966:135–37).

97. Roys (1962:43–77).

98. Cogolludo (1971, bk. 9, ch. 14). See Roys (1962:29).

99. It seems doubtful whether the details of this incident would have been recalled with such precision by the Itza if it had occurred during the Katun 8 Ahau which fell 256 years earlier.

100. Roys (1962:80); Tozzer (1957, 11:48).

101. Roys (1962:80).

102. Tozzer (1941:35–39); Landa (1978:16–18); Roys (1962:36) has suggested that the first group of Mexicans appear to have been the Canul mentioned as an affliction to the Maya in a Katun 1 Ahau which fell A.D. 1382–1401.

103. Codex Perez (126–727), quoted in Roys (1962:80–81).

104. Tozzer (1957, 11:49). Edmonson (1982:8–9) concurs in associating Hunac Ceel with the fall of Mayapan in Katun 8 Ahau (A.D. 1441–1461).

105. Roys (1962:34) suggests that there were Indian lords at Chichen Itza in post-Plumbate times, during the hegemony of Mayapan, "just as the Spaniards found a powerful Cupul chief at Chichen Itza in the sixteenth century."

106. Translation by Roys (1962:64). See Tozzer (1941:230–31, lacunae in parentheses from Cogolludo 1867–1868, bk. 4).

107. Roys (1962:53); *Relaciones de Yucatan* (1898, 1:156).

108. Tozzer (1957, 11:51, 56).

109. Tozzer (1957, 11:56); Roys (1962:50); Morley ([1941]:73–148).

110. Roys (1962:53).

111. Tozzer (1941:29–39); Roys (1962:49).

112. Tozzer (1941:vii).

113. Ciudad Real (1873, 2:470–71), quoted in Roys (1962:49), states: "In that *quardania* [Mani], near a mission town called Telchac, a very populous city once existed called Mayapan, in which (as if it were a court) all the caciques and lords of the province of Maya resided and then they came with their tribute. Among these were two principal ones, to whom the others acknowledged superiority and vassalage and for whom they had great respect, one was called Cocom and the other Xiu, and the old Indians say that the Xiu, helped by the other chiefs [principales], killed the Cocom, who was a greater and more important lord than he, . . ."

114. Roys (1962:46).

115. Edmonson (1982:8–9).

116. Tozzer (1941:29–33, 215).

117. Roys (1962:53); *Relaciones de Yucatan* (1898, 1:161).

118. Roys (1962:45–46).

119. *Relaciones de Yucatan* (1898, 1:176–77). Translation in Roys (1962:50).

120. Roys (1962:54).

121. Roys (1962:54–55).

122. Roys (1933:66–70); Roys (1962:78–79).

123. Morley ([1941]:69).

124. Roys (1949b:163–64).

125. Edmonson (1982:8–9).

126. *Relaciones de Yucatan* (1898, 1:192–94). Translation in Roys (1962:53).

127. Roys (1962:55).

128. Roys (1949b:177). This translation is from Roys's combined and annotated text of the Mani and Tizimin prophecies. For the translation from each source see p. 60 and Ch. 4 notes 71–73.

129. Morley ([1941]:69) suggested that they were about 15 and 17 years old, respectively, at the time of the destruction of Mayapan, but on fairly slim evidence.

130. Roys (1962:61–62); Tozzer (1941:216).

131. Roys (1966:171).

132. Stephens (1963, 1:197).

133. Foncerrada (1965:74).

134. Ruz Lhuillier (1955a:50–52, 66).

135. Davies (1977:25).

Chapter 5

1. Morley (1956:143); J. E. S. Thompson (1960:155).

2. Berlin (1958; 1959; 1968b; 1970); Proskouriakoff (1960; 1961a; 1963b; 1964); Kelley (1962); Coggins (1975); Jones (1977); Kubler (1969; 1972a); Mathews and Schele (1974); Lounsbury (1974); Schele (1976); Marcus (1976).

3. According to W. H. Holmes (1895–1897:96, pl. VII), this altar was discovered by E. H. Thompson "half a mile south and a little east of the Governor's Palace." See also Seler (1917: 153–154, taf. 35.1) and Pollock (1980:275), who identifies it as Uxmal Altar 10. The monument belongs to a group of Uxmal monuments designated as altars by Morley (1970). Riese and Mayer (1984:70–73) have contributed a recent study of Altar 10, based in part on my own work.

4. Berlin (1958:111).

5. J. E. S. Thompson (1960:276, fig. 43).

6. The water group includes affixes T32 through T41 in J. E. S. Thompson (1962:445).

7. A faint trace of this hook is visible in Holmes' photograph and on the monument as it now stands in the Ermita.

8. For an exhaustive study of the Ben-Ich prefix, wherein a reading of Ahpop, Ahpo or Ahau is proposed, see Lounsbury (1973).

9. J. E. S. Thompson (1960:38).

10. J. E. S. Thompson (1960:fig. 11; 19–21, 23–25, 28–29).

11. The dots originally may have been present, but have worn away.

12. J. E. S. Thompson (1962:119). The Muluc Variant glyph often occurs with the Ben-Ich superfix, but appears with water group prefixes suggestive of emblem glyph function only on Stela 5 from Tikal (at D10) and on Stela 3 from Caracol, Belize (at A16a; D12b). Both of these possible emblem glyphs have the same T130 postfix as the example from Uxmal.

13. J. E. S. Thompson (1962:198).

14. The diagonals of the Hel glyph normally curve and reach from the upper left to the lower right, the reverse of the Uxmal pattern.

15. I say "seems to have been" because the monument was cracked and repaired and is partly covered by cement in this and other points. For the original appearance of the glyph see Holmes (1895–1897:pl. VII), our fig. 36.

16. J. E. S. Thompson (1962:119).

17. David Kelley (personal communication) interprets the final emblem glyph at B5 as consisting of an emblem glyph prefix, perhaps T229, a main sign which may be a variant of the T683a moon sign, and no postfix. He also interprets the second emblem glyph main sign at A4 as an "earplug" glyph rather than a Muluc Variant (Kelley 1982:8, fig. 6). He does, however, agree that both are emblem glyphs.

18. Proskouriakoff (1961b:83).

19. The prefix has an upper and lower circle joined by striated lines, as in T110, but it also has a border at the left edge, which causes it to resemble T1 somewhat as well.

20. J. E. S. Thompson (1962:264–65).

21. See pages 30, 31, 34, 36, 37, 65, and 67 of the Dresden Codex in Villacorta and Villacorta (1930).

22. Proskouriakoff (1961b:84; 1963, 1964); Mathews and Schele (1974); Kelley (1962).

23. Jones (1977:35).

24. Kubler (1973).

25. Barrera Vasquez and Morley (1949:34–35).

26. Tozzer (1941:138); Roys (1967:67, note 1).

27. Roys (1967:67, note 5).

28. *Relaciones de Yucatan* (1898, 1:287); Tozzer (1941:15).

29. See chap. 4 for a consideration of these sources.

30. Roys (1943:177).

31. Roys (1943:175).

32. Roys (1967:67).

33. The last translation is my own, based on the following: (1) the word *hun* means one in Yucatec Maya (Tozzer 1921:99), and could express the concept "unique"; (2) the word *chac* can mean the rain god, as well as rain (Diccionario de Motul:240); and (3) the root word of *uitzil* is *uitz*, which means hill. It is combined with the suffix *il*, one function of which is to express national or ethnic identity, as in *Ho-il*, a "meridano" (Tozzer 1921:31).

34. J. E. S. Thompson (1960:fig. 27).

35. J. E. S. Thompson (1962:105).

36. The name "Chac-Uinal-Kan" was suggested by Floyd Lounsbury (personal communication), who also identified the uinal characteristics of the ear. He also points out possible glyphic and semantic connections between this Uxmal name and the names of three rulers at Palenque; the two figures known "cauac uinal" (Lounsbury 1974) and the ruler Lord Chaac (Mathews and schele 1974), who also has a uinal component in his name.

37. The compound could not signify marriage in this case, since it links two males. Another possibility would be that it names a relationship between close kin, such as a brother and sister, but this seem less likely.

38. Some evidence exists in the inscriptions of other sites supporting the idea that Lord Chac-Uinal-Kan and Lady Bone are the parents of Lord Chac, and that the distinctive Serpent Segment glyph names this relationship. See Kelley (1962:324; 1982:8), for identifications of similar relationship glyphs in the inscriptions of Quirigua and Chichen Itza. See also Pahl (1976: 35). The strongest evidence for the "parentage" meaning of this Serpent Segment glyph comes from its usage in the present context and from the structure of the passage. According to Lounsbury (personal communication) this is the standard format for a parentage statement as a part of the extended appellative phrase of the protagonist: Own Name=Relationship-=Father's Name=Relationship=Mother's name.

39. This Imix compound occurs as an introductory glyph

with some frequency in Yucatecan and other Maya inscriptions (J. E. S. Thompson (1962:88). Kelley (1976:fig. 83) has suggested that it is a title having the reading *batab*, but this is by no means certain. Riese and Mayer (1983:72), following Schele (1982:156–58), have suggested that it is a generalized introductory verb, perhaps with the reading *u'bah* (Yuc.), meaning "here is described."

40. Kelley (1968). Lounsbury (personal communication) has suggested that this inverted vase with prefixed flare, with crossed bands on the side of the vessel, and with three dots beneath it (or sometimes with a prefixed number nine) may be one of the appellative or attribute glyphs of the Maya sun god also used as a name or title by Maya rulers. He points out that on the second panel of alfardas of the Temple of the Sun at Palenque it is part of a two-glyph second appellative of GIII of the Triad. He identifies GIII as Ahaw K'in, who is equivalent to the Kekchi Xbalamq'e and the Xbalanque of the *Popol Vuh*. David Kelley (personal communication) also suggests that the T122:552/293:III glyph group at B1 is a title.

41. Morley (1970:fig. 21).

42. The Chac-Uinal main sign probably has the same T84 subfix (or possibly T87), and the T507 main sign has an added subfix of two circles and the T130 postfix.

43. A drawing by Ian Graham (personal communication) shows the outlines of a human face (possible female head?) on the interior of this main sign, but the carving is faint and the identification uncertain.

44. Lounsbury (1974a:ii).

45. A discussion of the following glyphs appears in Kowalski ([1981]:271; 1985b). A reference to fire (T565a:43?:122) occurs at position O, followed at P by a feminine head profile (T1000:16?). This glyph is probably also the personal name of some noble woman, but her relationship to the other figures is uncertain.

46. There are examples of recognizable emblem glyphs without the water group prefix in the inscriptions of other Maya sites. See Marcus (1976:10) and Kelley (1962:327).

47. Marcus (1976:fig. 1.6).

48. J. E. S. Thompson (1973a:62).

49. As noted in chap. 4, Kelley has objected to Thompson's methodology for the 10.3.18.9.12 date of the Building Y capstone. After a reexamination of the capstone in the East Structure of the Nunnery he also now rejects the Thompson date of 10.3.17.12.15 Imix 18 Kankin, and prefers a date of 11.12.17.11.1 5 Imix 19 Kankin—although he admits that this date cannot possibly be contemporary with the structure (Kelley 1982:16). This date was also proposed by Morley (1920:510–11) and Spinden (1920:379, 382). However, despite Kelley's arguments, considering the fact that the name glyphs of Lord Chac appear on Stela 14, which must be placed between about 10.0.0.0.0 and 10.5.0.0.0 on the basis of style, and on the rings of the Ball Court, for which Kelley (1982:15) himself has proposed a date of 10.3.15.16.14 2 Ix 17 (written 16) Pop, I am still inclined to accept Thompson's dates for the Nunnery capstones as most plausible. In addition, the glyphic monument ('Stela 17') at the base of the stairway of the North Structure of the Nunnery has a Tun-Ahau statement recording a Tun falling in a Katun 12 Ahau (Pollock 1980:274). This date must fall in the third katun of Cycle 10, and thus supports the Thompson interpretation.

50. Ruz Lhuillier (1958a:646, fig. 5).

51. J. E. S Thompson (1962:265).

52. J. E. S. Thompson (1962:265). Thompson identifies the subfix as T103.

53. Kelley (1982:15).

54. On the north side of the east ring a Calendar Round date occurs that has been identified as ? Ix 16 Pop. This is followed by 17 "winged" Cauac (naming a Tun 17) and a 12 Ahau (signifying a Katun ending on 12 Ahau). According to Thompson's (1937) method for reading Yucatecan dates this signifies a date? Ix 16 Pop (Puuc style) falling a Tun 17 of a Katun 12 Ahau. On the north side of the west ring the Calendar Round date is ?? 17 Pop, followed by a winged Cauac with a numeral 12 or 17 (Tun 12 or 17), in turn followed by a 12 prefixed to a destroyed daysign (probably Ahau).

The dates on the rings originally were read by Morley (1920:514–15), who interpreted the rings as marking a shift from Classical to Puuc-style dating. He thought that both of the rings recorded the same day, Ix, falling once on 16 Pop and once on 17 Pop. The "Tun-Ahau" statements were interpreted as referring to certain Tuns ending on certain Ahaus, rather than as Tuns within Katuns ending on a certain Ahau as in Thompson's (1937) later system. The only day on which a day Ix can fall in a 17th Tun ending on a day 12 Ahau is 11.15.16.12.14 10 Ix 17 Pop, which was Morley's accepted date for the rings.

In 1937 Thompson (193–94) read the dates of the west ring and east ring as 10.3.16.16.19 3 Cauac 17 Pop and 10.3.16.17.0 4 Ahau 18 Pop, respectively. Thompson (Proskouriakoff and Thompson 1947:146–47) later revised these readings and placed the dates at 9.10.16.6.14 9 Ix 17 (written 16) Pop for the east ring, and 9.10.16.6.15 10 Men 18 (written 17) Pop for the west ring. Ruz (1958a:644–50) accepted these Long Counts, but pointed out that Thompson made an error calculating the day numbers, which should be 6 Ix 17 (written 16) Pop and 7 Men 18 (written 17) Pop.

55. Ruz Lhuillier (1958a:656–57).

56. The masonry of the Ball Court is extremely fine and probably late.

57. Kelley (1982:15). Floyd Lounsbury (personal communication), before learning of the results of Hartig's inspection, also proposed that the Tun coefficient might be 16 rather than 17, which places the date at 10.3.15.16.14 2 Ix 17 (written 16) Pop.

58. Kelley (1982:fig. 6) identifies it as an earplug emblem glyph.

59. One of these appears in the upper register, followed by what looks like a moon sign (T683) glyph. Another occurs in the lower register with a T16/T17 "yax" postfix. For illustrations of the glyphs discussed see Kowalski (1986a).

60. Stephens (1963, 1:259); Kurjack, Garza T., and Lucas (1979:40) have recently confirmed the sacbe's existence and support the idea that it linked Kabah with Uxmal as a politically integrated community.

61. God B glyphs occur on Lintels 3A and 7A of the second story of the Monjas at Chichen Itza. Furthermore, at position B on Lintel 7A there is a female name with a T110 bone postfix resembling the prefixed element of Lady Bone's name on Uxmal Altar 10. These Monjas lintels have a Calendar Round date of 8 Manik 15 Uo which is placed at 10.2.10.11.7 (A.D. 880) in the Long Count (J. E. S. Thompson 1977:266).

Another possible God B glyph appears at position D4 on a drum from the south column of Structure 6E1 at Chichen Itza. Proskouriakoff (1970:462–65, fig. 17) has pointed out resemblances between the figures on this column and those of the Puuc area. The God B glyph names a figure wearing a broad-brimmed headdress somewhat similar to that worn by Lord Chac on Uxmal Stela 14. All four figures on the column war distinctive two-lobed chest pectorals like those worn by the male figure to the right of Lord Chac on Stela 14. These resemblances strongly suggest that the God B glyphs in the Cycle 10 inscriptions and late sculpture of Chichen Itza are references to Lord Chac of Uxmal. Contact between the two sites is also indicated by the fact that the Chichen ruler Kakupacal is mentioned on an inscription from the Chan Chimez Group at Uxmal (Kelley 1982:10).

Chapter 6

1. Evidence connecting Lord Chac with the House of the Governor is presented in chaps. 5 and 10.

2. Harrison (1971:62–63).

3. For example, if a deposit contains only ceremonial goods it implies that the structure was used for ceremonial activities. Conversely, a large proportion of domestic pottery and utilitarian artifacts would suggest a more secular use for a building.

4. Erosa Peniche ([1947a]:5–6).

5. Ruz Lhuillier (1955a). See chap. 14 for a discussion of the two-headed jaguar throne.

6. Ruz Lhuillier (1955a:62).

7. Ruz Lhuillier (1955a:fig. 6).

8. Ruz Lhuillier (1955a:64). An olla is a globular pot, while a cajete refers to a dish or bowllike vessel.

9. Gann (1918:140–42).

10. Saville (1921:126–27, pls. V–VII).

11. Tozzer (1941:151–52).

12. Harrison (1971:238) has suggested that such "house-cleaning" was a typical practice during the Classic period.

13. Harrison (1971:66).

14. Holmes (1895–1897:90); Morley (1946:330); Kubler (1962:148).

15. Cogolludo (1971:231).

16. Pollock (1965:409–411).

17. Harrison (1971:88); W. R. Coe (1967:55).

18. J. E. S. Thompson (1954a:57–58).

19. Tozzer (1941:130).

20. J. E. S. Thompson (1939:22) also put forward this position in his report on San José, British Honduras. In an earlier report Thompson (1931:237–48) described the type of architecture he believed to be residential. In the Mountain Cow district of British Honduras at the sites of Tizimin Kax, Cahal Cunil and Cahal Pichik he excavated several plazuelas that supported long, low platforms but no surviving buildings. Thompson interpreted these platforms as supports for the Maya noble's houses, whose form corresponds to the dwellings of Yucatec Maya lords described by Landa.

21. Satterthwaite (1937:20).

22. Satterthwaite (1937:19); Morley (1946:fig. 39, pls. 69–70a).

23. Harrison (1971:220).

24. Bullard (1960); Willey (1956).

25. Vogt (1964b:308).

26. Vogt (1964a:23).

27. Vogt's (1964a:29–30) work among the Maya of Zinacantan persuaded him that the cargo system of rotation of religious offices found today in highland Maya communities is so fundamental that it probably has pre-conquest roots. For a recent counterargument see M. J. Becker (1979).

28. Vogt (1964a:30). M. D. Coe (1966:94–95) also questioned the use of the palaces as dwelling places for the Maya rulers.

29. Tozzer (1911:96–98).

30. Spinden (1913:98).

31. Spinden (1913:101).

32. J. E. S. Thompson, Pollock, and Charlot (1932:111).

33. Pollock (1965:409).

34. Pollock (1965:382).

35. Morley (1956:322–23; 1946:table VIII).

36. Morley (1946:330, pl. 25a).

37. A. L. Smith (1950:26, 44, 70–73) noted that the architectural changes made at Uaxactun Structure A-V during the Classic period involved the replacement of temples by multi-roomed palaces. He concluded that "this clearly indicates that A-V complex changed from its purely ceremonial function to that of a palace or dwelling."

38. A. L. Smith (1962:165–330).

39. Tozzer (1941:85–86).

40. Bullard (1960:369).

41. Kubler (1975:131).

42. Kubler (1975:140, 142, 147) included Structure 1 at Quirigua, the Palace at Palenque, and several of the long, galleried palaces at Piedras Negras in this category.

43. Kubler (1975:1552).

44. Kubler (1975:152).

45. Kubler (1975:158).

46. Harrison (1971:298).

47. Harrison (1971:fig. 17).

48. Harrison (1971:299).

49. Harrison (1971:311).

50. Harrison (1971:186–87, 298–303).

51. Harrison (1971:313:16).

52. Potter (1977:16–45); Ruppert and Denison (1943:57–59, figs. 68–69, pls. 20–21).

53. Potter (1977:25–26).

54. Potter (1977:42–45).

55. Adams (1970:492).

56. Adams (1974:286).

57. Adams (1970:493). In addition to Harrison, Potter, and Adams, M. J. Becker (1979) recently has contributed an intellectual history and critique of the ceremonial-center concept, and its implications that the masonry buildings at the centers of Maya sites were uninhabited.

58. Means (1917:19).

59. More recently Villa Rojas (1945:52) observed that typical Maya houses in Quintana Roo had no windows, which caused the interiors to be dimly lit.

60. A. L. Smith (1950:55–56, 83, fig. 46).

61. For example, see Piedras Negras Stela 14 (Maler 1901: pl. XX, no. 2), the Initial Series Vase from Uaxactun (A. L. Smith 1932:fig. 9) and the Vase of the Seven Gods (no. 49) in M. D. Coe (1973:107).

62. Harrison (1971:286, 315). Landa (Tozzer 1941:86–87) reports that beds of small rods covered with sleeping mats were used in Yucatan at the time of the conquest. Examples of lashed wooden frameworks (e.g., litters, cages) appear on Lintel 3 of Temple IV at Tikal (W. R. Coe and Shook 1961:fig. 29) and the Art Institute of Chicago Vase (Paul 1976:120). See also Lounsbury and Coe (1968).

63. Tozzer (1941:85–86).

64. Tozzer (1941:171).

65. J. E. S. Thompson (1954b:71–72, 81).

66. E. H. Thompson (1886:252–53).

67. Ruppert and Smith (1957:580–84).

68. Ruppert and Smith (1957:580).

69. Ruppert and Smith (1957:581–82, fig. 3b, c, j).

70. Barrera Rubio (1978:fig. 1).

71. E. H. Thompson (1897:5–8, pls. 1–8); Pollock (1980:561).

72. Morley (1956:264:65).

73. Brainerd (1958:30).

74. Coggins (1967).

75. Satterthwaite (1935:7).

76. Satterthwaite (1935:29–30, 43; 1937); Morley (1946:pls. 69–70a, fig. 39).

77. Proskouriakoff (1960:459).

78. Proskouriakoff (1961a: 172, 175); Morley (1946:pl. 69).

79. Proskouriakoff (1960:460).

80. Coggins (1967:18).

81. Satterthwaite (1935:34–35); Maudslay (1889–1902, 4:23, pls. 41, 44).

82. Coggins (1967:19).

83. Aveni (1975:182).

84. Hartung (1971:51); Stephens (1963, 1:221).

85. According to Aveni (1975:table 5), the azimuth of the alignment perpendicular to the central doorway of the House of the Governor is 118°05′, while the azimuth of the alignment from the central doorway to Nohpat is 118°13′. These are very close to the Venus rise position at maximum southerly declination in A.D. 750, 118°03′.

86. Aveni (1975:184).

87. Seler (1906:414–20; 1917:135, abb. 115). Weldon Lamb (1980) recently has suggested that explicit Venus symbolism exists in the number of Xs (584 + 3 half Xs) found in the forty-eight serpent bars of the East Structure of the Nunnery. Since the Maya calculated the synodic period of Venus as 584 days, and since other Venus symbolism is evident in the art of Uxmal, Lamb's suggestions deserve serious consideration. However, his proposal ignores the fact that the Xs were originally covered with plaster and form a plaited lattice pattern. Hence they were not viewed separately, but as part of a unified field. See chap. 13 for a further consideration of such lattices.

Chapter 7

1. Morris, Charlot, and Morris (1931, 1:212, fig. 128).

2. Morris, Charlot, and Morris (1931, 1:213, fig. 129).

3. Morris, Charlot, and Morris (1931, 1:213:fig. 130).

4. Andrews IV and Rovner (1973:83, 85, fig. 4:10–13).

5. Andrews IV and Rovner (1973:85–86, figs. 7, 8:9).

6. Morris, Charlot, and Morris (1931, 1:214).

7. Andrews IV and Rovner (1973:86:87, fig. 8:10).

8. Morris, Charlot, and Morris (1931, 1:215).

9. Andrews IV and Rovner (1973:87, fig. 9:11). For a discussion of stone cutting techniques in Central Mexico see Outwater (1957). Holmes (1895–1897:198, fig. 62) mentions stone sawing as a possible technique at Palenque, but this does not seem to have been employed at the House of the Governor.

10. Andrews IV and Rovner (1973:89). See also Morris, Charlot, and Morris (1931, 1:210).

11. Morris, Charlot, and Morris (1931, 1:210); Andrews IV and Rovner (1973:89).

12. Andrews IV and Rovner (1973:83–91, figs. 1, 2, 3:7–8, 4:9, 6, 10, 11:4).

13. Morris, Charlot, and Morris (1931, 1:209).

14. The entire platform system of the House of the Governor was surveyed and mapped by the author and Roy Whitehead of Hingham, Massachusetts, in March, 1978. A Dietzgen engineer's transit was used, with a stadia constant of 0.77 feet from the center of the instrument, provided courtesy of the Middle American Research Institute center in Merida.

15. Morris, Charlot, and Morris (1931, 1:216) note the consistent variation from right angles on corner stones and facing stones at Chichen Itza. See also Morris, Charlot, and Morris (1931, 1:206–207). Satterthwaite (1935:1) notes the absence of the right angle at Piedras Negras. For a dissenting view see Hartung (1977:125), who asserts that "a precise (in-front-of-the-building) relation—that is, at 90 degrees to the façade—has been proved, and furthermore astronomically, in the case of the Palace of the Governor at Uxmal." Hartung is referring to the relationship between the House of the Governor and the mound at Nohpat mentioned in chap. 6 (Aveni 1975:184). A recent consideration of the problem appears in Aveni and Hartung (1982).

16. Morris, Charlot, and Morris (1931, 1:209–210); Pollock (1965:395–96).

17. For a further discussion of rope as a possible Maya measuring device see the section on proportion in chap. 9.

18. Morris, Charlot, and Morris (1931, 1:215).

19. Morris, Charlot, and Morris (1931, 1:215).

20. Morris, Charlot, and Morris (1931, 1:216). On quarrying see also Bullard (1960:363) and Pollock (1965:397).

21. Morris, Charlot, and Morris (1931, 1:221–23, figs. 133–37).

22. Morris, Charlot, and Morris (1931, 1:223). See note 20. According to Littmann (1960:409), the plasters of the Puuc region tend to rely heavily on sascab, and use only enough burned lime to insure rapid setting.

23. Morris, Charlot, and Morris (1931, 1:224).

24. Bolles (1977:246).

25. Andrews IV (1965a:310–311).

26. Sharp (1978:93).

27. Sharp (1978:93).

28. Sharp (1972:31–32).

29. Erasmus (1965:296–97).

30. For estimates of the man-hours required to complete various types of tasks involved in the construction of monumental architecture see Erasmus (1965). I simply applied these calculations to the amounts of masonry needed to complete the House of the Governor rather than the Nunnery Quadrangle.

31. Seler (1917:121) suggests that a natural hill determined the placement of the House of the Governor. See also Ruz Lhuiller (1959:33).

32. Pollock (1965:386). In the Puuc region, ruins near Uxmal such as Chacmultun, Tzula, Kom, Kiuic, and Itzimte make use of natural hills that have been artificially terraced to serve as substructures for palace-type structures. E. H. Thompson (1904:8–20, pls. I–III) provides descriptions of Chacmultun and Tzula. For Kiuic see Mariscal (1928:31–37). For Kom and Kiuic see Reygadas Vertiz (1928:187–97). Plans of Itzimte appear in Von Euw (1977:6–7).

33. Pollock (1970:66–78).

34. An excellent idea of the general form of this lowest platform can be gained from Frederick Catherwood's drawing of the front of the House of the Governor that appears as the frontispiece to Stephens (1963, 1:fig. 1). Unless otherwise stated, all measurements cited are by the author.

35. Pollock (1965:398) describes dirt, mud, stone, sascab, mortar, and habitation debris as the standard materials used for fill. Typical Maya platforms consist of a rough rubble fill within masonry retaining walls. Certain exceptions exist, such as platforms of dirt fill covered with stucco or more finished construc-

tions with a compact fill of stone and mortar. The terraces of the House of the Governor conform most closely to this last type.

36. This corresponds to the usual technique employed at Chichen Itza (Morris, Charlot, and Morris 1931, 1:205). This discussion of platform construction and surfacing is based on the composition of the building platform of the House of the Governor, where sections of the flooring still exist.

37. These measurements, determined by the author's survey, conform to those found on Merrill's (1930) map.

38. Friedrichstall (1841:308) gives the height as 26 feet. Stephens (1963, 1:103) and Seler (1917:121) give the height as 20 feet. Merrill's (1930) map indicates a height of 25 feet. The height varies from south to north and east to west.

39. Many of these corner stones are still in place at the southeast corner.

40. These corner stones are also about 3 feet 6 inches across the face.

41. Our measurements correspond to those on the Merrill (1930) map.

42. According to Morris, Charlot, and Morris (1931, 1:205), a similar construction method was used at Chichen Itza.

43. Stephens (1963, 1:106) describes this as "a grand staircase 130 feet broad, which once contained 35 steps." Seler (1917:123) gives the width as 40 meters (135 feet) and also mentions 35 steps. If the five steps of the smaller stairway of Platform 4 are added then the total number of steps is actually 33.

44. For the definition of a building platform see Satterthwaite (1943:16).

45. The lower part of the mask at the northeastern corner was revealed during excavations carried out in 1951–1952 under the direction of Alberto Ruz Lhuillier.

46. Alberto Ruz Lhuillier (personal conversation, 1976) concurred with this idea.

47. This lack of truly strong or especially supportive foundations is characteristic of Maya architecture. See Morris, Charlot, and Morris (1931, 1:206), L. Roys (1934:74–75), and Pollock, Roys, Proskouriakoff, and Smith (1962:62). Occasionally specially prepared masonry footings were incorporated in the substructure for the support of the building, as at the Mercado at Chichen Itza (Ruppert 1943:234–35, fig. 4a).

48. Some type of projecting base is a common feature in Maya architecture, though it is not invariably present. For plain basal zones typical of southern Maya buildings see Ruppert, Thompson, and Proskouriakoff (1955:figs. 3, 4, 8), Maler (1903:fig. 56), and Tozzer (1911:fig. 34). For the more elaborate multi-membered moldings of the northern area see Pollock (1965:fig. 21:1, 4–10).

49. See note 47.

50. Our measurements of this basal slope showed it to be irregular and not comparable to the precise entasis of the Parthenon.

51. Although they do not always occur, such steps up to a higher floor in the rear chambers of buildings are common in Maya architecture. See A. L. Smith (1937:pl. 23), Tozzer (1911:figs. 30, 42, 45), and Pollock (1965:400). In northern Yucatan such interior steps occur at Uxmal, notably in the East, West, and North Structures of the Nunnery Quadrangle, as well as at Kabah (Codz Poop), Labna, Chacmultun, and elsewhere.

52. It is interesting to speculate on the method used to mark the positions of the jambs and cornerstones. At Uaxactun there is an example of the walls of a building having been outlined on the plaster floor of a supporting platform prior to construction (A. L. Smith 1950:24), while a related working method was used

at Chichen Itza (Morris, Charlot, and Morris 1931, 1:146). An examination of the plaster floors of the House of the Governor failed to turn up any evidence of such incisions. Nevertheless, the architects and artists of Uxmal were well acquainted with both the incision and painting of stucco. It is possible that the positions of the cornerstones and jambs at the House of the Governor were marked originally by incising or painting the plaster floor, but that evidence was disturbed when the jambs were reset.

53. This practice is also visible in the columns of the Temple of the Warriors at Chichen Itza (Morris, Charlot, and Morris 1931, 1:206–207).

54. With the exception of the interior doorway of the central chamber, where the jambs have been reset and concrete lintels emplaced.

55. From the irregularity of the seams it is evident that the top of each layer was only roughly smoothed, undoubtedly so that the succeeding layer would have a better bonding surface. A similar course-by-course building procedure was used at Chichen Itza (Morris, Charlot, and Morris 1931, 1:206).

56. The wall construction of the House of the Governor falls within the general heading of "New Empire Lime Concrete" according to Lawrence Roys's (1934:62) analysis of Maya building techniques. This type of masonry differs from others in the Maya area in that the principal structural material is a concrete made of burnt and slaked lime mixed with sascab and broken or crushed limestone. Other descriptions of nothern Maya concrete and facing masonry appear in Shook (1940:169) and Andrews IV (1965a:307).

57. See Morris, Charlot, and Morris (1931, 1:205).

58. Morris, Charlot, and Morris (1931, 1:215).

59. L. Roys (1934:68–69).

60. L. Roys (1934:70, note 1).

61. At the time of Stephens's (1963, 1:101–103) and Catherwood's visit in 1841, all of the lintels in the exterior doorways had fallen and deteriorated. In some of the interior doorways the lintels were still in place, while others were lying on the floors. One of the lintels found in the south end apartment (Room 2) was sculptured with a hieroglyphic inscription. This zapote wood beam was 10 feet long, 1 foot 9 inches wide, and 10 inches thick. This beam was removed from Uxmal, taken to the United States of America, where it appeared in Catherwood's panorama. It was subsequently destroyed by fire.

62. The span of the central doorway is even greater—6 feet 8 inches.

63. Morris, Charlot, and Morris (1931, 1:220).

64. Morris, Charlot, and Morris (1931, 1:209).

65. Had the masons of the House of the Governor desired vents in these rooms they could have constructed them despite the thickness of the wall. That they did not suggests that the vents were intended to serve a functional purpose, such as admitting light and providing ventilation. Constructing narrow vents with a length of nine feet would have served neither of these purposes.

66. Ruz Lhuillier (1955a:58–59).

67. L. Roys (1934:75) notes that partition wall masonry is occasionally well bonded with that of the side walls, but the more common pattern is to have a clear overlap or vertical seam.

68. See L. Roys (1934:fig. 19).

69. Because the wall was capped with a smooth layer of stucco it can be assumed that the drying or setting time was expected to be lengthy, perhaps as long as a season or more. Maya architects apparently considered the strength of the

lower wall crucial for the support of the vaults and upper façades.

70. L. Roys (1934:69, note 2).

71. This type of offset is a characteristic feature of much Maya architecture. The offset that continues around all four sides of the room is typical of Puuc-style buildings, and has been used to distinguish them from the somewhat earlier Chenes style architecture to the south, where the offset is typically restricted to the long walls of the rooms (Pollock 1970:81).

72. Conversely, it is quite common to find vaulting in Puuc ruins where large sections of the boot-shaped facing stones have fallen, but where the concrete vault core still stands.

73. Presumably the end walls of the vault were constructed course by course with the rest of the vault.

74. Morris, Charlot, and Morris (1931, 1:216).

75. Holmes (1895–1897:49).

76. E. H. Thompson (1911:513).

77. L. Roys (1934:50).

78. L. Roys (1934:50); Roys (1934:50, figs. 15–16) also suggested the deep embedding of the beams indicated that they were used in some instances as tension members to prevent structural failure due to outward thrust, and that they served to support downward loading of masonry masses by transmitting their load to the vertical walls. He also suggested that the transverse beams may have supported a temporary framework of logs, laid horizontally, that served to guide and support the construction of the vaults. Spinden (1913:109) believed that impermanent wooden forms were used in vault construction. Morris (Morris, Charlot, and Morris 1931, 1:207–208), however, points out that the specialized shape of Yucatec boot-shaped vault stones indicates that the masons designed the stones so that gravity would hold them in position even before any mortar was applied to their tenons. By carrying the vaults upward only one course at a time, permitting them to set, and making sure that the courses projected equally on both sides of the supporting wall to maintain balance, vault construction could have progressed without the need of elaborate scaffolding or wooden forms. Simple lashed ladders may have provided the masons with access to the upper surfaces of the vaults. The use of such ladders in Late Classic times is illustrated by Maler (1911:figs. 9, 13; 1901:pls. XV–no. 3, XX–no. 1–2, XXII).

79. Maya masons often inclined the surface of rough masonry walls in this fashion (Morris, Charlot, and Morris 1931, 1:147).

80. For an account of excavations and reconstructions of the transverse vaults see Ruz Lhuillier (1955a:59–60, fig. 4). A synopsis of the building sequence also appears in Ruz Lhuillier (1959:33).

81. The stones of the central wall are larger, rougher, and have more chinking than those of the vault soffits.

82. Catherwood (1844:pl. 10).

83. Stephens (1963, 1:95) relates that the large section of the eastern façade had collapsed in 1825. Catherwood's drawing of the House of the Governor appears as the frontispiece to this volume. For early photographs of the east and west facades see Seler (1917:taf. XXIII).

84. Martínez Cantón ([1926]) reported that the cleavage was 8 cm. to 40 cm. wide at the top of the building.

85. Such sectional construction of the façade is also suggested by the construction technique used in the fill of the Temple of the Chac Mool at Chichen Itza, and on the core of the terraces of the Temple of the Warriors (Morris, Charlot, and Morris 1931, 1:146–47, 151, fig. 97).

86. L. Roys (1934:fig. 20).

87. L. Roys (1934:fig. 21). Morris, Charlot, and Morris (1931, 1:208).

88. L. Roys (1934:71) found this two-stage system of vault construction interesting because it showed that from a structural standpoint the principle of the mansard roof, characteristic of Palenque, was preserved and remained in use in northern Yucatan even at a time when concrete core and facing had replaced block or slab masonry. The retention of an inner mansard profile, however, does not imply that the House of the Governor, or other structures in this class, were originally planned with mansard roofs and only altered to vertical or negatively battered façades subsequently. Rather the roughly finished outer face of the vault mass indicates that the vertical or negatively battered façades were planned from the start.

89. L. Roys (1934:73) notes that "the usual building practice was to complete the walls and the vault sides up to the level of the peak of the vault and allow the mortar to harden before progressing upward. . . . The roof layer may be considered a separate section, especially during the aging period before the masonry of the entire building had developed the full strength of the final monolithic structure. This layer . . . sets heavily and firmly upon the walls and vault sides and holds them in place, . . ."

90. The roofing system at the House of the Governor parallels that employed at Chichen Itza (Morris, Charlot, and Morris 1931, 1:209).

91. Several large patches of smooth plaster still adhere to the soffits and capstones of the west side of the south transverse vault, as well as to the partition wall. A thick patch of creamy white plaster is found at the top of the southern vault on the east side. The west side of the north transverse vault has plaster adhering to the partition wall and vault soffits. Plaster also remains on the capstones of the east side of the north transverse vault. Much plaster is found on the exterior of the building in protected areas such as the eaves of cornices and moldings or within the cracks between facing stones. Traces of plaster exist beneath the offset at the spring of the vault and in the joints between wall stones in the central room of the House of the Governor.

92. Stephens (1963, 1:185).

93. J. E. S. Thompson (1973a:figs. 2–3).

94. Seler (1917:79, abb. 75b).

95. Kowalski (1985a).

96. Seler (1917:146, abb. 125).

Chapter 8

1. Kubler (1975:71–72). See also Kubler (1962b:33ff.) for an extended discussion of the notion of the "form-class" as a means of interpreting linked sequences of works of art.

2. G. Andrews (1975:6).

3. Kubler (1975:159).

4. Robertson (1963:27).

5. Kubler (1975:142); Andrews V (1974:139, fig. 4a).

6. Palladio (1965:38).

7. A. L. Smith (1950:fig. 106b3).

8. Harrison (1971:298, figs. 17, 18).

9. Harrison (1971:fig. 17).

10. G. Andrews (1975:fig. 15).

11. Tozzer (1913:170, fig. 55, pl. 32).

12. Tozzer (1913:189, fig. 82, pl. 33).

13. Kubler (1984:243); Pendergast (1980, 1:182).

14. Ruppert and Denison (1943:70, 91–92, fig. 85, pl. 74).

15. Pollock (1970:27–30, figs. 28–29).

16. Pollock (1970:fig. 56).

17. Andrews IV (1968:37); Kurjack (1974:table 7, index nos. 42, 27, table 9, index nos. 8, 50, 42).

18. Pollock (1980:567, fig. 672).

19. Pollock (1980:fig. 246).

20. Pollock (1980:fig. 581).

21. Pollock (1980:fig. 592).

22. Pollock (1980:figs. 290, 339).

23. Pollock (1980:fig. 338).

24. Morley (1910:pl. 1).

25. Eastern transverse rooms:ca. 16 feet 10 inches long; central rooms:ca. 20 feet 10 inches long; other rooms:ca 17 feet 2 inches long.

26. The central rooms of the West Structure are about 26 feet long, while the flanking rooms are about 20 feet to 21 feet long. The four smaller chambers at each end of the central rooms of the East Structure of the Nunnery are about 9 feet long, the flanking rooms are about 20 feet long, and the central rooms are about 33 feet long.

27. Seymour (1968:152).

28. Kubler (1975:92, pl. 61a); Hartung (1970:5).

29. Kubler (1975:158).

30. Kubler (1975:99, fig. 25).

31. W. R. Coe (1967:91); G. Andrews (1975:fig. 15a).

32. Pollock (1970:fig. 56).

33. Pollock (1970:40–41); Maler (1902:202–204).

34. Tozzer (1941:173–77).

35. Pollock (1980:294–301, figs. 507–509, 513, 515).

36. Ball and Andrews V (1975:243).

37. Pollock (1980:fig. 581).

38. Pollock (1980:fig. 338).

39. Pollock (1980:fig. 416).

40. Bullard (1960:357–59, figs. 2v, cc, dd, ff).

41. G. Andrews (1975:11–12).

42. Proskouriakoff (1963a:114); Kubler (1975:133, fig. 37).

43. Pollock (1965:fig. 6); Ricketson and Ricketson (1937:107); Ruppert (1940:fig. 14).

44. G. Andrews (1975:56–59, 291). See also Pollock (1965:389).

45. Willey and Bullard (1961); Willey and Smith (1963:86).

46. Ruppert (1940:222).

47. Pollock (1965:fig. 6b).

48. Ricketson (1928); Morley (1946:333–34); Aveni (1977:17–18).

49. Ruppert (1940:230).

50. Kubler (1975:147–49, fig. 45).

51. Resembling Calakmul Structure III in plan, but less large and complex in massing is Structure V of Group V at Rio Bec (Ruppert and Denison 1943:36, fig. 39).

52. Ruppert and Denison (1943:figs. 108, 110, frontispiece); Proskouriakoff (1963:53).

53. Ruppert and Denison (1943:87, fig. 108, pls. 38c, 39a).

54. Ruppert and Denison (1943:fig. 76–77).

55. Ruppert and Denison (1943:fig. 34).

56. Ruppert and Denison (1943:89, figs. 112–14).

57. Structure V at Culucbalom relates more closely to the three-unit façade of Xpuhil Structure 1 (Ruppert and Denison 1943:pl. 73).

58. Ruppert and Denison (1943:92, pls. 44c, 74).

59. Potter (1977:66–67, figs. 63–64).

60. On the basis of its ceramics, Structure II falls within the Chintok phase, ca. A.D. 750–830. Original radiocarbon dates from a sub-floor charcoal sample and a sliver of wooden lintel indicate dates of A.D. 670 ± 95 and A.D. 685 ± 95. These two dates, if converted on the basis of a 1.03 factor for the new half-life of C-14 isotope would be A.D. 632 ± 95 and A.D. 647 ± 95 (Potter 1977:62).

61. Seler (1916:abb. 11).

62. Pollock (1970:fig. 3).

63. Pollock (1970:57–58, fig. 78).

64. Pollock (1970:36–38, 64–66, figs. 41–45, 88); Seler (1916:65–67, taf. XII).

65. Pollock (1970:58, fig. 79).

66. Case (1911:facing 106); Rickards (1910:60 top, mislabeled Kewick, 66 top and middle).

67. Pollock (1970:58, fig. 79).

68. Structure 2 west of the House of the Governor is like Structure 1 in plan and may also have had a dragon mouth entrance (Pollock 1970:74–78).

69. Pollock (1970:78–80).

70. Pollock (1970:figs. 94–96).

71. Ruz Lhuillier (1959:39–40); Pollock (1970:73, 85); Seler (1917:16–19).

72. Ruz Lhuillier ([1947]:7).

73. Pollock (1970:83); Foncerrada (1965:161–61).

74. Kubler (1975:157–58).

75. Pollock (1980:220–23).

76. Kubler (1975:160).

77. Hartung (1971:56–57).

78. Kubler (1975:123–25).

79. According to W. R. Coe (1967:98), corbeled vaulted architecture appeared at Tikal by at least A.D. 250. Above-ground buildings were preceded by vaulted tombs, which have been dated to the Cauac phase (50 B.C.–A.D. 150).

80. A. L. Smith (1940:211–15) provides a discussion of the spread and distribution of the Maya vault. A few important sites such as Altar de Sacrificios in the Pasión River area are notable for their lack of vaulted architecture. See also Pollock (1965:423).

81. On the Twin-Pyramid Complexes of Tikal see W. R. Coe (1967:77–78, 82–87) and Jones (1969).

82. An important discussion of openings, or thresholds, as an element of existential and architectural space appears in Norberg-Schulz (1971:25, 58–59). The religious symbolism of the gate or threshold, and its paradoxical simultaneous function both as a boundary and as place "where passage from the profane to the sacred world becomes possible" is ably discussed by Eliade (1957:24–25).

83. Pollock (1970:47). Stephens (1963, 2:109). Plans and an elevation of the three-storied palace made by Maler appear in Seler's (1916:abbn 56a–56d) study of the Chenes region. See also Spinden (1913:fig. 143).

84. Seler (1916:64–65).

85. Freestanding gateways attained their greatest architectural development in northern Yucatan. Aside from those of Uxmal, Kabah, and Labna, another is known at Xculoc, situated some 25 kilometers south-southwest of Uxmal (Smith and Ruppert 1954:1). A portal vault also exists at Chichen Itza, where a small vaulted gateway formed the main entrance to the Initial Series Group from the north (Ruppert 1952:Appendix I, 157–62, 165, fig. 148a). The latest usage of an isolated portal vault occurs at Mayapan, where Structure Q-127 was comprised of a freestanding passageway and a portico, and clearly seems to have functioned as a gateway (Stromsvik 1953:137).

86. Stephens (1963, 1:247). See also Morley (1946:pl. 56b) and Smith and Ruppert (1954:1).

87. A. L. Smith and Ruppert (1954:1, fig. 1) provide a full description and plan of the Uxmal portal vault.

88. Stephens (1963, 1:259; 1963, 2:79). Landa provides an early reference to two heaps of stone placed at the entrances to Yucatecan towns, an architectural feature which may be a vestigial descendant of the monumental archways of the Puuc region (Tozzer 1941:139).

89. Marquina (1964:749–58, lam. 228); G. Andrews (1975: fig. 248). Pollock (1980:fig. 3).

90. Proskouriakoff (1963a:63); Marquina (1964:lam. 220).

91. G. Andrews (1975:344) suggests that the portal vault originally stood alone and that the other buildings were subsequently built around it.

92. The West Group at Uxmal lies some sixty meters west of the foot of the massive platform of the Pigeons Complex. It is entered on the east through a portal vault that passes through an extended palace. This portal was about the same size and design as that of the Nunnery Quadrangle (Hartung 1971:50, plan 6). A portal vault provides access to Structure 15, a quadrangle located south of the freestanding gateway of Uxmal (Blom 1934:59). North of the House of the Birds, and separated from the elevated courtyard of the Pyramid of the Magician by a narrow alley, is the Nunnery Annex or Northern Long Building, a long palace building with a tall portal vault at its center (Stephens 1963, 1:189; Seler 1917:119, abb. 104a; Pollock (1980:232–35, figs. 416–18).

93. Kubler (1975:158) places the Pigeons Group early in the Uxmal sequence. See also Seler (1917:20). The North Group portal vault passes through a Puuc-style building of simple design. The building has a simple string-course molding, rather than the more typical three-part Puuc moldings. Such simple moldings have been associated with early examples of Puuc architecture in chap. 3.

94. Morley (1910).

95. Morley (1910:7).

96. Morley (1910:14–15).

97. See G. Andrews (1975:67–71).

98. For more detailed descriptions of the Nunnery see Seler (1917:36–78), Kubler (1975:158–59, 174–75), and G. Andrews (1975:287–90). An analysis of significant alignments in the plan of the Nunnery is found in Hartung (1971:52–57).

99. Ruz Lhuillier (1958a:636).

100. Hartung (1971:52).

101. Hartung (1971:52) suggests that the placement of these crenellations was a consciously chosen feature of the Nunnery. He believes that the axis would have been accented too starkly if a mask tower rose directly above the portal vault.

102. Kubler (1975:159).

103. G. Andrews (1975:290, figs. 209–211).

104. Pollock (1970:59, fig. 56).

105. Pollock (1970:40–41); Ruz Lhuillier (1945:41).

106. Shook (1940:170 and map).

107. Tozzer (1941:173–77).

108. For an account of excavations and reconstructions at the transverse vaults see Ruz Lhuillier (1955a:59–60, fig. 4). A synopsis of the building sequence also appears in Ruz Lhuillier (1959:33) and in chap. 7.

109. The original height of the transverse vaults was approximately 8.3 meters, or 28 feet 2 inches.

110. Ruz Lhuillier (1955a:59–60).

111. The decorative panels flanking the portal vaults share a basic design, but differ slightly from the north to the south vault, and from one side of a vault to the other. A projecting cornice at the top of each panel bears long-snouted masks resembling those on the frieze of the three buildings of the House of the Governor. Below the masks, set against a background of lattice and diamond patterns, are large double-fret designs arranged in formats that vary slightly from vault to vault. These fretwork panels are framed by narrow bands of lattice, which are in turn separated from the plain face of the vault by a narrow channel.

The fretwork panels on the north and south vaults differ enough to suggest that they were the work of different designers, or of different crews interpreting a single design without regard for perfect congruence. The possibility that the differences may have been symbolic seems remote. On the eastern and western sides of the south vault the frets are constructed on two planes and are more broadly conceived. Their monumentality and two-planar form ties them to the frets on the frieze of the main buildings. The frets of the north vault are constructed on only one plane, permitting a more tightly coiled and delicate design. The northern frets relate more to the panel they occupy than to the larger frets of the House of the Governor as a whole.

The skillfully adjusted framing effect of these stepped, decorative panels recalls the balanced composition of several Maya sculptures, where glyphic texts frame figural panels (e.g., Morley 1937–1938, 5:pl. 126b).

112. The string-course also may have been employed simply as an unconscious archaism, or merely to articulate the break at the spring point.

113. Kubler (1975:160). It should be noted, however, that as originally planned and constructed the vault soffits did not continue nearly down to ground level. This low spring point was created only by the subsequent filling of the passageways to the level of the fourth platform.

Chapter 9

1. Stephens (1841, 2:422).

2. Morley (1956:294); Pollock (1965:431). Although it was common to leave the lower wall plain, there are various exceptions to the rule. At Uxmal the upper and lower façades of the Chenes-style Temple of the Pyramid of the Magician received mosaic sculpture.

3. Sharp (1972:21).

4. Kubler (1975:173).

5. Stierlin (1964:145); Kowalski (1985).

6. Spinden (1957:31).

7. Stephens (1963, 1:185); Totten (1926:36ff., Pls. 84–87); Hissink (1934:13).

8. Kubler (1975:171).

9. Sharp (1972–10).

10. Sharp (1972:209).

11. Kubler (1975:161).

12. Kubler (1975:161).

13. Foncerrada (1965:93–98).

14. Holmes (1895–1897:247–48); Saville (1909:188).

15. Kubler (1975:157).

16. Parsons (1969:157).

17. Sharp (1972:209). A somewhat similar view was expressed by J. W. Ball (1974:86).

18. Sharp (1970:2; 1978b:89). Such interregional contact is supported by finds at Lambityeco, Oaxaca, of a fine orange pottery resembling Balancan Fine Orangeware, produced in the Tabasco-Campeche region and imported by the Puuc sites.

The Oaxaca vessels are made with a different paste than those of the Maya area, and are probably local imitations of Balancan Fine Orangeware rather than imports (Paddock 1966:212; Sharp 1972:152). Sharp (1972:152) suggests that the imitations might have been made by itinerant Maya potters, but this is difficult to prove.

19. Sharp (1978b:97, note 3). See also Andrews (1975: 288–89) and Kubler (1975:100).

20. Oliver (1955:51).

21. Oliver (1955:60).

22. Oliver (1955:60).

23. Oliver (1955:60). On the Yagul Palace they begin .5 meters from the floor.

24. Oliver (1955:60, fig. 36).

25. Foncerrada (1965:96).

26. Oliver (1955:fig. 37d-e). At Mitla the Xs were also constructed of three separate stones.

27. Oliver (1955:fig. 36).

28. An example of figural sculpture in an architectural context does occur on the tablero friezes of the house patio of Mound 195-sub and on the façade of Tomb 6 at Lambityeco (Rabin 1970:figs. 3a, 18).

29. Sharp (1970–1972:35–76, 134–57).

30. Sharp (1972:89–104).

31. Potter (1977:87–88).

32. Potter (1977:89).

33. Blom (1930:207; 1932).

34. Blom (1932a:561).

35. Blom (1930:207).

36. Kubler (1975:158–59).

37. This was suggested to me in conversation with George Kubler.

38. Kubler (1975:157).

39. Hartung (1970:8).

40. Rabin (1970:15).

41. Sharp (1970:3).

42. Seler (1904:243–324); Kubler (1975:105–110, fig. 28); M. E. Smith (1973:19). Kubler (1975:106), however, suggests the paintings are additions to earlier buildings.

43. Hartung (1970:7).

44. Paddock, Mogor, and Lind (1968:23); Rabin (1970–15).

45. Pollock (1980:578).

46. Pollock (1980:570).

47. See chap. 3 and Pollock (1980:570, figs. 398–99, 437).

48. Pollock (1980:fig. 326).

49. Pollock (1980:fig. 143).

50. Pollock (1980:570).

51. Ruppert and Denison (1943:figs. 24, 32, pl. 5d).

52. Potter (1977:38, fig. 18).

53. Ruppert and Denison (1943:fig. 162, pl. 35b).

54. Potter (1977:table 1; 1976:444–45). Potter (1977:15 also reports radiocarbon dates of A.D. 683 ± 95 and A.D. 616 ± 95 for Structure IV at Becan.

55. Pollock (1970:fig. 15).

56. Pollock (1970:31–32, fig. 38a).

57. Pollock (1970:58, fig. 80).

58. Pollock (1970:59, fig. 84).

59. Pollock (1970:69).

60. Pollock (1970:78, fig. 106).

61. Pollock (1970:47). Stela 5 records 9.15.19.0.0, while Stela 7 records 9.15.19.17.14 according to Morley (1937–1938, 4:371).

62. Foncerrada (1965:fig. 43).

63. Pollock (1980:fig. 456).

64. Foncerrada (1965:fig. 47).

65. Pollock (1980:figs. 443, 449).

66. Pollock (1980:577) notes that moldings of three members are the most numerous in the Puuc region.

67. Pollock (1980:577).

68. Kubler (1975:153).

69. E. H. Thompson (1911:515).

70. Wauchope (1938:150).

71. The way in which atadura or double-atadura spindles serve to bind together groups of colonnettes can be appreciated on Structure 1B2 or on the second story of the Palace at Sayil. See Pollock (1980:figs. 167, 200) and Fig. 31.

72. Pollock (1970:fig. 10a); Seler (1916:abb. 27).

73. Pollock (1980:119, fig. 244).

74. G. Andrews ([1979]:fig. 5).

75. Pollock (1980:figs. 473, 551a–c, 552). Other Puuc altars have atadura moldings at the top but lack the braided rope and pleat pattern (Pollock 1980:figs. 890b, d, 866b, 763).

76. Pollock (1980:figs. 775, 777).

77. G. Andrews (1975:fig. 50).

78. Ruppert and Denison (1943:figs. 77–78).

79. Pollock (1970:fig. 55).

80. Pollock (1970:fig. 79).

81. Pollock (1970:fig. 63).

82. Pollock (1970:73, figs. 96, 103).

83. Pollock (1980:214, 359, figs. 359, 393–94, 601–603, 646, 663, 910, 929). Three-part moldings also occur in miniature on one of the stylized huts on the façade of the North Structure of the Nunnery (Seler 1917:abb. 69). The decorative binder on the façade of Room 15 of the Codz Poop at Kabah is a late usage (Pollock 1980:369).

84. Pollock (1980:573).

85. Pollock (1970:figs. 4, 41, 93).

86. Pollock (1980:figs. 282, 289).

87. Pollock (1980:fig. 444).

88. For example, on Structures 2D7 and 5C7 (Ruppert 1952:figs. 15, 88, 119b, 146a).

89. Indeed, Kubler (1962:150) has suggested that the House of the Governor has "overlapping and contrapuntal rhythms that recall the complexities of Maya time division."

90. Maudslay (1889–1902, 4:pls. 52, 84–85).

91. Ruppert and Denison (1943:fig. 67).

92. Ruppert and Denison (1943:fig. 112).

93. Pollock (1980:fig. 404).

94. Elsewhere in the Puuc area a doorway treatment like that of the Cemetery Temple occurs at the Adjacent Palace at Chunhuhub (Pollock 1980:fig. 672; Maler 1902:abb. 11).

95. Kubler (1975:159).

96. G. Andrews (1975:figs. 202–203).

97. Pollock (1965:395).

98. Green (n.d.); Maudslay (1889–1902, 2:pl. 85); Maler (1903:pl. 58); Proskouriakoff (1950:fig. 70c).

99. Green (n.d.:28) argued that such evenly spaced markers might have provided a standardized measurement. My own studies at the House of the Governor show close matching of geometric façade elements and an intention to match corresponding lengths of wall. No evidence for a truly standardized unit, such as might have been used in more than one site, was detected.

100. Roys (1967:82).

101. Recinos (1950:80).

102. Satterthwaite (1949:33).

103. The base of alternating smooth and colonnaded sections did not continue along the walls of the sides of the build-

ings that formed the original open passageways through the transverse vaults. Later, when the transverse vaults were walled and the small rooms and porticoes added, the panel and colonnette base was extended across the passageway.

104. This "standardization" of units of length, although consistent at the House of the Governor, does not necessarily apply to other structures at Uxmal. The East Structure of the Nunnery, for example, has plain panels at the corners of the base somewhat longer than those of the House of the Governor. At the House of the Governor itself there is only slightly longer section, 4 feet 1/2 inch, but this is part of the base in the later construction in the east side of the south transverse vault.

105. Numerological interpretation of the panels depends on the exemption of the shorter end panels. This seems reasonable on two counts. First, because their different lengths put them in a different class. Second, because the numerological explanation for each side rests on subtracting the end panels in each case.

106. J. E. S. Thompson (1960:53, 208–210; 1970:280–82).

107. J. E. S. Thompson (1960:53).

108. J. E. S. Thompson (1960:54). Other Maya deities with the number nine in their names include: Bolon Mayel, Bolon Hacmatz, Ah Bolon Yocte, Ah Bolon-Caan-Chac, Bolon Hobon, and Cit Bolon Tun in Yucatan.

109. Jones (1969:10). See also Morley (1937–1938, 2:517, fig. 76) for a ritualistic usage of nine at Yaxchilan.

110. J. E. S. Thompson (1960–10, 12; 1970:280–82). In the Chilam Balam of Chumayel there is an obscure reference to a cosmic battle between the Oxlahun-ti-ku and the Bolon-ti-ku (Roys 1967:99).

111. J. E. S. Thompson (1970:113); Redfield and Villa R. (1939:114).

112. J. E. S. Thompson (1960:10).

113. J. E. S. Thompson (1960:214).

114. Roys (1967:101); J. E. S. Thompson (1960:214).

115. J. E. S. Thompson (1960:276).

116. Kubler (1977:table 2, figs. 1–2, 8).

117. J. E. S. Thompson (1960:276; 1970:228).

118. Kubler (1977:9).

119. J. E. S. Thompson (1960:276) associates the Palenque head with the other examples, although it lacks the black prefix.

120. Kubler (1977:figs. 8, 13).

121. Sharp (1978a:167). There are thirteen large-scale frets on either side of the central motif, but there are also smaller frets and step quadrants as well. Stierlin (1981:145–48) recently has asserted that there were 260 mask panels and 104 key frets on the façades of the House of the Governor, that these are derived from the Tzolkin and the 52-year Calendar Round, and that they may symbolize the "alternation between rain (chac masks) and sun (key frets)." My own estimates of these numbers, based on Seler's diagrams and photographs, is that there were probably about 224 mask panels on the upper façades, and as many as 148 key frets, depending on whether smaller and incomplete frets on the east façade are included in the count.

122. Marquina (1964:87–88); Ruz Lhuillier (1965:22–23).

123. Sharp (1978a:167); Marquina (1964:886, fot. 457).

124. Ruz Lhuillier (1965:22–23).

125. Recently Weldon Lamb (1980) has suggested possible numerological significance for several of the Structures of the Nunnery Quadrangle at Uxmal as well.

126. Roys (1967:126).

127. Roys (1967:126, note 1).

128. Wittkower (1971:1–13).

129. Measurements of the curvature of the soffits were made by tightening a string straight between the offset at the capstones and the offset at the springline and taking the distance between the chord and soffit at one-foot intervals down from the top and up from the bottom.

130. We tested this by holding a rope at capstone level and springline of the north and south vaults. In each case, only slight variation in the tension on the rope produces either straight lines or curves that duplicated those of the vault soffits.

131. Cirerol Sansores ([1956]:126), who did not measure the vaults as carefully, suggested that the curvature may have been planned, but that it resulted in weakening the vaults, which necessitated the addition of a buttress wall.

Chapter 10

1. The earliest notice of these sculptured figures is provided by Fray Antonio Ciudad Real, who made a tour of inspection of Uxmal in 1586 (see chapter two). Stephens and Catherwood provided the first accurate descriptions and illustrations of some of these figures in 1843 (Stephens 1963, 1:95–96; Catherwood 1844:pl. IX). A much more thorough description of the human figures and their placement on the façade was then made by Eduard Seler (1917:131–41). In the present discussion of the figural sculptures I have relied heavily on Seler's account, supplementing his descriptions with my own photographs and notes.

2. This element seems to have been replaced during the reconstruction of the east façade, since Charnay's early photograph does not show it in place. See Fig. 18.

3. Apparently different sculptors or workshops were responsible for these two headdresses.

4. Seler (1917:abbn. 70, 105–125; schemata 1–5; tafn. XXII–XXVIII). For the placement and configuration of the central motif see particularly abbn. 114, 120a, 121, 122; tafn. XXIII-1, XXVIII.

5. Seler (1917:abb. 120a). The identification of the *kin* glyph was made by Seler (1917:141). For a discussion of the *kin* glyph, crossed bands, moon sign, and venus symbol see J. E. S. Thompson (1960:142–43, 260, 237–43, 220–21).

6. The sculpture is one of several which were brought to the United States of America by John Lloyd Stephens, and which are now in the American Museum of Natural History, New York City (Spinden 1920:382, 384–85).

7. All three of the torso sections have large shoulder collars. One has a fairly simple collar consisting of overlapping horizontal bands whose lower edges are decorated with striations (Fig. 130). This figure measures about 17½ inches at the widest part of the collar and is 14 inches high. Another figure, slightly larger, has a collar composed of large round beads with a lower edge trimmed by beads (Fig. 131). At the center of the collar is an elliptical medallion edged with small beads. At the rear of this figure is a long tenon that originally secured it to the façade. A third torso wears a similar beaded collar with elliptical medallion (Fig. 132). The lower section of a seated figure, consisting of trunk and crossed legs, wears a thick belt and a trapezoidal loincloth (Fig. 110). The midriff section of a standing? figure features a short kilt decorated with large circles, perhaps representing the spots on a jaguar pelt, and loincloth apron (Fig. 133).

8. Spinden (1920).

9. Pollock (1980:271, fig. 469c) illustrates a human head of stone now in the Museum of Archaeology in Mérida, Yucatan, which is supposed to have come from the House of the Governor. The face is broad and flat with low brow ridges.

10. Foncerrada (1965:148).

11. Foncerrada (1965:149) likens the collar to those on Stelae 9 and 11 at Seibal, the chest ornament to that on Stela 5 at Yaxchilan and the human face on the belt to one seen on Lintel 9 of Yaxchilan.

12. Rabin (1970:fig. 18).

13. Maler (1903:157).

14. Maler (1903:158–59). The left figure is almost entirely destroyed; the right figure is the best preserved.

15. Maler (1903:159).

16. Maler (1903:159). The rest of the roof comb is perforated with small, rectangular openings aligned in eight horizontal rows. The openings of the second row are T-shaped, perhaps a reference to the Maya sign *ik*, meaning "life, breath, or wind." See Marquina (1964:683).

17. Maler (1903:173, pl. XLIII-no. 1); Morley (1937–1938, 2:517).

18. Maler (1903:174) describes the ornament of the back and sides of Structure 40 as resembling that of the front.

19. Structure 1 dates from the fourth quarter of Cycle 9, probably about A.D. 790–800. See Ruppert, Thompson and Proskouriakoff (1955:11, 14, 34, 37, 40, 57, figs. 3, 13a).

20. Ruppert, Thompson, and Proskouriakoff (1955:17).

21. Ruppert and Denison (1943:70, figs. 85–86, pls. 27b, 27d, 28a). Similar sculptures are also found on the roof comb of a structure at La Muralla (Ruppert and Denison 1943:72–73, fig. 89, pls. 28c, 29a–b, 30a–b).

22. Ruppert and Denison (1943:fig. 103a, pl. 36b).

23. Seler (1916:taf. VI); Pollock (1970:13, fig. 4).

24. Stephens (1963, 2:30–32, pl. VI); G. Andrews (1975:figs. 258–59); Pollock (1965:431) includes the Mirador Temple as an example of Early -Puuc architecture.

25. At Sabacche, the Second Temple, a building with Early-Puuc stylistic traits, has a frieze and flying façade studded with projecting stone tenons of the type that support the human figures of modeled stucco at the Labna Mirador (Maler 1895:248, pl. 2).

26. Pollock (1980:253–56, figs. 444–47).

27. Stephens (1963, 1:193).

28. Seler (1917:22); Pollock (1980:247).

29. Maler (1902:200, abb. 2).

30. Maler (1902:214).

31. The Portal Vault had multi-member moldings and sharply cut masonry characteristic of Late-Puuc architecture.

32. Proskouriakoff (1963a:64).

33. See chap. 3.

34. Proskouriakoff (1963a:56).

35. Maler (1902:198).

36. Maler (1902:211–12, abb. 11). Pollock (1980:405, fig. 672).

37. Five of these figures remained in place when Maler (1902:211) visited the site.

38. Maler (1902:211); Pollock (1980:figs. 667, 669a).

39. Maler (1895:249; 1902:199, abb. 2); E. H. Thompson (1904:11, pls. 2–3).

40. One of these figures still exists (as of 1977) in the second room west of center on the south side. See Pollock (1980:fig. 611).

41. Bolles (1977:123–24, photo 113, drawing 115).

42. Bolles (1977:125).

43. The "constellation band" of the Monjas was supported at each end by a small figure on a pedestal. Bolles (1977:125) does not state what type of creature supports the band, but his photographs suggest it is a seated jaguar.

44. Bolles (1977:126).

45. Bolles (1977:126).

46. Bolles (1977:114); Seler (1960, 5:abb. 35). On the features of the Jaguar Lord of the Underworld, see J. E. S. Thompson (1960:134).

47. Sáenz (1969a:4, fig. 1, fots. 9–10; 1972:36, fot. 21).

48. The "Reina de Uxmal" was taken from the frieze of the Lower West Structure of the Pyramid of the Magician near the beginning of this century by Leopoldo Batres, and is now in the Museo Nacional de Antropologia e Historia, Mexico City. See Bernal (1969:pl. 96).

49. Seler (1917:abb. 47a).

50. Seler (1917:abb. 47b).

51. Seler (1917:abb. 52).

52. Seler (1917:abb. 53).

53. Seler (1917:abb. 55). Seler (1917:60, abb. 54) also illustrates a winged figure from the east end of the south façade of the North Structure. The figure carries an object which Seler identifies as a flute, but which may actually be a torch.

54. Foncerrada (1965:152).

55. Spinden (1920:382, 384–85).

56. Proskouriakoff (1951:fig. 2a, 2b wrongly labeled as Stela 26); Proskouriakoff (1950:fig. 88a).

57. Proskouriakoff (1950:fig. 104a).

58. Proskouriakoff (1950:fig. 81c).

59. Proskouriakoff (1950:fig. 88a).

60. Proskouriakoff (1950:fig. 87d).

61. See chap. 10, note 4.

62. As we can presume from the other extant heads from the frieze of the House of the Governor (Spinden 1920:382, 384–85; Pollock 1980:271, fig. 469c).

63. See chap. 10, note 5.

64. For a discussion of the ceremonial bar see Spinden (1913:49–50). Proskouriakoff (1950:88–89).

65. Proskouriakoff (1950:89).

66. Spinden (1913:50, 57). On Seibal Stela 10, the lower head of the bar is shown upside down and resembles the skeletalized rear head of the two-headed monster, with fleshless lower jaw, *kin* sign in the forehead, and tripartite badge headdress. For a discussion of the tripartite badge, also known as the Triadic Sign or the Quadripartite Badge (with the inclusion of the *kin* glyph), see Kubler (1969:33–46) and Robertson (1974).

67. Morley (1946:146).

68. Kubler (1962:152).

69. J. E. S. Thompson (1973c:65).

70. Piedras Negras lies some 250 miles from Uxmal, and the last securely dated monument at the site was dedicated in 9.19.0.0.0 9 Ahau 18 Mol, or A.D. 810 (Morley 1937–1938, 3:283–85), which is some 100 years before the estimated construction date of the House of the Governor.

71. Maler (1901:pls. XV–no. 3, XX, XXII).

72. See chapter 10, note 66. On the two-headed dragon, see Spinden (1913:53–56).

73. Satterthwaite (1943:178) suggested that Piedras Negras and Jonuta both participated in an extensive trade network that extended along the Usumacinta drainage and probably reached as far as the coasts of Veracruz and Yucatan. On the importance of the Chontal or Putun Maya see J. E. S. Thompson (1970:3–47).

74. Berlin (1956:126, fig. 10). Berlin (1956:132) places this type of figurine within his Jonuta Horizon, the major part of which dates to post-Tepeu II (Late Classic-Terminal Classic) time level.

75. See Corson (1976:67–72).

76. An earlier source for the mosaic serpent imagery is Teotihuacan, whence it spread to Maya sites such as Tikal (Stela 31) and Piedras Negras (Lintel 2, Stela 7) (Kubler 1976:172).

77. Ruz Lhuillier (1969:figs. LXVa, LXVb1–b2).

78. Corson (1976:fig. 24a, 24c).

79. Corson (1976:71).

80. Corson (1976:72) compares the figures with "several seated stelae figures from the middle Usumacinta, particularly at Piedras Negras." Speaking of Piedras Negras, he writes: "While that site cannot at present be identified as their source of manufacture, certainly many of the ideas they display (pose, headdress, and thrones with glyphic texts) are especially prominent there, and if the figurines were not actually made at Piedras Negras, there are, I think, strong indications that their stylistic development owed much to artistic achievements, recognizable principally in stone sculpture, at that center." See Corson (1976:151).

81. Maler (1901:pls. XVI, XXIII, XXV, XXXI). For variants of this headgear see Maler (1901:pls. XVII, XVIII–no. 1, XXVIII).

82. Corson (1976:51–54) provides a description and discussion of Jaina Group O.

83. Corson (1976:fig. 20d).

84. Butler (1935:fig. 31). Piña Chan (1968:1 am. 21).

85. Butler (1935:652).

86. Piña Chan (1968:1 am. 20).

87. Groth Kimball (1960:pl. 44).

88. Hellmuth (1976:pl. 16).

89. A photograph of this figure was provided to the author by Marilyn Goldstein.

90. Figurine in the Gilcrease Institute, Tulsa, Oklahoma.

91. Seler (1917:abbn. 63–67, 86). For the Pyramid of the Magician see also Sáenz (1969a:fot. 11).

92. For a discussion of the bicephalic jaguar throne see chap. 14.

93. Seler (1917:taf. VIII, abb. 28); Foncerrada (1965:145).

94. Proskouriakoff (1960:454–75).

95. Proskouriakoff (1960:455).

96. Proskouriakoff (1960:455).

97. J. E. S. Thompson (1962:289–90).

98. Proskouriakoff (1960:455–60). See also Roys (1967:75).

99. Maudslay (1889–1902, 4:pl. 43).

100. Maudslay (1889–1902, 1:pl. 12).

101. Foncerrada (1965:92).

102. Pollock (1970:83).

103. Kubler (1969:26, 39).

104. For the use of the "percentage sign" as a version of the death-associated glyph *cimi* see J. E. S. Thompson (1960:76).

105. Plans, illustrations, and photographs of the Chenes Temple of the Pyramid of the Magician appear in Marquina (1964:768–73).

106. Stephens (1963, 1:96).

107. Maudslay (1889–1902, 5:34).

108. Maler (1901:46ff., 59; 1903:117, 176).

109. J. E. S. Thompson (1960:64).

110. J. E. S. Thompson (1960:65).

111. Spinden (1916:442).

112. Spinden (1916:443).

113. Spinden (1916:444).

114. Gordon (1918:12, 15, 23, 25, fig. 7).

115. Butler (1937).

116. Butler (1937:19–23).

117. Proskouriakoff (1960; 1963; 1964).

118. Kelley (1962:323–35). For a more recent account of archaeology and epigraphy at Quirigua see Jones and Sharer (1980). The association between Quirigua and Copan does not seem to have been always peaceful, since the capture of Copan's ruler, 18 Rabbit, by the lord of Quirigua, Cauac Sky, in 9.15.6.14.6 (A.D. 737) is recorded several times in the Quirigua inscriptions.

119. Kubler (1969:16–17).

120. Maler (1908:18, 24); Morley (1937–1938, 2:263); Greene, Rands, and Graham (1972:222, 226, 234); Willey, Smith, Tourtellot III, and Graham (1975:31–32).

121. Spinden (1916:448–49).

122. Greene, Rands, and Graham (1972:234); Sanders (1977:78–86).

123. Harrison (1970:172).

124. Miller (1976:181).

125. Miller (1976:178).

126. Miller (1976:179).

127. Griffin (1976:141, fig. 10).

128. Griffin (1976:143, 147, fig. 12).

129. Willey (1982:31, fig. 47–47A).

130. Proskouriakoff (1963b; 1964); Ruppert, Thompson, and Proskouriakoff (1955). M. Miller ([1981]).

131. For descriptions and illustrations of this figure see Charnay (1887:440), Maler (1903:161–62, fig. 57), and Morley (1937–1938, 2:551–52; 1937–1938, 5:pl. 107a).

132. Maler describes the headdress as a "serpent's head," but it seems be basically feline, and to have the jaguar traits outlined by J. E. S. Thompson (1960:134).

133. Morley (1937–1938, 2:552) believes the collar and maskette medallions to be jade.

134. Maler (1903:161).

135. Maler (1903:162).

136. Quoted in Maler (1903:162); See also Tozzer (1907:80–83).

137. J. E. S. Thompson (1945:12–13, 23). Recently, however, Houston (1984:799–803) has argued that Kukulcan, the Maya version of the feathered serpent was occasionally pictured and referred to in the glyphic writing of the Classic period. Nevertheless, the cult was clearly not central at this point, and the Yaxchilan figure has no characteristics that would connect him with the feathered serpent.

138. Ruppert, Thompson, and Proskouriakoff (1955:3).

139. For a discussion of the life of Bird-Jaguar see Proskouriakoff (1964).

140. Proskouriakoff (1964:178).

141. Proskouriakoff (1964:190).

142. Maler (1903:pl. XLVI). See also Lintel 42 (9.16.1.2.0), depicting Bird-Jaguar in similar garb with a battle companion (Maler 1903:pl. LXVI; Proskouriakoff 1964:186).

143. Maler (1903:pls. XLVII–XLVIII); Morley (1937–1938, 5:pl. 115d). Proskouriakoff (1964:190, 194).

144. Maler (1903:pl. L).

145. Proskouriakoff (1964:189).

146. See Proskouriakoff (1964:189, 194), Maler (1903:pl. LXII) and Morley (1937–1938, 5:pl. 178Fd).

147. Morley (1937–1938, 2:552; 1937–1938, 5:178Fb).

148. Proskouriakoff (1964:178) says of Bird-Jaguar's name that it "includes the glyph 12 (or 229):683a:109 . . . , which is

almost always used in references to him."

149. It is surely not the shield affix (T152) of Shield-Jaguar's name glyph.

150. By "portrait" I do not imply a veristic record of facial features, but that the figure was intended to represent a single person, not to be confused with other rulers of Yaxchilan.

151. Spinden (1913:184) noted of the Yaxchilan sculptures that: "One of the persons represented is, as a rule, somewhat larger than the other. They commonly face each other, one being drawn in pure profile, while the other has the body in front view and the face in profile." The personage depicted in profile is apparently of subordinate rank.

152. As on Bonampak Stela 1 (Ruppert, Thompson and Proskouriakoff 1955:fig. 18) and Fig. 171.

153. As on Quirigua Stela I (Morley 1937–1938, 5:pl. 172).

154. Edmonson (1971:70, note 2037).

155. Satterthwaite (1937:18–23). See also chap. 6.

156. Morley (1937–1938, 2:517) believed that Structure 40 was dedicated at this time.

157. Proskouriakoff (1964:178, 180–81).

158. Proskouriakoff (1964:180–81).

159. Morley (1937–1938, 5:pl. 172); Kubler (1969:16).

160. This possibility was suggested by George Kubler in conversation.

161. Ruppert, Thompson, and Proskouriakoff (1955:fig. 28).

162. J. E. S. Thompson (Ruppert, Thompson, and Proskouriakoff 1955:52) suggests a raid on a village to determine territorial boundaries. Kubler (1975:180–81), on the other hand, favors a punitive action to redress grievances laid before the ruler in the arraignment scene. M. Miller ([1981]) provides a recent comprehensive discussion of the murals.

163. Proskouriakoff (Ruppert, Thompson, and Proskouriakoff 1955:42).

164. Proskouriakoff (1950:164). See chap. 3, pp. 000.

165. Graham (1974:216); Greene, Rands, and Graham (1972:220, 244, pls. 102, 115).

166. Proskouriakoff (1950:164).

167. Greene, Rands, and Graham (1972:pl. 112).

168. Kubler (1975:159). See chap. 3 for the dating of the House of the Governor.

169. See chap. 14 on the bicephalic jaguar throne.

170. J. E. S. Thompson (1973a:62). See chap. 3, pp. 000.

171. Kubler (1975:158–59).

172. Stephens (1963, 1:102–103).

173. Roys (1943:59–64).

Chapter 11

1. For a general discussion of mask panels see Spinden (1913:118–27), Hissink (1934) and Foncerrada (1965:98–118).

2. Seler (1917:135); J. E. S. Thompson (1960:220–21).

3. Seler (1917:136).

4. The bundle element has been variously interpreted. G. B. Gordon (1905:147) identified it as the xiuhmolpilli, the Mexican year bundle. Hissink (1934:82) more convincingly likened it to the nose ornaments worn by God B in the Maya codices.

5. Seler (1917:135).

6. For a complete discussion of the decoration of the frieze of the House of the Governor see Seler (1917:127–34). Two rhythms are produced: 1-3-1, corresponding to the building division; and 2-1-2, since the central canopy is two masks longer than the others.

7. Spinden (1913:118).

8. Proskouriakoff (1959:32).

9. Alternating feathered serpent heads and scaled reptilian heads adorn the tableros of the Pyramid of Quetzalcoatl at Teotihuacan (Marquina 1964:fot. 30), while large plaster sculptures of the Zapotec rain god Cocijo occur on the tablero of the Cocijo building at Lambityeco (Sharp 1970:fig. 14a). However, these architectural sculptures do not resemble the Maya masks closely.

10. Ricketson and Ricketson (1937); Proskouriakoff (1963a: 3–5). Kubler (1962:123, 161, pl. 65).

11. W. R. Coe (1965:11); Heyden and Gendrop (1973:96, 103, fig. 101). According to Coe (1965:11) masks of similar construction also adorned the Cauac phase Structure 5D-Sub. 3–5th.

12. Freidel (1979:45, fig. 7).

13. Merwin and Vaillant (1932:18–20).

14. At Nakum such masks occur on Structures F, G, L, and S (Tozzer 1913:172, 174, 183, figs. 59, 76, 79, pls. 51–1, 51–2).

15. The stucco modeling on a mask from Structure G shows a scroll form consisting of a suborbital bracket with attached dots, suggesting that in their original condition some of the Nakum masks may have resembled those of Yucatan more closely.

16. Satterthwaite (1939, 1940); Proskouriakoff (1963a:24).

17. Maler (1903:pl. XLII–2).

18. Maudslay (1889–1902, IV:pls. 20, 25, 38).

19. Ruz Lhuillier (1958b:69).

20. Marquina (1964:800–802, lam. 242).

21. Kubler (1975:132, 171).

22. Andrews V (1974:144).

23. Andrews V (1974:143).

24. A restoration drawing of the stucco façade of Structure 1-Sub (Temple of the Seven Dolls) appears in Andrews IV (1965:fig. 10).

25. Trik (1939:87–103, figs. 10–11, pl. 11a–b).

26. J. E. S. Thompson (1960:84).

27. Taylor (1978).

28. Trik (1939:101). At Temple 22 two large cauac heads project toward the central doorway from the inside faces of flanking piers (Trik 1939:pl. 11b). These masks are more anthropomorphic versions of those adorning the corners of the structure. The smaller, more rounded snout more closely resembles the fleshy proboscis of the codical God B.

29. Kubler (1975:171).

30. Kubler (1975:172).

31. Potter (1977:62, table 1).

32. Potter (1977:figs. 17–19).

33. Kubler supposes that the earlier Rio Bec masks were carved *in situ* on the façade. At Structure VI, Chicanna, it is difficult to tell whether this was the case. There a panel of three superimposed masks flanks the doorway (Potter 1977: figs. 66–67). The underlying framework is of stone, some pieces of which are plain and others having been cut fairly precisely to shape with grooves and hollows duplicating those in the stucco finish coat. These elements are standardized enough to suggest they were carved before being cemented to the wall. On the other hand, some passages, such as the falling scrolls behind each mask, relied on a rough stone base with all detail carried out in stucco. The stucco coat is heavy and the final effect would have been curvilinear. This building also dates to the Bejuco phase (Potter 1977:62). The stone and stucco sculpture of Becan Structure X conforms to Kubler's curvilinear type, and the detail in the stone seems to have been carved *in situ* (Potter 1977:fig. 54, table 1).

34. Pollock (1970: figs. 94–95); Kubler (1975: 172).
35. Pollock (1970: 13, fig. 7).
36. Andrews V (1974: 144, note 3).
37. Pollock (1980: 580) reports that cut-stone mask elements were observed only at Sisila, Halal, and Itzimte, which are located intermediate between east and west.
38. Kubler (1975: 173).
39. Díaz del Castillo (1956: 9–10).
40. See chap. 3 for the descriptions by these authors.
41. Waldeck (1838: 74).
42. Covarrubias (1957: 60, fig. 22).
43. Caso (1942: 42).
44. M. D. Coe (1966: 60–63); Quirarte (1973, 1977).
45. Spinden (1957: 33).
46. Spinden (1957: 38). Lamb (1980: 85) recently has again proposed that the Uxmal masks of the East and West Structures of the Nunnery may represent Quetzalcoatl-Kukulcan in a Venus manifestation. His astronomical-numerological interpretation of the latticework Xs of the East Structure is briefly considered in note 87 of chap. 6.
47. Foncerrada (1965: 105).
48. Foncerrada (1965: 103).
49. Seler (1917: 12ff.).
50. J. E. S. Thompson (1970: 252).
51. Seler (1917: 12–13).
52. Seler (1960, 1: 357–66).
53. Tozzer (1941: 161–64).
54. Roys (1967: 170–72).
55. Martínez Hernandez (1929: 290).
56. Martínez Hernandez (1929: 290).
57. J. E. S. Thompson (1970: 252, 260).
58. J. E. S. Thompson (1970: 252).
59. Seler (1960, 1: 357–66).
60. J. E. S. Thompson (1970: 253).
61. J. E. S. Thompson (1970: 253); Villacorta and Villacorta (1930).
62. Such world directional God Bs appear sitting in the tops of trees in the Dresden Codex (Villacorta and Villacorta (1930: 70–72).
63. J. E. S. Thompson (1970: 252).
64. J. E. S. Thompson (1970: 254–56).
65. Morley (1946: 225); Foncerrada (1965: 106); Ruz Lhuillier ([1945]: 80; 1959: 16).
66. Ruz Lhuillier (1959: 34).
67. J. E. S. Thompson (1966: 83–84).
68. J. E. S. Thompson (1966: 132).
69. J. E. S. Thompson (1966: 263–66).
70. Seler (1960, 4: 535–36). See also Hissink (1934: 78–80).
71. Morley (1946: 120).
72. Morley (1946: 123).
73. God B appears associated with the serpent on pages 33b, 34b, 35b, and 66a of the Dresden Codex, as well as on pages 9, 10b, 30a, and 31b of the Madrid Codex (Villacorta and Villacorta 1930: 76, 78, 80, 82, 142, 242, 244, 284, 286).
74. Spinden (1913: 40, fig. 30). See note 73.
75. Hissink (1934: 83–84).
76. J. E. S. Thompson (1970: 258).
77. Sahagún (1950–1971, Book 1: 21, 7).
78. Seler (1917: 14ff.).
79. Foncerrada (1965: 108–110).
80. Landa provides several references to rites aimed at promoting fertility and averting famine (Tozzer 1941: 54–56, 135–49, 161–64).
81. The glyph (T668) that identifies God B of the Chacs in

the Maya codices consists of the back of a clenched fist with a jade bead at the wrist. The fist is personified by being given a small mouth and nose as well as an eye that takes the form of a T-symbol. This T-symbol also serves to identify the Maya day sign ik, which has the meaning "breath, wind" or by extension "life" (J. E. S. Thompson 1970: 257; 1960: 73). Thompson (1970: 257) also believes that the ik sign may mean "germination," and that the glyph of God B refers to the Chacs as "causes of germination." The personified main sign is often accompanied by a T103 affix.
82. J. E. S. Thompson (1970: 259).
83. J. E. S. Thompson (1970: 260).
84. Roys (1967: 67, note 5).
85. Morley (1946: 95–96).
86. Morley ([1941]: 84). Quoted from the Xiu Family Papers, Document 54: 80.
87. Similar references appear in the Books of Chilam Balam of Mani, Tizimin, and Chumayel (Brinton 1882: 98, 103–104 [Mani], 142, 148–49 [Tizimin], 158, 161–62, 168, 172 [Chumayel]; Roys 1967: 49, 51, 138, 142–43 [Chumayel]).
88. Hissink (1934: 81).
89. J. E. S. Thompson (1970: 195).
90. Schellhas (1904: 34).
91. Seler (1917: 13).
92. Seler (1917: 99).
93. Hissink (1934: 78).
94. Seler (1960, 1: 367–89). Correspondences between the Dresden Codex and Landa include: God K-Bolon Dzacab; God G (sun god)-Kinich Ahau (sun god); God D (Itzamna)-Itzamna; and Death God-Uac Mitun Ahau (death god).
95. In a tzolkin on page 12 of the Dresden Codex, God K appears seated and holding a comal containing a food offering. In the glyphic text above, God K's name glyph appears with that of the Maize God (E) and the "good glyph" (Villacorta and Villacorta 1930: 34). J. E. S. Thompson (1960: 269) regards the good glyph as an augural glyph denoting the good luck of the day. He notes that it is often found associated with deities such as B, E, or K, who are generally well-disposed towards mankind. It is never found in association with the Death God (A). God K's name appears in texts with the good glyph on Dresden 3a, 7a, 10b, 12a, and on Madrid 16a, 17b? and 87a?
96. As on Dresden 12a, where the text juxtaposed to that associated with God K clearly concerns days of ill omen. The last glyph of the text (C4) is augural, conveying a sense of death of sickness (J. E. S. Thompson 1960: 268). A preceding glyph (C3) is a variant name for the sacred muan bird, a bird of ill omen (Schellhas 1904: 41; Tozzer and Allen 1910: 338; J. E. S. Thompson 1972b: 79). The glyph (C2) above the muan bird's is damaged, but may be that of the death god (Zimmerman 1956: 162). The general tenor of this text seems to be death-oriented and malevolent. Juxtaposing this text to a picture of God K emphasizes conversely, that he is a god of life. God K also appears between two malevolent deities on Dresden 7a.
97. As noted, on Dresden 12a, God K's name appears with that of God E, the maize god. God K's glyph is also found in conjunction with that of the maize god on Dresden 67a. J. E. S. Thompson (1970: 226) suggests the name Itzamna Kauil for God K, seeing him as a vegetal aspect of the god Itzam Na. Note that Landa mentions Itzamna Kauil in connection with the Kan years, which were under the patronage of Bolon Dzacab (God K) (Tozzer 1941: 142).
98. Pollock (1970: fig. 32). A similar representation of God K and God E occurs on a capstone probably from a site in Campeche (Jones 1975: fig. 1). The significance of these capstones

is discussed further by Kowalski (n.d. a).

99. God K appears on page 46c of the Dresden Codex in the Venus table. The possible iconographic correspondences between the Mexican and Maya Venus tables may be summarized as follows:

BORGIA	DRESDEN
Spearer	*Spearer*
Tlahuizcalpantecutli	Black God (God L)
Tlahuizcalpantecutli (as owl)	Lahun Chan (Venus)
Tlahuizcalpantecutli (as dog)	Xolotl?
Tlahuizcalpantecutli (as rabbit)	Quetzalcoatl-Kukulcan?
Tlahuizcalpantecutli (as death)	Ixquimilli
Victim	*Victim*
Chalchiuhtlicue	God K
Tezcatlipoca	Jaguar
Centeotl (maize god)	God E (maize god)
Rulers (jaguar seat)	Tortoise?
Warriors	Warrior?

Table adapted from Seler (1904:355–91) and J. E. S. Thompson (1960:218–20). Just as Chalchiuhtlicue is the speared victim on the first page of the Venus table in the Borgia Codex, so God K is the victim for the first Venus period in the Dresden Codex. The correspondences between Chalchiuhtlicue and God K, as well as the correspondences between the following two speared victims depicted in the Borgia and the Dresden Codices, suggested to Seler (1904:379) that there was a conceptual resemblance between the two deities. He writes of God K: "I consider it to be almost beyond doubt that he represents the water deity. On the stelae of Copan and Menche [Yaxchilan] he appears as a serpent. In the Troano Codex, page 26, he is the serpent on which Chac, the rain god, rides. . . ." For a variant interpretation of the Mexican and Maya Venus tables and deity correspondences, however, see Kelley (1976:82).

100. Proskouriakoff (1950:97, fig. 35l').

101. There are many instances in the codices where some sort of relationship is seen to exist between God K and God B. For example, on Dresden 3a God B's head glyph appears in a text above a scene featuring God K. The reverse occurs on Madrid 24a. God K's glyph also appears over depictions of God B on Madrid 63a and 94b. On Dresden 34b, God B wears a headdress that takes the form of God K. God K again appears as the headdress of God B on Dresden 65a, where God B is also holding the head of God K. Further connections between God B and God K are seen on Dresden 67a. On page 31b of the Madrid Codex, we see God B seated on God K in serpent form. For a discussion of parallels between the glyphic phrases on pages 30–31b of the Dresden Codex and the clauses dealing with the 819-day count in the inscriptions see Berlin and Kelley (1961:14–16). Whereas the god named in the inscriptions is God K, that named in the Dresden Codex is God B.

102. Villa Rojas (1945:102) says that among the Maya of Quintana Roo: "The chaacs, also called ahhoyas (the sprinklers), occupy first place among the Yuntzilob (lords) in the devotion of the natives. They are the gods who control the clouds and bring the rain. . . . First come the four *nucuch-chaacs* (great chaacs), who stand in the sky at the four cardinal points. They are: Chac-babatun-chaac (sometimes called Cangel) who occupies the east and is regarded as the most powerful; Kan-babatun-chaac to the north, Ek-babatun-chaac to the west, and Zac-babatun-chaac to the south." The use of the word *cangel* as an appellative of one of the rain gods of Yucatan has parallels in the mythologies of other Maya tribes. According to J. E. S. Thompson (1970:256) Anhel is used as a name for the rain gods of the Chorti Maya. See also p. 201 of this chapter, where it is shown that the name of the Tzotzil rain deities, Chauc, is merely another variant of Cauac. Evidence shows that there is a linguistic and conceptual link between the Chauc, who are also known as Anhel, and the Chacs, one of whom is known as Cangel.

The terms Anhel and Cangel were applied to various Maya rain deities. There is also evidence, however, supporting the use of such words in connection with God K. In the *Chilam Balam of Chumayel* a special type of portable insignia is referred to by the Maya word *canhel* (see p. 200 of this chapter). Roys (1967:67) has written of this reference: "There are reasons for believing that this *canhel* is the ceremonial staff carried by the God Impersonators of the fresco of the Chac Mool Temple. In the mixture of Christianity and paganism of page 110 of this present work [Chumayel] we read of God the father grasping in his hand his *canhel*, so it is evidently something that could be held in the hand." In Maya-Spanish dictionaries the word canhel is defined as "dragon" or "serpiente" (see page 200). Roys (1967:67) comments on this: "Again, the figure so obviously suggested by Beltran's dragon is the snakelike head of God K and as Ann Axtell Morris has conclusively shown in her analysis of the [Chac Mool] fresco, this ceremonial object is a vestigial form of the Manikin Scepter with its serpent handle and surmounted by the head or entire figure of God K."

The evidence illustrates that the word canhel was used to describe the Manikin Scepter or God K, while the chief rain deity of the Maya of Quintana Roo, Chac-babatun-chaac, also is known as Cangel (pronounced canhel). Other Maya rain gods are known by the similar name of Anhel. These correspondences strengthen the idea that God K is closely related to the Chacs or rain gods.

103. For a discussion of the Manikin Scepter see Spinden (1913:50–53).

104. Spinden (1913:fig. 30).

105. J. E. S. Thompson (1970:226) identified the tube and scrolls of the Manikin Scepter as "foliage emerging from the forehead. In some cases, this definitely takes the form of the *bil* (vegetal ornament) and may have maize grains." However, the identification of such scrolls as smoke or flame emerging from a smoke tube or axe seems more convincing, since similar scrolls are seen atop the fire glyph (T122:563a). See Kelley (1968). M. D. Coe (1973:116) has suggested that the sign (T617) in the Manikin Scepter's forehead may be a mirror seen in false three-quarter view, and that God K thus may be equated with the central Mexican deity Tezcatlipoca, or "Smoking Mirror." This challenging identification has recently been accepted by several other scholars (Schele 1976:24; Kelley 1976:133; Carlson 1980:125–30), and deserves serious consideration. However, there remain the close correspondences between God K and God B that are delineated in this chapter, and which are ignored by proponents of the God K-Tezcatlipoca identification. For further discussion see Kowalski (n.d. a).

106. J. E. S. Thompson (1970:224–25).

107. The combination of non-classic and decadent traits (e.g., the deep incision of feathers, general crudeness, and lack

of detail) seen on these lintels suggests a Late or Terminal Classic date—ca. A.D. 830–925—(Proskouriakoff 1950:168, fig. 102a–c). These Sayil lintels thus equate chronologically with the House of the Governor.

108. Proskouriakoff (1950:162, fig. 89b).

109. Proskouriakoff (1950:fig. 101c).

110. Kubler (1962:152).

111. For such representations as Tikal, Yaxchilan, and Copan see Spinden (1913:figs. 58, 62, 46). For representations at Naranjo and Bonampak see Proskouriakoff (1950:figs. 60b, 44c). Figures other than God K also appear in this position (e.g., Maudslay 1889–1902, 1:pl. 101).

112. Roys (1967:16, 67–68).

113. Beltrán de Santa Rosa (1859). See Roys (1967:67).

114. Pio Perez (1866–1877).

115. Roys (1967:67, note 5). See note 102 of this chapter.

116. J. E. S. Thompson (1960:87).

117. Schele (1974:43, 50–53). Cauac heads also appear on a limestone openwork relief said to have come from the lower Usamacinta Valley (Easby and Scott 1970:fig. 174).

118. J. E. S. Thompson (1970:267).

119. J. E. S. Thompson (1970:251–62, 267–70).

120. This correspondence was pointed out to me by Professor Lounsbury. He informs me that the linguistically correct form of these words is chahc (Chol) and chahac (Chorti), the h corresponding to the *hache simples* (the Maya have two "h" sounds, hache simples and hache recias). The hache recias more nearly corresponds to the Spanish jota (*j*).

121. Beekman (1963:37) and Ruano Suarez (1892:22).

122. Maudslay (1889–1902, 1:pls. 33, 36b, 38).

123. The notion of creating a supernatural locus was suggested to me by Professor Kubler.

124. Maler (1901:pl. XV–1). W. R. Coe, Shook, and Satterthwaite (1961:fig. 13).

125. For example, on the panel of the Temple of the Foliated Cross at Palenque (Maudslay 1889–1902, 4:pl. 76), Bonampak Stela 1 (Mathews 1980:fig. 3), Quirigua Stela I (Morley (1937–1938, 5:pl. 172), or Lintel 3 of Temple IV at Tikal (W. R. Coe, Shook and Satterthwaite 1961:fig. 29) (figs. 102, 171, 168).

126. Schele (1974:53).

127. Proskouriakoff (1950:50–58, figs. 17–18).

128. Maudslay (1889–1902, 2:pls. 22, 27, 36, 45, 48).

129. Proskouriakoff (1950:fig. 51a).

130. Greene, Rands, and Graham (1972:pl. 69).

131. Von Winning (n.d.:fig. 471). See also Stela 2 from Uxul (Ruppert and Denison 1943:pl. 58a).

132. Pollock (1980:fig. 386). See also the sculptured lintel from Xculoc, where a figure wears a Manikin headdress with a long, curved snout (Proskouriakoff 1950:fig. 101c).

133. Kubler (1962:143).

134. For a discussion of the two-headed monster see Spinden (1913:53–56). See also J. E. S. Thompson (1970:209–33).

135. Maler (1901:pls. XV, XX); Rands (1955:304).

136. Maudslay (1889–1902, 4:pl. 43; 1, pl. 12).

137. Proskouriakoff (1960:454–75). J. E. S. Thompson (1973c:67) sees the niche figures of these Piedras Negras stelae as representatives of the supreme Maya deity, Itzamna. The framing two-headed monster is interpreted as a symbolic depiction of the Maya universe or heavens.

138. Kubler (1969:26).

139. Aveni (1975:182). See chap. 6. Lamb (1980:85) considers the Venus glyphs on several Uxmal masks as evidence they represent Quetzalcoatl-Kukulcan as Venus. See note 46 of this chapter.

Chapter 12

1. For a diagram of the typical step-fret of the House of the Governor see Seler (1917:abb. 111).

2. Seler (1917:127–35) undertook the first thorough description of the frieze of the House of the Governor. The discussion in this chapter relies heavily on his work, and reproduces his diagrams of the frieze.

3. The question arises as to why the north frieze was maintained and not replaced when the second system was devised. Perhaps, having set in place a section of the frieze, the architect was daunted by the prospect of its dismantling and reconstruction. Another reason may have concerned the sacred qualities of the designs, which could not be tampered with once in place. A further possibility is that the potency of the individual design elements was considered more important than their conformation to a symmetrical pattern, particularly on the rear façade of the building.

4. Seler (1917:134).

5. According to Stephens (1963, 1:95), the frieze north of the central motif collapsed in 1825, but it was subsequently restored on the basis of the extant southern half.

6. An important early study of the step-fret is that of Beyer (1924). Sharp's studies incorporate much new data that was unavailable to Beyer.

7. Sharp (1972:38–39); Caso, Bernal, and Acosta (1967:70–71, lam. IX).

8. Rabin (1970:14).

9. Paddock (1966:111).

10. Brainerd (1953:470n; 1958:240–41, 49–50, fig. 64). This ware is now included in the Cochuah Complex, Valladolid Incised-Dichrome Type (R. E. Smith 1971:60).

11. Brainerd (1958:90); Andrews IV (1965b:62); Sharp (1972:37–38).

12. Sharp (1972:38).

13. Sharp (1972:42).

14. Paddock (1966:183; 1970:5, fig. 12).

15. e.g., Codex Nuttall (1975 ed.:26, 21, 5).

16. Kubler (1975:pl. 72a); Paddock (1966:pls. 18–21, 27, 30, 33, 35, 36, 38, 39); Bushnell (1965:fig. 84).

17. Sharp (1972:44); Kerr and Froom (1970:pls. 2, 5, 12, 14, 21, 30, 35, 44, 50).

18. *Ancient Art of Veracruz* (1971:fig. 61).

19. Séjourné (1966:fig. 175–6a).

20. Millon (1967:11); Acosta (1964:lams. 3, 7); Sharp (1972:43).

21. Millon (1967:11); Miller (1973:figs. 238–39).

22. Millon (1973:fig. 20b); Miller (1973:figs. 102–103).

23. Covarrubias (1957:fig. 143).

24. Anton (1969:pl. 194).

25. Brainerd (1958:90, fig. 64); Merwin and Vaillant (1932:pl. 18d).

26. Ruppert, Thompson, and Proskouriakoff (1955:fig. 28).

27. Greene, Rands, and Graham (1972:pl. 3); Proskouriakoff (1950:fig. 68).

28. Greene, Rands, and Graham (1972:pls. 36, 68). See also Morley (1937–1938, 2:301); Maler (1903:pl. 58).

29. Maler (1901:pl. XX); Proskouriakoff (1960:454–75).

30. Maudslay (1889–1902, 4:pls. 17b–18); Foncerrada (1965:125).

31. Ruppert, Thompson, and Proskouriakoff (1955:17).

32. R. E. Smith (1955, 2:figs. 2m, 24–a5, 24–b7, 25–a10, 26–b2, 56g, 57–a1, 57–b4, 57–b5, 57–b6).

33. R. E. Smith (1955, 1:67); Foncerrada (1965:126); Kid-

der, Jennings, and Shook (1946:236); Merwin and Vaillant (1932:pl. 18d).

34. At El Tajin, several buildings are adorned with running files of step-frets, recalling the horizontal sequences at Lambityeco, Oaxaca, but often embracing the building entirely, like a delicate necklace, rather than being limited to panels. See Sharp (1970:8, fig. 24) and Garcia Payon (1976:figs. 33–34, 57–58).

35. García Payon (1976:fig. 42).

36. Kubler (1975:81); García Payon (1976:figs. 60–61).

37. According to Garcia Payon's (1976:fig. 60) reconstruction of Edifice A, two horizontal sequences of step-frets also adorned the bases of the four L-shaped upper apartments, and their upper façades were completely covered with bilaterally symmetrical opposed meanders set in columns in shallow panels.

38. Foncerrada (1965:127–28).

39. Foncerrada (1965:128–29).

40. Saville (1909:188).

41. Kubler (1962:148). For further discussion of the negative batter and mosaic façade of the House of the Governor see chap. 9.

42. Sharp (1970:2, figs. 1–3).

43. Sharp (1970:fig. 4a).

44. Sharp (1970:3, fig. 46). See also Bernal (1966:fig. 19).

45. Sharp (1970:6, fig. 17).

46. Sharp (1970:figs. 5–6); Bernal (1966:357, fig. 13).

47. Wicke (1966:340, fig. 6); Oliver (1955:59, fig. 36b–no. 20).

48. Rabin (1970:15); Sharp (1970:3).

49. Sharp (1972:209).

50. The complex step-fret compositions of the second story of the Monjas are associated with hieroglyphic dates which fall in A.D. 880. See chap. 5, note 61. Although some of the Oaxaca designs probably predate this, there is fairly good evidence suggesting that the step-fret compositions related to those of the Monjas that appear on Buiding 1–N at Yagul and on one of the Mitla palaces date from the Post-Classic period (Rabin 1970:15; Sharp 1970:3).

51. Sharp (1970:5) has likened the doubled frets of the Yucatan step-frets to the frames of the Oaxaca tableros. This comparison is unconvincing, however, since the two-plane treatment was never used on a Oaxaca step-fret.

52. Ruppert and Denison (1943:31, fig. 25).

53. Ruppert and Denison (1943:82, fig. 102a–b, pl. 35a–b).

54. Ruppert and Denison (1943:83, fig. 103a, pl. 36).

55. As noted, Potter (1977:74) believes that Rio Bec style buildings were constructed for the most part between 9.8.0.0.0 and 10.0.0.0.0 in the Long Count, or between A.D. 600–830. See also Ball (1977:172–73). The architectural florescence of the Puuc region fell between about A.D. 770–975. See Ball and Andrews V (1975:235, 244) and chap. 3 of this book.

56. Maler (1902:230, abb. 22); Pollock (1970:23–24, fig. 20); Spinden (1913:fig. 179).

57. Maler (1895:25, fig. 6); Pollock (1970:25); Spinden (1913:fig. 170).

58. Pollock (1970:83–84).

59. For a general description of Xkichmook Structure 5 see E. H. Thompson (1898:221, pls. XVIII, XIX, XXVI).

60. Marquina (1964:fots. 349–50); Maler (1902:205–206).

61. Maler (1902:211, abb. 10); Pollock (1980:figs. 667, 669–70).

62. Maler (1902:211–12, abb. 11); Pollock (1980:figs. 672–73).

63. Maler (1902:abb. 13). The step-frets on the Portal Vault at Labna resemble those of the House of the Governor not only in their bold scale and sharp lines, but also in the concept of setting the steps against a textured background. It is probable that these step-frets at Labna provided an important model for those at Uxmal.

64. Maler (1902:204–205). Sáenz (1968:18–23, fots. 15–17).

65. At Chacmultun, a Puuc site southeast of Uxmal, step-frets do not occur in the architecture, but do appear in painted murals (E. H. Thompson 1904:pl. 8). Near Uxmal, at Kabah, step-fret designs appear on the roof combs of the Palace and the Codz Poop (Pollock 1980:figs. 341, 349, 357, 366).

66. Bolles (1977:150).

67. Sharp (1970:3).

68. The structure known as the Chimez, a two-storied palace located to the south of the main group of buildings at Uxmal, has a richly decorated façade composed of large angular frets. Here the frets are stacked vertically by twos, and alternate with rows of diamond-shaped stones (Pollock 1980:257–62, figs. 452–53, 455).

At the Great Pyramid both simple angular frets and step-frets were incorporated in the architectural sculpture (Sáenz 1975:fig. 6). Single step-frets, bilaterally symmetrical linked step-frets, and frets linked by a stepped diagonal also appear on the Pyramid of the Magician at Uxmal, where they adorn a complex medial molding on the Lower West Structure (Sáenz 1969a:fig. 2; Foncerrada 1965:lam. XIIf).

69. Foncerrada (1965:118).

70. Kubler (1975:174).

71. What the motif may have symbolized for the people of one time and place need not hold true for all. The history of art contains many examples of traditional forms that continued to be used but were invested with new meanings. See Panofsky (1960).

72. Foncerrada (1965:118).

73. Gordon (1905:119).

74. Gordon (1905:144, pl. VI).

75. Spinden (1913:49).

76. Beyer (1924:62).

77. Beyer (1924:61, 84).

78. Westheim (1965:102–103).

79. Foncerrada (1965:120).

80. Foncerrada (1965:120–21); Worringer (1967).

81. Foncerrada (1965:130).

82. Sharp (1972:54).

83. Sharp (1972:60).

84. Covarrubias (1957:113, fig. 50).

85. Sharp (1972:61, fig. 12). Sharp points out that Caso and Bernal (1952:111–12) also believe that the step-fret derives from the serpent head.

86. Kubler (1962:153).

87. Sharp (1972:65); Ho (1970).

88. Ho (1970:9).

89. Sharp (1972:66).

90. Sharp (1972:75).

91. Kubler (1973:33).

92. Various representations of what may be feathered serpents do occur in Olmec art (e.g., La Venta Monument 19, Chalcatzingo Relief V, Oxtotitlan Mural 1-c). Joralemon (1971:82–83) originally classified these images as his God VII of the Olmec. More recently, Joralemon (1976:37) has concluded that God VII should be included in his group of God I images. These define what he calls the Olmec Dragon, a "mythological beast with cayman, eagle, jaguar, human and serpent attributes.

Although feathered serpents possibly appear in Olmec art, they seem to represent a still fluid mythological concept that had not attained the degree of integration evident in later representations of the feathered serpent at Teotihuacan, Tula, and Tenochtitlan. Grove (1984:112) recently has argued that the feathered serpent images in Olmec art might be related more convincingly to the cipactli earth saurian.

93. M. D. Coe (1966:fig. 39).

94. Maler (1903:pl. LVIII).

95. Ruppert and Denison (1943:fig. 103).

96. The figures from the façade of the Figure Palace at Chunhuhub are clothed in birdlike disguise, wearing a beaked face mask and costume with wings. Since the costume is clearly worn by a human impersonator it need not mean that a ruler is not depicted. Various examples exist in Maya art where rulers conceal their identities behind a face mask. A notable case occurs on Yaxchilan Stela 11, where Bird Jaguar is depicted wearing the mask of GI of the Palenque Triad (Maler 1903:pl. LXXIV-no. 1).

97. Seler (1917:abb. 125).

Chapter 13

1. Spinden (1913:128). Kubler (1975:173).

2. Foncerrada (1965:134).

3. Kubler (1975:174–175) describes the lattice as the background in a planar façade organization. In reference to the frieze of the West Structure of the Nunnery he notes that "Three principal planes of relief are . . . established: the ground plane of lattice forms; the key frets of rectilinear units; and the rounded sculpture of serpent bodies and statues. A fourth plane is added by the over-door serpent masks in tiers near the ends of the building."

4. The lower wall is 8 feet 8 inches high, while the frieze between the medial and cornice moldings is 11 feet 5 inches.

5. Foncerrada (1965:132); Marquina (1964:443, fot. 199).

6. Foncerrada (1965:132).

7. García Payon (1976:10).

8. Foncerrada (1965:132).

9. Ruppert and Denison (1943:78, 83, figs. 96, 103, pls. 33a, 36b) provide descriptions, photographs, drawings and plans of these Rio Bec style buildings. The mat-weave structure of the lattice panels is also clear at Ramonal A, Building 1 (Merwin [1913]:fig. 21).

10. Potter (1977:74).

11. Pollock (1970:9–18, fig. 10a); Seler (1916:13–36, abb. 27).

12. Wauchope (1938:42, fig. 31).

13. Pollock (1970:73, 85).

14. Latticework designs carried out in stucco are also found in one of the late constructions of the southeast patio of the Palace at Palenque (Foncerrada 1965:135).

15. Maler (1902:203, abb. 4); Pollock (1980:424, fig. 707).

16. J. E. S. Thompson (1945:8).

17. The use of this type of lattice suggests that the Great Pyramid was constructed somewhat earlier than the House of the Governor. This is also supported by the fact that the second platform of the House of the Governor partly overlies the northeast corner of the Great Pyramid.

18. Bolles (1977:155–56).

19. Andrews IV (1965b:63, table 5).

20. Seler (1917:45).

21. Cirerol Sansores (1939–431).

22. J. E. S. Thompson (1966:84).

23. J. E. S. Thompson (1945:10).

24. J. E. S. Thompson (1973a:206). See also J. E. S. Thompson (1954a:73; 1970:215).

25. Sharp (1972:75).

26. Seler (1917:abbn. 88–89). There is one example of lattice strip with an attached serpent head at Ramonal A, Building 1 (Merwin [1913]:pl. 4, figs. 2, 5). However, these lattice strips have captive figures beneath them, and thus may be interpreted as mat-thrones terminating in serpent heads, somewhat similar in concept to the mat-throne seen in the Temple of the Sun at Palenque (Maudslay 1889–1902, 4:pl. 88).

27. Catherwood (1844:9–10).

28. Viollet-le-Duc (1863:64–69). E. H. Thompson (1911) similarly derived many architectural features of Maya buildings from the pole and thatch hut, but made no specific mention of latticework.

29. Viollet-le-Duc (1863:fig. 9).

30. Spinden (1913:132).

31. Spinden (1957:pl. 52).

32. Wauchope (1938:151).

33. Wauchope (1938:fig. 31).

34. Robicsek (1975:142). Villacorta and Villacorta (1930:26, 60, 62, 64, 66). This woven thatch design also appears in the glyph that Lounsbury (1973:119) has identified as signifying "dwelling place, house or temple," a good example of which appears following the name glyph of the death god on page 28c of the Dresden Codex.

35. E. H. Thompson (1904:pl. 4:2–3).

36. Maler (1895:abb. 6).

37. Villacorta and Villacorta (1930:356, 360).

38. Robicsek (1975:pl. 4).

39. Robicsek (1975:fig. 127).

40. Maudslay (1889–1902, 1:pl. 71).

41. Roys (1967:103, note 3).

42. Roys (1967:83).

43. Roys (1967:92).

44. Roys (1967:95).

45. Roys (1967:102).

46. J. E. S. Thompson (1960:181). Roys (1967:72, 77, 133).

47. Roys (1967:74).

48. Roys (1967:74, note 9).

49. Recinos (1950:207–208); Carmack (1973:19); Edmonson (1964:257–63).

50. Recinos (1950:207–208). This episode is also recounted in the *Titles of the Lords of Totonicapan* (Recinos and Goetz 1953:176–78).

51. Recinos and Goetz (1953:190, note 12).

52. J. E. S. Thompson (1960–107). The importance of the mat symbol can also be gauged by the role it plays in the Maya calendar. Plaited designs figure prominently as an element of the glyph for the Maya month *Pop, Huc Uincil, Nabich* or *Nichilkin.* The Yucatec name for this month, *Pop,* means straw mat in nearly every Maya dialect and language, and the plaited design undoubtedly refers to a mat-weave pattern. Thompson (1960:107–108) speculated that the month *Pop* may have been so named because it is the first month of the Maya year, and as carried natural connotations of elevated rank.

53. Morris, Charlot, and Morris (1931, 2:pl. 133). Variants of this type of jaguar-mat throne also support figures XII, XIII and XIV in the same mural (Morris, Charlot, and Morris 1931, 2:pl. 134).

54. Jones (1977:35–36, fig. 1).

55. W. R. Coe, Shook, and Satterthwaite (1961:figs. 18, 22).

56. Naranjo Stela 22 (Maler 1908:pl. 36–2); Piedras Negras Stela 33 (Proskouriakoff 1950:fig. 45a).

57. M. D. Coe (1975:11, vase no. 2); Kubler (1962:pl. 80A).

58. Schele (1976:25, fig. 12).

59. Maler (1903:pl. 50); Morley (1937–1938, 5:pl. 178b); Spinden (1913:147).

60. Morley (1937–1938, 2:410).

61. J. E. S. Thompson (1972a:125, 129, 138).

62. Villacorta and Villacorta (1930:92c).

63. Proskouriakoff (1950:50, figs. 17a, d, e, f, h, i, n, q, u. w, 18c, a).

64. Proskouriakoff (1950:fig. 23e, 1, m, p).

65. Proskouriakoff (1950:fig. 23m, d', e', f', g', h', k', l').

66. J. E. S. Thompson (1960:fig. 11:17–18, 20–21, 23–29).

67. Proskouriakoff (1950:fig. 22a, b, d, f, g, p). Maudslay (1889–1902, 4:pls. 76, 88).

68. Schele (1976:figs. 10, 12).

69. For a formal comparison see Robicsek (1975:fig. 183c).

Chapter 14

1. Stephens (1963, 1:104) describes the sculpture as a "double-headed cat or lynx." The monument was found complete except for a broken foot.

2. Stephens (1963, 1:104). At a later date the jaguar sculpture was carried to the Hacienda Uxmal, where it was built into a wall on the right side of the stairway that led to the gallery and the living quarters (Seler 1917:75).

3. During 1951–1952, excavation and restoration was conducted at the mound that held the bicephalic jaguar. Enough traces of the original platform were found, including corners and vestiges of the stairways, to determine the original form. The jaguar sculpture, which had been removed to the Hacienda, was replaced and aligned according to Catherwood's drawing (Stephens 1963, 1:fig. 10). Ceramics associated with the platform were of the Yucatan Florescent period. The presence of these Puuc-style ceramics suggests that the jaguar throne dates from the same chronological period as the House of the Governor (Ruz Lhuillier 1955a:49–67).

4. Robertson (1963:11).

5. The precision of this relationship was verified by Hartung (1971:51, 116, plan 6). Hartung (1971:51, 53) points out several other relationships involving the jaguar sculpture. A line with the orientation 20° east of north passes between the jaguar sculpture and a point directly in front of the doorway of the Chenes-style Temple of the Pyramid of the Magician. A line extended due north from the jaguar sculpture passes through the portal vault of the South Structure of the Nunnery.

6. Aveni (1975:183–184). The astronomical significance of this orientation is described in chapter 6.

7. Guggisberg (1975:247–65). Perry (1970:18–20).

8. M. D. Coe (1965:739–75). For the dating of Olmec civilization see M. D. Coe, Diehl, and Stuiver (1967:1399–1401) and M. D. Coe (1968a:41–71).

9. Saville (1929:266–99).

10. Drucker (1952:178). M. D. Coe (1965:752) suggested that the cleft in the head depicted a congenital birth defect. Furst (1968) originally stressed the strong jaguar component in Olmec art, but recently has suggested that some so-called jaguar traits may refer to characteristics of a toad-earth monster concept (Furst 1981:157).

11. Kubler (1972b:36); M. D. Coe (1968b:111–15). Joralemon (1971).

12. Fuente (1973:26–30, no. 5; 18–19, no. 2; 194–96, no. 137; 206–207, no. 145; 170–72, no. 124).

13. Benson (1976, 1:69).

14. M. D. Coe (1972:1–12).

15. Gay (1967:31–32); M. D. Coe (1972:10); Grove (1970:30, fig. 34).

16. Grove (1970:17–18, fig. 13).

17. Grove (1970:32) speculates that this apparent sexual union between the jaguar and the human being involves the theme of mythological origins, but that "since the jaguar is often a symbol of sovereignty, perhaps it is only the Olmec rulers who are the jaguar's children, born of an underworld union between man and jaguar." See also M. D. Coe (1972:10).

18. See p. 232.

19. Tozzer (1941:122).

20. Tozzer (1941:122, note 559); Roys (1943:66).

21. Quoted in Tozzer (1941:203, note 1132).

22. Ruppert, Thompson, and Proskouriakoff (1955:fig. 28).

23. Kubler (1975:180–81); Ruppert, Thompson and Proskouriakoff (1955:52). For a recent reconsideration of the Bonampak murals see Miller ([1981]).

24. Kelley (1965:97–106). For the motif see Maudslay (1889–1902, 4:pls. 87–88).

25. Kubler (1969:18–22).

26. Mathews and Schele (1974:63) and Lounsbury (1974a, 1974b) prefer the Chol Maya name Pacal for this ruler.

27. Schele (1976:25–26).

28. Proskouriakoff (1950:89, figs. 32k–s, 68).

29. J. E. S. Thompson (1960:134).

30. Caso (1958:90–97).

31. Ruppert, Thompson, and Proskouriakoff (1955:figs. 27–29); Greene, Rands, and Graham (1972:pl. 20).

32. Maler (1903:pl. LXXVIII).

33. Proskouriakoff (1950:fig. 70c); Maler (1901:fig. 45a).

34. A. L. Smith (1932:fig. 9); Kubler (1977:fig. 26); W. R. Coe, Shook, and Satterthwaite (1961:fig. 18).

35. Tozzer (1941:122).

36. Tozzer (1941:121–22).

37. Recinos and Goetz (1953:176–77).

38. Roys (1967:66, note 11).

39. Mathews and Schele (1973:66).

40. Maler (1908:pl. VII).

41. Morley (1937–1938, 5:pl. 95b).

42. Maudslay (1889–1902, 2:pl. 8); Maler (1901:pl. XIX).

43. Greene, Rands, and Graham (1972:178–81, pls. 82–83).

44. Robicsek (1975:110).

45. W. R. Coe, Shook, and Satterthwaite (1961:fig. 13).

46. Maler (1901:pl. 19).

47. Spinden (1913:pl. 17–10).

48. Roys (1967:66, note 11).

49. Tozzer (1941:35–39). See chap. 4.

50. J. E. S. Thompson (1960:105, 107).

51. Berlin (1968a:fig. 2, glyph G5); Mathews and Schele (1974:68).

52. This was pointed out to me by Floyd Lounsbury.

53. Morris, Charlot, and Morris (1931, 1:455–56, fig. 305a).

54. Morley (1937–1938, 5, part 1:pl. 146); Proskouriakoff (1961a:172, fig. 9).

55. Maler (1901:pl. XXII).

56. M. D. Coe (1973:70–71, vase no. 30).

57. Robicsek (1972:119, pl. 182).

58. Willey, Smith, Tourtellot, and Graham (1975:35).

59. M. D. Coe (1973:106–109, vase no. 49).
60. Groth-Kimball (1960:pl. 44).
61. Proskouriakoff (1950:fig. 60a).
62. Maler (1901:pl. 15); Proskouriakoff (1960:462).
63. Morris, Charlot, and Morris (1931, 2:pl. 135).
64. Morris, Charlot, and Morris (1931, 1:figs. 270a–b).
65. Ruz Lhuillier (1955a:66); Tozzer (1957, 11:103).
66. Ruz Lhuillier (1955a:66).
67. An original painting by Waldeck of the Palenque Beau Relief Panel is in the Newberry Library, Chicago (Graham 1971:fig. 38).
68. Maudslay (1889–1902, 4:pl. 44); Kubler (1969:26).
69. Seler (1917:abb. 69).
70. Proskouriakoff (1963a:64).
71. Ruz Lhuillier (1955a:50) describes the fragmentary remains of a stone jaguar sculpture that once rested on a low platform in the courtyard of the Nunnery Quadrangle. However, there is no clear evidence that this sculpture was two-headed.

Chapter 15

1. Ball (1974:85). For a recent discussion of the disintegration of Classic Maya civilization see *The Classic Maya Collapse* (T. Patrick Culbert, ed.), University of New Mexico Press, Albuquerque, 1973.
2. J. E. S. Thompson (1970:5).
3. J. E. S. Thompson (1970:7).
4. J. E. S. Thompson (1970:38–43).
5. Willey (1973:62).
6. Blom (1932b). On the importance of the salt trade from Yucatan see Anthony Andrews (1980:30–32). Ball (1974:87, 91) suggests that the coastal salt fields may have been a major impetus for the foundation of the Puuc centers. He also posits that they may have been settled by extra-peninsular groups of Chontal Maya, although also admitting the possibility that they developed as the result of Chontal-Yucatec alliances that were being formed at this time.
7. Kubler (1975:40–43, 81); Litvak King (1972); Foncerrada (1980). See Morley, Brainerd, and Sharer (1983:158).
8. Davies (1977:174–75). Matos Moctezuma (1978:176); Diehl and Benfer (1975:117); Diehl (1983:43–50).
9. Kurjack, Garza T., and Lucas (1979:38–39, 41).
10. J. E. S. Thompson (1970:12).
11. Ball (1979b:49–50). Recent studies by Kelley (1982), Davoust (1980), and Kowalski (1986b; n.d. b) discuss the references to Kakupacal and other historical individuals named in the Chichen Itza inscriptions. Two of these figures, named Jawbone-Longbone (T590b.110), and Yax Pul, also may be referred to on the contemporary (10.2.5.0.0, A.D. 874) Stela 1 from Sacchana [Quen Santo], Chiapas (Seler 1960, 2:figs. 4–5). This strongly suggests that members of the same Itza group who established themselves at Chichen Itza were moving southward simultaneously.
12. Andrews V and Sabloff (n.d.:15) have suggested that Toltec Chichen Itza coexisted with a limited part of the Copo 2 (Pure Florescent or Puuc) period at Dzibilchaltun, and that the two sites were probably competitors and antagonists. Although competition between centers undoubtedly existed, the occasional references to the rulers of one site in the inscriptions of another (e.g., Chichen Itza-Uxmal, Uxmal-Kabah) also suggest that diplomatic exchanges took place or that dynastic ties existed between some centers. See chap. 3, note 152, and chap. 5, note 61.

13. A. Andrews (1980:31–32) has suggested that control of the north coastal salt beds may have been the greatest economic attraction for the Toltecs.
14. J. E. S. Thompson (1970:10–11); Ball (1974:92); Proskouriakoff (1970:466). See the Synthesis section of chap. 3, where evidence is presented that some types of "Toltec" buildings (e.g. the patio-quadrangle Temple of the Hieroglyphic Jambs) may have been constructed prior to A.D. 900. Other possibilities are that several contingents of the Toltecs arrived in Chichen Itza at different times during the tenth century, or that some earlier Toltec traits represent the close alliance that existed between the Itza and Tula, Hidalgo at this time rather than indicating the physical presence of central Mexican Toltecs at Chichen Itza.
15. In this connection, Andrews V and Sabloff (n.d.:22) recently have suggested that the battle in the red hills depicted in the murals of the Upper Temple of the Jaguars at Chichen Itza might represent a conquest of peoples in the Puuc region. For a suggestion that some local rulers cooperated with the new, more highly Mexicanized groups see Morley, Brainerd, and Sharer (1983:158–160).
16. Ball (1974:56–57) and Sharp (1978b:92–96) both have suggested that the rulers of the Puuc centers may have been foreigners, specifically the Chontal or Putun Maya. However, the growing economic importance of the Puuc region during the Late and Terminal Classic periods could also have fostered the growth of strong local Yucatec Maya elites who allied themselves with the Chontal. See note 6.
17. Graham (1973:211–12). The Facies A group is associated with Stelae 8, 10, 11, 14, 20, and 21.
18. Graham (1973:216–17). Ball (1974:88), noting connections between Seibal and northern Yucatan at this time, suggests a "northern peninsular base for the Seibal intruders." Graham (1973:213) has suggested of the Facies A group that: "their derivation seems most likely to be found in the Northern Lowlands." Thompson (1970:41) and Sharer (Morley, Brainerd, and Sharer 1983:158), on the other hand, prefer to see Seibal's new rulers as stemming from the Chontal territory of southwestern Campeche or Tabasco.
19. Graham (1973:213). The later influences at Seibal are closely related to those found concurrently at Chichen Itza. They include the presence of a peculiar knife-wing bird as an iconographic motif (and personal name at Chichen Itza), as well as shared forms in art and architecture (e.g., prowling jaguar motif, round buildings similar ball court profiles). See A. L. Smith (1982:239–40), Kelley (1982:7, figs. 3–4), Greene, and Rands, and Graham (1972:pl. 101).
20. Indeed, as noted, (note 18) both Graham (1973:213) and Ball (1974:88) have suggested that the Facies A group actually came from the Northern Lowlands.

Appendix

1. Martínez Hernández ([1913]); John Lloyd Stephens (1963, 1:95).
2. Martínez Hernández ([1914]; [1918]).
3. Noguera ([1922]).
4. Martínez Cantón ([1926]).
5. Martínez Cantón ([1927]).
6. Martínez Cantón ([1928]).
7. Cirerol Sansores ([1936]).
8. Cirerol Sansores ([1937a]).

9. Cirerol Sansores ([1937b]).
10. Cirerol Sansores (1939).
11. Cirerol Sansores (1952; 1956).
12. Cirerol Sansores (1956:125–26).
13. Cirerol Sansores (1956:125).
14. Erosa Peniche ([1945a]).
15. Erosa Peniche ([1945b]; [1945c]; [1945d]).
16. Erosa Peniche ([1945e]).
17. Erosa Peniche ([1946a]; [1946b]).
18. Erosa Peniche ([1947a]).
19. Erosa Peniche ([1947b]).
20. Erosa Peniche ([1947a]; [1947b]).
21. Erosa Peniche (1947c).
22. Erosa Peniche (1947c:6).
23. Ruz Lhuillier ([1947]).
24. Ruz Lhuillier ([1948]; 1958).
25. Erosa Peniche ([1948a]).
26. Erosa Peniche ([1948b]; [1948c]; [1948d]).
27. Ruz Lhuillier ([1950]).
28. Ruz Lhuillier ([1950]:1–2).
29. Ruz Lhuillier (1955a).
30. Ruz Lhuillier (1955a:58).
31. Ruz Lhuillier (1955a:58–59).

32. Ruz Lhuillier (1955a:59). Ruz proposed that in order to restore the north vault to its original condition it would be necessary to remove the superimposed room on the west side of the passageway, as well and the central wall that closes off the vault. This project was never carried out.
33. Ruz Lhuillier (1955a:60).
34. Ruz Lhuillier (1955b:9). To replace some of the serpent-form guilloche of the middle course concrete molds of original pieces were used.
35. Ruz Lhuillier (1955b:9–10).
36. Ruz Lhuillier (1955b:10–11).
37. Ruz Lhuillier (1959).
38. Sáenz (1969a:5; [1969b]).
39. Konieczna and Mayer Guala (1976:6).
40. Barrera Rubio ([1978]).
41. Stephens (1963, 1:pl. II opposite p. 95). See also Sáenz (1972:36).
42. Barrera Rubio ([1978]:3). Similar walls, also of Pure Florescent date, have been reported from several sites in northwestern Yucatan, such as Ake, Muna, and Chunchucmil (Kurjack and Andrews V 1976:322).
43. Barrera Rubio ([1978]:4).

Bibliography

Acosta, Jorge R.
1964
El palacio de Quetzalpapalotl. *Memorias del Instituto Nacional de Antropología e Historia*, no. 10. Mexico, D.F.

Adams, R. E. W.
1970
Suggested Classic Period Occupational Specialization in the Southern Maya Lowlands. In *Monographs and Papers in Maya Archaeology*, ed. W. R. Bullard, Jr. *Papers of the Peabody Museum of Archaeology and Ethnology, Harvard University*, 61. Cambridge, Mass.
1971
The Ceramics of Altar de Sacrificios, Guatemala. *Papers of the Peabody Museum of Archaeology and Ethnology, Harvard University*, 63, no. 1. Cambridge, Mass.
1974
A Trial Estimation of Classic Maya Palace Populations at Uaxactun. In *Mesoamerican Archaeology, New Approaches*, ed. Norman Hammond, pp. 285–96. Austin, Texas.

Ancient Art of Veracruz
1971
Ancient Art of Veracruz. Exhibit sponsored by Ethnic Arts Council of Los Angeles. Los Angeles.

Andrews, Anthony P.
1980
The Salt Trade of the Ancient Maya. *Archaeology* 33 (4):24–33.

Andrews, E. Wyllys, IV
1960
Excavations at Dzibilchaltun, Northwestern Yucatan, Mexico. *Proceedings of the American Philosophical Society* 104:254–65.
1961
Preliminary Report on the 1959–60 Field Season, National Geographic-Tulane University Dzibilchaltun Program. *Tulane University, Middle American Research Institute, Miscellaneous Series*, 11, pp. 1–27. New Orleans, La.
1965a
Archaeology and Prehistory in the Northern Maya Lowlands: An Introduction. *Handbook of Middle American Indians*, 2:288–330. Austin, Texas.
1965b
Progress report on the 1960–1964 Field Seasons, National Geographic Society-Tulane University Dzibilchaltun Program. *Tulane University, Middle American Research Institute, Publication* 31, pp. 23–67. New Orleans, La.
1968
Dzibilchaltun, a Northern Maya Metropolis. *Archaeology* 21:36–47.
1973
The Development of Maya Civilization After the Abandonment of the Southern Cities. In *The Classic Maya Collapse*, ed. by T. P. Culbert, pp. 243–65. Albuquerque, N. Mex.

Andrews, E. Wyllys, IV, and E. Wyllys Andrews V
1980
Excavations at Dzibilchaltun, Yucatan, Mexico. *Tulane University, Middle American Research Institute, Publication* 48. New Orleans, La.

Andrews, E. Wyllys, IV, and Erwin Rovner
1973
Archaeological Evidence on Social Stratification and Commerce in the Northern Maya Lowlands: Two Mason's Tool Kits from Muna and Dzibilchaltun, Yucatan. *Tulane University, Middle American Research Institute, Publication* 31, pp. 81–102. New Orleans, La.

Andrews, E. Wyllys, V
1972
Comments on the Archaeological Sequence in the Northern Maya Lowlands. Paper prepared for the annual meeting of the American Association for the Advancement of Science.
1974
Some Architectural Similarities Between Dzibilchaltun and Palenque. In *Primera Mesa Redonda de Palenque*, ed. by Merle Greene Robertson, pp. 137–47. Pebble Beach, Calif.
1979

Some Comments on Puuc Architecture of the Northern Yucatan Peninsula. In *The Puuc: New Perspectives: Papers Presented at the Puuc Symposium, Central College, May, 1977,* ed. by Lawrence Mills, pp. 1–17. Pella, Iowa.

Andrews, E. Wyllys, V, and Jeremy A. Sabloff
n.d.
Classic to Postclassic: A Summary Discussion, draft of concluding chapter in *Late Lowland Maya Civilization: Classic to Postclassic.* School of American Research. University of New Mexico Press, Albuquerque. N. Mex.

Andrews, George
1975
Maya Cities, Placemaking and Urbanization. Norman, Okla.
[1979]
Early Puuc Architecture. Paper presented at the 43d International Congress of Americanists, Vancouver, B.C.

Anton, Ferdinand
1969
Ancient Mexican Art. New York.

Aveni, Anthony F.
1975
Possible Astronomical Orientations in Ancient Mesoamerica. In *Archaeoastronomy in Pre-Columbian America,* ed. Anthony F. Aveni, pp. 163–90. Austin, Texas.
1977
Concepts of Positional Astronomy employed in Ancient American Architecture. In *Native American Astronomy,* ed. Anthony F. Aveni, pp. 3–19. Austin, Texas.

Aveni, Anthony F., and Horst Hartung
1982
Precision in the Layout of Maya Architecture. *Annals of the New York Academy of Sciences.*

Ball, Joseph W.
1974
A Coordinate Approach to Northern Maya Prehistory: A.D. 700–1200. *American Antiquity* 39:85–93.
1977
The Archaeological Ceramics of Becan, Campeche, Mexico. *Tulane University, Middle American Research Institute, Publication* 43. New Orleans, La.
1979a
Ceramics, Culture History, and the Puuc Tradition: Some Alternative Possibilities. In *The Puuc: New Perspectives: Papers Presented at the Puuc Symposium, Central College, May, 1977,* ed. by Lawrence Mills, pp. 18–35. Pella, Iowa.
1979b
The 1977 Central College Symposium on Puuc Archaeology: A Summary View. In *The Puuc: New Perspectives: Papers Presented at the Puuc Symposium, Central College, May, 1977,* ed. by Lawrence Mills, pp. 46–51. Pella, Iowa.

Ball, Joseph W., and E. Wyllys Andrews V
1975
The Polychrome Pottery of Dzibilchaltun, Yucatan, Mexico: Typology and Architectural Context. *Tulane University, Middle American Research Institute, Publication* 31, pp. 227–47. New Orleans, La.

Bancroft, Hubert Howe
1875
The Native Races of the Pacific, Antiquities, vol. 4 New York, N.Y.

Barrera Rubio, Alfredo
1978
Settlement Patterns in the Uxmal Area, Yucatan, Mexico. Paper Presented at the 43d Annual Meeting of the Society for American Archaeology. Tucson, Az.
1979
Las Pinturas Murales del area Maya del Norte. In *Enciclopedia Yucatanense,* Edición Oficial del Gobierno de Yucatan, pp. 189–222. Mérida.

Barrera Vásquez, Alfredo, and S. G. Morley
1949
The Maya Chronicles. *Contributions to American Archaeology and History,* 10, no. 48. *Carnegie Institution of Washington, Publication* 585. Washington, D.C.

Becker, Marshall J.
1979
Priests, Peasants and Ceremonial Centers: The Intellectual History of a Model. *Maya Archaeology and Ethnology,* eds. Norman Hammond and Gordon R. Willey pp. 3–20. Austin, Texas.

Beekman, John, and Elaine Beekman
1963
Vocabulario Chol. Instituto Linguistico de Verano. Mexico, D.F.

Beltrán de Santa Rosa, P.
1859
Arte del idioma Maya reducido a sucintas reglas y semilexicon yucateco. Mérida.

Benson, Elizabeth P.
1976
Motifs in Olmec Sculpture. *Actas del XXIII Congreso Internacional de Historia del Arte, Granada,* 1973, vol. 1. Granada.

Berlin, Heinrich
1956
Late Pottery Horizons of Tabasco, Mexico. *Contributions to American Archaeology and History,* 12, no. 59. *Carnegie Institution of Washington, Publication* 606. Washington, D.C.
1958
El Glifo emblema en las inscripciones Mayas. *Journal de la Société des Américanistes de Paris,* n.s. 47: 111–19. Paris.
1959
Glifos Nominales en el Sarcófago de Palenque. *Humanidades* 2(10):1–8. Universidad de San Carlos, Guatemala.
1968a
The Tablet of the 96 Glyphs at Palenque, Chiapas, Mexico. *Tulane University, Middle American Research Institute, Publication* 26, pp. 135–49. New Orleans, La.
1968b
Estudios Epigráficos II. *Antropología e Historia de Guatemala,* 20, pp. 13–24. Guatemala.
1970

Miscelánea Palencana. *Journal de la Société des Américanistes de Paris*, n.s. 59:107–28. Paris.

Berlin, Heinrich, and David Kelley
1961
The 819-Day Count and Color-Direction Symbolism Among the Classic Maya. *Archaeological Studies in Middle America. Tulane University, Middle American Research Institute, Publication* 26. New Orleans, La.

Bernal, Ignacio
1966
The Mixtecs in the Archaeology of the Valley of Oaxaca. In *Ancient Oaxaca*, ed. by John Paddock, pp. 345–66. Stanford, Ca.
1969
100 Great Masterpieces of the Mexican National Museum of Anthropology. New York.

Beyer, Hermann
1924
El Origen, Desarrollo y Significado de la Greca Escalonada. *El México Antiguo* 2 (3–4): 1–121. Mexico, D.F.
1931
The Maya Hieroglyphs: The variable element of the introducing glyphs as month indicator. *Anthropos*, 26:99–108. Vienna.
1934
Ueber das Datum auf der Russelmaske von Labna. *El México Antiguo*, 3, (3–4): 9–13. Mexico, D.F.
1941
A Discussion of J. Eric Thompson's Interpretations of Chichen Itza hieroglyphs. *American Antiquity* 6: 327–38.

Blom, Frans
1930
Uxmal: The Great Capital of the Xiu Dynasty of the Maya. *Art and Archaeology*, 30(6): 199–209.
1931
Summary of Archaeological Work in the Americas during 1929 and 1930. *Pan-American Union, American Archaeological Series*, no. 5. Washington, D.C.
1932a
The "Negative Batter" at Uxmal. *Tulane University, Middle American Research Institute, Publication* 4, pp. 557–66. New Orleans, La.
1932b
Commerce, Trade and Monetary Units of the Maya. *Tulane University, Middle American Research Institute, Publication* 4, pp. 531–36. New Orleans, La.
1934
Short Summary of Recent Explorations in the Ruins of Uxmal, Yucatan. *Proceedings of the 24th International Congress of Americanists*, pp. 55–59. Hamburg.

Bolles, John
1977
Las Monjas, A Major Pre-Mexican Architectural Complex at Chichen Itza. Norman, Okla.

Bullard, William R., Jr.
1960
Maya Settlement Pattern in Northeastern Peten, Guatemala. *American Antiquity* 25:355–72.

Brainerd, George W.
1941
Fine Orange Pottery in Yucatan. *Revista Mexicana de Estudios Antropológicos* 5 (2–3): 163–83. Mexico, D.F.
1953
On the design of the Fine Orange pottery found at Chichen Itza, Yucatan. In *Huastecos, Totonacos y sus Vecinos. Revista Mexicana de Estudios Antropológicos* 13 (2–3): 463–73. Mexico, D.F.
1958
The Archaeological Ceramics of Yucatan. University of California, Anthropological Records, no. 19. Berkeley and Los Angeles.

Brasseur de Bourbourg, Charles Etienne
1858
Histoire des Nations Civilisées du Mexique et de l'Amérique Central, 2. Paris.
1867a
Extract from a letter written in Mexico, Jan. 27, 1865. *Archives de la Commission Scientifique du Mexique*, Tome I:457–60. Paris.
1967b
Essai historique sur le Yucatan et description des ruines de Ti-hoo (Mérida) et d'Izamal. *Archives de la Commission Scientifique du Mexique*, Tome II:18–64. Paris.
1867c
Rapport sur les ruines de Mayapan et d'Uxmal au Yucatan (Mexique). *Archives de la Commission Scientifique du Mexique*, Tome II:234–288. Paris.

Brine, Lindsay
1894
Travels amongst the American Indians, Their Ancient Earthworks and Temples, Including a Journey in Guatemala, Mexico and Yucatan, and a Visit to the Ruins of Patinamit, Palenque and Uxmal. London.

Brinton, Daniel G.
1882
The Maya Chronicles. Philadelphia.

Buchon, J. A.
1825
Atlas géographique, statistique, historique, et chronologique de deux Amériques et les îles adjacentes; traduit de l'atlas éxecuté en Amérique d'après Lesage. Paris.

Bushnell, Geoffrey
1965
Ancient Arts of the Americas. New York.

Butler, Mary
1935
A Study of Maya Moldmade Figurines. *American Anthropologist*, n.s. 37:636–72.
1937
Gods and Heroes on Maya Monuments. *Philadelphia Anthropological Society, Anniversary Volume*, ed. D. S. Davidson, pp. 13–26. Philadelphia, Pa.

Cabrera, Dr. Paul Felix
1822
Description of the Ruins of an Ancient city, Discovered near Palenque, in the Kingdom of Guatemala in Spanish America: Translated from the Original Manuscript Report of Captain Don Antonio del Rio. Followed by

Teatro Critico Americano: A Critical Investigation and Research into the History of Americans by Doctor Felix Cabrera of the city of Guatemala. London.

Carlson, John B.
1981
Olmec Concave Iron-Ore Mirrors: The Aesthetics of a Lithic Technology and the Lord of the Mirror (with an Illustrated Catalogue of Mirrors). *The Olmec and their Neighbors: Essays in Memory of Matthew W. Stirling*, ed. Elizabeth P. Benson, pp. 117–47. Dumbarton Oaks, Washington, D.C.

Carmack, Robert M.
1973
Quichean Civilization: The Ethnohistoric, Ethnographic, and Archaeological Sources. Berkeley and Los Angeles.

Case, Henry A.
1911
Views on and of Yucatan, Besides Notes upon the State of Campeche and the Territory of Quintana Roo. Mérida.

Caso, Alfonso
1942
Definición y extensión del complejo "Olmeca". In *Sociedad Mexicana de Antropología, Reuniones de Mesa Redonda: Mayas y Olmecas*, pp. 43–46. Tuxtla, Gutiérrez.
1958
The Aztecs: People of the Sun. Norman, Okla.

Caso, Alfonso, and Ignacio Bernal
1952
Urnas de Oaxaca. *Memorias del Instituto Nacional de Antropología e Historia*, no. 2. Mexico, D.F.

Caso, Alfonso, Ignacio Bernal and Jorge Acosta
1967
La Cerámica de Monte Alban. *Memorias del Instituto Nacional de Antropología e Historia*, no. 3.

Catherwood, Frederick
1844
Views of Ancient Monuments in Central America, Chiapas, and Yucatan. London.

Chandler, J. B., R. Kinningham and D. S. Massey
1963
Texas Bio-Nuclear Radiocarbon Measurements I. *Radiocarbon* 5:56–61.

Charnay, Desiré
1863
Cités et Ruines Americaines. Paris.
1887
The Ancient Cities of the New World. Trans. J. Gonino and Helen S. Conant. New York.

Chavero, Alfredo
1887
Mexico a través de los siglos, Tomo I, Primera Época, Historia Antigua. Mexico and Barcelona.

Cirerol Sansores, Manuel
[1936]
Informe final de las actividades desarrolladas en la zona arqueológica de Uxmal, Yuc. corresponde al mes de Junio de 1936. 27 de junio, 1936. Instituto Nacional de Antropología e Historia, Informes Inéditos, Estado de Yucatan—Uxmal, Tomo I. 1913–1937.
[1937a]
Se informa de los trabajos desarrollados en Uxmal, hasta el 30 de abril de 1937. 27 de Mayo, 1937. Instituto Nacional de Antropología e Historia, Informes Inéditos, Estado de Yucatan—Uxmal, Tomo I. 1913–1937.
[1937b]
Se informa de los trabajos desarrollados en la zona arqueológica de Uxmal durante el mes de mayo de 1937. 7 de junio, 1937. Instituto Nacional de Antropología e Historia, Informes Inéditos, Estado de Yucatan—Uxmal, Tomo I. 1913–1937.
1937c
Informe general de las restauraciónes arqueológicás en la zona de Uxmal, Yuc., durante la temporada de trabajos en el año de 1937. 14 de julio, 1937. Instituto Nacional de Antropología e Historia, Informes Inéditos, Estado de Yucatan—Uxmal, Tomo II. 1937–1942.
1939
La Realidad de las Fachadas Mayas. *Proceedings of the 22d International Congress of Americanists*. Mexico, D.F.
1952
Ushmal. Mérida.
1956
Guia de Ushmal (2nd ed.). Mérida.

Ciudad Real, Fray Antonio de
1872
Relacion breve y verdadera de algunas cosas de las muchas que sucedieron al Padre Fray Alonso Ponce de las provincias de la Nueva España, . . . *Colección de Documentos Inéditos para la Historia de España*, 57–58.

Codex, Nuttal
1975
The Codex Nuttall, A Picture Manuscript from Ancient Mexico. The Peabody Museum Facsimile, ed. Zelia Nuttall. Introductory text by Arthur G. Miller. New York.

Coe, Michael D.
1965
The Olmec Style and its Distributions. *Handbook of Middle American Indians*, 3:739–75. Austin, Texas.
1966
The Maya. New York. 2nd ed., 1980.
1968a
San Lorenzo and the Olmec Civilization. In *Dumbarton Oaks Conference on the Olmec*, ed. Elizabeth Benson. Washington, D.C.
1968b
America's First Civilization. New York and Washington.
1972
Olmec Jaguars and Olmec Kings. *The Cult of the Feline*, ed. Elizabeth Benson. Washington, D.C.
1973
The Maya Scribe and His World. New York.
1975
Classic Maya Pottery at Dumbarton Oaks. Washington, D.C.

Coe, Michael D., R. A. Diehl, and M. Stuiver

1967

Olmec Civilization, Veracruz, Mexico: Dating of the San Lorenzo Phase. *Science* 155 (3768): 1399–1401.

Coe, W. R.

1962

A Summary of Excavation and Research at Tikal, Guatemala: 1956–61. *American Antiquity* 27:479–507.

1965

Tikal, Guatemala, and Emergent Maya Civilization. *Science* 147 (3664): 1401–1419.

1967

Tikal, A Handbook of the Ancient Maya Ruins. The University Museum, University of Pennsylvania. Philadelphia, Pa.

Coe, William R., Edwin M. Shook, and Linton Satterthwaite

1961

The Carved Wooden Lintels of Tikal. *Museum Monographs, Tikal Reports,* no. 6. The University Museum, University of Pennsylvania. Philadelphia, Pa.

Coggins, Clemency C.

1967

Palaces and the Planning of Ceremonial Centers in the Southern Maya Lowlands. Unpublished paper.

1975

Painting and Drawing Styles at Tikal: an Historical and Iconographic Reconstruction. Ph.D. Dissertation, Harvard University. Ann Arbor.

Cogolludo, Diego Lopez de

1971

Los Tres Siglos de la Dominación Española en Yucatan o sea Historia de esta Provincia, 1. Graz, Austria.

Corson, Christopher.

1976

Maya Anthropomorphic Figurines from Jaina Island, Campeche. *Ballena Press Studies in Meso-american Art, Archaeology, and Ethnohistory,* no. 1. Ramona.

Covarrubias, Miguel

1957

Indian Art of Mexico and Central America. New York.

Crónica de Mani

1557–1813

Manuscript at the Middle American Research Institute at Tulane University. New Orleans, La.

Damon, P. E., C. W. Ferguson, A. Long, and E. I. Wallick

1974

Dendrochronologic Calibration of the Radiocarbon Time Scale. *American Antiquity* 39:350–66.

Davies, Nigel

1977

The Toltecs Until the Fall of Tula. Norman, Okla.

Deevey, E. S., J. S. Gralenski, and V. Hoffren

1959

Yale Natural Radiocarbon Dates II. *American Journal of Science, Radiocarbon Supplement* 1:144–72. New Haven, Conn.

De la Croix, H., and R. G. Tansey

1975

Gardner's Art through the Ages. New York.

De Vries, H., G. W. Barendson and H. T. Waterbolk

1958

Groningen radiocarbon dates II. *Science* 127:129–37.

De Vries, H., and H. T. Waterbolk

1958

Groningen radiocarbon dates III. *Science* 128.

Díaz del Castillo, Bernal

1956

The Discovery and Conquest of Mexico. Translated with an Introduction and Notes by Alfred P. Maudslay. New York, N.Y.

Dibble and Anderson. See Sahagún.

Diccionario de San Francisco

1976

Diccionario de San Francisco, ed. Oscar Michelson. Biblioteca Lingüística Americana, II. Graz, Austria.

Diehl, Richard A.

1983

Tula: The Toltec Capital of Ancient Mexico. London.

Diehl, Richard A., and Robert A. Benfer

1975

Tollan, the Toltec Capital. *Archaeology* 28 (2):112–24.

Drucker, Philip

1952

La Venta, Tabasco: A Study of Olmec Ceramics and Art. *Bureau of American Ethnology, Bulletin* 153. Washington, D.C.

Easby, Elizabeth K., and John K. Scott

1970

Before Cortes, Sculpture of Middle America. New York.

Edmonson, Munro S.

1965

Quiché-English Dictionary. *Tulane University, Middle American Research Institute, Publication* 30. New Orleans, La.

1971

The Book of Counsel: The Popol Vuh of the Quiché Maya of Guatemala. *Tulane University, Middle American Research Insittute, Publication* 35. New Orleans, La.

1982

The Ancient Future of the Itza: The Book of Chilam Balam of Tizimin. Austin, Texas.

Eliade, Mircea

1957

The Sacred and the Profane. New York, N.Y.

Erasmus, Charles J.

1965

Monument Building: Some Field Experiments. *Southwestern Journal of Anthropology* 21 (4):277–301. Albuquerque, N. Mex.

Erosa Peniche, José

[1945a]

Informe de las exploraciónes y restauraciónes arqueológicas verificadas en Uxmal, Yuc., del 26 de febrero al 31 de marzo de 1945. Informe num. 547. 16 de abril, 1945. Instituto Nacional de Antropología e Historia, Informes Inéditos, Estado de Yucatan—Uxmal, Tomo III. 1942–1947.

[1945b]

Informe de las exploraciónes y restauraciónes arqueológicas verificadas en Uxmal, Yuc., durante el mes de abril de 1945. Informe num. 585. 9 de mayo, 1945. Instituto Nacional de Antropología e Historia, Informes Inéditos, Estado de Yucatan—Uxmal, Tomo III. 1942–1947.

[1945c]
Informe de las exploraciónes y restauraciónes arqueológicas verificadas en Uxmal, Yuc., durante el mes de mayo de 1945. Informe num. 612. 8 de junio, 1945. Instituto Nacional de Antropología e Historia, Informes Inéditos, Estado de Yucatan—Uxmal, Tomo III. 1942–1947.

[1945d]
Informe de las exploraciónes y restauraciónes arqueológicas verificadas en Uxmal, Yuc., durante el mes de junio de 1945. Informe num. 645. 9 de julio, 1945. Instituto Nacional de Antropología e Historia, Informes Inéditos, Estado de Yucatan—Uxmal, Tomo III. 1942–1947.

[1945e]
Informe final de las exploraciónes y restauraciónes arqueológicas verificadas en Uxmal, Yuc. Informe num. 512. 31 de agosto, 1945. Instituto Nacional de Antropología e Historia, Informes Inéditos, Estado de Yucatan—Uxmal, Tomo III. 1942–1947.

[1946a]
Informe final de los trabajos de exploración y restauración verificadas en la zona arqueológica de Uxmal. Informe num. 284. 18 de julio, 1946. Instituto Nacional de Antropología e Historia, Informes Inéditos, Estado de Yucatan—Uxmal, Tomo III. 1942–1947.

[1946b]
Informe de las exploraciónes y restauraciónes arqueológicas verificadas en Uxmal, Yuc., durante el mes de abril de 1946. Informe num. 168. 8 de mayo, 1946. Instituto Nacional de Antropología e Historia, Informes Inéditos, Estado de Yucatan—Uxmal, Tomo III. 1942–1947.

[1947a]
Informe de las exploraciónes y restauraciónes verificadas en Uxmal, Yuc., durante los dias transcurridas del 17 de marzo al 30 de abril de 1947. Informe num. 166. 2 de mayo, 1947. Instituto Nacional de Antropología e Historia, Informes Inéditos, Estado de Yucatan—Uxmal, Tomo III. 1942–1947.

[1947b]
Informe de las exploraciónes arqueológicas y otros trabajos verificadas en Yucatan durante los meses de mayo y junio de 1947. Informe num. 241. 4 de julio, 1947. Instituto Nacional de Antropología e Historia, Informes Inéditos, Estado de Yucatan—Uxmal, Tomo III. 1942–1947.

1947c
Guia para visitar las Ruinas de Uxmal. Mérida.

[1948a]
Informe de las exploraciónes y restauraciónes arqueológicas verificadas en Uxmal, Yuc., del 5 al 30 de abril de 1948. Informe num. 179. 8 de mayo, 1948. Instituto Nacional de Antropología e Historia, Informes Inéditos, Estado de Yucatan—Uxmal, Tomo IV. 1948–1952.

[1948b]
Informe de las exploraciónes y restauraciónes arqueo-

lógicas verificadas en Uxmal, Yuc., durante el mes de mayo de 1948. Informe num. 318. 5 de junio, 1948. Instituto Nacional de Antropología e Historia, Informes Inéditos, Estado de Yucatan—Uxmal, Tomo IV. 1948–1952.

[1948c]
Informe sobre los trabajos de exploración y restauración en la zona arqueológica de Uxmal, Yuc. Informe num. 361. 5 de julio, 1948. Instituto Nacional de Antropología e Historia, Informes Inéditos, Estado de Yucatan—Uxmal, Tomo IV. 1948–1952.

[1948d]
Informe sobre las exploraciónes y restauraciónes arqueológicas en Uxmal, Yuc. Informe num. 411. 7 de agosto, 1948. Instituto Nacional de Antropología e Historia, Informes Inéditos, Estado de Yucatan—Uxmal, Tomo IV. 1948–1952.

1949
Guia para visitar las Ruinas de Uxmal (3rd ed.). Mérida.

Foncerrada de Molina, Marta
1964
Fechas de radiocarbono en el área Maya. *Estudios de Cultura Maya* 4:141–66. Mexico, D.F.

1965
La Escultura Arquitectónica de Uxmal. Mexico, D.F.

1980
Mural Painting in Cacaxtla and Teotihuacan Cosmopolitism. In *Third Palenque Round Table, 1978*, 5, pt. 2, ed. by Merle Green Robertson, pp. 183–98. Austin, Texas.

Freidel, David A.
1979
Culture Areas and Interaction Spheres: Contrasting Approaches to the Emergence of Civilization in the Maya Lowlands. *American Antiquity* 44 (1):36–54.

Freidel, David A., and Richard M. Leventhal
1975
The Settlement Survey. In *A Study of Changing pre-Columbian Commercial Systems*, ed. by Jeremy A. Sabloff and William L. Rathje, pp. 60–76. *Peabody Museum Monographs, Harvard University*, no. 3. Cambridge, Mass.

Friedrichsthall, Emmanuel de
1841
Les Monuments de l'Yucatan. *Nouvelles Annales des Voyages*, Tome quatrieme, année 1841, tome 92, pp. 291–314. Paris.

Fuente, Beatriz de la
1973
Escultura Monumental Olmeca. Mexico, D.F.

Furst, Peter T.
1968
The Olmec Were-Jaguar Motif in the Light of Ethnographic Reality. *Dumbarton Oaks Conference on the Olmec*, ed. Elizabeth P. Benson, pp. 143–78. Dumbarton Oaks, Washington, D.C.

1981
Jaguar Baby or Toad Mother: A New Look at an Old Problem in Olmec Iconography. *The Olmec and their Neighbors*, ed. Elizabeth P. Benson, pp. 149–62.

Dumbarton Oaks, Washington, D.C.

Gann, Thomas
1918
The Maya Indians of Southern Yucatan and Northern British Honduras. *Smithsonian Institution, Bureau of American Ethnology, Bulletin* 64. Washington, D.C.

Garcia Payon, José
1976
El Tajin: Official Guide. Institutio Nacional de Antropología e Historia. Mexico, D.F.

Gates, William
1937
Yucatan before and after the conquest, by Friar Diego de Landa, With other Related Documents, Maps and Illustrations. Translated with notes by William Gates. *Maya Society, Publication* 20. Baltimore, Md.

Gay, Carlo T. E.
1967
Oldest Paintings in the New World. *Natural History* 76 (4):28–35.

Gordon, George Byron
1905
The Serpent Motive in the Ancient Art of Central America and Mexico. *Transactions of the Department of Archaeology, University of Pennsylvania,* 1, pt. 3, pp. 131–63. Philadelphia, Pa.
1918
Native American Art. *The Museum Journal* 9 (1):7–28. The University Museum, University of Pennsylvania. Philadelphia, Pa.

Graham, Ian
1971
Art of Maya Hieroglyphic Writing. Catalogue of an Exhibition in the Art Gallery, Center for Inter-American Relations. New York.

Graham, John A.
1972
Aspects of Non-Classic Presences in the Inscriptions and Sculptural Art of Seibal. In *The Classic Maya Collapse,* ed. by T. P. Culbert, pp. 207–219. Albuquerque, N. Mex.

Green, Frank
[1952]
Unpublished Study of Maya Mensurational Systems. Copy in possession of author.

Greene, Merle, Robert L. Rands and John A. Graham
1972
Maya Sculpture from the Southern Lowlands, the Highlands, and Pacific Piedmont, Guatemala, Mexico, Honduras. Berkeley.

Griffin, Gillett
1976
Portraiture at Palenque. In *The Art, Iconography and Dynastic History of Palenque,* pt. 3, ed. Merle Greene Robertson, pp. 137–147. Pebble Beach, Calif.

Gropp, Alfred E.
1933
Manuscripts in the Department of Middle American Research. *Middle American Research Series, Tulane University, Publication* 5, pp. 217–97. New Orleans, La.

Groth Kimball, Irmgard
1960
Maya Terrakotten. Tübingen.

Grove, David C.
1970
The Olmec Paintings of Oxtotitlan Cave, Guerrero, Mexico. *Studies in Pre-Columbian Art and Archaeology,* no. 6. Dumbarton Oaks, Washington, D.C.
1984
Chalcatzingo: Excavations on the Olmec Frontier. Thames and Hudson, London and New York.

Guggisberg, C. A. W.
1975
Wild Cats of the World. New York.

Hammond, Norman
1982
Ancient Maya Civilization. New Brunswick, N.J.

Harrison, Peter D.
1970
Form and Function in a Maya "Palace" Group. *Verhandlungen des 38th Internationalen Amerikanistenkongresses* 1:165–72. Munich.
1971
The Central Acropolis, Tikal, Guatemala: A Preliminary Study of the Functions of its Structural Components During the Late Classic Period. Ph.D. Dissertation, University of Pennsylvania, 1970. Ann Arbor, Mich.

Hartung, Horst
1970
Notes on the Oaxaca Tablero. *Boletín de Estudios Oaxaqueños,* no. 27, pp. 2–8.
1971
Die Zeremonialzentren der Maya. Graz, Austria.
1977
Ancient Maya Architecture and Planning: Possibilities and Limitations for Astronomical Studies. In *Native American Astronomy,* ed. Anthony F. Aveni, pp. 111–29. Austin and London.

Hay, Clarence L.
1935
A Contribution to Maya Architecture. *Natural History* 36 (1):29–33.

Heller, Carl Bartholomaeus
1853
Reisen in Mexiko. Leipzig.

Hellmuth, Nicholas
1976
Maya Clay Sculpture of Pre-Columbian Mexico. *Apollo,* March.

Henderson, John M.
1981
The World of the Ancient Maya. Ithaca and London.

Heyden, Doris, and Paul Gendrop
1973
Pre-Columbian Architecture of Mesoamerica. Japan.

Hissink, Karin
1934
Masken als Fassadenschmuck. Untersucht an alten Bauten der Halbinsel Yukatan. Sammlung Heitz. Akademische Abhandlungen zur Kulturgeschichte, reihe III,

bd. 2. Strassburg.

Ho, Ting-jui
[1970]
The origin of some geometric designs: A Hypothesis. Paper read before the American Anthropological Association, San Diego, California.

Holmes, William H.
1895–1897
Archaeological Studies among the Ancient Cities of Mexico. Chicago.

Houston, Stephen A.
1984
An Example of Homophony in Maya Script. *American Antiquity* 49 (4):790–805.

Jimenez Moreno, Wigberto
1942
El enigma de los olmecas. *Cuadernos Americanos*, 5: 113–45.

Jones, Christopher
1969
The Twin Pyramid Group Pattern: A Classic Maya Architectural Assemblage at Tikal, Guatemala. Ph. D. Dissertation, University of Pennsylvania. Ann Arbor.
1975
A Painted Capstone from the Maya Area. *University of California Archaeological Research Facility Contributions*, no. 27. Berkeley.
1977
Inauguration Dates of Three Late Classic Rulers of Tikal, Guatemala. *American Antiquity* 42:28–60.

Jones, Christopher, and Robert J. Sharer
1980
Archaeological Investigations in the Site Core of Quirigua. *Expedition* 23, (1):11–19.

Joralemon, Peter David
1971
A study of Olmec iconography. *Studies in Pre-Columbian Art and Archaeology*, no. 7. Dumbarton Oaks, Washington, D.C.
1976
The Olmec Dragon: A Study in Pre-Columbian Iconography. In *Origins of Religious Art and Iconography in Preclassic Mesoamerica, ed. by H. B. Nicholson, pp. 27–71.* Los Angeles, Calif.

Kampen, Michael
1972
The Sculptures of El Tajin, Veracruz, Mexico. Gainesville, Fla.

Kelley, David
1962
Glyphic Evidence for a Dynastic Sequence at Quirigua, Guatemala. *American Antiquity* 27:323–35.
1965
The Birth of the Gods at Palenque. *Estudios de Cultura Maya*, 3:93–134. Mexico, D.F.
1968a
Kakupacal and the Itzas. *Estudios de Cultura Maya*, 7:255–68. Mexico, D.F.
1968b
Mayan Fire Glyphs. *Estudios de Cultura Maya* 8: 141–57. Mexico, D.F.

1976
Deciphering the Maya Script. Austin, Texas.
1982
Notes on Puuc Inscriptions and History. *The Puuc: New Perspectives. Papers presented at the Puuc Symposium, Central College, May, 1977,* ed. Lawrence Mills, publication 1, supplement. Pella, Iowa.

Kerr, J., and G. Froom
1970
Fifty figures from a site in Veracruz. Edward H. Merrin Gallery, New York.

Kidder, A. V., J. D. Jennings, and E. M. Shook
1946
Excavations at Kaminaljuyu, Guatemala. *Carnegie Institution of Washington, Publication* 561. Washington, D.C.

Konieczna, Barbara and Pablo Mayer Guala
1976
Uxmal, Yucatan. Informe de la Temporada 1973–1974. *Investigaciónes Arqueológicas en el sureste* 27:1–18. Mexico, D.F.

Kowalski, Jeff Karl
[1981]
The House of the Governor at Uxmal, Yucatan, Mexico. Doctoral Dissertation, Yale University.
1985a
Painted Architecture in the Northern Maya Area. *Painted Architecture and Polychrome Monumental Sculpture in Mesoamerica,* ed. Elizabeth H. Boone, Dumbarton Oaks, Washington, D.C.
1986a
A Historical Interpretation of the Inscriptions of Uxmal. Paper to be published in the Fourth Palenque Round Table Conference Volume ed. Merle G. Robertson, Precolumbian Art Research Center, San Francisco.
1986b
Lords of the Northern Maya: Dynastic History in the Inscriptions of Uxmal and Chichen Itza. Article to be published in *Expedition.*
n.d.a
Glyphic, Linguistic, Ethnographic and Iconographic Clues to the Identity of God K. Paper Presented at the Fifth Palenque Round Table Conference, Palenque, Chiapas, June 12–18, 1983.
n.d.b
Connections between Northern Yucatan, the Pasion Drainage, and the Comitan Valley during the Epi-Classic Period. Paper Delivered at the Society for American Archaeology Annual Meeting, Denver, May, 1985.

Krickeberg, Walter
1933
Los totonacs: contribución a la etnografía histórica de la Amearica Central. Talleres Graficos del Museo Nacional de Arqueología, Etnografía e Historia. Mexico, D.F.

Kubler, George
1961
The Shape of Time. New Haven, Conn.
1962

The Art and Architecture of Ancient America. Harmondsworth, Middlesex, England.
1969
Studies in Classic Maya Iconography. Memoirs of the Connecticut Academy of Arts and Sciences, 15. New Haven, Conn.
1972a
The Paired Attendants of the Temple Tablets at Palenque. *Religion en Mesoamerica. Sociedad Mexicana de Antropología, 12 Mesa Redonda.* Mexico, D.F.
1972b
Jaguars in the Valley of Mexico. *The Cult of the Feline,* ed. Elizabeth Benson, pp. 19–44. Washington, D.C.
1975
The Art and Architecture of Ancient America. (2nd ed.). Harmondsworth, Middlesex, England.
1976
The Doubled-Portrait Lintels of Tikal. *Actas del 23d Congreso Internacional de Historia del Arte,* 1:165–76. Granada.
1977
Aspects of Classic Maya Rulership on Two Inscribed Vessels. *Studies in Pre-Columbian Art and Archaeology,* no. 18. Dumbarton Oaks, Washington, D.C.

Kurjack, Edward B.
1974
Prehistoric Lowland Maya Community and Social Organization: A Case Study at Dzibilchaltun, Yucatan, Mexico. *Tulane University, Middle American Research Institute, Publication* 38. New Orleans, La.

Kurjack, Edward B., and E. Wyllys Andrews V
1976
Early Boundary Maintenance in Northwest Yucatan, Mexico. *American Antiquity* 41 (3):318–25.

Kurjack, Edward B., Silvia Garza T., and Jerry Lucas
1979
Archaeological Settlement Patterns and Modern Geography in the Hill Region of Yucatan. In *The Puuc: New Perspectives, Papers Presented at the Puuc Symposium, Central College,* May 1977, ed. Lawrence Mills, pp. 35–45. Pella, Iowa.

Lamb, Weldon
1980
The Sun, the Moon and Venus at Uxmal. *American Antiquity* 45 (1):79–86.

Landa, Fray Diego de
1978
Relación de las Cosas de Yucatan. Editorial Porrua. Mexico, D.F.

Lee, Thomas A., Jr.
1973
Secuencia de fases postformitivas en Izapa, Chiapas, Mexico. *Estudios de Cultura Maya* 9:75–84. Mexico, D.F.

Lehmann, Walter
1941
Una elegía tolteca. Publicaciónes de las Sociedad Alejandro Humboldt, Folleto No. 2. Mexico, D.F.

Le Plongeon, Alice D.
1885
The Old and the new in Yucatan. *Harper's Monthly*

(Feb. 1885): 372–86. New York, N.Y.

Lincoln, Charles
[1982]
Chichen Itza and the Total Overlap Model: An Attempt to Synthesize Archaeological and Monumental Data. Unpublished paper. Peabody Museum of American Archaeology and Ethnology, Harvard University.

Littmann, Edwin R.
1960
Ancient Mesoamerican Mortars, Plasters, and Stuccos: The Puuc Area. *American Antiquity* 25 (3):407–412.

Litvak King, Jaime
1972
Las relaciónes externas de Xochicalco: una evaluación de su significado. *Anales de Antropología* 9:49–77. Mexico, D.F.

Lounsbury, Floyd
1973
On the Derivation and Reading of the "Ben-Ich" prefix. In *Mesoamerican Writing Systems,* ed. Elizabeth P. Benson, pp. 99–143. Washington, D.C.
1974a
Pacal. In *Primera Mesa Redonda de Palenque,* pt. 1, ed. Merle Greene Robertson, p. ii. Pebble Beach, Calif.
1974b
The Inscription of the Sarcophagus Lid at Palenque. In *Primera Mesa Redonda de Palenque,* pt. 2, ed. Merle Greene Robertson, pp. 5–19. Pebble Beach, Calif.

Lounsbury, Floyd, and Michael D. Coe
1968
Linguistic and Ethnographic Data Pertinent to the "Cage" Glyph of Dresden 36c. *Estudios de Cultura Maya* 7:269–84. Mexico, D.F.

Maler, Teobert
1895
Yukatekische Forschungen. *Globus* 68:247–60, 277–92. Braunschweig.
1901
Researches in the Central Portion of the Usumacinta Valley. *Memoirs of the Peabody Museum of American Archaeology and Ethnology, Harvard University,* 2:1. Cambridge, Mass.
1902
Yukatekische Forschungen. *Globus* 82:197–230. Braunschweig.
1903
Researches in the Central Portion of the Usumacinta Valley. *Memoirs of the Peabody Museum of American Archaeology and Ethnology, Harvard University,* 2:2. Cambridge, Mass.
1908
Explorations of the Upper Usumatsintla and Adjacent Region: Altar de Sacrificios; Seibal; Itzimté-Sacluk; Cankuen. *Memoirs of the Peabody Museum of American Archaeology and Ethnology, Harvard University,* 4:1. Cambridge, Mass.
1908
Explorations in the Department of Peten Guatemala and Adjacent Region: Topoxté, Yǎxhá, Benque Viejo, Naranjo. *Memoirs of the Peabody Museum of Ameri-*

1968

Jaina, La Casa en el Agua. Mexico, D. F.

1972

Historia, Arqueología y Arte Prehispánico. Mexico, D. F.

n.d.

Edzna. Guía de la zona arqueológica. Mexico, D.F.

Pio Pérez, Juan

1866–1877

Diccionario de la lengua maya. Mérida.

Pollock, H. E. D.

1936

The Architectural Survey. *Carnegie Institution of Washington, Year Book* 35, pp. 122–25. Washington, D.C.

1940

The Architectural Survey of Yucatan. *Carnegie Institution of Washington, Year Book* 39, pp. 265–67. Washington, D.C.

1965

Architecture of the Maya Lowlands. *Handbook of Middle American Indians* 2:378–440. Austin, Texas.

1970

Architectural Notes on some Chenes Ruins. In *Monographs and Papers in Maya Archaeology,* ed. W. R. Bullard. *Papers of the Peabody Museum of Archaeology and Ethnology, Harvard University,* 61. Cambridge.

1980

The Puuc: an Architectural Survey of the Hill Country of Yucatan and Northern Campeche, Mexico. *Memoirs of the Peabody Museum of Archaeology and Ethnology, Harvard University,* 19. Cambridge, Mass.

Pollock, H. E. D., Ralph L. Roys, T. Proskouriakoff, and A. Ledyard Smith

1962

Mayapan, Yucatan, Mexico. Carnegie Institution of Washington, Publication 619. Washington, D.C.

Potter, David F.

1976

Prehispanic Architecture and Sculpture in Central Yucatan. *American Antiquity* 41:430–48.

1977

Maya Architecture of the Central Yucatan Peninsula, Mexico. *Tulane University, Middle American Research Institute, Publication* 44. New Orleans, La.

Proskouriakoff, Tatiana

1950

A Study of Classic Maya Sculpture. *Carnegie Institution of Washington, Publication* 593. Washington, D.C.

1951

Some Non-Classic Traits in the Sculpture of Yucatan. In *The Civilizations of Ancient America.* Selected papers of the 29th International Congress of Americanists, ed. Sol Tax, pp. 111–18. Chicago, Ill.

1959

Definitions of Maya Art and Culture. *Art Quarterly* 22 (2):110–122.

1960

Historical Implications of a Pattern of Dates at Piedras

Negras, Guatemala. *American Antiquity* 25:454–75.

1961a

The Lords of the Maya Realm. *Expedition Magazine* (Fall 1961), pp. 14–21.

1961b

Portraits of Women in Maya Art. In *Essays in Precolumbian Art and Archaeology,* ed. Samuel K. Lothrop, pp. 81–99. Cambridge, Mass.

1963a

An Album of Maya Architecture. Norman, Okla.

1963b

Historical Data in the Inscriptions of Yaxchilan. *Estudios de Cultura Maya,* 3:pp. 149–167. Mexico, D.F.

1964

Historical Data in the Inscriptions of Yaxchilan. *Estudios de Cultura Maya,* 3:149–67. Mexico, D.F.

1970

On Two Inscriptions at Chichen Itza. In *Monographs and Papers in Maya Archaeology,* ed. W. R. Bullard, pp. 457–67. *Papers of the Peabody Museum of Archaeology and History, Harvard University,* 61. Cambridge, Mass.

Proskouriakoff, Tatiana, and J. E. S. Thompson

1947

Maya Calendar Round Dates such as 9 Ahau 17 Mol. *Carnegie Institution of Washington, Notes on Middle American Archaeology and Ethnology,* no. 79, Cambridge, Mass.

Quirarte, Jacinto

1968

Differencias Arquitectónicas en dos Ciudades Mayas: Uxmal y Chichen. *University of Texas, Institute of Latin American Studies, Offprint,* 89, pp. 51–119.

1973

Izapan-Style Art: A Study of Its Form and Meaning. *Studies in Pre-Columbian Art and Archaeology,* no. 10. Dumbarton Oaks, Washington, D.C.

1977

Early Art Styles of Mesoamerica and Early Classic Maya Art. In *The Origins of Maya Civilization,* ed. by R. E. W. Adams, pp. 249–83. Albuquerque, N. Mex.

Rabin, Emily

1970

The Lambityeco Friezes: Notes on their content with an Appendix on C14 Dates. *Boletín de Estudios Oaxaqueños* 33:1–16.

Ralph, Elizabeth K.

1965

Review of Radiocarbon Dates from Tikal and the Maya Calendar Correlation Problem. *American Antiquity* 30:421–27.

Ramirez, José Fernando

1926

Viaje a Yucatán de 1865. Mérida.

Rands, Robert L.

1955

Some Manifestations of Water in Mesoamerican Art. *Bureau of American Ethnology Bulletin,* no. 157. Washington, D.C.

Recinos, Adrián

1950

The Popol Vuh: the Sacred Book of the Ancient Quiché Maya. Translated from the Spanish by S. G. Morley and Delia Goetz. Norman, Okla.

Recinos, Adrián, and Delia Goetz
1953
The Annals of the Cakchiquels and Title of the Lords of Totonicapán. Norman, Okla.

Redfield, Robert, and Alfonso Villa Rojas
1939
Notes on the Ethnography of Tzeltal Communities in Chiapas. *Contributions to American Anthropology and History*, 5 (28), *Carnegie Institution of Washington Publication 509*. Washington, D.C.

Relaciones de Yucatan
1898–1900
Coleción de documentos inéditos relativos al descubrimiento, conquista y organización de los antiguos posesiones Españoles de Ultramar. 2nd Serie, Vols. 11 and 13. Madrid.

Reygadas Vertiz, José
1928
Estado Actual de los Principales Edificios Arqueológicos de Mexico. Mexico, D.F.

Rickards, Constantine George
1910
The Ruins of Mexico. London.

Ricketson, O. G., Jr.
1928
Astronomical Observatories in the Maya Area. *Geographical Review* 18:215–25. New York, N.Y.

Ricketson, O. G., Jr., and E. B. Ricketson
1937
Uaxactun, Guatemala, Group E, 1926–1931. *Carnegie Institution of Washington, Publication 477.* Washington, D.C.

Riese, Berthold, and Karl Herbert Mayer
1984
Altar 10 von Uxmal, Yukatan, Mexiko. *Mexicon* 6 (5):70–73.

Robertson, Donald
1963
Pre-Columbian Architecture. New York, N.Y.

Robertson, Merle Greene
1974
The Quadripartite Badge—A Badge of Rulership. In *Primera Mesa Redonda de Palenque*, pt. 1, ed. Merle Greene Robertson, pp. 77–92. Pebble Beach, Calif.

Robicsek, Francis
1972
Copan, Home of the Mayan Gods. New York, N.Y.
1975
A Study in Maya Art and History: the Mat Symbol. New York: N.Y.

Roys, Lawrence
1934
The Engineering Knowledge of the Maya. *Contributions to American Archaeology 6, Carnegie Institution of Washington, Publication 436.* Washington, D.C.

Roys, Ralph L.
1933
The Book of Chilam Balam of Chumayel. *Carnegie Institution of Washington, Publication 438.* Washington, D.C.
1940
Personal Names of the Maya of Yucatan. *Contributions to American Anthropology and History*, 6 (31):31–48. *Carnegie Institution of Washington, Publication 523.* Washington, D.C.
[1941]
The Xiu Chronicle. Part II: The Xiu Chronicle. Manuscript in Peabody Museum, Harvard University, Cambridge, Mass.
1943
The Indian Background of Colonial Yucatan. *Carnegie Institution of Washington, Publication 548.* Washington, D.C.
1949a
Guide to the Codex Perez. *Contributions to American Archaeology and History*, 10:49. *Carnegie Institution of Washington, Publication 585.* Washington, D.C.
1949b
The Prophecies for the Maya Tuns or Years. In the Books of Chilam Balam of Tizimin and Mani. *Contributions to American Archaeology and History*, 10:51. *Carnegie Institution of Washington*, Publication 585. Washington, D.C.
1962
Literary Sources for the History of Mayapan. In Pollock, H. E. D., Ralph L. Roys, T. Proskouriakoff, and A. Ledyard Smith. *Mayapan, Yucatan, Mexico. Carnegie Institution of Washington*, Publication 619. Washington, D.C.
1966
Native Empires in Yucatan. *Revista Mexicana de Estudios Antropológicos* 20:155–78. Mexico, D.F.
1967
The Book of Chilam Balam of Chumayel. Norman, Okla.

Ruano, Suarez, A.
1892
Vocabulario de las lenguas pokoman y chorti. ms. 121 pp. Photostat in Peabody Museum, Harvard University. Cambridge, Mass.

Ruppert, Karl
1940
A Special Assemblage of Maya Structures. In *The Maya and their Neighbors*, ed. Clarence L. Hay, et. al., pp. 222–31. New York and London.
1943
The Mercado, Chichen Itza, Yucatan. *Contributions to American Anthropology and History*: 43. *Carnegie Institution of Washington, Publication 546.* Washington, D.C.
1952
Chichen Itza, Architectural Notes and Plans. *Carnegie Institution of Washington, Publication 595.* Washington, D.C.

Ruppert, Karl, and John H. Denison, Jr.
1943
Archaeological Reconnaissance in Campeche, Quintana Roo, and Peten. *Carnegie Institution of Washington, Publication 543.* Washington, D.C.

Ruppert, Karl, and A. L. Smith
1957
House Types in the Environs of Mayapan and at Uxmal, Kabah, Sayil, Chichen Itza, and Chacchob. *Current Report* 39, *Carnegie Institution of Washington, Department of Archaeology.* Cambridge, Mass.

Ruppert, Karl, J. E. S. Thompson, and Tatiana Proskouriakoff
1955
Bonampak, Chiapas, Mexico. *Carnegie Institution of Washington, Publication* 602. Washington, D.C.

Ruz Lhuillier, Alberto
1945
Campeche en la arqueológia Maya. *Acta Antropológica* 1:2–3. Mexico, D.F.

[1947]
Zona Maya. Temporada de 1947. Exploraciónes Arqueológicas en Uxmal, Yucatan. 7 de enero, 1947. Instituto Nacional de Antropología e Historia, Informes Inéditos, Estado de Yucatan—Uxmal, Tomo III. 1942–1947.

[1948]
Zona Maya. Temporada de 1948. El Juego de Pelota de Uxmal, Yucatan. 21 de diciembre, 1948. Instituto Nacional de Antropología e Historia, Informes Inéditos, Estado de Yucatan—Uxmal, Tomo IV. 1948–1952.

[1950]
Informe que rinde a la dirección de Monumentos Prehispánico del Instituto Nacional de Antropología e Historia, El Jefe de la oficina de Monumentos Prehispánicos en Yucatan, Arqueologo 'A' Alberto Ruz Lhuillier, con motive de las obras de restauración y consolidación que se llevaron a cabo en las Zonas Arqueológicas de Uxmal y Kabah en la Temporada de 1950. Diciembre, 1950. Instituto Nacional de Antropología e Historia, Informes Inéditos, Estado de Yucatan—Uxmal, Tomo IV. 1948–1952.

1953
Presencia atlántica en Palenque. *Revista Mexicana de Estudios Antropológicos* 13, (2–3):455–62. Mexico, D.F.

1955a
Uxmal: Temporada de Trabajos 1951–1952. *Anales del Instituto Nacional de Antropología e Historia,* 6 (34): 49–67.

1955b
Uxmal-Kabah-Zayil: Temporada 1953. *Instituto Nacional de Antropología e Historia, Dirección de Monumentos Prehispánicos, Informe* I.

1958a
El Juego de Pelota. *Miscellanea Paul Rivet, Octogenario Dictata.* Mexico, D.F.

1958b
Exploraciónes Arqueológicas en Palenque: 1953. *Anales del Instituto Nacional de Antropología e Historia,* 10 (39): 69–116. Mexico, D.F.

1959
Guía Oficial de Uxmal. Mexico, D.F.

1965
Chichen Itza: Official Guide. Mexico, D.F.

1969

La Costa de Campeche en los Tiempos Prehispánicos. Instituto Nacional de Antropología e Historia, Investigaciónes 18. Mexico, D.F.

Sabloff, Jeremy A.
1975
Excavations at Seibal, Department of Peten, Guatemala. Ceramics. *Memoirs of the Peabody Museum of Archaeology and Ethnology, Harvard University* 13:2. Cambridge, Mass.

Sáenz, César A.
1968
Exploraciónes y Restauraciónes en Yucatán. *Boletín del Instituto Nacional de Antropología e Historia* 31: 17–23. Mexico, D.F.

1969a
Exploraciónes y Restauraciónes en Uxmal, Yucatán. *Boletín del Instituto Nacional de Antropología e Historia* 36:5–13. Mexico, D.F.

[1969b]
Report on Excavations and Reconstructions Undertaken at Uxmal, dated April, 1969. Instituto Nacional de Antropología e Historia, Exploraciónes y Conservación en la Zona de Uxmal, Yuc.

1972
Exploraciónes y Restauraciónes en Uxmal (1970–1971). *Boletín del Instituto Nacional de Antropología e Historia,* Época II, 2, pp. 31–40. Mexico, D.F.

1975
Exploraciónes y Reconstrucciónes en la Gran Piramide de Uxmal, Yucatan. *Boletín del Instituto Nacional de Antropología e Historia,* Época II, no. 12, pp. 39–44. Mexico, D.F.

1976
Cerámica de Uxmal, Yucatan. *Anales del Instituto Nacional de Antropología e Historia,* Época 7, 5, 1974–1975, pp. 171–186. Mexico, D.F.

Sahagún, Fray Bernardino de
1950–1971
Florentine Codex. General History of the Things of New Spain. Translated by Charles E. Dibble and Arthur J. O. Anderson. 12 Vols. *Monographs of The School of American Research and The Museum of New Mexico.* Santa Fe, N. Mex.

Sanchez de Aguilar, Pedro
1937
Informe Contra Idolorum Cultores del Obispado de Yucatan. (3rd ed.) Mérida.

Sanders, Frank J.
1977
The "Twin Stelae" of Seibal. *American Antiquity* 42 (1):78–86.

Satterthwaite, Linton, Jr.
1935
Palace Structures J-2 and J-6. *Piedras Negras Preliminary Papers,* No. 3. The University Museum, University of Pennsylvania. Philadelphia, Pa.

1937
Thrones at Piedras Negras, *University Museum Bulletin* 7 (1):18–23. Philadelphia, Pa.

1939
Evolution of a Maya Temple—Part I. *University Mu-*

seum Bulletin 7 (4):3–14. The University Museum, University of Pennsylvania. Philadelphia, Pa.

1940

Evolution of a Maya Temple—Part II. *University Museum Bulletin* 8 (2–3):18–23. The University Museum, University of Pennsylvania. Philadelphia, Pa.

1943

Animal Head Feet and a Bark-beater in the Middle Usumacinta Region. *Carnegie Institution of Washington, Notes on Middle American Archaeology and Ethnology*, No. 27. Washington, D.C.

1944

Piedras Negras Archaeology: Architecture, pt. 4, Ball Courts. University Museum, University of Pennsylvania. Philadelphia, Pa.

Saville, Marshall H.

1909

The Cruciform structures of Mitla and vicinity. *Putnam Anniversary Volume*. New York, N.Y.

1921

Bibliographic Notes on Uxmal, Yucatan. *Museum of the American Indian, Heye Foundation, Indian Notes and Monographs* 9:2. New York, N.Y.

1929

Votive Axes from Ancient Mexico. Museum of the American Indian, Heye Foundation, Indian Notes and Monographs 6:266–99. New York, N.Y.

Schele, Linda

1974

Observations on the Cross Motif at Palenque. In *Primera Mesa Redonda de Palenque*, pt. 1, ed. Merle Greene Robertson, pp. 41–61. Pebble Beach, Calif.

1976

Accession Iconography of Chan-Bahlum in the Group of the Cross at Palenque. In *The Art, Iconography and Dynastic History of Palenque*, pt. 3, ed. Merle Greene Robertson, pp. 9–34. Pebble Beach, Calif.

1982

Maya Glyphs: The Verbs. Austin, Texas.

Schellhas, Paul

1904

Representation of Deities of the Maya Manuscripts. *Papers of the Peabody Museum of American Archaeology and Ethnology, Harvard University* 4:1. Cambridge, Mass.

Scholes, F. V., and Ralph Roys

1948

The Maya Chontal Indians of Acalan-Tixchel: a Contribution to the History and Ethnography of the Yucatán Peninsula. *Carnegie Institution of Washington, Publication* 560. Washington, D.C.

Séjourné, Laurette

1966

Arqueología de Teotihuacán, la cerámica. Fondo de Cultura Economica. Mexico, D.F.

Seler, Eduard

1904a

The Wall Paintings of Mitla. *Mexican and Central American Antiquities, Calendar Systems, and History. Bureau of American Ethnology Bulletin*, no. 28, pp. 243–324. Washington, D.C.

1904b

Venus Period in the Picture Writings of the Borgian Codex Group. *Mexican and Central American Antiquities, Calendar Systems, and History. Bureau of American Ethnology Bulletin*, no. 28. Washington, D.C.

1906

Studien in den Ruinen von Yucatan. *Proceedings of the 15th International Congress of Americanists*, 2:414–22. Quebec.

1913

Ueber einige Ältere Systeme in den Ruinen von Uxmal. *Proceedings of the 28th International Congress of Americanists, 1912*, pp. 220–35. London.

1916

Die Quetzalcouatl-Fassaden Yukatekischer Bauten. *Abhandlungen der Königlich Preussischen Akademie der Wissenschaften, Phil.-Hist. Klasse*, Nr. 3. Berlin.

1917

Die Ruinen von Uxmal. *Abhandlungen der Königlich Preussischen Akademie der Wissenschaften, Phil.-Hist. Klasse*, Nr. 3. Berlin.

1960

Gesammelte Abhandlungen zur Amerikanischen Sprach- und Altertumskunde. 5 vols. Graz, Austria.

Seymour, Charles, Jr.

1968

Notre-Dame of Noyon in the Twelfth Century. New York, N.Y.

Sharp, Rosemary

1970

Early architectural grecas in the Valley of Oaxaca. *Boletín de Estudios Oaxaqueños* 32:2–12.

1972

Greca: An Exploratory Study of Relationships between Art, Society, and Personality. Ph.D. Dissertation, University of North Carolina at Chapel Hill. Ann Arbor, Mich.

1978a

Architecture as Interelite Communication in Preconquest Oaxaca, Veracruz, and Yucatan. In *Middle Classic Mesoamerica: A.D. 400–700*, ed. Esther Pasztory, pp. 158–71. New York, N.Y.

1978b

Trading Chiefs to Warring Kings, The Political Nexus of Symbolic Forms During the Pure Florescent Period in Northern Yucatan, Mexico. In *Codex Wauchope; A Tribute Roll*, ed. Marco Giardino, Barbara Edmonson, and Winifred Creamer, pp. 89–100. New Orleans, La.

Shook, Edwin M.

1940

Exploration in the Ruins of Oxkintok, Yucatan. *Revista Mexicana de Estudios Antropológicos* 4:165–171. Mexico, D.F.

Shook, Edwin M., and Tatiana Proskouriakoff

1951

Yucatan. *Carnegie Institution of Washington, Year Book* 50:236–41. Washington, D.C.

Smith, A. Ledyard

1932

Two Recent Ceramic Finds at Uaxactun. *Contributions to American Archaeology* 2:5. *Carnegie Institution of*

Washington, Publication 436. Washington, D.C.

1937
Structure A-XVIII, Uaxactun. *Contributions to American Archaeology* 20. *Carnegie Institution of Washington, Publication* 483. Washington, D.C.

1940
The Corbeled Arch in the New World. In *The Maya and Their Neighbors*, ed. by Clarence L. Hay, et. al., pp. 202–231. New York, N.Y.

1950
Uaxactun, Guatemala: Excavations of 1931–1937. *Carnegie Institution of Washington, Publication* 588. Washington, D.C.

1962
Residential and Associated Structures at Mayapan. In Pollock, H. E. D., Ralph L. Roys, T. Proskouriakoff and A. Ledyard Smith. *Mayapan, Yucatan, Mexico. Carnegie Institution of Washington, Publication* 619. Washington, D.C.

1982
Major Architecture and Caches. Excavations at Seibal, Department of Peten, Guatemala. *Memoirs of the Peabody Museum of Archaeology and Ethnology, Harvard University* 15:1. Cambridge, Mass.

Smith, A. L., and Karl Ruppert

1954
Ceremonial or Formal Archway, Uxmal. *Carnegie Institution of Washington, Notes on Middle American Archaeology and Ethnology* 116. Cambridge, Mass.

Smith, Mary Elizabeth

1973
Picture Writing from Ancient Southern Mexico. Norman, Okla.

Smith, Robert E.

1955
Ceramic sequence at Uaxactun, Guatemala. 2 Vols. *Tulane University, Middle American Research Institute, Publication* 20. New Orleans, La.

1971
The Pottery of Mayapan, including Studies of Ceramic Material from Uxmal, Kabah, and Chichen Itza. 2 Vols. *Papers of the Peabody Museum of Archaeology and Ethnology, Harvard University* 66. Cambridge, Mass.

Spinden, Herbert J.

1913
A Study of Maya Art. *Memoirs of the Peabody Museum of American Archaeology and Ethnology, Harvard University* 6. Cambridge, Mass.

1916
Portraiture in Central American Art. *Holmes Anniversary Volume*, pp. 434–50. Washington, D.C.

1920
The Stephens Sculptures from Yucatan. *Natural History* 20:(4):378–89. New York, N.Y.

1957
Maya Art and Civilization. Indian Hills, Colorado.

Stephens, John Lloyd

1841
Incidents of Travel in Central America, Chiapas, and Yucatan. 2 Vols. New York, N.Y.

1963
Incidents of Travel in Yucatan. 2 Vols. Reissue, New York, N.Y.

Stierlin, Henri

1964
Living Architecture: Mayan. New York, N.Y.

1981
Art of the Maya. Rizzoli, New York.

Stromsvik, Gustav

1953
A Portal Vault at Mayapan. *Current Report* 8, *Carnegie Institution of Washington, Department of Archaeology.* Cambridge, Mass.

Tamers, M.A.

1969
Instituto Venezolano de Investigaciónes Cientificas Natural Radiocarbon Measurements IV. *American Journal of Science, Radiocarbon* 11:396–422. New Haven, Conn.

Taylor, Dicey

1978
The Cauac Monster. *Tercera Mesa Redonda de Palenque, Vol. IV* ed. Merle G. Robertson and Donnan C. Jeffers, pp. 79–89. Monterrey, Calif.

Thompson, Edward H.

1886
Archaeological research in Yucatan. *Proceedings of the American Antiquarian Society*, n.s. 4:248–54. Worcester, Mass.

1897
The Chultunes of Labna. *Memoirs of the Peabody Museum of American Archaeology and Ethnology, Harvard University* 1:3. Cambridge, Mass.

1898
Ruins of Xkichmook Yucatan. *Field Columbian Museum, Anthropological Series* 2:3. Chicago, Ill.

1904
Archaeological Researches in Yucatan. *Memoirs of the Peabody Museum of American Archaeology and Ethnology, Harvard University* 3:1. Cambridge, Mass.

1911
The Genesis of the Maya Arch. *American Anthropologist*, n.s., 13 (4):501–516.

Thompson, J. E. S.

1931
Archaeological Investigations in the Southern Cayo District, British Honduras. *Field Museum of Natural History, Publication* 301. *Anthropological Series* 17:3. Chicago, Ill.

1937
A new method of deciphering Yucatecan dates with special reference to Chichen Itza. *Contributions to American Archaeology, Contribution no.* 22. *Carnegie Institution of Washington, Publication* 483. Washington, D.C.

1939
Excavations at San José, British Honduras. *Carnegie Institution of Washington, Publication* 506. Washington, D.C.

1941
A coordination of the history of Chichen Itza with ceramic sequences in central Mexico. *Revista Mexicana*

de Estudios Antropològicos 56, 97–111. Mexico, D.F.

1945
A Survey of the Northern Maya Area. *American Antiquity* 11:2–24.

1954a
The Rise and Fall of Maya Civilization. Norman, Okla.

1954b
A presumed Residence of the Nobility at Mayapan. *Current Report* 19, *Carnegie Institution of Washington, Department of Archaeology.* Cambridge, Mass.

1960
Maya Hieroglyphic Writing: an Introduction. Norman, Okla.

1962
A Catalog of Maya Hieroglyphs. Norman, Okla.

1966
The Rise and Fall of Maya Civilization. (2nd. ed.). Norman, Okla.

1970
Maya History and Religion. Norman, Okla.

1972a
A commentary on the Dresden Codex: A Maya Hieroglyphic Book. Philadelphia, Pa.

1972b
Maya Hieroglyphs Without Tears. British Museum, London.

1973a
The Painted Capstone at Sacnicte, Yucatan, and two Others at Uxmal. *Indiana* 1:59–63. Berlin.

1973b
The Maya glyph for Capture or Conquest and an Iconographic Representation of Itzam Na on Yucatecan Facades. *Contributions of the University of California Archaeological Research Facility* 18:203–207. Berkeley, Calif.

1973c
Maya Rulers of the Classic Period and the Divine Right of Kings. In *The Iconography of Middle American Sculpture*, pp. 52–71. Metropolitan Museum of Art, New York, N.Y.

1977
Hieroglyphic Texts of Las Monjas and Their Bearing on Building Activities. In John Bolles. *Las Monjas, A Major Pre-Mexican Architectural Complex at Chichen Itza*, pp. 262–67. Norman, Okla.

Thompson, J. E. S., H. E. D. Pollock, and J. Charlot
1932
A Preliminary Study of the Ruins of Cobá. *Carnegie Institution of Washington, Publication* 424. Washington, D.C.

Toscano, Salvador
1970
Arte PreColombino de Mexico y de la América Central (3rd ed.). Mexico, D.F.

Totten, George Oakley
1926
Maya Architecture. Washington, D.C.

Tozzer, Alfred M.
1907
A comparative study of the Mayas and the Lacandones. New York, N.Y.

1911
A Preliminary Study of the Prehistoric Ruins of Tikal, Guatemala. *Memoirs of the Peabody Museum of American Archaeology and Ethnology, Harvard University* 5:2. Cambridge, Mass.

1913
A Preliminary Study of the Prehistoric Ruins of Nakum, Guatemala. *Memoirs of the Peabody Museum of American Archaeology and Ethnology, Harvard University* 5:3. Cambridge, Mass.

1921
A Maya Grammar. *Papers of the Peabody Museum of American Archaeology and Ethnology, Harvard University* 9. Cambridge, Mass.

1941
Landa's Relación de las cosas de Yucatan, a Translation. Edited with notes by A. M. Tozzer. *Papers of the Peabody Museum of Archaeology and Ethnology, Harvard University* 33. Cambridge, Mass.

1957
Chichen Itza and its Cenote of Sacrifice. A Comparative Study of Contemporaneous Maya and Toltec. *Memoirs of the Peabody Museum of Archaeology and History, Harvard University* 11–12. Cambridge, Mass.

Tozzer, Alfred M., and G. Allen
1910
Animal Figures in the Maya Codices. *Papers of the Peabody Museum of American Archaeology and Ethnology, Harvard University* 4:3. Cambridge, Mass.

Trik, Aubrey S.
1939
Temple XXII at Copan. *Contributions to American Archaeology and History*, 5:29. *Carnegie Institution of Washington, Publication* 509. Washington, D.C.

Villa Rojas, Alfonso
1945
The Maya of East Central Quintana Roo. *Carnegie Institution of Washington, Publication* 559. Washington, D.C.

Villacorta C., J. Antonio, and Carlos A.
1930
Codices Mayas. Guatemala, C.A.

Viollet-le-Duc, Eugène
1863
Antiquités Américaines. In Desiré Charnay's *Cités et Ruines Americaines.* Paris.

Vogel, J. C., and H. T. Waterbolk
1963
Groningen Radiocarbon Dates IV. *Radiocarbon,* 5:163–202.

Vogt, Evon Z.
1964a
The Genetic Model and Maya Cultural Development. In *Desarrollo Cultural de los Mayas*, ed. Evon Z. Vogt and Alberto Ruz Lhuillier, pp. 9–48. Universidad Autónoma de México. Mexico, D.F.

1964b
Some Implications of Zinacantan Social Structure for the Study of the Ancient Maya. *Actas y Memorias del 35th Congreso Internacional de Americanistas*, 1:307–319. Mexico, D.F.

Von Euw, Eric
    1977
        Itzimte, Pixoy, Tzum. *Corpus of Maya Hieroglyphic Inscriptions, Peabody Museum of Archaeology and Ethnology, Harvard University* 4, pt. 1. Cambridge, Mass.
Von Winning, Hasso
    n.d.
        Precolumbian Art of Mexico and Central America. New York, N.Y.
Waldeck, Jean Frederic M. de
    1838
        Voyage Pittoresque et archéologique dans la province d'Yucatan (Amérique Central) pendant les années 1834 et 1836. Paris.
Warden, David B.
    1825
        Description des ruines découvertes près de Palenque. *Recueil de Voyages et Mémoires publies par la Societé de Geographie,* Tome II. Paris.
Wauchope, Robert
    1938
        Modern Maya Houses: a Study of their Archaeological Significance. *Carnegie Institution of Washington, Publication* 502. Washington, D.C.
Westheim, Paul
    1965
        The Art of Ancient Mexico. New York, N.Y.
Westheim, Paul, Alberto Ruz, Pedro Armillas, Ricardo de Robina, and Alfonso Caso
    1972
        Prehispanic Mexican Art. New York, N.Y.
Wicke, C. R.
        Tomb 30 at Yagul and the Zaachila tombs. In *Ancient Oaxaca,* ed. John Paddock, pp. 336–44. Stanford, Calif.
Willey, Gordon
    1956
        The Structure of Ancient Maya Society: Evidence from the Southern Lowlands. *American Anthropologist* 58:777–82.
    1973
        The Altar de Sacrificios Excavations: General Summary and Conclusions. *Papers of the Peabody Museum of Archaeology and Ethnology, Harvard University*

64:3. Cambridge, Mass.
    1982
        Stucco Frieze. In A. L. Smith (1982:30–51).
Willey, Gordon R., and W.R. Bullard, Jr.
    1961
        Altar de Sacrificios, Guatemala: Mapa preliminar y resumen de las excavaciónes. *Estudios de Cultura Maya* 1:81–86. Mexico, D.F.
Willey, Gordon R., and Demitri B. Shimkin
    1973
        The Maya Collapse: A Summary View. In *The Classic Maya Collapse,* ed. by T. P. Culbert, pp. 457–501. Albuquerque, N. Mex.
Willey, Gordon R., and A. L. Smith
    1963
        New Discoveries at Altar de Sacrificios, Guatemala. *Archaeology* 16 (2):83–89.
Willey, Gordon R., A. L. Smith, G. Tourtellot III, and I. Graham
    1975
        Excavations at Seibal, Department of Peten, Guatemala. Introduction: The Site and its Setting. Memoirs of the Peabody Museum of Archaeology and Ethnology, Harvard University 13:1. Cambridge, Mass.
Wittkower, Rudolf
    1971
        Architectural Principles in the Age of Humanism. New York, N.Y.
Worringer, Wilhelm
    1967
        Abstraction and Empathy, a Contribution to the Psychology of Style. Cleveland, Ind.
Zavala, Lorenzo de
    1834
        Notice sur les monuments antiques d'Ushmal, dans la province de Yucatan, fournie par M. Lorenzo de Zavala, Ambassadeur du Mexique en France. *Antiquités Mexicaines, relation des trois expéditions du Captaine Dupaix, . . . ,* Premier partie, Notes et documents divers, Tome I, no. VI. Paris.
Zimmerman, Günter
    1956
        Die Hieroglyphen der Maya-Handschriften. Hamburg.

Index